MW01609970

ZAGAT®

Texas Restaurants 2008

LOCAL EDITOR
Claudia Alarcón, Mike Riccetti, Julia Celeste Rosenfeld and Kay Winzenried

STAFF EDITOR
Michelle Golden

Published and distributed by
Zagat Survey, LLC
4 Columbus Circle
New York, NY 10019
T: 212.977.6000
E: texas@zagat.com
www.zagat.com

ACKNOWLEDGMENTS

We thank Teresa Byrne-Dodge, Audrey Gerber, Valerie Jarvie, Will Larson, Annie and Brian Monahan, Mary Margaret Pack, Steven Shukow and Virginia B. Wood as well as the following members of our staff: Caitlin Eichelberger (editorial assistant), Stacey Slate (editorial assistant), Sean Beachell, Maryanne Bertollo, Sandy Cheng, Reni Chin, Larry Cohn, Alison Flick, Jeff Freier, Roy Jacob, Natalie Lebert, Mike Liao, Allison Lynn, Dave Makulec, Andre Pilette, Kimberly Rosado, Becky Ruthenburg, Sharon Yates, Anna Zappia and Kyle Zolner.

ISBN-13: 978-1-57006-961-1
ISBN-10: 1-57006-961-1
Printed in the
United States of America

Contents

Ratings & Symbols

Zagat Top Spot	Name	Symbols	Cuisine	Zagat Ratings: FOOD	DECOR	SERVICE	COST

Area, Address & Contact

Review, surveyor comments in quotes

Z **Tim & Nina's** ◐ *BBQ* ▽ 19 15 18 $195

Downtown | 1000 E. Salinas St. (Cecilia St.) | 210-555-1234 | www.zagat.com

"Deep in the heart of" Downtown, this "quirky winner" may be short on decor, but it's staffed by "hardworking folks" serving a "veggie version" of Texas BBQ, including a "to-die-for beet brisket sandwich" – though insiders insist it's the "outrageously delicious chicken-fried cabbage" that's "the lone star of the menu"; P.S. remember the "à la mode" for your parsnip-tofu cream pie.

Ratings

Food, Decor and **Service** are rated on the Zagat 0 to 30 scale.

0 – 9 poor to fair

10 – 15 fair to good

16 – 19 good to very good

20 – 25 very good to excellent

26 – 30 extraordinary to perfection

▽ low response | less reliable

Cost reflects our surveyors' average estimate of the price of a dinner with one drink and tip and is a benchmark only. Lunch is usually 25% less.

For **newcomers** or survey **write-ins** listed without ratings, the price range is indicated as follows:

I $25 and below

M $26 to $40

E $41 to $65

VE $66 or more

Symbols

Z Zagat Top Spot (highest ratings, popularity and importance)

◐ serves after 11 PM

S closed on Sunday

M closed on Monday

no credit cards accepted

About This Survey

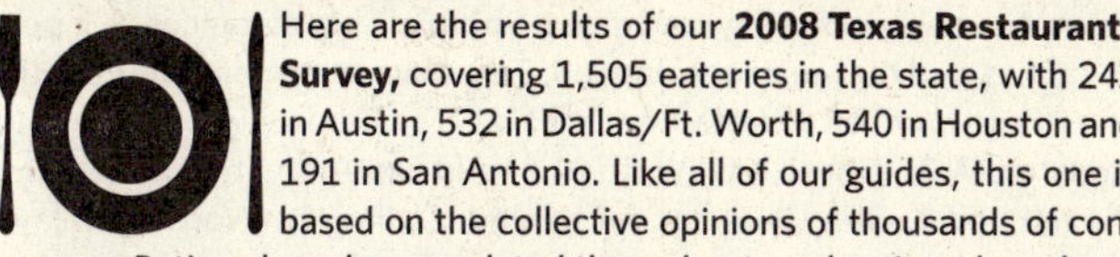

Here are the results of our **2008 Texas Restaurants Survey,** covering 1,505 eateries in the state, with 242 in Austin, 532 in Dallas/Ft. Worth, 540 in Houston and 191 in San Antonio. Like all of our guides, this one is based on the collective opinions of thousands of consumers. Ratings have been updated throughout, and reviews have been rewritten as needed to reflect significant changes since our last Survey.

WHO PARTICIPATED: Input from 5,039 frequent diners forms the basis for the ratings and reviews in this guide (their comments are shown in quotation marks within the reviews). Of these surveyors, 46% are women, 54% men; the breakdown by age is 7% in their 20s; 24%, 30s; 25%, 40s; 27%, 50s; and 17%, 60s or above. Collectively they bring roughly 1,050,000 annual meals worth of experience to this Survey. We sincerely thank each of these participants - this book is really "theirs."

HELPFUL LISTS: See top lists for Austin and the Hill Country (pages 11-16), Dallas/Ft. Worth (pages 76-82), Houston (pages 179-186) and San Antonio (pages 281-286). We've also provided 125 indexes.

OUR EDITORS: Special thanks go to our local editors, Claudia Alarcón, a contributor to the *Austin Chronicle* and to *Austin Monthly* magazine; Mike Riccetti, author of *Houston Dining on the Cheap* and a contributor to *My Table* magazine and to *Where the Locals Eat* guide; Julia Celeste Rosenfeld, the dining writer for *San Antonio Magazine*; and Kay Winzenried, a culinary/wine travel consultant and freelance writer.

ABOUT ZAGAT: This marks our 29th year reporting on the shared experiences of consumers like you. What started in 1979 as a hobby involving 200 of our friends has come a long way. Today we have well over 300,000 surveyors and now cover dining, entertaining, golf, hotels, movies, music, nightlife, resorts, shopping, spas, theater and tourist attractions worldwide.

SHARE YOUR OPINION: We invite you to join any of our upcoming surveys - just register at **ZAGAT.com,** where you can rate and review establishments year-round. Each participant will receive a free copy of the resulting guide when published.

AVAILABILITY: Zagat guides are available in all major bookstores, by subscription at **ZAGAT.com** and for use on web-enabled mobile devices via **ZAGAT TO GO** or **ZAGAT.mobi.** The latter two products allow you to contact any establishment by phone with one click.

FEEDBACK: There is always room for improvement, thus we invite your comments and suggestions about any aspect of our performance. Is there something more you would like us to include in our guides? We really need your input! Just contact us at **texas@zagat.com.**

New York, NY
March 20, 2008

Nina and Tim

Nina and Tim Zagat

What's New

Texas has always been synonymous with big – big distances, big personalities and big appetites. Indeed, Texas surveyors lead the country in average number of restaurant meals eaten per week, with those in Houston (4.2), Dallas/Ft. Worth (4.0) and San Antonio (4.0) topping the list and Austin (3.7) not far behind. Dallas/Ft. Worth also lays claim to the highest average Food and Service rating in the U.S. (though in Texas, as elsewhere, surveyors cite service as an overall weak link). And as Texas' five largest cities continue to expand, so do their dining options, bringing a bevy of new restaurants to both their recently revitalized Downtowns and their outskirts. Given that 87% of our surveyors say they'd drive at least a half-hour or more for a good meal, this sprawling setup suits most Texans just fine.

THE CREAM OF THE CAPITAL CITY CROP: While popular destinations like SoCo, Manor Road and Barton Springs' "Restaurant Row" continue to thrive, a new dining scene has developed around Northwest Austin's mammoth new retail and residential complex, The Domain, where openings include Daily Grill, Jasper's (from noted Dallas chef Kent Rathbun), Joe DiMaggio's Italian Chophouse and upscale tea shop The Steeping Room. Although many of those are chains, Austin also continues to nurture homegrown establishments, especially ones that make use of locally grown products, like Italian newcomer Sagra. Given that 59% of surveyors care whether food is locally grown and 51% are willing to pay more for sustainably raised food, expect more Austin chefs to follow the Green-centric lead of Wink's Mark Paul and Zoot's Stewart Scruggs, who nurture relationships with small suppliers and are often spotted shopping at the city's farmer's markets.

DALLAS AND FT. WORTH FIREWORKS: The Big D welcomed an influx of A-list chefs: Charlie Palmer debuted his New American namesake at the Joule Hotel, Laurent Tourondel opened a sleek new BLT Steak in the Galleria and Victory Park saw the arrival of Tom Colicchio's Craft. Dean Fearing (ex Mansion on Turtle Creek) reentered the scene with his eponymous restaurant at the new Ritz-Carlton, and soon to join him Uptown will be chef David Bull (ex Austin's Driskill Grill), who is opening Bolla, an Italian, at the Stoneleigh Hotel. Emerging neighborhoods in southern Dallas and Ft. Worth are also flourishing: Tillman's Roadhouse, a sassy American, is headlining in the Bishop Street Arts area, while the Italian Nonna Tata is drawing diners to Ft. Worth's Hospital District scene. Out in the suburbs, American venues like Olenjack's in Arlington and Michael Anthony's in Southlake are hitting their stride. As for cuisines, Japanese restaurants are now outscoring many Tex-Mex *cocinas,* BBQ joints and steakhouses that were long-reigning Dallas/Ft. Worth favorites, something unthinkable only a few years ago. For example, relative newcomer Yutaka has muscled its way into the top 10 for Food, where it joins established hits Tei Tei Robata Bar and Teppo Yakitori. Also fueling the trend are the Galleria's swanky new SushiSamba and Downtown Ft. Worth's plucky Piranha, where it seems impossible to snare a table – anytime.

HOUSTON HAPPENINGS: 2008 kicked off with one of Southwestern cuisine's founding stars, Robert Del Grande, opening The Grove in Downtown's Discovery Green development with Ryan Pera, formerly of 17, at the helm. Another highly anticipated newcomer, Reef, is delivering innovative seafood in a refreshingly unpretentious Midtown space, helping to reinforce the local trend of casualness in fine-dining restaurants. Washington Avenue continues to mature as an adult playground with more restaurants like Monica Pope's ambitious barbecue joint, Beaver's, and Soma, a new Japanese-French concept from the folks behind Azuma. The popular Uptown Sushi spawned a spin-off, Blue Fin, and just as the appetite for sushi continues unabated, so does the trend for small plates, exemplified by new wine bar SoVino. The suburbs welcomed a slew of stylish new eateries including Neapolitan-rooted Amici in Sugar Land with its Vallone family pedigree, French-influenced Aura in Missouri City and Pearland's Killen's Steakhouse. In Southwest Houston along Bellaire Boulevard in Alief, New Chinatown prospers with establishments like South Asians Jasmine and Tan Tan.

SAN ANTONIO EXPANSION: The ongoing progress in San Antonio's Northside neighborhoods has prompted some in-town haunts, such as Bistro Thyme, to pick up and move to outer Loop 1604, while others, like Aldaco's and Silo, are opening branches in the area. Joining them there this year will be La Frite chef Damien Watel, who promises a casual Continental bistro in the far northern reaches, and chef Scott Cohen (ex Las Canarias and Pesca) who is bringing his affinity for local ingredients to his new role as corporate chef for the Watermark Hotel Company.

MONEY MATTERS: Dallas diners spend an average of $34.61 per meal, considerably more than the average tabs in Austin ($26.74), Houston ($29.10) and San Antonio ($27.33) but not much higher than the U.S. average of $33.67. Overall, price increases since our last Survey were modest, ranging from 1.4% annualized in San Antonio to 3.8% in Houston. However, inflation at the top 20 most expensive eateries was more pronounced: 7.6% annualized in Austin, 3.8% in Dallas/Ft. Worth, 5.5% in Houston and 6.7% in San Antonio. Not surprisingly, 66% of Texas surveyors say they spend more per meal than they did two years ago. But high prices certainly haven't kept them home – 85% say they're still eating out as much or more than they did two years ago.

Austin, TX	Claudia Alarcón
Dallas, TX	Kay Winzenried
Houston, TX	Mike Riccetti
San Antonio, TX	Julia Celeste Rosenfeld
March 20, 2008	

AUSTIN AND THE HILL COUNTRY

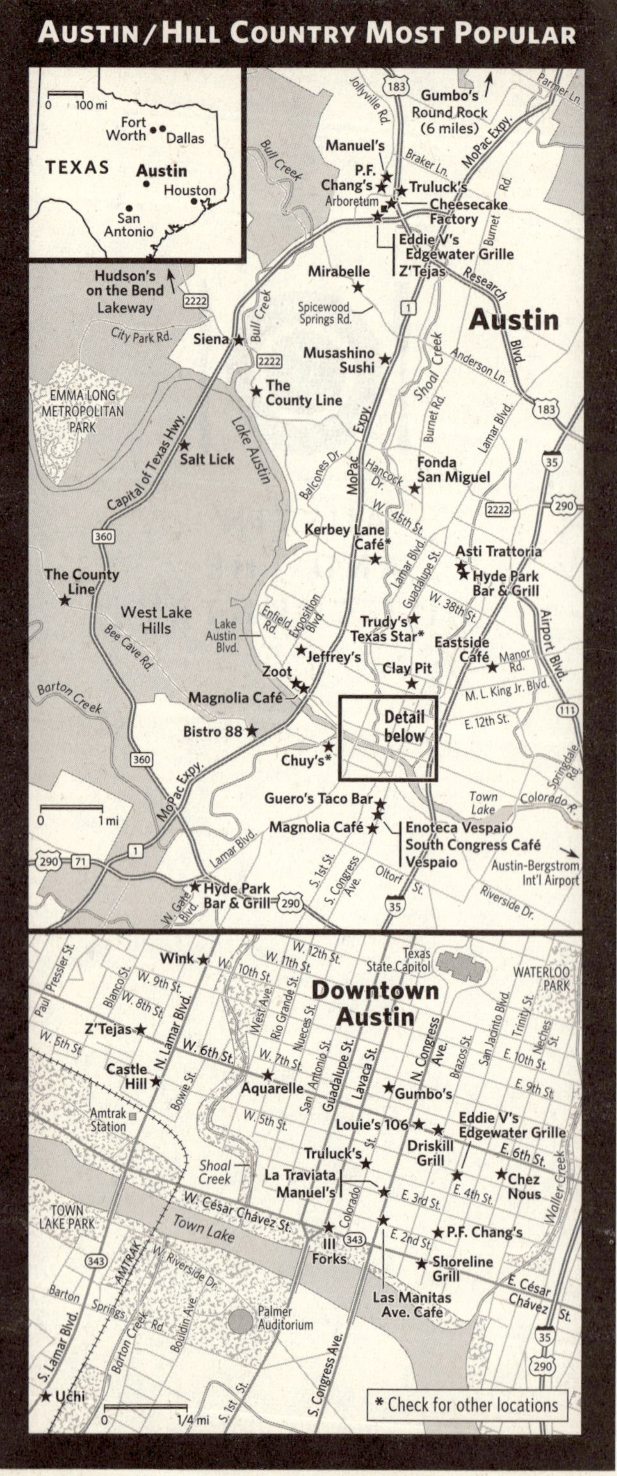
Austin / Hill Country Most Popular
TEXAS
Austin
Fort Worth
Dallas
Houston
San Antonio
Gumbo's Round Rock (6 miles)
Manuel's
P.F. Chang's
Truluck's
Arboretum
Cheesecake Factory
Eddie V's Edgewater Grille
Z'Tejas
Mirabelle
Hudson's on the Bend Lakeway
Siena
Musashino Sushi
The County Line
EMMA LONG METROPOLITAN PARK
Salt Lick
Fonda San Miguel
Kerbey Lane Café*
Asti Trattoria
Hyde Park Bar & Grill
The County Line
West Lake Hills
Trudy's Texas Star*
Jeffrey's
Eastside Café
Zoot
Clay Pit
Magnolia Café
Bistro 88
Detail below
Chuy's*
Guero's Taco Bar
Magnolia Café
Enoteca Vespaio
South Congress Café
Vespaio
Austin-Bergstrom Int'l Airport
Hyde Park Bar & Grill
Town Lake
Downtown Austin
Wink
Texas State Capitol
WATERLOO PARK
Z'Tejas
Castle Hill
Aquarelle
Gumbo's
Amtrak Station
Louie's 106
Eddie V's Edgewater Grille
Driskill Grill
Truluck's
La Traviata
Manuel's
Chez Nous
III Forks
P.F. Chang's
Shoreline Grill
Las Manitas Ave. Cafe
TOWN LAKE PARK
Town Lake
Palmer Auditorium
Uchi
* Check for other locations

Most Popular

1. Vespaio
2. Eddie V's
3. Chuy's
4. Uchi
5. Salt Lick
6. Fonda San Miguel
7. Wink
8. Driskill Grill
9. Hudson's
10. Clay Pit
11. Z'Tejas
12. Chez Nous
13. Castle Hill
14. Jeffrey's
15. Trudy's
16. Kerbey Ln. Café
17. Aquarelle
18. P.F. Chang's
19. County Line
20. Siena
21. Hyde Park B&G
22. Guero's
23. Truluck's
24. III Forks
25. Asti Trattoria
26. Eastside Café*
27. Gumbo's
28. Mirabelle*
29. Las Manitas Ave. Cafe
30. Manuel's*
31. Cheesecake Factory
32. Enoteca Vespaio*
33. Louie's 106
34. Musashino Sushi*
35. La Traviata
36. Magnolia Café*
37. Shoreline Grill
38. South Congress Café*
39. Bistro 88
40. Zoot

It's obvious that many of the above restaurants are among the Austin area's most expensive, but if popularity were calibrated to price, we suspect that a number of other restaurants would join their ranks. Thus, we have added a list of 40 Best Buys on page 16. These are restaurants that give real quality at extremely reasonable prices.

KEY NEWCOMERS

Our editors' take on the most notable new arrivals of the past year. For a full list, see the Noteworthy Newcomers index on page 68.

Daily Grill

Estancia Churrascaria

Jasper's

Joe DiMaggio's

NoRTH

Sagra

Steeping Room

III Forks

Trattoria Lisinia

TRIO

* Indicates a tie with restaurant above

Top Food (Based on a 30-pt. scale)

Excludes places with low votes, unless indicated by a ∇.

28 Uchi
Hudson's
Vespaio

27 Wink
TRIO
Cooper's
Musashino
Aquarelle

26 Fonda San Miguel
Driskill Grill
Eddie V's
Zoot
Kreuz Mkt.
Jeffrey's
Café Josie

25 Enoteca Vespaio
Tacodeli
Louie Mueller
Chez Nous
Ruth's Chris
Castle Hill
Bistro 88
Mirabelle
Roy's
Siena
Starlite
III Forks

24 Gumbo's
Jasper's
Eastside Café
Roaring Fork
Salt Lick
Southside Mkt.
Shoreline Grill
Louie's 106
Fleming's
Sullivan's
Vin Bistro
Asti Trattoria
Din Ho Chinese

BY CUISINE

AMERICAN (NEW)

28 Hudson's
27 Wink
TRIO
26 Driskill Grill
Zoot

AMERICAN (TRAD.)

23 Houston's
22 1886 Café
21 Magnolia Café
Dirty Martin's
Hyde Park

BARBECUE

27 Cooper's Old Time
26 Kreuz Mkt.
25 Louie Mueller BBQ
24 Salt Lick
Southside Mkt.

ITALIAN

28 Vespaio
25 Enoteca Vespaio
24 Asti Trattoria
La Traviata
23 Taverna Pizzeria

MEXICAN

26 Fonda San Miguel
25 Tacodeli
22 El Chile
Manuel's
21 Curra's

SEAFOOD

26 Eddie V's
23 Pappadeaux
Truluck's
Fin & Porter
21 McCormick & Schmick's

SOUTHWESTERN

24 Roaring Fork
23 Ranch 616
22 South Congress Café
Z'Tejas
19 Cool River Cafe

STEAKHOUSES

26 Eddie V's
25 Ruth's Chris
III Forks
24 Fleming's
Sullivan's

TEX-MEX

21 Chuy's
20 Trudy's
19 Vivo
18 Matt's El Rancho
Hula Hut

BY SPECIAL FEATURE

BREAKFAST

24 Judges' Hill
22 1886 Café
21 Magnolia Café
Curra's Grill
Taco Xpress

BRUNCH

26 Fonda San Miguel
25 Enoteca Vespaio
24 Eastside Café
Judges' Hill
23 Green Pastures

BUSINESS DINING

28 Uchi
Hudson's
27 Musashino
Aquarelle
24 Jasper's

CHILD-FRIENDLY

24 Eastside Café
Salt Lick
Din Ho Chinese
23 Hilltop Café
Ruby's

MEET FOR A DRINK

28 Vespaio
27 TRIO
26 Eddie V's
25 Starlite
24 Jasper's

NEWCOMERS (RATED)

27 TRIO
Estância▽
24 Jasper's
Daily Grill▽
20 Kona Grill

OFFBEAT

23 Ranch 616
Hut's
21 Magnolia Café
Taco Xpress
Chuy's

PEOPLE-WATCHING

25 Chez Nous
23 Home Slice
22 1886 Café
Z'Tejas
21 Frank & Angie's

POWER SCENES

27 TRIO
26 Driskill Grill
Eddie V's
25 Ruth's Chris
24 Jasper's

QUICK BITES

27 Cooper's
26 Kreuz Mkt.
25 Louie Mueller
24 Southside Mkt.
23 Home Slice

QUIET CONVERSATION

27 Aquarelle
26 Driskill Grill
Zoot
Jeffrey's
25 Chez Nous

SINGLES SCENES

26 Eddie V's
24 Sullivan's
23 Finn & Porter
22 South Congress Café
21 Chuy's

TRENDY

28 Uchi
Vespaio
27 Wink
TRIO
26 Eddie V's

WINNING WINE LISTS

28 Hudson's
Vespaio
27 Wink
Aquarelle
24 Vin Bistro

BY LOCATION

ARBORETUM

26 Eddie V's
23 Truluck's
22 P.F. Chang's
Z'Tejas
20 Kerbey Ln. Café

CAMPUS/WEST CAMPUS

24 Judges' Hill
23 Fino
21 Dirty Martin's
Madam Mam's
20 Kerbey Ln. Café

CHERRYWOOD/EAST AUSTIN

24 Eastside Café
22 El Chile
Ms. B's
21 Hoover's
19 Vivo

CLARKSVILLE/OLD WEST AUSTIN

27 Wink
26 Zoot
Jeffrey's
Café Josie
22 Z'Tejas

DOWNTOWN

27 TRIO
Aquarelle
26 Driskill Grill
Eddie V's
25 Chez Nous

NW AUSTIN/NW HILLS

27 Musashino
25 Tacodeli
Mirabelle
Siena
24 Jasper's

SOUTH CONGRESS (SOCO)

28 Vespaio
25 Enoteca Vespaio
23 Home Slice
22 South Congress Café
21 Magnolia Café

WAREHOUSE DISTRICT

25 Starlite
24 Sullivan's
23 Truluck's
22 Kenichi
21 219 West

WEST LAKE HILLS

25 Bistro 88
21 Las Palomas
20 County Line
Thai Kitchen
19 Suzi's

ZILKER

28 Uchi
21 Chuy's
19 Shady Grove
18 Green Mesquite
17 Romeo's

Top Decor (Based on a 30-pt. scale)

27 Fonda San Miguel
Siena
Driskill Grill

26 Uchi

25 Jasper's
Judges' Hill
Green Pastures

24 Shoreline Grill
Aquarelle
Roaring Fork
Hudson's
III Forks
Eddie V's
Fino
Oasis, The
Belmont, The
TRIO
1886 Café
Roy's
Fleming's

OUTDOORS

Fino
Jasper's
Joe DiMaggio's
Mars
Moonshine
NoRTH
Shady Grove
Shoreline Grill
Trattoria Lisina
TRIO

ROMANCE

Aquarelle
Bess
Carmelo's
Chez Nous
Driskill Grill
Sagra
Shoreline Grill
Siena
Starlite
Zoot

ROOMS

Aquarelle
Belmont, The
Bess
Driskill Grill
Fonda San Miguel
Joe DiMaggio's
Judges' Hill
Ranch 616
Siena
Woodland, The

VIEWS

County Line
Eddie V's
Hilltop Café
Hula Hut
Oasis, The
Salt Lick
Shoreline Grill
Trattoria Lisina
TRIO
Z'Tejas

Top Service (Based on a 30-pt. scale)

26 Hudson's
Driskill Grill
Jeffrey's
Wink
TRIO

25 Uchi
Zoot*
Eddie V's
Ruth's Chris
Aquarelle

24 Vespaio
Fonda San Miguel
Green Pastures
III Forks
Shoreline Grill
Louie's 106
Jasper's
Mirabelle

23 Roaring Fork
Sullivan's

Best Buys

In order of Bang for the Buck rating.

1. Tacodeli
2. Taco Xpress
3. Dirty Martin's
4. Hut's
5. Player's
6. Texas Chili
7. Mangieri's
8. Las Manitas Ave. Cafe
9. Meyer's
10. Ruby's BBQ
11. Frank & Angie's
12. Home Slice
13. Kreuz Mkt.
14. Golden Wok
15. Magnolia Café
16. Shady Grove
17. Kerbey Ln. Café
18. Pei Wei
19. Chuy's
20. El Sol y La Luna

OTHER GOOD VALUES

Alborz
Chez Nous
Crosstown BBQ
Din Ho Chinese
El Azteca
El Chile
El Mesón
Elsie's
Evangeline Café
Flip Happy Crepes
Gene's
Gypsy Italian Bistro
Hoover's
Korea House
Oaxacan Tamaleo
Opal Divine's
Quality Seafood
Sunflower
Ventana
Zax Pints

FOOD | DECOR | SERVICE | COST

Austin and the Hill Country

Abuelo's Mexican Food Embassy *Mexican* 19 | 21 | 19 | $21

Southwest Austin | Barton Creek Square Mall | 2901 Capital of Texas Hwy. (Mo-Pac Expwy.) | 512-306-0857 | www.abuelos.com

A "cut above" is how fans sum up this "better-than-typical chain Mexican" offering a few "unique items" along with the standards; some say the service is "hit-or-miss", but their "atmosphere is nicer than most" examples of the genre, with many branches boasting "interesting artwork" "for your viewing pleasure."

Alborz *Persian* 21 | 13 | 18 | $19

Northwest Austin | Shoal Creek Plaza | 3300 W. Anderson Ln. (Mo-Pac Expwy.) | 512-420-2222 | www.alborzpersiancuisine.com

The "authentic menu" of "delightfully different" Persian cuisine "with a focus on wonderfully spiced vegetable dishes" is "nicely served" by a "friendly staff" at this "relaxing spot" in Northwest Austin; perhaps the ambiance "isn't great" due to the "strip-mall location", but many "enjoy" the "tantalizing" scenery offered by the "occasional belly dancer" (Friday and Saturday evenings).

Aquarelle *French* 27 | 24 | 25 | $58

Downtown | 606 Rio Grande St. (6th St.) | 512-479-8117 | www.aquarellerestaurant.com

"Set in a lovely cottage", this "family-run" Downtown "oasis" is consistently called "the best French restaurant in town" thanks to its "impressive wine list" and "excellent", "creatively prepared and presented food"; add in service that most find "near-perfect" (a few dissenters say "arrogant") and an "upscale, enchanting" vibe, and you've got what may be "hands down the most romantic setting" for "special occasions"; P.S. the new adjacent wine bar is a "welcome development" for diners who want a lower-key, more affordable experience.

Artz Rib House *BBQ* 21 | 10 | 18 | $18

South Lamar | 2330 S. Lamar Blvd. (Bluebonnet Ln.) | 512-442-8283 | www.artzribhouse.com

"Authentic slow-smoked" meats and "lipsmacking" ribs please the masses at this "quintessential" South Lamar BBQ joint; "never mind the decor" that feels a bit "like a run-down shack" because fair prices, "cold beverages" and "live local music" make for an "enjoyable", "low-key" night out nonetheless.

Asti Trattoria *Italian* 24 | 19 | 22 | $31

Hyde Park | 408C E. 43rd St. (bet. Ave. H & Duval St.) | 512-451-1218 | www.astiaustin.com

This "happening" Hyde Park "neighborhood trattoria" is "not your grandma's spaghetti and meatballs kind of place", but instead serves an "innovative" menu featuring "organic, locally grown produce" alongside a "fabuloso" wine list, all at a "fair" price; a team of "attentive but not overbearing servers" works the "tiny" room, which is done up in "minimalist", "modern" decor.

August E's M *Steak* ▽ 27 | 23 | 24 | $50

Fredericksburg | 203 E. San Antonio St. (S. Llano St.) | 830-997-1585 | www.august-es.com

"Heavenly!" hail acolytes of this "upscale" Fredericksburg "gem" with "succulent steaks that melt in your mouth" and a wine list that's "fantastic"; its "lovely" "Western-elegant ambiance" is enhanced by "added touches" like servers who know "the proper way to pamper and make you feel special"; N.B. the Decor score may not fully reflect a recent move.

Austin Land & Cattle Co. *Steak* 22 | 17 | 21 | $39

Downtown | 1205 N. Lamar Blvd. (bet. Shoal Creek Blvd. & 12th St.) | 512-472-1813 | www.austinlandandcattlecompany.com

Long "a favorite of politicians and lobbyists", this "authentic Texan steakhouse" strikes supporters as "the real McCoy" - and a "great local" alternative to the "chain" spots - for its "savory" steaks, "consistent" side dishes (included in the "moderate prices") and "excellent" service; some find its Downtown location's "old Austin" atmosphere "dated, even by your parents standards", but most maintain it offers "more bang for the buck than the competitors."

Backstage Steakhouse M *Steak* ▽ 26 | 18 | 22 | $33

Spicewood | 21814 Hwy. 71 W. (Crawford Rd.) | 512-264-2223 | www.backstagesteakhouseaustin.com

A Hill Country "gem" "in the little town of Spicewood", this "high-quality" Southwestern steakhouse serves "creative, impressive" eats in a "casual setting" manned by a "comfortable, relaxed" crew; regulars "come back for the warmth and the food", ensuring a "laid-back Texas atmosphere" in which "everyone knows everyone else"; P.S. on weekends "be sure to eat outside under the oak tree" and listen to the "cool" "live music."

Bee Cave Bistro M *American* ▽ 20 | 16 | 19 | $24

Bee Cave | 11715 FM 2244 (Hwy. 71) | 512-263-1950

Nestled in the heart of Bee Cave, this neighborhood bistro dishes out "consistently scrumptious" American food with a "local" twist; the quaint, country-style quarters are "a good place for business" during lunchtime or quiet conversation at dinner, though a minority calls it "nothing special for the price."

Bellagio S *Italian* 21 | 19 | 23 | $39

Jester Village | 6507 Jester Blvd. (Rte. 2222) | 512-346-8228 | www.bellagioitalianbistro.com

Located in an "off-the-beaten-path" shopping center, this "upscale" Jester Village trattoria is an "island of Italian bliss in a suburban sea", offering "always consistent" cuisine served by "very attentive" waiters; even detractors who decry the "cramped" dining room that "feels like a senior citizens' home" insist that the staff's "food and wine recommendations make up for the lack in ambiance."

Belmont, The *American* 18 | 24 | 18 | $28

Downtown | 305 W. Sixth St. (Lavaca St.) | 512-457-0300 | www.thebelmontaustin.com

"Frank Sinatra would love this place" swoon acolytes of the "retro-cool", "swanky" Downtown "hangout" featuring "rooftop views" and a "sumptuous Rat Pack vibe"; although the midpriced, classic American fare is "pretty good" and "service is knowledgeable", most say that dinner here is "not the main draw" - people come "for cocktails" and to "see and be seen."

Bess *Eclectic* 17 | 23 | 18 | $32

Downtown | 500 W. Sixth St. (San Antonio St.) | 512-477-2377 | www.bessbistro.com

Sandra Bullock's "basement bistro" is a "Downtown jewel" serving "solid" Eclectic "comfort food" in a "cozy", "dark" and "romantic" setting that's "surprisingly casual and unpretentious"; fans fawn over the "beautiful" decor and "friendly, helpful staff", though a few gripe that it's "a bit noisy", "overpriced" and "popular more because of the famous owner than the food"; P.S. "go at lunch to skip the wait."

Billy's on Burnet ◐ *American* ∇ 20 | 13 | 19 | $14

Rosedale | 2105 Hancock Dr. (Burnet Rd.) | 512-407-9305 | www.billysonburnet.com

"Awesome burgers" plus "creative low-cal/veggie options" and other affordable American classics are the mainstay at this "great neighborhood bar" and "family-friendly tavern" in Rosedale, where the "patio is full of jovial locals from all walks of life"; though there's "no decor to write home about", it's a "good gathering spot" and a "great place to watch a game" or to "bring your dog and sit outside."

Bistro 88 *Asian/European* 25 | 20 | 23 | $41

West Lake Hills | 2712 Bee Caves Rd. (Edgegrove Dr.) | 512-328-8888 | www.bistro88austin.com

"Superior presentation and quality" mark the "interesting" Asian-European fusion menu at this West Lake Hills Asian favorite, featuring a "well-thought-out" wine list; behind its "nondescript strip-center" facade lies an "elegant", "comfortable" interior, presided over by "quick yet personalized" service, so it's no wonder that, despite somewhat "expensive" tabs, most voters vow it's "absolutely wonderful . . . every time."

Blue Star Cafeteria *American* 20 | 19 | 19 | $20

Rosedale | Rosedale Shopping Ctr. | 4800 Burnet Rd. (bet. 47th & 49th Sts.) | 512-454-7827 | www.bluestarcafeteria.com

This "nice neighborhood" relative newcomer in Rosedale is "far from a cafeteria", since "you get table service" and "good" affordable American "comfort food with a modern twist"; the staff is "competent" and "friendly", and the "retro" digs are "stylish", just know that the space is "usually crowded", meaning it can get "so loud at peak times that you can't even taste your food."

Brick Oven *Pizza* 19 | 14 | 18 | $17

Brykerwoods | 1608 W. 35th St. (Glenview Ave.) | 512-453-4330 | www.brickovenon35th.com
Downtown | 1209 Red River St. (12th St.) | 512-477-7006 | www.brickovenrestaurant.com
Great Hills | 10710 Research Blvd. (Braker Ln.) | 512-345-6181 | www.brickovenrestaurant.com
Southwest Austin | 9911 Brodie Ln. (Slaughter Ln.) | 512-292-3939 | www.brickovenrestaurant.com

"Tasty pizzas straight from the brick oven" make for "heavenly smells" at this local chain known for its "crispy-crusted" creations; as for the rest of its "basic Italian" fare, most surveyors find it "satisfying" (if somewhat "unexciting"), though the "spotty" service has fewer fans.

Buster's Bar-B-Que M *BBQ* ▽ 24 | 13 | 20 | $15

Bee Cave | 3927 R.R. 620 S. (Rte. 71) | 512-263-3999 | www.bustersbeecavebbq.com

Set inside an "old VFW hall" in Bee Cave , this unpretentious, friendly joint serves "innovative BBQ dishes" and "some of the best brisket in Central Texas"; stop by on your way to the lake to lap up the "authentic atmosphere", which is enlivened by "good music on Friday nights."

Café Josie S M *Caribbean* 26 | 20 | 23 | $34

Clarksville | Pecan Sq. | 1200 W. Sixth St. (Blanco Rd.) | 512-322-9226 | www.cafejosie.com

This "locally owned" "hidden gem" in Clarksville serves up "wonderful Caribbean creations" including "some of the best-dressed fish in town" and a "reasonable, eclectic wine list"; add in its "relaxing, slow-paced" atmosphere and "intimate", "beautiful space", and you get a "sublime blend" of food and decor, further complemented by "very good service."

Café 909 S M *American* ▽ 29 | 23 | 27 | $45

Marble Falls | 909 Second St. (Main St.) | 830-693-2126 | www.cafe909.com

"A real backstreet haute surprise", this "outstanding" Hill Country outpost set in the "sleepy fried-food/BBQ town of Marble Falls" is "worth the drive" thanks to an "exquisite menu" of "sophisticated" New American fare featuring "creative takes on Texas ingredients"; the staffers "take pride in their knowledge of wine pairings", leading devotees to say it sets "the new standard by which upscale restaurants should be measured."

Cantina Laredo *Mexican* 21 | 20 | 20 | $23

Downtown | 201 W. Third St. (Colorado St.) | 512-542-9670 | www.cantinalaredo.com

See review in Dallas/Ft. Worth Directory.

Carmelo's *Italian* 22 | 22 | 22 | $35

Downtown | 504 E. Fifth St. (Red River St.) | 512-477-7497 | www.carmelosrestaurant.com

The "smell of roasting garlic pervades the air" at this "family-owned" West Houston and Downtown Austin midpriced duo where "exquisitely prepared" "old-school" Italian cookery is served by a "very attentive" staff; the "romantic ambiance" is enhanced by "soft lighting" and live accordion music on some nights, making them a prime choice for "special occasions", "business lunches", "date-night dinners" or "to share an evening with one - or several friends."

Carrabba's Italian Grill *Italian* 22 19 22 $28

North Austin | 11590 Research Blvd. (Braker Ln.) | 512-345-8232
Travis Heights | 6406 I-35 N. (bet. Anderson & Koenig Lns.) | 512-419-1220
www.carrabbas.com
See review in Houston Directory.

Castle Hill 🅂 *Eclectic* 25 20 23 $32

Downtown | 1101 W. Fifth St. (Baylor St.) | 512-476-0728 | www.castlehillcafe.com

The Eclectic menu at this "nice but casual" Downtown Austin "institution" changes monthly, but always features "lots of original", "flavorful" fare served alongside a "great", "reasonably priced" wine list; "knowledgeable" servers work the "classy" yet "colorful" space, which regulars say is "great" for "power lunches" - so while it "can be loud during peak periods", most concur that it's "very inviting" all around.

Cedar Grove Steakhouse 🄼 *Steak* - - - M

Wimberley | 9595 R.R. 12 (R.R. 32) | 512-847-3113 | www.cedargrovesteakhouse.com

Fans toast this "fun and quirky" Wimberley Steakhouse as "one of the best, if not the best, in the Austin area" thanks to its "terrific food", "laid-back" vibe, and limestone building and terraces that scream 'Texas!'; the aged Angus steaks are cut in-house to guarantee quality, and are matched with serious sides and wines from an affordable, full-of-surprises list.

Cheesecake Factory *American* 20 20 18 $26

Arboretum | Arboretum Mall | 10000 Research Blvd. (bet. Capital of Dallas Hwy. & Great Hills Trail) | 512-241-0777 | www.thecheesecakefactory.com
See review in Houston Directory.

Chez Nous 🄼 *French* 25 18 22 $33

Downtown | 510 Neches St. (6th St.) | 512-473-2413

A "favorite" for over 25 years, this "tiny" Downtown French "keepsake", "run by true Parisians", offers "classic bistro food" and a "cleverly selected" wine list at "awesome prices" (including a "wonderful prix fixe deal"); "friendly, casual" waiters with accents oversee the "unpretentious" digs, where the decor may be "lacking", but still, there's always a "very vibrant, cozy vibe."

Chez Zee American Bistro *American* 21 20 20 $26

Northwest Hills | 5406 Balcones Dr. (Parkcrest Dr.) | 512-454-2666 | www.chezzee.com

"Zee best combination of quality" eats, "fair prices" and "warm service" is how supporters sum up this "attractive" "haunt" in the

Northwest Hills, "a fun family place" that's "great for groups" of any variety thanks to a "festive" feel and "reliable" New American menu; it's especially "popular for brunch" on the weekends, but whenever you go be sure to "save room for" the "marvelous desserts."

Chuy's *Tex-Mex* 21 | 19 | 19 | $18

Great Hills | 11680 Research Blvd. (Duval Rd.) | 512-342-0011
North Austin | 10520 N. Lamar Blvd. (Meadows Dr.) | 512-836-3218
Zilker | 1728 Barton Springs Rd. (Lamar Blvd.) | 512-474-4452
Round Rock | 2320 I-35 N. (Old Settlers Blvd.) | 512-255-2211
www.chuys.com

"Gargantuan" plates of "tasty" Tex-Mex fare come with a side of "kitsch" at this "lovable" "local" chain where "funky" "Elvis-obsessed" decor and "awesome margaritas" add to the "playful" atmosphere; in spite of "interminable waits", "cheap" prices make it a "favorite of university students", "singles" and "families" alike; P.S. the Zilker branch in Austin was "the site of the Bush daughters' underage drinking snafu."

Cibo *Italian* 20 | 18 | 19 | $38

Downtown | 918 Congress Ave. (10th St.) | 512-478-3663 | www.ciborestaurant.com

A "welcome addition" to Downtown's dining scene, chef Will Packwood's newest venture showcases "adventurous", "imaginative Italian" eats in a "high-style but relaxed", "arty" environment; critics complain that the "portions are small" and pricey, and the decor feels "really sterile", though few find fault with the "nice staff" that provides "simple but effective service."

City Market *BBQ* ▽ 24 | 8 | 13 | $15

Luling | 633 E. Davis St. (Magnolia St.) | 830-875-9019

A true "landmark" that's considered "Luling's claim to fame", this "BBQ mecca" is a "foodie wonderland" thanks to its "glorious sausage, ribs and brisket"; there's "no service" since you "order at the counter", and the "old general store" environs aren't much to look at, but still aficionados are willing to "fight any man who doesn't think this is Texas' best BBQ"; P.S. check out the "great play area outside for kids."

Clay Pit: Contemporary Indian Cuisine *Indian* 23 | 20 | 19 | $25

Downtown | 1601 Guadalupe St. (16th St.) | 512-322-5131 | www.claypit.com

"Traditional" Indian dishes are prepared with "modern" (some say "Americanized") "twists" at these "upscale" eateries where the "extensive wine and cocktail list" and "friendly", if sometimes "haphazard" service makes for an "overall satisfying experience"; the Addison branch features a waterwall and a dining room draped in saris, while the Downtown Austin outpost is housed in a "cool", "historic" building; the "reasonably priced lunch buffet" reigns at both locations.

Cool River Cafe *Southwestern/Steak* 19 21 20 $38

Northwest Austin | 4001 W. Parmer Ln. (Amherst Dr.) | 512-835-0010 | www.coolrivercafe.com

"Part restaurant, part singles pickup joint", this upscale Southwestern steakhouse chain is a "meat market in more ways than one" - thanks, no doubt, to the presence of a "loud and hopping bar" with cigar room, pool tables, live music (Thursday-Saturday) and "pretty people galore"; though "too pricey for everyday eating", the "great", "original food" is "actually a highlight", as it's "creatively and well prepared, while still managing to be hearty in size."

Cooper's Old Time Pit Bar-B-Que *BBQ* 27 11 17 $17

Llano | 604 W. Young St. (Ashley Ave.) | 325-247-5713 | www.coopersbbq.com

Look for the "smoke rising" and you'll know you're close to this "huge" "BBQ heaven" in Llano, where "selecting your meat from the outside pits" and eating at "picnic tables" is de rigueur; the food is "awesome", its no-frills atmosphere "ain't fancy but it's the real thing" and "cowboys and motorcycle dudes abound", so "get there early if you don't like waiting in line."

County Line, The *BBQ* 20 18 19 $23

Northwest Hills | 5204 Rte. 2222 (Capital of Texas Hwy.) | 512-346-3664

West Lake Hills | 6500 W. Bee Caves Rd. (Knollwood Dr.) | 512-327-1742

www.countyline.com

See review in San Antonio Directory.

Crosstown Bar-B-Q *BBQ* - - - I

Elgin | 202 S. Ave. C (Austin St.) | 512-281-5594

Funky and no-frills, this Downtown Elgin shack may not be the best known BBQ place in town, but it's possibly the most authentic; friendly counter folk serve up giant beef ribs, peppery pork ribs and brisket with all the classic sides, and there's tangy, spicy BBQ sauce on the table; N.B. locals suggest washing it down with sweet iced tea or an ice-cold Big Red.

Crú Wine Bar *American* 20 23 21 $34

Downtown | 238 W. Second St. (Lavaca St.) | 512-472-9463 | www.cruawinebar.com

See review in Dallas/Ft. Worth Directory.

Curra's Grill *Mexican* 21 14 16 $17

Travis Heights | 614 E. Oltorf St. (Eastside Dr.) | 512-444-0012 | www.currasgrill.com

There's "none of that Tex-Mex Velveeta baloney" at these "lively" "family" spots that feature "authentic" Mexican dishes, including "many veg options", and a "large variety of margaritas" ("the creamy, yummy avocado" variety is "a must-have"), all at a "fantastic value"; on the other hand, "decor is minimal - and not in a good way" - plus "service can be slow during peak hours"; N.B. a North Austin branch is currently in the works.

	FOOD	DECOR	SERVICE	COST
NEW Daily Grill *American*	▽ 24	25	26	$30

Northwest Austin | Domain, The | 11506 Century Oaks Terr. (Braker Ln.) | 512-836-4200 | www.dailygrill.com

"Simple" American food is "done extremely well" at this new outpost of the California-based chain in Northwest Austin's Domain shopping center; the 1930s-inflected atmosphere has a "fancy" feel befitting the relatively upmarket tabs and "great service"; N.B. the happy hour with $2 appetizers equals "happiness."

	FOOD	DECOR	SERVICE	COST
Din Ho Chinese BBQ *Chinese*	24	9	12	$15

North Austin | 8557 Research Blvd. (Fairfield Dr.) | 512-832-8788

"The first thing you notice is the BBQ stand with hanging ducks, chickens and pork" at this "good, cheap and fast" North Austin eatery whose "authentic Cantonese-style cuisine" is "about as real Chinese as it gets deep in the heart of Texas"; it may not be much to look at, but the "large round tables with lazy Susans are great for large parties" - and best of all it "stays open late."

	FOOD	DECOR	SERVICE	COST
Dirty Martin's Kum-Bak Place *Burgers*	21	12	16	$10

Campus | 2808 Guadalupe St. (28th St.) | 512-477-3173 | www.dirtymartins.com

"An Austin classic" since 1926, this inexpensive Campus-area "joint" is the epitome of a "greasy spoon" with "heavenly burgers", "hand-mixed" vanilla cokes and "some of the best malts and shakes" in town hustled by "friendly" counter staff; they've spiffed it up over the past few years, though it remains a "pre-game hangout" where "sports on the TVs" provides most of the atmosphere.

	FOOD	DECOR	SERVICE	COST
Doña Emilia's South American Bar & Grill M *S American*	20	18	19	$28

Downtown | 101 San Jacinto Blvd. (Cesar Chavez St.) | 512-478-2520 | www.donaemilias.com

"In a pretty setting" Downtown, this "upscale" spot dishes out a "wonderful blend" of South American dishes, including "delicious Colombian fare" and "selections you won't find anywhere else in Austin"; the wine list is interesting, and the "novel drinks" make it "a fun place for happy hour", plus there's "live music" on weekends; still, some suggest that the serving staff and kitchen "seem to have trouble handling large crowds"; N.B. reservations recommended.

	FOOD	DECOR	SERVICE	COST
Z Driskill Grill S M *American*	26	27	26	$63

Downtown | Driskill Hotel | 604 Brazos St. (6th St.) | 512-391-7162 | www.driskillgrill.com

"A sure winner" swear supporters of this Downtown destination inside the historic Driskill Hotel that "rivals the best restaurants of NY" with "amazing" New American cuisine, an "excellent wine list" and "solicitous service" to boot; the interior is "luxuriously appointed in true Texas style" with "rich woods" and portraits of politicians lining the walls setting an "elegant" scene for one of the "best dining experiences in Austin", and one that's well "worth" the "expensive" prices.

Eastside Café *American/Eclectic* 24 21 22 $26

Cherrywood | 2113 Manor Rd. (bet. Alamo & Coleto Sts.) | 512-476-5858 | www.eastsidecafeaustin.com

A "haven" for "wholesome" food, this Cherrywood "pioneer" "shows that healthy doesn't have to be boring" with an "amazing" menu of Eclectic-New American dishes featuring "fresh", organic produce and herbs harvested from their own gardens; it exudes a "homey" feel thanks to its "charming converted bungalow" setting, "friendly staff" and "fair prices."

Z Eddie V's Edgewater Grille *Seafood/Steak* 26 24 25 $49

Arboretum | 9400 Arboretum Blvd. (Capital of Texas Hwy.) | 512-342-2642

Downtown | 301 E. Fifth St. (San Jacinto Blvd.) | 512-472-1860 www.eddiev.com

Regulars "rave" about the "masterfully prepared" steaks and seafood presented by "professional" servers at these "high-end", "high-energy" Austin-area surf 'n' turfers; the Downtown branch boasts "great" live music and both cultivate a "clubby" atmosphere with leather booths and lots of wood that appeals to the "political crowd", "over-40 types" and "sorority girls" alike.

1886 Café *American* 22 24 21 $28

Downtown | Driskill Hotel | 604 Brazos St. (6th St.) | 512-391-7066 | www.driskillhotel.com

Enthusiasts attest this "lively and historic" Downtown destination "tucked into a corner" of The Driskill Hotel is "a must" for "classic" American cuisine with a "Texas twist", including "decadent" breakfasts, "civilized" lunches and "fantastic" pastries that sate any "sweet tooth"; though a few find it a little "pricey", insiders insist "it's worth a visit" even if just to gaze at the "palatial" "cattle baronesque" decor.

El Azteca ☒ *Tex-Mex* ▽ 18 12 15 $15

East Austin | 2600 E. Seventh St. (Calles St.) | 512-477-4701

For a true "mom-and-pop experience" or "one last Tex-Mex fix on the way to the airport", duck into this inexpensive, "small, family-owned" institution - "the only one of its kind in East Austin" - where "home-cooked flavors" abound (cabrito, or roasted goat, is a specialty) and "service is warm and friendly"; as for the "funky decor", think "Neo-Aztec warriors" and "virgin volcano sacrifice posters."

El Chile *Mexican* 22 17 17 $21

Cherrywood | 1809 Manor Rd. (Chicon St.) | 512-457-9900 | www.elchilecafe.com

"A standout among the plethora of Mexican restaurants in town", this small Cherrywood eatery serves "great drinks" and "superb, delicately prepared entrees" in a "cool, hip, fun" environment - and at "best-value" prices; critics complain that it gets "way too noisy" and say the staffers "try hard but are easily overwhelmed when it's crowded", yet all "enjoy" alfresco dining on the "nice deck" ("blankets are provided on cooler nights").

El Mercado *Tex-Mex* 15 | 14 | 16 | $15

Allandale | 7414 Burnet Rd. (Richcreek Rd.) | 512-454-2500
Bouldin Creek | 1302 S. First St. (Gibson St.) | 512-447-7445
Downtown | 1702 Lavaca St. (17th St.) | 512-477-7689
Northwest Austin | 13776 Hwy. 183 N. (Lake Creek Pkwy.) | 512-219-0232
www.elmercadorestaurant.com

Supporters of this "casual" local Tex-Mex chain favor its "reasonable" tabs, "large portions" and "good margaritas"; still, foes fault the "unspectacular" eats, "unmemorable decor" and "sketchy service", recommending you "go for drinks but dine elsewhere" – though at the Downtown and Northwest Austin branches you can do both via a "substantial appetizer buffet" that's "free during happy hour" with the purchase of an alcoholic beverage.

El Meson Taqueria *Mexican* ▽ 27 | 7 | 14 | $15

Southeast Austin | 5808 Burleson Rd. (Montopolis Dr.) | 512-416-0749

Intrepid eaters insist you "don't miss" this tiny, no-frills spot in Southeast Austin dishing out "delicious" "handmade" Mexican specialties like squash blossom quesadillas and boasting one of "the best breakfasts" around all at an "unbelievable price"; though it's "basically self service" (you pick up your order at the counter), all agree it's "worth the trip"; N.B. lunch only.

Elsi's *Mexican/Salvadoran* - | - | - | I

Brentwood | 6601 Burnet Rd. (Twin Oaks Dr.) | 512-454-0747 | www.elsisrestaurant.com

This colorful family-owned Brentwood eatery specializes in homey Mexican and Salvadoran staples – like pupusas and tacos ahogados – that keep devoted regulars coming back; tabs are cheap, especially during happy hour (3–7 PM) when domestic beers and margaritas are priced even lower.

El Sol y La Luna *Mexican* 19 | 13 | 18 | $15

SoCo | 1224 S. Congress Ave. (Academy Dr.) | 512-444-7770 | www.elsolylalunaaustin.com

First the "fresh, filling" fare (including "wonderful veggie" items) and then the check will "put a smile on your face" at this long-time SoCo Mexican eatery that predates the area's hipness; the decor "treads the line between funky and junky", but a "relaxed vibe", "live music" (weekends only) and a patio overlooking the "parade" of passersby add to the "fun atmosphere"; N.B. they now have a full bar.

Enoteca Vespaio *Italian* 25 | 19 | 22 | $26

SoCo | 1610 S. Congress Ave. (Monroe St.) | 512-441-7672 | www.austinvespaio.com

"Fabulous" panini, 50 "well-priced" wines by the glass and an "amazing Sunday brunch" lure local foodies to this "more affordable" SoCo alternative to "big brother" Vespaio; with "knowledgeable servers", "casual" cafelike digs with a "nice small patio" and a "gourmet" take-out counter stocked with cheeses and housemade charcuterie, it's no wonder it's so "well-liked."

NEW Estância Churrascaria *Brazilian/Steak* ▽ 27 | 19 | 25 | $37

Southwest Austin | 4894 Hwy. 290 W. (bet. Brodie Ln. & Westgate Blvd.) | 512-892-1225 | www.estanciachurrascaria.com

"Beef lovers" bring a "hearty appetite" to this moderately priced Brazilian newcomer in Southwest Austin where "roving" "gaucho" waiters dole out an "expertly prepared" array of sirloin, ribs, pork and lamb that "just keeps coming and coming" until you cry uncle; as for the "crowded" interior done up in an earthy style with exposed ceiling beams, most are "so busy eating", they "don't even notice."

European Bistro M *E European* ▽ 24 | 20 | 21 | $30

Pflugerville | 111 E. Main St. (Railroad Ave.) | 512-835-1919 | www.european-bistro.com

"Well worth the drive" out of Austin, this bastion of Central/Eastern European "bliss" "in a quaint jewel of a historic building" in Downtown Pflugerville offers a "unique menu" that "reflects a love for old-world cuisine" with its "wide variety of German, Hungarian, Russian", Czech and French dishes; the "tasty food" is both "delightful and authentic", but be sure to save "room for the housemade desserts."

Evangeline Café $ *Cajun/Creole* ▽ 19 | 11 | 20 | $18

Southwest Austin | 8106 Brodie Ln. (Thomas Kincheon St.) | 512-282-2586 | www.evangelinecafe.com

"Friendly and homey", this Southwest Austin spot sports a "great" staff serving up "some of the best authentic Cajun-Creole" "vittles" "this side of the Mississippi"; the "casual atmosphere" really hops in the evenings (Monday-Friday) when the tunes of "rousing bands" "go with the spicy food", adding to its status as a "really special place."

Finn & Porter *Seafood/Steak* 23 | 21 | 22 | $41

Downtown | Hilton Downtown | 500 E. Fourth St. (Neches St.) | 512-493-4900 | www.finnandporter.com

Ensconced within the Hilton hotel Downtown, this surf 'n' turf-style establishment features a "talented chef" who oversees everything from the "excellent steaks" to the "fabulous sushi" (complemented by a "good sake list"); the "gorgeous", "large dining room" can be "a bit noisy", but it has an "urbane", "cool", "big-city feel", and the two bars are a popular stop for cocktails.

Fino $ *Mediterranean* 23 | 24 | 23 | $36

West Campus | 2905 San Gabriel St. (29th St.) | 512-474-2905 | www.finoaustin.com

"Inventive small plates", "exciting" wines and "fabulous" cocktails are the standouts on the "eclectic" midpriced Mediterranean menu at this West Campus "winner" (and sister to Asti) set in "stylish", "airy" digs and serviced by a "knowledgeable" staff; insiders insist that a seat on the "wonderful patio" is the "perfect ending to the workday"; N.B. the Food score may not fully reflect a 2007 chef change.

FOOD | DECOR | SERVICE | COST

Fleming's Prime Steakhouse & Wine Bar *Steak* 24 | 24 | 23 | $54

Downtown | 320 E. Second St. (San Jacinto Blvd.) | 512-457-1500 | www.flemingssteakhouse.com

See review in Houston Directory.

Flip Happy Crepes ⊠ Ⓜ ≠ *French* - | - | - | I

Zilker | 401 Jessie St. (Butler Rd.) | 512-552-9034 | www.fliphappycrepes.com

Operating out of a cutely refurbished Airstream trailer in Zilker, Nessa Higgins and Andrea Dayboykin turn out toothsome homemade crêpes stuffed to the brim with savory and sweet fillings (like shredded pork with cheddar cheese or lemon curd with blueberries for dessert); although there's no indoor seating, the picnic area strung with Christmas lights and mismatched tables and chairs suits the steady stream of regulars just fine; N.B. breakfast and lunch only with evening hours in the spring.

Z Fonda San Miguel *Mexican* 26 | 27 | 24 | $37

Highland Park | 2330 W. North Loop Blvd. (Hancock Dr.) | 512-459-4121 | www.fondasanmiguel.com

"Nothing misses a beat" at this "long-running", "high-end" Highland Park "favorite" that's "truly a feast for the senses" with "lovingly prepared" Mexican cuisine "made from the best ingredients", "killer margaritas" and a "Sunday brunch that's not to be missed"; it's ranked No. 1 for Decor in Austin thanks to the "gorgeous, old-world" hacienda setting that's enhanced by a staff that "treats you like royalty."

Frank & Angie's *Pizza* 21 | 13 | 18 | $14

Downtown | 508 West Ave. (6th St.) | 512-472-3534

"Austin ain't no pizza mecca", but this "fun *Lady and the Tramp*-style" Downtown "dive" "might just be the pie enthusiast's best bet"; its "great thin-crust" version is accompanied by "reasonably priced", "classic homestyle" dishes "named after famous Italians" and "served with a bit of nostalgic attitude", making it "great for a casual date" – especially for those "on a budget."

Gene's ⊠ *Cajun/Soul Food* ▽ 25 | 6 | 17 | $14

East Austin | 1209 E. 11th St. (Wheeless St.) | 512-477-6600 | www.genesrestaurant.com

"You can't go wrong with a seafood po' boy" at this East Austin "find" turning out "authentic" Cajun dishes from a lineup of "comfort food" (like smothered pork chops and fried chicken) that "varies daily"; service is "friendly" and prices are cheap, though the "down-home" cafe-style setting has some customers clamoring for "takeout."

Golden Wok Chinese Restaurant *Chinese* 22 | 19 | 19 | $17

North Austin | Tech Ridge Ctr. | 500 Canyon Ridge (I-35) | 512-228-3688 | www.golden-wok.com

See review in San Antonio Directory.

Gonzales Food Market ☒ *BBQ* | - | - | - | I |

Gonzales | 311 St. Lawrence St. (St. James St.) | 830-672-3156 | www.gonzalesfoodmarket.com

The historic town of Gonzales is home to this no-frills, family-owned and -run BBQ mecca that started as a Downtown grocery store/ meat market in 1959; these days, three pits can barely keep up with demand for its mesquite-smoked sausage, brisket, chicken and ribs (including a house-specialty lamb version); it's no wonder the small dining room is usually full of locals and visitors from around the country; N.B. save room for dessert.

Green Mesquite *BBQ* | 18 | 13 | 17 | $16 |

Zilker | 1400 Barton Springs Rd. (Lamar Blvd.) | 512-479-0485 | www.greenmesquite.net

Specializing in "everything the cow and pig have to offer", this "Texas roadhouse BBQ joint" "conveniently" located just down the road from Zilker Park also offers "down-home flavors ranging from burgers to crispy catfish"; it's a "fun, boisterous" kind of place, with a "great patio" for anyone wanting "to listen to local music" (Thursday–Sunday); P.S. ask about the "all-you-can-eat special."

Green Pastures *Continental* | 23 | 25 | 24 | $38 |

Bouldin Creek | 811 W. Live Oak St. (3rd St.) | 512-444-4747 | greenpasturesrestaurant.com

"A longtime favorite" for "weddings" and "celebrations", this "beautiful" Bouldin Creek destination is set in a "delightful", "rambling" 19th-century home with peacocks roaming free on the "peaceful grounds"; though a few find it "staid", most marvel at the "delicious" Continental cuisine and "thoughtful staff" and say the "cost is in line" with what they deem a "special" place that "stands alone in its class"; P.S. there's also an "excellent Sunday brunch."

Guero's Taco Bar *Mexican* | 20 | 18 | 17 | $19 |

SoCo | 1412 S. Congress Ave. (Elizabeth St.) | 512-447-7688 | www.guerostacobar.com

"Always crowded", this "loud and energetic" SoCo Mexican conjures up "the quintessential Austin experience" with "tourists", "under-35" locals and "the occasional celebrity" all chowing down on "killer tacos" and "fantastic" salsas in a "funky" converted feed store with an enclosed patio and local bands playing Fridays and Saturdays; margaritas "on the deck" help alleviate "long waits" on weekend nights as well as "surly" service from the "too cool" staff.

Gumbo's ☒ *Cajun/Creole* | 24 | 20 | 22 | $34 |

Downtown | Brown Bldg. | 710 Colorado St. (7th St.) | 512-480-8053 | www.gumbosaustin.com

Round Rock | 901 Round Rock Ave. (Chisholm Trail) | 512-671-7925 | www.gumbosroundrock.com

It "feels and tastes like New Orleans" at this "upscale" Downtown Cajun-Creole, where visitors "enjoy the contrast between" the "elegant" interior and "the spice-a-thon on your plate"; not only is the food "fantastic" and the service "refined", but the "cozy, intimate atmosphere" complete with "dim lighting" makes it quite the "romantic hangout"; P.S. be sure to "visit the Round Rock location up north."

NEW Gypsy Italian Bistro *Italian* — | — | — | M

Bouldin Creek | 1025 Barton Springs Rd. (Dawson Rd.) | 512-499-0200 | www.go2gypsy.com

Owned and operated by recent graduates from the Texas Culinary Academy, this Bouldin Creek trattoria fuses old and new with modern takes on traditional Northern Italian dishes - like lamb chops with orzo pesto - served up in a cozy stone-accented setting; though prices can feel high for the area, wallet-watchers find brunch a less-expensive option.

Habana *Cuban* 21 | 15 | 15 | $23

Downtown | 709 E. Sixth St. (Colorado St.) | 512-443-4252
South Austin | 2728 S. Congress Ave. (Cumberland Rd.) | 512-443-4253
www.habana.com

The "massive portions" of "great Cuban" fare will "make your taste buds sing" at this "small" spot (and its South Austin offshoot) with a "fun atmosphere" and tropical, earthy decor "off the beaten path" Downtown; some say the staff can get "overwhelmed" at times, but most predict you'll get "satisfaction for your dining dollar" - especially if you sample the "wonderful array of mojitos" and "really good tres leches cake."

Hilltop Café M *Eclectic* 23 | 20 | 20 | $29

Fredericksburg | 10661 Hwy. 87 N. (Rte. 648) | 830-997-8922 | www.hilltopcafe.com

"In the middle of nowhere", this "wonderful find", an "old gas station"-turned-cafe near Fredericksburg, is an "authentic Texas roadhouse with urban eats" thanks to a menu on which "Cajun meets cowboy" "meets Greek" - with "a punch of down-home thrown in"; the "funky", "casual" space is often full of "interesting characters", and "you never know when the cook (and owner) will leave his kitchen and start playing music", making for "a real Hill Country experience" that's "well worth the trip."

Hoffbrau Steakhouse S M *Steak* 16 | 11 | 19 | $22

Downtown | 613 W. Sixth St. (Nueces St.) | 512-472-0822 | www.originalhoffbrausteaks.com

"It's all about nostalgia" at this "old-timey" Downtown steakhouse from 1936 that still holds strong with "decent" cuts of meat and salads served up "quickly" "on the cheap" to a motley crew of "politicians" and other assorted "regulars"; the location is "dilapidated" and decor is "nonexistent", but insiders insist "that's the charm" of this "beloved" "landmark."

Home Slice Pizza *Pizza* 23 | 14 | 17 | $15

SoCo | 1415 S. Congress Ave. (bet. Elizabeth & Gibson Sts.) | 512-444-7437 | www.homeslicepizza.com

Fans of "authentic" "NY-style" pizza head to this "friendly" SoCo "hangout" where "hipsters" and "families" munch on "crispy crust" pies and sip "affordable wines" in a "funky", "noisy" setting; "if it's late and you're hungry, this is the place to go", since you can order slices "from the walk-up to-go window" until 3 AM on weekends.

Hoover's *Southern* 21 | 10 | 17 | $18

Cherrywood | 2002 Manor Rd. (Alamo St.) | 512-479-5006
Jollyville | 13376 Research Blvd. (Anderson Mill Rd.) | 512-335-0300
www.hooverscooking.com

Get ready for "a belt-busting meal" of "excellent down-home Southern cooking" (including "better meatloaf than mother ever could have made") and "great soul food" - all "for a good price" - at this Cherrywood favorite near the University of Texas campus and its Jollyville sib; despite the "utilitarian", "cafeterialike atmosphere" and "friendly" but "often very busy" service, devotees declare it the place to go "when you need a comfort-food fix."

Houston's *American* 23 | 20 | 22 | $30

Northwest Austin | 2408 W. Anderson Ln. (Burnet Rd.) | 512-451-7333 | www.hillstone.com

See review in Houston Directory.

Z Hudson's on the Bend *American* 28 | 24 | 26 | $56

Lakeway | 3509 Ranch Rd. 620 N. (McCormick Mountain Dr.) | 512-266-1369 | www.hudsonsonthebend.com

"Meat eaters" marvel at the "memorable" game choices - like venison, bison, elk and rattlesnake - that come "artfully prepared" at this Lakeway New American set in a "quaint" old cottage with a "lovely", "romantic patio" and "five-star service" that's ranked No. 1 in Austin; in all, it's a "truly unique" "special treat" that surveyors swear is "easily worth" the 30 minute drive from Downtown, not to mention the "splurge"-worthy prices.

Hula Hut *Tex-Mex* 18 | 21 | 16 | $21

Old West Austin | 3825 Lake Austin Blvd. (Enfield Rd.) | 512-476-4852 | www.hulahut.com

"Beautiful lake views" and a "good variety of margaritas" make this "charmingly kitschy" "tiki hut"-esque spot an Old West "Austin summertime must" for the "under-25" set; some say the "unique" fare "isn't great", but others find it a "nice Polynesian twist on Tex-Mex" food - plus, the fact that "you can arrive by boat" adds to the "cool factor"; still, critics claim that the "unyielding crowds are intolerable", making the atmosphere "noisy" and service "erratic."

Hut's *Burgers* 23 | 16 | 19 | $13

Downtown | 807 W. Sixth St. (West Ave.) | 512-472-0693

Proponents "pity the person who's never had a burger" from this "legendary" "longtime favorite", a Downtown "hole-in-the-wall" serving a "wide variety of tasty" patties along with "rich, thick shakes and huge onion rings" in a "fun, relaxing environment" (think "diner with checkered floors and a bunch of tables jammed in"); insider's tip: the two-for-one nights (Monday, Wednesday and Thursday) "are the way to go."

Hyde Park Bar & Grill *American* 21 | 18 | 19 | $20

Hyde Park | 4206 Duval St. (Park Blvd.) | 512-458-3168 ◐
Southwest Austin | 4527 W. Gate Blvd. (Lamar Blvd.) | 512-899-2700
www.hydeparkbarandgrill.com

Surveyors say this "cheery" Hyde Park "hangout" – a "favorite of old-time Austinites" – "still does a fine job" with "simple" "all-American" dishes that "aren't too expensive" set down by "pleasant" servers in "comfy" quarters with local artwork on the walls; the newer outpost on West Gate may "lack the funky ambiance of the original", but it offers "more room" and "better parking" while maintaining the same "home cooking'" and "legendary french fries."

Iron Cactus *Tex-Mex* 18 | 19 | 18 | $25

Downtown | 606 Trinity St. (6th St.) | 512-472-9240
North Austin | 10001 Stonelake Blvd. (Capital of Texas Hwy.) | 512-794-8778
www.ironcactus.com

The "well-priced" "Tex-Mex fare is "tasty" enough, but connoisseurs claim the real appeal" of this Austin-based chain are the "70+ tequila choices vying for your attention" and served up in a "mind-boggling array" of flights or in "specialty margaritas"; service varies by location, though all boast "comfortable" quarters that get a boost from patio seating.

Iron Works ☒ *BBQ* 22 | 15 | 13 | $15

Downtown | 100 Red River St. (1st St.) | 512-478-4855 |
www.ironworksbbq.com

Set in a "historic" "restored ironworks factory" with "lovely creek-side seating" and an "awesome" Downtown location "right next to the Convention Center", this "great BBQ" place dishes out "huge portions" (including "ribs the size of Texas") in a "funky Western atmosphere"; you have to "order at the counter" from "indifferent", even "grumpy servers", but supporters swear that "just makes it taste better"; P.S. "there's no air-conditioning, so beware of the heat!"

Z NEW Jasper's *American* 24 | 25 | 24 | $42

Northwest Austin | Domain, The | 11506 Century Oaks Terr. (Braker Ln.) | 512-834-4111 | www.jaspers-restaurant.com

"Foodies rejoice" over this "lively" New American "standout" with branches in Austin, Plano and The Woodlands dishing up "inventively prepared" "comfort food" (the Maytag blue cheese chips are "worth the trip alone") courtesy of "incredible" chef-owner Kent Rathbun of Dallas' Abacus; the atmosphere is "casually elegant" with "modern" decor and patios that are "great for people-watching", so even if some feel it's "not a great value", it's a "winner" nonetheless.

Z Jeffrey's *American/Continental* 26 | 22 | 26 | $53

Clarksville | 1204 W. Lynn St. (12th St.) | 512-477-5584 |
www.jeffreysofaustin.com

"An old standard that hasn't lost a step", this Clarksville "wonder" "continues its great traditions" with "divine" Continental-New American cuisine and "wonderful wines" presented in "elegant", but "simple", flower-filled rooms that loyalists liken to "eating at a chef's home"; add in "solicitous" servers cherished by some as "the best staff in town", and it's no wonder it's often considered a "first choice" for "special occasions."

NEW Joe DiMaggio's Italian Chophouse *Italian/Steak* - | - | - | M

Northwest Austin | Domain, The | 11410 Century Oaks Terr. (Braker Ln.) | 512-835-5633 | www.joedimaggiosrestaurant.com

The latest addition to the burgeoning dining scene at The Domain in Northwest Austin, this swank chophouse serves a solid lineup of steaks alongside pizzas and pastas in a 1940s-style setting decorated with memorabilia paying homage to the namesake Yankee legend; those seeking an expertly made cocktail can settle in at the ample bar area or sink into a seat in front of the fire pit on the lighted patio.

Judges' Hill Restaurant *American* 24 | 25 | 21 | $46

West Campus | Mansion at Judges' Hill Hotel | 1900 Rio Grande St. (Martin Luther King Blvd.) | 512-495-1800 | www.judgeshillrestaurant.com

"An old, beautifully restored" West Campus mansion that's been turned into "an elegant inn" is the "lovely" setting of this "intimate dining room", "a well-kept secret" that's "great for cocktails and hors d'oeuvres", a "discreet power business dinner" or a "romantic meal"; though the "ambiance is old-world", the menu is New American, managing to "cover the basics" while also offering "unique food" that "doesn't lack creativity."

Katz's Deli & Bar ◐ *Deli* 19 | 15 | 16 | $18

Downtown | 618 W. Sixth St. (Rio Grande St.) | 512-472-2037 | www.katzneverkloses.com

These 24/7 Austin and Houston-area delis are "all-night traditions" for "tastes of New York in the heart of Texas", offering "monstrous portions" at "reasonable prices" from an "extensive menu"; detractors declare that the "quality is variable", the "service is spotty" and the atmosphere is "nightmarishly kitschy", but they're always "really loud and busy on weekends", making them "fun places to people-watch."

Kenichi *Pan-Asian* 22 | 22 | 19 | $43

Warehouse District | 419 Colorado St. (4th St.) | 512-320-8883 | www.kenichirestaurants.com

"The beautiful people love to eat" at this "swanky spot" in Austin's Warehouse District (and its newer Victory Park twin in Dallas) with "chic" "modern" decor and a Pan-Asian menu sporting a "great variety of sushi, rolls and sashimi" and "melt-in-your-mouth seafood" dishes, accompanied by a wide "range of sakes"; still, protesters pan the "pretentiously hip" vibe and certain staffers who are "more snobby than a Rockefeller at Tiffany's."

Kerbey Lane Café ◐ *Eclectic* 20 | 14 | 16 | $15

Arboretum | 12602 Research Blvd. (Barrington Way) | 512-258-7757

Brykerwoods | 3704 Kerbey Ln. (35th St.) | 512-451-1436 S M

Campus | 2606 Guadalupe St. (26th St.) | 512-477-5717 S M

(continued)

(continued)

Kerbey Lane Café

South Lamar | 2700 S. Lamar Blvd. (Dickson Dr.) | 512-445-4451 ⓢ Ⓜ
www.kerbeylanecafe.com

"An eclectic clientele" enjoys the "Eclectic menu of fresh cooking" at this "home-grown" mini-chain of "24-hour heavens", the original "located in a charming midcentury bungalow" in Brykerwoods that boasts a "bohemian flavor"; regulars who revel in its "famously funky vibe" love having "breakfast any time of day" ("legendary pancakes"), though some say the "hippie-student" servers are a bit too "laid-back", "usually acting like you're interrupting their smoke break."

NEW Kona Grill *American* 20 | 21 | 18 | $27

Northwest Austin | Domain, The | 11410 Century Oaks Terr. (Braker Ln.) | 512-835-5900 | www.konagrill.com

See review in Houston Directory.

Korea House *Korean* 21 | 9 | 16 | $17

Northwest Austin | 2700 W. Anderson Ln. (Northcross Dr.) | 512-458-2477

This "authentic Korean hangout" in Northwest Austin serves "enjoyable" "traditional dishes" accompanied by "lots of interesting sides" (including "a wonderful range of fresh pickled vegetables"), as well as "good sushi"; the service is "attentive" and the prices are "great", making it "a fave for lunch", but "no-frills" decor "leaves much to be desired", so surveyors suggest sitting by the window and "looking out over the water feature in the courtyard."

Kreuz Market ⓢ ≠ *BBQ* 26 | 12 | 15 | $15

Lockhart | 619 N. Colorado St. (bet. Cemetery & Flores Sts.) | 512-398-2361 | www.kreuzmarket.com

"One of the greatest in the state" attest those "amazed" by this "German-style" BBQ "mecca" in Lockhart that's well "worth the drive" for "tender" smoked meats – like "standout" brisket and pork chops – served "right off the pit", without sauce, and tied up in butcher paper ("don't look for a fork", just unwrap and eat); no one minds the "huge rustic building" that "leaves much to be desired" or market-style sevice, since it's ultimately a "pure Texas" experience where "all that really matters is the meat."

Lambert's Downtown Barbecue *BBQ* 23 | 21 | 21 | $29

Downtown | Schneider Brothers Bldg. | 401 W. Second St. (Guadalupe St.) | 512-494-1500 | www.lambertsaustin.com

Barbecue gets an "upscale" twist at chef Lou Lambert's "sophisticated" Downtown arrival turning out "delectable" oak-smoked and wood-grilled meats, "delicious" "nontraditional" sides and a "great Sunday brunch" all ferried to your table by a staff that "treats you like kin"; the setting in the "wonderfully restored" Schneider Brothers Building features "whitewashed brick walls" and "loud" live music Tuesday–Saturday confirming this "popular" destination is "as much about the scene" as the "awesome" food.

Las Manitas Avenue Cafe *Mexican* 20 | 11 | 17 | $13

Downtown | 211 Congress Ave. (2nd St.) | 512-472-9357

"A local favorite" with "tons of personality", this "iconic" Downtown diner draws "crowds" of "Texas legislators", "hungover partyers" and other assorted "loyal locals" gathering in the "no-frills" interior (or on the "ample" back patio) for "lovingly prepared" Mexican breakfasts and lunches; add in "fast-paced" service and tabs that tally to "next to nothing" and it "may not be fine dining", but it sure is "fine eating."

Las Palomas Ⓢ Ⓜ *Mexican* 21 | 14 | 19 | $22

West Lake Hills | West Woods Shopping Ctr. | 3201 Bee Caves Rd. (Old Walsh Tarlton) | 512-327-9889 | www.laspalomasrestaurant.com

"Tucked in the corner of a strip mall" in West Lake Hills is this "fabulous, sophisticated" little gem with an unexpectedly "excellent menu" of "authentic and delicious" Mexican fare "at reasonable prices"; an "inviting atmosphere" (including "nice patio seating") and "great service" from a staff that "always treats you like part of the family" are more reasons it's been a favorite since 1983.

La Traviata Ⓢ *Italian* 24 | 20 | 21 | $35

Downtown | 314 Congress Ave. (3rd St.) | 512-479-8131 | www.latraviata.net

Downtowners are delighted by this "lovely" little midpriced trattoria offering "straightforward" Italian dishes like "heavenly" pastas that really let the "fresh ingredients" shine; regulars recommend you "make reservations" because the "cozy" (some say "cramped") "NYC-like setting" with whitewashed brick and red accents "fills up quickly."

Louie Mueller BBQ Ⓢ *BBQ* 25 | 10 | 14 | $16

Taylor | 206 W. Second St. (Talbot St.) | 512-352-6206 | www.louiemuellerbarbeque.com

"There is a God and his name is Louie" proclaim proponents of this decades-old Taylor BBQ institution famed for its "outstanding brisket", "tender" ribs and "fantastic" sausages presented with white bread on a "tray with butcher paper"; "barn"-like decor is strictly "no-frills", but the "years of real smoke" on the walls "has to count for something."

Louie's 106 *Mediterranean* 24 | 23 | 24 | $41

Downtown | Littlefield Bldg. | 106 E. Sixth St. (Congress Ave.) | 512-476-1998 | www.louies106.net

A "dependable" Downtown "favorite", this "lively" Mediterranean features "fabulous tapas", a "reasonable wine list" and solid service all coming together in a "lovely" space with marble floors and redwood accents; regulars remark it works both for business lunches or a "romantic" meal and is "always popular" with "guests from out of town."

Madam Mam's *Thai* 21 | 11 | 14 | $14

Campus | 2514 Guadalupe St. (Dean Keaton Pkwy.) | 512-472-8306
Southwest Austin | 4514 W. Gate Blvd. (Ben White Blvd.) | 512-899-8525
www.madammam.com

This "budget"-friendly "Campus favorite" boasting the "best Thai food in town" and its West Gate offshoot offer the same "consistent authentic provincial dishes" from "spicy to subtle" with "crisp flavors" as "exotic and succulent as the entertainers at a Bangkok cabaret"; the newer location has better parking and a space featuring bright colors, Thai art and a beautiful rose garden, which stand in stark contrast with the original's "strip-mall" setup.

Madras Pavilion *Indian* 22 | 11 | 14 | $17

North Austin | Colonnade Shopping Ctr. | 9025 Research Blvd. (Burnet Rd.) | 512-719-5575 | www.madraspavilion.us

See review in Houston Directory.

Magnolia Café ◐ *American* 21 | 14 | 19 | $16

Old West Austin | 2304 Lake Austin Blvd. (Veterans Dr.) | 512-478-8645
SoCo | 1920 S. Congress Ave. (Mary St.) | 512-445-0000
www.cafemagnolia.com

"Peace, love" and pancakes abound at this "cheap", "funky" local "institution" with outposts in SoCo and Old West Austin dishing out "great breakfasts" served "any time of day" as well as an "eclectic" array of "hearty" "wholesome" American food with lots of choices for "vegetarians"; open 24/7, it's "always crowded" with a "diverse" crowd while the "artist and musician" staff provides proficient if sometimes "snobby" service.

Málaga Tapas & Bar Ⓢ *Spanish* 20 | 20 | 19 | $31

Warehouse District | 208 W. Fourth St. (bet. Colorado & Lavaca Sts.) | 512-236-8020 | www.malagatapasbar.com

The destination for "moderately priced" tapas in the Warehouse District, this Spaniard eatery sports "something for everyone": its "informal, barlike setting" is "perfect" for everything from "mingling" during the "great happy hour" to "a light, casual meal", as diners "feel just as comfortable sitting alone with a glass of wine" from the "immense list" as they do "having a full-course dinner with a group"; still, surveyors are less smitten with the service; N.B. they plan to move to 440 West Second Street this spring.

Mandola's Italian Market *Italian* 22 | 18 | 15 | $17

North Central | 4700 W. Guadalupe St. (Lamar Blvd.) | 512-419-9700 | www.mandolasmarket.com

Chowhounds hail this "nice addition" to the North Central Austin dining scene – a "charming" Italian market stocked with breads, meats, cheeses, "amazing gelato" and assorted "gourmet products" and featuring a counter-service eatery offering "freshly made" pastas, panini and pizzas alongside a "great selection" of wines; the mood is one of "slightly organized chaos", but "if you can handle the wait to place your order", "you'll be rewarded with terrific food at a reasonable price"; P.S. there's also a small patio that's a "wonderful setting" for an alfresco meal.

Mangieri's Pizza Cafe *Pizza* 22 | 16 | 20 | $15

Circle C | 5900 W. Slaughter Ln. (Escarpment Blvd.) | 512-301-0063 | www.mangieris.com

"Locals" "love" this counter-service Italian "hidden away" on a strip mall in Circle C for its "irresistible" "thin-crust" pizzas with "delicious" toppings and "good variety" of inexpensive pastas and salads; "it's a nice option when you don't feel like cooking", and though the casually rustic setting is well-suited for families, delivery and takeout are also available.

Manuel's *Mexican* 22 | 20 | 19 | $24

Downtown | 310 Congress Ave. (bet. 3rd & 4th Sts.) | 512-472-7555
Great Hills | 10201 Jollyville Rd. (Great Hills Trail) | 512-345-1042
www.manuels.com

"Imaginative" Mexican fare is "prepared well" with "fresh ingredients" and served by an "attentive staff" at these "affordable" eateries; regulars report the Great Hills Arboretum outpost is famed for its tree-shaded patio (a "great place" to enjoy an "inventive margarita") while the Downtown location is more of a "see-and-be-seen place" that "can be a bit loud especially at lunch."

Mars *Asian Fusion* 20 | 21 | 18 | $33

SoCo | 1400 S. Congress Ave. (Gibson St.) | 512-472-3901 | www.marsaustin.com

Now ensconced in "hip", new SoCo digs trimmed in reds and golds, this "happening" Asian fusion is brimming with a "see-and-be-seen crowd" munching on "unusual" "eclectic" dishes and indulging in "cocktails" and "people-watching" on the "fab" oak-shaded patio; a number of naysayers think the "menu isn't keeping pace" with the scene and claim that "apathetic" service and "too noisy" digs are additional causes for complaint.

Matt's El Rancho *Tex-Mex* 18 | 17 | 19 | $19

South Lamar | 2613 S. Lamar Blvd. (bet. Bluebonnet Ln. & Manchaca Rd.) | 512-462-9333 | www.mattselrancho.com

A "local favorite with a loyal following" for more than half a century, this huge South Lamar "temple of Tex-Mex" still serves classic dishes from "1950s recipes", providing "a 'retro' experience" to "generations of regulars" in a "loud" but "comfortable setting" ideal for "families and large groups"; because it's "crowded and popular", though, "waits can be wicked" - especially "after Texas football."

McCormick & Schmick's *Seafood* 21 | 21 | 20 | $41

Downtown | Frost Bank Tower | 401 Congress Ave. (4th St.) | 512-236-9600
NEW **North Austin** | 11600 Century Oaks Terr. (Burnet Rd.) | 512-836-0500
www.mccormickandschmicks.com

Unless you "get a booth and draw the curtain", it's sea and be seen at this "upscale" chain known for its "succulent seafood" (especially the "impressive" variety of oysters), "ample" wine list and "helpful" staff; revelers reveal "real fun" can be had at the bar, home to "great happy-hour specials", but landlubbers lament it's a "typical chain" - "seen one, seen 'em all."

Melting Pot, The *Fondue* 21 | 20 | 21 | $43

NEW **Downtown** | 305 E. Third St. (bet. San Jacinto Blvd. & Trinity St.) | 512-401-2424

(continued)

(continued)

Melting Pot, The

Northwest Austin | 13343 Hwy. 183 N. (Anderson Mill Rd.) | 512-401-2424
www.meltingpot.com

"Change-of-pace" mavens and "do-it-yourself" types are fond of this "novel" fondue franchise for its "interactive" approach, i.e. the chance to "cook your own dinner"; the "long, slow meals" make it appropriate for "first dates" or "large crowds", and although the morsels are "tasty", you'll "end up spending a lot of money" for them.

Meyer's Elgin Smokehouse *BBQ* 21 | 10 | 15 | $12

Elgin | 188 Hwy. 290 E. (County Line Rd.) | 512-281-3331 |
www.meyerselginsausage.com

"First-class Texas BBQ" including "amazing brisket" and "wonderful" housemade sausages are the pride and joy of this "mom-and-pop smokehouse" in the middle of Elgin - a small town just 30 minutes east of Austin; boosters boast it "takes you back to the bygone days" with "order-at-the-counter" service and a "plain" setting with picnic-style seating adding to the overall "authentic" experience.

Mikado Ryotei ☒ *Japanese* ▽ 24 | 22 | 22 | $35

North Austin | 9033 Research Blvd. (Burnet Rd.) | 512-833-8188 |
www.mikadoryotei.com

Though set in an "unassuming" North Austin strip mall, this Japanese "favorite" "soars above fancier Downtown places" with a mix of "traditional and inventive" fare including charcoal-grilled robata dishes and "top-grade" sushi all set down in "stylish" quarters; a "black-clad" staff provides proficient service, but those in-the-know sit at the bar where you're "treated like a king."

Mirabelle ☒ *American* 25 | 19 | 24 | $35

Northwest Hills | 8127 Mesa Dr. (bet. Spicewood Springs Rd. & Steck Ave.) | 512-346-7900 | www.mirabellerestaurant.com

"Inspired" New American cuisine keeps Northwest Hills crowds coming to this "favorite" "neighborhood" "bistro" where the "creative" plates are "perfectly paired" with "reasonably priced, high-quality" vintages; devotees don't mind the "plain decor" with wood tables and floors because the "stunning food" plus "knowledgeable staff" guarantee it as "a safe bet for a quality meal"; P.S. their twice-monthly wine dinners are a "great value" too

Moonshine *American* 20 | 20 | 19 | $28

Downtown | 303 Red River St. (3rd St.) | 512-236-9599 |
www.moonshinegrill.com

The "upscale, creative" American "comfort food" features "cutting-edge twists on some Southern mainstays" at this "quaint", "old rock house" Downtown, a "historic landmark" from the 1850s that's "elegantly comfy" and "romantic, without being stuffy"; highlights include its "generous" Sunday brunch, a "relaxed, breezy patio", drinks from the old carriage house bar that are "like candy in a glass" and a "caring staff that's anxious to please."

FOOD	DECOR	SERVICE	COST

Ms. B's Authentic Creole Restaurant *Creole*

22	17	21	$23

East Austin | 1050 E. 11th St. (Waller St.) | 512-542-9143
Northwest Hills | 8105 Mesa Dr. (Spicewood Springs) | 512-372-9529 Ⓢ
www.msbscreole.com

Surveyors swear they'd "died and gone to heaven (or at least New Orleans)" after a taste of the "fabulous" Creole dishes like seafood gumbo and shrimp étouffée at these "lovely", "comfortable" eateries offering "good value" for the money; "friendly owners and staff" provide "leisurely service" at both the Northwest Hills original and the more "upscale" offshoot in East Austin on a revitalized stretch of 11th Street.

Musashino Sushi Dokoro Ⓜ *Japanese*

27	18	19	$38

Northwest Hills | 3407 Greystone Dr. (Mo-Pac Expwy.) | 512-795-8593 | www.musashinosushi.com

Connoisseurs claim "you'd be hard-pressed to find a more authentic Japanese menu" than the one at this Northwest Hills "gem" "hidden" beneath a Chinese restaurant where the "knowledgeable chefs" craft an "amazing selection" of Tokyo-style sushi from "fresh" fish flown in daily from the Tsukiji market; considering it's "one of the best in the city", supporters say it's "easy to go overboard" and end up "spending too much" here.

NEW NoRTH *Italian*

-	-	-	M

Northwest Austin | Domain, The | 11506 Century Oaks Terr. (Braker Ln.) | 512-339-4400 | www.foxrc.com

Another Domain newcomer, this Northwest Austin outpost of a Scottsdale-based chain marries contemporary design with a modern menu of Northern Italian dishes (think wood-fired pizzas and innovative pasta dishes); it's already drawing a crowd of hip mall-goers who stop in for a post-shopping boost or a cocktail out on the lively patio.

North by Northwest *American*

18	19	17	$24

Great Hills | 10010 N. Capital of Texas Hwy. (Stonelake Blvd.) | 512-467-6969 | www.nxnwbrew.com

"Catering to the Northwest Austin young professional set", this Great Hills American bistro/microbrewery is known as the spot "for after-work drinks" and "singles mingling" in a "Pacific Northwestern" "mountain-lodge" setting; folks enjoy "sitting by the fireplace in the winter" or listening to "live music on the patio" (Thursday–Saturday) while noshing on "upscale pub grub" washed down with "great house brews" at "reasonable prices", even if the "service can be cranky."

Oasis, The *Tex-Mex*

11	24	14	$24

Lakeway | 6550 Comanche Trail (Rte. 620) | 512-266-2442 | www.oasis-texas.com

The "stunning views" of Lake Travis are best admired from the "great patio" at this Lakeway Tex-Mex where locals label the food "underwhelming", the drinks "watered down" and the service "marginal"; yet in spite of that and a "crowded", "touristy" "atmosphere that feels like you're at a frat amusement park", most maintain you have to go "at least once" and bask in the "terrific sunsets" on "a warm Friday night."

NEW Oaxacan Tamaleo *Mexican* - | - | - | I

Cedar Creek | 1634 Hwy. 71 (FM 1209) | 512-289-9262 | www.tamaleo.com

Though recently relocated to larger digs in Cedar Creek, the authentic Oaxacan fare remains the focus of Leonor and Bill Stoude's homey Mexican joint turning out a variety of moles and tamales all made from scratch and based on family recipes; although it's no longer BYO only (they now offer beer and wine), tabs are kept as low as ever.

Opal Divine's ◐ *American* 14 | 15 | 16 | $16

Downtown | 700 W. Sixth St. (Rio Grande St.) | 512-477-3308
North Austin | 12709 N. Mo-Pac Expwy. (Parmer Ln.) | 512-733-5353
South Austin | 3601 S. Congress Ave. (Ben White Blvd.) | 512-707-0237
www.opaldivines.com

"Popular for it extensive scotch and beer selections", this locally owned American trio serves "good", "standard pub grub"; regulars "quaff quality pints" on "the best patio on lower Sixth Street" at the Downtown original, on the "great deck" at the Penn Field location or on the boardwalklike setting at The Marina, but all boast a "laid-back ambiance" that's ideal "for big groups" - from the "fun happy hour" to late-night.

Opie's Barbecue *BBQ* ▽ 23 | 6 | 14 | $17

Spicewood | 9504 Hwy. 71 E. (Spur 191) | 830-693-8660

"Like the many other famous destination BBQ joints" in Central Texas, chowhounds claim this "friendly, family-owned" Spicewood staple is definitely "worth the drive" for "fantastic" smoked meats, chops, sausages and babyback ribs; patrons pick their grub "off the pit" then head inside the roomy new space (which still packs loads of good ol' country style) for side dishes and fixin's off the all-you-can-eat bean and condiment bar; N.B. save room for their fab homemade cobbler!

Pappadeaux *Seafood* 23 | 19 | 20 | $29

North Austin | 6319 I-35 N. (Hwy. 290) | 512-452-9363 | www.pappadeaux.com

See review in Houston Directory.

Patton's On Main *Eclectic* - | - | - | M

Marble Falls | 201 Main St. (2nd St.) | 830-693-8664 | www.pattonsonmain.com

Marble Falls, in the heart of the Hill Country, is quickly becoming a fine-dining destination thanks to the likes of this elegantly relaxed establishment ensconced in a historic, renovated filling station, serving a fine Eclectic menu that chef Patton Roberts calls 'Texas fusion'; besides boasting one of the most extensive wine lists in town, it also has a sports bar that mixes mean martinis and an outdoor patio with live music Thursday-Saturday.

Pei Wei Asian Diner *Pan-Asian* 19 | 15 | 16 | $15

Hyde Park | Hancock Shopping Ctr. | 1000 E. 41st St. (I-35) | 512-382-3860
North Austin | Shops at Tech Ridge | 12901 I-35 N. (Parmer Ln.) | 512-691-3060
Southwest Austin | Brodie Oaks Shopping Ctr. | 4200 S. Lamar Blvd. (Capital of Texas Hwy.) | 512-382-2990
www.peiwei.com
See review in Dallas/Ft. Worth Directory.

P.F. Chang's China Bistro *Chinese* 22 | 22 | 20 | $27

Arboretum | 10114 Jollyville Rd. (Great Hills Trail) | 512-231-0208
Downtown | 201 San Jacinto Blvd. (2nd St.) | 512-457-8300
www.pfchangs.com
See review in Dallas/Ft. Worth Directory.

Player's ◐ *Burgers* 19 | 9 | 14 | $10

Campus | 300 W. Martin Luther King Jr. Blvd. (Guadalupe St.) | 512-478-9299

"Just a hop, skip and a jump from Campus", this "shrine to grease (the liquid, not the musical)" is a "longtime" "favorite" of "starving students", who love to "hang out" here, bolting "some of the best burgers in town" and "not-to-be-missed shakes" while "watching games" on the big-screen TV or playing "horseshoes in the back"; "there may not be decor" and service is "counter-style", but it's a cool "dive" – and it's open "late at night."

Polvo's *Mexican* 21 | 12 | 15 | $16

Bouldin Creek | 2004 S. First St. (bet. Johanna & Live Oaks Sts.) | 512-441-5446

A "change of pace from Tex-Mex", this "classic Mexican dive (right down to the hideous pastel plastered walls)" in Bouldin Creek is chock-full of "hipsters" in their "thrift-store trendiest" tucking into "tasty" dishes, "housemade salsas" and "downright lethal margaritas", served on the "cool patio" or within its "funky South Austin" interior – "all of which is worth" putting up with "the neglect you'll receive" from the "slow", "occasionally snide" staff.

Quality Seafood Restaurant & Oyster Bar *Seafood* - | - | - | I

Hyde Park | 5621 Airport Blvd. (FM 2222) | 512-454-5827 | www.qualityseafoodmarket.com

Ensconced in a historic North Hyde Park fish market, this inexpensive Cajun-inflected seafooder serves up heaping plates of shrimp, deep-fried catfish fillets and hearty bowls of gumbo available to eat in the no-frills interior or packaged to go; there's also a full oyster bar that's the perfect place to wait out rush hour traffic while relaxing with a pile of bivalves and an icy cold beer.

Ranch 616 *Southwestern* 23 | 22 | 20 | $35

Downtown | 616 Nueces St. (7th St.) | 512-479-7616

The "impressive menu" of "unique", "savory" dishes features plenty of "local ingredients" at this "small, locally owned" Downtown

Southwestern serving what many call "cowboy cuisine at its best" - and "at a great price"; "cool", "quirky decor", "friendly owners" and staff and a "deft hand in the kitchen" add up to a "wonderful experience", even if the "live country music" (Tuesdays and Thursdays) sometimes "gets too loud for conversation."

Rather Sweet Bakery & Café ☒ *Bakery* ▽ 26 | 17 | 20 | $15

Fredericksburg | 249 E. Main St. (Lincoln St.) | 830-990-0498 | www.rathersweet.com

"The bread alone is worth driving 100 miles for" declare devotees of chef-owner Rebecca Rather's "small, simply decorated" Fredericksburg cafe where a "light" menu of soups, salads and sandwiches are a "good prelude" to her "fantastic" sweets like decadent chocolate buttercream cake and fruity tarts; early birds applaud the "breakfast items" too, with cinnamon rolls, bacon and cheddar scones and other modestly priced items available till they close at 5 PM.

Reale's Pizza & Cafe ☒ *Pizza* 23 | 13 | 19 | $18

Jollyville | Plaza 183 | 13450 Hwy. 183 N. (Anderson Mill Rd.) | 512-335-5115 | www.realespizzaandcafe.com

"Genuine New York-style thin-crust pizza" and "down-home Italian fare" can be found at this "family-run business" "somewhat hidden in a strip mall" in Jollyville; its "devoted following of expat Easterners" flocks for its "excellent" veal, chicken and pasta dishes, which are served "at reasonable prices" within a homey atmosphere (right "down to the checkered tablecloths") and can be wonderfully paired with offerings from their "decent wine list."

Real New Orleans Restaurant, The ☒ *Creole* - | - | - | I

Round Mountain | 10541 Hwy. 281 N. (R.R. 962) | 830-825-3600 | www.therealneworleansstylerestaurant.com

In the tiny hamlet of Round Mountain (between Marble Falls and Johnson City), this former failing truck stop has been taken over by members of a New Orleans congregation whose church and homes were destroyed by Hurricane Katrina; they're bringing Creole cooking and a dash of Big Easy style to the Hill Country, much to the delight of locals and travelers; N.B. it's closed on Sundays, when the staff is 'on fire for the Lord, and smokin' for Jesus.'

Restaurant Jezebel ☒ *American* ▽ 27 | 21 | 23 | $52

Downtown | 914 Congress Ave. (9th St.) | 512-499-3999 | www.restaurantjezebel.com

Enthusiasts assert the food is "first rate" at this relative newcomer "in the heart of Downtown Austin" whose "interesting" New American menu draws inspiration from a variety of international cuisines and solicitous servers help diners navigate the 1,400-label wine list; decor is done up in "dark", deep burgundy and mustard colors, but some critics challenge that the "TV screens" depicting the chef in action in the open kitchen detract from the otherwise "romantic" atmosphere.

Roaring Fork *Southwestern* — 24 | 24 | 23 | $38

Downtown | InterContinental Stephen F. Austin Hotel | 701 Congress Ave. (7th St.) | 512-583-0000 | www.roaringforkaustin.com

"Hearty" "haute cowboy cuisine" like green chile pork stew and Dr. Pepper-braised short ribs sates the appetites of "congressmen", "lobbyists" and other "businesspeople" at this "convivial" Downtown hangout done up in an "elegant" Old-West style with wrought-iron accents and rustic wood floors; service is suitably "professional", and those who find the tab "a bit high" may want to visit the "inviting" bar where you can make a "whole meal" on reduced-price drinks and apps during the "great happy hour."

Rocco's Grill *Italian* — ▽ 20 | 22 | 20 | $30

Lakeway | Lakeway Commons | 900 Ranch Road 620 S. (Lakeway Blvd.) | 512-263-8204 | www.roccosgrill.com

Patrons praise the "beautiful" golf-course views and "nice deck" at this Lakeway eatery offering midpriced Italian specialties as well as mesquite-grilled meats ferried by servers who are generally "up to par"; cons counter that the cuisine is "run of the mill" adding that "the murals on the wall are the most colorful part of the experience" here.

Romeo's *Italian* — 17 | 17 | 19 | $22

Zilker | 1500 Barton Springs Rd. (Lamar Blvd.) | 512-476-1090 | www.austinromeos.com

"Large portions" of "homestyle Italian" at "reasonable prices" are served by a "friendly staff" at this "cozy spot" on Zilker's Restaurant Row; despite its "kitschy" decor - "grapes growing out of the ceiling" and "fake, plastic flowers" - fans feel the "dimly lit" space manages to be "charming and intimate", with "romantic touches" like "live piano music" Thursday-Saturday that make it "perfect for a cheap date-night"; P.S. ask to be "seated out on the patio."

R.O.'s Outpost ☒ ⊭ *BBQ* — - | - | - | I

Spicewood | 22112 Hwy. 71 W. (bet. Crawford Rd. & Hazy Hills Dr.) | 512-264-1169

This tiny, funky shack on Highway 71 in Spicewood (17 miles west of Austin) teems with Texas hospitality and some of the most ardent BBQ fans around; its hickory-smoked brisket, pork ribs, sausage, ham and chicken - not to mention housemade pies - are legendary, as the walls covered in autographed photos of Texas musicians suggest; chicken-fried steak and other Southern dishes round out the menu.

Roy's *Hawaiian* — 25 | 24 | 23 | $48

Downtown | 340 E. Second St. (Trinity St.) | 512-391-1500 | www.roysrestaurant.com

See review in Dallas/Ft. Worth Directory.

Ruby's BBQ ◐ *BBQ* — 23 | 13 | 17 | $14

North Campus | 512 W. 29th St. (Guadalupe St.) | 512-477-1651 | www.rubysbbq.com

"Some of the yummiest (and most PC) barbecue in town" can be found at this "quirky", "unpretentious" North Campus "joint" whose "beef is billed as hormone-free" with "no antibiotics"; the "tender" cuts are "smoked to perfection" and served by a "friendly counter" staff with "numerous healthy sides" and "divine desserts", plus its selection of "tasty veg" dishes means it's the "place for carnivores to take vegetarians and make everyone happy."

Ruth's Chris Steak House *Steak* 25 | 22 | 25 | $57

Downtown | 107 W. Sixth St. (Congress Ave.) | 512-477-7884 | www.ruthschris.com

See review in San Antonio Directory.

Saba Blue Water *Eclectic* 18 | 19 | 16 | $28

Warehouse District | 208D W. Fourth St. (bet. Colorado & Lavaca Sts.) | 512-478-7222 | www.sabacafe.com

"It's hard to be blue" at this Warehouse District destination where the modern space with aquatic details sets the tone for an "inventive" menu of Pacific- and Caribbean-influenced plates and creative cocktails; filled with a "lively crowd", it "can get a bit loud, especially later at night" when it morphs into more of a "club"-like environment; P.S. wallet-watchers insist the "happy-hour specials" are a great deal.

NEW Sagra ⊠ *Italian* - | - | - | I

Downtown | 1610 San Antonio St. (17th St.) | 512-535-5988 | www.sagrarestaurant.net

Occupying a refurbished cottage Downtown, this Italian newcomer turns out affordable regional dishes made from local, seasonal ingredients in a simple, candlelit space with white linen tablecloths; inspired by the food festivals for which it's named, it also plays host to special monthly dinners based around a single ingredient.

Z Salt Lick ≠ *BBQ* 24 | 18 | 20 | $21

Driftwood | 18300 FM 1826 (FM 967) | 512-858-4959 | www.saltlickbbq.com

"The mother of all Texas BBQ places" swear surveyors sweet on this Driftwood "landmark" famed for its "tender", "flavorful" brisket and "rustic" Hill Country setting with "communal" "picnic tables" and live music on weekends; be forewarned, it's BYO (and located in a dry county), so grab a cooler and "pick up a six-pack" of Shiner Bock before you "mosey on over."

Sampaio's Restaurant *Brazilian* 20 | 20 | 19 | $27

Rosedale | 4800 Burnet Rd. (bet. 47th & 49th Sts.) | 512-469-9988 | www.sampaiosrestaurant.com

Locals laud this "welcome addition" to Rosedale where moderately priced "nouveau" Brazilian" fare and "tasty" cocktails come together in a "stylish" setting awash in yellows and greens; "top-notch" service adds to the appeal, as does a "quiet", plant-filled patio that proves the perfect escape from the sometimes "noisy" interior.

São Paulo's ⊠ *Brazilian* ▽ 21 | 14 | 18 | $20

Campus | 2809 San Jacinto Blvd. (bet. Elmwood & Park Pls.) | 512-473-9988

"Brazil meets Tex-Mex" at this "groovy little joint" near Campus that's "popular with university" sorts for its "varied" menu of "authentic" and "tasty" dishes from its namesake city along with some local offerings, all served with "terrific" tropical cocktails like caipirinhas and mojitos by a staff that's "always friendly"; P.S. "great Brazilian music performed on weekends" (Thursday-Saturday nights) is a bonus.

Sarovar Indian Cuisine *Indian* ▽ 21 | 12 | 15 | $18

North Austin | 8440 Burnet Rd. (Penny Ln.) | 512-454-8636 | www.sarovar.net

See review in San Antonio Directory.

Satay *Pan-Asian* 21 | 15 | 17 | $20

Northwest Austin | 3202 W. Anderson Ln. (Shoal Creek Blvd.) | 512-467-6731 | www.satayusa.com

"Fresh, flavorful fare" at a "great price point" characterizes this longtime Northwest Austin favorite that's earned a loyal following with its "good presentations" of "spicy", "interesting" Southeast Asian dishes (mostly Thai, with some Malaysian, Indonesian and Vietnamese dishes), including "daily specials that are always winners"; though "the owner makes you feel like one of the family", some still suggest that the "service can vary considerably."

Scholz Garten *German* 13 | 16 | 15 | $15

Downtown | 1607 San Jacinto Blvd. (17th St.) | 512-474-1958 | www.scholzgarten.net

Offering "a bit of Austin as our great-grandparents knew it", this "real 19th-century German biergarten" Downtown, just south of Campus, "creates a decent Oktoberfest atmosphere" within its "beer-hall" interior and out on its "picnic table-studded patio"; perhaps people "don't come here for the food or the service" but it's nevertheless a popular "hangout for students and politicos", and "the UT football game-day tailgate" headquarters.

Serranos *Tex-Mex* 16 | 14 | 17 | $17

Arboretum | 10000 Research Blvd. (Great Hills Trail) | 512-250-9555
Downtown | Symphony Sq. | 1111 Red River St. (11th St.) | 512-322-9080
Southwest Austin | Best Buy Shopping Ctr. | 5030 Hwy. 290 W. (Mo-Pac Expwy.) | 512-891-7592
Cedar Park | 11100 Pecan Park Blvd. (Lakeline Blvd.) | 512-258-3441
Round Rock | La Frontera Shopping Ctr. | 2701 Parker Rd. (I-35) | 512-218-4888
www.serranos.com

"Popular" for its "two-for-one specials" on Mondays, this "local" chain serves up "huge portions" of "standard Tex-Mex" fare that tends toward the "run-of-the-mill"; although the Downtown location's "great outdoor setting" with "terraced stone steps overlooking the creek" make it a destination to "grab a few margaritas", patrons of the other branches wish they'd "work on that decor, please."

Shady Grove *American* 19 | 21 | 17 | $17

Zilker | 1624 Barton Springs Rd. (Lamar Blvd.) | 512-474-9991 | www.theshadygrove.com

A "laid-back, relaxed atmosphere" characterizes this "trailer-themed" spot, a "true Austin-style hangout" in Zilker with "something to please everyone" on its "interesting" classic American menu; the "unique decor is just too cool" but the main draw is the "outside seating under the pecan trees", where diners dig "fab margaritas" and "live music under the stars" on Thursdays – but "expect long waits during peak times."

NEW Shanghai Restaurant *Chinese* - | - | - | I

North Central | 6718 Middle Fiskville Rd. (Huntland Dr.) | 512-458-8088

This family-owned emporium in North Central Austin features an extensive menu of inexpensive Chinese standards set down in spacious bamboo-accented surroundings; it's a favorite for dim sum on weekends, with a mind-boggling array of offerings brought to your table by friendly cart-pushing servers.

Shoal Creek Saloon *Cajun* 18 | 15 | 18 | $16

Downtown | 909 N. Lamar Blvd. (9th St.) | 512-474-0805 | www.shoalcreeksaloon.com

Often "overlooked", this "Louisiana-inspired" "hole-in-the-wall" "hangout" offers "a little New Orleans in Downtown Austin"; it's a spot "to watch sports" or "sit out back" on the patio "overlooking Shoal Creek" while having a "cheap" "cold beer" and "good Cajun" fare such as "fried seafood" and "po' boys that easily serve two"; P.S. the Wednesday and Friday "all-you-can-eat lunchtime fish fry is popular with the locals."

Shoreline Grill *Continental* 24 | 24 | 24 | $44

Downtown | San Jacinto Ctr. | 98 San Jacinto Blvd. (Cesar Chavez St.) | 512-477-3300 | www.shorelinegrill.com

An "appealing" menu with "a wide variety" of "exceptional" and "artfully presented" Continental dishes and a "fantastic wine selection" are staples at this Downtown mainstay, which also offers "splendid service that's a perfect balance of professionalism, warmth and courteousness"; further enhancing the experience are the "gorgeous views" from its "lovely room" and "outdoor seating along Lady Bird Lake", making it the ideal place to "watch the bats fly at sunset."

Z Siena *Italian* 25 | 27 | 22 | $41

Northwest Hills | 6203 N. Capital of Texas Hwy. (Rte. 2222) | 512-349-7667 | www.sienarestaurant.com

Set in a "lovely" stone building that evokes an "old Italian villa", this Northwest Hills "favorite" charms customers with "scrumptious", "rustic" Tuscan cuisine (think bistecca alla florentina and "lots of wild boar") and an "expansive" regional wine list; service is "attentive, but not hovering", ensuring a "delightful", if "expensive", experience that works for a "quiet lunch" or "romantic dinner."

Silver K Cafe *American* - | - | - | M

Johnson City | 209 E. Main St. (F Ave.) | 830-868-2911 | www.silverkcafe.com

Housed in a "pretty" historic building with exposed-wood beams and antique light fixtures, this Johnson City cafe proves a "must-visit" in Hill Country for its "inspired" takes on traditional American fare (signatures include honey-pecan fried chicken and buttermilk pie) and its well-considered selection of Texas wines; service is "good" too, leading regulars to recommend it as a "nice place to stop in" - you'd never expect such a "jewel" "given the small-town location."

Smitty's Market ⊭ *BBQ* ▽ 19 | 10 | 12 | $16

Lockhart | 208 S. Commerce St. (Prairie Lea St.) | 512-398-9344 | www.smittysmarket.com

Another "darn good" BBQ "joint" in Lockhart, this "top-tier" contender occupies the historic building where Kreuz Market once stood (the two institutions are run by different branches of the same family); fans line up for "wonderful" smoked meats and links served cafeteria-style and then hunker down at one of the long pine tables for an old-fashioned chowdown.

South Congress Café *Southwestern* 22 | 20 | 21 | $28

SoCo | 1600 S. Congress Ave. (Monroe St.) | 512-447-3905 | www.southcongresscafe.com

"Clever" takes on Southwestern cuisine, "great cocktails" and a "knockout brunch" are the hallmarks of this fairly priced SoCo spot set in "bright", "stylish" digs with alligator-skin booths and retro light fixtures; service is "top-notch", but regulars warn of "long waits" to be seated and suggest you "go at off hours because this place is mighty popular."

Southside Market & BBQ *BBQ* 24 | 10 | 14 | $15

Elgin | 1212 Hwy. 290 E. (Hwy. 95) | 512-281-4650 | www.southsidemarket.com

Supporters salivate over the "excellent sausage" at this family-owned BBQ fixture in Elgin that's been turning out their "spicy" signature links since 1882; a selection of slow-cooked meats, "homemade" sides and hand-dipped ice cream cones round out the inexpensive offerings served up "Texas-style" in a "down-home" setting with communal tables and a full-service butcher shop on-site.

Starlite *American* 25 | 21 | 22 | $42

Warehouse District | 407 Colorado St. (4th St.) | 512-374-9012 | www.starliteaustin.net

This Warehouse District "star" "shines" thanks to a seasonal New American menu showcasing "innovative" dishes plus handcrafted cocktails all served up in an "elegant and modern" interior with vaulted ceilings and an Italian crystal chandelier; "professional" servers and all-around "attention to detail" make it a favorite "date spot."

NEW **Steeping Room, The** *Tearoom* ▽ 21 | 22 | 19 | $16

Northwest Austin | Domain, The | 11410 Century Oaks Terr. (Braker Ln.) | 512-977-8337 | www.thesteepingroom.com

Northwest Austinites applaud this "charming" newcomer, a "cute little tearoom" ensconced in The Domain shopping center serving a long list of drinks alongside "delicious" sandwiches "with the crusts cut off", as well as reasonably priced soups, salads and a selection of sweets; even if service sometimes hits a snag, the soothing "Zen atmosphere" makes it "a pleasant place for lunch", a hot drink or a glass of wine at one of the outdoor tables.

Stubb's M *BBQ* 20 | 17 | 16 | $18

Downtown | 801 Red River Rd. (8th St.) | 512-480-8341 | www.stubbsaustin.com

"Beer, barbecue and bands" are the mainstays of this Downtown temple to "live music" and "hearty meals" that are a "fine example of" the genre, featuring "many more options of sides than most joints" of its ilk, all dished out with "fast service" in a "lively, rustic atmosphere"; P.S. "the gospel Sunday brunch is a treat."

Sullivan's Steakhouse ◐ *Steak* 24 | 23 | 23 | $53

Warehouse District | 300 Colorado St. (3rd St.) | 512-495-6504 | www.sullivansteakhouse.com

"If you're in the mood for steak" but "don't want a $300 bill", these "dependable" links in an "Austin-based chain" prove some of "the better chophouses" around given their "excellent cuts of beef", "attentive" staffers and retro "big-city" vibe; the "lively" bars are a "swinging" "place to mingle" and are typically "crowded and noisy" after dark.

Sunflower Vietnamese *Vietnamese* ▽ 23 | 8 | 13 | $15

North Austin | 8557 Research Blvd. (Fairfield Dr.) | 512-339-7860

"Someone in the kitchen truly knows what he's doing" at this "find" "in the Little Saigon area" of North Austin featuring "delightful" Vietnamese dishes that are "fresh, hot and well-seasoned"; most don't fret about the "slow service" (or the "strip-mall" location), insisting that "every dish is worth the wait", because "dollar for dollar it's one of the best values in town."

Suzi's China Grill *Chinese* 19 | 17 | 18 | $20

Allandale | 7858 Shoal Creek Blvd. (Anderson Ln.) | 512-302-4600

West Lake Hills | 2745 Bee Caves Rd. (Edgegrove Dr.) | 512-347-7077

Suzi's China Kitchen S *Chinese*

South Lamar | 1152 S. Lamar Blvd. (Barton Springs Rd.) | 512-441-8400

www.suzischinagrill.com

"Old standbys that never fail to please", these "upscale Chinese" outposts appeal to those craving "fresh", "fast", "elegant" fare (the "specials are tempting") served in a "pleasant" "friendly atmosphere"; the "effervescent" owner has created three distinct eateries: the South Lamar original has a "neighborhood feel", the Allandale location is "a hot spot for those weekday lunches", while the West Lake Hills branch is "spiffier."

Tacodeli *Mexican* 25 | 13 | 20 | $9

Northwest Austin | 12001 Burnet Rd. (Mo-Pac Expwy.) | 512-339-1700

Southwest Austin | 1500 Spyglass Dr. (Mo-Pac Expwy.) | 512-732-0303

www.tacodeli.com

"Crave-worthy tacos", "mouthwatering" daily specials and other inexpensive "authentic" Mexican eats make these area "standouts" Austin's No. 1 Bang-for-the Buck in this year's Survey ("talk about a great meal at a great price"); both the Northwest and Southwest locations offer "order-at-the-counter" service and "cool", "casual" settings, which are "overflowing with regulars" whose only complaint is that they "wish" these "gems" "were open for dinner."

Taco Xpress ⊄ *Mexican* 21 | 16 | 15 | $10

South Lamar | 2529 S. Lamar Blvd. (Montclaire St.) | 512-444-0261 | www.tacoxpress.com

The epitome of "Austin", this "funky" South Lamar "joint" run by local "icon" Maria Corbalan turns out "yummy" tacos in a "kitschy", "convivial" atmosphere enhanced by "live music" on the "great patio"; though a recent move imparted a "more modern" look, it remains as "busy" as ever thanks to the "same wonderful food" at "unbeatable" prices.

Taverna Pizzeria & Risotteria *Italian* 23 | 20 | 20 | $30

Downtown | 258 W. Second St. (Lavaca St.) | 512-477-1001 | www.tavernabylombardi.com

See review in Dallas/Ft. Worth Directory.

Texas Chili Parlor ◐ *American* 20 | 18 | 20 | $14

Downtown | 1409 Lavaca St. (15th St.) | 512-472-2828

This "dark", "grungy" "Capitol-area" Downtown "hangout" is famed for its "hellfire hot chili", juicy burgers and other "cheap" American grub accompanied by "heavy pours" of "good cold beer"; even if connoisseurs claim the food's "not that great", old-timers insist it's "a must-visit for tradition's sake" thanks to an "authentically Texas" vibe and "gruff service [that's] part of the charm."

Thai Kitchen *Thai* 20 | 7 | 16 | $14

Campus | 3009 Guadalupe St. (30th St.) | 512-474-2575 ◐
South Austin | 801 E. William Cannon Dr. (I-81) | 512-445-4844
West Lake Hills | 3437 Bee Caves Rd. (Blue Ridge Trail) | 512-328-3538 Ⓢ

"Good, cheap" Thai fare (and some Chinese dishes) – including a "wide selection" of "blissful soups" – is on the menu at these branches of a locally owned chain; still, some say the "service and food quality can be hit-or-miss" and the "slit-your-wrists decor" "could use a lot of help", especially at the West Lake Hills and South Austin outposts, which are each "marred by a crummy location."

Thai Noodle House *Thai* ▽ 17 | 7 | 14 | $11

Campus | 2602 Guadalupe St. (26th St.) | 512-494-1011

"Don't expect fancy dining" at this "simple, reliable" Campus noodle house that's frequented by "die-hard fans" (many from "the college set"), despite being "tucked away a bit from The Drag"; its "repeat customers" report that it's "worth the effort to find" for its menu of "basic Thai options" featuring food that's "humble" but full of "flavor", while detractors are "not happy with the service" or similarly "no-frills" decor; N.B. the Decor score may not fully reflect a recent expansion.

Thai Passion ◐ *Thai* 20 | 16 | 19 | $19

Downtown | 620 Congress Ave. (7th St.) | 512-472-1244 | www.thaipassion.com

"Beautifully plated" and "tasty" cuisine is "attentively served" by a "gracious" staff in a "serene setting" (especially the glass-topped "courtyard dining room") at this Downtown Thai eatery with "historic ambiance"; its "good value" makes it a "favorite lunch spot", and its "late-night hours" (open nightly till 3 AM) are another plus.

Thistle Café *American* 18 | 18 | 16 | $24

Downtown | 300 W. Sixth St. (Lavaca St.) | 512-275-9777
West Lake Hills | Davenport Vill. | 3801 N. Capital of Texas Hwy. (Westlake Dr.) | 512-347-1000
www.thistlecafe.com

A varied menu of "healthy" American options prove "more than acceptable" to local lunchers at these order-at-the-counter twins Downtown (sleeker with more space) and in West Lake Hills (offering full dinner service); yet while some regulars report they've had "good" experiences, the majority maintains it "could be a lot better" and add that "unconcerned" service and "soulless" decor leads them to seek options elsewhere.

Threadgill's *Southern* 19 | 19 | 18 | $18

Crestview | 6416 N. Lamar Blvd. (bet. Hwy. 183 & Rte. 2222) | 512-451-5440
Downtown South | 301 W. Riverside Dr. (Barton Springs Rd.) | 512-472-9304
www.threadgills.com

"You'll think you're at grandma's" when you visit these "homestyle Southern" spots that are "legendary for live music" ("most nights") and "old-fashioned comfort food that makes mouths happy"; "history was made at the original" Crestview site (Janis Joplin got her start here in the early 1960s), while the newer Downtown South branch is "filled to the rafters with rock memorabilia", and features a "fine Sunday gospel brunch."

III Forks ☒ *Steak* 25 | 24 | 24 | $60

Downtown | 111 Lavaca St. (1st St.) | 512-474-1776 | www.3forks.com

Bring "a full wallet and an empty stomach" to these Austin and Dallas-area "temples of beef" searing "excellent steaks" "cooked to perfection" and accompanied by "fabulous fixin's" like duchess potatoes and "the best creamed corn ever"; a "gracious" staff and "over-the-top" marble and dark-wood decor "give it an elegant" feel, so even if critics cry it's "gaudy" and "overhyped", it still ranks as a "favorite" for "special occasions."

NEW Trattoria Lisina *Italian* - | - | - | M

Driftwood | Mandola Estate Winery | 13308 FM 150 W. (FM 1826) | 512-894-3111 | www.trattorialisina.com

Resembling a Tuscan stone villa, this lovely Driftwood Italian from chef Damian Mandola proffers a variety of moderately priced rustic specialties like osso buco and roast suckling pig; the romantic interior features well-worn concrete floors, wooden chairs and copper accents while the breezy patio perched on the edge of the family's adjacent vineyard offers a superb seat for taking in a Hill Country sunset.

Z NEW TRIO *American* 27 | 24 | 26 | $52

Downtown | Four Seasons Hotel | 98 San Jacinto Blvd. (1st St.) | 512-685-8300 | www.fourseasons.com

It's "not just 'hotel food'" insist enthusiasts of the "delicious" fare at this reinvented dining room in Downtown's Four Seasons where the New American menu focuses on premium steaks, seafood and wine (60 available by the glass) and the "elegant" interior is dressed in warm red tones and outfitted with mahogany tables; considering it still offers a luxurious Sunday brunch and a "fab view" of Lady Bird Lake, it's no wonder some suggest it "reflects the best of the 'new' Austin."

Trudy's *Tex-Mex* 20 | 16 | 18 | $17

North Austin | 8820 Burnet Rd. (Hwy. 183) | 512-454-1474 ◐
North Campus | 409 W. 30th St. (Guadalupe St.) | 512-477-2935 ◐
South Austin | 901 Little Texas Ln. (I-35) | 512-326-9899
www.trudys.com

"Still going strong after more than 25 years", this "popular" Tex-Mex mini-chain "hits the spot" with "fresh" south-of-the-border eats and a handful of Southern specialties served in a "crowded", "family-friendly" atmosphere; some diners demur on the "fraternity party" bar scene and service that can be "variable", but most misgivings are pushed aside once you toss back one of their famously "potent" Mexican martinis (only two per customer because "they'll really knock you on your you-know-what").

Truluck's *Seafood* 23 | 22 | 23 | $44

Arboretum | 10225 Research Blvd. (Great Hills Trail) | 512-794-8300
Warehouse District | 400 Colorado St. (4th St.) | 512-482-9000
www.trulucks.com

See review in Dallas/Ft. Worth Directory.

Turtle Restaurant, The *American* - | - | - | M

Brownwood | 514 Center Ave. (Chandler St.) | 325-646-8200 | www.theturtlerestaurant.com

The quaint Hill Country town of Brownwood is home to this inviting BYO where chef Eric Aldis pays homage to the Slow Food movement with New American dishes he crafts from local Texas ingredients, including herbs and veggies from the back garden; the small, candlelit room is decorated with a turtle theme, though the most appealing feature may be the adjacent gelateria turning out 16 seasonal homemade flavors.

219 West *American* 21 | 19 | 18 | $26

Warehouse District | 219 W. Fourth St. (Colorado St.) | 512-474-2194 | www.219west.com

"Upscale bar food" plus "a darn good wine list" lure "trendy" tipplers to this "hip" Warehouse District New American featuring one of "the best happy hours in town", with deals on drinks and small plates from 5-9 PM daily; "service can slow", but plasma TVs and a "cool singles scene" provide ample distraction.

Z Uchi *Japanese* 28 | 26 | 25 | $48

Zilker | 801 S. Lamar Blvd. (Barton Springs Rd.) | 512-916-4808 | www.uchiaustin.com

"Prepare to be dazzled" at this "chic" Zilker destination that surveyors say is "about as close to perfect as it gets" thanks to "incredible young chef" Tyson Cole's "brilliant" creations that take Japanese cuisine "to a new level" and earn this "jewel" the No. 1 Food score in Austin; a "top-notch" staff "goes out of its way to please" in the "charming, little" space, so even if "endless waits" and "expensive" tabs are par for the course, it all adds up to a "wonderful experience" nonetheless.

Ventana S M *French* ▽ 23 | 17 | 18 | $30

North Austin | Texas Culinary Academy | 11400 Burnet Rd. (Duval Rd.) | 512-339-3850 | www.tca.edu/restaurant.asp

Staffed by the students and teachers of the Texas Culinary Academy, this North Austin fine-dining room features a "wonderful" "sampling" of classical and contemporary French "delights" accompanied by well-chosen wines all at more-than-reasonable prices; even if a few note the modern space is "too stark" and service sometimes hits a snag, consensus is that "when the students hit it right, it's as good or better than anything else in the city"; N.B. open Tuesdays-Fridays.

Z Vespaio *Italian* 28 | 23 | 24 | $43

SoCo | 1610 S. Congress Ave. (Monroe St.) | 512-441-6100 | www.austinvespaio.com

Equal parts "unpretentious" "neighborhood" hangout and "elegant" "big-city" joint, this "upscale" SoCo "mainstay" - and Austin's Most Popular restaurant - is "almost impossible to get into" thanks to its "fantastic", "rustic" Italian cuisine ("delicious homemade pastas", "tempting specials") and "great wines" brought from the open kitchen by an "outstanding" staff; because of a no-reservations policy on weekends, there's "always a line", but those in-the-know "steal a seat at the bar" and pass the "interminable waits" with some stellar "people-watching."

Vin Bistro S *American* 24 | 20 | 23 | $37

Brykerwoods | 1601 W. 38th St. (Kerbey Ln.) | 512-377-5252 | www.vinbistro.com

"The wine shines" at this "hidden gem" in Brykerwoods that "hits the mark every time" with "perfect pairings" matching "inventive" New American dishes with two- and five-oz pours from "a fine selection" of international vintages; given the "knowledgeable staff", "pleasant" patio for "outside dining" and "great" drink specials on various nights, it's no wonder "neighborhood" denizens hail it as a "sleeper on the Austin eating scene."

Vivo *Tex-Mex* 19 | 21 | 17 | $21

Cherrywood | 2015 Manor Rd. (Poquito St.) | 512-482-0300 | www.vivo-austin.com

A "cool" crimson interior and paintings of voluptuous nudes set a "sexy" scene at this "crowded" Cherrywood hideaway that's "great for a date" thanks to "fab margaritas", a "beautiful" plant-filled patio and "complimentary roses for each lady"; "fresh" Tex-Mex fare includes "delicious" deep-fried puffy tacos as well as a smattering of "healthy options" all at moderate prices.

Waterloo Ice House *Burgers* 16 | 14 | 16 | $15

Downtown | 600 N. Lamar Blvd. (6th St.) | 512-472-5400
NEW **Jollyville** | 14900 Avery Ranch Blvd. (Parmer Ln.) | 512-255-4873
North Austin | 8600 Burnet Rd. (Hwy. 183) | 512-458-6544
Northwest Hills | 6203 N. Capital of Texas Hwy. (Rte. 2222) | 512-418-9700
Rosedale | 1106 W. 38th St. (Medical Pkwy.) | 512-451-5245
www.waterlooicehouse.com

"Juicy", "loaded burgers" and "crispy housemade fries" are the staples at this "fast, friendly", "family-oriented" chain where small fry get their own menu; "typical", "bland decor" and "inconsistent service" are drawbacks, but the Downtown location has "good live music" on weekends, while "parents can have a beer" from the "extensive selection" as "kids play in the sandbox" at the Northwest Hills branch.

Wildfire *Southwestern* ▽ 22 | 17 | 19 | $25

Georgetown | 812 S. Austin Ave. (bet. 8th & 9th Sts.) | 512-869-3473

"A pleasant surprise in Georgetown", this upscale-casual Southwestern in an "interesting location" across the street from the courthouse offers a "creative menu" showcasing succulent meats (including wild game) cooked in an "oak-fired grill", plus "an excellent selection of fine appetizers" and "Texas wines" at "great prices"; with dark woods and low lighting, the space is "quaint", but it's the "smell of the wood fire burning that brings folks back every time."

Z **Wink** **S** *American* 27 | 21 | 26 | $54

Old West Austin | 1014 N. Lamar Blvd. (11th St.) | 512-482-8868 | www.winkrestaurant.com

A "temple for foodies" in Old West Austin, this "super-small" strip-mall eatery "delights" diners with an "amazing" New American menu that shows a "fanatical devotion to fresh, local ingredients" while the equally "wonderful" wine list is loaded with "little-known gems"; on the downside are "small portions", "big prices" and a "cramped" "seating plan that would make a Parisian cafe proud", but "personalized service" means most "can't wait to go back"; P.S. the adjacent wine bar "is worth a visit on its own."

Woodland, The **M** *American* 18 | 17 | 18 | $24

SoCo | 1716 S. Congress Ave. (Annie St.) | 512-441-6800 | www.woodlandaustin.com

American "home cooking" is updated for "hipsters" at this SoCo spot that mixes gently priced "comfort" classics with "retro" cocktails; the "cute" "sylvan setting" ("yes, that is a tree in there") is trimmed in greens while a "friendly staff" tends to a customer base culled from "neighborhood" "students" and "families."

Zax Pints & Plates *Pub Food* 19 17 19 $25

Downtown South | 312 Barton Springs Rd. (Riverside Dr.) | 512-481-0100 | www.zaxaustin.com

You'll find "more than just pints" at this "sleek" "yet comfortable" spot south of Downtown serving "upscale pub grub" and "a decent wine list" at an "excellent value"; it's ideal for "burgers for the kids and something a little better for the parents", or for "a nice lunch with clients", and there's "live jazz" and a "pint-night happy hour" on Wednesdays and a "lovely courtyard."

Zoot M *American* 26 22 25 $48

Old West Austin | 509 Hearn St. (Lake Austin Blvd.) | 512-477-6535 | www.zootrestaurant.com

"Beautifully prepared" dishes from an "imaginative" market-driven New American menu "attract a great mix" of customers to this Old West Austin "favorite" set in an "elegant", "well-appointed" bungalow exuding a "quiet, relaxing" atmosphere; "unhurried" service from a "first-class" staff means "you can always count on it" for a "romantic" date or any other "special occasion" that calls for a "near-perfect meal"; P.S. insiders say the tasting menus - especially the "amazing" vegetarian one - are "excellent" options.

Z'Tejas *Southwestern* 22 20 19 $26

Arboretum | 9400 Arboretum Blvd. (Capital of Texas Hwy.) | 512-346-3506
Clarksville | 1110 W. Sixth St. (Lamar Blvd.) | 512-478-5355
Jollyville | 10525 W. Parmer Ln. (Avery Ranch Blvd.) | 512-388-7772
www.ztejas.com

"A loyal following" means "tables are scarce" at these "convivial" "hot spots" offering "delicious" Southwestern fare, "festive" environments (complete with "terrific outside dining") and "friendly staffers"; the Clarksville "original is a hodgepodge of linked 1940s cottages", while the Arboretum offshoot is housed in a "Colorado lodge-style" building that's "big, airy and spacious"; N.B. the Cedar Park branch opened post-Survey.

AUSTIN AND THE HILL COUNTRY INDEXES

Cuisines

Includes restaurant names, locations and Food ratings. Z indicates places with the highest ratings, popularity and importance.

AMERICAN (NEW)

Blue Star | **Rosedale** 20
Café 909 | **Marble Falls** 29
Chez Zee | **NW Hills** 21
Crú Wine Bar | **Downtown** 20
Z Driskill Grill | **Downtown** 26
Eastside Café | **Cherrywood** 24
Z Hudson's | **Lakeway** 28
Z Jasper's | **NW Austin** 24
Z Jeffrey's | **Clarksville** 26
Judges' Hill | **W Campus** 24
Kona Grill | **NW Austin** 20
Mirabelle | **NW Hills** 25
Rest. Jezebel | **Downtown** 27
Starlite | **Warehouse Dist** 25
Z NEW TRIO | **Downtown** 27
Turtle, The | **Brownwood** -
219 West | **Warehouse Dist** 21
Vin Bistro | **Brykerwoods** 24
Z Wink | **Old W Austin** 27
Woodland, The | **SoCo** 18
Zoot | **Old W Austin** 26

AMERICAN (TRADITIONAL)

Bee Cave | **Bee Cave** 20
Belmont, The | **Downtown** 18
Billy's/Burnet | **Rosedale** 20
Cheesecake Factory | **Arboretum** 20
NEW Daily Grill | **NW Austin** 24
Dirty Martin's | **Campus** 21
1886 Café | **Downtown** 22
Houston's | **NW Austin** 23
Hyde Park | **multi.** 21
Magnolia Café | **multi.** 21
Moonshine | **Downtown** 20
North by NW | **Great Hills** 18
Opal Divine's | **multi.** 14
Shady Grove | **Zilker** 19
Silver K | **Johnson City** -
Texas Chili | **Downtown** 20
Thistle Café | **multi.** 18
Zax Pints | **Downtown S** 19

ASIAN FUSION

Bistro 88 | **West Lake** 25
Mars | **SoCo** 20

BAKERIES

1886 Café | **Downtown** 22
Rather Sweet | **Fredericksburg** 26

BARBECUE

Artz Rib Hse. | **S Lamar** 21
Buster's | **Bee Cave** 24
City Market | **Luling** 24
Cooper's | **Llano** 27
County Line | **multi.** 20
Crosstown BBQ | **Elgin** -
Gonzales | **Gonzales** -
Green Mesquite | **Zilker** 18
Iron Works | **Downtown** 22
Kreuz Mkt. | **Lockhart** 26
Lambert's | **Downtown** 23
Louie Mueller | **Taylor** 25
Meyer's | **Elgin** 21
Opie's BBQ | **Spicewood** 23
R.O.'s Outpost | **Spicewood** -
Ruby's | **N Campus** 23
Z Salt Lick | **Driftwood** 24
Smitty's Mkt. | **Lockhart** 19
Southside Mkt. | **Elgin** 24
Stubb's | **Downtown** 20

BRAZILIAN

NEW Estância | **SW Austin** 27
Sampaio's | **Rosedale** 20
São Paulo's | **Campus** 21

BURGERS

Billy's/Burnet | **Rosedale** 20
Dirty Martin's | **Campus** 21
Hut's | **Downtown** 23
Player's | **Campus** 19
Shady Grove | **Zilker** 19
Waterloo Ice Hse. | **multi.** 16

CAJUN

Evangeline Café | **SW Austin** 19
Gene's | **E Austin** 25
Gumbo's | **multi.** 24
Hilltop Café | **Fredericksburg** 23
Pappadeaux | **N Austin** 23
Shoal Creek | **Downtown** 18

CARIBBEAN

Café Josie | **Clarksville** 26

CHINESE

Din Ho Chinese | **N Austin** 24
Golden Wok* | **N Austin** 22
P.F. Chang's | **multi.** 22
NEW Shanghai Rest. | **N Central** -
Suzi's | **multi.** 19

CONTINENTAL

Green Pastures | **Bouldin Creek** 23
Z Jeffrey's | **Clarksville** 26
Shoreline Grill | **Downtown** 24

CREOLE

Evangeline Café | **SW Austin** 19
Gumbo's | **multi.** 24
Ms. B's | **multi.** 22
Real New Orleans | **Round Mtn** -

CUBAN

Habana | **multi.** 21

DELIS

Katz's Deli | **Downtown** 19

DESSERT

Aquarelle | **Downtown** 27
Asti Trattoria | **Hyde Pk** 24
Austin Land | **Downtown** 22
Cheesecake Factory | **Arboretum** 20
Chez Zee | **NW Hills** 21
Z Driskill Grill | **Downtown** 26
1886 Café | **Downtown** 22
Enoteca Vespaio | **SoCo** 25
European Bistro | **Pflugerville** 24
Fino | **W Campus** 23
Moonshine | **Downtown** 20
Starlite | **Warehouse Dist** 25
NEW Steeping Room | **NW Austin** 21
Z NEW TRIO | **Downtown** 27
Z Vespaio | **SoCo** 28

EASTERN EUROPEAN

European Bistro | **Pflugerville** 24

ECLECTIC

August E's | **Fredericksburg** 27
Bess | **Downtown** 17
Castle Hill | **Downtown** 25
Eastside Café | **Cherrywood** 24
Hilltop Café | **Fredericksburg** 23
Kerbey Ln. Café | **multi.** 20
Patton's | **Marble Falls** -
Saba Blue | **Warehouse Dist** 18

EUROPEAN

Bistro 88 | **West Lake** 25

FONDUE

Melting Pot | **multi.** 21

FRENCH

Aquarelle | **Downtown** 27
Chez Nous | **Downtown** 25
Flip Happy Crepes | **Zilker** -
Ventana | **N Austin** 23

GERMAN

Scholz Garten | **Downtown** 13

HAWAIIAN

Kona Grill | **NW Austin** 20
Roy's | **Downtown** 25

INDIAN

Clay Pit | **Downtown** 23
Madras Pavilion | **N Austin** 22
Sarovar Indian | **N Austin** 21

ITALIAN

(N=Northern)

Asti Trattoria | **Hyde Pk** 24
Bellagio | **Jester Vill** 21
Brick Oven | **multi.** 19
Carmelo's | **Downtown** 22
Carrabba's | **multi.** 22
Cibo | **Downtown** 20
Enoteca Vespaio | **SoCo** 25
Frank & Angie's | **Downtown** 21
NEW Gypsy Italian | **Bouldin Creek** -
La Traviata | **Downtown** 24
Mandola's | **N Central** 22
Mangieri's | **Circle C** 22
NEW NoRTH | **NW Austin** -
Reale's | **Jollyville** 23
Rocco's Grill | **Lakeway** 20
Romeo's | **Zilker** 17
NEW Sagra | **Downtown** -
Z Siena | N | **NW Hills** 25
Taverna Pizzeria | **Downtown** 23
NEW Trattoria Lisina | **Driftwood** -
Z Vespaio | **SoCo** 28

JAPANESE

(* sushi specialist)

Kenichi* | **Warehouse Dist** 22
Mikado Ryotei* | **N Austin** 24
Musashino* | **NW Hills** 27
Z Uchi* | **Zilker** 28

JEWISH

Katz's Deli | **Downtown** 19

KOREAN

Korea Hse. | **NW Austin** 21

KOSHER

Madras Pavilion | **N Austin** 22

MEDITERRANEAN

Fino | **W Campus** 23
Louie's 106 | **Downtown** 24

MEXICAN

Abuelo's | **SW Austin** 19
Cantina Laredo | **Downtown** 21
Curra's Grill | **Travis Hts** 21
El Chile | **Cherrywood** 22
El Meson | **SE Austin** 27
Elsi's | **Brentwood** -
El Sol y La Luna | **SoCo** 19
Z Fonda San Miguel | **Highland Pk** 26
Guero's | **SoCo** 20
Las Manitas | **Downtown** 20
Las Palomas | **West Lake** 21
Manuel's | **multi.** 22
NEW Oaxacan Tamaleo | **Cedar Creek** -
Polvo's | **Bouldin Creek** 21
Tacodeli | **multi.** 25
Taco Xpress | **S Lamar** 21

NOODLE SHOPS

Thai Noodle Hse. | **Campus** 17

PAN-ASIAN

Kenichi | **Warehouse Dist** 22
Pei Wei | **multi.** 19
Satay | **NW Austin** 21

PERSIAN

Alborz | **NW Austin** 21

PIZZA

Brick Oven | **multi.** 19
Frank & Angie's | **Downtown** 21
Home Slice | **SoCo** 23
Mangieri's | **Circle C** 22
Reale's | **Jollyville** 23
Taverna Pizzeria | **Downtown** 23

PUB FOOD

Zax Pints | **Downtown S** 19

SALVADORAN

Elsi's | **Brentwood** -

SEAFOOD

Z Eddie V's | **multi.** 26
Finn & Porter | **Downtown** 23
McCormick/Schmick | **multi.** 21
Pappadeaux | **N Austin** 23
Quality Seafood | **Hyde Pk** -
III Forks | **Downtown** 25
Z NEW TRIO | **Downtown** 27
Truluck's | **multi.** 23

SMALL PLATES

(See also Spanish tapas specialist)
Fino | Med. | **W Campus** 23
Louie's 106 | Med. | **Downtown** 24
219 West | Amer. | **Warehouse Dist** 21

SOUL FOOD

Gene's | **E Austin** 25
Hoover's | **multi.** 21

SOUTH AMERICAN

Café Josie | **Clarksville** 26
Doña Emilia's | **Downtown** 20

SOUTHERN

Hoover's | **multi.** 21
Threadgill's | **multi.** 19

SOUTHWESTERN

Backstage | **Spicewood** 26
Cool River | **NW Austin** 19
Patton's | **Marble Falls** -
Ranch 616 | **Downtown** 23
Roaring Fork | **Downtown** 24
South Congress | **SoCo** 22
Wildfire | **Georgetown** 22
Z'Tejas | **multi.** 22

SPANISH

(* tapas specialist)
Málaga* | **Warehouse Dist** 20

STEAKHOUSES

August E's | **Fredericksburg** 27
Austin Land | **Downtown** 22
Backstage | **Spicewood** 26
Cedar Grove | **Wimberley** -
Cool River | **NW Austin** 19
Z Eddie V's | **multi.** 26
NEW Estância | **SW Austin** 27
Finn & Porter | **Downtown** 23
Fleming's Prime | **Downtown** 24
Hoffbrau Steak | **Downtown** 16
NEW Joe DiMaggio's | **NW Austin** -

Ruth's Chris | **Downtown** 25
Sullivan's | **Warehouse Dist** 24
Ill Forks | **Downtown** 25
Z NEW TRIO | **Downtown** 27

TEAROOMS

NEW Steeping Room | **NW Austin** 21

TEX-MEX

Z Chuy's | **multi.** 21
El Azteca | **E Austin** 18
El Mercado | **multi.** 15
Hula Hut | **Old W Austin** 18
Iron Cactus | **multi.** 18
Matt's El Rancho | **S Lamar** 18
Oasis | **Lakeway** 11
Serranos | **multi.** 16
Trudy's | **multi.** 20
Vivo | **Cherrywood** 19

THAI

Madam Mam's | **multi.** 21
Thai Kitchen | **multi.** 20
Thai Noodle Hse. | **Campus** 17
Thai Passion | **Downtown** 20

VEGETARIAN

Madras Pavilion | **N Austin** 22

VIETNAMESE

Sunflower | **N Austin** 23

Locations

Includes restaurant names, cuisines and Food ratings. Z indicates places with the highest ratings, popularity and importance.

Austin

ALLANDALE

El Mercado | *Tex-Mex* 15
Suzi's | *Chinese* 19

ARBORETUM

Cheesecake Factory | *Amer.* 20
Z Eddie V's | *Seafood/Steak* 26
Kerbey Ln. Café | *Eclectic* 20
P.F. Chang's | *Chinese* 22
Serranos | *Tex-Mex* 16
Truluck's | *Seafood* 23
Z'Tejas | *SW* 22

BEE CAVE

Bee Cave | *Amer.* 20
Buster's | *BBQ* 24

BOULDIN CREEK

El Mercado | *Tex-Mex* 15
Green Pastures | *Continental* 23
NEW Gypsy Italian | *Italian* -
Polvo's | *Mex.* 21

BRENTWOOD

Elsi's | *Mex./Salvadoran* -

BRYKERWOODS

Brick Oven | *Pizza* 19
Kerbey Ln. Café | *Eclectic* 20
Vin Bistro | *Amer.* 24

CAMPUS

Dirty Martin's | *Burgers* 21
Kerbey Ln. Café | *Eclectic* 20
Madam Mam's | *Thai* 21
Player's | *Burgers* 19
São Paulo's | *Brazilian* 21
Thai Kitchen | *Thai* 20
Thai Noodle Hse. | *Thai* 17

CEDAR CREEK

NEW Oaxacan Tamaleo | *Mex.* -

CEDAR PARK

Serranos | *Tex-Mex* 16

CHERRYWOOD

Eastside Café | *Amer./Eclectic* 24
El Chile | *Mex.* 22
Hoover's | *Southern* 21
Vivo | *Tex-Mex* 19

CIRCLE C

Mangieri's | *Pizza* 22

CLARKSVILLE

Café Josie | *Carib.* 26
Z Jeffrey's | *Amer./Continental* 26
Z'Tejas | *SW* 22

CRESTVIEW

Threadgill's | *Southern* 19

DOWNTOWN

Aquarelle | *French* 27
Austin Land | *Steak* 22
Belmont, The | *Amer.* 18
Bess | *Eclectic* 17
Brick Oven | *Pizza* 19
Cantina Laredo | *Mex.* 21
Carmelo's | *Italian* 22
Castle Hill | *Eclectic* 25
Chez Nous | *French* 25
Cibo | *Italian* 20
Clay Pit | *Indian* 23
Crú Wine Bar | *Amer.* 20
Doña Emilia's | *S Amer.* 20
Z Driskill Grill | *Amer.* 26
Z Eddie V's | *Seafood/Steak* 26
1886 Café | *Amer.* 22
El Mercado | *Tex-Mex* 15
Finn & Porter | *Seafood/Steak* 23
Fleming's Prime | *Steak* 24
Frank & Angie's | *Pizza* 21
Gumbo's | *Cajun/Creole* 24
Habana | *Cuban* 21
Hoffbrau Steak | *Steak* 16
Hut's | *Burgers* 23
Iron Cactus | *Tex-Mex* 18
Iron Works | *BBQ* 22
Katz's Deli | *Deli* 19
Lambert's | *BBQ* 23
Las Manitas | *Mex.* 20
La Traviata | *Italian* 24
Louie's 106 | *Med.* 24
Manuel's | *Mex.* 22
McCormick/Schmick | *Seafood* 21
Melting Pot | *Fondue* 21

Moonshine | *Amer.* 20
Opal Divine's | *Amer.* 14
P.F. Chang's | *Chinese* 22
Ranch 616 | *SW* 23
Rest. Jezebel | *Amer.* 27
Roaring Fork | *SW* 24
Roy's | *Hawaiian* 25
Ruth's Chris | *Steak* 25
NEW Sagra | *Italian* -
Scholz Garten | *German* 13
Serranos | *Tex-Mex* 16
Shoal Creek | *Cajun* 18
Shoreline Grill | *Continental* 24
Stubb's | *BBQ* 20
Taverna Pizzeria | *Italian* 23
Texas Chili | *Amer.* 20
Thai Passion | *Thai* 20
Thistle Café | *Amer.* 18
III Forks | *Steak* 25
Z NEW TRIO | *Amer.* 27
Waterloo Ice Hse. | *Burgers* 16

DOWNTOWN SOUTH

Threadgill's | *Southern* 19
Zax Pints | *Pub* 19

EAST AUSTIN

El Azteca | *Tex-Mex* 18
Gene's | *Cajun/Soul Food* 25
Ms. B's | *Creole* 22

ELGIN

Crosstown BBQ | *BBQ* -
Meyer's | *BBQ* 21
Southside Mkt. | *BBQ* 24

GEORGETOWN

Wildfire | *SW* 22

GONZALES

Gonzales | *BBQ* -

GREAT HILLS

Brick Oven | *Pizza* 19
Z Chuy's | *Tex-Mex* 21
Manuel's | *Mex.* 22
North by NW | *Amer.* 18

HIGHLAND PARK

Z Fonda San Miguel | *Mex.* 26

HYDE PARK

Asti Trattoria | *Italian* 24
Hyde Park | *Amer* 21
Pei Wei | *Pan-Asian* 19

Quality Seafood | *Seafood* -

JESTER VILLAGE

Bellagio | *Italian* 21

JOLLYVILLE

Hoover's | *Southern* 21
Reale's | *Pizza* 23
Waterloo Ice Hse. | *Burgers* 16
Z'Tejas | *Southwestern* 22

LAKEWAY

Z Hudson's | *Amer.* 28
Oasis | *Tex-Mex* 11
Rocco's Grill | *Italian* 20

LOCKHART

Kreuz Mkt. | *BBQ* 26
Smitty's Mkt. | *BBQ* 19

LULING

City Market | *BBQ* 24

NORTH AUSTIN

Carrabba's | *Italian* 22
Z Chuy's | *Tex-Mex* 21
Din Ho Chinese | *Chinese* 24
Golden Wok | *Chinese* 22
Iron Cactus | *Tex-Mex* 18
Madras Pavilion | *Indian* 22
Mikado Ryotei | *Japanese* 24
Opal Divine's | *Amer.* 14
Pappadeaux | *Seafood* 23
Pei Wei | *Pan-Asian* 19
Sarovar Indian | *Indian* 21
Sunflower | *Viet.* 23
Trudy's | *Tex-Mex* 20
Ventana | *French* 23
Waterloo Ice Hse. | *Burgers* 16

NORTH CAMPUS

Ruby's | *BBQ* 23
Trudy's | *Tex-Mex* 20

NORTH CENTRAL

Mandola's | *Italian* 22
NEW Shanghai Rest. | *Chinese* -

NORTHWEST AUSTIN

Alborz | *Persian* 21
Cool River | *SW/Steak* 19
NEW Daily Grill | *Amer.* 24
El Mercado | *Tex-Mex* 15
Houston's | *Amer.* 23
Z Jasper's | *Amer.* 24

NEW Joe DiMaggio's | *Italian/Steak* –

Kona Grill | *Amer.* 20

Korea Hse. | *Korean* 21

McCormick/Schmick | *Seafood* 21

Melting Pot | *Fondue* 21

NEW NoRTH | *Italian* –

Satay | *Pan-Asian* 21

NEW Steeping Room | *Tea* 21

Tacodeli | *Mex.* 25

NORTHWEST HILLS

Chez Zee | *Amer.* 21

County Line | *BBQ* 20

Mirabelle | *Amer.* 25

Ms. B's | *Creole* 22

Musashino | *Japanese* 27

Z Siena | *Italian* 25

Waterloo Ice Hse. | *Burgers* 16

OLD WEST AUSTIN

Hula Hut | *Tex-Mex* 18

Magnolia Café | *Amer.* 21

Z Wink | *Amer.* 27

Zoot | *Amer.* 26

PFLUGERVILLE

European Bistro | *E Euro.* 24

ROSEDALE

Billy's/Burnet | *Amer.* 20

Blue Star | *Amer.* 20

Sampaio's | *Brazilian* 20

Waterloo Ice Hse. | *Burgers* 16

ROUND ROCK

Z Chuy's | *Tex-Mex* 21

Gumbo's | *Cajun/Creole* 24

Serranos | *Tex-Mex* 16

SOCO

El Sol y La Luna | *Mex.* 19

Enoteca Vespaio | *Italian* 25

Guero's | *Mex.* 20

Home Slice | *Pizza* 23

Magnolia Café | *Amer.* 21

Mars | *Asian Fusion* 20

South Congress | *SW* 22

Z Vespaio | *Italian* 28

Woodland, The | *Amer.* 18

SOUTH AUSTIN

Habana | *Cuban* 21

Opal Divine's | *Amer.* 14

Thai Kitchen | *Thai* 20

Trudy's | *Tex-Mex* 20

SOUTHEAST AUSTIN

El Meson | *Mex.* 27

SOUTH LAMAR

Artz Rib Hse. | *BBQ* 21

Kerbey Ln. Café | *Eclectic* 20

Matt's El Rancho | *Tex-Mex* 18

Suzi's | *Chinese* 19

Taco Xpress | *Mex.* 21

SOUTHWEST AUSTIN

Abuelo's | *Mex.* 19

Brick Oven | *Pizza* 19

NEW Estância | *Brazilian/Steak* 27

Evangeline Café | *Cajun/Creole* 19

Hyde Park | *Amer.* 21

Madam Mam's | *Thai* 21

Pei Wei | *Pan-Asian* 19

Serranos | *Tex-Mex* 16

Tacodeli | *Mex.* 25

TAYLOR

Louie Mueller | *BBQ* 25

TRAVIS HEIGHTS

Carrabba's | *Italian* 22

Curra's Grill | *Mex.* 21

WAREHOUSE DISTRICT

Kenichi | *Pan-Asian* 22

Málaga | *Spanish* 20

Saba Blue | *Eclectic* 18

Starlite | *Amer.* 25

Sullivan's | *Steak* 24

Truluck's | *Seafood* 23

219 West | *Amer.* 21

WEST CAMPUS

Fino | *Med.* 23

Judges' Hill | *Amer.* 24

WEST LAKE HILLS

Bistro 88 | *Asian/Euro.* 25

County Line | *BBQ* 20

Las Palomas | *Mex.* 21

Suzi's | *Chinese* 19

Thai Kitchen | *Thai* 20

Thistle Café | *Amer.* 18

WIMBERLEY

Cedar Grove | *Steak* –

ZILKER

Z Chuy's | *Tex-Mex* 21

Flip Happy Crepes | *French* –

Green Mesquite | *BBQ* 18

Romeo's | *Italian* 17

Shady Grove | *Amer.* 19

Z Uchi | *Japanese* 28

Hill Country

BROWNWOOD

Turtle, The | *Amer.* -

DRIFTWOOD

Z Salt Lick | *BBQ* 24

NEW Trattoria Lisina | *Italian* -

FREDERICKSBURG

August E's | *Steak* 27

Hilltop Café | *Eclectic* 23

Rather Sweet | *Bakery* 26

JOHNSON CITY

Silver K | *Amer.* -

LLANO

Cooper's | *BBQ* 27

MARBLE FALLS

Café 909 | *Amer.* 29

Patton's | *Eclectic* -

ROUND MOUNTAIN

Real New Orleans | *Creole* -

SPICEWOOD

Backstage | *Steak* 26

Opie's BBQ | *BBQ* 23

R.O.'s Outpost | *BBQ* -

Special Features

Listings cover the best in each category and include names, locations and Food ratings. Multi-location restaurants' features may vary by branch. Z indicates places with the highest ratings, popularity and importance.

BREAKFAST

(See also Hotel Dining)

Curra's Grill | **Travis Hts** 21
El Mercado | **multi.** 15
El Meson | **SE Austin** 27
El Sol y La Luna | **SoCo** 19
Guero's | **SoCo** 20
Hoover's | **Cherrywood** 21
Katz's Deli | **Downtown** 19
Kerbey Ln. Café | **multi.** 20
Las Manitas | **Downtown** 20
Magnolia Café | **multi.** 21
Taco Xpress | **S Lamar** 21
Trudy's | **multi.** 20
Waterloo Ice Hse. | **multi.** 16

BRUNCH

Chez Zee | **NW Hills** 21
Eastside Café | **Cherrywood** 24
1886 Café | **Downtown** 22
Enoteca Vespaio | **SoCo** 25
Z Fonda San Miguel | **Highland Pk** 26
Green Pastures | **Bouldin Creek** 23
Hyde Park | **Hyde Pk** 21
Judges' Hill | **W Campus** 24
Katz's Deli | **Downtown** 19
Manuel's | **multi.** 22
Moonshine | **Downtown** 20
Oasis | **Lakeway** 11
South Congress | **SoCo** 22
Thistle Café | **West Lake** 18
Threadgill's | **Downtown S** 19
Trudy's | **N Campus** 20
Wildfire | **Georgetown** 22

BUFFET SERVED

(Check availability)

Alborz | **NW Austin** 21
Clay Pit | **Downtown** 23
El Mercado | **Downtown** 15
Green Pastures | **Bouldin Creek** 23
Iron Cactus | **multi.** 18
Lambert's | **Downtown** 23
Madras Pavilion | **N Austin** 22
Sarovar Indian | **N Austin** 21
Silver K | **Johnson City** -
Threadgill's | **Downtown S** 19
Trudy's | **N Austin** 20

BUSINESS DINING

Aquarelle | **Downtown** 27
Asti Trattoria | **Hyde Pk** 24
August E's | **Fredericksburg** 27
Bee Cave | **Bee Cave** 20
Belmont, The | **Downtown** 18
Blue Star | **Rosedale** 20
Carmelo's | **Downtown** 22
Castle Hill | **Downtown** 25
Cedar Grove | **Wimberley** -
Cibo | **Downtown** 20
Cool River | **NW Austin** 19
Z Driskill Grill | **Downtown** 26
Z Eddie V's | **multi.** 26
1886 Café | **Downtown** 22
Finn & Porter | **Downtown** 23
Fino | **W Campus** 23
Fleming's Prime | **Downtown** 24
Z Fonda San Miguel | **Highland Pk** 26
Gumbo's | **Downtown** 24
NEW Gypsy Italian | **Bouldin Creek** -
Z Hudson's | **Lakeway** 28
Z Jasper's | **NW Austin** 24
Z Jeffrey's | **Clarksville** 26
NEW Joe DiMaggio's | **NW Austin** -
Judges' Hill | **W Campus** 24
Kenichi | **Warehouse Dist** 22
Louie's 106 | **Downtown** 24
Manuel's | **multi.** 22
McCormick/Schmick | **multi.** 21
Mikado Ryotei | **N Austin** 24
Mirabelle | **NW Hills** 25
Musashino | **NW Hills** 27
NEW NoRTH | **NW Austin** -
Rather Sweet | **Fredericksburg** 26
Rest. Jezebel | **Downtown** 27
Roaring Fork | **Downtown** 24
Roy's | **Downtown** 25
Ruth's Chris | **Downtown** 25
NEW Shanghai Rest. | **N Central** -
Shoreline Grill | **Downtown** 24
Z Siena | **NW Hills** 25

- Silver K | **Johnson City** –
- Starlite | **Warehouse Dist** 25
- Sullivan's | **Warehouse Dist** 24
- Suzi's | **multi.** 19
- Texas Chili | **Downtown** 20
- Thistle Café | **Downtown** 18
- Z NEW TRIO | **Downtown** 27
- Z Uchi | **Zilker** 28
- Ventana | **N Austin** 23
- Wildfire | **Georgetown** 22
- Woodland, The | **SoCo** 18
- Zax Pints | **Downtown S** 19
- Zoot | **Old W Austin** 26

CELEBRITY CHEFS

- Cibo | *Will Packwood* | **Downtown** 20
- Z Fonda San Miguel | *Miguel Ravago* | **Highland Pk** 26
- Z Hudson's | *Jeff Blank* | **Lakeway** 28
- Rather Sweet | *Rebecca Rather* | **Fredericksburg** 26
- NEW Trattoria Lisina | *Damian Mandola* | **Driftwood** –
- Z Uchi | *Tyson Cole* | **Zilker** 28

CHEF'S TABLE

- Cibo | **Downtown** 20

CHILD-FRIENDLY

(Alternatives to the usual fast-food places; * children's menu available)

- Billy's/Burnet* | **Rosedale** 20
- Brick Oven* | **multi.** 19
- County Line* | **multi.** 20
- Curra's Grill* | **Travis Hts** 21
- Din Ho Chinese | **N Austin** 24
- El Azteca* | **E Austin** 18
- El Mercado* | **multi.** 15
- El Meson | **SE Austin** 27
- El Sol y La Luna* | **SoCo** 19
- Evangeline Café* | **SW Austin** 19
- Frank & Angie's | **Downtown** 21
- Green Mesquite* | **Zilker** 18
- Guero's* | **SoCo** 20
- Hilltop Café* | **Fredericksburg** 23
- Hoover's* | **Cherrywood** 21
- Hut's | **Downtown** 23
- Hyde Park* | **Hyde Pk** 21
- Iron Works | **Downtown** 22
- Kerbey Ln. Café* | **multi.** 20
- Las Manitas | **Downtown** 20
- Las Palomas* | **West Lake** 21
- Magnolia Café* | **multi.** 21
- Matt's El Rancho* | **S Lamar** 18
- Oasis* | **Lakeway** 11
- Pei Wei* | **multi.** 19
- Player's | **Campus** 19
- Polvo's* | **Bouldin Creek** 21
- Rocco's Grill* | **Lakeway** 20
- Romeo's* | **Zilker** 17
- Ruby's* | **N Campus** 23
- Z Salt Lick* | **Driftwood** 24
- Scholz Garten* | **Downtown** 13
- Serranos* | **multi.** 16
- Shady Grove* | **Zilker** 19
- Stubb's* | **Downtown** 20
- Suzi's | **multi.** 19
- Taco Xpress | **S Lamar** 21
- Threadgill's | **Downtown S** 19
- Trudy's* | **S Austin** 20
- Waterloo Ice Hse. | **multi.** 16
- Z'Tejas* | **multi.** 22

DELIVERY/TAKEOUT

(D=delivery, T=takeout)

- Alborz | T | **NW Austin** 21
- Billy's/Burnet | T | **Rosedale** 20
- Brick Oven | D, T | **multi.** 19
- Chez Zee | T | **NW Hills** 21
- Z Chuy's | D | **multi.** 21
- County Line | T | **multi.** 20
- Curra's Grill | T | **Travis Hts** 21
- Din Ho Chinese | T | **N Austin** 24
- 1886 Café | T | **Downtown** 22
- El Meson | T | **SE Austin** 27
- Frank & Angie's | T | **Downtown** 21
- Hoover's | T | **Cherrywood** 21
- Hut's | T | **Downtown** 23
- Iron Works | T | **Downtown** 22
- Katz's Deli | T | **Downtown** 19
- Kerbey Ln. Café | T | **multi.** 20
- Las Manitas | T | **Downtown** 20
- Louie's 106 | T | **Downtown** 24
- Madam Mam's | T | **Campus** 21
- Madras Pavilion | T | **N Austin** 22
- Magnolia Café | T | **multi.** 21
- Manuel's | T | **multi.** 22
- Matt's El Rancho | T | **S Lamar** 18
- North by NW | D, T | **Great Hills** 18
- Pei Wei | T | **multi.** 19
- P.F. Chang's | T | **Downtown** 22
- Player's | T | **Campus** 19
- Ruby's | T | **N Campus** 23
- Z Salt Lick | D, T | **Driftwood** 24
- Satay | D, T | **NW Austin** 21
- Shoal Creek | T | **Downtown** 18
- Stubb's | T | **Downtown** 20

Sunflower | T | **N Austin** 23
Suzi's | T | **multi.** 19
Taco Xpress | T | **S Lamar** 21
Thai Kitchen | T | **multi.** 20
Thai Noodle Hse. | D, T | **Campus** 17
Thai Passion | T | **Downtown** 20
Thistle Café | T | **multi.** 18
Threadgill's | D, T | **multi.** 19
Waterloo Ice Hse. | T | **multi.** 16

DESSERT

Aquarelle | **Downtown** 27
Asti Trattoria | **Hyde Pk** 24
Austin Land | **Downtown** 22
Chez Zee | **NW Hills** 21
Z Driskill Grill | **Downtown** 26
1886 Café | **Downtown** 22
European Bistro | **Pflugerville** 24
Fino | **W Campus** 23
Moonshine | **Downtown** 20
Starlite | **Warehouse Dist** 25
NEW Steeping Room | **NW Austin** 21
Z NEW TRIO | **Downtown** 27
Z Vespaio | **SoCo** 28

DINING ALONE

(Other than hotels and places with counter service)

Bee Cave | **Bee Cave** 20
Billy's/Burnet | **Rosedale** 20
Chez Nous | **Downtown** 25
Z Eddie V's | **Downtown** 26
Enoteca Vespaio | **SoCo** 25
Fino | **W Campus** 23
Fleming's Prime | **Downtown** 24
Z Jasper's | **NW Austin** 24
La Traviata | **Downtown** 24
Louie's 106 | **Downtown** 24
Málaga | **Warehouse Dist** 20
Opal Divine's | **Downtown** 14
Pei Wei | **multi.** 19
Ranch 616 | **Downtown** 23
Tacodeli | **multi.** 25
Z Uchi | **Zilker** 28
Z Vespaio | **SoCo** 28
Waterloo Ice Hse. | **Jollyville** 16
Zax Pints | **Downtown S** 19

ENTERTAINMENT

(Call for days and times of performances)

Alborz | belly dancers | **NW Austin** 21
Backstage | varies | **Spicewood** 26
Chez Zee | jazz/piano/pop | **NW Hills** 21
Cool River | varies | **NW Austin** 19
County Line | guitar | **NW Hills** 20
Z Driskill Grill | jazz/piano | **Downtown** 26
Z Eddie V's | varies | **Downtown** 26
El Mercado | varies | **Bouldin Creek** 15
El Sol y La Luna | Latin | **SoCo** 19
European Bistro | piano | **Pflugerville** 24
Frank & Angie's | mandolin | **Downtown** 21
Green Mesquite | blues/country/folk | **Zilker** 18
Green Pastures | piano | **Bouldin Creek** 23
Guero's | varies | **SoCo** 20
Habana | varies | **Downtown** 21
Hilltop Café | blues/jazz | **Fredericksburg** 23
Las Palomas | jazz/Latin | **West Lake** 21
Manuel's | jazz/Latin | **multi.** 22
Matt's El Rancho | jazz/Latin | **S Lamar** 18
McCormick/Schmick | jazz | **Downtown** 21
Mirabelle | jazz | **NW Hills** 25
North by NW | varies | **Great Hills** 18
Oasis | jazz/rock | **Lakeway** 11
Opal Divine's | blues/folk/rock | **multi.** 14
Ranch 616 | country | **Downtown** 23
Romeo's | piano | **Zilker** 17
Z Salt Lick | varies | **Driftwood** 24
Shady Grove | varies | **Zilker** 19
Shoal Creek | varies | **Downtown** 18
Stubb's | varies | **Downtown** 20
Sullivan's | bands/jazz | **Warehouse Dist** 24
Threadgill's | varies | **multi.** 19
Truluck's | jazz/piano | **Arboretum** 23
Vivo | DJ | **Cherrywood** 19
Waterloo Ice Hse. | varies | **multi.** 16
Z'Tejas | varies | **Clarksville** 22

GAME IN SEASON

Asti Trattoria | **Hyde Pk** 24
August E's | **Fredericksburg** 27

Backstage | **Spicewood** 26
Cedar Grove | **Wimberley** -
Chez Nous | **Downtown** 25
Cool River | **NW Austin** 19
Z Driskill Grill | **Downtown** 26
Fino | **W Campus** 23
Green Pastures | **Bouldin Creek** 23
Z Hudson's | **Lakeway** 28
Z Jeffrey's | **Clarksville** 26
Meyer's | **Elgin** 21
Ranch 616 | **Downtown** 23
Rest. Jezebel | **Downtown** 27
Sampaio's | **Rosedale** 20
Z Siena | **NW Hills** 25
Turtle, The | **Brownwood** -
Ventana | **N Austin** 23
Wildfire | **Georgetown** 22
Z Wink | **Old W Austin** 27

HISTORIC PLACES

(Year opened; * building)

1830 | Stubb's* | **Downtown** 20
1850 | Moonshine* | **Downtown** 20
1859 | Thai Passion* | **Downtown** 20
1866 | Scholz Garten* | **Downtown** 13
1882 | Southside Mkt. | **Elgin** 24
1886 | Driskill Grill* | **Downtown** 26
1886 | 1886 Café* | **Downtown** 22
1894 | Green Pastures* | **Bouldin Creek** 23
1900 | Guero's* | **SoCo** 20
1900 | Hudson's* | **Lakeway** 28
1900 | Judges' Hill* | **W Campus** 24
1900 | Kreuz Mkt. | **Lockhart** 26
1904 | European Bistro* | **Pflugerville** 24
1918 | Bess* | **Downtown** 17
1920 | Eastside Café* | **Cherrywood** 24
1920 | Green Mesquite* | **Zilker** 19
1920 | Zoot* | **Old W Austin** 26
1926 | Dirty Martin's* | **Campus** 21
1930 | Hyde Park* | **Hyde Pk** 21
1930 | Iron Works* | **Downtown** 22
1933 | Threadgill's | **Crestview** 19
1934 | Hoffbrau Steak* | **Downtown** 16
1938 | Quality Seafood | **Hyde Pk** -
1939 | Hut's* | **Downtown** 23
1949 | Louie Mueller | **Taylor** 25
1952 | Matt's El Rancho | **S Lamar** 18
1957 | City Market | **Luling** 24

HOTEL DINING

Driskill Hotel
Z Driskill Grill | **Downtown** 26
1886 Café | **Downtown** 22
Four Seasons Hotel
Z NEW TRIO | **Downtown** 27
Hilton Downtown
Finn & Porter | **Downtown** 23
InterContinental Stephen F. Austin Hotel
Roaring Fork | **Downtown** 24
Mansion at Judges' Hill
Judges' Hill | **W Campus** 24

LATE DINING

(Weekday closing hour)

Billy's/Burnet | 12 AM | **Rosedale** 20
Hyde Park | 12 AM | **Hyde Pk** 21
Katz's Deli | 24 hrs. | **Downtown** 19
Kerbey Ln. Café | 24 hrs. | **multi.** 20
Magnolia Café | 24 hrs. | **multi.** 21
Opal Divine's | 1 AM | **multi.** 14
Player's | 3 AM | **Campus** 19
Ruby's | 12 AM | **N Campus** 23
Texas Chili | 12 AM | **Downtown** 20
Thai Kitchen | 12 AM | **Campus** 20
Thai Passion | 3 AM | **Downtown** 20
Trudy's | 12 AM | **multi.** 20

MEET FOR A DRINK

Belmont, The | **Downtown** 18
Bess | **Downtown** 17
Billy's/Burnet | **Rosedale** 20
Z Chuy's | **multi.** 21
Cibo | **Downtown** 20
Cool River | **NW Austin** 19
Curra's Grill | **Travis Hts** 21
Doña Emilia's | **Downtown** 20
Z Eddie V's | **multi.** 26
El Chile | **Cherrywood** 22
Fino | **W Campus** 23
Fleming's Prime | **Downtown** 24
Guero's | **SoCo** 20
Habana | **Downtown** 21
Hula Hut | **Old W Austin** 18
Z Jasper's | **NW Austin** 24
NEW Joe DiMaggio's | **NW Austin** -

Louie's 106 | **Downtown** 24
Málaga | **Warehouse Dist** 20
Manuel's | **multi.** 22
Mars | **SoCo** 20
Matt's El Rancho | **S Lamar** 18
McCormick/Schmick | **NW Austin** 21
Moonshine | **Downtown** 20
NEW NoRTH | **NW Austin** -
North by NW | **Great Hills** 18
Oasis | **Lakeway** 11
Opal Divine's | **multi.** 14
Quality Seafood | **Hyde Pk** -
Ranch 616 | **Downtown** 23
Roaring Fork | **Downtown** 24
Saba Blue | **Warehouse Dist** 18
NEW Sagra | **Downtown** -
Sampaio's | **Rosedale** 20
Scholz Garten | **Downtown** 13
Serranos | **multi.** 16
Shady Grove | **Zilker** 19
Shoal Creek | **Downtown** 18
South Congress | **SoCo** 22
Starlite | **Warehouse Dist** 25
NEW Steeping Room | **NW Austin** 21
Texas Chili | **Downtown** 20
Threadgill's | **Downtown S** 19
Z NEW TRIO | **Downtown** 27
Trudy's | **multi.** 20
Turtle, The | **Brownwood** -
Z Vespaio | **SoCo** 28
Waterloo Ice Hse. | **multi.** 16
Woodland, The | **SoCo** 18
Zax Pints | **Downtown S** 19
Z'Tejas | **multi.** 22

NOTEWORTHY NEWCOMERS

Daily Grill | **NW Austin** 24
Estância | **SW Austin** 27
Gypsy Italian | **Bouldin Creek** -
Z Jasper's | **NW Austin** 24
Joe DiMaggio's | **NW Austin** -
Kona Grill | **NW Austin** 20
NoRTH | **NW Austin** -
Oaxacan Tamaleo | **Cedar Creek** -
Sagra | **Downtown** -
Shanghai Rest. | **N Central** -
Steeping Room | **NW Austin** 21
Trattoria Lisina | **Driftwood** -
Z TRIO | **Downtown** 27

OUTDOOR DINING

(G=garden; P=patio; S=sidewalk; T=terrace; W=waterside)

Abuelo's | G | **SW Austin** 19
Backstage | P | **Spicewood** 26
Billy's/Burnet | P | **Rosedale** 20
Brick Oven | P | **multi.** 19
Chez Zee | G | **NW Hills** 21
Z Chuy's | P | **multi.** 21
Cool River | P | **NW Austin** 19
County Line | P | **West Lake** 20
Crú Wine Bar | P | **Downtown** 20
Curra's Grill | P | **Travis Hts** 21
Doña Emilia's | P | **Downtown** 20
1886 Café | P | **Downtown** 22
El Azteca | P | **E Austin** 18
El Chile | P | **Cherrywood** 22
El Mercado | P | **multi.** 15
El Sol y La Luna | P | **SoCo** 19
Evangeline Café | S | **SW Austin** 19
Fino | T | **W Campus** 23
Frank & Angie's | P | **Downtown** 21
Green Mesquite | P | **Zilker** 18
Guero's | P | **SoCo** 20
Habana | P | **Downtown** 21
Hoffbrau Steak | P | **Downtown** 16
Z Hudson's | G, P | **Lakeway** 28
Hula Hut | P, W | **Old W Austin** 18
Iron Works | P | **Downtown** 22
Z Jasper's | P | **NW Austin** 24
NEW Joe DiMaggio's | P | **NW Austin** -
Kerbey Ln. Café | P | **multi.** 20
Las Manitas | P | **Downtown** 20
Las Palomas | P | **West Lake** 21
Manuel's | P | **Great Hills** 22
Mars | P | **SoCo** 20
Matt's El Rancho | P | **S Lamar** 18
Moonshine | G, P | **Downtown** 20
NEW NoRTH | P | **NW Austin** -
North by NW | P, T | **Great Hills** 18
Oasis | P, T | **Lakeway** 11
Opal Divine's | P, T | **multi.** 14
Pei Wei | P | **SW Austin** 19
P.F. Chang's | P | **Arboretum** 22
Player's | G | **Campus** 19
Polvo's | P | **Bouldin Creek** 21
Rocco's Grill | P, W | **Lakeway** 20
Romeo's | P | **Zilker** 17
Ruby's | P | **N Campus** 23
Z Salt Lick | P | **Driftwood** 24
São Paulo's | S | **Campus** 21
Satay | G, P | **NW Austin** 21

Scholz Garten | P | **Downtown** 13
Serranos | P | **multi.** 16
Shady Grove | P | **Zilker** 19
Shoal Creek | P | **Downtown** 18
Shoreline Grill | P, W | **Downtown** 24
Z Siena | P | **NW Hills** 25
Taco Xpress | P | **S Lamar** 21
Thai Noodle Hse. | P | **Campus** 17
Thistle Café | P | **West Lake** 18
NEW Trattoria Lisina | P | **Driftwood** -
Z NEW TRIO | T, W | **Downtown** 27
Trudy's | P, T | **multi.** 20
Truluck's | P | **Arboretum** 23
Vin Bistro | P | **Brykerwoods** 24
Vivo | P | **Cherrywood** 19
Waterloo Ice Hse. | P | **NW Hills** 16
Zax Pints | P | **Downtown S** 19
Z'Tejas | P | **multi.** 22

POWER SCENES

August E's | **Fredericksburg** 27
Austin Land | **Downtown** 22
Belmont, The | **Downtown** 18
Bess | **Downtown** 17
Carmelo's | **Downtown** 22
Cedar Grove | **Wimberley** -
Cool River | **NW Austin** 19
Z Driskill Grill | **Downtown** 26
Z Eddie V's | **Downtown** 26
Finn & Porter | **Downtown** 23
Fleming's Prime | **Downtown** 24
Z Jasper's | **NW Austin** 24
NEW Joe DiMaggio's | **NW Austin** -
Lambert's | **Downtown** 23
Las Manitas | **Downtown** 20
McCormick/Schmick | **multi.** 21
NEW NoRTH | **NW Austin** -
Rest. Jezebel | **Downtown** 27
Roaring Fork | **Downtown** 24
Ruth's Chris | **Downtown** 25
Sullivan's | **Warehouse Dist** 24
Texas Chili | **Downtown** 20
Z NEW TRIO | **Downtown** 27

PRIX FIXE MENUS

(Call for prices and times)

Aquarelle | **Downtown** 27
Chez Nous | **Downtown** 25
Z Driskill Grill | **Downtown** 26
Z Jeffrey's | **Clarksville** 26
Z Salt Lick | **Driftwood** 24
Z Siena | **NW Hills** 25
Thai Passion | **Downtown** 20
Threadgill's | **Downtown S** 19
Vin Bistro | **Brykerwoods** 24
Z Wink | **Old W Austin** 27
Zoot | **Old W Austin** 26

QUIET CONVERSATION

Aquarelle | **Downtown** 27
August E's | **Fredericksburg** 27
Backstage | **Spicewood** 26
Bee Cave | **Bee Cave** 20
Bess | **Downtown** 17
Café 909 | **Marble Falls** 29
Carmelo's | **Downtown** 22
Cedar Grove | **Wimberley** -
Chez Nous | **Downtown** 25
Cibo | **Downtown** 20
Z Driskill Grill | **Downtown** 26
Eastside Café | **Cherrywood** 24
1886 Café | **Downtown** 22
European Bistro | **Pflugerville** 24
NEW Gypsy Italian | **Bouldin Creek** -
Z Jeffrey's | **Clarksville** 26
Judges' Hill | **W Campus** 24
Mars | **SoCo** 20
McCormick/Schmick | **NW Austin** 21
Mirabelle | **NW Hills** 25
Ms. B's | **multi.** 22
Patton's | **Marble Falls** -
Rather Sweet | **Fredericksburg** 26
NEW Sagra | **Downtown** -
Shoreline Grill | **Downtown** 24
Z Siena | **NW Hills** 25
Silver K | **Johnson City** -
Starlite | **Warehouse Dist** 25
NEW Steeping Room | **NW Austin** 21
Thistle Café | **Downtown** 18
Z NEW TRIO | **Downtown** 27
Turtle, The | **Brownwood** -
Ventana | **N Austin** 23
Vin Bistro | **Brykerwoods** 24
Woodland, The | **SoCo** 18
Zoot | **Old W Austin** 26

ROMANTIC PLACES

Aquarelle | **Downtown** 27
August E's | **Fredericksburg** 27
Backstage | **Spicewood** 26
Bee Cave | **Bee Cave** 20

Belmont, The | **Downtown** 18
Bess | **Downtown** 17
Bistro 88 | **West Lake** 25
Café 909 | **Marble Falls** 29
Carmelo's | **Downtown** 22
Cedar Grove | **Wimberley** -
Chez Nous | **Downtown** 25
Cibo | **Downtown** 20
Clay Pit | **Downtown** 23
Z Driskill Grill | **Downtown** 26
Eastside Café | **Cherrywood** 24
European Bistro | **Pflugerville** 24
Z Fonda San Miguel | **Highland Pk** 26
NEW Gypsy Italian | **Bouldin Creek** -
NEW Joe DiMaggio's | **NW Austin** -
Judges' Hill | **W Campus** 24
Mirabelle | **NW Hills** 25
Ms. B's | **E Austin** 22
Patton's | **Marble Falls** -
Rest. Jezebel | **Downtown** 27
Romeo's | **Zilker** 17
NEW Sagra | **Downtown** -
Shoreline Grill | **Downtown** 24
Z Siena | **NW Hills** 25
Silver K | **Johnson City** -
Starlite | **Warehouse Dist** 25
Z NEW TRIO | **Downtown** 27
Turtle, The | **Brownwood** -
Wildfire | **Georgetown** 22
Zoot | **Old W Austin** 26

SENIOR APPEAL

Aquarelle | **Downtown** 27
Austin Land | **Downtown** 22
Bee Cave | **Bee Cave** 20
Carmelo's | **Downtown** 22
Cedar Grove | **Wimberley** -
City Market | **Luling** 24
Cooper's | **Llano** 27
County Line | **multi.** 20
Crosstown BBQ | **Elgin** -
Z Driskill Grill | **Downtown** 26
1886 Café | **Downtown** 22
European Bistro | **Pflugerville** 24
Gonzales | **Gonzales** -
Green Pastures | **Bouldin Creek** 23
Z Hudson's | **Lakeway** 28
Z Jasper's | **NW Austin** 24
NEW Joe DiMaggio's | **NW Austin** -
Judges' Hill | **W Campus** 24
Kreuz Mkt. | **Lockhart** 26
Lambert's | **Downtown** 23
Louie Mueller | **Taylor** 25
Mandola's | **N Central** 22
Mangieri's | **Circle C** 22
McCormick/Schmick | **NW Austin** 21
Melting Pot | **multi.** 21
Meyer's | **Elgin** 21
Ms. B's | **multi.** 22
Opie's BBQ | **Spicewood** 23
Patton's | **Marble Falls** -
Rather Sweet | **Fredericksburg** 26
Real New Orleans | **Round Mtn** -
R.O.'s Outpost | **Spicewood** -
Ruth's Chris | **Downtown** 25
Shoreline Grill | **Downtown** 24
Smitty's Mkt. | **Lockhart** 19
Southside Mkt. | **Elgin** 24
NEW Steeping Room | **NW Austin** 21
Threadgill's | **multi.** 19
NEW Trattoria Lisina | **Driftwood** -
Z NEW TRIO | **Downtown** 27
Turtle, The | **Brownwood** -
Ventana | **N Austin** 23
Woodland, The | **SoCo** 18

SINGLES SCENES

Belmont, The | **Downtown** 18
Bess | **Downtown** 17
Blue Star | **Rosedale** 20
Z Chuy's | **multi.** 21
Cool River | **NW Austin** 19
Z Eddie V's | **multi.** 26
Finn & Porter | **Downtown** 23
Habana | **Downtown** 21
Hula Hut | **Old W Austin** 18
NEW Joe DiMaggio's | **NW Austin** -
Málaga | **Warehouse Dist** 20
NEW NoRTH | **NW Austin** -
North by NW | **Great Hills** 18
Saba Blue | **Warehouse Dist** 18
Serranos | **multi.** 16
South Congress | **SoCo** 22
Sullivan's | **Warehouse Dist** 24

SLEEPERS

(Good to excellent food, but little known)

August E's | **Fredericksburg** 27
Backstage | **Spicewood** 26

Buster's | **Bee Cave** 24
Café 909 | **Marble Falls** 29
City Market | **Luling** 24
NEW Daily Grill | **NW Austin** 24
Din Ho Chinese | **N Austin** 24
El Meson | **SE Austin** 27
NEW Estância | **SW Austin** 27
European Bistro | **Pflugerville** 24
Finn & Porter | **Downtown** 23
Gene's | **E Austin** 25
Golden Wok | **N Austin** 22
Hilltop Café | **Fredericksburg** 23
Judges' Hill | **W Campus** 24
Louie Mueller | **Taylor** 25
Mangieri's | **Circle C** 22
Mikado Ryotei | **N Austin** 24
Ms. B's | **multi.** 22
Opie's BBQ | **Spicewood** 23
Rather Sweet | **Fredericksburg** 26
Reale's | **Jollyville** 23
Rest. Jezebel | **Downtown** 27
Southside Mkt. | **Elgin** 24
Sunflower | **N Austin** 23
Tacodeli | **multi.** 25
Ventana | **N Austin** 23
Wildfire | **Georgetown** 22

TRANSPORTING EXPERIENCES

Aquarelle | **Downtown** 27
Carmelo's | **Downtown** 22
County Line | **multi.** 20
Din Ho Chinese | **N Austin** 24
NEW Estância | **SW Austin** 27
European Bistro | **Pflugerville** 24
Z Fonda San Miguel | **Highland Pk** 26
Green Pastures | **Bouldin Creek** 23
Hula Hut | **Old W Austin** 18
Z Siena | **NW Hills** 25

TRENDY

Asti Trattoria | **Hyde Pk** 24
August E's | **Fredericksburg** 27
Belmont, The | **Downtown** 18
Bess | **Downtown** 17
Blue Star | **Rosedale** 20
Castle Hill | **Downtown** 25
Cibo | **Downtown** 20
Z Eddie V's | **multi.** 26
Finn & Porter | **Downtown** 23
Fino | **W Campus** 23
Z Jasper's | **NW Austin** 24
NEW Joe DiMaggio's | **NW Austin** -
Lambert's | **Downtown** 23
Mars | **SoCo** 20
McCormick/Schmick | **Downtown** 21
NEW NoRTH | **NW Austin** -
Rest. Jezebel | **Downtown** 27
Roy's | **Downtown** 25
Saba Blue | **Warehouse Dist** 18
Starlite | **Warehouse Dist** 25
Thistle Café | **Downtown** 18
Z NEW TRIO | **Downtown** 27
Z Uchi | **Zilker** 28
Z Vespaio | **SoCo** 28
Vin Bistro | **Brykerwoods** 24
Z Wink | **Old W Austin** 27
Zoot | **Old W Austin** 26

VIEWS

Cedar Grove | **Wimberley** -
County Line | **NW Hills** 20
Z Eddie V's | **multi.** 26
Hilltop Café | **Fredericksburg** 23
Hula Hut | **Old W Austin** 18
Oasis | **Lakeway** 11
Rocco's Grill | **Lakeway** 20
Z Salt Lick | **Driftwood** 24
Shoreline Grill | **Downtown** 24
NEW Trattoria Lisina | **Driftwood** -
Z NEW TRIO | **Downtown** 27
Z'Tejas | **multi.** 22

VISITORS ON EXPENSE ACCOUNT

Aquarelle | **Downtown** 27
Carmelo's | **Downtown** 22
Cibo | **Downtown** 20
Cool River | **NW Austin** 19
Finn & Porter | **Downtown** 23
Fleming's Prime | **Downtown** 24
Z Hudson's | **Lakeway** [illegible]
Z Jeffrey's | **Clarksville** 26
NEW Joe DiMaggio's | **NW Austin** -
Judges' Hill | **W Campus** 24
Kenichi | **Warehouse Dist** 22
McCormick/Schmick | **Downtown** 21
Rest. Jezebel | **Downtown** 27
Roy's | **Downtown** 25
Ruth's Chris | **Downtown** 25
Z NEW TRIO | **Downtown** 27

Z Uchi | **Zilker** 28
Z Vespaio | **SoCo** 28
Z Wink | **Old W Austin** 27
Zoot | **Old W Austin** 26

WINNING WINE LISTS

Aquarelle | **Downtown** 27
Asti Trattoria | **Hyde Pk** 24
August E's | **Fredericksburg** 27
Belmont, The | **Downtown** 18
Bess | **Downtown** 17
Blue Star | **Rosedale** 20
Café 909 | **Marble Falls** 29
Carmelo's | **Downtown** 22
Castle Hill | **Downtown** 25
Cedar Grove | **Wimberley** -
Cibo | **Downtown** 20
Doña Emilia's | **Downtown** 20
Z Driskill Grill | **Downtown** 26
Enoteca Vespaio | **SoCo** 25
NEW Estância | **SW Austin** 27
Finn & Porter | **Downtown** 23
Fino | **W Campus** 23
Fleming's Prime | **Downtown** 24
Z Hudson's | **Lakeway** 28
Z Jasper's | **NW Austin** 24
Z Jeffrey's | **Clarksville** 26
NEW Joe DiMaggio's | **NW Austin** -
La Traviata | **Downtown** 24
Louie's 106 | **Downtown** 24
Mirabelle | **NW Hills** 25
Ms. B's | **E Austin** 22
Roaring Fork | **Downtown** 24
Roy's | **Downtown** 25
Ruth's Chris | **Downtown** 25
Z Siena | **NW Hills** 25
Z NEW TRIO | **Downtown** 27
Z Uchi | **Zilker** 28
Z Vespaio | **SoCo** 28
Wildfire | **Georgetown** 22
Z Wink | **Old W Austin** 27
Zoot | **Old W Austin** 26

WORTH A TRIP

Driftwood
Z Salt Lick 24
Fredericksburg
Hilltop Café 23
Georgetown
Wildfire 22
Marble Falls
Café 909 29
Pflugerville
European Bistro 24
Spicewood
Backstage 26
Opie's BBQ 23

DALLAS/FT. WORTH

Dallas/Ft. Worth Most Popular

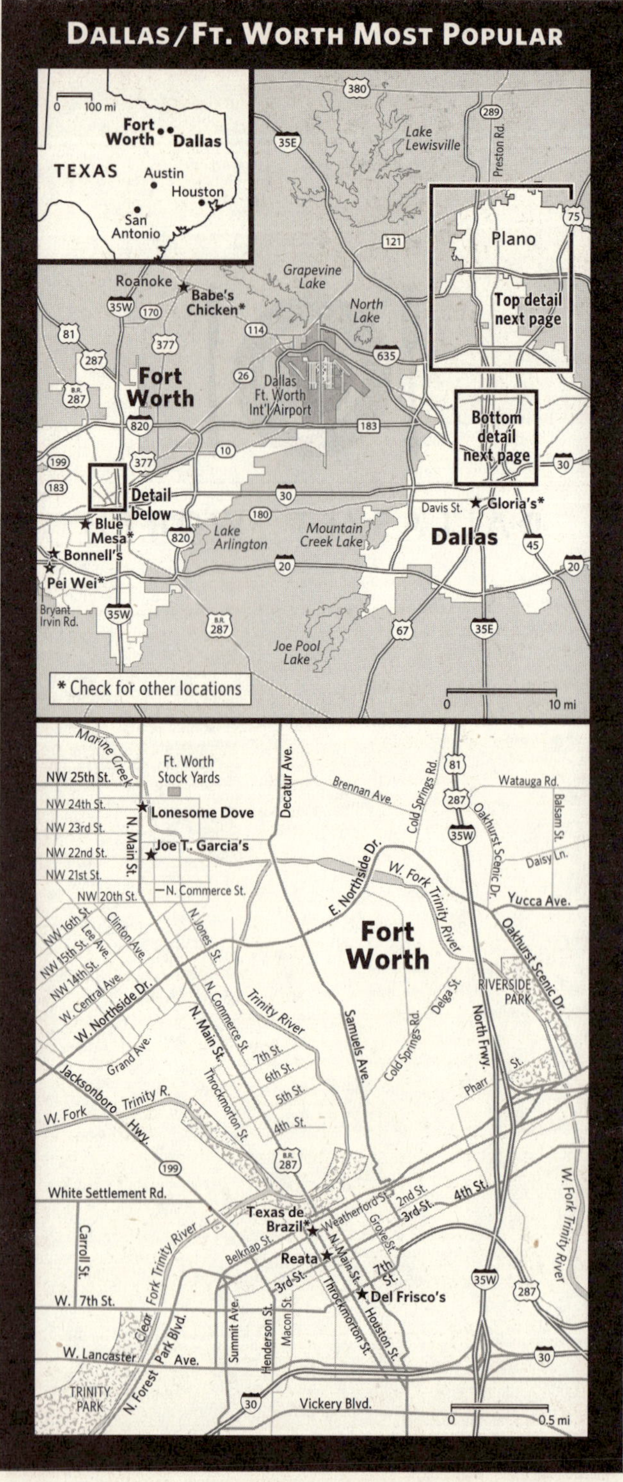

Dallas/Ft. Worth Most Popular

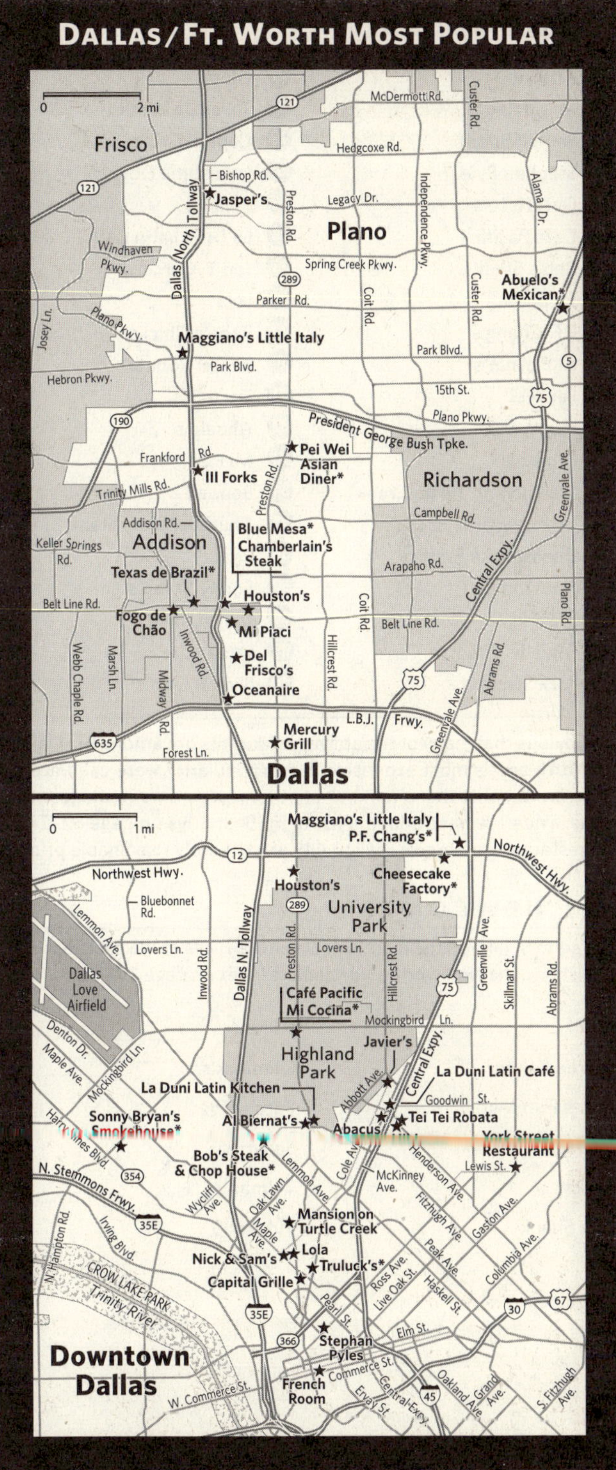

Most Popular

1. Abacus
2. Mi Cocina
3. French Room
4. Stephan Pyles*
5. Del Frisco's
6. Café Pacific
7. Bob's Steak
8. Jasper's
9. P.F. Chang's
10. Al Biernat's
11. Pei Wei*
12. Blue Mesa
13. Hibiscus*
14. Mansion on Turtle Creek
15. Mercury Grill
16. Cheesecake Factory
17. Houston's*
18. III Forks
19. Fogo de Chão
20. York Street
21. Gloria's
22. Texas de Brazil
23. Capital Grille
24. Lonesome Dove
25. Javier's
26. La Duni Latin Cafe
27. Joe T. Garcia's
28. Lola
29. Babe's Chicken
30. Tei Tei Robata*
31. Truluck's
32. Abuelo's
33. Mi Piaci*
34. Bonnell's
35. Chamberlain's Steak
36. Reata*
37. Sonny Bryan's
38. Maggiano's
39. Oceanaire
40. Nick & Sam's

It's obvious that many of the above restaurants are among the Dallas/Ft. Worth area's most expensive, but if popularity were calibrated to price, we suspect that a number of other restaurants would join their ranks. Thus, we have added a list of 40 Best Buys on page 82. These are restaurants that give real quality at extremely reasonable prices.

KEY NEWCOMERS

Our editors' take on the most notable new arrivals of the past year. For a full list, see the Noteworthy Newcomers index on page 171.

ALÓ

Charlie Palmer

Dallas Fish Mkt.

Fearing's

Kenichi

Love Shack

N9ne

Olenjack's

Porch, The

Sangria

Tillman's

Yutaka

* Indicates a tie with restaurant above

Top Food (Based on a 30-pt. scale)

Excludes places with low votes, unless indicated by a ∇.

28 French Room
Tei Tei Robata
Local
Teppo Yakitori
Abacus

27 York Street
Saint-Emilion
Yutaka Sushi
Bonnell's
Lanny's Alta Cocina
Aurora
Bijoux
Stephan Pyles
Del Frisco's
Mercury Grill
Amici
Nana*
Lola
Pappas Bros.
62 Main

26 Mercury Chop
Lonesome Dove
Suze
Café Pacific
Ristorante La Piazza
Mansion on Turtle Creek
Al Biernat's
Fearing's
Bistro Louise
St. Martin's
Fogo de Chão
Michael Anthony's

25 Hibiscus
Chamberlain's Steak
First Chinese BBQ
Hattie's
Piranha
Nick & Sam's
Capital Grille
Babe's Chicken

BY CUISINE

AMERICAN (NEW)

28 Local
27 York Street
Aurora
Mercury Grill
Nana

AMERICAN (TRAD.)

25 Babe's Chicken
23 Houston's
Sevy's
Paris Coffee Shop
22 Porch, The

BARBECUE

24 Angelo's BBQ
22 Railhead Smokehouse
Peggy Sue BBQ
Sonny Bryan's
21 Cousin's BBQ

CHINESE

25 First Chinese BBQ
22 P.F. Chang's
20 Howard Wang's
Szechuan Chinese*
19 Empress of China

ECLECTIC

28 Abacus
27 Lanny's Alta Cocina
24 Sapristi!
23 2900
22 Café Modern

FRENCH

28 French Room
27 Saint-Emilion
26 St. Martin's
25 Cacharel
24 Lavendou

INDIAN

23 India Palace
Clay Pit
22 Madras Pavilion
18 Roti Grill
Masala

ITALIAN

27 Amici
26 Ristorante La Piazza
24 Mi Piaci
Nicola's
Danielle

JAPANESE

28 Tei Tei Robata
Teppo Yakitori
27 Yutaka Sushi
25 Piranha
Steel

MEDITERRANEAN

26 Canary Cafe▽
Suze
Bistro Louise
25 Parigi
23 Olea

MEXICAN

27 Lanny's Alta Cocina
24 Esperanza's
La Familia
Veracruz
22 Javier's

SEAFOOD

26 Café Pacific
24 Oceanaire
23 Chamberlain's Fish
Truluck's
S&D Oyster Co.

SOUTHWESTERN

27 Bonnell's
Stephan Pyles
26 Lonesome Dove
Fearing's
24 Reata

STEAKHOUSES

27 Del Frisco's
Pappas Bros.
26 Mercury Chop
Al Biernat's
Fogo de Chão

TEX-MEX

24 Mia's
21 Cantina Laredo
Matt's Rancho Martinez
Mi Cocina
Chuy's

THAI

24 Samui Thai
23 Royal Thai
Chow Thai
Asian Mint
21 Mango Thai

BY SPECIAL FEATURE

BREAKFAST

23 Main St. Bistro
23 Paris Coffee Shop
22 Bread Winners Cafe
21 Mama's Daughters
19 Café Brazil

BRUNCH

27 Mercury Grill
26 Bistro Louise
St. Martin's
25 Hattie's
Parigi

BUSINESS DINING

28 Abacus
27 Saint-Emilion
Stephan Pyles
Del Frisco's
Pappas Bros.

CHILD-FRIENDLY

25 Babe's
21 Mi Cocina
19 H.P. Pharmacy
17 Zoe's Kitchen
14 Purple Cow

HOTEL DINING

28 French Room
(Hotel Adolphus)
27 Nana (Hilton Anatole)
26 Mansion on Turtle Creek
Fearing's (Ritz-Carlton)
25 Craft Dallas (W Hotel)

MEET FOR A DRINK

27 Stephan Pyles
Mercury Grill
26 Mansion on Turtle Creek
24 Reata
21 Fuse

NEWCOMERS (RATED)

26 Fearing's
22 Kenichi
Love Shack
N9ne
Porch, The

OFFBEAT

25 Babe's
23 Spiral Diner
22 Cosmic Café
21 Fuse
19 Trader Vic's

PEOPLE-WATCHING

- 28 French Room
- Abacus
- 26 Fearing's
- Lonesome Dove
- 25 Craft

QUICK BITES

- 23 Kincaid's
- 19 H.P. Pharmacy
- Tio's Torta's
- Pei Wei
- 17 Zoe's Kitchen

QUIET CONVERSATION

- 28 French Room
- 27 Saint-Emilion
- Bonnell's
- Nana
- 25 Grape, The

TRENDY

- 27 Lanny's
- 26 Fearing's
- 24 ALÓ
- 22 Kenichi
- 21 Trece

WINNING WINE LISTS

- 28 French Room
- Abacus
- 27 Pappas Bros
- Del Frisco's
- Lola

WORTH A TRIP

- 27 62 Main
  - Colleyville
- 26 Michael Anthony's
  - Southlake
- 25 Hattie's
  - Oak Cliff
- 24 Jasper's
  - Plano
- Culpepper
  - Rockwall

BY LOCATION

DALLAS

DOWNTOWN

- 28 French Room
- 25 Morton's
- 24 Zodiac, The
- 23 Amuse
- 21 Fuse

GREENVILLE AVENUE

- 28 Teppo Yakitori
- 26 St. Martin's
- 25 Grape, The
- 24 Kirby's
- 23 Royal Thai

KNOX-HENDERSON

- 28 Tei Tei Robata
- Abacus
- 25 Hibiscus
- 24 ALÓ
- La Duni Latin Cafe

LOVE FIELD AREA

- 27 Pappas Bros.
- 23 Avila's
- 22 Sonny Bryan's
- 21 Mama's Daughters'
- Celebration

NORTH DALLAS

- 27 Del Frisco's
- 25 Ruth's Chris
- III Forks
- 24 Oceanaire
- Lavendou Bistro

NORTHPARK

- 22 P.F. Chang's
- 21 McCormick & Schmick's
- 20 Blue Mesa
- Luna de Noche
- Maggiano's

OAK LAWN

- 27 Aurora
- 26 Al Biernat's
- 25 Parigi
- Steel
- 24 Silver Fox

UPTOWN

- 27 Yutaka Sushi
- Lola
- 26 Mansion on Turtle Creek
- Fearing's
- 25 Nick & Sam's

WEST LOVERS LANE

27 Bijoux
25 Shinsei
22 Bread Winners Cafe
Sonny Bryan's
21 Café Istanbul

WEST VILLAGE

23 Campania
21 Mi Cocina
Ferre
20 Taco Diner
Crú Wine Bar

FT. WORTH

CULTURAL DISTRICT

27 Saint-Emilion
Lanny's Alta Cocina
24 Michaels
Buffet at the Kimbell
22 Café Modern

SOUTHWEST

27 Bonnell's
26 Bistro Louise
21 Keg Steak
Cousin's BBQ
20 Szechuan Chinese

OTHER AREAS

ADDISON

26 Fogo de Chão
25 Chamberlain's Steak
24 Texas de Brazil
Mi Piaci
23 Houston's

FRISCO

24 Silver Fox
21 Cantina Laredo
Gloria's
Jinbeh
20 Terilli's

GRAPEVINE

25 Bob's Steak
24 Silver Fox
Boi Na Braza
23 Main St. Bistro
Ferrari's

LAS COLINAS

24 Café on the Green
23 Blue Fish
Via Reál
22 I Fratelli
21 Café Cipriani

PLANO

25 Bob's Steak
Roy's
24 Jasper's
Samui Thai
Kirby's

RICHARDSON

25 First Chinese BBQ
24 Silver Fox
23 Pappadeaux
Main St. Bistro
22 Madras Pavilion

Top Decor (Based on a 30-pt. scale)

29 French Room

28 Stephan Pyles

27 Nana
Fearing's
Mansion on Turtle Creek

26 Café Modern
ALÓ Cena Duria
Abacus
Mercy
Trader Vic's

25 Reata
Café on the Green
Lanny's Alta Cocina
Jasper's
Tillman's
Craft Dallas
Bijoux
Nicola's
Capital Grille
Ristorante La Piazza

24 Bistro Louise
Café Ashton
Saint-Emilion
Café Pacific
III Forks
St. Martin's
Del Frisco's
Mi Piaci
Nobu
Pappas Bros.
Local
Nove Italiano
N9ne Steak
Old Warsaw
Roy's
Buffet at the Kimbell
Aurora
Landmark*
Michael Anthony's*

23 Arthur's

OUTDOORS

Coal Vines
Dakota's
Ferre's
Fuse
Joe T. Garcia's
Mansion on Turtle Creek
Nove
Patrizio's
Reata
Rough Creek Lodge

ROMANCE

Aurora
Bijoux
French Room
Grape, The
Hotel St. Germain
Lola
Lonesome Dove
Mansion on Turtle Creek
Nana
Saint-Emilion

ROOMS

Abacus
Central 214
City Cafe
Maggiano's
Mansion on Turtle Creek
Mercury Grill
Nana
Pappas Bros.
Reata
Stephan Pyles

VIEWS

Amuse
Cacharel
Café Modern
Chaparral
Mansion on Turtle Creek
Mi Piaci
Nana
Nove
Reata
Rough Creek Lodge

Top Service (Based on a 30-pt. scale)

29 French Room

27 Nana
Saint-Emilion
Aurora
Abacus

26 Stephan Pyles
Bonnell's
Café Pacific
Mansion on Turtle Creek
Café on the Green
Old Warsaw
La Familia
Lanny's Alta Cocina
York Street
62 Main
Fogo de Chão

25 Del Frisco's
Local
Capital Grille
Lola
Teppo Yakitori
Bijoux
Michael Anthony's*
Pappas Bros.
Al Biernat's
St. Martin's
Ruth's Chris
Fearing's
Nick & Sam's
Boi Na Braza
Rick Stein's

24 Chamberlain's Steak
Palm, The
Mercury Grill
Bugatti
Suze*
Landmark
Texas de Brazil
Hattie's
Amici

Best Buys

In order of Bang for the Buck rating.

1. Highland Park
2. Paris Coffee Shop
3. Kincaid's
4. Buffet at the Kimbell
5. Esperanza's
6. Love Shack
7. Cousin's BBQ
8. La Familia
9. Carshon's Deli
10. Babe's Chicken
11. Bubba's
12. Mama's Daughters'
13. Angelo's BBQ
14. Cosmic Café
15. Railhead Smokehouse
16. Billy Miner's
17. Benito's
18. Main St. Bistro
19. Greenz
20. Masala

OTHER GOOD VALUES

Amici
Breadwinner's
Café Brazil
Celebration
Charleston's
Chic of Barcelona
First Chinese BBQ
Gloria's
Green Papaya
Kathleen's Sky Diner
Kuby's
Maggiano's
Mango Thai
Mia's
Neuhaus Cafe
Peggy Sue BBQ
Pei Wei
Roti Grill
Taco Diner
Zeke's

FOOD	DECOR	SERVICE	COST

Dallas/Ft. Worth

Z Abacus ⊠ *Eclectic* 28 | 26 | 27 | $66

Knox-Henderson | 4511 McKinney Ave. (Armstrong Ave.) | Dallas | 214-559-3111 | www.abacus-restaurant.com

"Hands down one of the best restaurants in town" hail fans of this "inventive" Knox-Henderson Eclectic (indeed it's Dallas/Ft. Worth's Most Popular) helmed by Kent Rathbun whose "truly memorable" "Californian, French and Asian"-style dishes - including signature lobster shooters that "deserve the hype" - "never fail to delight or impress"; "meticulous" servers work the "noisy", "trendy, neo-industrial" dining room, where the only downside is that it's so "expensive", you may "need an abacus to total the bill."

Abuelo's Mexican Food Embassy *Mexican* 19 | 21 | 19 | $21

Plano | 3420 N. Central Expwy. (Parker Rd.) | 972-423-9290
Plano | 3701 Dallas Pkwy. (Parker Rd.) | 972-781-1613
Lewisville | 2520 S. Stemmons Frwy. (Rte. 121) | 972-315-6057
Arlington | 1041 I-20 W. (Matlock Rd.) | 817-468-2622
Hurst | 824 Airport Frwy. (Precinct Line Rd.) | 817-514-9355
www.abuelos.com

See review in Austin and the Hill Country Directory.

Addison Cafe *American* 23 | 20 | 24 | $39

Addison | 5290 Belt Line Rd. (Montfort Dr.) | 972-991-8824 | www.addisoncafe.com

After "many years in business", this "quaint little bistro" in Addison is "still a wonderful experience", with a "solid, steady" "French-themed" New American menu and servers so "attentive" that, after you dine there "only a couple times", they'll "know your name and favorite drink"; "best for business lunches and dates", it has a "cozy", "classy" interior that takes some "back to the elegance of the '50s and '60s" - and even those who can't "get over" the location concede it's "nice for a shopping-strip" venue.

Adelmo's ⊠ *Italian* 23 | 18 | 22 | $42

Knox-Henderson | 4537 Cole Ave. (Knox St.) | Dallas | 214-559-0325 | www.adelmos.com

Adelmo Banchetti's eatery in Knox-Henderson is "just what a good Italian neighborhood restaurant ought to be": "unpretentious", with "no gimmicks - just a nice place to enjoy good food" and wines that "will satisfy the most particular connoisseur without emptying the bank account"; backed by a "staff-to-diner ratio" that's "insane" (in a good way), Adelmo "tends bar and greets you" within the "cozy" interior of a "lovely, charming old house" with "lace curtains" that feels "like grandma's."

Aija ⊠ *American* ▽ 19 | 15 | 19 | $20

Arts District | Trammell Crow Ctr. | 2001 Ross Ave. (bet. Harwood & Olive Sts.) | Dallas | 214-979-3111 | www.artsdistrictbanquets.com

Downtowners in-the-know scamper to this "great bargain", lunch-only eatery in a "beautiful setting" at the Trammel Crow Center in the Arts District, where the all-buffet offerings include a "nice variety" of "innovative" Asian-influenced American dishes; locals eat their "quick bite" at tables that are decked in white linen, backdropped by a stunning museum-quality mural.

Z Al Biernat's *Steak* 26 | 23 | 25 | $57

Oak Lawn | 4217 Oak Lawn Ave. (Herschel Ave.) | Dallas | 214-219-2201 | www.albiernats.com

A "magnet for the rich and famous", this "always-crowded" Oak Lawn steakhouse is a "loud but welcoming" "classic" that proffers "very solid" "power lunches and dinners"; advocates admire the "social" ambiance that's encouraged by owner Al Biernat as he works the room and greets guests by name, and if the "prices set your heart aflame", given the "outstanding" service and "snazzelicious" vibe, they're "worth the hole they burn in your pocket."

Z NEW ALÓ Cena Duria & Piqueos *Mexican/Peruvian* 24 | 26 | 19 | $34

Knox-Henderson | 4447 N. Central Expwy. (Garrett Ave.) | Dallas | 214-520-9711 | www.alodallas.com

The La Duni duo bring "fabulously unique" "Peruvian-Mexican fusion" and other Pan-Latin flavors to Knox-Henderson with this "delightful" cantina and its "clever, unusual" "small plates"; the cool modern surroundings (complete with flat-screen cooking demos and stone accents) win raves, though a few frugal-minded feasters argue that it's "supposed to be street food, but the cost is out of proportion", especially given the sometimes "haphazard" service.

Ama Lur *Southwestern* ▽ 23 | 23 | 23 | $51

Grapevine | Gaylord Texan Resort | 1501 Gaylord Trail (Rte. 26) | 817-778-2340 | www.gaylordhotels.com

Though the fare at this "expensive" Southwestern restaurant in Grapevine's Gaylord Texan Resort is "still good", disappointed sorts bemoan that it's slipped since "many of the faves were taken off the menu", making it "not nearly as good as when it first opened"; still, it's a popular gathering spot, set under an atrium, and the margarita bar and salsa band distract from a somewhat "inconsistent" staff.

Amici B M *Italian* 27 | 17 | 24 | $42

Carrollton | 1022 S. Broadway Rd. (Belt Line Rd.) | 972-245-3191 | www.amicisignature.com

A "delightful find" rave fans of this Carrollton "hideaway" overseen by a "charming chef-owner" who sends out "first-class" French-inflected Italian cuisine with "excellent game specials"; the dining room is "dark" and modern (and, it's worth noting, located up a "steep flight of stairs"), and because it's BYO, prices are a relative "bargain."

Amuse B *American* 23 | 17 | 18 | $34

Downtown Dallas | 1326 S. Lamar St. (bet. Belleview & Powhattan Sts.) | Dallas | 214-428-7300 | www.amusedallas.com

This "easy, comfortable, reliable" New American south of Downtown is so "funky" that it "feels like San Francisco", complete with an "inventive" menu featuring enough choices to "satisfy everyone"; "reasonable" prices and a dramatic "skyline view" from the patio bar round out the experience.

Andiamo ☒ *Italian* — 21 | 17 | 20 | $31

Addison | 4151 Belt Line Rd. (Midway Rd.) | 972-233-1515 | www.andiamogrill.com

"For many years", enthusiasts have enjoyed "pleasant" "repeat visits" to this "cozy" "neighborhood restaurant" in Addison, where "moderately priced" and "well-prepared classic Italian" fare is served by an "attentive staff" amid "charming" (if "typical") decor; though it's "free from the usual North Dallas hype", "do call ahead" since "without a reservation, you may not get a table."

Angela's Bistro 51 ☒ *American* — ▽ 22 | 19 | 21 | $46

Uptown | 2701 Guillot St. (Boll St.) | Dallas | 214-979-0051 | www.angelasbistro51.com

Expect "well-executed", "upscale home cooking" at this Uptown New American that's a "great neighborhooder", serving fast-paced pre-theater dinners as well as leisurely lunches; surveyors "love the art" on the walls (made by local talent) and the polish that radiates from the restored hardwood floors inside this "hidden treasure."

Angelo's Barbecue ☒⊘ *BBQ* — 24 | 14 | 15 | $13

Near West | 2533 White Settlement Rd. (University Dr.) | Ft. Worth | 817-332-0357 | www.angelosbbq.com

This "classic" Near West Ft. Worth spot is "a longtime institution" and an "almighty shrine to smoked meat", dishing up "Texas beef at its very finest" along with "schooners of cold draft beer"; with its "authentic Texana surroundings", including a weathered wood interior and an infamous "big bear in the foyer" that "kids love", it "may look like a hole-in-the-wall, but isn't that usually where one finds the best BBQ?"

Arcodoro & Pomodoro [M] *Italian* — 21 | 21 | 19 | $43

Uptown | 2708 Routh St. (McKinney Ave.) | Dallas | 214-871-1924 | www.arcodoro.com

The "authentic Sardinian" cuisine is a departure "from standard Italian fare" at this Uptown "see-and-be-seen" spot that gets special nods for its "awesome pastas" and "delicious thin-crust pizza" made in a "wood-burning oven"; it also boasts "beautiful villa decor" and a "romantic outdoor patio", but surveyors are split on the "well-dressed staff" – some finding it "snooty", others "as enchanting as the food"; N.B. there's a Houston sib named Arcodoro.

Arthur's Prime Steaks & Seafood ☒ *Seafood/Steak* — 23 | 23 | 21 | $53

Addison | 15175 Quorum Dr. (Belt Line Rd.) | 972-385-0800 | www.arthursdallas.com

Take "a step into the past" at this "elegant" steak-and-seafood house in Addison, whose "dark and quiet" interior is a "good place for a special dinner or just treating yourself" to a "nice all-around meal" accompanied by a "well-made" cocktail; its "huge bar" is "a gathering place for mature adults", with an "active lounge" featuring "great bands" (Monday-Saturday) and a dance floor that affords prime "people-watching."

Asian Mint *Pan-Asian/Thai* 23 | 14 | 18 | $23

Medical City | 11617 N. Central Expwy. (Forest Ln.) | Dallas | 214-363-6655 | www.asianmint.com

An "oasis" tucked into an "unattractive shopping center", this local "treasure" near Medical City charms chowhounds with "wonderful", "affordable" Thai and Pan-Asian dishes plus "inventive cocktails" and desserts you'll want to "leave room for"; though a few find the "trendy" quarters don't offer "much ambiance for dinner", "smooth service" ensures a pleasant time nonetheless.

Z Aurora ☒ *American* 27 | 24 | 27 | $89

Oak Lawn | 4216 Oak Lawn Ave. (Wycliff Ave.) | Dallas | 214-528-9400 | www.auroradallas.com

Diners don't hesitate to "max out [their] credit cards" at this "over-the-top" Oak Lawn New American that "stands out among the many temples of haute cuisine" thanks to "master" chef Avner Samuel, who serves up "beautifully presented" plates matched with wine from an "outstanding" 500-label list; bejeweled cognoscenti fill the art deco-inspired space and coo over its "luxury, sophistication and polish", though some find the "strip center" drive-up an incongruous welcome.

Avanti *Italian/Mediterranean* 20 | 19 | 19 | $35

Downtown Dallas | Fountain Pl. | 1445 Ross Ave. (Field St.) | Dallas | 214-965-0055 ☒

Uptown | 2720 McKinney Ave. (Worthington St.) | Dallas | 214-871-4955

Addison | Addison Circle | 5001 Addison Circle (bet. Airport Pkwy. & McEntire Pl.) | 972-386-7800 ☒

www.avantirestaurants.com

A "charming" trio, these "reliable" eateries offer "very good Italian-Med food" in a variety of "intimate", "sophisticated" atmospheres; big-city émigrés find the Uptown branch "a great place to go for late evenings" on weekends, with a "fabulous after-hours breakfast" for "in-the-know" eaters, and there's "good live music" at the Addison and McKinney Avenue locations.

Avila's ☒ *Mexican* 23 | 15 | 21 | $18

Love Field | 4714 Maple Ave. (Kings Rd.) | Dallas | 214-520-2700

"Don't go for the ambiance - go for" the "fresh", "authentic" fare at this "awesome hole-in-the-wall Mexican" near Love Field, where "you feel like family" thanks to the welcoming Avila clan; it's "beer and wine" only ("no hard liquor"), "but the food's so good you won't miss it" - or if you do, go ahead and "bring your own favorite margarita" over which you can "enjoy the serenade by guitar" on weekends.

Awaji *Japanese* 24 | 15 | 21 | $33

Plano | Berkley Sq. | 4701 W. Park Blvd. (Preston Park Blvd.) | 972-519-1688 | www.awajirestaurant.com

"Spectacular" sushi crafted from "quality fish" is the draw at this Japanese in western Plano also featuring "fairly creative" specialty dishes; moderate tabs and a "warm" welcome from the "polite" staff overcome its strip-center setting and "long-in-the-tooth" decor.

Babe's Chicken Dinner House *American* 25 | 17 | 22 | $16

Carrollton | 1006 W. Main St. (Denton Dr.) | 972-245-7773
Garland | 1456 Belt Line Rd. (Garland Ave.) | 972-496-1041
Sanger | 204 N. Fourth St. (Cherry St.) | 940-458-0000 M
Roanoke | 104 N. Oak St. (Main St.) | 817-491-2900
Burleson | 120 S. Main St. (Ellison St.) | 817-447-3400
www.babeschicken.com

The "fried chicken puts your mother's to shame" at this "kitschy" homegrown Texas chain where the "old-fashioned" American cooking comes with "all-you-can-eat" "fixings" (like "great" homemade biscuits) passed "family-style"; regulars report the Roanoke original reigns, but all outposts offer the same modest tabs plus plenty of "kids", "noise" and occasional "waits"; N.B. they're BYO.

Bagelstein's *Deli* 15 | 8 | 13 | $14

Preston Royal | 6025 Royal Ln. (Preston Rd.) | Dallas | 214-360-9925 | www.bagelsteinsdeli.com

East coast expats seek out this "casual" Preston Royal deli dishing out "solid" "NY"-style fare like Reubens and matzo-ball soup (though "with bagels in Dallas, don't expect miracles"); even if foes find it's "not the real deal", it still remains "crowded on weekends."

Bavarian Grill S M *German* 20 | 18 | 20 | $23

Plano | Ruisseau Vill. | 221 W. Parker Rd. (Central Expwy.) | 972-881-0705 | www.bavariangrill.com

"Come hungry, as the portions are huge" at this east Plano parlor - one of the few area German spots - whose popular biergarten boasts "all the basics: brats, schnitzels" and a "great selection of draft beers"; perhaps the "decor is a bit worn", but "you can have a fine, if somewhat hokey, meal" - as long as "you don't mind the accordion, ever-present chicken dance" and "fun polka bands" that "add to the atmosphere" of "good cheer."

Bella Italia West S *Italian* ∇ 24 | 17 | 24 | $34

West | 5139 Camp Bowie Blvd. (Neville St.) | Ft. Worth | 817-738-1700

"If you like game, this is your place" say fans of this "neighborhood gem", a quaint, homey hideaway in West Ft. Worth that's one of the rare Italian places to specialize in that wild provender; regulars insist that the "specials are always the best" bet (some would "have them every night"), and other attractions are an "excellent wine list" and a personable staff that makes you feel "like you're eating at home."

Benihana *Japanese/Steak* 20 | 18 | 21 | $32

Oak Lawn | 3848 Oak Lawn Ave. (bet. Blackburn St. & Irving Ave.) | Dallas | 214-559-3450
Medical City | 7775 Banner Dr. (Merit Dr.) | Dallas | 972-387-4404
Las Colinas | 5400 Whitehall St. (Walnut Hill Ln.) | Irving | 972-550-0060
www.benihana.com

They "have a good sense of humor" at this "kitschy" national Japanese steakhouse chain "where the personable staff cooks your food in front of you on giant grills"; "fun with a group", they're "great places to entertain 13-year-old boys who love to see food thrown" ("the flying shrimp" that "go from the grill to the chef's toque" or are "flipped into a pocket" are particular favorites), but the fare's also "tasty" – "good lunch specials too."

Benito's *Mexican* 18 | 12 | 19 | $13

Hospital District | 1450 W. Magnolia Ave. (Fairmount Ave.) | Ft. Worth | 817-332-8633

It's "nothing fancy", but this "authentic" Mexican in Ft. Worth's Hospital District pleases local lunchers with "solid" fare at reasonable prices (you'll have to pay for your chips and salsa, though); the "old-school" atmosphere "hasn't changed in years", but is enlivened on weekends when it draws a "late-night" crowd till 2 AM.

Bice *Italian* 21 | 23 | 21 | $56

Uptown | Crescent Shops & Galleries | 100 Crescent Ct. (bet. Maple & McKinney Aves.) | Dallas | 214-922-9055 | www.bicedallas.com

"Trendy and lively", this upmarket Northern Italian chain "without the chain feel" was born in Milan in 1926 and now boasts "nicely decorated" satellites around the globe, including these Dallas and Houston outposts; "snooty service" seems to be its weak link (they "only treat you well if you're a regular"), but overall the dining's "consistently good" and the tabs consistently "pricey."

Big Buck Brewery & Steakhouse *Steak* 19 | 21 | 20 | $36

Grapevine | 2501 Bass Pro Dr. (Hwy. 121) | 214-513-2337 | www.bigbuck.com

Hunters are in heaven at this larger-than-life lodge-themed steakhouse adjacent to the Bass Pro sporting goods shop in Grapevine featuring "cowboy"-sized steaks and house brews on tap all at moderate prices; the "festive" atmosphere makes it especially "good for groups."

Z **Bijoux** S M *French* 27 | 25 | 25 | $77

West Lovers Lane | 5450 W. Lovers Ln. (bet. Inwood Rd. & Preston Park Dr.) | Dallas | 214-350-6100 | www.bijouxrestaurant.com

Expect "impeccable everything" at Scott Gottlich's "consistently superb" West Lovers Lane "star that has not lost its luster", luring foodies and "special-occasion" celebrators with "ultrarefined" French food and "fabulous, attentive service"; the "tables are spaced nicely" in the artful, "sedate" space, so your conversation is your own, just know that prix fixe menus (which can be paired with "affordable wines") are the only dining option.

Billy Miner's *Burgers* 19 | 15 | 15 | $13

Sundance Square | 150 W. Third St. (bet. Houston & Main Sts.) | Ft. Worth | 817-877-3301 | www.cyberrodeo.com

Locals laud the "delicious burgers" and solid American grub at this "friendly" saloon in Downtown Ft. Worth's Sundance Square; "cheap" prices pull in local "families", while "drink specials" and plenty of "ice-cold beer" draw a rowdier bar crowd later on.

	FOOD	DECOR	SERVICE	COST

Bistro Louise *American/Mediterranean* 26 | 24 | 22 | $43

Southwest | Stonegate Commons | 2900 S. Hulen St. (Oak Park Ln.) | Ft. Worth | 817-922-9244 | www.bistrolouise.com

"Marvelous" New American-Med cuisine served in "pretty" surroundings by "attentive" servers make chef-owner Louise Lamensdorf's "expensive" Southwest Ft. Worth boîte a "wonderful find" that's "worth returning" to; it's especially favored by "ladies who lunch" while denizens declare that brunch is "exquisite" too.

NEW **Blackfinn** *Pub Food* 13 | 17 | 13 | $21

Addison | 4440 Beltline Rd. (Midway Rd.) | 469-374-7667 | www.blackfinndallas.com

The "lively bar scene" is the best thing going for this "friendly" Addison chain link catering to a "younger crowd" with "happy-hour" specials, TV screens blaring and "eye candy" galore; considering the Irish-American pub grub is only "ok", most patrons propose you "go for a drink, but pass on the food."

NEW **BLT Steak** *Steak* - | - | - | E

Galleria | 5301 Alpha Rd. (Noel Rd.) | Dallas | 972-726-9200 | www.bltrestaurants.com

In a city with a plethora of beloved steakhouses, newcomers must be overachievers, and this chichi Galleria-area outpost of Laurent Tourondel's bistro empire pulls out all the stops with sleek cream-colored suede decor and a magnetic bar scene attracting throngs of chic Dallasites; yet even with Gruyère popovers, a sensational raw bar and prime cuts of Kobe and Black Angus, hard-to-win-over beef eaters may be hard-pressed to change their allegiance just yet.

Blue Fish *Japanese* 23 | 18 | 19 | $33

Greenville Avenue | 3519 Greenville Ave. (McCommas Blvd.) | Dallas | 214-824-3474

North Dallas | 18149 N. Dallas Pkwy. (Frankford Rd.) | Dallas | 972-250-3474

Las Colinas | Las Colinas Vill. | 925 W. John Carpenter Frwy. (Walnut Hill Ln.) | Irving | 972-385-3474

www.thebluefishsushi.com

With three branches (in Dallas, North Dallas and Las Colinas), this Japanese micro-chain is a "surprising find", a "hip, happening kind of place" with "creative" fin fare, "fusion-type rolls", and "tempura and bento boxes" that are "right on"; thanks to its "bustling" "club-like atmosphere with thumping music and intimate lighting" and "Asian-eclectic decor", it's "not your typical, quiet sushi place."

Z **Blue Mesa** *Southwestern* 20 | 19 | 19 | $24

NorthPark | Lincoln Park | 7700 W. Northwest Hwy. (Central Expwy.) | Dallas | 214-378-8686

Addison | Village on the Pkwy. | 5100 Belt Line Rd. (Dallas N. Tollway) | 972-934-0165

Plano | Granite Park | 8200 N. Dallas Pkwy. (Hwy. 121) | 214-387-4407

University Area | University Park Vill. | 1600 S. University Dr. (bet. Old University Dr. & River Run) | Ft. Worth | 817-332-6372

(continued)

(continued)

Blue Mesa

Southlake | Southlake Town Sq. | 1586 E. Southlake Blvd. (Carroll Ave.) | 817-416-0055
www.bluemesagrill.com

"A taste of Santa Fe" comes to Texas via this "popular" mini-chain drawing plenty of "crowds" for "affordable", "palate-pleasing" Southwestern dishes, "addictive sweet potato chips", "killer" blue margaritas and a "fantastic Sunday brunch buffet"; the vibe is "comfortable" and staff "accommodating to large groups", so the only downside is that it "can be hard to get in."

Z Bob's Steak & Chop House S *Steak* 25 | 20 | 23 | $59

Lemmon Avenue | 4300 Lemmon Ave. (Wycliff Ave.) | Dallas | 214-528-9446
Plano | Shops at Legacy | 5760 Legacy Dr. (Bishop Rd.) | 972-608-2627
NEW Grapevine | 1255 South Main St. (Hwy. 114) | 817-481-5555
www.bobs-steakandchop.com

"Manly high-end dining" is alive and well at these "clubby" chophouse "institutions" where "yuppies" on "expense accounts" "tackle" "perfectly seared" steaks garnished with an "enormous" signature glazed carrot; all locations feature "noisy" environs, while the Lemmon Avenue branch offers "frequent Dallas Cowboy sightings" as an added appeasement.

Boi Na Braza *Brazilian/Steak* 24 | 22 | 25 | $55

Grapevine | 4025 William D. Tate Ave. (Hall Johnson Rd.) | 817-329-5514 | www.boinabraza.com

Those "hungry for meat" march over to this all-you-can-eat Grapevine churrascaria where gaucho-clad waiters "carve" "delicious" morsels from a "mind-boggling" array of skewered cuts while an extensive salad bar satisfies grazers; it's "top-shelf" all the way from the handsome wood-accented decor to cigar-friendly bar and "expensive" prices.

Z Bonnell's S M *Southwestern* 27 | 23 | 26 | $44

Southwest | 4259 Bryant Irvin Rd. (Southwest Blvd.) | Ft. Worth | 817-738-5489 | www.bonnellstexas.com

"A safari of fine foods" is rounded up by "wonderfully inventive" chef Jon Bonnell who is "true to Texas cuisine" at this moderately priced Southwestern "favorite" where "innovative" wild game preparations wow "adventurous" and timid types alike; "don't be fooled by the outside appearance" "next to the freeway" on the Southwest side of town, "inside is cozier", trimmed in stylish "cowboy and Western motifs", and serviced by a "top-quality" staff.

Bread Winners Cafe & Bakery *American/Bakery* 22 | 18 | 17 | $21

West Lovers Lane | Inwood Vill. | 5560 W. Lovers Ln. (Inwood Rd.) | Dallas | 214-351-3339
Uptown | 3301 McKinney Ave. (N. Hall St.) | Dallas | 214-754-4940

FOOD	DECOR	SERVICE	COST

(continued)

Bread Winners Cafe & Bakery

NEW **Plano** | Lakeside Mkt. | 4021 Preston Rd. (bet. Parker Rd. & Spring Creek Pkwy.) | 972-312-9300
www.breadwinnerscafe.com

"Fabulous lunches and brunches" are the main event at this trio of cafes that "also presents a delicious dinner"; each sports a "huge menu" of "amazing bakery items" plus "consistently good" New American salads, sandwiches and soups; still, some say their "lively atmosphere" can translate into a vibe that's "rushed" and "loud", and on weekends when it's a mob scene, "the wait could kill your appetite."

Brio Tuscan Grille *Italian* — 21 | 23 | 20 | $31

Southlake | Southlake Town Sq. | 1431 Plaza Pl. (Grand Ave.) | 817-310-3136 | www.brioitalian.com

A "wide selection" of "simple" Tuscan fare makes these "lively", "child-friendly" chain links in Dallas and Houston "dependable" picks for a "reasonably priced" meal; spacious, "high-style" decor gets a boost from "fabulous" outdoor seating at both locations, though regulars report service that swings between "sometimes great and sometimes not."

Bruno's ☒ *Italian* — 22 | 17 | 21 | $31

Irving | 9462 N. MacArthur Blvd. (Santa Fe Trail) | 972-556-2465 | www.brunosristorante.com

The "warm welcome" from owner Bruno Ceka adds to the "homey" feel of this "local" Italian in the Valley Ranch section of Irving; with "wonderful" food, moderate prices and a view of the canals, "it's particularly nice for a romantic evening" with live music on weekends as an added virtue.

Bubba's *Southern* — 23 | 10 | 15 | $12

Park Cities | Snider Plaza | 6617 Hillcrest Rd. (bet. Lovers & Mockingbird Lns.) | Dallas | 214-373-6527 | www.babeschicken.com

"Skip the Colonel" and head straight to this Snider Plaza "comfort-food" joint (and sib of Babe's) for "damn good fried chicken", "huge yeast rolls" and other rib-sticking dishes at appropriately down-home prices; though many opt for takeout or drive-thru, inside has a "retro" feel thanks to order-at-the-counter service and its setting in a converted 1920s service station.

Buffet at the Kimbell Ⓜ *American* — 24 | 24 | 16 | $15

Cultural District | Kimbell Art Museum | 3333 Camp Bowie Blvd. (University Dr.) | Ft. Worth | 817-332-8451 | www.kimbellart.org

"As classy and refined as" the Kimbell Art Museum that houses it, this Traditional American in Ft. Worth's Cultural District features an "excellent buffet" comprising a "lovely selection of salads, sandwiches, soups, quiches and desserts"; though some see the menu as "limited", all agree it's "carefully prepared", and "to top it off, you're surrounded by some of the finest artworks in the world"; N.B. dinner on Fridays only.

	FOOD	DECOR	SERVICE	COST

Bugatti Ristorante *Italian* 21 | 17 | 24 | $30

Love Field | 3802 W. Northwest Hwy. (Lemmon Ave.) | Dallas | 214-350-2470 | www.bugattis.com

"They always remember your name" at this Love Field "neighborhood restaurant" where the faithful flock for "inspiring" Italian food at moderate prices; the "quiet" Mediterranean-styled quarters with adjoining patio work for business meetings and "romantic" interludes alike.

Byblos Lebanese ☒ *Lebanese* 21 | 15 | 17 | $23

North Side | 1406 N. Main St. (Central Ave.) | Ft. Worth | 817-625-9667 | www.byblostx.com

Befitting a member of the Hedary family of Med eateries, the "delectable" "traditional" Lebanese fare "does not disappoint" at this "informal and cheap" North Sider with a "wonderful buffet" at lunch (Monday–Saturday) and one night a week (Thursday) – plus "available hookahs" and "belly dancing on certain nights" add to a "fun experience" that's "certainly different from most in Ft. Worth"; N.B. open till 2 AM on weekends.

Cacharel ☒ *French* 25 | 23 | 24 | $54

Arlington | Brookhollow Tower Two | 2221 E. Lamar Blvd., 9th fl. (Ballpark Way) | 817-640-9981

"Everything a French restaurant should be" avow admirers of this longtime Arlington eatery nestled on the ninth floor of an office building where "excellent", "classic" cuisine is delivered by an equally "top-notch" staff; it's "perfect for that special night out" with "elegant" provincial decor heightened by "fantastic" panoramic views.

Cadillac Bar *Mexican* 18 | 18 | 18 | $25

West End | 1800 North Mkt. (Corbin St.) | Dallas | 214-999-0662 | www.cadillacbar.com

See review in Houston Directory.

Café Ashton *American* 24 | 24 | 21 | $46

Downtown Ft. Worth | Ashton Hotel | 610 Main St. (6th St.) | Ft. Worth | 817-332-0100 | www.theashtonhotel.com

A "charming" respite in Downtown Ft. Worth's historic Ashton Hotel, this "intimate" New American delights diners with a "romantic" ambiance enhanced by live piano (Thursday–Saturday) and a fireplace; service can be "slightly slow" but "consistently good" fare redeems, making it a "lovely" choice for dinner or an "elegant" afternoon tea.

Cafe Aspen ☒ *American* 21 | 17 | 21 | $32

West | 6103 Camp Bowie Blvd. (Bryant Irvin Rd.) | Ft. Worth | 817-738-0838 | www.cafeaspen.com

How nice for West Ft. Worth to have this "popular spot" with "consistently" "excellent" New American fare, a "knowledgeable staff" and a "wonderful community feeling, where people know one another and the owner knows everyone" – be it the "blue-haired ladies at lunch" or those seeking "a great place for a business or pleasure" meal; some say the "setting leaves a bit to be desired", but more find the "nice, soothing decor" "charming."

Café Brazil *Coffeehouse/Tex-Mex* 19 | 14 | 17 | $17

Deep Ellum | 2815 Elm St. (Malcolm X Blvd.) | Dallas | 214-747-2730 ◐
Greenville Avenue | 2900 Greenville Ave. (Goodwin Ave.) | Dallas | 214-841-0900 ◐
Park Cities | 6420 N. Central Expwy. (Fondren Dr.) | Dallas | 214-691-7791 ◐
Oak Lawn | 3847 Cedar Springs Rd. (Oak Lawn Ave.) | Dallas | 214-461-8762 ◐
NEW Addison | Quorum II Plaza | 4930 Belt Line Rd. (Addison Rd.) | 972-386-7966 ◐
Richardson | 2071 N. Central Expwy. (Campbell Rd.) | 972-783-9011 ◐
McKinney | 3190 S. Central Expwy. (Eldorado Pkwy.) | 972-984-1259
Carrollton | 2510 N. Josey Ln. (Trinity Mills Rd.) | 972-242-8228
NEW Plano | 200 Coit Rd. (President George Bush Tpke.) | 469-229-9140
www.cafebrazil.com

An "eclectic" mix of "hipsters", "students" and "typical Dallas yuppies" come together at these "funky" Tex-Mex coffeehouses to "hang out" and fill up on "exceptional" java and "hearty breakfasts" or "sober up" after a night out (some branches are open 24/7); the "tattooed" staff is "friendly, if not always professional", but a little "quirkiness" is no matter when prices are this "affordable."

Café Cipriani Ⓢ *Italian* 21 | 17 | 22 | $41

Las Colinas | 220 E. Las Colinas Blvd. (O'Connor Blvd.) | Irving | 972-869-0713 | www.cafecipriani.com

You'll be "treated as a regular, even if it's your first time" at this "dependable" Northern Italian in Las Colinas, where the modus operandi is to lavish the customer with "warm, personal attention"; the "homestyle food" is both "affordable" and "very good", making it a popular "business-lunch" spot, but the big curiosity is the "elevator you take down to" the "basement dining room."

Café Express *Eclectic* 18 | 14 | 14 | $15

Mockingbird Station | Mockingbird Station | 5307 E. Mockingbird Ln. (I-75) | Dallas | 214-841-9444
West Lovers Lane | Pavilion Ctr. | 5600 W. Lovers Ln. (Inwood Rd.) | Dallas | 214-352-2211
Uptown | 3230 McKinney Ave. (Bowen St.) | Dallas | 214-999-9444
Plano | Shops at Legacy | 5800 Legacy Dr. (Bishop Rd.) | 972-378-9444
Southlake | Southlake Town Sq. | 1472 Main St. (Fountain Pl.) | 817-251-0063
www.cafe-express.com

See review in Houston Directory.

Café Istanbul Ⓜ *Turkish* 21 | 15 | 18 | $24

West Lovers Lane | Inwood Vill. | 5450 W. Lovers Ln. (Inwood Rd.) | Dallas | 214-902-0919 | www.cafe-istanbul.net

"Seductive flavors" "tickle the tongue" at this "authentic" Turkish "favorite" on West Lovers Lane where "inexpensive" prices (including "affordable wines") and a "warm" welcome from the staff increase the appeal; those craving quiet may want to "watch out for weekends" when belly dancers enhance the already "lively" atmosphere.

FOOD	DECOR	SERVICE	COST

Café Italia *Italian* 21 | 19 | 20 | $31

Love Field | 4615 W. Lovers Ln. (bet. Inwood & Midway Rds.) | Dallas | 214-357-4200

The idiosyncrasy at this "Italian bistro" near Love Field is the "Texan twist" to its "inventive menu", but regulars advise "don't laugh at the odd combos until you try some"; some say its offbeat site (a former motorcycle rental place) lacks appeal, and the "tables are a little close", but "chandeliers and a glowing interior" help smooth edges.

Café Lago *Eclectic* - | - | - | I

Lake Highlands | 9219 Garland Rd. (Lunar Ln.) | Dallas | 214-320-0726 | www.cafe-lago.com

Regulars of this "quaint", "unexpectedly good" Lake Highlands cantina "really like" it as a "fun little spot" for breakfast or a lunch of "great sandwiches and salads" or a "casual dinner", saying they've "yet to find something they don't like" on its Eclectic menu.

Café Madrid *Spanish* 21 | 16 | 19 | $28

Knox-Henderson | 4501 Travis St. (Armstrong Ave.) | Dallas | 214-528-1731 [S]

Oak Cliff | 408 N. Bishop Ave. (8th St.) | Dallas | 214-942-8272 www.cafemadrid-dallas.com

"Hang for a couple hours and dine on wonderful tapas", a "traditional" "taste of Spain", paired with "pitchers of sangria" or "inexpensive" Iberian wines served "in ordinary glasses (very European)" at these Knox-Henderson and Oak Cliff snackeries; its "warm, inviting vibe", "efficient service" and a hopping patio-and-bar scene that "allows you to ogle the beautiful people" make it a favorite "gathering place" that's "fun for a party or date."

[Z] **Café Modern** [M] *Eclectic* 22 | 26 | 20 | $25

Cultural District | Modern Art Museum | 3200 Darnell St. (University Dr.) | Ft. Worth | 817-840-2157 | www.themodern.org

Gallery-goers make a beeline for this "chic" canteen with "cool" "water views" housed in the "magnificent" Tadao Ando-designed Modern Art Museum in Ft. Worth's Cultural District; the seasonal Eclectic menu offers "creative" midpriced lunch and brunch options as well as a selection of coffees and sandwiches available for those on the go; N.B. dinner is served the first Friday of every month.

Café Nasher by Wolfgang Puck [M] *American* 18 | 22 | 16 | $24

Arts District | Nasher Sculpture Ctr. | 2001 Flora St. (Pearl St.) | Dallas | 214-242-5118 | www.nashersculpturecenter.org

The "spacious and airy" digs overlooking the grounds of the "stunning" Nasher Sculpture Center in the Arts District win raves from those who say it's a "nice place" for New American "comfort food" like signature salads and "soup and sandwich fare" after "checking out some great work"; others opine it "doesn't deserve Wolfgang Puck's name" with "not-that-great" fare, cafeteria-style service and tabs they find "expensive"; N.B. admission to the museum is required to dine here.

Café on the Green *American* 24 | 25 | 26 | $59

Las Colinas | Four Seasons Resort & Club | 4150 N. MacArthur Blvd. (Northgate Dr.) | Irving | 972-717-2420 | www.fourseasons.com

"As if you needed another reason to stay at the Four Seasons" in Las Colinas, you'll find it in the "great overall experience" at this "elegant hotel restaurant": between its "wonderful service", "serene atmosphere", "beautiful vistas" and "enticing" American menu of "excellent, innovative" dishes, it's no wonder it's a pick for a "business power dinner", "romantic evening" or "excellent Sunday brunch."

Z Café Pacific *Seafood* 26 | 24 | 26 | $51

Park Cities | 24 Highland Park Vill. (Mockingbird Ln.) | Dallas | 214-526-1170

"Rub elbows" with "old money" matrons and a "who's who" of "society" types at this "tony" Highland Park Village eatery ensconced in "clubby" quarters with polished marble floors and a "classic 1920s feel"; "top-tier" seafood plates are set down by a staff that "caters to your every need", though a few critics charge it's "stuffy" and add "you better be a regular if you want even average service."

Campania *Pizza* 23 | 12 | 14 | $18

West Village | Mondrian | 3800 McKinney Ave. (Blackburn St.) | Dallas | 214-780-0605

Southlake | 291 Grand Ave. (Civic Pl.) | 817-310-3116 S M

www.campaniapizza.com

Pieheads praise the "amazing" Neapolitan pizza made from "imported Italian ingredients" at this well-priced West Village BYO with "funky mosaic tables", a streetside patio and a "laid-back" vibe; even with "mediocre" service, converts claim it's "definitely worth a visit"; N.B. the Southlake branch is newer and unrated.

Campisi's *Pizza* 19 | 14 | 17 | $19

Downtown Dallas | Stone Street Gdns. | 1520 Elm St. (bet. Akard & Erway Sts.) | Dallas | 214-752-0141 S

Greenville Avenue | Kroger's Food Court | 5665 E. Mockingbird Ln. (Greenville Ave.) | Dallas | 214-821-4741

West Lovers Lane | 5405 W. Lovers Ln. (Inwood Rd.) | Dallas | 214-350-2595 S

North Dallas | 7632 W. Campbell Rd. (Coit Rd.) | Dallas | 972-931-2267

Plano | 3115 W. Parker Rd. (Independence Pkwy.) | 972-612-1177

Plano | 8100 N. Dallas Pkwy. (Granite Pkwy.) | 214-387-0233

Campisi's Egyptian *Pizza*

Greenville Avenue | 5610 E. Mockingbird Ln. (Greenville Ave.) | Dallas | 214-827-0355

www.campisis.us

"A mainstay since the 1940s", this "landmark" near Greenville Avenue has appeal that goes beyond its "unique", "thin, rectangular pizza"; yes, it's "dated inside", but its "funky" interior, "like walking onto the set of a Scorsese movie", is "filled with character" - and characters, such as its "old-school waitresses", who are "part of the charm"; there are several newer outposts, but enthusiasts attest "the original has the best atmosphere."

	FOOD	DECOR	SERVICE	COST

Canary Cafe *Mediterranean* ▽ 26 | 18 | 24 | $36

Addison | Village on the Pkwy. | 5100 Belt Line Rd. (Dallas N. Tollway) | 972-503-7080 | www.canarycafeaddison.com

Enthusiasts applaud the evening-only performances at this moderately priced Addison Mediterranean where chef-owner Mansour Gorji "is always there" turning out "delicious" dishes that play off of "unusual combinations of ingredients"; though it's set in a strip mall, the "candlelit" room creates a "cozy" atmosphere that's "perfect" for a "relaxed" meal or "special occasion."

Cantina Laredo *Mexican* 21 | 20 | 20 | $23

Lakewood | 2031 Abrams Rd. (Gaston Ave.) | Dallas | 214-821-5785
Preston Royal | 6025 Royal Ln. (Preston Rd.) | Dallas | 214-265-1610
West Lovers Lane | 165 Inwood Vill. (Lovers Ln.) | Dallas | 214-350-5227
Addison | 4546 Belt Line Rd. (Beltway Dr.) | 972-458-0962
North Dallas | 17808 Dallas Pkwy. (Briargrove Ln.) | Dallas | 469-828-4818
Frisco | 1125 Legacy Dr. (Hwy. 121) | 214-618-9860
Sundance Square | 530 Throckmorton St. (bet. 4th & 5th Sts.) | Ft. Worth | 817-810-0773
Lewisville | 2225 S. Stemmons Frwy. (bet. Corporate Dr. & Hebron Pkwy.) | 972-315-8100
Grapevine | 4020 William D. Tate Ave. (Hall Johnson Rd.) | 817-358-0505
www.cantinalaredo.com

"Creative" Mexican fare including "guacamole made tableside" "satisfies cravings" and elevates these "reliable" south-of-the-border outposts "a step above" the typical chain experience; the decor is "upscale" too, though some sticklers suggest they're "overpriced" and add that "service can be lacking" as well.

Capital Grille *Steak* 25 | 25 | 25 | $58

Uptown | Crescent Shops & Galleries | 500 Crescent Ct. (Cedar Springs Rd.) | Dallas | 214-303-0500 | www.thecapitalgrille.com

"Everything a steakhouse ought to be", this decidedly "upscale" chain lures "buttoned-down" "power" players with "flavorful", "artfully presented" chops; the "low-lit, dark-wood" digs and "attentive" service are "ideal for a special occasion or a business dinner", and even though the bill can be "way expensive", "you get what you pay for" here.

Carrabba's Italian Grill *Italian* 22 | 19 | 22 | $28

North Dallas | 17548 Dallas Pkwy. (Trinity Mills Rd.) | Dallas | 972-732-7752
Plano | 3400 N. Central Expwy. (Parker Rd.) | 972-516-9900
Rockwall | 1599 Laguna Dr. (I-30) | 972-722-4304
Hurst | 1101 Melbourne Rd. (bet. Bedford Euless & Pipeline Rds.) | 817-595-3345
Grapevine | 1701 Crossroads Dr. (Hwy. 114) | 817-410-8461
www.carrabbas.com

See review in Houston Directory.

Carshon's Delicatessen *Deli* 23 | 12 | 18 | $13

University Area | 3133 Cleburne Rd. (bet. 8th & McCart Aves.) | Ft. Worth | 817-923-1907

Corned beef connoisseurs head to this "classic" (circa 1929) deli in Ft. Worth's University Area for "great sandwiches" and other "top-quality" noshes like bagels and soups with a "New York feel"; "proficient service" keeps the line moving at the counter while the seating area is decked out with "vintage chrome and Formica decor" and historic photos of the city.

Catalina Room M *American* 18 | 23 | 20 | $34

Lemmon Avenue | 4218 Lemmon Ave. (bet. Douglas & Wycliff Aves.) | Dallas | 214-526-5411

The "swanky" decor with a mahogany bar and plush booths wired with "flat-screen TVs" creates a backdrop for "consistently good" Traditional American "comfort food" at this moderately priced Lemmon Avenue eatery; service can be "inconsistent", but little touches like patio seating and live music on weekends make it a "comfortable" place for those in the "neighborhood."

Cattlemen's Steakhouse *Steak* 23 | 18 | 21 | $36

Stockyards | 2458 N. Main St. (Exchange Ave.) | Ft. Worth | 817-624-3945 | www.cattlemenssteakhouse.com

"If nostalgia counts for anything" this Ft. Worth "classic" from 1947 set in the historic Stockyards District is "still worth a visit" claim "cowboys" clamoring for "outrageous" charbroiled steaks and sides rustled to the table by "sweet waitresses with big hair"; even if a few find there are "better beef options" elsewhere, it's still "worth a visit" if only for a beer and to soak in the "old-style" decor with "pictures of cattle" plastered on the walls.

Celebration *American* 21 | 15 | 20 | $21

Love Field | 4503 W. Lovers Ln. (bet. Inwood Rd. & Lemmon Ave.) | Dallas | 214-358-0612 | www.celebrationrestaurant.com

"The granddaddy of all Dallas home-cooking restaurants", this "old standby" has been serving generous portions of "solid, consistent" "comfort food" "in a homey setting" for over 30 years; set "in a series of houses" near Love Field (like "grandma's house, without the grandma"), it's a "great" spot for "large groups", a "post-finals hangout for SMU students" and a "quaint place to slow down with family" "after church on Sundays."

Central 214 *American* 24 | 23 | 21 | $50

Park Cities | Hotel Palomar | 5680 N. Central Expwy. (Mockingbird Ln.) | Dallas | 214-443-9339 | www.central214.com

A "cool Beverly Hills vibe" emanates from this "sleek, modern" venue in Park Cities' "trendy" Hotel Palomar where "hipsters" and blue bloods are "blown away by" the "excellent" New American cuisine from chef Tom Fleming; "the staff aims to please", though you'll pay for it with prices that several diners dub "expensive."

Chamberlain's Fish Market Grill *Seafood* 23 | 21 | 23 | $44

Addison | 4525 Belt Line Rd. (bet. Dallas N. Tollway & Midway Rd.) | 972-503-3474 | www.chefchamberlain.com

Sister to Chamberlain's Steak & Chop House down the street, this "outstanding (and busy) seafood" spot in Addison features "nicely cooked and presented" fin fare "so fresh, you'd think you were in Cape Cod instead of Texas"; some say it lacks "the flair you'd expect, given the prices", but most maintain it's simply "superior", plus the "pleasant (if not fancy)" setting and "super, laid-back service" elevate it "beyond the standard fish house."

Chamberlain's Steak & Chop House *Steak* 25 | 22 | 24 | $54

Addison | 5330 Belt Line Rd. (Montfort Dr.) | 972-934-2467 | www.chamberlainsrestaurant.com

"A standout among the many cow palaces of Dallas" proclaim patrons of this big-ticket Addison chophouse (and sister to Chamberlain's Fish Market Grill) searing "fine" dry-aged steaks so "succulent", it "should be a crime" not to order one; it's a "class act" all around, from the "top-notch" service to the "quiet, clubby atmosphere" that makes for "a most enjoyable evening on every occasion."

Chaparral S M *Steak* ▽ 21 | 25 | 22 | $50

Downtown Dallas | Adams Mark Hotel | 400 Olive St. (Live Oak St.) | Dallas | 214-777-6539 | www.adamsmark.com

"Ask for a window table" if you want to enjoy the "breathtaking" view of the city at this "commendable" steakhouse set atop Downtown's Adams Mark Hotel; though deep-pocketed diners deem it a "pleasant", "low-key" spot, the less-impressed proclaim it "long in the tooth"; N.B. a concept revamp is reportedly in the works for 2008.

Charleston's *American* 18 | 18 | 19 | $23

Southwest | 3020 S. Hulen St. (Bellaire Dr.) | Ft. Worth | 817-735-8900 | www.charlestons.com

Whether "for lunch" or "a quick dinner with family", you'll find "consistently good food and service" at this "casual American" on Ft. Worth's Southwest Side, a branch of an Oklahoma-based chain; its menu of steaks, seafood and other basics is "varied for all tastes" – in fact, its "mac 'n' cheese is big with the adults as well as the preschool set."

NEW Charlie Palmer at the Joule *American* - | - | - | VE

Downtown Dallas | Joule Hotel | 1530 Main St. (bet. Akard & Ervay Sts.) | Dallas | 214-261-4600 | www.charliepalmer.com

Acclaimed chef Charlie Palmer adds star power to this vibrant Downtown venue in the Joule Hotel; though the Adam Tihany-designed decor is themed on wind energy (with an earthy color scheme and turbine ceiling features to convey the message), it's the New American food that makes the bolder statement, along with an exceptional wine list that comes to the table in an electronic tablet; prices are high, but appropriate, given the top-tier experience; N.B. the adjacent wine shop features selections from the restaurant.

Cheesecake Factory *American* 20 | 20 | 18 | $26

NorthPark | Lincoln Park | 7700 W. Northwest Hwy. (bet. Boedeker St. & Hwy. 75) | Dallas | 214-373-4844

Frisco | Stonebriar Ctr. | 2601 Preston Rd. (Rte. 121) | 972-731-7799

Southlake | Southlake Town Sq. | 1440 Plaza Pl. (Grand Ave.) | 817-310-0050

www.thecheesecakefactory.com

See review in Houston Directory.

Chic from Barcelona *Spanish* 18 | 18 | 18 | $22

Preston Forest | Preston Forest Vill. | 11909 Preston Rd. (Forest Ln.) | Dallas | 972-239-2442 | www.chicbarcelona.com

The "fantastic" rotisserie chicken alone is "worth the trip" to this "cheap" Preston Forest "find" featuring a "limited" menu of "unusual" Catalan choices served by a "friendly" (if sometimes "slow") staff; the "strip-center" space is "big on charm" with the "cool decor" cast in upbeat yellow tones and adorned with customer decorated plates while there's a "nice patio" outside too.

Chow Thai *Thai* 23 | 19 | 19 | $25

Addison | 5290 Belt Line Rd. (Montfort Dr.) | 972-960-2999
Plano | 3309 Dallas Pkwy. (Parker Rd.) | 972-608-1883
www.chowthai.com

"Go once and you'll be hooked" by these "upscale" spots owned by West Coast transplants Vinnie and Sam Virasin, a husband-and-wife duo that delivers with "wonderful" food that's a "fresh, Californian-style Thai (i.e. don't expect authentic)"; "despite the strip-mall location" at both the Addison and Plano branches, each is a "quiet place, perfect for lunch or dinner", with "lightning-fast service" and "fun decor."

Chubby's *Diner* ▽ 18 | 11 | 19 | $12

Lake Highlands | 11331 E. Northwest Hwy. (Jupiter Rd.) | Dallas | 214-348-6065
Lancaster | 3307 W. Pleasant Run Rd. (I-35) | 972-228-4101
Plano | 910 W. Parker Rd. (bet. Alma & Premier Drs.) | 972-881-1348
www.chubbysfamilyrestaurant.com

"No frills here", just "hearty", "home-cooked" all-day breakfasts plus "standard" American lunches and dinners doled out by "friendly" waitresses at these "old-fashioned diners" in Lake Highlands, Lancaster and Plano; all deliver "quick" in-and-out service "even on busy weekends" with prices so "affordable" there's enough left for the "don't-miss cakes and pies."

Chuy's *Tex-Mex* 21 | 19 | 19 | $18

Knox-Henderson | 4544 McKinney Ave. (bet. Armstrong Ave. & Knox St.) | Dallas | 214-559-2489 | www.chuys.com

See review in Austin and the Hill Country Directory.

Cindi's New York Style Deli *Deli* 17 | 9 | 16 | $15

Medical City | 11111 N. Central Expwy. (Northhaven Rd.) | Dallas | 214-739-0918
Richardson | 7522 Campbell Rd. (Lauder Ln.) | 972-248-0608
www.cindisnydeli.com

Its menu may be "more Midwest than Midtown", but this "NY-style deli" duo in Richardson and Medical City still satisfies with "credible bagels", "matzo ball soup" and other "solid", "home-style" fare all at "reasonable" prices; waitresses may be "sassy", but they let you "stay and chat" even when there's a "long wait" during "Sunday brunch."

FOOD | DECOR | SERVICE | COST

City Café *American* — - | - | - | M

West Lovers Lane | 5757 W. Lovers Ln. (Dallas N. Tollway) | Dallas | 214-351-2233 | www.thecitycafedallas.com

Tucked into a multistory shopping center in the shadow of the Tollway, this West Lovers Lane landmark proves its staying power with an approachable, if pricey, menu of New American dishes; the simple-yet-elegant white-tablecloth decor suits the well-heeled locals who find the adjacent casual take-out shop (with tables for daytime service) and wine boutique a fabulous alternative when they are too hurried to linger.

Classic Cafe at Roanoke, The ☒ *American* — ▽ 28 | 21 | 27 | $40

Roanoke | 504 N. Oak St. (Denton St.) | 817-430-8185 | www.theclassiccafe.com

"A small-town jewel", this "intimate" New American is where "haute cuisine meets Texas - and with great success"; though some say its upscale profile seems "kind of out of place in Roanoke", and its old converted house is somewhat "underwhelming from the outside", the "inviting atmosphere" within complements the "wonderful staff and exquisite food", making it a keeper, especially for "special occasions"; N.B. a patio and wine cellar are new additions.

Clay Pit: Contemporary Indian Cuisine *Indian* — 23 | 20 | 19 | $25

Addison | 4460 Belt Line Rd. (Midway Rd.) | 972-233-0111 | www.claypit.com

"Traditional" Indian dishes are prepared with "modern" (some say "Americanized") "twists" at these "upscale" eateries where the "extensive wine and cocktail list" and "friendly", if sometimes "haphazard" service makes for an "overall satisfying experience"; the Addison branch features a waterwall and a dining room draped in saris, while the Downtown Austin outpost is housed in a "cool", "historic" building; the "reasonably priced lunch buffet" reigns at both locations.

NEW Club, The *American/Italian* — - | - | - | E

Oak Lawn | Centrum Bldg. | 3102 Oak Lawn Ave. (Cedar Springs Rd.) | Dallas | 214-526-3100 | www.theclub-dallas.com

An international marriage of American and Italian cuisines draws the pretty, powerful and oft photographed to restaurateur Robert Colombo's tony new den in Oak Lawn's Centrum Building; the decor is swanky with tartan banquets and polished brass accents while pampering service is overseen by manager Enam Chowdhury (ex Mansion on Turtle Creek).

Coal Vines *Italian* — 24 | 19 | 18 | $25

Uptown | 2404 Cedar Springs Rd. (Maple Ave.) | Dallas | 214-855-4999 ◐

NEW Southlake | 1251 E. Southlake Blvd. (Carroll Ave.) | 817-310-0850

www.coalvines.com

"New York transplants" tout the "delectable thin-crust" pies, "fresh salads" and "affordable wines" at this "trendy" Uptown Italian catering to a "yuppie" crowd with "late" hours on weekends and a "lively" bar scene; for those who complain they feel "stuffed" into the rustic, brick-walled quarters, good news - a new branch in Southlake offers an alternative to the Cedar Springs Road location's "uncomfortable" seating and "annoying waits."

Cool River Cafe *Southwestern/Steak* 19 21 20 $38

Las Colinas | 1045 Hidden Ridge (MacArthur Blvd.) | Irving | 972-871-8881 | www.coolrivercafe.com

See review in Austin and the Hill Country Directory.

Cosmic Café *Eclectic* 22 19 17 $15

Oak Lawn | 2912 Oak Lawn Ave. (Cedar Springs Rd.) | Dallas | 214-521-6157 | www.cosmiccafedallas.com

"One of the few all vegetarian/vegan places in Dallas", this "fun" spot "in an old home" in Oak Lawn features an Eclectic menu of physically and "metaphysically pleasing food" enlivened by "Indian spices throughout" and served within a "quaint, quirky setting"; a "Nepali hippie Zen-yoga feel" that "defines laid-back" adds to the "mystical, surreal experience", prompting patrons to proclaim that "just being there calms your soul" - and also provides some correspondingly "great people-watching."

Cousin's Bar-B-Q ☒ *BBQ* 21 15 17 $13

Southwest | 5125 Bryant Irvin Rd. (bet. Overton Ridge Blvd. & Trailview Dr.) | Ft. Worth | 817-346-3999
South Side | 6262 McCart Ave. (Westcreek Dr.) | Ft. Worth | 817-346-2511
Keller | 535 Keller Pkwy. (Cindy St.) | 817-379-0306
www.cousinsbbq.com

"Tender" brisket and ribs plus plentiful sides and sweet tea await at this "family-owned" chain of "hometown" BBQ joints scattered around Tarrant County; a "friendly staff", "fast" "cafeteria line" service and a "relaxed atmosphere" with "middle-of-the-road prices" make it "a great place to take the kids" or pick up some solid takeout; N.B. the Keller branch is drive-thru only.

Craft Dallas *American* 25 25 23 $67

Victory Park | W Hotel | 2440 Victory Park Ln. (Olive St.) | Dallas | 214-397-4111 | www.craftrestaurant.com

"Deceptively simple" New American dishes showcasing "sublime" ingredients win the favor of "foodies" at this Victory Park outpost from NYC chef-owner Tom Colicchio that's set in a "glossy, sumptuous" ground-floor space with a beige and black color scheme in the W Hotel; though a "trendy" crowd thrives on the "buzz" and "swank atmosphere", detractors declare "some of the adventure doesn't quite work out" with "snooty service" and "outrageous prices" leaving "much to be desired."

Cristina's *Mexican* 18 17 17 $15

Addison | 4021 Beltline Rd. (Runyon Rd.) | 972-386-0082
McKinney | 2811 Craig Dr. (Eldorado Pkwy.) | 214-544-2800
Frisco | 8210 Hwy. 121 (Parkwood Blvd.) | 214-618-8230
Garland | 4107 Lavon Dr. (Firewheel Pkwy.) | 972-476-7555

(continued)

(continued)

Cristina's

Plano | 3432 Hebron Pkwy. (Park Blvd.) | 972-380-8844
Flower Mound | 6424 Cross Timbers Rd. (Shiloh Rd.) | 817-430-3669
Lewisville | 360 E. Round Grove Rd. (Rockbrook Dr.) | 972-315-3126
Trophy Club | 2003 Hwy. 114 (Trophy Club Dr.) | 817-430-4545
Grapevine | 2707 E. Southlake Blvd. (Nolan Dr.) | 817-488-2095
www.cristinasmex.com

"Just one will do it" toast tequila lovers sipping the "biggest margaritas you ever saw" at this "reliable" chain with an "extensive menu" of "well-made" dishes from Central Mexico brought out by "attentive servers"; all locations thrive on inexpensive prices and a casual atmosphere brightened with sun-themed Latin art.

Crú Wine Bar *American* 20 | 23 | 21 | $34

West Village | West Vill. | 3699 McKinney Ave. (Lemmon Ave.) | Dallas | 214-526-9463
Plano | Shops at Legacy | 7201 Bishop Rd. (Legacy Dr.) | 972-312-9463 ◐
www.cruawinebar.com

Oenophiles "enjoy a glass of vino", indulge in "creative" New American snacks "after shopping or a movie" or perch on a seat and "people-watch" at these "atmospheric" outposts of a Dallas-based wine bar chain; they're "sophisticated", candlelit spots with a "swanky library" feel, though some detractors demur on tabs they find "pricey" and say there's "room for improvement" when it comes to service too.

Cuba Libre *Caribbean* 20 | 19 | 18 | $26

Knox-Henderson | 2822 N. Henderson Ave. (Milam St.) | Dallas | 214-827-2820 | www.cubalibredallas.com

"Be ready for a wait" at this "lively" Caribbean in Knox-Henderson, as its "large portions" of "fun, flirty food" (at "easy-on-the-pocket prices"), "tasty Cuban-inspired cocktails" and "vibrant atmosphere" preserve its position as a "perennial hot spot" that attracts an "eclectic crowd", with "lots of hotties" and "beautiful people" among its "young professionals, families and sophisticated seniors"; another "bonus - the kitchen is open late" Thursdays-Saturdays.

Culpepper Steakhouse *Steak* 24 | 21 | 23 | $47

Rockwall | 309 I-30 E. (Horizon Rd.) | 972-771-1001 | www.culpeppersteakhouse.com

The venerable Rockwall beef emporium fires up "excellent" steaks and teams them with "fantastic wines" in "Texas-themed" surroundings decked out in animal hides and outfitted with a huge fireplace; add in solid service, moderate prices and live music on weekends and it's no wonder converts count on it as a "place to bring visitors" for a "traditional" Lone Star state experience.

Dakota's Steakhouse Ⓢ *Steak* 22 | 21 | 20 | $50

Arts District | 600 N. Akard St. (Ross Ave.) | Dallas | 214-740-4001 | www.dakotasrestaurant.com

While acknowledged as "another great steakhouse" - with "big, juicy" cuts of meat, "excellent" seafood and an "attentive staff" -

what sets apart this "upscale" "gem" is its "unique" underground setting, with a "dark, elegant" atmosphere and "romantic patio" complete with "waterfall and hanging plants"; it's a "place to take tourists" or "special dates", and its Arts District location Downtown makes it "very good for business lunches" as well.

NEW Dallas Fish Market ⊠ *American/Seafood* ▽ 24 | 22 | 24 | $48

Downtown Dallas | 1501 Main St. (Akard St.) | Dallas | 214-744-3474 | www.dallasfishmarket.com

Seafood comes to "meat country" via this swank Downtown arrival ensconced in an "airy, modern" space with a sushi bar and wine room filled with a "well-edited" selection of boutique vinos (24 are available by the glass); patrons proclaim the sea-centric New American cuisine "creative" and "fresh", and if it's "too soon to know" how it'll all shape up, it certainly "has potential."

Daniele Osteria M *Italian* 24 | 17 | 23 | $39

Oak Lawn | 3300 Oak Lawn Ave. (Hall St.) | Dallas | 214-443-9420 | www.danieleosteria.com

Local gastronomes are grateful this midpriced Oak Lawn hideaway "remains under the radar" (it's quite literally "hidden away" below street level) so they can enjoy "simple", "flavorful" Sicilian meals with "no delays" in a "romantic" candlelit setting; "personable" chef-owner Daniele Puleo packs the place with a "posh mixed crowd" that practices its "Texas-accented Italian" with the "friendly" staff.

Z Del Frisco's Double Eagle Steak House *Steak* 27 | 24 | 25 | $69

North Dallas | 5251 Spring Valley Rd. (Dallas N. Tollway) | Dallas | 972-490-9000

Downtown Ft. Worth | 812 Main St. (8th St.) | Ft. Worth | 817-877-3999 www.delfriscos.com

Born in Dallas, this "high-end" franchise attracts a "see-and-be-seen" crowd with its "Texas-size" steaks and sides backed up by a "fantastic wine list"; sure, it's "way expensive", but in return you get sleek settings, "flawless service" from "attractive" staffers and "no chain feeling."

Deli-News *Deli* 22 | 13 | 17 | $17

North Dallas | 17062 Preston Rd. (Campbell Rd.) | Dallas | 972-733-3354

This "really good" "New York-style deli" in North Dallas offers "outstanding meats and desserts" plus "bagels flown in from New York", specifically H&H of *Sex and the City* fame; it features a "crowded, dinerlike atmosphere", providing a "valid option for" Manhattan expats - well, "almost", quip those who say the "servers are too polite."

Dixie House *Southern* 18 | 14 | 18 | $15

Lakewood | 6400 Gaston Ave. (Abrams Pkwy.) | Dallas | 214-826-2412 | www.theblackeyedpea.com

Lakewood's "comfort-food headquarters", this "authentic" Southerner still feels like a "neighborhood venue" in spite of its kinship with the Black-Eyed Pea restaurant chain (it's the original outpost); supporters say it's a "reliable family place" with fried and grilled specialties to fit every diet and a "friendly atmosphere" with sweet service, and gentle pricing.

Dragonfly *American* 19 | 23 | 18 | $47

Uptown | Hotel ZaZa | 2332 Leonard St. (McKinney Ave.) | Dallas | 214-468-8399 | www.hotelzaza.com

"You can't beat the people-watching" at this "Uptown hot spot" in the "sexy" Hotel ZaZa, a "happening" New American eatery with an "awesome interior"and "a fantastic wine list"; still, some can't get past the "stereotypical Dallas pretty people" peopling the place, quipping that it's "better known for what celebrity is falling into the pool "than for its food."

Dream Café *American* 18 | 13 | 15 | $19

Uptown | Quadrangle | 2800 Routh St. (Howell St.) | Dallas | 214-954-0486
Addison | Village on the Pkwy. | 5100 Belt Line Rd. (Dallas N. Tollway) | 972-503-7326
www.thedreamcafe.com

Bringing an "Austin attitude to Dallas", this pair of "healthy alternatives" purveys "cheap, casual" New American eats, including "lots of choices for vegetarians"; its forte is its "hectic" Sunday brunch, when families descend on the "kid-friendly", "dog-friendly" Addison branch with its patio and jungle gym, and "large crowds" throng the the Quadrangle location, "as hippie a setting as possible in Uptown."

Duce [S] [M] *Eclectic* 20 | 23 | 18 | $39

West | 6333 Camp Bowie Blvd. (bet. Bernie Anderson & Fairfield Aves.) | Ft. Worth | 817-377-4400 | www.eatdrinkliveduce.com

An "upbeat" vibe prevails at chef Tim Love's rambunctious outpost that "fills a huge void" on the West side of Ft. Worth with "inventive, well-presented" Eclectic small-plates - prices "add up fast so watch out" - plus a full lineup of steaks appealing to an "upscale young crowd"; a "disappointed" few note that it's "not as good as its older brother", Lonesome Dove, while others grumble about "weak service" too.

East Wind *Pan-Asian* 21 | 18 | 21 | $28

Uptown | Quadrangle | 2800 Routh St. (Howell St.) | Dallas | 214-745-5554 | www.eastwinddallas.com

"There's always a warm reception from the gracious owner" at this Uptown Pan-Asian featuring a "treasure trove" of well-priced Eastern specialties that go "far beyond the typical Thai" with sushi, Chinese and Vietnamese dishes rounding out the offerings; lunches are "busy", but the vibe is "soothing" thanks to a warm interior with fresh flowers on the tables and paintings on the walls.

Edelweiss [S] [M] *German* 20 | 20 | 24 | $25

West | 3801 Southwest Blvd. (Desert Ridge Dr.) | Ft. Worth | 817-738-5934 | www.edelweissrestaurant.com

Don the lederhosen and head to the West side of Ft. Worth for this "old-world" eatery that satisfies schnitzel lovers with "hearty"

German "grub" and pitchers of imported brews; an "oompah band" every night adds to the authenticity of the "mountain lodge" setting.

Ed's Deli *Deli* 23 | 15 | 19 | $19

(fka Deli News Too)

Preston Forest | 12817 Preston Rd. (Lyndon B. Johnson Frwy.) | Dallas | 972-386-0300 | www.edsdeli.com

"Plentiful" portions of "authentic" "NYC"-style deli fare keeps the "neighborhood crowd" "coming back" to this BYO noshers nook in Preston Forest for a mind-boggling array of "old-school" delicacies like "succulent" corned beef; the staff is "friendly" while the "beyond casual" atmosphere is always bustling, especially on weekends.

8.0 Restaurant & Bar ☒ *American* 14 | 17 | 15 | $27

Sundance Square | Sundance Sq. | 111 E. Third St. (bet. Commerce & Houston Sts.) | Ft. Worth | 817-336-0880 | www.eightobar.com

"Grab a quick bite" at this "casual" "hangout" that "draws a hip crowd" of "lively post-work" "professionals" and "singles" who "enjoy the live music", "great drinks" and American "bar staples"; some deem the eats "average" and say the staffers are "hired only on the basis of their good looks", but the "popular patio" provides some of the "best people-watching in Sundance Square."

El Rancho Grande ☒ *Mexican* 20 | 15 | 21 | $18

North Side | 1400 N. Main St. (Central Ave.) | Ft. Worth | 817-624-9206

"Ignore the decor and focus on the food" at this no-frills Mexican on the North Side of Ft. Worth where the "great" housemade chips are the perfect prelude to "traditional" dishes like fajitas and chalupas; service is swift, but those in-the-know insist you "come early" since "there's always a lineup" on "weekends" and at "lunch."

Empress of China *Chinese* 19 | 14 | 19 | $18

Las Colinas | Grande Shopping Ctr. | 2648 N. Belt Line Rd. (Grande Bulevar) | Irving | 972-252-7677

Flower Mound | 1913 Justin Rd. (Valley Ridge Ln.) | 972-691-1628

Grapevine | 2030 Glade Rd. (bet. Hwy. 360 & W. Airfield Dr.) | 817-442-0088

It may not rival "NYC or San Francisco", but this trio of "dependable" Chinese eateries does a "pretty darn good" job serving Flower Mound, Grapevine and Las Colinas with "tasty" dishes made from "fresh" "top-quality ingredients"; as a welcome "change from mega-buffets" nearby, the "waiters remember your favorites" here – a personal touch that overcomes the "spartan atmosphere" and strip-mall locations without leaving you with a higher tab.

Esperanza's Mexican Bakery & Café *Mexican* 24 | 14 | 19 | $14

Hospital District | 1109 Hemphill St. (Rosedale St.) | Ft. Worth | 817-332-3848

North Side | 2122 N. Main St. (21st St.) | Ft. Worth | 817-626-5770 ⊄

www.joets.com

Part of "the famous Joe T. Garcia-LanCarte family", this pair of "Ft. Worth staples" has long been serving up "no-frills", "authentic

Mexican dishes" at an "affordable price"; its Hospital District location "is not the prettiest" (the Main Street branch is nicer), but both get the thumbs-up for their "great breakfasts" and "excellent bakery items."

Z NEW Fearing's *Southwestern* 26 | 27 | 25 | $77

Uptown | Ritz-Carlton Hotel | 2121 McKinney Ave. (Olive St.) | Dallas | 214-922-4848 | www.fearingsrestaurant.com

Chef-owner Dean Fearing (ex Mansion on Turtle Creek) takes Southwestern cuisine "to a new level" claim those who "can't get enough" of his "fantastic" food at this "much anticipated" arrival in Uptown's new Ritz-Carlton Hotel, where the "mesmerizing interior" is separated into seven "chic" areas abuzz with a glittery crowd and some of "Dallas' finest plastic surgery on display"; some find the prices "excessive" and note a few "kinks" with the otherwise "courteous" service, but insiders insist it's "destined to become a destination."

Ferrari's Italian Villa *Italian* 23 | 18 | 23 | $37

Addison | 14831 Midway Rd. (bet. Belt Line & Spring Valley Rds.) | 972-980-9898

NEW Grapevine | 1200 William D. Tate Ave. (Ira E. Woods Ave.) | 817-251-2525 S

www.ferrarisrestaurant.com

The Secchis "make you feel like you're family" at their Sardinia-themed Italian in Addison, where "extraordinarily talented chef" Stefano turns out "fresh, delicious pasta" and "outstanding bread", baked in an "open-hearth" "wood-burning oven strategically positioned" in the center of the dining room; "tableside creations" and an impressive antipasto table contribute to the "charming atmosphere"; N.B. the Grapevine location is newer and unrated.

Ferre Ristorante e Bar *Italian* 21 | 21 | 19 | $38

West Village | West Vill. | 3699 McKinney Ave. (Lemmon Ave.) | Dallas | 214-522-3888

Sundance Square | Sundance Sq. | 215 E. Fourth St. (bet. Calhoun & Commerce Sts.) | Ft. Worth | 817-332-0033 S

www.ferredallas.com

You'll find "surprisingly good food at this hip spot in West Village" (and its Sundance Square sib), a "see-and-be-seen" scene with "creative" Northern Italian fare and a "very good wine list"; regulars also "love" the "Manhattan-like" vibe and "attentive staff", but its "popularity" means it "can be louder than a rock concert", so "sit outside" on the "wonderful patio" where people-watching is its own entertainment.

Fireside Pies *Pizza* 23 | 17 | 18 | $24

Knox-Henderson | 2820 N. Henderson Ave. (Milam St.) | Dallas | 214-370-3916 ●

NEW West Lovers Lane | 7709 Inwood Rd. (W. Lover's Ln.) | Dallas | 214-357-3800 S M

Plano | Shops at Legacy | 5417 Legacy Dr. (Hedgcoxe Rd.) | 972-398-2700

NEW Grapevine | 1285 S. Main St. (Hwy. 114) | 817-416-1285

www.firesidepies.com

"Fantastic, gourmet pizzas" coupled with "creative salads" "make it worth" the sometimes "two-hour wait" at these "hip" spots (at least "they don't rush you once you've been seated"); some sigh it's "too bad" the "cramped inside spaces" are "so small", though, suggesting you "sit on the patio if you can - it's even heated during the winter."

First Chinese BBQ ⊭ *Chinese* | 25 | 9 | 12 | $15

Richardson | 111 S. Greenville Ave. (Belt Line Rd.) | 972-680-8216
Plano | 3304 Coit Rd. (Parker Rd.) | 972-758-2988
Arlington | 2214 S. Collins St. (Pioneer Pkwy.) | 817-469-8876
www.firstchinesebbq.com

"You'll be eating leftover pork for days" after a visit to these "authentic" Cantonese standbys attracting a steady stream of chowhounds and the occasional celeb chef for roast meats and "awesome" noodles at "bargain prices"; never mind that there's no alcohol, "service could be better" and decor doesn't amount to much more than the "ducks hanging in the window", insiders insist "you will not be disappointed" with your meal; N.B. cash only.

NEW Fish, The *Japanese* | 20 | 17 | 15 | $37

West Village | 3636 McKinney Ave. (Cityplace West Blvd.) | Dallas | 214-522-0071 | www.thefishhouston.com

See review in Houston Directory.

Fogo de Chão *Brazilian/Steak* | 26 | 22 | 26 | $55

Addison | 4300 Belt Line Rd. (Midway Rd.) | 972-503-7300 | www.fogodechao.com

See review in Houston Directory.

Franki's Li'l Europe *E European* | ▽ 21 | 15 | 19 | $33

Lake Highlands | Casa Linda Plaza | 362 Casa Linda Plaza (Garland Rd.) | Dallas | 214-320-0426

Though ex-owner Franc Kovacic sold out to former manager Jeffrey Batt in 2005, his "neighborhood cafe" in Lake Highlands still boasts a "delicious" "varied menu", expanded from its original Eastern European roots with "additions" "from all over the continent"; with an "inexpensive wine list", "personable service" and a "cozy" ambiance, it's no wonder the "area's best-kept secret isn't so secret anymore."

Z French Room S M *American/French* | 28 | 29 | 29 | $87

Downtown Dallas | Hotel Adolphus | 1321 Commerce St. (Field St.) | Dallas | 214-742-8200 | www.hoteladolphus.com

"Smitten" surveyors salute an "off-the-charts experience" at this Downtown "icon", voted No. 1 for Food, Decor and Service in Dallas/Ft. Worth, where "stupendous" French-New American cuisine is served with "unparalleled attention to detail" inside the "opulent" crystal-chandeliered and marble-columned dining room of the Hotel Adolphus; sure, it's "expensive", but "close to perfect" for a "good old-fashioned splurge" - especially if you opt for the tasting menu with "excellent" wine pairings.

Fuji Steakhouse & Sushi Bar *Japanese* | ▽ 20 | 15 | 19 | $26

North Dallas | 12817 Preston Rd. (Linden Ln.) | Dallas | 972-661-5662

The hibachi takes center stage at this North Dallas "favorite" where knife-wielding chefs "put on a show for the kids" and expertly cook up an array of seafood and beef dishes; a "surprisingly good neighborhood sushi bar" in the back pleases finicky fish fiends while all are appeased by modest tabs, if not the simply decorated surroundings.

Fuse ⊠ *Pan-Asian/Southwestern* 21 22 20 $42

Downtown Dallas | Dallas Power and Light Bldg. | 1512 Commerce St. (Akard St.) | Dallas | 214-742-3873 | www.fusedallas.com

This "hip", high-wattage Downtown hub reengineered from a space once home to Dallas Power and Light boasts a "cool layout" of multi-level eating spaces capped by a "rooftop, pool-side bar" proffering "fanciful drinks"; the wild mix of Pan-Asian and Southwestern cuisine "sounds strange, but works well", though service strikes some as "spotty" while tabs can feel "overpriced" too.

Gloria's *Salvadoran* 21 18 19 $21

Greenville Avenue | 3715 Greenville Ave. (bet. Martel & Matalee Aves.) | Dallas | 214-874-0088

Lemmon Avenue | 4140 Lemmon Ave. (Douglas Ave.) | Dallas | 214-521-7576

Oak Cliff | 600 W. Davis St. (bet. Bishop Ave. & Tyler St.) | Dallas | 214-948-3672

Addison | Village on the Pkwy. | 5100 Belt Line Rd. (Dallas N. Tollway) | 972-387-8442

Frisco | 8600 Gaylord Pkwy. (Preston Rd.) | 972-668-1555

Garland | Firewheel Town Ctr. | 360 Coneflower Dr. (Town Center Blvd.) | 972-526-5290

Rockwall | 2079 Summer Lee Dr. (Rockwall Pkwy.) | 972-772-4088

Near West | Montgomery Plaza | 2600 W. Seventh St. (Lancaster Ave.) | Ft. Worth | 817-332-8800

Colleyville | 5611 Colleyville Blvd. (Church St.) | 817-656-1784

www.gloriasrestaurants.com

Fanatics "can't get enough" of the complimentary warm black bean dip at this "popular" chain of cantinas with a menu that marries "authentic Salvadoran" cuisine with "solid Tex-Mex" cooking; the "friendly", "tropical atmosphere" and "excellent happy-hour prices" make it a "festive place to kick off the night" though some opt to "stick around for the salsa dancing" ("it's quite a show") or the live entertainment that varies by location.

Go Fish *American/Seafood* 21 17 19 $37

Addison | 4950 Belt Line Rd. (Quorum Dr.) | 972-980-1919 | www.gofishrestaurants.com

Afishonados applaud the "flavorful" New American dishes that come in "imaginative" presentations at this "upscale" seafooder in landlocked Addison; the granite-and-wood decor is deemed "attractive" and "comfortable" by most, but surveyors split on service with pros calling it "super-smart" and cons contending it "inattentive" at best.

Goodhues Wood Fired Grill ⊠ *American* ▽ 24 21 20 $39

McKinney | 204 W. Virginia St. (Wood St.) | 972-562-7570 | www.goodhuesgrill.com

Ensconced in a historic neighborhood "just off the square in McKinney", this upmarket eatery conjures up a "nice atmosphere" thanks to its setting in a 1920s building with lots of brick and exposed wood beams; the midpriced New American menu showcases "great" signatures like ribs, steaks and seafood grilled over pecan and mesquite wood, but regulars report the "specials rock" too.

Grand Lux Cafe *Eclectic* 19 | 22 | 18 | $29

Galleria | Galleria | 13420 N. Dallas Pkwy. (Alpha Rd.) | Dallas | 972-385-3114 | www.grandluxcafe.com

With an Eclectic menu so "amazingly long" it "takes 15 minutes to read", this Galleria "spin-off of the ever-popular Cheesecake Factory" is "good for kids, picky eaters and those with huge appetites"; foes say that the portions are "obscenely large", the "cavernous space" is "loud" and the "over-enthusiastic service" gets "a little annoying" - but none of that stops it from getting "crazy on the weekends."

Grape, The *American* 25 | 20 | 23 | $35

Greenville Avenue | 2808 Greenville Ave. (Vickery Blvd.) | Dallas | 214-828-1981 | www.thegraperestaurant.com

"One of the darkest and oldest wine bars in Dallas", this "intimate" Greenville Avenue "neighborhood bistro" is a "foodie favorite", boasting "terrific" New American fare that's "consistently good, even with different chefs over the years"; "comparatively low markups" on its vino and an "educated, attentive staff" are other selling points, and the "romantic atmosphere" with its "cozy, close quarters" makes it a "perfect place to get engaged."

Green Papaya *Vietnamese* 21 | 12 | 18 | $21

Oak Lawn | 3211 Oak Lawn Ave. (Cedar Springs Rd.) | Dallas | 214-521-4811 | greenpapayarestaurants.com

"Excellent Vietnamese at a reasonable price" is the draw at this Oak Lawn storefront specializing in "good, healthy Asian" fare; other than a "beautiful fish tank set in the wall like a picture frame", the feel of this "tiny, crowded place" is "no-frills", but the smitten shrug "so what?"

Greenz 🅂 *American* 20 | 13 | 16 | $14

NEW **Preston Forest** | Preston Forest Vill. | 11661 Preston Rd. (Forest Ln.) | Dallas | 214-691-7770

Uptown | 2808 McKinney Ave. (Allen St.) | Dallas | 214-720-7788

Addison | 15615 Quorum Dr. (Addison Circle) | 972-385-7721

www.greenzsalads.com

As the name suggests, "the major attraction is salads" - and "inventive" ones too - at this trio of "quick, healthy" New Americans; they may be "small and crowded", but they're still "lunch favorites", whether "on the run or at your desk", a status abetted by the fact that "any salad can be rolled into a wrap" for maximum portability; P.S. the Uptown location has "a definite parking problem."

Grill on the Alley, The *American* 21 | 23 | 22 | $50

Galleria | Galleria | 13270 N. Dallas Pkwy. (Alpha Rd.) | Dallas | 214-459-1601 | www.thegrill.com

Dealmakers declare the tony Galleria outpost of this Beverly Hills original a "convenient" option for "power lunching" on an "expense account" in appropriately handsome dark-wood surroundings; the "professional" staff dispatches traditional cocktails and an "expansive" selection of "perfectly executed" American dishes on cue, so even though some beef "it's a bit pricey" most maintain, "if you can afford it", "it's a sure bet."

Grotto Ristorante *Italian* 19 | 19 | 18 | $30

Uptown | Uptown Park | 2222 McKinney Ave. (Pearl St.) | Dallas | 214-954-4461 | www.grottorestaurants.com

This Houston-based chain trattoria Uptown has a "casual and easy" "neighborhood feel" thanks to "abundant" quantities of "affordable" food served up by an "accommodating" staff in a "comfortable atmosphere" with a fireplace and Tuscan murals; foes find it "not memorable", and add that like a big Italian family it's "a little on the loud side."

Hattie's *American* 25 | 23 | 24 | $32

Oak Cliff | 418 N. Bishop Ave. (8th St.) | Dallas | 214-942-7400 | www.hatties.net

"A place with character in a sea of urban sprawl" this "contemporary Southern" belle housed in a "quaint" 1920s Oak Cliff storefront charms customers with "inventive" New American "home cooking" like "shrimp and grits to die for" and "addictive pecan-crusted catfish"; the "reasonably priced" dishes all come with a side of "fabulous service", keeping this "popular" spot "packed every night" (in other words: "make a reservation").

Hector's on Henderson [S] *American* 22 | 18 | 21 | $47

Knox-Henderson | 2929 N. Henderson Ave. (bet. Miller & Willis Aves.) | Dallas | 214-821-0432 | www.hectorsonhenderson.com

Diners "thankful for the exploding Knox-Henderson food scene" consider this "snappy, fun place" "another top-notch example" of the trend; the New American cuisine "with a Texas accent" is "memorable", and owner Hector Garcia is "the ultimate host", and "quite the singer" too – he sometimes "spontaneously belts out a song" with musicians who play nightly in its "noisy, lively" space.

Hedary's Mediterranean [M] *Mediterranean* ▽ 22 | 17 | 15 | $24

West | 6323 Shopping Ctr. | 3308 Fairfield Ave. (Camp Bowie Blvd.) | Ft. Worth | 817-731-6961 | www.hedarys.com

Those with a hankering for "authentic" Lebanese specialties head to this family-owned West Ft. Worth stalwart where the Middle Eastern "food is always good" (and cheap) and has been for decades; it recently benefited from a "much-needed face-lift" reenergizing the interior, yet followers fume that "uneven" service could use a similar boost; N.B. lunch served only on Sunday.

[Z] Hibiscus [S] *American* 25 | 23 | 24 | $54

Knox-Henderson | 2927 N. Henderson Ave. (Central Expwy.) | Dallas | 214-827-2927 | www.hibiscusdallas.com

"No meal is complete" without a helping of the "amazing mac 'n' cheese" at this "happening" Knox-Henderson New American where the "dark", "swanky" decor "is a mere backdrop for some of the best food in the city"; the service team "works very hard to make you feel special", so even if the prices are "expensive", it still "lives up to every penny"; P.S. if there's no room for dessert, satisfy your sweet tooth with "great eye candy" in all flavors.

Highland Park Cafeteria *American* - - - I

Lake Highlands | Casa Linda Plaza | 1200 N. Buckner Blvd. (Garland Rd.) | Dallas | 214-324-5000 | www.highlandparkcafeteria.com

Though shuttered for over a decade, this Dallas institution reopened in 2007 in Lake Highlands' Casa Linda Plaza; traditionalists take comfort in the well-stocked cafeteria line of homestyle American entrees, salads (with Jell-O, natch) and an endless array of veggies, breads and desserts; the Kelly green-and-white dining room attracts a wide range of customers from old folks to young families and professionals enjoying a square meal at a reasonable price; N.B. takeaway is also available via a separate entrance.

Highland Park Pharmacy *American* 19 16 19 $10

Knox-Henderson | 3229 Knox St. (Travis St.) | Dallas | 214-521-2126

You "never know who you might sit next to" at this "classic soda fountain", "a staple of life" in Knox-Henderson since 1912 that's ranked Best Bang for the Buck among Dallas/Ft. Worth restaurants; it's a "throwback to the days before automation and sensitive staffs", "so don't expect gourmet, but do expect to be called 'hon'" as you "enjoy the meanest milkshake and grilled cheese sandwich in town"; N.B. the Decor score may not fully reflect a 2007 expansion.

Hola! *Spanish* 23 19 20 $29

Knox-Henderson | 4831 McKinney Ave. (Knox St.) | Dallas | 214-522-0505

"Authentic" "tapas, tapas, tapas" along with "good sangria and an extensive wine list" are the main event at this Spanish spot "set in a refurbished garage" in Knox-Henderson; some say it's "more a neighborhood bar than a restaurant", but whatever you call it, its "small space" (complete "with a great patio") feels "kinda romantic", and its "friendly atmosphere" makes it "perfect for chatting and having a good time."

Hot Damn, Tamales! ⓢ *Tex-Mex* ▽ 26 9 19 $13

Hospital District | 713 W. Magnolia Ave. (Hemphill St.) | Ft. Worth | 817-926-9909 | www.hotdamntamales.com

"Hot damn, these are good tamales!" exclaim fans of these "mighty tasty" hand-pressed treats that "great people" turn out of a Hospital District storefront in an "unbelievable selection of flavors" from poblano chicken to chocolate cherry; with just a few booths and cafeteria-style service, it's "not primarily a dine-in place" but locals are more than content to grab one (or a "dozen") to take on the go; P.S. the "lard-free" recipes mean even "vegetarians" can indulge.

Hôtel St. Germain ⓢ Ⓜ *Continental/French* ▽ 25 26 26 $132

Uptown | Hôtel St. Germain | 2516 Maple Ave. (bet. Cedar Springs Rd. & McKinney Ave.) | Dallas | 214-871-2516 | www.hotelstgermain.com

Set within a "beautiful hotel" "in an old Victorian house" Uptown, this "romantic getaway" is a "perfect" "place to celebrate" any "special occasion" thanks to a "well-thought-out" prix fixe French-

Continental menu of "fantastic food" served by a host of "waiters in white gloves"; reserve "weeks in advance" and your reward will be an "elegant", "formal dining experience" (jacket and tie required).

NEW House of Blues ◐ *Southern* 19 | 23 | 19 | $30

Victory Park | White Swan Bldg. | 2200 N. Lamar St. (Houston St.) | Dallas | 214-978-2583 | www.hob.com

This "down-home, feel-good" chain link in Victory Park purveys a "standard" selection of "Southern comfort-food" items in faux honky-tonk settings goosed up by "live band performances"; "loud, bustling" and always jammed with "tourists", it may be "nothing to write home about", though disciples sing "hallelujah for the Sunday gospel brunch."

Houston's *American* 23 | 20 | 22 | $30

Preston Center | 8300 Preston Rd. (Wentwood Dr.) | Dallas | 214-691-8991

Addison | 5318 Belt Line Rd. (Dallas N. Tollway) | 972-960-1752

www.hillstone.com

See review in Houston Directory.

Howard Wang's China Grill *Chinese* 20 | 15 | 18 | $21

Preston Hollow | Villages of Preston Hollow | 4343 W. Northwest Hwy. (Midway Rd.) | Dallas | 214-366-1606 | www.hwchinagrill.com

"Little brother to the Empress of China", this Preston Hollow eatery serves "very good Chinese food" - "not the traditional American" version, but a "sleek, modern" interpretation "with a cosmopolitan twist" "as well as some of the old favorites" - "in a contemporary setting"; some suggest the "service veers between rushed and lackadaisical at times", but those who "make it a regular stop" report it's "improving with each visit."

H3 Ranch *Steak* 20 | 21 | 18 | $29

Stockyards | 109 E. Exchange Ave. (Main St.) | Ft. Worth | 817-624-1246 | www.h3ranch.com

This Stockyards steakhouse is a "pretty darn good pardner" for roping up "awesome steaks" with all the "trimmings" as well as "rockin' breakfasts" on weekends; the "Texas-themed environment" complete with saddle-topped stools and "stuffed buffalo heads on one side and buffalo butts on the other" make it a "must-go" "tourist attraction" for "out-of-towners" who also appreciate the moderate prices.

I Fratelli Ristorante & Wine Bar *Italian* 22 | 19 | 19 | $21

Las Colinas | 7701 N. MacArthur Blvd. (Lyndon B. Johnson Frwy.) | Irving | 972-501-9700 | www.ifratelli.net

Piezanos praise the "killer pizzas" with "excellent thin crusts" and "just the right amount of toppings" at this "suburban oasis" in Las Colinas also offering "traditional" Italian "comfort food" paired with wines from a "well-thought-out" list; it packs a crowd with "nice ambiance" and "bargain" lunch specials while the delivery outlets from Grapevine to Lewisville are on everyone's speed dial.

	FOOD	DECOR	SERVICE	COST

Il Sole *Italian* 22 | 20 | 20 | $40

Knox-Henderson | Travis Walk | 4514 Travis St. (Knox St.) | Dallas | 214-559-3888 | www.ilsole-dallas.com

Surveyors are smitten with the "wonderful rooftop patio" affording "romantic" sunset views at this polished Knox-Henderson Italian; the "cozy" ambiance inside, "solid food" with a "wonderful mix of flavors" and a "large selection of reasonably priced wine" make it a "must" for "date night" even if some say service provided by an "eye-candy staff" doesn't always shine.

India Palace *Indian* 23 | 17 | 22 | $27

Preston Forest | 12817 Preston Rd. (Lyndon B. Johnson Frwy.) | Dallas | 972-392-0190 | www.indiapalacedallas.com

"One of the most reliable Indian places" in the area, this "traditional establishment" in Preston Forest "has been around a long time" thanks to "authentic" "flavorful and fragrant" fare ferried by "servers who are very nice about explaining the choices"; "white tablecloths and quiet, subdued lighting" exhibit a flair for atmosphere not seen at some of its competitors.

Iron Cactus *Tex-Mex* 18 | 19 | 18 | $25

Downtown Dallas | 1520 Main St. (Akard St.) | Dallas | 214-749-4766 | www.ironcactus.com

See review in Austin and the Hill Country Directory.

NEW **Isabella's** *Italian* ▽ 21 | 24 | 23 | $32

Frisco | Stonebriar Commons | 1279 Legacy Dr. (Hwy. 121) | 214-618-3384 | www.isabellasfrisco.com

You'll feel as if you've "stepped out of Frisco and into Italy" at this upscale eatery in Stonebriar Commons ensconced in a tasteful setting enlivened by "wonderful contemporary art" and an active fountain outside; admirers applaud the "excellent" menu items that hail from Lombardy, Piedmont, Tuscany and the Veneto Region while "accommodating" "individualized" service adds a "warm" touch to the evening.

J & J Oyster Bar *Cajun/Creole* ▽ 21 | 10 | 18 | $16

Cultural District | 612 N. University Dr. (Rockwood Ln.) | Ft. Worth | 817-335-2756 | www.jjbluesbar.com

For more than 30 years, this "hole-in-the-wall" "dive" in Ft. Worth's Cultural District has been dishing up "great" Cajun-Creole seafood "at a reasonable price", along with "cold beer or iced tea"; with "rolls of paper towels on every table to make cleanup easy", it's strictly a "no-frills" vibe, but "if you like things fried this is the place for you."

Japanese Palace *Japanese* ▽ 26 | 18 | 23 | $33

West | 8445 Camp Bowie W. (Brandon Ln.) | Ft. Worth | 817-244-0144

Noble flavors reign at this midpriced West Ft. Worth Japanese where chefs behind hibachi tables cook up "stellar" sukiyaki and the sushi bar sends out a wide variety of fresh fin fare; some say the decor's a bit dated, but even if the "bar feels like a relic from the *Love Boat*", the "attentive" staff makes it a "fun" place for "kids and adults" alike.

	FOOD	DECOR	SERVICE	COST

Z Jasper's *American* | 24 | 25 | 24 | $42 |

Plano | Shops at Legacy | 7161 Bishop Rd. (Legacy Dr.) | 469-229-9111 | www.jaspers-restaurant.com

See review in Austin and the Hill Country Directory.

Javier's *Mexican* | 22 | 21 | 21 | $39 |

Knox-Henderson | 4912 Cole Ave. (Harvard Ave.) | Dallas | 214-521-4211 | www.javiers.net

An "old Dallas hangout" for over 30 years, this "established" temple of "haute Mexican" cuisine on the edge of Knox-Henderson presents "top-notch margaritas" and "wonderfully authentic" fare to a "clubby", "loud-voiced" crowd; some wags warn it's "pricey" and "overrated", but the "zigzag maze" of "dark" "well-decorated dining rooms" and cigar bar filled with "old-timers and their trophies" mean it's "hard to beat" "for drinks, apps and people-watching"; P.S. "have a reservation or plan to wait."

Jinbeh *Japanese* | 21 | 18 | 20 | $29 |

Frisco | Shafer Plaza | 2693 Preston Rd. (Warren Pkwy.) | 214-619-1200
Las Colinas | 301 E. Las Colinas Blvd. (O'Connor Blvd.) | Irving | 972-869-4011
Lewisville | 2440A S. Stemmons Frwy. (Vista Ridge Blvd.) | 214-488-2224
www.jinbeh.com

A "very good local" mini-chain, this "solid performer" is "popular" for its "excellent sushi", all the more noteworthy since its audience consists mostly of "families with kids" who come for the "great hibachi"; perhaps the "decor is a little lacking", but the "theatrics" of the "tableside cooking", such as the "fire-blowing onions", are "worth the price of admission" alone – so expect "some long waits."

Joe T. Garcia's ⊭ *Tex-Mex* | 19 | 22 | 20 | $21 |

North Side | 2201 N. Commerce St. (22nd St.) | Ft. Worth | 817-626-4356 | www.joets.com

An "awesome patio" overlooking a "beautiful garden" and "tranquil" fountain make this rambling North Side Ft. Worth hacienda a "perennial favorite", especially for "out-of-town guests" (translation: beware of "long lines"); yet in spite of the "delightful atmosphere" and "friendly service", a number of naysayers label the Tex-Mex fare only "ok", though they admit that after a couple of the "potent margaritas", even the pickiest patron "may not care"; N.B. cash only.

Jorg's Café Vienna S M *Austrian* | ▽ 25 | 17 | 22 | $22 |

Plano | 1037 E. 15th St. (K Ave.) | 972-509-5966 | www.cafevienna.us

"A slice of Vienna" comes to Plano via this "real nice neighborhood spot" where a basket of homemade pretzels sets the mood for a full array of well-priced "down-home" Austrian specialties paired with a "great" selection of brews on tap; brick walls and checkered tablecloths conjure up old-world charm while the beer garden proves a festive respite especially during Oktoberfest; N.B. open Wednesday–Saturday.

	FOOD	DECOR	SERVICE	COST
Josephine's Wine Bar & Bistro Ⓜ *Italian*	∇ 24	22	23	$32

Frisco | 6959 Lebanon Rd. (Dallas Pkwy.) | 972-712-4343 | www.josephineswinebar.com

Oenophiles applaud the "fantastic selection of wines" - over 40 available by the glass - at this "wonderful" Frisco "neighborhood find" where the "creative Italian cooking" comes at "reasonable prices"; the "quaint" arched-stone decor features rustic wood tables and a painting of the owner's 14th-century ancestral hometown in Sicily while live jazz on Wednesdays adds to the "great atmosphere."

J. R.'s Steakhouse ☒ *Steak* — 23 | 21 | 23 | $59

(fka J. R.'s Fine Dining)

Colleyville | 5400 Hwy. 121 (Hall Johnson St.) | 817-355-1414 | www.jrssteaks.com

Carnivores claim "everything is done well" at this "pricey" Colleyville chophouse where "prime" steaks and "excellent" American dishes are kicked into high gear by an extensive martini selection; a "pleasant" staff warms up the sophisticated setting as does a working fireplace and "good jazz at the right volume" Thursdays-Saturdays.

Kathleen's Sky Diner *Eclectic* — 20 | 16 | 17 | $24

(fka Kathleen's Art Café)

Park Cities | 4424 Lovers Ln. (Armstrong Pkwy.) | Dallas | 214-691-2355 | www.kathleensartcafe.com

You'll find "some very original food" on the "varied" Eclectic menu at this "convenient", inexpensive Park Cities restaurant, including "delicious desserts" and an "awesome Sunday brunch"; still, some surveyors say the "quality depends on what you order", adding that "service is unfortunately slow"; N.B. the Plano location has closed.

Keg Steakhouse & Bar, The *Steak* — 21 | 20 | 22 | $38

Las Colinas | 859 W. John Carpenter Frwy. (MacArthur Blvd.) | Irving | 972-556-9188

Plano | Shops at Willow Bend | 6101 W. Park Blvd. (Dallas Pkwy.) | 972-403-0430

Southwest | 5760 SW Loop 820 (Bryant Irvin Rd.) | Ft. Worth | 817-731-3534

www.kegsteakhouse.com

Bravely venturing into well-trodden territory with "steaks substantially cheaper than" some of their competitors', these outposts of a steakhouse chain can claim quality that's "surprisingly good" - "without the à la carte sky-high prices and snootiness"; their classy lodge decor and good bars make for a "fun environment" that's also fine "for a business lunch."

NEW Kenichi *Pan-Asian* — 22 | 22 | 19 | $43

Victory Park | 2400 Victory Park Ln. (Museum Way) | Dallas | 214-871-8883 | www.kenichirestaurants.com

See review in Austin and the Hill Country Directory.

	FOOD	DECOR	SERVICE	COST

Kincaid's Hamburgers *Burgers* 23 13 16 $11

NEW **Southwest** | 4825 Overton Ridge Blvd. (Hulen St.) | Ft. Worth | 817-370-6400
West | 4901 Camp Bowie Blvd. (Eldridge St.) | Ft. Worth | 817-732-2881 ☒
Southlake | 100 N. Kimball Ave. (Southlake Blvd.) | 817-416-2573
Occupying a "former small grocery store" since 1946, this "landmark" brings foodies to West Ft. Worth (and to Southlake and Southwest Ft. Worth) for "gooey, juicy, melt-in-your-mouth burgers" made from "fresh" beef, "not frozen premade patties"; sitting communally "at long picnic tables, next to people getting just as messy as you, somehow adds to the flavor"; N.B. you no longer have to stop at the ATM first as they now accept credit cards.

Kirby's Steakhouse *Steak* 24 22 23 $50

Greenville Avenue | 3525 Greenville Ave. (McCommas Blvd.) | Dallas | 214-821-2122
Plano | 3408 Preston Rd. (Parker Rd.) | 972-867-2122
Southlake | 3305 E. Hwy. 114 (Southlake Blvd.) | 817-410-2221
www.kirbyssteakhouse.com
Enjoy "excellent steaks", "fresh seafood", "strong cocktails and great service" from an "accommodating staff" within the "laid-back atmosphere" of these outposts of a "great medium-priced steakhouse" micro-chain; their decor is done "in the style of the old supper clubs", with "tasteful wood paneling", and don't forget the "great bar" ("with piano music" at the Plano and Southlake branches) - plus they're "open Sunday when many others aren't."

Kitchen 1924 ☒ *Eclectic* 20 15 20 $37

Lakewood | 1924 Abrams Pkwy. (Gaston Ave.) | Dallas | 214-821-1924 | www.kitchen1924.com
A "hip crowd of thirtysomethings" fills up this "noisy" Lakewood eatery decorated in a minimalist style with white walls and a slate floor and offering an "imaginative", "affordable" Eclectic menu that "changes daily"; though some say the food is "inconsistent" and "service is variable", most maintain it's a "refreshing" addition to the neighborhood; P.S. "call ahead" if you'd rather not sit at the communal table.

Kona Grill *American* 20 21 18 $27

NorthPark | NorthPark Ctr. | 8687 N. Central Expwy. (Park Ln.) | Dallas | 214-369-7600 | www.konagrill.com
See review in Houston Directory.

Kozy Kitchen *Eclectic* ▽ 25 12 24 $24

Knox-Henderson | 4433 McKinney Ave. (bet. Armstrong Ave. & Oliver St.) | Dallas | 214-219-5044 | www.thekozy.net
Those seeking "good, healthy food" find it at this Knox-Henderson BYO "jewel" serving up "fresh and delicious" Eclectic dishes that make use of grass-fed meat, wild seafood and organic produce (they also offer a full line of gluten-free baked goods); colorful quarters and a "friendly" vibe make it a "favorite", especially for lunch.

Kuby's Sausage House *German* 22 11 17 $18

Park Cities | Snider Plaza | 6601 Snider Plaza (Daniel Ave.) | Dallas | 214-363-2231 | www.kubys.com

"If you're a fan of German food, you'll find all the standards and then some" at this "small, modest" "neighborhood place" in the Snider Plaza area of Park Cities "with a great butcher and gourmet shop attached"; specializing in "awesome sausages", it's a Teutonic "food lover's heaven", and regulars report that "the hearty breakfast is even better than dinner" ("get there when it opens or you'll wait in line"), though some say service is nicer when "they know you."

La Calle Doce *Mexican* 21 16 19 $19

Lakewood | 1925 Skillman St. (Las Vista Dr.) | Dallas | 214-824-9900
Oak Cliff | 415 W. 12th St. (Bishop Ave.) | Dallas | 214-941-4304

Serving "Veracruz-style seafood at its best", this "modest" Mexican "hole-in-the-wall" in Oak Cliff has been in business for more than 25 years, and since 1999 has had a sibling in Lakewood; both family-owned and -operated locations have a "casual and crowded" vibe that can sometimes tax the servers, resulting in "slow service", "but they're friendly", nonetheless.

La Duni Latin Cafe M *Pan-Latin* 24 21 19 $30

Knox-Henderson | 4620 McKinney Ave. (Knox St.) | Dallas | 214-520-7300

La Duni Latin Kitchen *Pan-Latin*

Oak Lawn | 4264 Oak Lawn Ave. (Herschel Ave.) | Dallas | 214-520-6888
www.laduni.com

Supporters swoon over chef-owners Espartaco and Dunia Borga's "cosmopolitan" Pan-Latin cuisine, "fabulous coffee drinks" and "magnificent desserts" ("don't leave without a piece of the quatro leches cake") at this "lively" Oak Lawn and Knox-Henderson cafe duo; in spite of "spotty" service and a "noisy" setting, regulars report it's a solid "bet for budget challenged foodies"; N.B. a new outpost at NorthPark Center is reportedly in the works.

La Familia S *Mexican* 24 22 26 $18

Near West | 841 Foch St. (1 block west of Carroll St.) | Ft. Worth | 817-870-2002 | www.lafamilia-fw.com

"You're always greeted with a handshake" from owner Al Cavazos at this Near West Ft. Worth Mexican offering "excellent" dishes like enchiladas that are "spiced just right"; dark, "cozy" decor decked out with family photos and cowhides on display brightens up when flaming margaritas are brought over by the "friendly" staff.

L'Ancestral S *French* 23 20 24 $43

Knox-Henderson | Travis Walk | 4514 Travis St. (Knox St.) | Dallas | 214-528-1081

"Nostalgic" Francophiles favor this "romantic" Knox-Henderson "staple" serving up "consistently wonderful" Gallic classics like escargots and steak frites in a "low-key" setting decorated in a "cozy" country style; even if a few find it's "showing its age", it's a "charming" spot enhanced by "professional" if "slightly gruff waiters who are actually softies."

Landmark, The *American* 23 | 24 | 24 | $51

Oak Lawn | Warwick Melrose Hotel | 3015 Oak Lawn Ave. (Cedar Springs Rd.) | Dallas | 214-224-3152 | www.warwickmelrosedallas.com

Though ratings may not fully reflect a 2007 chef and management change, this new American in Oak Lawn's Warwick Melrose Hotel retains its "peaceful" ambiance and "old-school classy decor", making it suitable for anything from "power breakfasts" to a "romantic" dinner; P.S. regulars suggest a stop in the Library Bar "to round out the evening."

Z Lanny's Alta Cocina Mexicana S M *Eclectic/Mexican* 27 | 25 | 26 | $56

Cultural District | 3405 W. Seventh St. (Boland St.) | Ft. Worth | 817-850-9996 | www.lannyskitchen.com

"Simply awesome" declare those dazzled by chef Lanny Lancarte's "haute" Eclectic-Mexican eatery in Ft. Worth's Cultural District offering "clever takes" on south-of-the-border classics (like elk mole in spring and pomegranate margaritas) plus "inventive" international dishes all served by a "friendly and efficient" staff; yes, it's "expensive" but an "inviting" atmosphere with a "beautiful patio" make it all "worth it."

La Paesana *Italian* ▽ 15 | 14 | 18 | $31

Park Cities | 4326 Lover's Ln. (bet. Preston Rd. & Tollway) | Dallas | 214-890-1811 | www.lapaesanarestaurant.com

"You're greeted by the owner with a kiss on each cheek" at Luciana Cola's small, brick-walled Italian venue set in one of the many strip centers on Park Cities' Miracle Mile; proponents praise the "classics" from the northern region of The Boot (think risotto and veal piccata), and though detractors declare it's only "average", at least prices are comparable with other family-oriented trattorias.

La Playa Maya *Mexican* 23 | 17 | 20 | $20

West | 6209 Sunset Dr. (bet. Bernie Anderson & Westridge Aves.) | Ft. Worth | 817-738-3329

South Side | 3200 Hemphill St. (Devitt St.) | Ft. Worth | 817-924-0698

North Side | 1540 N. Main St. (14th St.) | Ft. Worth | 817-624-8411

North Side | 202 W. Central Ave. (Main St.) | Ft. Worth | 817-626-8720

Weatherford | 1445 Ft. Worth Hwy. (Hazel Hwy.) | 817-613-8686

www.laplayamaya.com

"Go for" the "authentic ceviche" and other "Mexican seafood specialties" at these "popular" "bright" spots on the Texas horizon, outposts of a "local semi-chain" that also feature a few "great Tex-Mex" dishes; all offer a "fun atmosphere", and they're "quick at lunch" too.

Lavendou S *French* 24 | 23 | 22 | $42

North Dallas | 19009 Preston Rd. (bet. Frankford Rd. & President George Bush Tpke.) | Dallas | 972-248-1911 | www.lavendou.com

For "a touch of France", visit this far North Dallas bistro, a "lovely, serene place" offering "the feel and taste of Provence", with a "nice country interior" and "plants on the patio that screen the traffic noise and view of the parking lot well enough that you can forget you are in a strip shopping center"; some say the staff "occasionally exhibits a little bit of attitude", but the service is generally "caring."

Lawry's The Prime Rib *Steak* 24 21 24 $53

North Dallas | 14655 Dallas Pkwy. (Spring Valley Rd.) | Dallas | 972-503-6688 | www.lawrysonline.com

Like the name says, it's all about the "first-class prime rib" at this "old-fashioned", "high-quality" steakhouse chain where the signature dish is "carved tableside" by an "attentive" crew; what with the "1970s-all-over-again vibe", it's a magnet for the "senior set", though folks of all ages agree its "quaint style" makes for a "unique dining experience."

Little Katana *Asian Fusion* 23 15 18 $33

Knox-Henderson | 4527 Travis St. (Knox St.) | Dallas | 214-443-9600

Little Katana Sushi Bar *Japanese*

Galleria | Galleria | 13350 N. Dallas Pkwy. (Noel Rd.) | Dallas | 972-991-1122

www.littlekatana.com

"Shhh - don't tell anybody" say secretive supporters of this "small" Asian fusion bôite in Knox-Henderson offering a "diverse menu" drawing from Japanese, Korean, Thai and American cuisines plus a "great" 40-plus bottle sake list; in spite of the "very good food", the less starry-eyed claim that "cramped" conditions and "slow service" prompt them to seek out "lower priced options" elsewhere; N.B. the Galleria original offers sushi only.

Z Local S M *American* 28 24 25 $51

Deep Ellum | 2936 Elm St. (1 block west of Hall St.) | Dallas | 214-752-7500 | www.localdallas.com

A "hidden gem" in Deep Ellum, chef Tracy Miller's "funky, modern" venue set in the historic Boyd Hotel building charms connoisseurs with "great wines" and a "zingy, fresh-flavored" New American menu that utilizes "local, seasonal ingredients" with fans calling it "one of the few places in Dallas where it's possible to eat both healthy and well"; solid service is a plus, though some find the tabs "pretty pricey" for the area; N.B. there's private parking adjacent to the restaurant.

Lola S M *American* 27 23 25 $67

Uptown | 2917 Fairmount St. (Cedar Springs Rd.) | Dallas | 214-855-0700 | www.lola4dinner.com

"Romantics", "out-of-towners" and busienss execs all adore this "quaint old house" Uptown where "outstanding" New American cuisine is presented in "exquisite" prix fixe menus and matched with wines from an "incredible", "reasonably priced" list; add in high-level service, and it's the "perfect spot for a special evening"; P.S. the separate chef's tasting room with a 10-course menu is "one of the city's great fine-dining experiences."

Lonesome Dove Western Bistro Ⓢ Ⓜ *Southwestern* 26 | 23 | 23 | $51

Stockyards | 2406 N. Main St. (24th St.) | Ft. Worth | 817-740-8810 | www.lonesomedovebistro.com

Celebrity chef-owner Tim Love's "haute cowboy cuisine" earns legions of fans at this fine-dining "treasure" in Ft. Worth's Stockyards that "hits the mark" with "huge portions" of "impressive", "experimental" Southwestern specialties like braised wild boar ribs and buffalo rib-eye; given the "sophisticated" saloon setting and staff that lays on the "Texas charm", it's "a must" for visitors, especially those on an "expense account."

Love & War in Texas *Southwestern* 16 | 17 | 16 | $24

Plano | 601 E. Plano Pkwy. (Rte. 75) | 972-422-6201

Grapevine | Grapevine Mills | 2505 E. Grapevine Mills Circle (Hwy. 121) | 972-724-5557

www.loveandwarintexas.com

Boot-scooting types gather at these "funky roadhouses" in east Plano and Grapevine for "gargantuan portions" of regional-style "cowboy food" like chicken-fried steak and fajitas and kick up their heels on weekends to "live music"; the "down-home atmosphere" at both locations is "loud" and "energetic" making it a good fit for large groups.

NEW Love Shack ⊄ *American* 22 | 14 | 13 | $12

Stockyards | 110 E. Exchange Ave. (Main St.) | Ft. Worth | 817-740-8812 | www.shakeyourloveshack.com

"Burgers and music" come together at Lonesome Dove chef-owner Tim Love's "quirky" new venture in Ft. Worth's Stockyards offering "memorable" patties crafted from ground brisket and tenderloin plus hot dogs, hand-cut onion rings, ice-cold beer and a rotating selection of milkshakes; the "open-air" setting plays host to live bands at lunch and on weekends, though folks can also opt to "grab [their] grub to go."

Lucile's *American* 18 | 16 | 17 | $23

West | 4700 Camp Bowie Blvd. (Hulen St.) | Ft. Worth | 817-738-4761

West Ft. Worthers appreciate the "convenience" of this "venerable" favorite featuring "excellent" American cuisine and "friendly" service – "the way things used to be"; it's a "casual" kind of "place for simple, straightforward, slightly Southern-inspired dishes", and it wins special raves for its "great lobster dishes", "wood-oven pizzas" and "nice brunch" on Saturdays and Sundays.

Lucky's Café *American* 20 | 14 | 19 | $16

Oak Lawn | 3531 Oak Lawn Ave. (Lemmon Ave.) | Dallas | 214-522-3500 | www.croinc.com

When you're "craving" "a hearty breakfast" after a night on the town or "classic diner-type" fare and "mom's not cooking", drop into this Oak Lawn Traditional American where the "comfort food" is "simple but great" and "service can be slow if they are busy"; its "gay-friendly" milieu showcases the "scene, truly a mix of all walks of life" who chat it up in line together on the weekends.

Luna de Noche *Tex-Mex* 20 | 18 | 19 | $23

Medical City | 7927 Forest Ln. (Central Expwy.) | Dallas | 972-233-1880
NorthPark | NorthPark Ctr. | 8687 N. Central Expwy. (Park Ln.) | Dallas | 214-389-9520
NEW Victory Park | 2300 Victory Park Ln. (Lamar St.) | Dallas | 214-420-3050
Garland | 7602 N. Jupiter Rd. (Lookout Dr.) | 972-414-3616
Plano | 1401 Preston Rd. (Plano Pkwy.) | 972-509-5757
www.lunadenoche.net

"Creative" Tex-Mex cuisine draws in Dallas denizens at this "fancy" (read: "pricey") chain of cantinas seeded across town where diners devour "heavenly guacamole" prepared tableside and "delicious salsa"; though service can be "uneven", the "inviting" contemporary digs with "twinkling lights" draw crowds for "romantic" dates and happy-hour margaritas.

Madras Pavilion *Indian* 22 | 11 | 14 | $17

Richardson | Dalrich Shopping Ctr. | 101 S. Colt Rd. (Belt Line Rd.) | 972-671-3672 | www.madraspavilion.us

See review in Houston Directory.

Maggiano's Little Italy *Italian* 20 | 20 | 20 | $30

NorthPark | NorthPark Ctr. | 8687 N. Central Expwy. (Park Ln.) | Dallas | 214-360-0707
Plano | Shops at Willow Bend | 6001 W. Park Blvd. (Dallas Pkwy.) | 972-781-0776
www.maggianos.com

You almost "expect to see Sinatra walk in behind you" at this "1940s-esque", checkered-tablecloth chain where "monster portions" of "red-sauce" Italiana are dished out in "enjoyably hectic" surroundings; some dub it a "mixed bag", citing a "mass-production", "quantity-trumps-quality" approach, but fans tout this "crowd-pleaser" as a "big night out" for "not a lot of money."

Maguire's *American* 23 | 21 | 22 | $36

North Dallas | 17552 Dallas Pkwy. (Trinity Mills Rd.) | Dallas | 972-818-0068 | www.maguiresdallas.com

"Always reliable", this North Dallas clubhouse is "a habit" with area residents, the kind of "place the locals call home" thanks to "always-great" Traditional American fare and "dependable service" offered in a "casual yet trendy setting" - plus a "big bar that's a gathering place for mature adults"; clearly, "they're doing something right."

Mainstream Fish House *Seafood* 20 | 18 | 20 | $27

Preston Forest | Preston Forest Vill. | 11661 Preston Rd. (Forest Ln.) | Dallas | 214-739-3474 | www.mcrowd.com

A sea of supporters rank this Preston Forest strip-mall eatery from the M Crowd Restaurant Group (Mi Cocina, Taco Diner, Mercury Grill) a "reliable" source for "numerous choices" of "fresh", "healthy" fish grilled, fried or broiled to your taste and sided with sauces and veggies; the airy, casual space caters to "families", seniors and other bargain-hunters who "go there regularly" and find the "midrange prices" especially appealing.

Main Street Bistro & Bakery *French* 23 | 17 | 17 | $15
(fka Main Street Bread Baking Co.)
Richardson | Shire, The | 3600 Shire Blvd. (Jupiter Rd.) | 972-578-0294
Plano | Shops at Legacy | 7200 Bishop Rd. (Legacy Dr.) | 972-309-0404
Grapevine | 316 S. Main St. (bet. Dallas Rd. & Northwest Hwy.) | 817-424-4333
www.themainbakery.com
Set "in historic Downtown Grapevine", this "intimate sidewalk cafe" is "good for salad and sandwiches", with a "casual French bakery" component that "smells of fresh baked bread and has beautiful pastries"; its younger sibling is also a "popular place", and "a little slice of Europe in Plano", but "be prepared to wait in line" and endure "disappointing service" at both branches; N.B. a third location in Richardson opened post-Survey.

Mama's Daughters' Diner *Diner* 21 | 11 | 20 | $13
Market Center | 2014 Irving Blvd. (bet. Turtle Creek Blvd. & Wycliff Ave.) | Dallas | 214-742-8646 | www.mamasdaughtersdiner.com
Love Field | 2610 Royal Ln. (Harry Hines Blvd.) | Dallas | 972-241-8646 | www.mamasdiner.com
Irving | 2412 W. Shady Grove Rd. (Story Rd.) | 972-790-2778 | www.mamasdaughtersdiner.com
Lewisville | 1288 W. Main St. (Old Orchard Ln.) | 972-353-5955 | www.mamasdaughtersdiner.com
"Down-home cookin'" "just like mama makes" keeps this chain of "old-fashioned" diners "packed" with patrons praising the "rib-sticking" breakfasts and "homemade pies" not to mention the "good value for the money"; decor is "simple", so most of the local color comes from "veteran waitresses" who take no sass ("they're ornery and proud of it") and provide "efficient", "to the point" service.

Mamma Emilia's *Italian* 18 | 20 | 20 | $28
McKinney | 119 W. Virginia St. (Wood St.) | 972-562-1102
"Nice Italian fare" "fits the bill" for "neighborhood" denizens at this "attractive eatery" on the Square in McKinney, presenting solid, moderately priced cuisine from staff and owners who "take pride in what they do"; the old-world decor prompts a mixed response with the dining room deemed "charming" and "comfortable" for some, and a bit too "dark" and "moody" for others.

Mango Thai *Thai* 21 | 15 | 19 | $23
Park Cities | 4448 E. Lovers Ln. (Dallas North Tollway) | Dallas | 214-265-9996
Plano | 4701 W. Park Blvd. (bet. Ohio Dr. & Preston Rd.) | 972-599-0289
www.chowthai.com
Surveyors salute these "solidly performing" Thai "staples" in Park Cities and Plano (sibs of Chow Thai) offering "consistently good" – if "Americanized" – South Asian specialties as well as some Chinese and Japanese dishes; decor is "casual" and "modern" though insiders insist it's a "go-to place for takeout" too.

Mansion on Turtle Creek *American* 26 | 27 | 26 | $77

Uptown | Mansion on Turtle Creek | 2821 Turtle Creek Blvd. (Gillespie St.) | Dallas | 214-559-2100 | www.mansiononturtlecreek.com

"Still the grande dame of Dallas" proclaim proponents of this Uptown "institution" helmed by chef John Tesar, who turns out "superb" New American dishes that make use of locally sourced ingredients; a major renovation completed post-Survey divided the "elegant" interior into three rooms done up in dark woods with contemporary art on the walls, added a bar menu and relaxed the dress code (except in the more formal 20-seat Chef's Room); "extremely accommodating service" and "upscale" pricing, however, remain constants.

Margaux's *Cajun/Creole* ▽ 25 | 22 | 24 | $38

Market Center | 150 Turtle Creek Blvd. (Irving Blvd.) | Dallas | 214-740-1985 | www.margauxsdallas.com

A "charming" detour ensconced in Dallas's Design District, this "quirky local place" draws a loyal lunchtime following for contemporary Cajun-Creole cuisine (think crawfish and shrimp enchiladas) that "never disappoints"; white-walled decor is enhanced by enormous floral prints, fresh flowers on each table as well as "friendly" service; N.B. open for dinner Saturdays only.

Mariposa *American* ▽ 23 | 23 | 22 | $27

Plano | Shops at Willow Bend | 2201 Dallas Pkwy. (Park Blvd.) | 972-629-1718 | www.neimanmarcus.com

A "jewel in the crown of Neiman Marcus", this upscale daytime-only New American noshery inside the store at Plano's Shops at Willow Bend offers an "excellent repast", with "food and service that rank with the quality of the merchandise" nearby; it's a "lovely place to lunch with the ladies" and a "great end to a fun day of shopping", and high points include "real Texas women with big hair and big jewels, and the best popovers in the world."

Masala *Chinese/Indian* 18 | 12 | 15 | $13

Irving | 7447 N. MacArthur Blvd. (Mimosa Dr.) | 972-409-0000

Masala Wok *Chinese/Indian*

Richardson | 1310 W. Campbell Rd. (Coit Rd.) | 972-644-9000

Plano | 8404 Preston Rd. (Route 121) | 469-362-5586

www.masalawok.com

"Mix and match" at these links in a regional chain, a "quick", "casual" stop for a "cheap" and "satisfying" fix of Indian and Chinese (with more weight on the former); the "concept" yields some "unusual combinations" and "oddball seasonings", but the "servers are helpful with first-timers."

Matt's Rancho Martinez *Tex-Mex* 21 | 16 | 19 | $20

Lakewood | 6332 La Vista Dr. (Gaston Ave.) | Dallas | 214-823-5517 | www.thetexmexchef.com

"When you want some carb loading, there's nothing like a meal" at this "good Lakewood spot" that "has grown into an East Dallas staple" for "fab" Tex-Mex fare; perhaps the "space isn't very inviting" (some say it feels "almost like eating in a warehouse") and the service is just "good", "not great" - but ya "gotta love" "grabbing a table on the patio and enjoying" a few of their "strong margaritas" "while kicking back with friends."

McCormick & Schmick's *Seafood* 21 | 21 | 20 | $41

NorthPark | NorthPark Ctr. | 307 Northpark Ctr. (bet. Central Expwy. & Northwest Hwy.) | Dallas | 214-891-0100 | www.mccormickandschmicks.com

See review in Austin and the Hill Country Directory.

Melting Pot, The *Fondue* 21 | 20 | 21 | $43

Addison | Quorum II Plaza | 4900 Belt Line Rd. (Addison Rd.) | 972-960-7028 | www.meltingpot.com

See review in Austin and the Hill Country Directory.

Mercury Chophouse *Steak* 26 | 23 | 23 | $43
(fka Fort Worth Chophouse)

Sundance Square | 301 Main St. (2nd St.) | Ft. Worth | 817-336-4129 | www.mcrowd.com

There's "never a bad meal" at this "solid" Downtown steakhouse in Sundance Square (recently taken over by the M Crowd restaurant group) that's "excellent for a business lunch" and "one of the best in Ft. Worth for conversation"; the "great" fare features a "perfect filet", and the "intimate" room is both "comfortable and luxurious", with "velvety drapes" and "club chairs" to bring you "back to the '40s."

Z Mercury Grill *American* 27 | 23 | 24 | $50

Preston Forest | Preston Forest Vill. | 11909 Preston Rd. (Forest Ln.) | Dallas | 972-960-7774 | www.mcrowd.com

"Talented" chef Chris Ward "gets it right" at this "fashionable" Preston Forest "place to be seen" with his "sublime" New American menu from which loyalists recite their litany of "favorites" ("heavenly mushroom risotto", braised short ribs); despite the fact that it's "tucked into a strip center", this is "one happening spot", with a staff so personable "we wished our waiter could have joined us for the meal" - just "watch out for the tab."; N.B there's an expanded lounge and rooms for private groups.

Z Mercy, A Wine Bar Ⓢ *French* 19 | 26 | 22 | $36

Addison | Village on the Pkwy. | 5100 Belt Line Rd. (Dallas N. Tollway) | 972-702-9463 | www.mercywinebar.com

You'll need to "elbow your way through the young and beautiful" at this Addison "oasis" where the "dark", "loungey" room and "extensive" wine selection (over 100 available by the glass) is conducive to sipping and lingering "all night long"; "knowledgeable" servers pair your vinos with "tasty" shareable French plates, but wallet-watchers should be aware of a "pricey" tab that can creep up on you.

Mia's Ⓢ *Tex-Mex* 24 | 13 | 19 | $17

Lemmon Avenue | 4322 Lemmon Ave. (Wycliff Ave.) | Dallas | 214-526-1020 | www.miastexmex.com

Groupies "guarantee a good night out" at this "quintessential" Tex-Mexer on Lemmon Avenue where the "nuclear-strength margaritas" and "justifiably famous brisket tacos" come at prices that won't bust your budget; "service is fast" while the "cramped", "casual" quarters have been known to include a "Dallas Cowboy" or two.

Michael Anthony's ☒ *American* 26 | 24 | 25 | $52

Southlake | 2750 E. Southlake Blvd. (Nolan Dr.) | 817-749-0377

Southlakers swoon over this "fantastic" entry offering "fine dining so close to home" with an "outstanding" New American menu and "top-of-the-line" service; it's a fine choice for a "celebratory dinner or special occasion" with the "intimate" wood-trimmed dining room striking the right "balance of elegance and comfort"; N.B. there's also live music Friday and Saturday nights.

Michaels ☒ *Southwestern* 24 | 18 | 19 | $37

Cultural District | 3413 W. Seventh St. (Montgomery St.) | Ft. Worth | 817-877-3413 | www.michaelscuisine.com

"Those who like it hot" say chef-owner Michael Thompson's namesake restaurant "tucked away in a shopping center" in Ft. Worth's Cultural District sizzles with "inventive" "Southwestern ranch" dishes like chipotle-honey brined pork, an "excellent wine" list and solid service; the sleek low-lit dining room features Andy Warhol's Cowboys and Indians series on the walls while the adjacent Ancho Chili Bar is a "late-night hangout" where "over-30" singles and cigar smokers are well received.

Z Mi Cocina *Tex-Mex* 21 | 19 | 20 | $23

Galleria | Galleria | 13350 N. Dallas Pkwy. (Lyndon B. Johnson Frwy.) | Dallas | 972-239-6426

Lake Highlands | 7201 Skillman St. (Kingsley Rd.) | Dallas | 214-503-6426

Park Cities | Highland Park Vill. | 77 Highland Park Vill. (bet. Mockingbird Ln. & Preston Rd.) | Dallas | 214-521-6426

Preston Forest | Preston Forest Vill. | 11661 Preston Rd. (Forest Ln.) | Dallas | 214-265-7704

West Village | West Vill. | 3699 McKinney Ave. (Lemmon Ave.) | Dallas | 469-533-5663

Las Colinas | 7750 N. MacArthur Blvd. (Lyndon B. Johnson Frwy.) | Irving | 469-621-0452

Plano | Lakeside Mkt. | 4001 Preston Rd. (Lorimar Dr.) | 469-467-8655

Plano | Shops at Legacy | 5760 Legacy Dr. (Parkwood Blvd.) | 972-473-8777

Sundance Square | Sundance Sq. | 509 Main St. (bet. 4th & 5th Sts.) | Ft. Worth | 817-877-3600

Southlake | Southlake Town Sq. | 1276 S. Main St. (Carroll Ave.) | 817-410-6426

www.mcrowd.com

Additional locations throughout the Dallas/Ft. Worth area

Admirers assert this "upscale" chain with locations in Highland Park, North Dallas and all the nearby suburbs is the "standard setter" for Tex-Mex cuisine with "light", "fresh-tasting" "contemporary" fare and "killer 'ritas" attracting a "noisy" crowd of "pretty folk" and their offspring; "modern" atmosphere (no "south-of-the-border clichés" here) plus "solid value", even considering the "expensive drinks", mean you can "go to any of them and leave satisfied."

	FOOD	DECOR	SERVICE	COST
Mignon *French*	22	22	20	$48

Plano | Lakeside Mkt. | 4005 Preston Rd. (Lorimar Dr.) | 972-943-3372 | www.mignonplano.com

Locals label this Plano bistro a "fine place for impressing your client as well as your date" with "excellent" "real" French fare delivered to your table by a staff that "tries hard"; curved booths and mod wood decor evoke "early 1960s" Paris, though "high" prices are a more modern touch.

	FOOD	DECOR	SERVICE	COST
Mi Piaci Ristorante *Italian*	24	24	22	$44

Addison | 14854 Montfort Dr. (Belt Line Rd.) | 972-934-8424 | www.mipiaci-dallas.com

For "a business dinner or a special date", diners declare this longstanding "favorite" "in the heart of Addison" proves "never less than wonderful" with "refined" Northern Italian cuisine, a "terrific" from-The-Boot wine list and "attentive" service from a "caring" staff; the "luxurious" setting includes a "gorgeous" patio overlooking a pond and trees, which is a "nice" respite from the sometimes "noisy" interior.

	FOOD	DECOR	SERVICE	COST
Mirabelle 🅂 🄼 *American*	▽ 28	23	28	$64

North Dallas | 17610 Midway Rd. (Trinity Mills Rd.) | Dallas | 972-733-0202

Chef Joseph Maher "attends to you personally" at this "extraordinary" North Dallas "neighborhood" spot serving "perfectly executed" New American dishes from a "small, but always innovative menu"; add in a "quiet", "intimate" space accented with an aquarium and colorful art, and it "feels like dining in a private home", in spite of its "strip-mall" location.

	FOOD	DECOR	SERVICE	COST
Momo's Pasta *Italian*	19	14	18	$26

Knox-Henderson | 3312 Knox St. (Travis St.) | Dallas | 214-521-3009
Addison | 5290 Belt Line Rd. (Montfort Dr.) | 972-386-7373
www.momospasta.com

"Long established", this duo in Addison and Knox-Henderson offers "consistent", "good Italian comfort food" that is "not overpriced" (another "plus": "you can bring your own wine" for a $10 corkage fee) and is ferried by a "fast, friendly" staff; with decor that's just "ok", their interiors are "nothing fancy", but many say they're still "worth" a visit.

	FOOD	DECOR	SERVICE	COST
Monica's Aca y Alla *Mexican*	23	19	21	$24

Deep Ellum | 2914 Main St. (bet. Hall St. & Malcolm X Blvd.) | Dallas | 214-748-7140 | www.monicas.com

"Monica Greene is a Dallas original", and her cosmopolitan Mexican restaurant in Deep Ellum is an "institution" with a "creative" menu featuring lots of "fantastic specials" to sweeten the deal (plus "fabulous margaritas"); there's "great people-watching" every night, but the "cozy, comfortable and fun" atmosphere is "especially enjoyable with the live music" on weekends.

	FOOD	DECOR	SERVICE	COST
Morton's, The Steakhouse *Steak*	25	21	23	$62

Downtown Dallas | 501 Elm St. (Houston St.) | Dallas | 214-741-2277 | www.mortons.com

See review in Houston Directory.

My Martini Wine & Bistro *Eclectic* ▽ 23 | 22 | 20 | $33

Arlington | 859 NE Green Oaks Blvd. (Collins St.) | 817-461-4424 | www.mymartinibistro.com

"As the name suggests", "delish" martinis - along with "excellent" small plates of multiethnic fusion fare and a selection of updated chophouse entrees - are on offer at this Arlington Eclectic; though most are "impressed with the quality of food and the service", some think of the "classy" hipster "mostly for the wine" and as "a place to be seen", since it's "one of the coolest in the mid-cities."

Naan *Japanese/Korean* 22 | 20 | 18 | $35

Plano | Shops at Legacy | 7161 Bishop Rd. (Legacy Dr.) | 972-943-9288 | www.naan-restaurant.com

"A departure from the usual", this "upscale" "combo Korean-Japanese place" situated within Plano's tony Shops at Legacy features an "interesting" menu with a "totally original" "twist on Asian fusion" fare, including unique "sushi creations" that are "unavailable at most run-of-the-mill" raw-fisheries; a "helpful" staff and a "nice-looking space" with "cool modern decor" and "a large bar" also add appeal, even if the "food is a little over the edge" for less adventurous eaters.

Nakamoto Japanese Cuisine *Japanese* ▽ 24 | 18 | 25 | $38

Plano | 3309 N. Central Expwy. (Parker Rd.) | 972-881-0328

Sushi mavens maintain this east Plano Japanese is the "preferred" "local" "choice" for "creative" fin fare and cooked dishes at moderate prices; though dissenters decry the "drab" "1980s decor", "friendly" service and moderate prices have kept the customers coming back "for over 20 years."

Z Nana *American* 27 | 27 | 27 | $73

Market Center | Hilton Anatole Hotel | 2201 Stemmons Frwy. (Market Center Blvd.) | Dallas | 214-761-7470 | www.nanarestaurant.com

It's tough to compete with "absolutely stunning" "panoramic" views of Downtown Dallas, yet chef Anthony Bombaci captivates diners with equally "amazing" New American dishes prepared in "imaginative" ways (think ahi tuna tartare with wasabi ice cream) at this elegant aerie atop the Hilton Anatole Hotel in Market Center; prices are "expensive", but the "superb" staff "executes at a high level", making it a top ticket for "special occasions."

Neuhaus Café *American/Dessert* 17 | 10 | 15 | $17

Preston Royal | 626 Preston Royal Shopping Ctr. (Royal Ln.) | Dallas | 214-739-4600 | www.neuhauscafe.com

Chocoholics claim they "just can't resist" the assorted Belgian bon bons and "wonderful desserts" at this coffee shop/"neighborhood sandwich and salad place" in the Preston Royal shopping area; it's "solid in all the basics", so even if the brightly lit quarters could stand to be "toned down a bit", it still works for an inexpensive meal or a quick snack.

Newport's Seafood *Seafood* 21 | 20 | 20 | $42

West End | 703 McKinney Ave. (I-35) | Dallas | 214-954-0220 | www.newports.us

"Even people who are on the fence about seafood" rave about the "reasonably priced", "fresh" fare at this "hard-to-find" but "delightful place" in the touristy West End that's "great for power lunches or intimate dinners"; lauders also "love the brick interior" of its "converted-brewery" setting "with an old well" "in the center of the dining room" that "makes for unique decor."

Nick & Sam's *Seafood/Steak* 25 | 23 | 25 | $61

Uptown | 3008 Maple Ave. (Carlisle St.) | Dallas | 214-871-7444 | www.nick-sams.com

Surveyors salute this Uptown meat "mecca" – the "standard bearer" for Dallas beeferies – where "sublime seafood and steaks" come together with "waistline-busting" sides and a 500-label wine list in "dark", "clubby" quarters with a baby grand piano and "great bar" adding to the palpable "buzz"; the "knowledgeable staff" elevates it to among "the best in town" – "just be prepared for a bill as big as the bone-in rib-eye."

Nicola's *Italian* 24 | 25 | 22 | $40

Plano | Shops at Legacy | 5800 Legacy Dr. (Bishop Rd.) | 972-608-4455 | www.nicolaslegacy.com

Plano patrons "find *amore*" at this "sophisticated" spot where the "customer is always taken care of" and the "handmade pastas" win raves, as do more "innovative" offerings on the "pricey" Northern Italian menu; the "beautiful" two-story space is dressed in burgundy tones and accented with a wrought-iron chandelier, but the "energetic vibe" means that sometimes "it can be so noisy you can't hear yourself think."

NEW N9ne Steakhouse ☒ *Steak* 22 | 24 | 22 | $66

Victory Park | 3090 Olive St. (Houston St.) | Dallas | 214-720-9901 | www.n9negroup.com

A "sceney" take on the classic steakhouse, this Victory Park "hot spot" (with outposts in Chicago and Sin City) piles on the "Vegas glitz" with "swanky" contemporary decor with suede booths, a "very noisy" clublike ambiance and a young "see-and-be-seen" crowd; yet while highrollers hail the "high-quality beef" and "inventive sides", the less starry-eyed claim it's "all hype" and "overpriced" to boot.

Nobu Dallas *Japanese* 24 | 24 | 20 | $67

Uptown | Hotel Crescent Ct. | 400 Crescent Ct. (bet. Cedar Springs Rd. & Maple Ave.) | Dallas | 214-252-7000 | www.noburestaurants.com

Dallas foodies feel "lucky to have this" "world-class" restaurant in Uptown's Crescent Court complex, an outpost of Nobu Matsuhisa's "famous" Peruvian-influenced Japanese chain and a "true dining experience" thanks to "fabulous food" (including "awesome" "melt-in-your-mouth sushi") and "way-cool decor"; be warned, though, that the "noise" from the "trendy" clientele can make it "hard to converse", while the "outrageous" "expense-account pricing" has some insisting that "better value can be found elsewhere."

Nonna Tata *Italian* | - | - | - | M

Hospital District | 1400 W. Magnolia Ave. (6th Ave.) | Ft. Worth | 817-332-0250

It's nearly impossible to snag one of the dozen tables at this no-reservations, cash-only, BYO trattoria in Ft. Worth's Hospital District; armed with no prior experience but a passion for cooking, chef-owner Donatella Trotti draws a loyal following thanks to her homey Italian cooking created from recipes handed down from her *nonna.*

NEW Nove Italiano *Italian* | 19 | 24 | 20 | $57

Victory Park | 3090 Olive St. (Houston St.) | Dallas | 214-720-9903 | www.n9negroup.com

"Eye-popping", "Vegas-style" decor with "Swarovski chandeliers" and classic artwork displayed on plasma TVs creates a "flashy" backdrop for the contemporary Italian cuisine at this "hip" sib of a Sin City original in Victory Park; yet in spite of an "attentive" staff, foes find "the food is not as good as the scenery" and complain it's "overpriced"and way too "loud" ("my ears are still ringing").

Nuevo Leon *Mexican* | 22 | 13 | 20 | $20

Farmers Branch | 12895 Josey Ln. (Valley View Ln.) | 972-488-1984 | www.nuevoleonrestaurant.net

"Buried in a Farmers Branch shopping center", this "locals" cantina "doesn't look like much", but customers claim the inexpensive, "authentic" Mexican dishes have had them "coming back for years"; though "nostalgics" "miss the original location" (lost in a fire some years ago), the "small" Josey Lane outpost decorated with Frida Kahlo paintings gets a boost from friendly service.

Oceanaire Seafood Room *Seafood* | 24 | 23 | 23 | $51

Galleria | Westin Galleria Hotel | 13340 N. Dallas Pkwy. (bet. Dallas N. Tollway & Lyndon B. Johnson Frwy.) | Dallas | 972-759-2277 | www.theoceanaire.com

See review in Houston Directory.

Old Hickory Steakhouse *Steak* | ▽ 21 | 21 | 22 | $73

Grapevine | Gaylord Texan Resort | 1501 Gaylord Trail (Rte. 26) | 817-778-1000 | www.gaylordhotels.com

Conventioneers corralled at the Gaylord Texan, a megaresort in Grapevine, chow down at this top-of-the-line steakhouse where chef Joanne Bondy (ex Ciudad) turns out "excellent" filets and a selection of seafood in a wood-paneled salon overlooking a tiny vineyard; though it's "not that popular with locals", it holds it own "in its category" with courteous service and live piano pleasing most patrons.

Old Warsaw, The *Continental/French* | 24 | 24 | 26 | $67

Uptown | 2610 Maple Ave. (bet. Cedar Springs Rd. & McKinney Ave.) | Dallas | 214-528-0032 | www.theoldwarsaw.com

This 60-year-old Uptown bastion of "fine dining" continues to hold court in a "romantic" "old-world" setting with a tuxedo-clad staff and nightly piano and violin music adding to the overall "impeccable" level of service; even if it's not exactly "on the cutting-edge", it still "serves up some of the best food in Dallas" with "exquisite" Continental-French cuisine complemented by "wonderful wines"; N.B. jacket required.

NEW Olea Mediterranean Bistro *Mediterranean*

∇ 23 | 21 | 19 | $34

Plano | 5809 Preston Rd. (bet. Parker & Spring Creek Rds.) | 972-378-0203 | www.oleabistro.com

"Simple", "well-made" "traditional" Mediterranean fare including "creative" tapas is washed down with homemade sangria at this western Plano newcomer from Pascal Cayet just up the road from his long-popular Provençal eatery, Lavendou; service rates as solid, and the warmly lit, white-tablecloth space wins fans, as does the shaded patio.

NEW Olenjack's Grille *American*

∇ 26 | 18 | 26 | $31

Arlington | Lincoln Sq. | 770 E. Road to Six Flags (Collins St.) | 817-226-2600 | www.olenjacksgrille.com

"A winner!" proclaim patrons of this Arlington arrival where chef-owner Brian Olenjack (of Reata) "takes pride in his food and it shows" in the "creative" American cuisine that emphasizes local ingredients; add in "kid-friendly" service and fans find it's an "excellent value", even if some note the "shopping-center" setting doesn't do it justice.

NEW Olivella's *Pizza*

22 | 12 | 16 | $20

Park Cities | 3406 McFarlin Blvd. (Hillcrest Rd.) | Dallas | 214-528-7070 | www.olivellas.com

"Finally, real pizza in Dallas" sigh those savoring the "superb" "thin-crust" Neapolitan-style pies crafted from "fresh" ingredients and fired in a wood-burning brick oven at this "welcome addition" to Park Cities; "cute SMU" waitresses work the "crowded", "quirky" slice of a restaurant, but with only seven tables of seating inside (plus extras on the sidewalk) takeout is sometimes the best option.

On Broadway Ristorante *Italian*

∇ 19 | 17 | 22 | $25

Southwest | 6306 Hulen Bend Blvd. (Hulen St.) | Ft. Worth | 817-346-8841 | www.onbroadwayrestaurant.com

If you're looking for a "nice local place to take a date or the family" in Southwest Ft. Worth, you'll find it at this "basic" Northern Italian, where the "friendly folks" ensure that diners receive "attentive service" and "consistently good" food ("the tableside Ceasar salad rocks") - and all "at an affordable price"; P.S. it's "a bit difficult to find, so first-timers should call ahead for directions."

Opa! Grille *Greek*

∇ 19 | 13 | 21 | $21

Preston Forest | 12829 Preston Rd. (Lyndon B. Johnson Frwy.) | Dallas | 972-661-0134

The "tasty Greek dishes are prepared with care" and "reasonably priced" at this "delightful mom and pop" near Preston Forest that caters to those who "just want a good meal"; some suggest "the decor is bizarre", but most say the "casual" space has a "coffee-shop appeal", and it earns more points still among the thrifty for its BYO policy.

Original Market Diner *Diner* ∇ 20 | 16 | 22 | $13

Market Center | 4434 Harry Hines Blvd. (Market Center Blvd.) | Dallas | 214-521-0992

"If you're on a budget and don't care about calories", this Market Center fixture is "the place to go" for "true Texas" staples – "from grits to chicken-fried steak" – dished out daily for breakfast and lunch; the "authentic" experience is further enhanced by "sassy" "beehived" waitresses providing sweet service.

Palm, The *Seafood/Steak* 24 | 19 | 24 | $56

West End | 701 Ross Ave. (Market St.) | Dallas | 214-698-0470 | www.thepalm.com

See review in San Antonio Directory.

Palomino *American/Mediterranean* 21 | 21 | 21 | $39

Uptown | 500 Crescent Ct. (bet. Cedar Springs Rd. & Maple Ave.) | Dallas | 214-999-1222 | www.palomino.com

"You'll never get a bad meal" at this national chain link, a New American-Med powerhouse at Uptown's Crescent Court complex, where all the "anything-but-commonplace" menu items "sound delicious – and are"; perhaps it's "not the scene" it once was, "but it's still a beautiful room" with "dependable service" and a "contemporary" feel that's ideal "for a power lunch" (and for happy hour too).

Pan Acean *Pan-Asian* 20 | 18 | 18 | $19

Coppell | 777 S. MacArthur Blvd. (Belt Line Rd.) | 972-745-7788 | www.panaceancoppell.com

"A smorgasbord" of "affordable" Asian options is what you'll find at this Coppell canteen catering to "neighborhood" denizens with a plethora of "fresh" options from Korea, Japan, Thailand and Vietnam; a "friendly" staff "makes [you] feel at home" in the "small", casual "strip-mall" space while "delivery service" is a convenient bonus.

Pappadeaux *Seafood* 23 | 19 | 20 | $29

Oak Lawn | 3520 Oak Lawn Ave. (Lemmon Ave.) | Dallas | 214-521-4700
Duncanville | 800 E. Hwy. 67 (Cockrell Hill Rd.) | 972-572-0580
North Dallas | 10428 Lombardy Ln. (Northwest Hwy.) | Dallas | 214-358-1912
North Dallas | 18349 Dallas Pkwy. (Frankford Rd.) | Dallas | 972-447-9616
Richardson | 725 S. Central Expwy. (Floyds Rd.) | 972-235-1181
Forest Park | 2708 West Frwy. (Park View Dr.) | Ft. Worth | 817-877-8843
Arlington | 13004 Copeland Rd. (Six Flags Dr.) | 817-543-0545
Bedford | 2121 Airport Frwy. (Central Dr.) | 817-571-4696
www.pappadeaux.com

See review in Houston Directory.

Pappas Bros. Steakhouse ☒ *Steak* 27 | 24 | 25 | $62

Love Field | 10477 Lombardy Ln. (Northwest Hwy.) | Dallas | 214-366-2000 | www.pappasbros.com

See review in Houston Directory.

Parigi *American/Mediterranean* 25 22 23 $39

Oak Lawn | 3311 Oak Lawn Ave. (Hall St.) | Dallas | 214-521-0295 | www.parigirestaurant.com

"On the cutting-edge for over 20 years" this "urban" Oak Lawn boîte has a name that conjures up "gay Paree", but the "wonderful" menu actually tilts toward "unique" New American-Mediterranean dishes like grilled quail with espresso glaze; it "packs a crowd" of "longtime residents" (some trying to "impress a date") thanks to servers who "make you feel like family" and a "charming" interior decorated with paintings by local artists.

Paris Coffee Shop ⊠ *American* 23 12 22 $11

Hospital District | 704 W. Magnolia Ave. (Hemphill St.) | Ft. Worth | 817-335-2041

"Basic diner food and decor, but good value" – that's how to become a "Ft. Worth institution", and this "legendary" "Traditional" American in the Hospital District has been doing just that since the 1920s, serving up "excellent old-fashioned, down-home cooking for breakfast and lunch" (sorry – no dinner service); when you're gorging on those "favorite chicken 'n' dumplings", though, "be sure to leave room for the sinful home-baked pies."

NEW Park Cities Prime ⊠ *Steak* ▽ 16 21 22 $56

Preston Center | 8411 Preston Rd. (Villanova Dr.) | Dallas | 214-691-7763 | www.parkcitiesprime.com

Maybe it's not quite "prime", but some surveyors say they still like this "pleasant" new steakhouse in Preston Center (from the same owners of PoPoLos Cafe) set in a "beautifully" decorated space done up in a "clubby", "masculine" style; so even if regulars report the food is only "average", "live piano" (Monday–Saturday) and "attentive" barkeeps have turned it into a "local hangout" all the same.

Pasand Indian Cuisine *Indian* ▽ 21 11 15 $18

Richardson | 1377 W. Campbell Rd. (Coit Rd.) | 972-644-4447
Irving | 2600 N. Belt Line Rd. (Hwy. 183) | 972-594-0693
www.pasand.net

With branches in Irving and Richardson, this pair has "earned a reputation" for "excellent", "expertly spiced" North and South Indian offerings; the "popular" "places are packed every lunch"-time since the "extensive buffet" is "a fabulous value", boasting a "good selection of both meat and vegetable dishes" and "flavorsome naan."

Pastazio's *Pizza* 22 12 17 $16

Uptown | 3028 N. Hall St. (McKinney Ave.) | Dallas | 214-969-5959
Addison | Addison Circle | 5026 Addison Circle (Spectrum Dr.) | 972-386-9200
www.pastazios.com

It's all about the pizza at this Addison and Uptown counter-service duo where boosters boast the "huge", "thin-crust" slices taste like they came "right off the streets of Manhattan"; prices are "inexpensive" and delivery is a plus, so some say the biggest drawback is that it's "not open late" "after the bars close."

Patrizio *Italian* 21 | 20 | 19 | $28

Park Cities | Highland Park Vill. | 25 Highland Park Vill. (bet. Livingston Ave. & Mockingbird Ln.) | Dallas | 214-522-7878
Plano | 1900 Preston Park Blvd. (Park Blvd.) | 972-964-2200
Highland Village | Shops at Highland Vlg. | 4131 Deer Creek (2499 & FM 407) | 972-966-0809
www.patrizios.net

"Amazing pasta at surprisingly reasonable prices", and in portions that "could almost serve two people", draws crowds to this Italian trio, the original a "favorite spot in Highland Park Village" and younger siblings in Park Cities and Plano that present solid "value"; each is "popular at both lunch and dinner", so "be prepared for a wait" (and "sometimes slow service"), and if you find them too "noisy" inside, "sit out on" their "fabulous patios."

Peggy Sue BBQ *BBQ* 22 | 13 | 19 | $18

Park Cities | Snider Plaza | 6600 Snider Plaza (Daniel Ave.) | Dallas | 214-987-9188 | www.peggysuebbq.com

BBQ fans find the "down-home" grub "very tasty" at this "local" "fixture" in Snider Plaza specializing in oak-smoked meats enhanced with "spicy sauce" and offering a salad bar and a full lineup of veggies and sides; the "small", "homey" "'50s-flashback"-style space with red-checked tablecloths is "always crowded" with "families, students and couples" who appreciate the friendly "sit-down service" and "cheap" prices.

Z Pei Wei Asian Diner *Pan-Asian* 19 | 15 | 16 | $15

Knox-Henderson | 3001 Knox St. (N. Central Expwy.) | Dallas | 214-219-0000
Preston Center | Preston Center Pavilion | 8305 Westchester Dr. (Luther Ln.) | Dallas | 214-765-9911
Addison | 4801 Belt Line Rd. (Addison Rd.) | 972-764-0844
North Dallas | 18204 Preston Rd. (Frankford Rd.) | Dallas | 972-985-0090
Allen | 1008 W. McDermott Dr. (I-75) | 469-675-2266
Irving | 7600 N. MacArthur Blvd. (bet. I-635 & President George Bush Tpke.) | 972-373-8000
Cultural District | Montgomery Plaza | 2600 W. Seventh St. (Carroll St.) | Ft. Worth | 817-806-9950
Southwest | 5900 Overton Ridge Rd. (Bryant Irvin Rd.) | Ft. Worth | 817-294-0808
Arlington | Village by the Parks | 4133 E. Cooper St. (Pleasant Ridge Rd.) | 817-466-4545
Southlake | 1582 E. Southlake Blvd. (Central Ave.) | 817-722-0070
www.peiwei.com
Additional locations throughout the Dallas/Ft. Worth area

There's "always a crowd" at this Pan-Asian chain (a "downscale" "little cousin" of P.F. Chang's), where the chow is "tasty", the menu "limited" and the service primarily "cafeteria-style"; a few sigh "boring", but "kids like it", the food "seems healthy" and, not incidentally, the "prices are really good."

FOOD | DECOR | SERVICE | COST

Penne Pomodoro *Italian* 19 | 15 | 17 | $23

Park Cities | Snider Plaza | 6815 Snider Plaza (Lovers Ln.) | Dallas | 214-373-9911

Preston Forest | Preston Forest Vill. | 11661 Preston Rd. (Forest Ln.) | Dallas | 214-373-9911

www.pennepomodoro.com

A "variety" of "reliable" (if "Americanized") Italian dishes attracts couples and "kids" to Alberto Lombardi's "down-to-earth" duo in the Park Cities and Preston Forest where "quality" wood-fired pizzas and pastas are turned out in "comfortable" shopping-center settings; "prompt service" and "low prices" make them a "solid option for a casual night out."

Pepe & Mito's Mexican Café *Mexican* ▽ 22 | 16 | 25 | $15

Deep Ellum | 2911 Elm St. (bet. Malcolm X Blvd. & Walton St.) | Dallas | 214-741-1901

Supporters say this "locals'" cantina in Deep Ellum cooks up "tasty" Mexican and Tex-Mex specialties that keep them "coming back" for more; it's a "favorite" thanks to gentle prices, a colorful setting outfitted with a patio and a warm welcome from the family owners ("the nicest people you'll meet").

Perry's ⊠ *Steak* 24 | 22 | 23 | $57

Uptown | 2911 Routh St. (Cedar Springs Rd.) | Dallas | 214-871-9991 | www.perrys-dallas.com

Chef Travis Henderson is the "wizard in the kitchen" of this Uptown steakhouse, a "favorite" of many thirtysomethings, and his "expertise shines in both the seafood and beef departments"; the "clubby, dark and romantic" atmosphere makes it "better for intimate dinners than most" competitors, plus the "excellent bar" is a "great place to take a date or meet colleagues" - "without the noise and pretense" of the "singles scene that flocks to similar restaurants."

Z P.F. Chang's China Bistro *Chinese* 22 | 22 | 20 | $27

NorthPark | NorthPark Ctr. | 225 Northpark Ctr. (Northwest Hwy.) | Dallas | 214-265-8669

North Dallas | 18323 N. Dallas Pkwy. (Frankford Rd.) | Dallas | 972-818-3336

NEW Allen | Watters Crossing at Montgomery Farm | 915 W. Bethany Dr. (Rte. 198) | 972-390-1040

Sundance Square | Bank One Bldg. | 400 Throckmorton St. (3rd St.) | Ft. Worth | 817-840-2450

NEW Arlington | Arlington Highlands | 215 I-20 E. (Matlock Rd.) | 817-375-8690

Grapevine | 650 Hwy. 114 (bet. Main St. & William D. Tate Ave.) | 817-421-6658

www.pfchangs.com

Expect "major hustle-bustle" at this "noisy" Chinese chain where the "sanitized", "mass-produced" menus "aren't really authentic" yet do "appeal to most palates" (when in doubt, the "lettuce wraps rule"); no one minds the "spotty" service and "ersatz" Sino decor since they "have the formula down" - starting with "nothing-fancy" prices and an overall "fun" vibe.

	FOOD	DECOR	SERVICE	COST

Piccolo Mondo *Italian* ▽ 21 | 19 | 22 | $32

Arlington | Parkway Central Ctr. | 829 E. Lamar Blvd. (Collins St.) | 817-265-9174 | www.piccolomondo.com

Regulars report they're "never disappointed" at this "longtime" Arlington Italian turning out "well-prepared" dishes at moderate prices; in spite of its "nondescript strip-mall location", it remains a "neighborhood" standby thanks to "witty waiters", fair prices and live piano (Tuesday–Saturday).

Piranha *Japanese* 25 | 21 | 20 | $36

Sundance Square | 335 W. Third St. (Throckmorton St.) | Ft. Worth | 817-348-0200

Arlington | 851 NE Green Oaks Blvd. (Collins St.) | 817-261-1636

www.piranhakillersushi.com

"Killer sushi" is bested only by the "imaginative" maki in "wild" combinations (like shrimp tempura with avocado and pico de gallo) at these "lively" Japanese twins that converts claim serve "the best" fish around; the "trendy" Sundance Square outpost boasts a "hip" scene for "twenty to thirtysomethings" that's as "vibrant" as the food while the Arlington branch is more of an understated "find"; both boast the same "great" (if sometimes "slow") service and somewhat "pricey" tabs.

Poor Richard's Café *American* ▽ 20 | 9 | 21 | $11

Plano | 2442 K Ave. (Park Blvd.) | 972-423-1524 | www.poorrichardscafe.com

"Down-home" American cooking hits the spot for fans of this east Plano "classic" serving "tasty" breakfasts and lunches in a "noisy" setting decorated with "cute quotes" from Poor Richard's Almanac; it's a "friendly, hometown place" enhanced by "old-fashioned" touches like cheap tabs and "fast" service from "waitresses who call you 'hon.'"

PoPoLos Cafe *Italian* 20 | 18 | 21 | $38

Preston Royal | Preston Royal Shopping Ctr. | 5959 Royal Ln. (Preston Rd.) | Dallas | 214-692-5497 | www.popolos.com

A "convenient" stop for Preston Royal locals for more than a decade, this "neighborhood" Italian is "good for dates, business dinners or a family night out"; with its Med touches, the food is "reliably good" (if "not memorable"), plus the room is "seldom overcrowded" and there's "jazz to accompany the meal" Tuesday–Saturday nights.

NEW Porch, The *American* 22 | 20 | 22 | $31

Knox-Henderson | 2912 N. Henderson Ave. (Willis Ave.) | Dallas | 214-828-2916 | www.theporchrestaurant.com

A "young, hip" flock roosts at this Knox-Henderson "hot spot" from restaurateur Tristan Simon (Hibiscus and Cuba Libre) turning out "edgy" American "comfort food" – like brisket sliders and short-rib stroganoff – at prices so "affordable" habitués have adopted it as their new "casual" hangout; it can be "loud" and there are frequent "waits", so some suggest you pass the time with an "innovative" cocktail and some "great people-watching."

Positano *Italian* ▽ 22 | 22 | 23 | $40

North Dallas | 18111 Preston Rd. (Frankford Rd.) | Dallas | 972-407-9180 | www.positanodallas.com

A warm "welcome" from chef-owner Antonio Avona kicks off an "enjoyable experience" at this "excellent" midpriced North Dallas eatery featuring a wide-ranging Italian menu; the "fabulous staff" adds to the appeal as does the warm interior with tile floors and vaulted ceilings that manages to be both "elegant" and "comfortable" at the same time.

Primo's Bar & Grille ◐ *Tex-Mex* 18 | 13 | 16 | $19

Uptown | 3309 McKinney Ave. (Hall St.) | Dallas | 214-220-0510 | www.primosdallas.com

While its "dependable Tex-Mex" fare is certainly "good", this Uptown "hangout" "is all about getting to know your table-neighbor" – hence its rep as a "happenin' spot" for "twentysomethings who conduct mating rituals" "while sipping potent Meltdown margaritas" on the "popular patio" ("comb your hair and smile pretty"); still, those who find the grub "standard", the service "iffy" and the decor "lacking" see "no apparent reason" for its perpetually "packed" state.

Purple Cow Diner *Diner* 14 | 15 | 15 | $14

Preston Royal | Preston Royal Shopping Ctr. | 110 Preston Royal Shopping Ctr. (Royal Ln.) | Dallas | 214-373-0037

Plano | Lakeside Mkt. | 5809 Preston Rd. (bet. Parker Rd. & Spring Creek Pkwy.) | 972-473-6100

West | 4601 West Frwy. (Rte. 30) | Ft. Worth | 817-737-7177

It's "kiddie city" at this "family"-oriented mini-chain styled after a "1950s soda shop" with a jukebox spinning vintage tunes and a somewhat "generic" selection of American grub (burgers, chicken fingers) plus "decadent" "signature" milkshakes with "liquored up" versions for the adults; prices are "inexpensive", and though service may be "slow", at least they handle the young 'uns with "humor and patience."

Z Railhead Smokehouse ⊠ *BBQ* 22 | 14 | 14 | $14

Cultural District | 2900 Montgomery St. (I-30) | Ft. Worth | 817-738-9808 | www.railheadonline.com

"Bikers", "attorneys" and other assorted "Tuppies (Texas urban professionals)" converge on this "lively" BBQ "institution" in Ft. Worth's Cultural District for "fallin'-off-the-bone-good" ribs and "tender" brisket washed down with "very cold beer"; "long" cafeteria-style "lines are typical, but flow quickly", even on Thursdays, when the bar fills up and this meat market quite literally turns into a "meet market"; N.B. drive-thru is also available.

Reata *Southwestern* 24 | 25 | 23 | $43

Sundance Square | 310 Houston St. (3rd St.) | Ft. Worth | 817-336-1009 | www.reata.net

"No cowboy ever ate so good" say those savoring the "fancied up ranch cuisine" at this "unique" eatery in Downtown Ft. Worth's

Sundance Square where the "superb" Southwestern cuisine (especially "the to-die-for" tenderloin tamales) represents "upscale" "camp cooking at its best"; loads of "out-of-towners" fill the "over-the-top" cowhide-appointed interior rendering it rather "loud", so those in-the-know scamper to the rooftop bar for a quieter atmosphere in addition to "remarkable views" of the city skyline.

Red's Patio Grill *American* 20 | 18 | 19 | $22

Plano | 4005 Preston Rd. (Lorimar Dr.) | 469-229-0098 | www.redspatiogrill.com

The "excellent margaritas" take center stage at this western Plano yearling boasting a collection of over 100 tequilas and a "lovely" "lakeside" patio that's the perfect spot for sipping; Traditional American entrees include rotisserie chicken and "great burgers" all at prices low enough to make it an easy pick for friends and "families" on the run.

Remington's Seafood Grill *Seafood* 21 | 15 | 20 | $30

Addison | 4580 Belt Line Rd. (Addison Rd.) | 972-386-0122 | www.remingtonseafoodgrill.com

For more than a quarter century, the Remington family has been serving "consistently" "excellent" "fresh-fish" fare at this Addison "standby" favored by an "older" clientele; the decor may be "a bit tired", but "for the hungry seafood lover looking for value", such things pale next to "classic" cuisine, "friendly" service and "reasonable prices."

Riccardi's Italian Dining ☒ *Italian* ▽ 20 | 18 | 20 | $62

Uptown | Quadrangle | 2800 Routh St. (Howell St.) | Dallas | 214-303-0881 | www.riccardis-dallas.com

Deep-pocketed pastaphiles say owner Anita Riccardi "makes you feel extra special" at her thoroughly "enjoyable" Italian in Uptown's Quadrangle serving up Northern-style specialties like veal Gaetano and risotto Milanese with wines from her family's vineyard; the "romantic" room accented with chandeliers and frescos (there's even a replica of the Sistine Chapel ceiling in the entryway) comes alive with music on weekends while a lounge tucked in the back draws cigar-smoking patrons who settle in for a martini in front of the three flat-screen TVs.

NEW Rick's Chop House *Southern/Steak* ▽ 21 | 25 | 21 | $49

McKinney | Grand Hotel | 107 N. Kentucky St. (Louisianna St.) | 214-726-9251

Champions cheer this "great addition" to Downtown McKinney, the Grand Hotel's upscale new steakhouse with a Southern-leaning menu featuring fried green tomatoes and shrimp and andouille beignets plus a full lineup of steaks; set in the space that was once an opera house (circa 1885), it features a pressed tin ceiling and gas lanterns illuminating the "beautiful" room while it hangs onto a "small-town feel" thanks to a "knowledgeable staff" offering "accommodating" service.

Rick Stein's ☒ *Steak* 22 | 22 | 25 | $64

North Dallas | 18020 N. Dallas Pkwy. (Frankford Rd.) | Dallas | 972-713-9999 | www.ricksteins.com

Owner Rick Stein "is a master", and it shows in the "personal touch" he brings to his eponymous North Dallas chophouse, where the "steaks sizzle and are served perfectly" and there's also an "innovative menu" of other offerings - and let's hear it for the "great wine list"; the lighting is "dim", making for a "warm ambiance" with nightly live piano music and a covered patio.

Ristorante La Piazza ☒ *Italian* 26 | 25 | 22 | $49

University Area | University Park Vill. | 1600 S. University Dr. (bet. Old University Dr. & River Run) | Ft. Worth | 817-334-0000

"A feast for the senses" awaits at this "elegant" University Area enclave where Ft. Worth's "upper crust" gathers for "incredible" "classic Italian" cuisine in a "transporting" setting with "opera playing quietly in the background"; though regulars report "marvelous" treatment, those not on the A-list find service "pretentious" and say the "stuffy" attitude "spoils" an otherwise pleasant experience; N.B. jacket suggested.

Roti Grill *Indian* 18 | 10 | 15 | $15

Knox-Henderson | 4438 McKinney Ave. (bet. Armstrong Ave. & Oliver St.) | Dallas | 214-521-3655

Plano | 6509 W. Park Blvd. (Midway Blvd.) | 972-403-7600

www.freshindianfood.com

An "oasis" in the "virtual desert" of Dallas-area Indian options, this "casual" order-at-the-counter duo curries favor with fans thanks to "quality" "low-cost" masalas and tandooris served up "fast"; it works "in a pinch", though "nondescript" environs mean many opt for "takeout"; P.S. the Plano branch is BYO and has a "great lunch buffet."

Rough Creek Lodge *American* ▽ 27 | 28 | 28 | $60

Glen Rose | Rough Creek Lodge & Resort | County Rd. 2013 (U.S. 67) | 254-918-2550 | www.roughcreek.com

The "dramatic contemporary Western setting" of the Rough Creek Lodge & Resort affords "breathtaking views" of the landscape, but it's really the "superb" food that's "worth the trip" to this New American in Glen Rose; of course, there's also "excellent service" from an "attentive", "tireless staff", as well as the "rustic elegance" of its "wonderful atmosphere", which reminds some "of a secluded hunting lodge" where "nobility coming in from the hunt celebrate in grand style."

Royal Thai *Thai* 23 | 19 | 21 | $23

Greenville Avenue | 5500 Greenville Ave. (Lovers Ln.) | Dallas | 214-691-3555

This Greenville Avenue Thai temple is "different from a lot of others" - "more of an elegant sit-down-and-linger-over-dinner kind of place"; we're talking "top-notch food at an incredibly inexpensive price" and "well presented" by a "wonderful restrained" staff, so "prepare to wait during prime hours on a Friday or Saturday."

Roy's *Hawaiian* 25 | 24 | 23 | $48

Plano | 2840 Dallas Pkwy. (bet. Park Blvd. & Parker Rd.) | 972-473-6263 | www.roysrestaurant.com

The "next best thing to being oceanside in Maui", this "haute Hawaiian" chain via celeb chef Roy Yamaguchi is "fine dining" personified thanks to a "top-shelf" fusion menu that's as "eye-pleasing as it is palate-pleasing"; "great" service and "upscale-casual" atmospheres add to its luster, though given the "upmarket pricing", it does "taste better when someone else is paying."

Ruffino's Ristorante Italiano ⊠ *Italian* 22 | 18 | 23 | $30

Forest Park | 2455 Forest Park Blvd. (Park Hill Dr.) | Ft. Worth | 817-923-0522 | www.ruffinosfinedining.com

"After many years", this "old-world" "romantic Italian bistro" in Ft. Worth's Forest Park section "still doesn't disappoint" thanks to an "authentic menu" including "housemade pastas with fresh ingredients"; "its fine-dining atmosphere belies the casual, friendly service" of staffers who are so diligent "they practically greet you at your car."

Ruggeri's *Italian* 20 | 19 | 21 | $47

Preston Royal | 5950 Royal Ln. (Preston Rd.) | Dallas | 214-750-0111 | www.ruggerisrestaurant.net

Colleyville | 32 Village Ln. (Main St.) | 817-503-7373

NEW **Grapevine** | Residence Inn | 2020 State Hwy. 26 (Grapevine Mills Circle) | 972-539-8989

"Reborn" in rustic Preston Royal digs in 2006, this "neighborhood" Italian from "friendly" owner Tom Ruggeri pleases loyal patrons who praise the "well-executed" cuisine, which they deem "worth it" even if it "won't knock your socks off"; still, some longtimers lament they miss the "old" incarnation and label the menu "mediocre" and the tabs "pricey" too; N.B. scores may not reflect the independently operated Grapevine and Colleyville addresses.

Ruth's Chris Steak House *Steak* 25 | 22 | 25 | $57

North Dallas | 17840 Dallas Pkwy. (Trinity Mills Rd.) | Dallas | 972-250-2244 | www.ruthschris.com

See review in San Antonio Directory.

Saffron House *Indian* ▽ 20 | 21 | 18 | $25

Addison | Village on the Pkwy. | 5100 Belt Line Rd. (Dallas N. Tollway) | 972-239-1800 | www.thesaffronhouse.com

This Addison entry "raises the bar" for "Dallas-area" Indian food with "perfectly seasoned" curries in addition to an array of more "refined" dishes; diners deem the vividly colored decor "exotic without venturing toward tacky" and service seems "genuinely helpful", so the only downside, say sticklers, is "inconsistency."

Z **Saint-Emilion** ⊠ M *French* 27 | 24 | 27 | $54

Cultural District | 3617 W. Seventh St. (Montgomery St.) | Ft. Worth | 817-737-2781

A "country French delight" in Ft. Worth's Cultural District, this "small jewel" warmed by brick walls and a wood-beamed ceiling is "perfect for dates" and "special occasions", presenting "amazing" "daily blackboard specials" matched by a "fabulous" wine list and "hospitality on the same delicious level as the food"; fans say the prix fixe option offers a real "value in fine dining" and, as tables are limited, recommend making "reservations on peak nights."

Salum ☒ *American* 25 | 22 | 22 | $54

Uptown | 4152 Cole Ave. (Fitzhugh Ave.) | Dallas | 214-252-9604 | www.salumrestaurant.com

Admirers adore this "friendly, little" Uptown bistro helmed by "gracious chef-owner" Abraham Salum whose "sophisticated" takes on "seasonal" New American cooking come at "pretty reasonable" prices making it a "wonderful neighborhood spot"; don't be "deterred" by the strip-mall location because supporters say the "nondescript" exterior doesn't do justice to the "lovely", "understated room", not to mention the "terrific" food.

Sambuca *Eclectic* 21 | 23 | 19 | $38

Uptown | 2120 McKinney Ave. (Pearl St.) | Dallas | 214-744-0820

Addison | 15207 Addison Rd. (Belt Line Rd.) | 972-385-8455 www.sambucarestaurant.com

"Unwind" with "classy jazz" at this Dallas-based "supper club" chain, where "super" "live entertainment" enhances a "something-for-everyone" lineup of "fusion-style" Eclectic cuisine; "lounge" habitués laud the "sophisticated" (if "loud") atmosphere, though some who claim it's "a little expensive for what you get" foodwise swing by solely "for the music" and "lively" "bar scene."

Sammy's Bar-B-Q ☒ *BBQ* - | - | - | I

Preston Center | 6100 Luther Ln. (Westchester Dr.) | Dallas | 214-360-9064

Uptown | 2126 Leonard St. (Woodall Rodgers Frwy.) | Dallas | 214-880-9064 | www.sammysbbq.com

When it comes to slow-smoked meats slathered in piquant sauce, this lunch-only duo is a top choice among local 'cue critics; the Uptown campsite (in the shadows of the Federal Reserve Bank) caters to power brokers who fling their Hermès neckwear over their shoulder to avoid telltale grease stains while Preston Center attracts a not-as-fastidious family crowd that appreciates the tidy prices.

Samui Thai *Thai* 24 | 23 | 23 | $25

Allen | Twin Creek Shopping Ctr. | 906 W. McDermott Dr. (I-75) | 972-747-7452

Plano | 5700 Legacy Dr. (Dallas N. Tollway) | 972-398-2807 www.samuithai.com

"Good enough to convert the picky", this pair of "friendly seafood-themed Thai places" in Allen and Plano features an "incredible menu with more choices than" many in the genre, all with "nary a trace of grease and oil"; it's "amazing what they did with strip-mall spaces", and the "great lunch specials" add to their "reasonable" rep.

	FOOD	DECOR	SERVICE	COST

S & D Oyster Company ⊠ *Seafood* 23 16 22 $25

Uptown | 2701 McKinney Ave. (Boll St.) | Dallas | 214-880-0111 | www.sdoyster.com

"For a bit of nostalgia, try this holdout" Uptown that's been serving "New Orleans-style" "seafood and oysters on the half shell" for 30-plus years; though it's a "no-frills place", the "loud" room's "unpretentious, old-timey" vibe is definitely part of the "fun", and the "superb staff" will really make "you feel at home."

NEW Sangria Tapas y Bar *Spanish* 17 19 17 $31

Knox-Henderson | 4524 Cole Ave. (Knox St.) | Dallas | 214-520-4863 | www.sangriatapasybar.com

"Trendy" foodies cram into this "noisy" Knox-Henderson newcomer for a "little taste of Spain" thanks to "innovative" tapas and a festive, "crowded" interior decked out in imported Iberian tiles; yet while some customers cheer the "happening" scene, critics knock "inconsistent" fare that "costs too much" and say they "should have better sangria given their name."

Sapristi! M *Eclectic* 24 20 21 $31

Forest Park | 2418 Forest Park Blvd. (Park Hill Dr.) | Ft. Worth | 817-924-7231 | www.sapristibistro.com

"Cheery" and "relaxed", this "cute neighborhood bistro" is a "venerable" part of Ft. Worth's Forest Park district, with "fabulous, European-inspired" Eclectic cuisine that tastes "homemade"; "service can be a little slow for some city folks", but the "friendly and knowledgeable" staff will help you navigate the "ever-changing" list of "fantastic, inexpensive" wines "selected for quality and value, and available for chump change."

Sardines Ristorante Italiano *Italian* 18 15 19 $27

Cultural District | 509 University Dr. (5th St.) | Ft. Worth | 817-332-9937

"Surprisingly good" Italian food is jazzed up by live music nightly at this "old mainstay" in Ft. Worth's Cultural District; "very dark" ("some say cozy") digs feature lots of "memorabilia" on the walls, though grousers who gripe they "can't see the menu" find the patio a more agreeable and less "noisy" solution.

Seventeen Seventeen ⊠ M *Eclectic* 22 21 20 $35

Arts District | Dallas Museum of Art | 1717 N. Harwood St. (Ross Ave.) | Dallas | 214-880-0158 | www.wynnwood.com

As "you'd expect", this "great place" in the Dallas Museum of Art is known for the "artfully" presented and "well-prepared Eclectic choices" on its "seasonal menu"; "relaxed service" is also a plus, but in the end, it's the "stylish decor" that makes it "very, very special" – perhaps even the "most elegant lunch spot in town"?

Sevy's Grill *American* 23 22 23 $40

Preston Center | 8201 Preston Rd. (Sherry Ln.) | Dallas | 214-265-7389 | www.sevys.com

Chef Jim 'Sevy' Severson is an "independent who excels at his work", namely creating "stellar food" at this "upscale-casual" Preston

Center "neighborhood hangout" that fans feel is "the definition of what an American bistro should be"; regulars are also "fond of" the "even-keeled service" from the "professional" staff, including "bartenders who remember your name" and "really know how to pour a drink" - one reason for the "active bar scene."

Shinsei ⊠ *Pan-Asian* 25 | 23 | 22 | $49

West Lovers Lane | 7713 Inwood Rd. (Lovers Ln.) | Dallas | 214-352-0005 | www.shinseirestaurant.com

"Sexy atmosphere, sexy people, sexy food" sum up surveyors who "dress to the nines" for this "beautifully decorated" West Lovers Lane boîte backed by Lynae Fearing and Tracy Rathbun (wives of Dean and Kent) and helmed by "top chef" and *Top Chef* finalist Casey Thompson; sure, it's a "swanky" scene, but surveyors swear the food is "phenomenal" too with "artfully presented" Pan-Asian dishes showcasing "brilliant flavors" plus "amazing service" and "designer libations" adding up to a "don't-miss" experience.

Silver Fox Steakhouse *Steak* 24 | 22 | 23 | $54

NEW **Oak Lawn** | Centrum Bldg. | 3102 Oak Lawn Ave. (Cedar Springs Rd.) | Dallas | 214-559-2442
Richardson | 3650 Shire Blvd. (Jupiter Rd.) | 972-423-8121 ⊠
NEW **Frisco** | 1303 Legacy Dr. (Hwy. 121) | 214-618-5220
University Area | 1651 S. University Dr. (I-30) | Ft. Worth | 817-332-9060 ⊠
Grapevine | 1235 William D. Tate Ave. (Hwy. 114) | 817-329-6995 ⊠
www.silverfoxsteakhouse.com

"If you want a fancy steak dinner without being expected to dress up", these "crowded" younger siblings of III Forks do the trick; with an "impeccable menu, superior service" and a "dark, romantic atmosphere", they offer a "more modern Texas steakhouse" experience, and their "value" also sets them apart - "side dishes are included with the price of the meal."

62 Main Restaurant ⊠ Ⓜ *American* 27 | 23 | 26 | $50

Colleyville | 62 Main St. (bet. Hwy. 26 & Main St.) | 817-605-0858 | www.62mainrestaurant.com

It's "big-city dining in the 'burbs" proclaim chain-weary fans who flock to chef-owner David McMillan's "upscale" New American spot that serves "inventive" "masterpieces" with "sauces and flavors that are right on"; "tucked away" on the second floor of the Village at Colleyville development, the rustic room has a Napa feel, enhanced by "friendly" service and costs that are "a bit pricey, but an overall fair value", causing most to concur that it's "worth the drive."

Sonny Bryan's Smokehouse *BBQ* 22 | 12 | 16 | $16

Downtown Dallas | Republic Ctr. | 325 N. St. Paul St. (Pacific Ave.) | Dallas | 214-979-0102 ⊠
West End | 302 N. Market St. (Pacific Ave.) | Dallas | 214-744-1610
Galleria | 13375 Noel Rd. (bet. James Temple Dr. & Peterson Ln.) | Dallas | 972-851-5131 ⊠
Love Field | 2202 Inwood Rd. (Harry Hines Blvd.) | Dallas | 214-357-7120 ⊠

(continued)

Sonny Bryan's Smokehouse

Preston Forest | Preston Forest Vill. | 11661 Preston Rd. (Forest Ln.) | Dallas | 214-234-0888

West Lovers Lane | 5519 W. Lovers Ln. (Inwood Rd.) | Dallas | 214-351-2024

North Dallas | 4701 Frankford Rd. (Dallas N. Tollway) | Dallas | 972-447-0102

Richardson | Pavilion Park Ctr. | 1251 W. Campbell Rd. (Coit Rd.) | 972-664-9494

Las Colinas | Las Colinas Plaza | 4030 N. MacArthur Blvd. (Northgate Dr.) | Irving | 972-650-9564

Alliance | Alliance Ctr. | 2421 Westport Pkwy. (I-35) | Ft. Worth | 817-224-9191

www.sonnybryans.com

Additional locations throughout the Dallas/Ft. Worth area

"It'd be hard to find better BBQ" – "served without decor or great service, just like it should be" – than at this Love Field–area "institution" that's spawned a slew of satellites; "a true melting pot of Dallas", it's peopled by everyone "from day laborers to billionaires", all tucking into "reliable beef sandwiches, monster onion rings" and "ice-cold beers" plunked down on "grease-stained picnic tables" by servers "with an attitude" in "a shack right out of central casting."

Sonoma Grill & Wine Bar *American* ▽ 22 | 19 | 19 | $37

Flower Mound | Parker Sq. | 380 Parker Sq. (Main St.) | 972-899-8989 | www.sonomagrillandwinebar.com

"Lucky" Flower Mound is home to this "little gem" in the Parker Square shopping center where the "fabulous" New American fare is bested only by the "strong selection" of Northern California vinos; regulars who bask on the covered patio insist you'll "feel you've been whisked off to wine country" with coddling service adding to the appeal.

Spiral Diner M *Diner/Vegetarian* ▽ 23 | 22 | 21 | $14

Hospital District | 1314 W. Magnolia Ave. (6th Ave.) | Ft. Worth | 817-332-8834 | www.spiraldiner.com

"Vegetarians", "your friends from California" and even "carnivores" all appreciate the "imaginative", "delicious" vegan fare and "socially conscious" vibe at this "funky" outpost in an "up-and-coming" area around Ft. Worth's Hospital District; 1950s-style diner digs get a modern kick from the tattooed staff, while prices remain delightfully retro; N.B. a Dallas location is reportedly in the works.

State & Allen Lounge ◐ *American* ▽ 19 | 16 | 19 | $22

(fka Taste)

Uptown | 2400 Allen St. (State St.) | Dallas | 214-239-1990 | www.noblerot.net

Chef-owners Jonathan Calabrese and Joseph Hickey migrated from their shuttered Savory in Lakewood to launch this New American bistro in Uptown, featuring "delicious" "cutting-edge creations" and a broad wine list boasting "all kinds and all prices"; adding to the allure are a "friendly, fun staff" and a "charming atmosphere", all of which makes many willing to overlook the fact that it's "expensive."

Steel *Japanese/Vietnamese* 25 | 23 | 21 | $50

Oak Lawn | Centrum Bldg. | 3102 Oak Lawn Ave. (Cedar Springs Rd.) | Dallas | 214-219-9908 | www.steeldallas.com

Yes, this "trendy" Oak Lawn "place to be seen" is filled with "sports figures" and "young", "beautiful people", but supporters insist its "sexy", "urban-chic decor", "fantastic wine list" and "amazing" Japanese-Vietnamese cuisine (including "creatively presented sushi") "back up the flash"; a few find it "pretentious" and "noisy", but more maintain it's "a favorite place to take out-of-towners, who are surprised to find something other than steak in Dallas."

Z Stephan Pyles S *Southwestern* 27 | 28 | 26 | $65

Arts District | 1807 Ross Ave. (St. Paul St.) | Dallas | 214-580-7000 | www.stephanpyles.com

"Father of Southwestern cuisine" Stephan Pyles "has his groove back" say fans of this "elegant but relaxed" Dallas Arts District "hot spot" where he reprises some of his "classic" menu items while also "branching out into newer territory", mixing ingredients "you never expect to mesh"; though some say it can get "way too noisy", most concur that the "great lighting and architecture" create a "beyond phenomenal" package that's "classy down to the waiter's attire", making it "worth every cent and more."

Steve Fields Steak & Lobster Lounge *Seafood/Steak* 23 | 22 | 23 | $52

Plano | 5013 W. Park Blvd. (Preston Rd.) | 972-596-7100 | www.stevefieldsrestaurant.com

Carnivores claim this western Plano beefery lives up to "everything a steak place should be" with "first-rate" filets and seafood sent out in a "smart" space hosted by namesake Steve Fields who "personally drops by your table" ensuring an "all-around" "great experience"; despite a few quibbles about "noise level", the white-tablecloth setting fits the bill for an adult night out with "premium" prices to match.

St. Martin's Wine Bistro *American/French* 26 | 24 | 25 | $39

Greenville Avenue | 3020 Greenville Ave. (Monticello Ave.) | Dallas | 214-826-0940 | www.stmartinswinebistro.com

Regulars report this "elegant" hideaway "tucked in an unassuming row of shops on Lower Greenville" "has it all" from a "delightful" French-accented American menu to a "romantic" "softly lit" mahogany-trimmed room where live "piano is a plus"; a "welcoming" team ensures a "pleasant" atmosphere, making it a "reliable" well-priced pick for "anniversary dinners" or for a "nice", leisurely brunch.

Sullivan's Steakhouse *Steak* 24 | 23 | 23 | $53

North Dallas | 17795 Dallas Pkwy. (Briargrove Ln.) | Dallas | 972-267-9393 | www.sullivansteakhouse.com

See review in Austin and the Hill Country Directory.

FOOD | DECOR | SERVICE | COST

NEW SushiSamba *Japanese* 20 | 22 | 19 | $42

Galleria | Galleria | 13270 N. Dallas Pkwy. (Alpha Rd.) | Dallas | 214-866-0214 | www.sushisamba.com

Japanese cuisine gets a South American spin at this sceney Galleria newcomer proffering "tasty", "artfully" presented fusion creations and "interesting" libations in a fabulously "modern" space that's become a "meet scene" for North Dallas denizens; servers "really know their stuff" but the place is "so lively" and loud ("I couldn't hear a thing the waitress said") that the whole "concept" strikes cynical surveyors as a bit "silly and insincere."

Sushi Zushi *Japanese* 21 | 20 | 17 | $29

Oak Lawn | Turtle Creek Shopping Ctr. | 3858 Oak Lawn Ave. (Blackburn St.) | Dallas | 214-522-7253 | www.sushizushi.com

See review in San Antonio Directory.

Suze S M *Mediterranean* 26 | 19 | 24 | $41

Preston Hollow | Villages of Preston Hollow | 4345 W. Northwest Hwy. (Midway Rd.) | Dallas | 214-350-6135

"Expertly prepared" dishes from a "frequently changing" Mediterranean menu keep crowds coming to this "upscale" "little neighborhood jewel" "hidden" in a Preston Hollow strip center; it "never fails to deliver" thanks to "quiet", "cozy digs", a "courteous" staff and "personal attention" from chef-owner Gilbert Garza.

Sweet Basil *Italian* ▽ 23 | 19 | 24 | $24

North Dallas | 17610 Midway Rd. (Trinity Mills Rd.) | Dallas | 972-733-1500 | www.sweetbasilitalian.com

A "rare find" in North Dallas, this family-friendly Italian standby differentiates itself from the nearby chains with "attentive" servers who always "remember you" and solid takes on old-school "classics" like shrimp scampi and eggplant parmigiana; a few find it "bland", but the "affordable" prices usually win them over.

Szechuan Chinese *Chinese* 20 | 14 | 19 | $18

Southwest | 4750 Bryant Irvin Rd. (I-20) | Ft. Worth | 817-346-6111

West | 5712 Locke Ave. (bet. Camp Bowie Blvd. & Horne St.) | Ft. Worth | 817-738-7300

Aficionados aver "you can't go wrong" at this Chinese staple in West Ft. Worth or its Southwest spin-off, each of which has a "long track record" for "reliable food", "consistent service" and a "quiet" setting that's "good for the soul"; modernists might fault the fare as "not cutting-edge", but traditionalists testify that it's "excellent Sichuan"; P.S. don't miss the "value-priced lunches."

Taco Diner *Mexican* 20 | 17 | 18 | $20

Preston Center | 4011 Villanova St. (Preston Center Pl.) | Dallas | 214-696-4944

West Village | 3699 McKinney Ave. (Lemmon Ave.) | Dallas | 214-521-3669

Las Colinas | 5904 N. MacArthur Blvd. (Hwy. 114) | Irving | 972-401-2691

Plano | Shops at Legacy | 7201 Bishop Rd. (Legacy Dr.) | 469-241-9945

(continued)

(continued)

Taco Diner

Southlake | Southlake Town Sq. | 432 Grand Ave. W. (Southlake Blvd.) | 682-651-6426
www.mcrowd.com

Brought to you by the M Crowd, who also own Mi Cocina and Mercury Grill, these members of an "authentic Mexico City taqueria" family bring "a citified and healthful flair" to the "pretty food" they purvey to "pretty people" within a "modern atmosphere" that's "more upscale than your typical Mexican place"; perhaps the "service could be better at times", but not to worry – "the people-watching is superb."

Taverna Pizzeria & Risotteria *Italian* 23 20 20 $30

Knox-Henderson | 3210 Armstrong Ave. (Travis St.) | Dallas | 214-520-9933

Sundance Square | Sundance Sq. | 450 Throckmorton St. (4th St.) | Ft. Worth | 817-885-7502
www.tavernabylombardi.com

"The Lombardi family really got it right" with these "hip, upscale" "favorites" focused on "fantastic Italian food" including "to-die-for risotto" and "tasty, thin-crust pizza"; the "bustling urban-style setting" and "cute, attentive waiters" make it "wonderful for meeting friends and lovers" – "the only problems are the wait" and "noise."

Z Tei Tei Robata Bar M *Japanese* 28 23 23 $48

Knox-Henderson | 2906 N. Henderson Ave. (Willis Ave.) | Dallas | 214-828-2400 | www.teiteirobata.com

"Some of the best sushi in Dallas" shout aficionados at this "noisy" Knox-Henderson Japanese (and sib of Teppo) catering to a "hip" crowd with "fantastic" fish and a "wonderful" selection of grilled dishes served by a "warm" staff; it's "often very crowded", but fans find it's "worth the wait" and the somewhat "pricey" tabs.

Z Teppo Yakitori & Sushi Bar M *Japanese* 28 22 25 $45

Greenville Avenue | 2014 Greenville Ave. (Prospect Ave.) | Dallas | 214-826-8989 | www.teppo.com

It's "like a top yakitori restaurant in Tokyo" rave devotees of this "real-deal" Japanese, a Greenville Avenue sibling of Tei Tei Robata, that dishes out "killer sushi" and "great grilled" meats by chefs who clearly show "care in the preparation" of "fresh, fresh, fresh" food; adding to the "wonderful experience", its minimally decorated space (with semi-private tatami rooms for parties) feels "swanky yet comfortable", prices are "reasonable" and the staff is "welcoming" – just "be prepared for a long wait."

Terilli's *Italian* 20 18 19 $31

Greenville Avenue | 2815 Greenville Ave. (Vickery Blvd.) | Dallas | 214-827-3993 ◐

Frisco | 4226 Preston Rd. (bet. Lebanon Rd. & Warren Pkwy.) | 214-387-4600
www.terillis.com

"Heavenly" signature "Italian nachos" stand out among the "down-to-earth Italian fare" at Jeannie Terilli's twin "standbys" in Frisco and the Greenville Avenue area; served by staffers "you can depend on", the eats are complemented by the "coldest martinis in town" and "reasonably priced" wines, while "live jazz music" ("a great bonus", if sometimes "a little loud") and breezy patios augment the "intimate" feel of the dark, candlelit interiors.

Texas de Brazil *Brazilian/Steak* 24 | 23 | 24 | $52

Uptown | 2727 Cedar Springs Rd. (bet. Carlisle & Woodrow Sts.) | Dallas | 214-720-1414
Addison | 15101 Addison Rd. (Belt Line Rd.) | 972-385-1000
Downtown Ft. Worth | 101 N. Houston St. (Weatherford St.) | Ft. Worth | 817-882-9500
www.texasdebrazil.com

Bring a "Texas-sized appetite" to these all-you-can-eat Brazilian steakhouses - a veritable "meat orgy" where an "unending" parade of "delicious" cuts are proffered by "gaucho"-clad servers and "even a vegetarian" "won't leave hungry" thanks to the "huge" salad bar stocked with "fabulous" goodies; though the less-impressed label them "gimmicky" and "overpriced", backers boast that "considering the amount you get for your money" "at least you won't leave hungry."

III Forks *Steak* 25 | 24 | 24 | $60

North Dallas | 17776 Dallas Pkwy. (bet. Frankford & Trinity Mills Rds.) | Dallas | 972-267-1776 | www.3forks.com

See review in Austin and the Hill Country Directory.

Tillman's Roadhouse S M *American* 23 | 25 | 22 | $33

Oak Cliff | 324 W. Seventh St. (Madison Ave.) | Dallas | 214-942-0988 | www.tillmansroadhouse.com

"Diners south of the Trinity" are singing praises for "roadhouse mama" Sarah Tillman's "sassy" Oak Cliff creation - a revamp of her original Tillman's Corner - that's "getting better all the time" thanks to chef Dan Landsberg's "adventurous" American comfort food and equally "daring", "over-the-top" Western-style decor fancied up with crystal chandeliers; though lauded as a "breath of fresh air" in the emerging Bishop Arts District, wallet-watchers lament it's "more expensive" than they were expecting given the "funky" setting.

NEW **Tio's Tortas** *Mexican* ∇ 19 | 13 | 16 | $11

Lemmon Avenue | 4015 Lemmon Ave. (Throckmorton St.) | Dallas | 214-526-4846 | www.tiostortas.com

"Amazing" Mexican grilled sandwiches are constructed from a variety of meats and fresh veggies at this Lemmon Avenue establishment where "a dozen different" varieties come on freshly baked bread accompanied by fries, beans and "an interesting selection of authentic agua frescas"; given such "cheap prices", no one minds much about the cafeteria-style service or rather basic decor.

Tipperary Inn *Pub Food* ∇ 18 | 22 | 19 | $17

Lakewood | 5815 Live Oak St. (Skillman St.) | Dallas | 214-821-6500 | www.tippinn.com

More a "great bar" than an eatery, this classic-looking, dark-wood Emerald Isle pub in Lakewood gets its patrons' Irish up with the help of an "international beer selection", live Celtic music, dartboards and a "lively atmosphere"; still, tasters attest that downing "a pint of Guinness" and a "heaping helping of fish 'n' chips" will make you "feel like you're no longer in Dallas."

Tom Tom Asian Grill & Sushi Bar *Pan-Asian* 20 18 16 $26

West Village | West Vill. | 3699 McKinney Ave. (Lemmon Ave.) | Dallas | 214-522-9866 | www.tomtomasiangrill.com

Devotees beat the drum for this "trendy" boîte in McKinney Avenue's "über-hip West Village" shopping center, calling its Pan-Asian provender "tasty, easy on the wallet" and fine for a "quick bite"; the modern, "minimalist-Zen" interiors are "pleasant" but alfresco fans particularly recommend "dining on the patio" (now covered) and "watching the cool crowd walk by"; disappointed dissenters dis "declining" service and "wish their food were as hot as their spot."

Toulouse Café & Bar *French* 19 20 18 $35

Knox-Henderson | 3314 Knox St. (Travis St.) | Dallas | 214-520-8999 | www.toulousecafeandbar.com

"Very Parisian" proclaim patrons of this "bustling" bistro nestled in Knox-Henderson that buzzes with "beautiful people" munching "well-prepared" French specialties (like mussels cooked five different ways) in a "noisy" space outfitted with cushy red booths and a lively streetside patio; despite some quibbles about "inconsistent" service, most diners deem it "quite enjoyable" for a leisurely brunch, an "afternoon drink" or an "easy night out."

Z NEW Trader Vic's *Polynesian* 19 26 20 $46

Park Cities | 5330 E. Mockingbird Ln. (Homer St.) | Dallas | 214-823-0600 | www.tradervicsdallas.com

"Shuttered for 20 years", this "kitschy" Polynesian paradise recently reopened in its original location adjacent to Park Cities' Hotel Palomar and was immediately embraced by nostalgic Dallasites delighting in the "overflowing rum drinks" and "glorious faux-island decor"; a few pooh-pooh the "mediocre" food (although "the pupu platter is a must"), but supporters swear they "love" this "tiki time warp" that takes you "back to the '60s", that is, at least "until you get the check."

Tramontana S M *American* 23 19 22 $47

Preston Center | Preston Center Pavilion | 8220 Westchester Dr. (bet. Luther & Sherry Lns.) | Dallas | 214-368-4188 | www.mybistro.net

A "wonderful, intimate dining experience" awaits at this "charming" "chef-owned neighborhood" bistro "tucked away" in Preston Center with a "creative menu" of New American fare featuring "refined country-style French" and Italian influences, along with a list of "well-priced wines"; its dark, casual environment is "without pretense", plus the "attentive service" makes eating here "like dining in the home of good friends."

Trece *Mexican/Southwestern* 21 21 20 $41

Knox-Henderson | 4513 Travis St. (bet. Armstrong Ave. & Knox St.) | Dallas | 214-780-1900 | www.trecerestaurant.com

It's "quite the scene" at this "chic" Knox-Henderson hangout catering to a "chichi crowd" with "innovative" Southwestern and Mexican dishes (the lobster nachos are a "favorite") and "enticing cocktails" crafted from a selection of over 100 tequilas; some diners demur on "uneven service" and "expensive" tabs, but "trendy" types tout it as a "fun" experience as long as you're prepared for the "ear-splitting" acoustics.

Truluck's *Seafood* 23 22 23 $44

Uptown | 2401 McKinney Ave. (Maple Ave.) | Dallas | 214-220-2401
Addison | 5001 Belt Line Rd. (Quorum Dr.) | 972-503-3079
NEW **Southlake** | 1420 Plaza Pl. (Grand Ave.) | 817-912-0500
www.trulucks.com

Those in need of a "stone crab fix" seek out this "popular" chain of upscale seafood specialists where the "incredible" crustaceans are "the highlight" of a "satisfying" lineup of "fresh fish", "quality steaks" and a "marvelous" collection of wines; "handsome" decor and "attentive" service add to the appeal, though a chorus of critics claim it's "not impressed" with what it dubs "mediocre" eats and an overall "formulaic" experience.

Tucker S M *American* 21 20 20 $42

Downtown Dallas | 3113 Ross Ave. (I-75) | Dallas | 214-389-1313 | www.tuckeraoc.com

"Located in an old car dealership" rich in "warm" woods, this "fun and quirky" "hidden treasure" "off the beaten path" Downtown "has an atmosphere like no other restaurant in the area"; it also has "a worldly chef" in "friendly Australian owner" Andrew Ormsby, who whips up "excellent" New American dishes, which are accompanied by wines from a global list.

2900 S M *American/Eclectic* 23 18 20 $44

Uptown | 2900 Thomas Ave. (Allen St.) | Dallas | 214-303-0400 | www.2900restaurant.com

Behind this unadorned Uptown facade lies one of the "best moderately priced" restaurants around exclaim enthusiasts who "absolutely love the manchego stuffed beef tenderloin" and other "unique, high-end" New American–Eclectic eats; with a "quaint" interior, "friendly" service and "good-value" tabs, it's "great before the symphony", with a "date" or on a casual night out.

Veracruz Café *Mexican* 24 21 21 $25

Oak Cliff | 408 N. Bishop St. (8th St.) | Dallas | 214-948-4746

"Excellent, original Mexican cuisine" "with a twist" is on the menu at this Oak Cliff spot in the Bishop Arts district, where "everything tastes homemade", including "coastal dishes that are a refreshing change" of pace; a limited number of seats makes it "perennially packed" - and leads some to sigh that it's just "too small" - but at least you get "nice, personal service from the owners."

Via Reál *Mexican* 23 | 20 | 21 | $34

Las Colinas | 4020 N. MacArthur Blvd. (Byron Nelson Way) | Irving | 972-650-9001 | www.viareal.com

It's "not just the standard Mexican cuisine" among the "novel offerings" at this "classy" cantina that's "still a favorite" after more than 20 years, as the "nice variety" on its menu also includes "wonderful Southwestern cuisine"; its "nice, tableclothed" Las Colinas setting is "relaxing and attractive", with a distinct Santa Fe vibe, and the "so-attentive" staffers ensure a "perfect work lunch or special meal."

NEW **Victory Tavern** S *American* 15 | 18 | 17 | $29

Victory Park | 3030 Olive St. (Houston St.) | Dallas | 214-432-1900 | www.victorytavern.com

"Much nicer" looking than the name suggests, this sleek, minimalist eatery in Victory Park from Patrick Colombo (Nick & Sam's, Ferre) proffers "solid", "upscale" takes on American "bar food" and pairs them with an "excellent" selection of wines by the glass; yet "save for the gorgeous decor" several sum up the experience as "disappointing" though they admit it works for "a quick bite" "before or after one of the events at the American Airlines center."

Watel's Allen Street Cottage M *French* 24 | 20 | 21 | $47

Uptown | 2207 Allen St. (bet. Hallsville & Thomas Sts.) | Dallas | 214-720-0323 | www.watels.com

Tucked into a charming cottage, this "traditional" country French "is a nice change of pace" in trendy Uptown, and the "perfect romantic date" spot; "chef-owner René Peeters knows his stuff for sure", turning out a "great variety" of "consistently delicious dishes", including "to-die-for sweetbreads" (it's "the place for offal"); some cluck that he "should learn how to do more vegetables", but factor in "nice service" and it all adds up to "real value."

Who's Who Burgers *Burgers* 18 | 9 | 13 | $14

Park Cities | Highland Park Vill. | 69 Highland Park Vill. (Preston Rd.) | Dallas | 214-522-1980 | www.whoswhoburgers.com

"Kobe beef" patties clinch it for the "well-heeled clientele" at this Highland Park Village "gourmet" burger "joint" with a plethora of "tasty" between-the-bun offerings plus sea-salt sprinkled fries and thick shakes all at "expensive" prices befitting its ritzy address; order-at-the-counter service is "fast", but with only a smattering of stools inside, many maintain it's "better for takeout."

Y.O. Ranch Steakhouse *Steak* ▽ 19 | 21 | 19 | $41

West End | 702 Ross Ave. (Market St.) | Dallas | 214-744-3287 | www.yoranchsteakhouse.com

Branded with the name of a "famous" Kerrville ranch, this "upscale" West End steakhouse is "the place to go for game" (buffalo, elk, quail), prime cuts of beef and other "creative cowboy" dishes served in a "nostalgic, chuck wagon" setting decorated with artifacts from its namesake inspiration; prices are comparable to other cow palaces making it a concierge's choice for conventiongoers and other "tourists"; N.B. patio seating was recently added.

	FOOD	DECOR	SERVICE	COST

Z York Street S M *American* — 27 | 20 | 26 | $58

Lakewood | 6047 Lewis St. (Skillman St.) | Dallas | 214-826-0968 | www.yorkstreetdallas.com

Chef-owner Sharon Hage's "artistry" makes for "world-class", "beautifully conceived and executed" New American dishes incorporating "locally fresh" ingredients at this "teeny-tiny", hard-to-find "old house" on the outskirts of Lakewood; while some find the space "sparse" and "cramped", most agree the servers are "wonderful" (even if they sometimes "concentrate on regulars") and the food offers "substantial rewards" at "fair prices" for those willing to "reserve well in advance."

Z Yutaka Sushi & Bistro *Japanese* — 27 | 19 | 22 | $45

Uptown | 2633 McKinney Ave. (Routh St.) | Dallas | 214-969-5533 | www.yutakasushibistro.com

"Locals" lament "the secret is out" at this Uptown Japanese that's "packed" with fin-addicts feasting on "outstanding sushi" and "phenomenal grilled dishes", all best appreciated via an "omakase meal" that's "to die for"; the space is "small", but "down-to-earth prices" and a "friendly" staff compensate for occasional "waits."

Zander's House *Vietnamese* — ▽ 23 | 18 | 23 | $24

Plano | 2300 N. Central Expwy. (Park Blvd.) | 972-943-9199 | www.zandershouse.com

Relocated from the Big Apple, this relative newcomer to the Plano dining scene captures a neighborhood crowd with an "interesting variety" of "well-done" Vietnamese dishes ("beautifully cooked fish", "excellent appetizers") tagged with prices that won't bust your budget; though it's set off of I-75, it cultivates a "nice atmosphere" thanks to its whitewashed setting and "friendly service" from the family owners.

Zeke's *Seafood* — ▽ 24 | 13 | 14 | $13

West | 5920 Curzon Ave. (Bryant Irvin Rd.) | Ft. Worth | 817-731-3321

Fry fetishists seek out this "hole-in-the-wall" seafooder in West Ft. Worth where the "crisp", "nongreasy" fish 'n' chips earn raves from even the pickiest Brit; prices are cheap, and order-at-the-counter and drive-thru service efficient, so even if it may not be the most "healthy" experience (though they do offer some "good" clam chowder and shrimp gumbo), converts claim you'll always leave here "happy and full"; N.B. there's also an outdoor beer garden.

Ziziki's Restaurant & Bar *Greek* — 24 | 19 | 21 | $32

Knox-Henderson | Travis Walk | 4514 Travis St. (Knox St.) | Dallas | 214-521-2233

Preston Forest | Preston Forest Vill. | 11661 Preston Rd. (Forest Ln.) | Dallas | 469-232-9922

www.zizikis.com

It's a consensus: "excellent Greek cuisine" blesses both the original Knox-Henderson location and the Preston Forest spin-off of this "always-reliable" pair whose "upbeat" environments are "great for a big group"; the "warm", "friendly staffers" provide "attentive" service, but be warned that the spaces are so "small" that "you might get to know the folks at the next table before the night's over."

Zodiac, The *American* 24 | 22 | 23 | $30

Downtown Dallas | Neiman Marcus | 1618 Main St. (bet. Akard & Ervay Sts.) | Dallas | 214-573-5800 | www.neimanmarcus.com

"A Dallas institution inside a Dallas institution", this "elegant" dining room in Downtown's Neiman Marcus department store attracts a crowd of blue bloods and "blue hairs" with a "truly great" New American menu that works for lunch, a "late afternoon meal" or a post-shopping pick-me-up; the "famous" "popovers with strawberry butter" and "consommé" alone are "reason enough to go", but "gracious service" and "people-watching" supply added enticement.

Zoë's Kitchen *American* ▽ 17 | 12 | 15 | $17

NEW **Park Cities** | Snider Plaza | 6800 Snider Plaza (Milton Ave.) | Dallas | 214-987-1020

West Lovers Lane | 5710 Lovers Ln. (Eastern Ave.) | Dallas | 214-357-0100

www.zoeskitchen.com

This bevy of "cute", "very basic" kitchens are linked to a Southeastern chain specializing in "quality" casual New American cuisine – like soups, sandwiches, salads and take-out chicken dinners – dispensed fast and with a healthy twist; "loud enough for kids" and priced for the family budget, they "hit the spot" for perpetually pressed moms.

Zoom *Thai/Vietnamese* ▽ 21 | 14 | 21 | $28

North Dallas | 4727 Frankford Rd. (Dallas N. Tollway) | Dallas | 972-713-8884 | www.zoomvietthai.com

Diners find an "extensive" array of traditional and "creative" Thai and Vietnamese dishes at this quirky strip-mall Asian set in colorful quarters in North Dallas; though only a smattering of surveyors have discovered it thus far, fair prices (including lunch specials) place it on the "favorites" list for chain-averse eaters.

DALLAS/FT. WORTH INDEXES

Cuisines

Includes restaurant names, locations and Food ratings. Z indicates places with the highest ratings, popularity and importance.

AMERICAN (NEW)

Addison Cafe | **Addison** 23
Aija | **Arts Dist** 19
Amuse | **Downtown D** 23
Angela's | **Uptown** 22
Z Aurora | **Oak Lawn** 27
Bistro Louise | **SW** 26
Bread Winners | **multi.** 22
Café Ashton | **Downtown FW** 24
Cafe Aspen | **West** 21
Café Nasher | **Arts Dist** 18
Central 214 | **Park Cities** 24
NEW Charlie Palmer | **Downtown D** –
City Café | **W Lovers Ln** –
Classic Cafe | **Roanoke** 28
NEW Club, The | **Oak Lawn** –
Craft Dallas | **Victory Pk** 25
Crú Wine Bar | **multi.** 20
NEW Dallas Fish | **Downtown D** 24
Dragonfly | **Uptown** 19
Dream Café | **multi.** 18
Z French Room | **Downtown D** 28
Go Fish | **Addison** 21
Goodhues | **McKinney** 24
Grape, The | **Greenville Ave** 25
Greenz | **multi.** 20
Hattie's | **Oak Cliff** 25
Hector's | **Knox-Henderson** 22
Z Hibiscus | **Knox-Henderson** 25
Z Jasper's | **Plano** 24
Kitchen 1924 | **Lakewood** 20
Kona Grill | **NorthPark** 20
Landmark | **Oak Lawn** 23
Z Local | **Deep Ellum** 28
Lola | **Uptown** 27
Z Mansion/Turtle Creek | **Uptown** 26
Mariposa | **Plano** 23
Z Mercury Grill | **Preston Forest** 27
Michael Anthony's | **Southlake** 26
Mirabelle | **N Dallas** 28
Z Nana | **Market Ctr** 27
Palomino | **Uptown** 21
Parigi | **Oak Lawn** 25
Rough Creek | **Glen Rose** 27
Salum | **Uptown** 25
62 Main | **Colleyville** 27
Sonoma Grill | **Flower Mound** 22
State & Allen | **Uptown** 19
Tramontana | **Preston Ctr** 23
Tucker | **Downtown D** 21
2900 | **Uptown** 23
NEW Victory Tavern | **Victory Pk** 15
Z York St. | **Lakewood** 27
Zodiac, The | **Downtown D** 24
Zoë's Kitchen | **multi.** 17

AMERICAN (TRADITIONAL)

Babe's | **multi.** 25
Billy Miner's | **Sundance Sq** 19
Buffet/Kimbell | **Cultural Dist** 24
Café on Green | **Las Colinas** 24
Catalina Room | **Lemmon Ave** 18
Celebration | **Love Field** 21
Charleston's | **SW** 18
Cheesecake Factory | **multi.** 20
Chubby's | **multi.** 18
Cindi's | **multi.** 17
Deli-News | **N Dallas** 22
8.0 | **Sundance Sq** 14
Grill/Alley | **Galleria** 21
H.P. Cafeteria | **Lake Highlands** –
H.P. Pharmacy | **Knox-Henderson** 19
Houston's | **multi.** 23
NEW Love Shack | **Stockyards** 22
Lucile's | **West** 18
Lucky's | **Oak Lawn** 20
Maguire's | **N Dallas** 23
Mama's Daughters' | **multi.** 21
Neuhaus Café | **Preston Royal** 17
NEW Olenjack's Grille | **Arlington** 26
Paris Coffee | **Hospital Dist** 23
Poor Richard's | **Plano** 20
NEW Porch, The | **Knox-Henderson** 22
Purple Cow | **multi.** 14
Red's | **Plano** 20
Sevy's | **Preston Ctr** 23
St. Martin's | **Greenville Ave** 26
Tillman's | **Oak Cliff** 23

ASIAN FUSION

Little Katana | **Knox-Henderson** 23

AUSTRIAN

Jorg's | **Plano** 25

BAKERIES

- Bread Winners | **multi.** 22
- Esperanza's | **multi.** 24
- Main St. Bistro | **multi.** 23

BARBECUE

- Angelo's | **Near W** 24
- Cousin's | **multi.** 21
- Peggy Sue BBQ | **Park Cities** 22
- Z Railhead Smokehse. | **Cultural Dist** 22
- Sammy's BBQ | **multi.** -
- Sonny Bryan's | **multi.** 22

BRAZILIAN

- Boi Na Braza | **Grapevine** 24
- Fogo de Chão | **Addison** 26
- Texas de Brazil | **multi.** 24

BURGERS

- Billy Miner's | **Sundance Sq** 19
- Kincaid's | **multi.** 23
- NEW Love Shack | **Stockyards** 22
- Red's | **Plano** 20
- Who's Who | **Park Cities** 18

CAJUN

- J&J Oyster | **Cultural Dist** 21
- Margaux's | **Market Ctr** 25
- Pappadeaux | **multi.** 23

CARIBBEAN

- Cuba Libre | **Knox-Henderson** 20

CHINESE

- Empress of China | **multi.** 19
- First Chinese BBQ | **multi.** 25
- Howard Wang's | **Preston Hollow** 20
- Masala Wok | **multi.** 18
- Z P.F. Chang's | **multi.** 22
- Szechuan Chinese | **multi.** 20

COFFEE SHOPS/DINERS

- Café Brazil | **multi.** 19
- Chubby's | **multi.** 18
- H.P. Cafeteria | **Lake Highlands** -
- Mama's Daughters' | **multi.** 21
- Original Mkt. | **Market Ctr** 20
- Poor Richard's | **Plano** 20
- Purple Cow | **multi.** 14
- Spiral Diner | **Hospital Dist** 23

CONTINENTAL

- Hôtel St. Germain | **Uptown** 25
- Old Warsaw | **Uptown** 24

CREOLE

- J&J Oyster | **Cultural Dist** 21
- Margaux's | **Market Ctr** 25

DELIS

- Bagelstein's | **Preston Royal** 15
- Carshon's | **University Area** 23
- Cindi's | **multi.** 17
- Deli-News | **N Dallas** 22
- Ed's | **Preston Forest** 23

DESSERT

- Cheesecake Factory | **multi.** 20
- La Duni | **multi.** 24
- Neuhaus Café | **Preston Royal** 17

EASTERN EUROPEAN

- Franki's | **Lake Highlands** 21

ECLECTIC

- Z Abacus | **Knox-Henderson** 28
- Café Express | **multi.** 18
- Café Lago | **Lake Highlands** -
- Z Café Modern | **Cultural Dist** 22
- Cosmic Café | **Oak Lawn** 22
- Duce | **West** 20
- Grand Lux Cafe | **Galleria** 19
- Kathleen's Sky Diner | **Park Cities** 20
- Kitchen 1924 | **Lakewood** 20
- Kozy Kitchen | **Knox-Henderson** 25
- Z Lanny's | **Cultural Dist** 27
- My Martini | **Arlington** 23
- Sambuca | **multi.** 21
- Sapristi! | **Forest Pk** 24
- Seventeen Seventeen | **Arts Dist** 22
- 2900 | **Uptown** 23

FONDUE

- Melting Pot | **Addison** 21

FRENCH

- Z Bijoux | **W Lovers Ln** 27
- Cacharel | **Arlington** 25
- Z French Room | **Downtown D** 28
- Hôtel St. Germain | **Uptown** 25
- L'Ancestral | **Knox-Henderson** 23
- Lavendou | **N Dallas** 24
- Main St. Bistro | **multi.** 23
- Z Mercy | **Addison** 19
- Mignon | **Plano** 22
- Old Warsaw | **Uptown** 24
- Z Saint-Emilion | **Cultural Dist** 27
- St. Martin's | **Greenville Ave** 26
- Toulouse | **Knox-Henderson** 19
- Watel's | **Uptown** 24

GERMAN

Bavarian Grill | **Plano** 20
Edelweiss | **West** 20
Kuby's | **Park Cities** 22

GREEK

Opa! Grille | **Preston Forest** 19
Ziziki's | **multi.** 24

HAWAIIAN

Kona Grill | **NorthPark** 20
Roy's | **Plano** 25

HEALTH FOOD

(See also Vegetarian)
Kozy Kitchen | **Knox-Henderson** 25
Zoë's Kitchen | **multi.** 17

ICE CREAM PARLORS

H.P. Pharmacy | **Knox-Henderson** 19
Purple Cow | **multi.** 14

INDIAN

Clay Pit | **Addison** 23
India Palace | **Preston Forest** 23
Madras Pavilion | **Richardson** 22
Masala Wok | **multi.** 18
Pasand Indian | **multi.** 21
Roti Grill | **multi.** 18
Saffron Hse. | **Addison** 20

IRISH

Tipperary Inn | **Lakewood** 18

ITALIAN

(N=Northern; S=Southern)
Adelmo's | **Knox-Henderson** 23
Amici | **Carrollton** 27
Andiamo | **Addison** 21
Arcodoro/Pomodoro | **Uptown** 21
Avanti | **multi.** 20
Bella Italia | **West** 24
Bice | **Uptown** 21
Brio | **Southlake** 21
Bruno's | **Irving** 22
Bugatti | **Love Field** 21
Café Cipriani | N | **Las Colinas** 21
Café Italia | S | **Love Field** 21
Campisi's | **multi.** 19
Carrabba's | **multi.** 22
NEW Club, The | **Oak Lawn** -
Coal Vines | **multi.** 24
Daniele Osteria | S | **Oak Lawn** 24
Ferrari's | **multi.** 23
Ferre | N | **multi.** 21
Grotto Rist. | **Uptown** 19
Il Sole | **Knox-Henderson** 22
NEW Isabella's | **Frisco** 21
Josephine's | **Frisco** 24
La Paesana | **Park Cities** 15
Maggiano's | **multi.** 20
Mamma Emilia's | **McKinney** 18
Mi Piaci | N | **Addison** 24
Momo's Pasta | **multi.** 19
Nicola's | N | **Plano** 24
Nonna Tata | **Hospital Dist** -
NEW Nove | **Victory Pk** 19
On Broadway | N | **SW** 19
Pastazio's | **multi.** 22
Patrizio | **multi.** 21
Penne Pomodoro | **multi.** 19
Piccolo Mondo | **Arlington** 21
PoPoLos | **Preston Royal** 20
Positano | N | **N Dallas** 22
Riccardi's | N | **Uptown** 20
Rist. La Piazza | **University Area** 26
Ruffino's | **Forest Pk** 22
Ruggeri's | N | **multi.** 20
Sardines | **Cultural Dist** 18
Sweet Basil | **N Dallas** 23
Taverna Pizzeria | **multi.** 23
Terilli's | **multi.** 20

JAPANESE

(* sushi specialist)
Awaji* | **Plano** 24
Benihana | **multi.** 20
Blue Fish* | **multi.** 23
East Wind* | **Uptown** 21
NEW Fish, The* | **W Vill** 20
Fuji Steak* | **N Dallas** 20
Japanese Palace* | **West** 26
Jinbeh* | **multi.** 21
NEW Kenichi* | **Victory Pk** 22
Little Katana* | **multi.** 23
My Martini* | **Arlington** 23
Naan* | **Plano** 22
Nakamoto | **Plano** 24
Nobu* | **Uptown** 24
Piranha* | **multi.** 25
Shinsei* | **W Lovers Ln** 25
Steel | **Oak Lawn** 25
NEW SushiSamba | **Galleria** 20
Sushi Zushi* | **Oak Lawn** 21
Z Tei Tei Robata* | **Knox-Henderson** 28
Z Teppo* | **Greenville Ave** 28
Z Yutaka | **Uptown** 27

KOREAN

Naan | **Plano** 22

KOSHER

Madras Pavilion | **Richardson** 22

LEBANESE

Byblos | **N Side** 21
Hedary's | **West** 22

MEDITERRANEAN

Avanti | **multi.** 20
Bistro Louise | **SW** 26
Canary Cafe | **Addison** 26
Hedary's | **West** 22
NEW Olea | **Plano** 23
Palomino | **Uptown** 21
Parigi | **Oak Lawn** 25
Suze | **Preston Hollow** 26

MEXICAN

Abuelo's | **multi.** 19
Z NEW ALÓ | **Knox-Henderson** 24
Avila's | **Love Field** 23
Benito's | **Hospital Dist** 18
Cadillac Bar | **W End** 18
Cantina Laredo | **multi.** 21
Cristina's | **multi.** 18
El Rancho Grande | **N Side** 20
Esperanza's | **multi.** 24
Javier's | **Knox-Henderson** 22
La Calle Doce | **multi.** 21
La Familia | **Near W** 24
Z Lanny's | **Cultural Dist** 27
La Playa Maya | **multi.** 23
Z Mi Cocina | **Galleria** 21
Monica's Aca | **Deep Ellum** 23
Nuevo Leon | **Farmers Branch** 22
Pepe & Mito's | **Deep Ellum** 22
Taco Diner | **multi.** 20
NEW Tio's Tortas | **Lemmon Ave** 19
Trece | **Knox-Henderson** 21
Veracruz | **Oak Cliff** 24
Via Reál | **Las Colinas** 23

PAN-ASIAN

Asian Mint | **Medical City** 23
East Wind | **Uptown** 21
Fuse | **Downtown D** 21
NEW Kenichi | **Victory Pk** 22
Pan Acean | **Coppell** 20
Z Pei Wei | **multi.** 19
Shinsei | **W Lovers Ln** 25
Tom Tom Asian | **W Vill** 20

PAN-LATIN

La Duni | **multi.** 24

PERUVIAN

Z NEW ALÓ | **Knox-Henderson** 24

PIZZA

Arcodoro/Pomodoro | **Uptown** 21
Campania | **multi.** 23
Campisi's | **multi.** 19
Coal Vines | **multi.** 24
Fireside Pies | **multi.** 23
I Fratelli | **Las Colinas** 22
NEW Olivella's | **Park Cities** 22
Pastazio's | **multi.** 22
Taverna Pizzeria | **multi.** 23

POLYNESIAN

Z Trader Vic's | **Park Cities** 19

PUB FOOD

NEW Blackfinn | **Addison** 13
NEW Porch, The | **Knox-Henderson** 22
Tipperary Inn | **Lakewood** 18

SALVADORAN

Gloria's | **multi.** 21

SEAFOOD

Arthur's | **Addison** 23
Z Café Pacific | **Park Cities** 26
Chamberlain's Fish | **Addison** 23
NEW Dallas Fish | **Downtown D** 24
Go Fish | **Addison** 21
J&J Oyster | **Cultural Dist** 21
Mainstream Fish | **Preston Forest** 20
McCormick/Schmick | **NorthPark** 21
Newport's | **W End** 21
Nick & Sam's | **Uptown** 25
Oceanaire | **Galleria** 24
Palm, The | **W End** 24
Pappadeaux | **multi.** 23
Remington's | **Addison** 21
S&D Oyster | **Uptown** 23
III Forks | **N Dallas** 25
Truluck's | **multi.** 23
Zeke's | **West** 24

SMALL PLATES

(See also Spanish tapas specialist)
Café Madrid | Spanish | **multi.** 21
Duce | Eclectic | **West** 20
Hola! | Spanish | **Knox-Henderson** 23
Z Mercy | French | **Addison** 19
My Martini | Eclectic | **Arlington** 23
NEW Sangria Tapas | Spanish | **Knox-Henderson** 17

SOUTHERN

- Bubba's | **Park Cities** 23
- Dixie House | **Lakewood** 18
- NEW House of Blues | **Victory Pk** 19
- NEW Rick's | **McKinney** 21

SOUTHWESTERN

- Ama Lur | **Grapevine** 23
- Z Blue Mesa | **multi.** 20
- Z Bonnell's | **SW** 27
- Cool River | **Las Colinas** 19
- Z NEW Fearing's | **Uptown** 26
- Fuse | **Downtown D** 21
- Lonesome Dove | **Stockyards** 26
- Love & War | **multi.** 16
- Michaels | **Cultural Dist** 24
- Reata | **Sundance Sq** 24
- Z Stephan Pyles | **Arts Dist** 27
- Trece | **Knox-Henderson** 21
- Via Reál | **Las Colinas** 23

SPANISH

(* tapas specialist)

- Café Madrid* | **multi.** 21
- Chic from Barcelona | **Preston Forest** 18
- Hola!* | **Knox-Henderson** 23
- NEW Sangria Tapas* | **Knox-Henderson** 17

STEAKHOUSES

- Z Al Biernat's | **Oak Lawn** 26
- Arthur's | **Addison** 23
- Benihana | **multi.** 20
- Big Buck Brew. | **Grapevine** 19
- NEW BLT Steak | **Galleria** -
- Z Bob's Steak | **multi.** 25
- Boi Na Braza | **Grapevine** 24
- Capital Grille | **Uptown** 25
- Cattlemen's | **Stockyards** 23
- Chamberlain's Steak | **Addison** 25
- Chaparral | **Downtown D** 21
- Cool River | **Las Colinas** 19
- Culpepper Steak | **Rockwall** 24
- Dakota's Steak | **Arts Dist** 22
- Z Del Frisco's | **multi.** 27
- Fogo de Chão | **Addison** 26
- H3 Ranch | **Stockyards** 20
- J.R.'s Steak | **Colleyville** 23
- Keg Steak | **multi.** 21
- Kirby's | **multi.** 24
- Lawry's | **N Dallas** 24
- Mercury Chophse. | **Sundance Sq** 26
- Morton's Steak | **Downtown D** 25
- Nick & Sam's | **Uptown** 25
- NEW N9ne | **Victory Pk** 22
- Old Hickory | **Grapevine** 21
- Palm, The | **W End** 24
- Pappas Bros. | **Love Field** 27
- NEW Park Cities Prime | **Preston Ctr** 16
- Perry's | **Uptown** 24
- NEW Rick's | **McKinney** 21
- Rick Stein's | **N Dallas** 22
- Ruth's Chris | **N Dallas** 25
- Silver Fox | **multi.** 24
- Sullivan's | **N Dallas** 24
- Texas de Brazil | **multi.** 24
- III Forks | **N Dallas** 25
- Y.O. Ranch | **W End** 19

TEX-MEX

- Café Brazil | **multi.** 19
- Chuy's | **Knox-Henderson** 21
- Hot Damn, Tamales! | **Hospital Dist** 26
- Iron Cactus | **Downtown D** 18
- Joe T. Garcia's | **N Side** 19
- Luna de Noche | **multi.** 20
- Matt's Rancho | **Lakewood** 21
- Mia's | **Lemmon Ave** 24
- Z Mi Cocina | **multi.** 21
- Primo's B&G | **Uptown** 18

THAI

- Asian Mint | **Medical City** 23
- Chow Thai | **multi.** 23
- Mango Thai | **multi.** 21
- Royal Thai | **Greenville Ave** 23
- Samui Thai | **multi.** 24
- Zoom | **N Dallas** 21

TURKISH

- Café Istanbul | **W Lovers Ln** 21

VEGETARIAN

(* vegan)

- Cosmic Café* | **Oak Lawn** 22
- Madras Pavilion | **Richardson** 22
- Spiral Diner* | **Hospital Dist** 23

VIETNAMESE

- Green Papaya | **Oak Lawn** 21
- Steel | **Oak Lawn** 25
- Zander's Hse. | **Plano** 23
- Zoom | **N Dallas** 21

Locations

Includes restaurant names, cuisines and Food ratings. **Z** indicates places with the highest ratings, popularity and importance.

Dallas

ARTS DISTRICT

Aija | *Amer.* 19
Café Nasher | *Amer.* 18
Dakota's Steak | *Steak* 22
Seventeen Seventeen | *Eclectic* 22
Z Stephan Pyles | *SW* 27

DEEP ELLUM/ DOWNTOWN/MARKET CENTER/WEST END

Amuse | *Amer.* 23
Avanti | *Italian/Med.* 20
Cadillac Bar | *Mex.* 18
Café Brazil | *Coffee/Tex-Mex* 19
Campisi's | *Pizza* 19
Chaparral | *Steak* 21
NEW Charlie Palmer | *Amer.* -
NEW Dallas Fish | *Amer./Seafood* 24
Z French Room | *Amer./French* 28
Fuse | *Pan-Asian/SW* 21
Iron Cactus | *Tex-Mex* 18
Z Local | *Amer.* 28
Mama's Daughters' | *Diner* 21
Margaux's | *Cajun/Creole* 25
Monica's Aca | *Mex.* 23
Morton's Steak | *Steak* 25
Z Nana | *Amer.* 27
Newport's | *Seafood* 21
Original Mkt. | *Diner* 20
Palm, The | *Seafood/Steak* 24
Pepe & Mito's | *Mex.* 22
Sonny Bryan's | *BBQ* 22
Tucker | *Amer.* 21
Y.O. Ranch | *Steak* 19
Zodiac, The | *Amer.* 24

GALLERIA

NEW BLT Steak | *Steak* -
Grand Lux Cafe | *Eclectic* 19
Grill/Alley | *Amer.* 21
Little Katana | *Japanese* 23
Z Mi Cocina | *Tex-Mex* 21
Oceanaire | *Seafood* 24
Sonny Bryan's 22
NEW SushiSamba | *Japanese* 20

GREENVILLE AVE./ LAKE HIGHLANDS/ LAKEWOOD

Blue Fish | *Japanese* 23
Café Brazil | *Coffee/Tex-Mex* 19
Café Lago | *Eclectic* -
Campisi's | *Pizza* 19
Cantina Laredo | *Mex.* 21
Chubby's | *Diner* 18
Dixie House | *Southern* 18
Franki's | *E Euro.* 21
Gloria's | *Salvadoran* 21
Grape, The | *Amer.* 25
H.P. Cafeteria | *Amer.* -
Kirby's | *Steak* 24
Kitchen 1924 | *Eclectic* 20
La Calle Doce | *Mex.* 21
Matt's Rancho | *Tex-Mex* 21
Z Mi Cocina | *Tex-Mex* 21
Royal Thai | *Thai* 23
St. Martin's | *Amer./French* 26
Z Teppo | *Japanese* 28
Terilli's | *Italian* 20
Tipperary Inn | *Pub* 18
Z York St. | *Amer.* 27

HIGHLAND PARK VILL./ MOCKINGBIRD STA./ PARK CITIES

Bubba's | *Southern* 23
Café Brazil | *Coffee/Tex-Mex* 19
Café Express | *Eclectic* 18
Z Café Pacific | *Seafood* 26
Central 214 | *Amer.* 24
Kathleen's Sky Diner | *Eclectic* 20
Kuby's | *German* 22
La Paesana | *Italian* 15
Mango Thai | *Thai* 21
Z Mi Cocina | *Tex-Mex* 21
NEW Olivella's | *Pizza* 22
Patrizio | *Italian* 21
Peggy Sue BBQ | *BBQ* 22
Penne Pomodoro | *Italian* 19
Z Trader Vic's | *Polynesian* 19
Who's Who | *Burgers* 18
Zoë's Kitchen | *Amer.* 17

KNOX-HENDERSON

Z Abacus | *Eclectic* 28
Adelmo's | *Italian* 23
Z NEW ALÓ | *Mex./Peruvian* 24
Café Madrid | *Spanish* 21
Chuy's | *Tex-Mex* 21
Cuba Libre | *Carib.* 20
Fireside Pies | *Pizza* 23
Hector's | *Amer.* 22

Z Hibiscus | *Amer.* 25
H.P. Pharmacy | *Amer.* 19
Hola! | *Spanish* 23
Il Sole | *Italian* 22
Javier's | *Mex.* 22
Kozy Kitchen | *Eclectic* 25
La Duni | *Pan-Latin* 24
L'Ancestral | *French* 23
Little Katana | *Asian Fusion* 23
Momo's Pasta | *Italian* 19
Z Pei Wei | *Pan-Asian* 19
NEW Porch, The | *Amer.* 22
Roti Grill | *Indian* 18
NEW Sangria Tapas | *Spanish* 17
Taverna Pizzeria | *Italian* 23
Z Tei Tei Robata | *Japanese* 28
Toulouse | *French* 19
Trece | *Mex./SW* 21
Ziziki's | *Greek* 24

LEMMON AVE./ OAK LAWN

Z Al Biernat's | *Steak* 26
Z Aurora | *Amer.* 27
Benihana | *Japanese/Steak* 20
Z Bob's Steak | *Steak* 25
Café Brazil | *Coffee/Tex-Mex* 19
Catalina Room | *Amer.* 18
NEW Club, The | *Amer./Italian* -
Cosmic Café | *Eclectic* 22
Daniele Osteria | *Italian* 24
Gloria's | *Salvadoran* 21
Green Papaya | *Viet.* 21
La Duni | *Pan-Latin* 24
Landmark | *Amer.* 23
Lucky's | *Amer.* 20
Mia's | *Tex-Mex* 24
Pappadeaux | *Seafood* 23
Parigi | *Amer./Med.* 25
Silver Fox | *Steak* 24
Steel | *Japanese/Viet.* 25
Sushi Zushi | *Japanese* 21
NEW Tio's Tortas | *Mex.* 19

LOVE FIELD AREA/ NORTHPARK/PRESTON/ WEST LOVERS LN. (SOUTH OF LBJ)

Asian Mint | *Pan-Asian/Thai* 23
Avila's | *Mex.* 23
Bagelstein's | *Deli* 15
Benihana | *Japanese/Steak* 20
Z Bijoux | *French* 27
Z Blue Mesa | *SW* 20
Bread Winners | *Amer./Bakery* 22
Bugatti | *Italian* 21
Café Express | *Eclectic* 18
Café Istanbul | *Turkish* 21
Café Italia | *Italian* 21
Campisi's | *Pizza* 19
Cantina Laredo | *Mex.* 21
Celebration | *Amer.* 21
Cheesecake Factory | *Amer.* 20
Chic from Barcelona | *Spanish* 18
Cindi's | *Deli* 17
City Café | *Amer.* -
Ed's | *Deli* 23
Fireside Pies | *Pizza* 23
Greenz | *Amer.* 20
Houston's | *Amer.* 23
India Palace | *Indian* 23
Kona Grill | *Amer.* 20
Luna de Noche | *Tex-Mex* 20
Maggiano's | *Italian* 20
Mainstream Fish | *Seafood* 20
Mama's Daughters' | *Diner* 21
McCormick/Schmick | *Seafood* 21
Z Mercury Grill | *Amer.* 27
Z Mi Cocina | *Tex-Mex* 21
Neuhaus Café | *Amer./Dessert* 17
Opa! Grille | *Greek* 19
Pappas Bros. | *Steak* 27
NEW Park Cities Prime | *Steak* 16
Z Pei Wei | *Pan-Asian* 19
Penne Pomodoro | *Italian* 19
Z P.F. Chang's | *Chinese* 22
PoPoLos | *Italian* 20
Purple Cow | *Diner* 14
Ruggeri's | *Italian* 20
Sammy's BBQ | *BBQ* -
Sevy's | *Amer.* 23
Shinsei | *Pan-Asian* 25
Sonny Bryan's | *BBQ* 22
Taco Diner | *Mex.* 20
Tramontana | *Amer.* 23
Ziziki's | *Greek* 24
Zoë's Kitchen | *Amer.* 17

MCKINNEY AVE./ QUADRANGLE/ UPTOWN/WEST VILLAGE (NORTH OF DOWNTOWN)

Angela's | *Amer.* 22
Arcodoro/Pomodoro | *Italian* 21
Avanti | *Italian/Med.* 20
Bice | *Italian* 21
Bread Winners | *Amer./Bakery* 22
Café Express | *Eclectic* 18
Campania | *Pizza* 23
Capital Grille | *Steak* 25
Coal Vines | *Italian* 24

Crú Wine Bar | *Amer.* 20
Dragonfly | *Amer.* 19
Dream Café | *Amer.* 18
East Wind | *Pan-Asian* 21
Z NEW Fearing's | *SW* 26
Ferre | *Italian* 21
NEW Fish, The | *Japanese* 20
Greenz | *Amer.* 20
Grotto Rist. | *Italian* 19
Hôtel St. Germain | *Continental/French* 25
Lola | *Amer.* 27
Z Mansion/Turtle Creek | *Amer.* 26
Z Mi Cocina | *Tex-Mex* 21
Nick & Sam's | *Seafood/Steak* 25
Nobu | *Japanese* 24
Old Warsaw | *Continental/French* 24
Palomino | *Amer./Med.* 21
Pastazio's | *Pizza* 22
Perry's | *Steak* 24
Primo's B&G | *Tex-Mex* 18
Riccardi's | *Italian* 20
Salum | *Amer.* 25
Sambuca | *Eclectic* 21
Sammy's BBQ | *BBQ* -
S&D Oyster | *Seafood* 23
State & Allen | *Amer.* 19
Taco Diner | *Mex.* 20
Texas de Brazil | *Brazilian/Steak* 24
Tom Tom Asian | *Pan-Asian* 20
Truluck's | *Seafood* 23
2900 | *Amer./Eclectic* 23
Watel's | *French* 24
Z Yutaka | *Japanese* 27

PRESTON HOLLOW

Howard Wang's | *Chinese* 20
Suze | *Med.* 26

VICTORY PARK

Craft Dallas | *Amer.* 25
NEW House of Blues | *Southern* 19
NEW Kenichi | *Pan-Asian* 22
Luna de Noche | *Tex-Mex* 20
NEW N9ne | *Steak* 22
NEW Nove | *Italian* 19
NEW Victory Tavern | *Amer.* 15

South Dallas

DUNCANVILLE

Pappadeaux | *Seafood* 23

LANCASTER

Chubby's | *Diner* 18

OAK CLIFF

Café Madrid | *Spanish* 21
Gloria's | *Salvadoran* 21
Hattie's | *Amer.* 25
La Calle Doce | *Mex.* 21
Tillman's | *Amer.* 23
Veracruz | *Mex.* 24

Outlying Dallas

ADDISON/NORTH DALLAS/RICHARDSON (NORTH OF LBJ)

Addison Cafe | *Amer.* 23
Andiamo | *Italian* 21
Arthur's | *Seafood/Steak* 23
Avanti | *Italian/Med.* 20
NEW Blackfinn | *Pub* 13
Blue Fish | *Japanese* 23
Z Blue Mesa | *SW* 20
Café Brazil | *Coffee/Tex-Mex* 19
Campisi's | *Pizza* 19
Canary Cafe | *Med.* 26
Cantina Laredo | *Mex.* 21
Carrabba's | *Italian* 22
Chamberlain's Fish | *Seafood* 23
Chamberlain's Steak | *Steak* 25
Chow Thai | *Thai* 23
Cindi's | *Deli* 17
Clay Pit | *Indian* 23
Cristina's | *Mex.* 18
Z Del Frisco's | *Steak* 27
Deli-News | *Deli* 22
Dream Café | *Amer.* 18
Ferrari's | *Italian* 23
First Chinese BBQ | *Chinese* 25
Fogo de Chão | *Brazilian/Steak* 26
Fuji Steak | *Japanese* 20
Gloria's | *Salvadoran* 21
Go Fish | *Amer./Seafood* 21
Greenz | *Amer.* 20
Houston's | *Amer.* 23
Lavendou | *French* 24
Lawry's | *Steak* 24
Madras Pavilion | *Indian* 22
Maguire's | *Amer.* 23
Main St. Bistro | *French* 23
Masala Wok | *Chinese/Indian* 18
Melting Pot | *Fondue* 21
Z Mercy | *French* 19
Mi Piaci | *Italian* 24
Mirabelle | *Amer.* 28
Momo's Pasta | *Italian* 19
Pappadeaux | *Seafood* 23
Pasand Indian | *Indian* 21

DALLAS/FT. WORTH

LOCATIONS

Pastazio's | *Pizza* 22
Pei Wei | *Pan-Asian* 19
P.F. Chang's | *Chinese* 22
Positano | *Italian* 22
Remington's | *Seafood* 21
Rick Stein's | *Steak* 22
Ruth's Chris | *Steak* 25
Saffron Hse. | *Indian* 20
Sambuca | *Eclectic* 21
Silver Fox | *Steak* 24
Sonny Bryan's | *BBQ* 22
Sullivan's | *Steak* 24
Sweet Basil | *Italian* 23
Texas de Brazil | *Brazilian/Steak* 24
III Forks | *Steak* 25
Truluck's | *Seafood* 23
Zoom | *Thai/Viet.* 21

ALLEN/MCKINNEY

Café Brazil | *Coffee/Tex-Mex* 19
Cristina's | *Mex.* 18
Goodhues | *Amer.* 24
Mamma Emilia's | *Italian* 18
Pei Wei | *Pan-Asian* 19
P.F. Chang's | *Chinese* 22
NEW Rick's | *Southern/Steak* 21
Samui Thai | *Thai* 24

CARROLLTON/ FARMERS BRANCH

Amici | *Italian* 27
Babe's | *Amer.* 25
Café Brazil | *Coffee/Tex-Mex* 19
Nuevo Leon | *Mex.* 22

FRISCO

Cantina Laredo | *Mex.* 21
Cheesecake Factory | *Amer.* 20
Cristina's | *Mex.* 18
Gloria's | *Salvadoran* 21
NEW Isabella's | *Italian* 21
Jinbeh | *Japanese* 21
Josephine's | *Italian* 24
Silver Fox | *Steak* 24
Terilli's | *Italian* 20

GARLAND/MESQUITE

Babe's | *Amer.* 25
Cristina's | *Mex.* 18
Gloria's | *Salvadoran* 21
Luna de Noche | *Tex-Mex* 20

IRVING/LAS COLINAS

Benihana | *Japanese/Steak* 20
Blue Fish | *Japanese* 23
Bruno's | *Italian* 22
Café Cipriani | *Italian* 21
Café on Green | *Amer.* 24
Cool River | *SW/Steak* 19
Empress of China | *Chinese* 19
I Fratelli | *Italian* 22
Jinbeh | *Japanese* 21
Keg Steak | *Steak* 21
Mama's Daughters' | *Diner* 21
Masala Wok | *Chinese/Indian* 18
Mi Cocina | *Tex-Mex* 21
Pasand Indian | *Indian* 21
Pei Wei | *Pan-Asian* 19
Sonny Bryan's | *BBQ* 22
Taco Diner | *Mex.* 20
Via Reál | *Mex.* 23

PLANO

Abuelo's | *Mex.* 19
Awaji | *Japanese* 24
Bavarian Grill | *German* 20
Blue Mesa | *SW* 20
Bob's Steak | *Steak* 25
Bread Winners | *Amer./Bakery* 22
Café Brazil | *Coffee/Tex-Mex* 19
Café Express | *Eclectic* 18
Campisi's | *Pizza* 19
Carrabba's | *Italian* 22
Chow Thai | *Thai* 23
Chubby's | *Diner* 18
Cristina's | *Mex.* 18
Crú Wine Bar | *Amer.* 20
Fireside Pies | *Pizza* 23
First Chinese BBQ | *Chinese* 25
Jasper's | *Amer.* 24
Jorg's | *Austrian* 25
Keg Steak | *Steak* 21
Kirby's | *Steak* 24
Love & War | *SW* 16
Luna de Noche | *Tex-Mex* 20
Maggiano's | *Italian* 20
Main St. Bistro | *French* 23
Mango Thai | *Thai* 21
Mariposa | *Amer.* 23
Masala Wok | *Chinese/Indian* 18
Mi Cocina | *Tex-Mex* 21
Mignon | *French* 22
Naan | *Japanese/Korean* 22
Nakamoto | *Japanese* 24
Nicola's | *Italian* 24
NEW Olea | *Med.* 23
Patrizio | *Italian* 21
Poor Richard's | *Amer.* 20
Purple Cow | *Diner* 14
Red's | *Amer.* 20
Roti Grill | *Indian* 18
Roy's | *Hawaiian* 25

Samui Thai | *Thai* 24
Steve Fields | *Seafood/Steak* 23
Taco Diner | *Mex.* 20
Zander's Hse. | *Viet.* 23

ROCKWALL

Carrabba's | *Italian* 22
Culpepper Steak | *Steak* 24
Gloria's | *Salvadoran* 21

SANGER

Babe's | *Amer.* 25

Ft. Worth

CULTURAL DISTRICT/ NEAR WEST/ SOUTHWEST/WEST

Angelo's | *BBQ* 24
Bella Italia | *Italian* 24
Bistro Louise | *Amer./Med.* 26
Z Bonnell's | *SW* 27
Buffet/Kimbell | *Amer.* 24
Cafe Aspen | *Amer.* 21
Z Café Modern | *Eclectic* 22
Charleston's | *Amer.* 18
Cousin's | *BBQ* 21
Duce | *Eclectic* 20
Edelweiss | *German* 20
Gloria's | *Salvadoran* 21
Hedary's | *Med.* 22
J&J Oyster | *Cajun/Creole* 21
Japanese Palace | *Japanese* 26
Keg Steak | *Steak* 21
Kincaid's | *Burgers* 23
La Familia | *Mex.* 24
Z Lanny's | *Eclectic/Mex.* 27
La Playa Maya | *Mex.* 23
Lucile's | *Amer.* 18
Michaels | *SW* 24
On Broadway | *Italian* 19
Z Pei Wei | *Pan-Asian* 19
Purple Cow | *Diner* 14
Z Railhead Smokehse. | *BBQ* 22
Z Saint-Emilion | *French* 27
Sardines | *Italian* 18
Szechuan Chinese | *Chinese* 20
Zeke's | *Seafood* 24

DOWNTOWN/ SUNDANCE SQUARE

Billy Miner's | *Burgers* 19
Café Ashton | *Amer.* 24
Cantina Laredo | *Mex.* 21
Z Del Frisco's | *Steak* 27
8.0 | *Amer.* 14
Ferre | *Italian* 21
Mercury Chophse. | *Steak* 26
Z Mi Cocina | *Tex-Mex* 21
Z P.F. Chang's | *Chinese* 22
Piranha | *Japanese* 25
Reata | *SW* 24
Taverna Pizzeria | *Italian* 23
Texas de Brazil | *Brazilian/Steak* 24

FOREST PARK/ HOSPITAL DISTRICT/ SOUTH SIDE/ UNIVERSITY AREA

Benito's | *Mex.* 18
Z Blue Mesa | *SW* 20
Carshon's | *Deli* 23
Cousin's | *BBQ* 21
Esperanza's | *Mex.* 24
Hot Damn, Tamales! | *Tex-Mex* 26
La Playa Maya | *Mex.* 23
Nonna Tata | *Italian* -
Pappadeaux | *Seafood* 23
Paris Coffee | *Amer.* 23
Rist. La Piazza | *Italian* 26
Ruffino's | *Italian* 22
Sapristi! | *Eclectic* 24
Silver Fox | *Steak* 24
Spiral Diner | *Diner/Veg.* 23

NORTH SIDE/ STOCKYARDS

Byblos | *Lebanese* 21
Cattlemen's | *Steak* 23
El Rancho Grande | *Mex.* 20
Esperanza's | *Mex.* 24
H3 Ranch | *Steak* 20
Joe T. Garcia's | *Tex-Mex* 19
La Playa Maya | *Mex.* 23
Lonesome Dove | *SW* 26
NEW Love Shack | *Amer.* 22

Denton County

FLOWER MOUND

Cristina's | *Mex.* 18
Empress of China | *Chinese* 19
Sonoma Grill | *Amer.* 22

HIGHLAND VILLAGE

Patrizio | *Italian* 21

LEWISVILLE

Abuelo's | *Mex.* 19
Cantina Laredo | *Mex.* 21
Cristina's | *Mex.* 18
Jinbeh | *Japanese* 21
Mama's Daughters' | *Diner* 21

ROANOKE

Babe's | *Amer.* 25
Classic Cafe | *Amer.* 28

TROPHY CLUB

Cristina's | *Mex.* 18

Mid-Cities

ARLINGTON

Abuelo's | *Mex.* 19
Cacharel | *French* 25
First Chinese BBQ | *Chinese* 25
My Martini | *Eclectic* 23
NEW Olenjack's Grille | *Amer.* 26
Pappadeaux | *Seafood* 23
Z Pei Wei | *Pan-Asian* 19
Z P.F. Chang's | *Chinese* 22
Piccolo Mondo | *Italian* 21
Piranha | *Japanese* 25

BEDFORD

Pappadeaux | *Seafood* 23

HURST

Abuelo's | *Mex.* 19
Carrabba's | *Italian* 22

Northeast Tarrant County

ALLIANCE

Sonny Bryan's | *BBQ* 22

COLLEYVILLE

Gloria's | *Salvadoran* 21
J.R.'s Steak | *Steak* 23
Ruggeri's | *Italian* 20
62 Main | *Amer.* 27

COPPELL

Pan Acean | *Pan-Asian* 20

GRAPEVINE

Ama Lur | *SW* 23
Big Buck Brew. | *Steak* 19
Z Bob's Steak | *Steak* 25
Boi Na Braza | *Brazilian/Steak* 24
Cantina Laredo | *Mex.* 21
Carrabba's | *Italian* 22
Cristina's | *Mex.* 18
Empress of China | *Chinese* 19
Ferrari's | *Italian* 23
Fireside Pies | *Pizza* 23
Love & War | *SW* 16
Main St. Bistro | *French* 23
Old Hickory | *Steak* 21
Z P.F. Chang's | *Chinese* 22
Ruggeri's | *Italian* 20
Silver Fox | *Steak* 24

KELLER

Cousin's | *BBQ* 21

SOUTHLAKE

Z Blue Mesa | *SW* 20
Brio | *Italian* 21
Café Express | *Eclectic* 18
Campania 23
Cheesecake Factory | *Amer.* 20
Coal Vines | *Italian* 24
Kincaid's | *Burgers* 23
Kirby's | *Steak* 24
Michael Anthony's | *Amer.* 26
Z Mi Cocina | *Tex-Mex* 21
Z Pei Wei | *Pan-Asian* 19
Taco Diner | *Mex.* 20
Truluck's | *Seafood* 23

Rural

BURLESON

Babe's | *Amer.* 25

GLEN ROSE

Rough Creek | *Amer.* 27

WEATHERFORD

La Playa Maya | *Mex.* 23

Special Features

Listings cover the best in each category and include names, locations and Food ratings. Multi-location restaurants' features may vary by branch. **Z** indicates places with the highest ratings, popularity and importance.

BREAKFAST

(See also Hotel Dining)

Bagelstein's | **Preston Royal** 15
Bread Winners | **multi.** 22
Café Brazil | **multi.** 19
Café Lago | **Lake Highlands** -
Deli-News | **N Dallas** 22
Dream Café | **multi.** 18
H.P. Pharmacy | **Knox-Henderson** 19
H3 Ranch | **Stockyards** 20
Kathleen's Sky Diner | **Park Cities** 20
Kuby's | **Park Cities** 22
La Duni | **Oak Lawn** 24
Lucky's | **Oak Lawn** 20
Main St. Bistro | **multi.** 23
Mama's Daughters' | **multi.** 21
Opa! Grille | **Preston Forest** 19
Original Mkt. | **Market Ctr** 20
Paris Coffee | **Hospital Dist** 23
Poor Richard's | **Plano** 20

BRUNCH

Bistro Louise | **SW** 26
Z Blue Mesa | **multi.** 20
Bread Winners | **multi.** 22
Café on Green | **Las Colinas** 24
Carshon's | **University Area** 23
Cheesecake Factory | **NorthPark** 20
City Café | **W Lovers Ln** -
Cool River | **Las Colinas** 19
Z NEW Fearing's | **Uptown** 26
Ferre | **W Vill** 21
Grand Lux Cafe | **Galleria** 19
Hattie's | **Oak Cliff** 25
Hedary's | **West** 22
NEW House of Blues | **Victory Pk** 19
Kuby's | **Park Cities** 22
La Calle Doce | **multi.** 21
La Duni | **multi.** 24
Landmark | **Oak Lawn** 23
Lawry's | **N Dallas** 24
Lucile's | **West** 18
Maguire's | **N Dallas** 23
Mamma Emilia's | **McKinney** 18
Z Mercury Grill | **Preston Forest** 27
Monica's Aca | **Deep Ellum** 23
Palomino | **Uptown** 21
Parigi | **Oak Lawn** 25
PoPoLos | **Preston Royal** 20
Reata | **Sundance Sq** 24
Rough Creek | **Glen Rose** 27
Saffron Hse. | **Addison** 20
Sapristi! | **Forest Pk** 24
St. Martin's | **Greenville Ave** 26
Terilli's | **multi.** 20
Texas de Brazil | **Addison** 24
Veracruz | **Oak Cliff** 24
Via Reál | **Las Colinas** 23
Watel's | **Uptown** 24
Ziziki's | **multi.** 24

BUFFET SERVED

(Check availability)

Aija | **Arts Dist** 19
Z Blue Mesa | **multi.** 20
Buffet/Kimbell | **Cultural Dist** 24
Café on Green | **Las Colinas** 24
Clay Pit | **Addison** 23
Hedary's | **West** 22
H.P. Cafeteria | **Lake Highlands** -
India Palace | **Preston Forest** 23
Iron Cactus | **Downtown D** 18
Madras Pavilion | **Richardson** 22
Mamma Emilia's | **McKinney** 18
Pasand Indian | **multi.** 21
Roti Grill | **Plano** 18
Saffron Hse. | **Addison** 20

BUSINESS DINING

Z Abacus | **Knox-Henderson** 28
Z Al Biernat's | **Oak Lawn** 26
Z Bob's Steak | **multi.** 25
Brio | **Southlake** 21
Cacharel | **Arlington** 25
Café Ashton | **Downtown FW** 24
Café on Green | **Las Colinas** 24
Z Café Pacific | **Park Cities** 26
Capital Grille | **Uptown** 25
Chamberlain's Steak | **Addison** 25
NEW Charlie Palmer | **Downtown D** -
City Café | **W Lovers Ln** -
NEW Club, The | **Oak Lawn** -
Cool River | **Las Colinas** 19
Dakota's Steak | **Arts Dist** 22

Z Del Frisco's | **multi.** 27
Z NEW Fearing's | **Uptown** 26
Grill/Alley | **Galleria** 21
Z Jasper's | **Plano** 24
NEW Kenichi | **Victory Pk** 22
Lavendou | **N Dallas** 24
Lola | **Uptown** 27
Z Mansion/Turtle Creek | **Uptown** 26
Mercury Chophse. | **Sundance Sq** 26
Z Mercury Grill | **Preston Forest** 27
Michael Anthony's | **Southlake** 26
Mi Piaci | **Addison** 24
Z Nana | **Market Ctr** 27
Nick & Sam's | **Uptown** 25
NEW N9ne | **Victory Pk** 22
Nobu | **Uptown** 24
Oceanaire | **Galleria** 24
NEW Olenjack's Grille | **Arlington** 26
Palm, The | **W End** 24
Palomino | **Uptown** 21
Pappas Bros. | **Love Field** 27
Perry's | **Uptown** 24
PoPoLos | **Preston Royal** 20
Reata | **Sundance Sq** 24
Rist. La Piazza | **University Area** 26
Z Saint-Emilion | **Cultural Dist** 27
Sevy's | **Preston Ctr** 23
Silver Fox | **multi.** 24
Sonny Bryan's | **Love Field** 22
Steel | **Oak Lawn** 25
Z Stephan Pyles | **Arts Dist** 27
Steve Fields | **Plano** 23
III Forks | **N Dallas** 25

CELEBRITY CHEFS

Z Abacus | *Kent Rathbun* | **Knox-Henderson** 28
Z Aurora | *Avner Samuel* | **Oak Lawn** 27
Z Bijoux | *Scott Gottlich* | **W Lovers Ln** 27
Bistro Louise | *Louise Lamensdorf* | **SW** 26
NEW BLT Steak | *Laurent Tourondel* | **Galleria** -
Z Bonnell's | *Jon Bonnell* | **SW** 27
NEW Charlie Palmer | *Charlie Palmer* | **Downtown D** -
Craft Dallas | *Tom Colicchio* | **Victory Pk** 25
Duce | *Tim Love* | **West** 20
Z NEW Fearing's | *Dean Fearing* | **Uptown** 26
Z Lanny's | *Lanny Lancarte* | **Cultural Dist** 27
Lonesome Dove | *Tim Love* | **Stockyards** 26
Z Mansion/Turtle Creek | *John Tesar* | **Uptown** 26
Mercury Chophse. | *Chris Ward* | **Sundance Sq** 26
Z Mercury Grill | *Chris Ward* | **Preston Forest** 27
Z Nana | *Anthony Bombaci* | **Market Ctr** 27
Nobu | *Nobu Matsuhisa* | **Uptown** 24
NEW Olenjack's Grille | *Brian Olenjack* | **Arlington** 26
Shinsei | *Casey Thompson* | **W Lovers Ln** 25
Z Stephan Pyles | *Stephan Pyles* | **Arts Dist** 27
Z York St. | *Sharon Hage* | **Lakewood** 27

CHEF'S TABLE

Z Abacus | **Knox-Henderson** 28
Daniele Osteria | **Oak Lawn** 24
Z NEW Fearing's | **Uptown** 26
Kitchen 1924 | **Lakewood** 20
Michael Anthony's | **Southlake** 26
Tramontana | **Preston Ctr** 23

CHILD-FRIENDLY

(Alternatives to the usual fast-food places; * children's menu available)

Avila's* | **Love Field** 23
Babe's* | **multi.** 25
Benihana* | **multi.** 20
Benito's* | **Hospital Dist** 18
Big Buck Brew.* | **Grapevine** 19
Z Blue Mesa* | **multi.** 20
Bread Winners* | **multi.** 22
Café Brazil* | **multi.** 19
Café Express* | **multi.** 18
Campisi's* | **Greenville Ave** 19
Celebration* | **Love Field** 21
Charleston's* | **SW** 18
Cheesecake Factory | **multi.** 20
Classic Cafe* | **Roanoke** 28
Cousin's* | **multi.** 21
Deli-News* | **N Dallas** 22
Dream Café* | **multi.** 18
Edelweiss* | **West** 20
El Rancho Grande* | **N Side** 20
Ferrari's* | **Addison** 23
Fireside Pies* | **multi.** 23
Fuji Steak* | **N Dallas** 20
Gloria's* | **multi.** 21
Hedary's | **West** 22

H.P. Cafeteria | **Lake Highlands** –
H.P. Pharmacy | **Knox-Henderson** 19
Houston's* | **multi.** 23
Howard Wang's* | **Preston Hollow** 20
H3 Ranch* | **Stockyards** 20
I Fratelli* | **Las Colinas** 22
India Palace* | **Preston Forest** 23
Japanese Palace* | **West** 26
Joe T. Garcia's* | **N Side** 19
Keg Steak* | **multi.** 21
Kincaid's | **multi.** 23
La Familia* | **Near W** 24
Lucile's* | **West** 18
Maggiano's* | **multi.** 20
Maguire's | **N Dallas** 23
Main St. Bistro* | **multi.** 23
Mama's Daughters'* | **multi.** 21
Mamma Emilia's* | **McKinney** 18
Z Mi Cocina* | **multi.** 21
Nuevo Leon* | **Farmers Branch** 22
Pasand Indian | **multi.** 21
Z Pei Wei* | **multi.** 19
Z P.F. Chang's | **multi.** 22
Purple Cow* | **multi.** 14
Z Railhead Smokehse. | **Cultural Dist** 22
Roti Grill* | **multi.** 18
Samui Thai* | **multi.** 24
Sevy's* | **Preston Ctr** 23
Sonny Bryan's* | **multi.** 22
Sonoma Grill* | **Flower Mound** 22
Sweet Basil* | **N Dallas** 23
Via Reál* | **Las Colinas** 23
Y.O. Ranch* | **W End** 19
Zeke's | **West** 24
Zoë's Kitchen* | **multi.** 17
Zoom | **N Dallas** 21

CIGARS WELCOME

Boi Na Braza | **Grapevine** 24
Chamberlain's Steak | **Addison** 25
Cool River | **Las Colinas** 19
Javier's | **Knox-Henderson** 22
Michaels | **Cultural Dist** 24
Z Railhead Smokehse. | **Cultural Dist** 22
Riccardi's | **Uptown** 20

DELIVERY/TAKEOUT

(D=delivery, T=takeout)

Abuelo's | D, T | **multi.** 19
Amici | T | **Carrollton** 27
Andiamo | T | **Addison** 21
Angelo's | T | **Near W** 24
Asian Mint | D, T | **Medical City** 23
Avila's | T | **Love Field** 23
Babe's | T | **Roanoke** 25
Bagelstein's | T | **Preston Royal** 15
Z Blue Mesa | D, T | **multi.** 20
Bread Winners | T | **multi.** 22
Byblos | T | **N Side** 21
Café Ashton | T | **Downtown FW** 24
Café Express | T | **multi.** 18
Café Lago | T | **Lake Highlands** –
Campania | D, T | **multi.** 23
Campisi's | D, T | **multi.** 19
Carshon's | D, T | **University Area** 23
Celebration | T | **Love Field** 21
Chamberlain's Fish | T | **Addison** 23
Charleston's | T | **SW** 18
Cheesecake Factory | T | **multi.** 20
Chow Thai | T | **multi.** 23
Chuy's | D | **Knox-Henderson** 21
City Café | D, T | **W Lovers Ln** –
Classic Cafe | T | **Roanoke** 28
Clay Pit | D, T | **Addison** 23
Coal Vines | D, T | **multi.** 24
Cosmic Café | T | **Oak Lawn** 22
Cousin's | T | **multi.** 21
Deli-News | D, T | **N Dallas** 22
Dixie House | T | **Lakewood** 18
Dream Café | T | **multi.** 18
East Wind | T | **Uptown** 21
8.0 | D, T | **Sundance Sq** 14
El Rancho Grande | T | **N Side** 20
Empress of China | D, T | **Las Colinas** 19
Esperanza's | T | **multi.** 24
Fireside Pies | T | **Knox-Henderson** 23
First Chinese BBQ | D | **multi.** 25
Gloria's | T | **multi.** 21
Grand Lux Cafe | T | **Galleria** 19
Green Papaya | T | **Oak Lawn** 21
Greenz | T | **multi.** 20
H.P. Cafeteria | T | **Lake Highlands** –
Howard Wang's | D, T | **Preston Hollow** 20
H3 Ranch | T | **Stockyards** 20
I Fratelli | T | **Las Colinas** 22
India Palace | T | **Preston Forest** 23
Z Jasper's | T | **Plano** 24
Jinbeh | T | **multi.** 21
Kincaid's | T | **multi.** 23
Kuby's | T | **Park Cities** 22
La Calle Doce | T | **multi.** 21
Lucky's | D, T | **Oak Lawn** 20

Maggiano's | T | **multi.** 20
Maguire's | D, T | **N Dallas** 23
Main St. Bistro | D, T | **multi.** 23
Mama's Daughters' | T | **multi.** 21
Mamma Emilia's | T | **McKinney** 18
Mariposa | D, T | **Plano** 23
Matt's Rancho | T | **Lakewood** 21
Z Mi Cocina | T | **multi.** 21
Monica's Aca | T | **Deep Ellum** 23
Nuevo Leon | T | **Farmers Branch** 22
NEW Olivella's | D | **Park Cities** 22
On Broadway | D, T | **SW** 19
Opa! Grille | D, T | **Preston Forest** 19
Original Mkt. | D, T | **Market Ctr** 20
Palomino | T | **Uptown** 21
Pan Acean | D, T | **Coppell** 20
Paris Coffee | T | **Hospital Dist** 23
Pasand Indian | T | **multi.** 21
Pastazio's | T | **multi.** 22
Z Pei Wei | T | **multi.** 19
Z P.F. Chang's | T | **multi.** 22
Purple Cow | D, T | **multi.** 14
Z Railhead Smokehse. | T | **Cultural Dist** 22
Roti Grill | D, T | **Knox-Henderson** 18
Royal Thai | D, T | **Greenville Ave** 23
Samui Thai | T | **multi.** 24
S&D Oyster | T | **Uptown** 23
Sapristi! | T | **Forest Pk** 24
Sardines | D, T | **Cultural Dist** 18
Sonny Bryan's | D, T | **multi.** 22
Sonoma Grill | T | **Flower Mound** 22
Spiral Diner | T | **Hospital Dist** 23
State & Allen | T | **Uptown** 19
Sushi Zushi | D, T | **Oak Lawn** 21
Suze | T | **Preston Hollow** 26
Szechuan Chinese | D, T | **multi.** 20
Taco Diner | T | **multi.** 20
Taverna Pizzeria | T | **Knox-Henderson** 23
NEW Tio's Tortas | D | **Lemmon Ave** 19
Via Reál | T | **Las Colinas** 23
Y.O. Ranch | T | **W End** 19
Zeke's | D, T | **West** 24
Ziziki's | T | **multi.** 24
Zoë's Kitchen | D | **multi.** 17
Zoom | T | **N Dallas** 21

DESSERT

Bistro Louise | **SW** 26
Z Bonnell's | **SW** 27
Bread Winners | **multi.** 22
Capital Grille | **Uptown** 25
Cheesecake Factory | **multi.** 20
Dream Café | **multi.** 18
Grand Lux Cafe | **Galleria** 19
Z Hibiscus | **Knox-Henderson** 25
La Duni | **multi.** 24
Main St. Bistro | **multi.** 23
Z Mansion/Turtle Creek | **Uptown** 26
Z Nana | **Market Ctr** 27
Pappas Bros. | **Love Field** 27
Z Saint-Emilion | **Cultural Dist** 27

DINING ALONE

(Other than hotels and places with counter service)

Z NEW ALÓ | **Knox-Henderson** 24
Asian Mint | **Medical City** 23
Bread Winners | **multi.** 22
Buffet/Kimbell | **Cultural Dist** 24
Cafe Aspen | **West** 21
Café Brazil | **multi.** 19
Campisi's | **multi.** 19
Chic from Barcelona | **Preston Forest** 18
City Café | **W Lovers Ln** -
Classic Cafe | **Roanoke** 28
Coal Vines | **multi.** 24
Cosmic Café | **Oak Lawn** 22
Deli-News | **N Dallas** 22
Dream Café | **multi.** 18
Ed's | **Preston Forest** 23
Ferre | **multi.** 21
Fireside Pies | **multi.** 23
First Chinese BBQ | **Richardson** 25
Gloria's | **multi.** 21
Greenz | **multi.** 20
H.P. Pharmacy | **Knox-Henderson** 19
H3 Ranch | **Stockyards** 20
I Fratelli | **Las Colinas** 22
Kincaid's | **multi.** 23
Kitchen 1924 | **Lakewood** 20
La Familia | **Near W** 24
L'Ancestral | **Knox-Henderson** 23
La Paesana | **Park Cities** 15
Lavendou | **N Dallas** 24
Little Katana | **multi.** 23
Luna de Noche | **multi.** 20
Mainstream Fish | **Preston Forest** 20
Mango Thai | **Park Cities** 21
Masala Wok | **multi.** 18
Mia's | **Lemmon Ave** 24
Neuhaus Café | **Preston Royal** 17

Nonna Tata | **Hospital Dist** –
NEW Olea | **Plano** 23
NEW Olenjack's Grille | **Arlington** 26
NEW Olivella's | **Park Cities** 22
Z Pei Wei | **multi.** 19
Penne Pomodoro | **multi.** 19
Z Railhead Smokehse. | **Cultural Dist** 22
Reata | **Sundance Sq** 24
Sonny Bryan's | **multi.** 22
Z Stephan Pyles | **Arts Dist** 27
NEW Tio's Tortas | **Lemmon Ave** 19
Tramontana | **Preston Ctr** 23
Z Yutaka | **Uptown** 27
Zander's Hse. | **Plano** 23
Zoë's Kitchen | **W Lovers Ln** 17

ENTERTAINMENT

(Call for days and times of performances)

Ama Lur | salsa | **Grapevine** 23
Arthur's | bands | **Addison** 23
Avanti | jazz/Latin | **multi.** 20
Bavarian Grill | varies | **Plano** 20
Bella Italia | guitar | **West** 24
Bread Winners | jazz | **Uptown** 22
Bruno's | piano | **Irving** 22
Buffet/Kimbell | jazz | **Cultural Dist** 24
Byblos | belly dancers | **N Side** 21
Café Ashton | piano | **Downtown FW** 24
Cafe Aspen | jazz/piano | **West** 21
Café Istanbul | belly dancers | **W Lovers Ln** 21
Café Madrid | flamenco | **Knox-Henderson** 21
Café on Green | saxophonist | **Las Colinas** 24
Celebration | jazz | **Love Field** 21
Clay Pit | varies | **Addison** 23
Cool River | varies | **Las Colinas** 19
Cosmic Café | varies | **Oak Lawn** 22
Culpepper Steak | varies | **Rockwall** 24
Z Del Frisco's | piano | **N Dallas** 27
Edelweiss | German | **West** 20
8.0 | varies | **Sundance Sq** 14
Z French Room | jazz | **Downtown D** 28
Gloria's | varies | **multi.** 21
Hector's | varies | **Knox-Henderson** 22
Joe T. Garcia's | mariachi | **N Side** 19
J.R.'s Steak | blues/jazz | **Colleyville** 23
Kirby's | jazz | **multi.** 24
Kuby's | accordion | **Park Cities** 22
La Calle Doce | varies | **multi.** 21
Maggiano's | piano/vocals | **NorthPark** 20
Maguire's | jazz | **N Dallas** 23
Main St. Bistro | varies | **Plano** 23
Z Mansion/Turtle Creek | jazz | **Uptown** 26
Monica's Aca | jazz/Latin | **Deep Ellum** 23
My Martini | jazz | **Arlington** 23
Z Nana | jazz | **Market Ctr** 27
Nick & Sam's | piano | **Uptown** 25
Old Hickory | piano | **Grapevine** 21
Old Warsaw | piano/violin | **Uptown** 24
On Broadway | varies | **SW** 19
Pappas Bros. | piano | **Love Field** 27
PoPoLos | jazz | **Preston Royal** 20
Reata | gospel | **Sundance Sq** 24
Riccardi's | vocals | **Uptown** 20
Rick Stein's | piano | **N Dallas** 22
Ruffino's | piano | **Forest Pk** 22
Sambuca | varies | **multi.** 21
Sardines | jazz | **Cultural Dist** 18
St. Martin's | piano | **Greenville Ave** 26
Sullivan's | bands/jazz | **N Dallas** 24
Terilli's | jazz | **multi.** 20
III Forks | varies | **N Dallas** 25
Tipperary Inn | Irish | **Lakewood** 18
Watel's | jazz | **Uptown** 24
Zeke's | bands | **West** 24

GAME IN SEASON

Z Abacus | **Knox-Henderson** 28
Addison Cafe | **Addison** 23
Adelmo's | **Knox-Henderson** 23
Amici | **Carrollton** 27
Arcodoro/Pomodoro | **Uptown** 21
Arthur's | **Addison** 23
Z Aurora | **Oak Lawn** 27
Bella Italia | **West** 24
Big Buck Brew. | **Grapevine** 19
Z Bijoux | **W Lovers Ln** 27
Bistro Louise | **SW** 26
Z Bonnell's | **SW** 27
Bruno's | **Irving** 22
Cacharel | **Arlington** 25
Café Madrid | **multi.** 21
Chamberlain's Steak | **Addison** 25
Classic Cafe | **Roanoke** 28
Culpepper Steak | **Rockwall** 24

Franki's | **Lake Highlands** 21
Gloria's | **multi.** 21
Grape, The | **Greenville Ave** 25
Hattie's | **Oak Cliff** 25
Hôtel St. Germain | **Uptown** 25
Il Sole | **Knox-Henderson** 22
Kuby's | **Park Cities** 22
Z Lanny's | **Cultural Dist** 27
Lonesome Dove | **Stockyards** 26
Mi Piaci | **Addison** 24
Mirabelle | **N Dallas** 28
Riccardi's | **Uptown** 20
Rough Creek | **Glen Rose** 27
Z Saint-Emilion | **Cultural Dist** 27
Sapristi! | **Forest Pk** 24
62 Main | **Colleyville** 27
State & Allen | **Uptown** 19
Watel's | **Uptown** 24
Y.O. Ranch | **W End** 19
Z York St. | **Lakewood** 27

HISTORIC PLACES

(Year opened; * building)

1885 | Rick's* | **McKinney** 21
1891 | S&D Oyster* | **Uptown** 23
1903 | Hola!* | **Knox-Henderson** 23
1906 | Hôtel St. Germain* | **Uptown** 25
1908 | Local* | **Deep Ellum** 28
1912 | French Room* | **Downtown D** 28
1912 | H.P. Pharmacy | **Knox-Henderson** 19
1920 | Goodhues* | **McKinney** 24
1920 | Hattie's* | **Oak Cliff** 25
1926 | Lucile's* | **West** 18
1926 | Paris Coffee | **Hospital Dist** 23
1929 | Carshon's | **University Area** 23
1930 | Fuse* | **Downtown D** 21
1932 | Spiral Diner* | **Hospital Dist** 23
1935 | Joe T. Garcia's | **N Side** 19
1946 | Campisi's | **multi.** 19
1946 | Kincaid's | **West** 23
1946 | Tucker* | **Downtown D** 21
1947 | Cattlemen's | **Stockyards** 23
1948 | Arthur's | **Addison** 23
1948 | Old Warsaw | **Uptown** 24
1954 | Kirby's | **Greenville Ave** 24
1957 | Zodiac, The | **Downtown D** 24
1958 | Angelo's | **Near W** 24
1958 | Mama's Daughters' | **Market Ctr** 21
1958 | Sonny Bryan's | **multi.** 22

HOTEL DINING

Adams Mark Hotel
Chaparral | **Downtown D** 21
Adolphus Hotel
Z French Room | **Downtown D** 28
Ashton Hotel
Café Ashton | **Downtown FW** 24
Crescent Ct. Hotel
Nobu | **Uptown** 24
Four Seasons Resort & Club
Café on Green | **Las Colinas** 24
Gaylord Texan Resort
Ama Lur | **Grapevine** 23
Old Hickory | **Grapevine** 21
Grand Hotel
NEW Rick's | **McKinney** 21
Hilton Anatole Hotel
Z Nana | **Market Ctr** 27
Hotel Palomar
Central 214 | **Park Cities** 24
Z Trader Vic's | **Park Cities** 19
Joule Hotel
NEW Charlie Palmer | **Downtown D** -
Mansion on Turtle Creek
Z Mansion/Turtle Creek | **Uptown** 26
Residence Inn
Ruggeri's | **Grapevine** 20
Ritz-Carlton Hotel
Z NEW Fearing's | **Uptown** 26
Rough Creek Lodge
Rough Creek | **Glen Rose** 27
St. Germain Hôtel
Hôtel St. Germain | **Uptown** 25
Warwick Melrose Hotel
Landmark | **Oak Lawn** 23
Westin Galleria Hotel
Oceanaire | **Galleria** 24
W Hotel
Craft Dallas | **Victory Pk** 25
ZaZa Hotel
Dragonfly | **Uptown** 19

JACKET REQUIRED

(* Tie also required)

Z French Room | **Downtown D** 28
Hôtel St. Germain* | **Uptown** 25
Old Warsaw | **Uptown** 24

LATE DINING

(Weekday closing hour)

Café Brazil | 12 AM | **multi.** 19
Coal Vines | varies | **Uptown** 24
Crú Wine Bar | 12 AM | **Plano** 20

Fireside Pies | 12 AM | **Knox-Henderson** 23
NEW House of Blues | 12 AM | **Victory Pk** 19
Primo's B&G | 1 AM | **Uptown** 18
State & Allen | varies | **Uptown** 19
Terilli's | 12 AM | **Greenville Ave** 20

MEET FOR A DRINK

Z NEW ALÓ | **Knox-Henderson** 24
Ama Lur | **Grapevine** 23
Amuse | **Downtown D** 23
NEW Blackfinn | **Addison** 13
NEW BLT Steak | **Galleria** -
Brio | **Southlake** 21
Z Café Pacific | **Park Cities** 26
Capital Grille | **Uptown** 25
Catalina Room | **Lemmon Ave** 18
Central 214 | **Park Cities** 24
NEW Charlie Palmer | **Downtown D** -
Chuy's | **Knox-Henderson** 21
NEW Club, The | **Oak Lawn** -
Cool River | **Las Colinas** 19
Cristina's | **multi.** 18
Crú Wine Bar | **multi.** 20
Cuba Libre | **Knox-Henderson** 20
NEW Dallas Fish | **Downtown D** 24
Z Del Frisco's | **multi.** 27
Duce | **West** 20
El Rancho Grande | **N Side** 20
Z NEW Fearing's | **Uptown** 26
Ferre | **multi.** 21
Fireside Pies | **W Lovers Ln** 23
Fuse | **Downtown D** 21
Grape, The | **Greenville Ave** 25
Grill/Alley | **Galleria** 21
Hola! | **Knox-Henderson** 23
NEW House of Blues | **Victory Pk** 19
H3 Ranch | **Stockyards** 20
Il Sole | **Knox-Henderson** 22
Iron Cactus | **Downtown D** 18
Z Jasper's | **Plano** 24
Joe T. Garcia's | **N Side** 19
Josephine's | **Frisco** 24
Keg Steak | **SW** 21
NEW Kenichi | **Victory Pk** 22
Landmark | **Oak Lawn** 23
NEW Love Shack | **Stockyards** 22
Luna de Noche | **Victory Pk** 20
Maguire's | **N Dallas** 23
Z Mansion/Turtle Creek | **Uptown** 26
Mercury Chophse. | **Sundance Sq** 26
Z Mercury Grill | **Preston Forest** 27
Z Mercy | **Addison** 19
Michael Anthony's | **Southlake** 26
Z Mi Cocina | **multi.** 21
Monica's Aca | **Deep Ellum** 23
Z Nana | **Market Ctr** 27
Nick & Sam's | **Uptown** 25
NEW N9ne | **Victory Pk** 22
NEW Nove | **Victory Pk** 19
NEW Olenjack's Grille | **Arlington** 26
Palm, The | **W End** 24
Palomino | **Uptown** 21
NEW Porch, The | **Knox-Henderson** 22
Primo's B&G | **Uptown** 18
Reata | **Sundance Sq** 24
Sambuca | **multi.** 21
NEW Sangria Tapas | **Knox-Henderson** 17
Sapristi! | **Forest Pk** 24
Sevy's | **Preston Ctr** 23
Steel | **Oak Lawn** 25
Z Stephan Pyles | **Arts Dist** 27
Sullivan's | **N Dallas** 24
NEW SushiSamba | **Galleria** 20
Tipperary Inn | **Lakewood** 18
Z Trader Vic's | **Park Cities** 19
Trece | **Knox-Henderson** 21
NEW Victory Tavern | **Victory Pk** 15

NOTEWORTHY NEWCOMERS

Z ALÓ | **Knox-Henderson** 24
Blackfinn | **Addison** 13
BLT Steak | **Galleria** -
Charlie Palmer | **Downtown D** -
Club, The | **Oak Lawn** -
Dallas Fish | **Downtown D** 24
Z Fearing's | **Uptown** 26
Fish, The | **W Vill** 20
House of Blues | **Victory Pk** 19
Isabella's | **Frisco** 21
Kenichi | **Victory Pk** 22
Love Shack | **Stockyards** 22
N9ne | **Victory Pk** 22
Nove | **Victory Pk** 19
Olea | **Plano** 23
Olenjack's Grille | **Arlington** 26
Olivella's | **Park Cities** 22
Park Cities Prime | **Preston Ctr** 16
Porch, The | **Knox-Henderson** 22
Rick's | **McKinney** 21
Sangria Tapas | **Knox-Henderson** 17

SushiSamba | **Galleria** 20
Tillman's | **Oak Cliff** 23
Tio's Tortas | **Lemmon Ave** 19
Z Trader Vic's | **Park Cities** 19
Victory Tavern | **Victory Pk** 15

OUTDOOR DINING

(G=garden; P=patio; S=sidewalk; T=terrace; W=waterside)

Abuelo's | P | **multi.** 19
Amuse | P | **Downtown D** 23
Angela's | P | **Uptown** 22
Arcodoro/Pomodoro | P | **Uptown** 21
Bavarian Grill | G | **Plano** 20
Bread Winners | G, P | **multi.** 22
Brio | T | **Southlake** 21
Bruno's | P, W | **Irving** 22
Buffet/Kimbell | G | **Cultural Dist** 24
Cafe Aspen | P | **West** 21
Café Express | G, P, S | **multi.** 18
Café Lago | P | **Lake Highlands** -
Z Café Modern | P | **Cultural Dist** 22
Celebration | P | **Love Field** 21
Chuy's | P | **Knox-Henderson** 21
Clay Pit | P | **Addison** 23
Coal Vines | P | **multi.** 24
Cosmic Café | P | **Oak Lawn** 22
Cousin's | P, S | **multi.** 21
Crú Wine Bar | P | **multi.** 20
Cuba Libre | P | **Knox-Henderson** 20
Culpepper Steak | G, T | **Rockwall** 24
Dakota's Steak | P | **Arts Dist** 22
Dragonfly | P, W | **Uptown** 19
Dream Café | P | **multi.** 18
8.0 | P | **Sundance Sq** 14
Z NEW Fearing's | P | **Uptown** 26
Ferre | P | **multi.** 21
Fireside Pies | P | **Knox-Henderson** 23
Fuse | P | **Downtown D** 21
Gloria's | P | **multi.** 21
Hola! | P | **Knox-Henderson** 23
Z Jasper's | P | **Plano** 24
Joe T. Garcia's | P | **N Side** 19
La Calle Doce | P | **multi.** 21
Lavendou | P | **N Dallas** 24
Z Mansion/Turtle Creek | T | **Uptown** 26
Mignon | W | **Plano** 22
Mi Piaci | P, W | **Addison** 24
Nonna Tata | S | **Hospital Dist** -
NEW Nove | P | **Victory Pk** 19
NEW Olea | P | **Plano** 23
Parigi | P | **Oak Lawn** 25
Patrizio | G, P | **multi.** 21
Primo's B&G | P | **Uptown** 18
Reata | P | **Sundance Sq** 24
Red's | P, W | **Plano** 20
Rough Creek | T, W | **Glen Rose** 27
Sambuca | P | **Uptown** 21
Sapristi! | P | **Forest Pk** 24
Sardines | P | **Cultural Dist** 18
State & Allen | S | **Uptown** 19
Taco Diner | P | **multi.** 20
Taverna Pizzeria | P | **Knox-Henderson** 23
Terilli's | P | **multi.** 20
Tipperary Inn | P | **Lakewood** 18
Tom Tom Asian | P | **W Vill** 20
Watel's | P | **Uptown** 24

POWER SCENES

Z Abacus | **Knox-Henderson** 28
Z Al Biernat's | **Oak Lawn** 26
Z Bijoux | **W Lovers Ln** 27
Z Bob's Steak | **multi.** 25
Z Café Pacific | **Park Cities** 26
Capital Grille | **Uptown** 25
NEW Charlie Palmer | **Downtown D** -
NEW Club, The | **Oak Lawn** -
Craft Dallas | **Victory Pk** 25
Z Del Frisco's | **multi.** 27
Z NEW Fearing's | **Uptown** 26
Z French Room | **Downtown D** 28
Z Jasper's | **Plano** 24
NEW Kenichi | **Victory Pk** 22
Z Lanny's | **Cultural Dist** 27
Lola | **Uptown** 27
Lonesome Dove | **Stockyards** 26
Z Mansion/Turtle Creek | **Uptown** 26
Z Mercury Grill | **Preston Forest** 27
Mi Piaci | **Addison** 24
Morton's Steak | **Downtown D** 25
Z Nana | **Market Ctr** 27
Nick & Sam's | **Uptown** 25
NEW N9ne | **Victory Pk** 22
Nobu | **Uptown** 24
Oceanaire | **Galleria** 24
Palm, The | **W End** 24
Pappas Bros. | **Love Field** 27
Rist. La Piazza | **University Area** 26
Z Saint-Emilion | **Cultural Dist** 27
Sammy's BBQ | **Uptown** -
Shinsei | **W Lovers Ln** 25
Silver Fox | **multi.** 24

- 62 Main | **Colleyville** 27
- Steel | **Oak Lawn** 25
- Z Stephan Pyles | **Arts Dist** 27

PRIX FIXE MENUS

(Call for prices and times)

- Z Abacus | **Knox-Henderson** 28
- Z Bijoux | **W Lovers Ln** 27
- Cacharel | **Arlington** 25
- Fogo de Chão | **Addison** 26
- Z French Room | **Downtown D** 28
- Hector's | **Knox-Henderson** 22
- Hôtel St. Germain | **Uptown** 25
- Il Sole | **Knox-Henderson** 22
- Landmark | **Oak Lawn** 23
- Lola | **Uptown** 27
- Z Mansion/Turtle Creek | **Uptown** 26
- Z Nana | **Market Ctr** 27
- Nobu | **Uptown** 24
- Old Warsaw | **Uptown** 24
- Palm, The | **W End** 24
- Z Saint-Emilion | **Cultural Dist** 27
- Tramontana | **Preston Ctr** 23

QUIET CONVERSATION

- Adelmo's | **Knox-Henderson** 23
- Z Bijoux | **W Lovers Ln** 27
- Bistro Louise | **SW** 26
- Z Bonnell's | **SW** 27
- Bugatti | **Love Field** 21
- Cacharel | **Arlington** 25
- Café Cipriani | **Las Colinas** 21
- Café on Green | **Las Colinas** 24
- Chaparral | **Downtown D** 21
- City Café | **W Lovers Ln** -
- Classic Cafe | **Roanoke** 28
- Daniele Osteria | **Oak Lawn** 24
- Z French Room | **Downtown D** 28
- Grape, The | **Greenville Ave** 25
- Hôtel St. Germain | **Uptown** 25
- Josephine's | **Frisco** 24
- L'Ancestral | **Knox-Henderson** 23
- Landmark | **Oak Lawn** 23
- Lavendou | **N Dallas** 24
- Lonesome Dove | **Stockyards** 26
- Z Mansion/Turtle Creek | **Uptown** 26
- Michael Anthony's | **Southlake** 26
- Mi Piaci | **Addison** 24
- Z Nana | **Market Ctr** 27
- Old Warsaw | **Uptown** 24
- NEW Olea | **Plano** 23
- Riccardi's | **Uptown** 20
- Rist. La Piazza | **University Area** 26
- Rough Creek | **Glen Rose** 27
- Ruffino's | **Forest Pk** 22
- Ruggeri's | **Preston Royal** 20
- Z Saint-Emilion | **Cultural Dist** 27
- Sapristi! | **Forest Pk** 24
- Seventeen Seventeen | **Arts Dist** 22
- Tramontana | **Preston Ctr** 23
- Zodiac, The | **Downtown D** 24

ROMANTIC PLACES

- Addison Cafe | **Addison** 23
- Z Aurora | **Oak Lawn** 27
- Z Bijoux | **W Lovers Ln** 27
- Cacharel | **Arlington** 25
- Café Ashton | **Downtown FW** 24
- Classic Cafe | **Roanoke** 28
- Z French Room | **Downtown D** 28
- Grape, The | **Greenville Ave** 25
- Hôtel St. Germain | **Uptown** 25
- Il Sole | **Knox-Henderson** 22
- NEW Isabella's | **Frisco** 21
- Josephine's | **Frisco** 24
- L'Ancestral | **Knox-Henderson** 23
- Z Local | **Deep Ellum** 28
- Lola | **Uptown** 27
- Lonesome Dove | **Stockyards** 26
- Z Mansion/Turtle Creek | **Uptown** 26
- Michael Anthony's | **Southlake** 26
- Mi Piaci | **Addison** 24
- Z Nana | **Market Ctr** 27
- Old Warsaw | **Uptown** 24
- Perry's | **Uptown** 24
- Riccardi's | **Uptown** 20
- Rough Creek | **Glen Rose** 27
- Ruffino's | **Forest Pk** 22
- Ruggeri's | **Preston Royal** 20
- Z Saint-Emilion | **Cultural Dist** 27
- Sapristi! | **Forest Pk** 24
- Watel's | **Uptown** 24
- Z York St. | **Lakewood** 27

SENIOR APPEAL

- Adelmo's | **Knox-Henderson** 23
- Babe's | **multi.** 25
- Bagelstein's | **Preston Royal** 15
- Bistro Louise | **SW** 26
- Bubba's | **Park Cities** 23
- Cacharel | **Arlington** 25
- Café Ashton | **Downtown FW** 24
- Z Café Modern | **Cultural Dist** 22
- Z Café Pacific | **Park Cities** 26
- Celebration | **Love Field** 21
- Chubby's | **multi.** 18
- City Café | **W Lovers Ln** -
- Deli-News | **N Dallas** 22

H.P. Cafeteria | **Lake Highlands** -
H.P. Pharmacy | **Knox-Henderson** 19
Kuby's | **Park Cities** 22
L'Ancestral | **Knox-Henderson** 23
La Paesana | **Park Cities** 15
Lawry's | **N Dallas** 24
Mainstream Fish | **Preston Forest** 20
Mama's Daughters' | **multi.** 21
Old Warsaw | **Uptown** 24
NEW Olea | **Plano** 23
Patrizio | **multi.** 21
Poor Richard's | **Plano** 20
Ruggeri's | **Preston Royal** 20
Zodiac, The | **Downtown D** 24

SINGLES SCENES

Z NEW ALÓ | **Knox-Henderson** 24
Amuse | **Downtown D** 23
NEW Blackfinn | **Addison** 13
Z Blue Mesa | **Southlake** 20
Catalina Room | **Lemmon Ave** 18
Chuy's | **Knox-Henderson** 21
Cool River | **Las Colinas** 19
Cristina's | **multi.** 18
Crú Wine Bar | **multi.** 20
Cuba Libre | **Knox-Henderson** 20
NEW Dallas Fish | **Downtown D** 24
Z Del Frisco's | **multi.** 27
Dragonfly | **Uptown** 19
Fireside Pies | **multi.** 23
Fuse | **Downtown D** 21
Gloria's | **multi.** 21
Hola! | **Knox-Henderson** 23
NEW House of Blues | **Victory Pk** 19
Il Sole | **Knox-Henderson** 22
Iron Cactus | **Downtown D** 18
NEW Kenichi | **Victory Pk** 22
Z Mercy | **Addison** 19
Z Mi Cocina | **multi.** 21
NEW Nove | **Victory Pk** 19
NEW Porch, The | **Knox-Henderson** 22
Primo's B&G | **Uptown** 18
Red's | **Plano** 20
Sambuca | **multi.** 21
NEW Sangria Tapas | **Knox-Henderson** 17
Sevy's | **Preston Ctr** 23
Steel | **Oak Lawn** 25
Sullivan's | **N Dallas** 24
NEW SushiSamba | **Galleria** 20
Z Teppo | **Greenville Ave** 28
Texas de Brazil | **Downtown FW** 24
Tom Tom Asian | **W Vill** 20
Z Trader Vic's | **Park Cities** 19
Trece | **Knox-Henderson** 21
NEW Victory Tavern | **Victory Pk** 15

SLEEPERS

(Good to excellent food, but little known)

Addison Cafe | **Addison** 23
Adelmo's | **Knox-Henderson** 23
Amici | **Carrollton** 27
Amuse | **Downtown D** 23
Arthur's | **Addison** 23
Awaji | **Plano** 24
Bella Italia | **West** 24
Campania | **multi.** 23
Canary Cafe | **Addison** 26
Classic Cafe | **Roanoke** 28
NEW Dallas Fish | **Downtown D** 24
Daniele Osteria | **Oak Lawn** 24
Ed's | **Preston Forest** 23
First Chinese BBQ | **multi.** 25
Goodhues | **McKinney** 24
Hot Damn, Tamales! | **Hospital Dist** 26
India Palace | **Preston Forest** 23
Jorg's | **Plano** 25
Josephine's | **Frisco** 24
J.R.'s Steak | **Colleyville** 23
Kozy Kitchen | **Knox-Henderson** 25
L'Ancestral | **Knox-Henderson** 23
Little Katana | **multi.** 23
Main St. Bistro | **multi.** 23
Margaux's | **Market Ctr** 25
Michael Anthony's | **Southlake** 26
Mirabelle | **N Dallas** 28
My Martini | **Arlington** 23
NEW Olea | **Plano** 23
NEW Olenjack's Grille | **Arlington** 26
Parigi | **Oak Lawn** 25
Rist. La Piazza | **University Area** 26
Rough Creek | **Glen Rose** 27
Royal Thai | **Greenville Ave** 23
Salum | **Uptown** 25
Spiral Diner | **Hospital Dist** 23
Sweet Basil | **N Dallas** 23
Tramontana | **Preston Ctr** 23
2900 | **Uptown** 23
Watel's | **Uptown** 24
Zander's Hse. | **Plano** 23

TRANSPORTING EXPERIENCES

Z Abacus | **Knox-Henderson** 28
Z Aurora | **Oak Lawn** 27

Z Café Modern | **Cultural Dist** 22
NEW Charlie Palmer | **Downtown D** -
Z French Room | **Downtown D** 28
Lola | **Uptown** 27
Z Nana | **Market Ctr** 27
Nobu | **Uptown** 24
NEW Nove | **Victory Pk** 19
Reata | **Sundance Sq** 24
Rough Creek | **Glen Rose** 27
Z Saint-Emilion | **Cultural Dist** 27
Seventeen Seventeen | **Arts Dist** 22
Z Stephan Pyles | **Arts Dist** 27
Z Trader Vic's | **Park Cities** 19

TRENDY

Z Abacus | **Knox-Henderson** 28
Z NEW ALÓ | **Knox-Henderson** 24
Amuse | **Downtown D** 23
Brio | **Southlake** 21
Central 214 | **Park Cities** 24
NEW Charlie Palmer | **Downtown D** -
NEW Club, The | **Oak Lawn** -
Craft Dallas | **Victory Pk** 25
NEW Dallas Fish | **Downtown D** 24
Z Del Frisco's | **multi.** 27
Duce | **West** 20
Z NEW Fearing's | **Uptown** 26
Fireside Pies | **multi.** 23
Fuse | **Downtown D** 21
Hattie's | **Oak Cliff** 25
Z Hibiscus | **Knox-Henderson** 25
NEW House of Blues | **Victory Pk** 19
NEW Kenichi | **Victory Pk** 22
Z Lanny's | **Cultural Dist** 27
Little Katana | **multi.** 23
NEW Love Shack | **Stockyards** 22
Z Mercy | **Addison** 19
NEW N9ne | **Victory Pk** 22
Nobu | **Uptown** 24
Nonna Tata | **Hospital Dist** -
NEW Nove | **Victory Pk** 19
NEW Olivella's | **Park Cities** 22
NEW Porch, The | **Knox-Henderson** 22
NEW Sangria Tapas | **Knox-Henderson** 17
Shinsei | **W Lovers Ln** 25
Z Stephan Pyles | **Arts Dist** 27
NEW SushiSamba | **Galleria** 20
Tillman's | **Oak Cliff** 23
Z Trader Vic's | **Park Cities** 19
Trece | **Knox-Henderson** 21
Z Yutaka | **Uptown** 27

VIEWS

Aija | **Arts Dist** 19
Amuse | **Downtown D** 23
Cacharel | **Arlington** 25
Z Café Modern | **Cultural Dist** 22
Chaparral | **Downtown D** 21
Il Sole | **Knox-Henderson** 22
Iron Cactus | **Downtown D** 18
Z Mansion/Turtle Creek | **Uptown** 26
Mia's | **Lemmon Ave** 24
Mignon | **Plano** 22
Mi Piaci | **Addison** 24
Z Nana | **Market Ctr** 27
NEW Nove | **Victory Pk** 19
Reata | **Sundance Sq** 24
Rough Creek | **Glen Rose** 27

VISITORS ON EXPENSE ACCOUNT

Z Abacus | **Knox-Henderson** 28
Z Al Biernat's | **Oak Lawn** 26
Z Aurora | **Oak Lawn** 27
Bice | **Uptown** 21
Z Bijoux | **W Lovers Ln** 27
NEW BLT Steak | **Galleria** -
Z Bob's Steak | **multi.** 25
Z Café Pacific | **Park Cities** 26
Capital Grille | **Uptown** 25
NEW Charlie Palmer | **Downtown D** -
Craft Dallas | **Victory Pk** 25
Z Del Frisco's | **multi.** 27
Z NEW Fearing's | **Uptown** 26
Z French Room | **Downtown D** 28
Grill/Alley | **Galleria** 21
Hôtel St. Germain | **Uptown** 25
NEW Kenichi | **Victory Pk** 22
Lola | **Uptown** 27
Z Mansion/Turtle Creek | **Uptown** 26
Z Mercury Grill | **Preston Forest** 27
Mi Piaci | **Addison** 24
Z Nana | **Market Ctr** 27
Nick & Sam's | **Uptown** 25
NEW N9ne | **Victory Pk** 22
Nobu | **Uptown** 24
NEW Nove | **Victory Pk** 19
Oceanaire | **Galleria** 24
Old Hickory | **Grapevine** 21
Pappas Bros. | **Love Field** 27
Perry's | **Uptown** 24
Z Saint-Emilion | **Cultural Dist** 27
Silver Fox | **multi.** 24
Steel | **Oak Lawn** 25

- Z Stephan Pyles | **Arts Dist** 27
- Texas de Brazil | **multi.** 24
- III Forks | **N Dallas** 25
- Z York St. | **Lakewood** 27

WINNING WINE LISTS

- Z Abacus | **Knox-Henderson** 28
- Adelmo's | **Knox-Henderson** 23
- Z Al Biernat's | **Oak Lawn** 26
- Arcodoro/Pomodoro | **Uptown** 21
- Z Aurora | **Oak Lawn** 27
- NEW BLT Steak | **Galleria** -
- Café on Green | **Las Colinas** 24
- Z Café Pacific | **Park Cities** 26
- Capital Grille | **Uptown** 25
- Chamberlain's Steak | **Addison** 25
- NEW Charlie Palmer | **Downtown D** -
- NEW Club, The | **Oak Lawn** -
- Craft Dallas | **Victory Pk** 25
- Crú Wine Bar | **multi.** 20
- Dakota's Steak | **Arts Dist** 22
- Z Del Frisco's | **multi.** 27
- Z NEW Fearing's | **Uptown** 26
- Ferre | **multi.** 21
- Z French Room | **Downtown D** 28
- Grape, The | **Greenville Ave** 25
- Houston's | **Addison** 23
- Il Sole | **Knox-Henderson** 22
- Josephine's | **Frisco** 24
- NEW Kenichi | **Victory Pk** 22
- Landmark | **Oak Lawn** 23
- Lawry's | **N Dallas** 24
- Lola | **Uptown** 27
- Maguire's | **N Dallas** 23
- Z Mansion/Turtle Creek | **Uptown** 26
- Z Mercury Grill | **Preston Forest** 27
- Z Mercy | **Addison** 19
- Michael Anthony's | **Southlake** 26
- Mi Piaci | **Addison** 24
- Morton's Steak | **Downtown D** 25
- My Martini | **Arlington** 23
- Z Nana | **Market Ctr** 27
- Newport's | **W End** 21
- Nick & Sam's | **Uptown** 25
- NEW N9ne | **Victory Pk** 22
- Oceanaire | **Galleria** 24
- Old Hickory | **Grapevine** 21
- Old Warsaw | **Uptown** 24
- Palm, The | **W End** 24
- Pappas Bros. | **Love Field** 27
- Perry's | **Uptown** 24
- PoPoLos | **Preston Royal** 20
- Riccardi's | **Uptown** 20
- Rough Creek | **Glen Rose** 27
- Ruth's Chris | **N Dallas** 25
- Z Saint-Emilion | **Cultural Dist** 27
- Sapristi! | **Forest Pk** 24
- Sonoma Grill | **Flower Mound** 22
- State & Allen | **Uptown** 19
- Steel | **Oak Lawn** 25
- Z Stephan Pyles | **Arts Dist** 27
- St. Martin's | **Greenville Ave** 26
- Sullivan's | **N Dallas** 24
- III Forks | **N Dallas** 25
- Truluck's | **Uptown** 23
- Z York St. | **Lakewood** 27
- Ziziki's | **multi.** 24

WORTH A TRIP

Colleyville
- 62 Main 27

Glen Rose
- Rough Creek 27

McKinney
- Goodhues 24

Oak Cliff
- Hattie's 25

Plano
- Z Jasper's 24

Roanoke
- Classic Cafe 28

Rockwall
- Culpepper Steak 24

Southlake
- Michael Anthony's 26

HOUSTON

Houston Most Popular

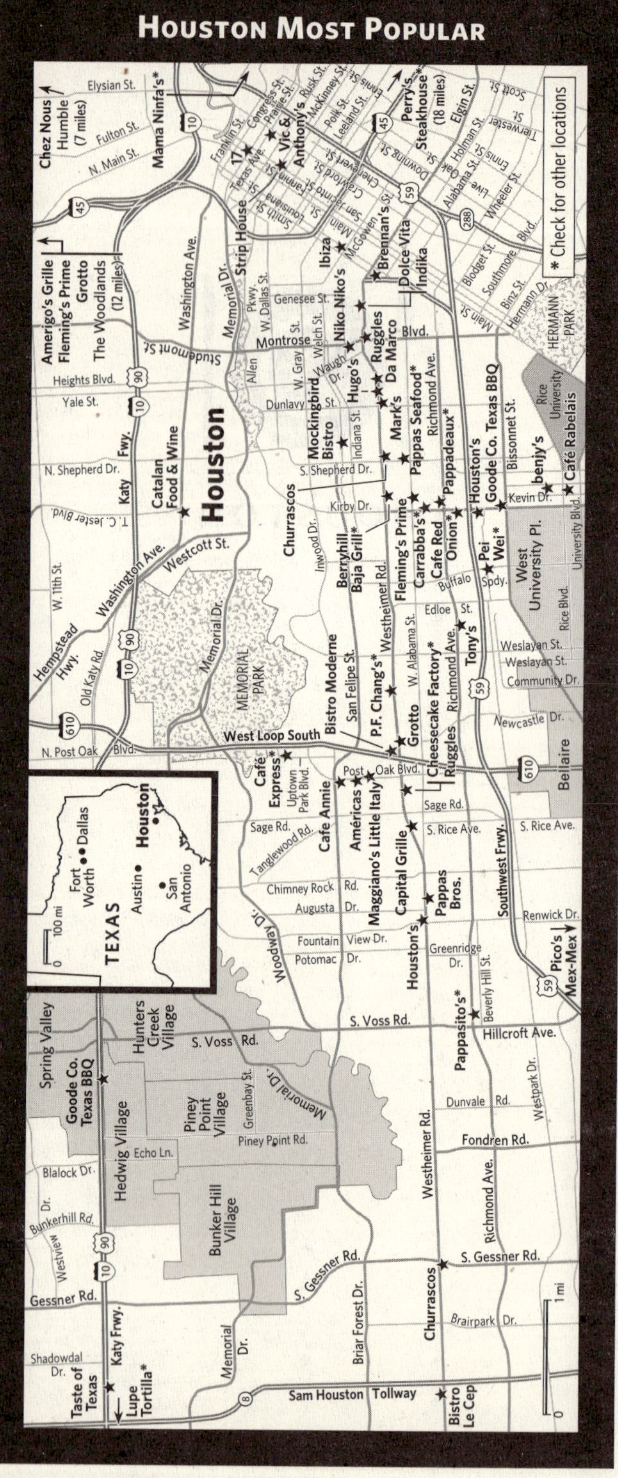

Most Popular

1. Mark's
2. Carrabba's
3. Cafe Annie
4. Perry's Steak
5. Da Marco
6. Pappasito's
7. Pappadeaux
8. Brennan's
9. Américas
10. Pappas Bros.
11. P.F. Chang's
12. Lupe Tortilla
13. Churrascos
14. Hugo's
15. Goode Co. Texas BBQ
16. Tony's
17. Fleming's
18. Ibiza
19. Cafe Red Onion
20. Cheesecake Factory
21. Grotto*
22. Vic & Anthony's
23. Capital Grille
24. Taste of Texas*
25. Café Rabelais
26. Ruggles*
27. Pappas Seafood
28. Niko Niko's
29. Mockingbird Bistro
30. Berryhill Baja Grill
31. Indika
32. Mama Ninfa's/Original Ninfa's
33. 17
34. Chez Nous
35. Dolce Vita
36. Bistro Moderne
37. Catalan*
38. Pico's
39. Café Express
40. Pei Wei*
41. Strip House*
42. Amerigo's
43. Bistro Le Cep*
44. benjy's
45. Houston's*
46. Maggiano's

It's obvious that many of the above restaurants are among the Houston area's most expensive, but if popularity were calibrated to price, we suspect that a number of other restaurants would join their ranks. Thus, we have added a list of 80 Best Buys on page 186. These are restaurants that give real quality at extremely reasonable prices.

KEY NEWCOMERS

Our editors' take on the most notable new arrivals of the past year. For a full list, see the Noteworthy Newcomers index on page 274.

Amici
Armandos
Au Petit Paris
Aura
Bob's Steak
Brasserie Max & Julie
Danton's
Del Frisco's
Grove, The
Monarch
Polo's
Reef

* Indicates a tie with restaurant above

Top Food (Based on a 30-pt. scale)

Excludes places with low votes, unless indicated by a ∇.

28 Mark's
Da Marco

27 Tony's
Kanomwan
China View
Pappas Bros.

26 Cafe Annie
Vic & Anthony's
Nielsen's Deli
Japaneiro's
Chez Nous
Brennan's
Hugo's
Lynn's Steak
Fogo de Chão
Jimmy Wilson's
Red Onion*
Café Rabelais
Le Mistral
Uptown Sushi

25 Brenner's
Churrascos
Bistro Le Cep
Indika
Kubo's
Capital Grille
Reef
Fung's Kitchen
Ruth's Chris
t'afia
Mockingbird Bistro
Remington
Ibiza
Kiran's
17
Bob's Steak
Glass Wall
Goode Co. Texas BBQ
Shade
Artista

BY CUISINE

AMERICAN (NEW)

28 Mark's
25 t'afia
Mockingbird Bistro
Remington
17

AMERICAN (TRAD.)

23 Houston's
Cleburne Cafeteria
Lankford Grocery
Breakfast Klub
22 Dessert Gallery

BARBECUE

25 Goode Co. Texas BBQ
24 Swinging Door
Pizzitola's BBQ∇
23 Luling City Mkt.
Thelma's BBQ∇

BURGERS

23 Pappas Burgers
Lankford Grocery
22 Becks Prime
Goode Co. Hamburgers
21 Bellaire Burger

CHINESE

27 China View
25 Fung's Kitchen
23 Yum Yum Cha
Daniel Wong's
Kim Son

CREOLE/CAJUN

26 Brennan's
Jimmy Wilson's
24 Tony Mandola's
Treebeards
23 Pappadeaux

ECLECTIC

21 Barnaby's Café
Hobbit Cafe
Sambuca
Raven Grill
Max's

FRENCH

26 Chez Nous
Café Rabelais
Le Mistral
25 Bistro Le Cep
24 Chez Georges

INDIAN

- 25 Indika
- Kiran's
- 24 Ashiana
- 23 Khyber North Indian
- 22 Madras Pavilion

ITALIAN

- 28 Da Marco
- 27 Tony's
- 25 Piatto
- 24 Dolce Vita
- Nino's

JAPANESE

- 26 Japaneiro's
- Uptown Sushi
- 25 Kubo's
- 23 Sushi King
- Azuma/Azumi

MEDITERRANEAN

- 25 Ibiza
- 23 Phoenicia Deli
- Café Benedicte∇
- 21 Fadi's
- 18 Dimassi's

MEXICAN

- 26 Hugo's
- 24 Pico's Mex-Mex
- 22 Irma's
- 21 Tila's
- 20 Las Alamedas

SEAFOOD

- 26 Jimmy Wilson's
- Red Onion Seafood
- 25 Reef
- Fung's Kitchen
- 24 Oceanaire

SOUTH AMERICAN

- 26 Japaneiro's
- Red Onion Seafood
- 25 Churrascos
- 24 Américas
- Café Red Onion

SOUTHERN/ SOUTHWESTERN

- 26 Brennan's
- 24 Treebeards
- 23 Cleburne Cafeteria
- Burning Pear
- Ouisie's Table

STEAKHOUSES

- 27 Pappas Bros.
- 26 Vic & Anthony's
- Lynn's Steak
- Fogo de Chão
- 25 Brenner's

TEX-MEX

- 23 Pappasito's
- 22 Mama Ninfa's/Original Ninfa's
- El Tiempo
- 21 Sylvia's
- Chuy's

THAI

- 27 Kanomwan
- 24 Thai Gourmet
- 23 Mai Thai
- 21 Nit Noi
- 18 Thai Pepper

VIETNAMESE

- 23 Mai's
- 22 Kim Son
- Miss Saigon
- 20 Mo Mong
- Vietopia

BY SPECIAL FEATURE

BREAKFAST

- 25 Remington
- 17
- 24 Pico's
- Kenny & Ziggy's
- 23 Lankford Grocery

BRUNCH

- 26 Brennan's
- Hugo's
- 25 Bistro Le Cep
- Shade
- 24 Ashiana

BUSINESS DINING

- 28 Mark's
- 27 Tony's
- Pappas Bros.
- 26 Cafe Annie
- Vic & Anthony's

CHILD-FRIENDLY

- 25 Goode Co. Texas BBQ
- 24 Swinging Door
- Taste of Texas
- Pico's
- Cafe Red Onion

HOTEL DINING

25 Remington (St. Regis)
17 (Alden Houston)
24 Hotel Icon
23 Quattro (Four Seasons)
21 Rio Ranch (Westchase Hilton)

MEET FOR A DRINK

26 Uptown Sushi
25 t'afia
Remington
Ibiza
17

NEWCOMERS (RATED)

27 Del Frisco's
25 Reef
24 Amici
20 Polo's

OFFBEAT

25 Goode Co. Texas BBQ
24 Swinging Door
23 Yum Yum Cha
Niko Niko's
Star Pizza

PEOPLE-WATCHING

28 Mark's
27 Tony's
26 Vic & Antony's
Uptown Sushi
25 t'afia

POWER SCENES

28 Mark's
27 Tony's
Pappas Bros.
26 Cafe Annie
Vic & Anthony's

QUICK BITES

24 Frenchie's
23 Kahn's Deli
Lankford Grocery
Ruggles Café Bakery
22 Becks Prime

TRENDY

28 Mark's
26 Uptown Sushi
25 Reef
t'afia
Mockingbird Bistro

WINNING WINE LISTS

28 Mark's
Da Marco
27 Tony's
Pappas Bros.
26 Cafe Annie

WORTH A TRIP

26 Chez Nous
Humble
24 Swinging Door
Richmond
Frenchie's
Clear Lake
22 Amerigo's
The Woodlands
Gaido's
Galveston

BY LOCATION

DOWNTOWN

26 Vic & Anthony's
25 17
Artista
Morton's
24 Strip House

GALLERIA

27 Pappas Bros.
26 Cafe Annie
Nielsen's Deli
25 Capital Grille
Ruth's Chris

HEIGHTS

25 Glass Wall
Shade
24 Catalan
23 Star Pizza
Rainbow Lodge

LOWER SHEPHERD

25 Churrascos
23 Star Pizza
22 divino
Mission Burritos
21 Hobbit Cafe

MEMORIAL

25 Brenner's
Goode Co. Texas BBQ
Perry's Steakhouse
24 Taste of Texas
23 Pappadeaux

MIDTOWN

26 Brennan's
25 Reef
t'afia
Ibiza
23 Charivari

MONTROSE

28 Mark's
Da Marco
26 Hugo's
25 Indika
24 Dolce Vita

RICE VILLAGE

26 Café Rabelais
25 Kubo's
23 Yum Yum Cha
Prego
Kahn's Deli

RIVER OAKS

25 Brenner's
Mockingbird Bistro
24 Fleming's
23 Tony Mandola's
Andre's

SUGAR LAND

26 Japaneiro's
25 Perry's Steak
24 Amici
23 Pappasito's
22 Carrabba's

SW HOUSTON

25 Churrascos
Fung's Kitchen
23 Rudi Lechner's
21 Rio Ranch
Ragin' Cajun

THE WOODLANDS

25 Perry's Steak
24 Jasper's
Kirby's Steak
Fleming's
23 Pappadeaux

UPPER KIRBY DISTRICT

24 Cafe Red Onion
23 Houston's
Pappadeaux
Mai Thai
Sushi King

WEST HOUSTON

27 China View
26 Lynn's Steak
Le Mistral
25 Bistro Le Cep
24 Ashiana

WEST U

25 Goode Co. Texas BBQ
24 Antica Osteria
23 Cleburne Cafeteria
Goode Co. Texas Seafood
22 Goode Co. Hamburgers

Top Decor (Based on a 30-pt. scale)

27
La Colombe d'Or
Tony's

26
17
Rainbow Lodge
Brennan's
Mark's
Café Le Jadeite

25
Hotel Icon
Artista
Américas
Jasper's
Strip House
Perry's Steak
Las Alamedas
Remington*
Vic & Anthony's
Capital Grille
Trevisio

24
Vargo's
Brenner's
Brownstone
Uptown Sushi*
Zula*
Cafe Annie
Amici
Masraff's
Pappas Bros.
Sorrento
Fleming's

23
Hugo's
Oceanaire
Sambuca
Lynn's Steak
Bice
Quattro
Crú Wine Bar
Brio
Sullivan's Steak*
Grappino di Nino
Pesce

OUTDOORS

Baba Yega
Backstreet Café
Bistro Vino
Brasil
Brennan's
Daily Review
Empire Café
Grappino di Nino
Grove, The
Hugo's

ROMANCE

Artista
Brennan's
Café Annie
Café Le Jadeite
Chez Nous
Da Marco
La Colombe d'Or
Mark's
Rainbow Lodge
Tony's

ROOMS

Arcodoro
Brennan's
Café Annie
Mark's
Masraff's
Ouisie's Table
Pappas Bros.
Quattro
Rainbow Lodge
Smith & Wollensky's

VIEWS

Artista
Brenner's
Del Friscco's
Grove, The
Las Alamedas
Monarch
Rainbow Lodge
Skyline Bar & Grill
Trevisio
Vargo's

Top Service (Based on a 30-pt. scale)

27 Tony's
Mark's

26 Brennan's
Cafe Annie
Chez Nous
Da Marco
Fogo de Chão

25 Capital Grille
Pappas Bros.
Remington, The
Ruth's Chris

24 Vic & Anthony's
Charivari
Lynn's Steak
Palm, The
Masraff's
Rudi Lechner's
La Colombe d'Or
Brenner's
Perry's Steak
Jasper's

23 Churrascos
Kirby's Steak
Sullivan's Steak
Bistro Le Cep
Jimmy Wilson's*
Michelangelo's*
Rioja Tapas*
Bob's Steak
Fleming's Prime
Morton's Steak
Mockingbird Bistro
Hotel Icon
17
Amerigo's
Taste of Texas
Quattro
Strip House
Oceanaire
Reef

Best Buys

In order of Bang for the Buck rating.

1. Bellaire Burger
2. Mission Burritos
3. Nielsen's Deli
4. 100% Taquito
5. Kahn's Deli
6. Treebeards
7. Lankford Grocery
8. Becks Prime
9. Cleburne Cafeteria
10. Chinese Café
11. Swinging Door
12. Jax Grill
13. Goode Co. Texas BBQ
14. Dessert Gallery
15. Fadi's
16. Daniel Wong's
17. China View
18. Mama's Café
19. 59 Diner
20. Leibman's
21. Sylvia's Enchilada
22. Niko Niko's
23. Avalon Drug Co.
24. Breakfast Klub
25. Buffalo Grille
26. Barnaby's
27. Masala
28. Black Walnut Café
29. Istanbul Grill
30. Empire Café
31. Pappas Burgers
32. Star Pizza
33. Berryhill Baja
34. Pei Wei
35. Van Loc
36. Chuy's
37. McGonigel's
38. Christian's Tailgate
39. Barry's Pizza
40. Phoenicia Deli

OTHER GOOD VALUES

Baba Yega
Blue Nile
Brasil
Café Artiste
Café Express
Café Malay
Dimassi's
Don Carlos
Droubi's
Empanadas by Marini
Goode Co. Hamburgers
Himalaya
Hobbit Café
Jarro Café
Jasmine
Jenni's Noodle Hse.
Kasra
Kenneally's
La Mexicana
Luling City Mkt.
Lyndon's Pit BBQ
Market Sq. B&G
Mexico's Deli
Noemi's Tacos
Otilia's
Phoenicia Deli
Pizzitola's
Saigon Pagolac
San Dong
Sawadee
Sichuan Cuisine
Spanish Flowers
Tan Tan
Taydo
Teotihuacan
Thelma's
This is It
Vieng Thai
Vietopia
Zabak's

Houston

Aka Japanese Cuisine *Japanese* ▽ 23 | 21 | 17 | $27

West Houston | 1460 Eldridge Pkwy. (bet. Forkland & Westerloch Drs.) | 281-558-8900 | www.akasushi.net

Aka Sushi House *Japanese*

Upper Kirby District | 2390 W. Alabama St. (bet. Kirby & Shepherd Drs.) | 713-807-7875

This pleasantly plush West Houston eatery is the sushi spot of choice and convenience for nearby Energy Corridor executives seeking "innovative" Japanese dishes at lunch; after dark, happy-hour specials and flat-screen TVs at the bar draw post-work revelers for fruity sake cocktails, snacks and more substantial meals; N.B. a smaller Upper Kirby District sibling opened post-Survey.

Alexander the Great *Greek* 24 | 17 | 21 | $27

Galleria | 3055 Sage Rd. (Hidalgo St.) | 713-622-2778 | www.alexanderthegreat.cc

Supporters say it's worth seeking out this "hard-to-find" Hellenic where the "tasty", "well-priced" food is served in "large portions" and sets the "gold standard" for Galleria-area Greek; traditional decor may be "underwhelming" but it gets a boost from live music and belly dancing Thursday–Saturday.

Amazon Grill *S American* 18 | 15 | 14 | $16

West U | 5114 Kirby Dr. (Bissonnet St.) | 713-522-5888

Southwest Houston | 9600 Westheimer Rd. (Tanglewilde Ave.) | 713-933-0980

www.cordua.com

Another "home run" for the Cordúa family (Churrascos, Américas), this counter-service, family-friendly Southwest Houston and West U duo is "fun for a casual meal" thanks to "inexpensive" and "unusual" South American dishes in a "carefree" environment; many deem it "one of Houston's best bargains", though a few holdouts aren't bananas about the "screaming kids and funny food."

Américas *S American* 24 | 25 | 22 | $42

Galleria | Pavilion, The | 1800 Post Oak Blvd. (bet. San Felipe St. & Westheimer Rd.) | 713-961-1492 | www.cordua.com

"Whimsical" doesn't even begin to describe the "over-the-top" decor at this Cordúa family Galleria-area "mainstay" where the "dark, cavernous" interior conjures up a "psychedelic" fantasyland that diners liken to a "full-scale production at Disney World"; "imaginative" South American cuisine is "well done" too and service "surpasses your expectations", so the "only complaint" is that the "noise level is extremely high."

Amerigo's Grille *Italian* 22 | 22 | 23 | $51

The Woodlands | Grogan's Park | 25250 Grogan's Park Dr. (Sawdust Rd.) | 281-362-0808 | www.amerigos.com

A comparative "oldie in The Woodlands" (since 1994) amid a host of "high-end" "chain" newcomers, this rustic-looking "hometown fave" is still respected for its "attractive, tasty" Italian eats and "excellent wine selections", all enhanced by "first-class service"; locals label it "lovely for special lunches or dinners" and a "nice break from the suburban sprawl"; N.B. there's also occasional live music.

NEW Amici *Italian* 24 | 24 | 23 | $38

Sugar Land | Sugar Land Town Sq. | 16089 City Walk (Plaza Dr.) | 281-242-2800 | www.amicitownsquare.com

"Excellent" Italian entrees with a Neapolitan "twist" plus "outstanding antipasto" and plenty of "traditional favorites" make the Vallone family's moderately priced Sugar Land venture "a big hit" with local "families"; though critics call it "too loud", the outdoor patio is a quieter respite where "great people-watching" is a plus.

Antica Osteria ☒ *Italian* 24 | 19 | 21 | $40

West U | 2311 Bissonnet St. (Greenbriar Dr.) | 713-521-1155 | www.anticarestaurant.com

Set in a "cozy" space that was once a rare-books shop, this rustic West U trattoria has become a best-seller among the "local power crowd" for its "authentic Italian cuisine" and "nice owners"; fans find it a "romantic fave" but critics claim it's nothing novel ("you can do better for your money in the area"); P.S. "eat early" before the "awesome specials" "get erased from the chalkboard."

Arcodoro *Italian* 20 | 20 | 19 | $44

Galleria | 5000 Westheimer Rd. (Post Oak Blvd.) | 713-621-6888 | www.arcodoro.com

"Actual Italians would approve" of the "friendly service" and "reliable" dishes (including "exotic Sardinian specialties") at this "upmarket" - read: "expensive" - ristorante near the Galleria; during the day it's a "convenient" haven for "business-lunchers" and "shopping tourists", while the "hopping" bar is popular "after work" and as a "late-night watering hole for Gen-Xers"; N.B. there's a Dallas sibling named Arcodoro & Pomodoro.

Armadillo Palace ◐ *Pub Food* ▽ 21 | 23 | 18 | $17

West U | 5015 Kirby Dr. (Bartlett St.) | 713-526-9700 | www.thearmadillopalace.com

A giant stainless-steel armadillo out front welcomes folks to this "energetic" West U eatery, an "Old West-type saloon" with "casual" Traditional American fare and "better-than-average live country music"; pleased pardners like to "hang out after work" on the patio, but if the "mayhem" gets "maddening" or the food seems "off" it's easy to mosey across the street to corporate sibling Goode Co. Texas BBQ.

NEW Armandos *Tex-Mex* 14 | 18 | 15 | $40

River Oaks | 2630 Westheimer Rd. (Kirby Dr.) | 713-520-1738 | www.armandoshouston.com

After a seven-year hiatus, "local celebrity" Armando Palacios has re-created his eponymous Tex-Mex hangout, now in River Oaks digs decked out with gilded mirrors, Hispanic art and "loud music" on the speakers; it's "popular with the social set", even if critics maintain it's "more about the 'scene' than the food", pointing to "uninspired" fare, "expensive" tabs and "mediocre service."

Z Artista ⊠ *American* — 25 | 25 | 22 | $43

Downtown | Hobby Center for the Performing Arts | 800 Bagby St. (Walker St.) | 713-278-4782 | www.cordua.com

Another Cordúa family "favorite", this "theater district" "standout" features a "creative" New American menu that allows patrons to "mix-and-match sides and sauces" adding a "fun element of experimentation" to any meal; it may be "pricey", and "service can be hit-or-miss", but the "elegant" setting on the second floor of the Hobby Center offers a "glorious view" of the Downtown skyline making it "perfect before a show" or "an excellent place to impress out-of-towners"; N.B. outdoor terrace seating is also available.

Arturo's Uptown Italiano ⊠ *Italian* — 19 | 22 | 21 | $42

Uptown | Uptown Park | 1180 Uptown Park Blvd. (San Felipe St.) | 713-621-1180 | www.arturosuptown.com

Arturo Boada's (ex Beso) "inviting" Uptowner thrives on a "lively" atmosphere thanks to an "elegant" interior done up in warm Tuscan tones and an active bar scene "for the well-heeled, over-40 set"; prices are "reasonable" considering the posh address and "parking lot dotted with Ferraris and Rolls-Royces", but a number of skeptics say they're left disappointed" by Italian cuisine that doesn't "live up to its surroundings" or its noted chef; N.B. jacket suggested.

Ashiana *Indian* — 24 | 18 | 20 | $29

West Houston | 12610 Briar Forest Dr. (Dairy Ashford Rd.) | 281-679-5555 | www.ashiana.cc

Even "dedicated Inner-Loopers" readily trek out to West Houston for the "superb variety" of "excellent" Indian eats at this "fine" establishment, where there's an "incredible lunch buffet" and staffers can "recommend the right wine" from an "impressive" list; sticklers suggest "don't show up in jeans" because atmosphere is on the "upscale" side.

NEW Au Petit Paris ⊠ *French* — - | - | - | M

Lower Shepherd | 2048 Colquitt St. (Shepherd Dr.) | 713-524-7070 | www.aupetitparisrestaurant.com

Tucked into a converted bungalow on a gentrified strip of Lower Shepherd, this midpriced French newcomer echoes Paris with a classic menu featuring foie gras made in-house and duck confit; the appropriately *petit* interior is divided into three cream-colored dining rooms and includes a charming bar area that seats five.

NEW Aura ⊠ *American* — - | - | - | M

Missouri City | 3340 FM 1092 Rd. (Highway Six) | 281-403-2872 | www.aura-restaurant.com

Frédéric Perrier (ex Ruggles Grille 5115) has resurfaced in a Missouri City strip mall with this French-influenced New American eatery that exhibits modern sensibilities both in its sleek setting and innovative menu featuring enticing dishes like bison sliders with seared foie gras; it's already drawing a loyal local following thanks to its moderate prices and eager-to-please staff.

FOOD | DECOR | SERVICE | COST

Avalon Drug Co. & Diner *American* 16 | 12 | 15 | $12

River Oaks | 2417 Westheimer Rd. (Revere St.) | 713-527-8900
Stafford | The Fountains, Stafford | 12810 Southwest Frwy. (Fountain Lake Circle) | 281-240-0213

"Generations" have "savored" the "great old drugstore food" (e.g. "hearty" American breakfasts) at this River Oaks institution, which also has a licensed namesake in Stafford; you'll "rub shoulders" with "people you read about in *Texas Monthly*" but you may also get "service with a grimace."

Azuma *Japanese* 23 | 20 | 18 | $32

Downtown | 909 Texas St. (909 Texas Ave.) | 713-223-0909
Rice Village | 5600 Kirby Dr. (Nottingham St.) | 713-432-9649

Azumi *Japanese*

Medical Center | Baylor College of Medicine | 1709 Dryden Rd. (Main St.) | 713-790-9997

Sushi-seekers say this "upmarket" threesome "really works" thanks to "fabulously fresh fish", a list of "exotic rolls" that "reads like 31 Flavors" and the "unusual" opportunity to "cook your own meat on hot rocks"; "contemporary" Asian-inflected decor and "mean martinis" attract "trendies" and "couples on dates" who'll overlook the "pricey" tabs and sometimes "slow" service; N.B. the scaled-down Azumi, in the Medical Center, is the most take-out oriented.

Baba Yega *American* 20 | 19 | 18 | $20

Montrose | 2607 Grant St. (Missouri St.) | 713-522-0042 | www.babayega.com

"Flamboyant staffers" and "Montrose characters" make for "good people-watching" at this "funky" "house-turned-restaurant" that's become a "local institution" in Houston; denizens dig into "deliciously fresh", vegetarian-friendly Traditional American fare and find "comfort" in the "cozy" setting that "looks like your great-aunt's living room"; bonus: a patio overlooking lush, "tranquil" gardens.

Backstreet Café *American* 22 | 20 | 21 | $37

River Oaks | 1103 S. Shepherd Dr. (Clay St.) | 713-521-2239 | www.backstreetcafe.net

Loyalists "love everything about" this River Oaks "neighborhood bistro" from the "well-prepared" New American cuisine with a Southern "kick" to the "lovely", "shaded" patio where you can enjoy a "romantic dinner" attended by a "knowledgeable" staff; though it's generally quiet ("you can actually have a conversation here"), "brunch is prime time" with live jazz music bringing in a "more festive crowd."

Barnaby's Café *American/Eclectic* 21 | 16 | 20 | $16

Midtown | 414 W. Gray St. (bet. Stanford & Taft Sts.) | 713-522-8898
Montrose | 604 Fairview St. (Hopkins St.) | 713-522-0106
River Oaks | 1701 S. Shepherd Dr. (Haddon St.) | 713-520-5131

(continued)

Baby Barnaby's *American/Eclectic*

Montrose | 602 Fairview St. (Hopkins St.) | 713-522-4229
www.barnabyscafe.com

"Salads bigger than most gardens" and "excellent meatloaf" are among the "hearty" Eclectic-Traditional American eats served at this "colorful", canine-themed local chain ("too nice to be called a dive, but just as comfortable"); best friends say "super prices" make it a "no-brainer" for "fun" family meals, even if, like dogs, the service is "friendly" yet "spotty"; N.B. Baby Barnaby's in Montrose serves only breakfast; its big brother next door handles lunch and dinner.

Barry's Pizza *Pizza* 20 | 12 | 17 | $15

Southwest Houston | 6003 Richmond Ave. (Fountain View Dr.) | 713-266-8692

Stafford | The Fountains, Stafford | 11303 Fountain Lake Dr. (Fountain Lake Circle) | 281-494-0666
www.barryspizza.com

This duet of extremely casual, "user-friendly" parlors in Southwest Houston and Stafford is best known for its "good" pizza, including a thick-crusted Sicilian pie that some say is the "best deep-dish" in the area; with cheap prices and TVs on-site, these are also "terrific places to watch sports."

NEW Beaver's M *BBQ* - | - | - | M

Heights | 2310 Decatur St. (Washington Ave.) | 713-864-2328 | www.beavershouston.com

Monica Pope (t'afia) takes on Texas BBQ at her casual new joint near the Heights offering a wide-ranging menu featuring smoked brisket and shredded pork shoulder alongside more unusual selections like quail stuffed with jalapeño-cream cheese and bison meatloaf; with unusual cocktails and 65 varieties of beer, the modern roadhouse setting plays host to a busy bar scene as well.

Becks Prime *Burgers* 22 | 13 | 17 | $13

Briargrove | 2615 Augusta Dr. (Westheimer Rd.) | 713-266-9901

Downtown | 919 Milam St. (Walker St.) | 713-659-6122 ☒

Memorial | Memorial Park Golf Course Clubhouse | 1001 E. Memorial Loop (Westcott St.) | 713-863-8188

Upper Kirby District | 2902 Kirby Dr. (Kipling St.) | 713-524-7085

West Houston | 11000 Westheimer Rd. (Wilcrest Dr.) | 713-952-2325

West Houston | 1202 Dairy Ashford St. (Katy Frwy.) | 281-493-3806

Sugar Land | 1822 Hwy. 6 S. (Southwest Frwy.) | 281-242-6300

The Woodlands | Grogan's Mill Village Ctr. | 2120 Buckthorne Pl. (Grogans Mill Rd.) | 281-367-3600
www.becksprime.com

Patty people "can't drive by" any of this local chain's locations "without salivating" for "the best burgers, bar none" ("juicy, flavorful and perfectly cooked"), "real" fries and "heavenly", "thick" milkshakes; interiors are "zero"-frills but outdoor seating draws kudos, especially Augusta's "giant oak tree" and Memorial Park's "lovely golf-course views"; wallet-watchers warn it's "pricey for fast food."

Bellaire Broiler Burger ⊠ *Burgers* 21 | 6 | 16 | $9

Bellaire | 5216 Bellaire Blvd. (Bissonnet St.) | 713-668-8171 | www.houstonbizdir.com/bbb/

This "Bellaire institution" has been "pumping out" "flavorful and juicy" flame-broiled burgers for the past half-century; sure, it's "a dive" with "decor that time warps to the '50s" and service that's sometimes "unpleasant", but it remains a "favorite" among "locals" who rank it as the No. 1 Best Buy in the Houston area.

Benihana *Japanese/Steak* 20 | 18 | 21 | $32

Downtown | 1318 Louisiana St. (bet. Cray & Polk Sts.) | 713-659-8231

Southwest Houston | 9707 Westheimer Rd. (Gessner Rd.) | 713-789-4962

The Woodlands | Pinecroft Town Ctr. | 1720 Lake Woodlands Dr. (Six Pines Dr.) | 281-292-0061

www.benihana.com

See review in Dallas/Ft. Worth Directory.

benjy's *American* 23 | 19 | 21 | $32

Rice Village | 2424 Dunstan St. (Kelvin Dr.) | 713-522-7602 | www.benjys.com

A "stark"-looking space in Rice Village, this New American retains its "devoted following" with a "classy" menu of "creative", "tasty" multinational munchies (including a "terrific" weekend brunch) and a "cool lounge" upstairs; still, some say the eats are "overshadowed" by the "see-and-be-seen" scene ("the better you look, the better time you'll have") and that servers, though "knowledgeable" and "cheerful", can be "detached."

Berryhill Baja Grill *Mexican* 19 | 15 | 15 | $15

West U | 5110 Buffalo Spdwy. (Westpark Dr.) | 713-667-8226

Champions | Champions Forest | 5482 FM 1960 W. (Champions Vill.) | 281-444-8844

Galleria | 1717 Post Oak Blvd. (San Felipe St.) | 713-871-8226

Heights | 702 E. 11th St. (Beverly St.) | 713-225-2252

Montrose | Hawthorne Sq. | 3407 Montrose Blvd. (Hawthorne St.) | 713-523-8226

River Oaks | 2639 Revere St. (Westheimer Rd.) | 713-526-8080

Royal Oaks | Royal Oaks Plaza | 11660 Westheimer Rd. (bet. Hayes Rd. & Kirkwood Dr.) | 281-759-2242

Kingwood | 716 Kingwood Dr. (Chestnut Ridge Dr.) | 281-359-8226

Sugar Land | 13703 Southwest Frwy. (Sugar Creek Blvd.) | 281-313-8226

The Woodlands | Market St. | 9595 Six Pines Dr. (Lake Woodlands Dr.) | 281-298-8226

www.berryhillbajagrill.com

Additional locations throughout the Houston area

"Phenomenal fish tacos" are the main draw at this "popular" local chain offering "tasty" Mexican eats, "casual" digs and "quick" order-at-the-counter service; insiders insist that "some locations" – like "the original on Revere" – are better than others, but all "still get packed", especially at "happy hour."

Bibas Greek Pizza *Greek/Pizza* ▽ 18 | 7 | 19 | $17

Heights | 5526 Memorial Dr. (bet. Shepherd Dr. & Westcott St.) | 713-861-2266

"Unique" pizzas plus "some of the best gyros in town" head up the menu at this inexpensive Greek in the lower Heights; nondescript digs are elevated by a friendly staff that makes it a "great place to stop after a softball game" at nearby Memorial Park.

Bibas One's A Meal Restaurant ◐ Ⓢ Ⓜ *Greek* 18 | 10 | 17 | $14

Montrose | 607 W. Gray St. (bet. Stanford & Taft Sts.) | 713-523-0425

An "unpretentious' spot for "solid" Greek "standbys", this "homey" Montrose "joint" draws a "line out the door" at lunch, when "Houstonians" crowd in for a cheap and "filling" meal served by longtime waiters ("John is a gem"); it's open 24/7, meaning it works for "post-drinking munchies" "after a night out" as well.

Bice *Italian* 21 | 23 | 21 | $56

Galleria | Galleria | 5175 Westheimer Rd. (Sage Rd.) | 713-622-2423 | www.bicehouston.com

See review in Dallas/Ft. Worth Directory.

Bistro Calais Ⓜ *French* ▽ 23 | 22 | 21 | $32

River Oaks | 2811 Bammel Ln. (Westheimer Rd.) | 713-529-1314 | www.bistrocalais.com

Supporters say this "quiet, little" bistro in River Oaks "keeps getting better" with country-style French fare and a "great" Sunday buffet brunch plus a well-priced selection of wines to match; servers "who care" tend to customers in the light-filled converted cottage setting while live jazz on Wednesdays and Thursday add additional appeal.

Bistro Lancaster *American* 20 | 20 | 20 | $42

Downtown | Lancaster Hotel | 701 Texas Ave. (Louisiana St.) | 713-228-9500 | www.thelancaster.com

It's an "easy walk to all live performance" venues from this Downtown Lancaster Hotel longtimer, but that's not the only thing that has admirers applauding - they also laud its "unpretentious, fresh and well-prepared" New American cuisine, "comfortable" "old-world charm" and "cool" jazz piano music on weekends; trendier types term it "stuffy", though, and add that "service should be faster."

Bistro Le Cep *French* 25 | 21 | 23 | $34

West Houston | 11112 Westheimer Rd. (Wilcrest Dr.) | 713-783-3985 | www.bistrolecep.com

"Amiable" chef-owner Joe Mannke "makes everyone feel welcome" at his "charming" West Houston bistro where "delicious", "beautifully presented" French dishes and "wonderful" wines (30 by the glass) come at "moderate prices"; "quaint" "country" quarters may get "a might crowded", but it's all so "delightful" that no one seems to mind.

Bistro Provence ⊠ *French* 23 | 20 | 23 | $32

West Houston | 13616 Memorial Dr. (bet. Wilcrest & Yorkchester Drs.) | 713-827-8008 | www.bistroprovence.us

"Comfort food" for Francophiles wins raves at this "family-run" "gem" set in a West Houston strip mall where "first-rate bread from a wood-burning oven" proves a promising start to a meal of "scrumptious" bistro classics; the "cozy" digs get a "rustic" feel from exposed wood beams, and while a few fret over "crowded" conditions and a no-reservations policy, gentle prices keep everything "*très bien.*"

Bistro Toulouse ⊠ *American* 20 | 15 | 19 | $27

Briargrove | 5750 Woodway Dr. (bet. Bering Dr. & Chimney Rock Rd.) | 713-977-6900 | www.bistrotoulousehouston.com

"Tucked away on a side street", this "quaint" Briargrove bistro serves up "flavorful" New American dishes with a "snappy" Louisiana French twist (think Creole spiced salmon and apple beignets); "attentive" service, modest tabs and "casual" surroundings decorated with local artwork make it feel like "the kind of place one can become a regular."

Bistro Vino ◐⊠ *French/Italian* 20 | 21 | 20 | $37

Montrose | 819 W. Alabama St. (Stanford St.) | 713-526-5500 | www.bistrovino.net

A "beautifully romantic setting" in a converted 19th-century mansion creates the backdrop for a "lovely dinner" at this venerable Montrose "hideaway" proffering "classic" French and Italian cuisine; though some diners declare the decor outshines the food, others insist it's a "favorite" "as long as someone else is paying" the bill.

Black Labrador Pub *Pub Food* 17 | 21 | 18 | $20

Montrose | 4100 Montrose Blvd. (W. Main St.) | 713-529-1199 | www.blacklabradorpub.com

Expats and Tex-pats alike patronize this "proper pub" in Montrose for the sake of its "authentic", "warming" British "comfort food" (shepherd's pie, fish 'n' chips, trifle) and "great selection" of draft beers and scotches; it's a "charming" (if slightly "stereotypical") "bit of Merrie Olde England" replete with a "friendly staff", a "cozy fireplace" and an attractive patio with a giant chess set - now "all they need is cricket on the telly."

Black Walnut Café *Eclectic/Italian* 20 | 20 | 16 | $16

Rice Village | 5510 Morningside Dr. (University Blvd.) | 713-526-5551

NEW **Sugar Land** | First Colony Mall | 16535 Southwest Frwy. (Hwy. 6) | 281-565-7800

The Woodlands | 2520 Research Forest Dr. (Grogans Mill Rd.) | 281-362-1678

www.bwcafe.com

These self-styled 'fast-casual' Eclectic-Italians in Rice Village, Sugar Land and The Woodlands proffer a "fun" menu of "consistent" fare (including "excellent" all-day breakfasts) for "every kind of appetite"; their wood-paneled "conversation areas" are a "pleasant" compensation for the "informal" counter service.

NEW Blue Fin *Japanese* | - | - | - | M |

West Houston | 12225 Westheimer Rd. (Shadowbriar Dr.) | 281-493-1244

"Fancy" raw fare made from "good-quality fish" is the focus of this West Houston Japanese and moderately priced offshoot of Uptown Sushi; though it resides in a nondescript strip mall, it boasts a "hip decor" with shimmery beaded curtains as well as "attentive service."

Blue Nile *Ethiopian* | - | - | - | I |

Southwest Houston | 9400 Richmond (Westerland Dr.) | 713-782-6882 | www.bluenilerestaurant.com

"What an experience for the taste buds!" exclaim admirers of this Southwest Houston "destination" featuring "exotic" Ethiopian dishes presented with spongy injera bread; bright-colored decor may not be much to speak of, but with a cordial staff there to "guide you" through the menu, it's a "favorable" experience overall.

Bob's Steak & Chop House ☒ *Steak* | 25 | 20 | 23 | $59 |

Galleria | 1801 Post Oak Blvd. (bet. San Felipe St. & Westheimer Rd.) | 713-877-8325 | www.bobs-steakandchop.com

See review in Dallas/Ft. Worth Directory.

Bombay Brasserie *Indian* | 18 | 14 | 17 | $23 |

Rice Village | Rice Village Arcade | 2414 University Blvd. (Morningside Dr.) | 713-355-2000 | www.thebombaybrasserie.com

Locals laud the "authentic" "mix of old standards and a wildcard dish or two" at this modestly priced Rice Village Indian featuring a lunch buffet that some say is "the best in the area"; white-walled mahogany-accented decor isn't fancy, but has a "pleasant", "neighborhood" feel nonetheless.

Brasil ◐ *Coffeehouse* | 20 | 19 | 16 | $17 |

Montrose | 2604 Dunlavy St. (Westheimer Rd.) | 713-528-1993

This "bohemian", "funky" Montrose hangout caters to an "arty crowd" - "cool tattoos and piercings" abound - with "great" vegetarian-friendly sandwiches and salads, well-chosen bottled beers and wines and what many deem "the best house coffee around"; it's dished up in art-filled, bare-brick quarters boasting live music and movies; P.S. just "people-watch and pretend you're studying."

NEW Brasserie Max & Julie ☒ *French* | - | - | - | M |

Montrose | 4315 Montrose Blvd. (Richmond Ave.) | 713-524-0075 | www.caferabelais.com

Set in the Montrose spot that acclaimed Aires previously occupied, this moderately priced newcomer from the owners of Café Rabelais dishes up comforting Gallic cooking like cassoulet and boeuf bourguignon; the wine list is all-French, as is the homey decor with its lace curtains and polished brass fixtures.

Breakfast Klub, The *Soul Food* 23 | 12 | 19 | $15

Midtown | 3711 Travis St. (Alabama St.) | 713-528-8561 | www.thebreakfastklub.com

Don't you "forget about" this "funky" Midtown "hot spot", which "outguns IHOP and Denny's" with "housemade soul food" (i.e. "real-deal" "chicken wings and waffles, catfish and grits") that's so "excellent" the "nonexistent decor" hardly matters - witness the "enormous lines on weekends"; so what if these folks "kan't spell, they sure kan kook!"

Z Brennan's *Creole* 26 | 26 | 26 | $57

Midtown | 3300 Smith St. (Stuart St.) | 713-522-9711 | www.brennanshouston.com

"Truly a Houston classic", this "elegant" Midtowner from New Orleans' Brennan family brings together "impeccably prepared" Creole-Southwestern cuisine and "wines galore" in a "delightful" atmosphere well-suited for a "special occasion" or an "outstanding brunch" with live jazz; "gracious servers" and a "charming" patio add to the appeal of what supporters swear is "one of Houston's best"; N.B. jackets preferred.

Brenner's *Steak* 25 | 24 | 24 | $55

Memorial | 10911 Katy Frwy. (bet. Brittmoore Rd. & Wilcrest Dr.) | 713-465-2901 | www.brennerssteakhouse.com

NEW River Oaks | 1 Birdsall St. (Memorial Dr.) | 713-868-4444 | www.brennersonthebayou.com

Longtime fans laud this "traditional", "high-end" Memorial steakhouse that's "held true" since 1936 (despite its acquisition by the Landry's empire) with "wonderfully aged" beef and "impeccable" service; prices may be high, but "inviting" decor with a working fireplace and a "pretty garden" make it a "memorable" pick for "special occasions"; N.B. scores may not reflect the newer River Oaks branch.

Brio Tuscan Grille *Italian* 21 | 23 | 20 | $31

The Woodlands | Woodlands Mall | 1201 Lake Woodlands Dr. (I-45) | 281-465-8993 | www.brioitalian.com

See review in Dallas/Ft. Worth Directory.

Brownstone, The ☒ *Continental* 22 | 24 | 21 | $47

Upper Kirby District | 2736 Virginia St. (Westheimer Rd.) | 713-520-5666 | www.brownstone-houston.com

"Antiques adorn every room" of this "lovely" Upper Kirby District dowager that lures a "middle-aged" clientele for "gourmet" Continental cuisine; a few diners find it "stuffy", but the majority maintains this "elegant" entry is "worth every cent" of its price for "romantic outings" or a "luncheon with the gals"; P.S. regulars report most of the "quaint" furnishings are "available for purchase."

Buffalo Grille, The *American* 20 | 13 | 15 | $14

West U | 3116 Bissonnet St. (Buffalo Spdwy.) | 713-661-3663

(continued)

Buffalo Grille, The

Memorial | 1301 S. Voss Rd. (bet. San Felipe St. & Woodway Dr.) | 713-784-3663
www.thebuffalogrille.com

"Unbelievable breakfasts" (especially the "plate-sized flapjacks") dished up all day long bring "white-collar yuppies", "dreadlocked college students" and "kids, parents and grandparents" to this "hectic but friendly" Tex-Mex-flavored American duo in West U and Memorial; given these spots' "affordable" tabs and "neighborhoody" vibe, it's no surprise there are "lines out the door" on weekends; P.S. "good buffalo burgers too", natch.

Burning Pear, The *Southwestern/Steak* ▽ 23 | 18 | 21 | $34

Sugar Land | Sugar Land Marriott Hotel | 16090 City Walk (Alvin-Sugar Land Rd.) | 281-275-5925 |
www.theburningpear.com

This "really creative" Southwestern steakhouse in Sugar Land gets burned by hotelophobes who claim "this place is great, shame it's in the Marriott", but thanks to "excellent" personnel proffering "Texas grub at its best" - including a "lovely Sunday brunch buffet" - most munchers don't mind the somewhat impersonal earth-toned environs.

Cabo Mix-Mex Grill ◐ *Tex-Mex* 14 | 14 | 12 | $17

Downtown | 419 Travis St. (Prairie St.) | 713-225-2060 |
www.cabomixmex.com

"Average" Tex-Mex meals and "hit-or-miss" service "much slower than the pickup scene" don't dissuade loyalists from mixing it up at this "cool hangout spot" Downtown, especially if they can sit on the "great balcony" while downing "fresh-squeezed margaritas" ("imbibe with caution!") and "nice cold beers"; baseball fans find it a convenient stop "before an Astros game."

Cadillac Bar *Mexican* 18 | 18 | 18 | $25

Heights | 1802 Shepherd Dr. (I-10) | 713-862-2020
Kemah | 100 Bradford St. (3rd St.) | 281-334-9049 Ⓜ
www.cadillacbar.com

Strong margaritas fuel the "incredible bar scene" at these "boisterous" Landry's-owned cantinas in Dallas and Houston serving up solid, if not exactly "authentic" Mexican eats; the "lively" atmosphere plus spacious seating and reasonable prices make it "perfect for large groups."

Z Cafe Annie ⊠ *Southwestern* 26 | 24 | 26 | $60

Galleria | 1728 Post Oak Blvd. (San Felipe St.) | 713-840-1111 |
www.cafe-annie.com

Robert Del Grande "still has it" declare devotees of his "fabulous" Galleria-area destination where "businessmen" and "Chanel-clad ladies" sup on "exquisite" Southwestern cuisine ferried by "impeccable" servers in an "elegant" high-ceilinged dining room; though the less starry-eyed declare it "overpriced" and "overrated", most maintain that even with "occasional lapses", this is still among "the best in the city."

Café Artiste *Coffeehouse/Eclectic* 16 | 14 | 16 | $19

Montrose | 1601 W. Main St. (Mandell St.) | 713-528-3704

As much "coffeehouse" as a restaurant, this "tucked-away", moderately priced Eclectic Montrose mainstay serves "home cooking" with a Louisiana bent, including "surprisingly good" breakfasts; though detractors note that the "interior is deteriorating, as is the service", it remains a favorite with "students working away on laptops."

Café Benedicte *Continental* 23 | 20 | 21 | $30

West Houston | 15455 Memorial Dr. (bet. Eldridge Pkwy. & Hwy. 6) | 281-558-6607 | www.cafebenedicte.com

This West Houston "neighborhood favorite" proffers well-prepared dishes from just about "any country bordering the [Mediterranean] Sea" - including Spain, France, Italy, Morocco and Greece - in a "very pleasing atmosphere" that includes a "quaint view" of a small pond; it shares French owners with Lynn's Steakhouse, so diners can expect "nice wine flights", plus service that's "personable", if sometimes "uneven."

Café Caspian M *Persian* 22 | 18 | 20 | $23

West Houston | Gray Falls | 12126 Westheimer Rd. (Gray Falls Dr.) | 281-493-4000 | www.cafecaspian.com

"Reliably" well-prepared meals begin with freshly made taftoon, a "wonderful bread", that's pared with bountiful herbs and a fetalike cheese at this West Houston Persian; "friendly service" and modest tabs boost the appeal of the casual, cafe-style setting in a strip mall off busy Westheimer.

Café Chino *Chinese* 22 | 17 | 20 | $22

Rice Village | 6140 Village Pkwy. (bet. Amherst St. & Times Blvd.) | 713-524-4433 | www.cafechinohouston.com

Comparatively "attractive decor" helps make this Chinese in Rice Village a "favorite" for folks craving "fresh", "consistent" and "relatively inexpensive" eats served by "quick, friendly" staffers with "never a wait"; N.B. the Downtown branch has closed.

Café Express *Eclectic* 18 | 14 | 14 | $15

Champions | Champions Vill. | 5311 FM 1960 W. (Champions Vill.) | 832-484-9222

Downtown | 650 Main St. (bet. Capitol St. & Texas Ave.) | 713-237-9222 S

Uptown | Uptown Park | 1101 Uptown Park Blvd. (Post Oak Blvd.) | 713-963-9222 ●

Meyerland | Meyerland Plaza | 210 Meyerland Plaza (I-610) | 713-349-9222

Montrose | Museum of Fine Arts, Houston | 5601 S. Main St. (Binz St.) | 713-639-7370 M

River Oaks | 1422 W. Gray St. (Waugh Dr.) | 713-522-3100

Upper Kirby District | 3200 Kirby Dr. (Main St.) | 713-522-3994

(continued)

Café Express

West Houston | 6570 Woodway Dr. (Voss Rd.) | 713-935-9222
Webster | 19443 Gulf Frwy. (Bay Area Blvd.) | 281-554-6999
Sugar Land | First Colony Mall | 15930 City Walk Blvd. (bet. Rte. 6 & Sweetwater Blvd.) | 281-980-9222
www.cafe-express.com
Additional locations throughout the Houston area

Surveyors salute the "fresh, healthy meals" at these chain links that kick "fast food" "up a notch" with a "wholesome" array of Eclectic sandwiches and salads plus a "large condiment bar" to customize your order and "happy-hour specials" on wine too; prices are "cheap", though "noisy" digs and order-at-the-counter service have some relegating it to "take-ut" only; N.B. longtime fans "are glad that the original owners" bought them back from Wendy's in July 2007.

Café Japon ◐ *Japanese* 22 | 18 | 18 | $23

West U | 3915 Kirby Dr. (bet. Richmond Ave. & Southwest Frwy.) | 713-529-1668 | www.cafejapon.com

This long-running West U Japanese remains "a favorite" for its "good-value" sushi ("the jazz roll deserves homage"); however, aesthetes assert the "somewhat run-down" furnishings "need remodeling" and the servers, though "nice", can be slow ("are there staffers in the building?"); N.B. open till 2 AM on weekends.

Z Café Le Jadeite *Pacific Rim* 22 | 26 | 22 | $36

River Oaks | River Oaks Ctr. | 1952 W. Gray St. (Driscoll St.) | 713-528-4288 | www.cafelejadeite.biz

"Sublime" Pacific Rim cuisine awaits at this "top-notch" Asian eatery in River Oaks; loyalists liken the "over-the-top" decor decked out with lacquer, jade and "ancient treasures" to "eating in a museum", creating an "elegant" atmosphere aided by live piano (Tuesday-Saturday) and a "wonderful staff."

Cafe Lili ☒ *Lebanese* 24 | 12 | 21 | $19

Galleria | 5757 Westheimer Rd. (Bering Dr.) | 713-952-6969 | www.cafelili.com

"The hosts make everyone feel at home" at this "mom-and-pop" Galleria Lebanese "favorite" turning out "fantastic", "authentic" food like "top-quality grilled meats" and especially "addictive" appetizers; there may not be "much in the way of decor" (service is order-at-the-counter too) but supporters swear that for an "inexpensive" meal, "it can't be beat."

Café Malay *Malaysian* - | - | - | I

West Houston | 10234 Westheimer Rd. (Beltway 8) | 713-785-7915

"Wonderfully authentic Malaysian food" lures intrepid eaters to this inexpensive West Houston eatery where beef rending and roti cani (a puffy, freshly baked bread) are standouts on the expansive menu; service is friendly, but for those who find the banquet-style quarters rather sparse, delivery is also an option.

Café Montrose Ⓢ *Belgian* 22 | 11 | 17 | $27

Montrose | 1609 Westheimer Rd. (Mandell St.) | 713-523-1201 | www.cafemontrose.com

Anchored in a Montrose strip center, this "inexpensive Belgian" flexes its mussels - its most popular dish, deemed by some "the stuff of myth and legend" - and "impresses" fans with its array of ales and "perfectly crispy pommes frites"; surroundings are "modest", but this "homey" place is "authentically Euro" enough to draw an "international crowd."

Cafe Piquet *Cuban* ▽ 21 | 17 | 19 | $16

Bellaire | 5757 Bissonnet St. (Chimney Rock Rd.) | 713-664-1031

This Bellaire mainstay (now in its third location on Bissonnet) pleases local patrons with "outstanding Cuban food" like long-cooked roast pork, ropa vieja and whole fried red snapper; even if prices have been "raised", tabs are still quite reasonable while service remains "pleasant" and efficient.

Ⓩ Café Rabelais Ⓢ *French* 26 | 20 | 22 | $36

Rice Village | 2442 Times Blvd. (bet. Kelvin St. & Morningside Dr.) | 713-520-8841 | www.caferabelais.com

"Authentic" bistro cooking like "amazing mussels" and frites "to die for" "transport" diners to "Paris" at this "charming" Rice Village French that also pleases with "phenomenal wines" and a "knowledgeable" staff; "tables are tight, but the crowd is friendly" and prices a "great value", but they don't take reservations, so "get there early or expect to wait."

Ⓩ Cafe Red Onion Ⓢ *Pan-Latin* 24 | 17 | 19 | $23

Northwest Houston | 12440 Northwest Frwy. (43rd St.) | 713-957-0957

Upper Kirby District | 3910 Kirby Dr. (bet. Richmond Ave. & Southwest Frwy.) | 713-807-1122

West Houston | 1111 Eldridge Pkwy. (Enclave Pkwy.) | 281-293-7500

www.caferedonion.com

It's "always a fiesta" at this trio of "festive", "casual" "favorites" featuring "imaginative" "Latin fusion" cuisine plus South/Central American standards set out in "beautiful presentations" (also notable are the "wonderful chips and pineapple salsa to munch on"); in spite of a few grumbles about "noisy" environs and "sometimes slow" service, they remain "unique" spots "worth a visit."

Cantina Laredo *Mexican* 21 | 20 | 20 | $23

West Houston | 11129 Westheimer Rd. (Wilcrest Dr.) | 713-952-3287 | www.cantinalaredo.com

See review in Dallas/Ft. Worth Directory.

Capital Grille *Steak* 25 | 25 | 25 | $58

Galleria | 5365 Westheimer Rd. (Yorktown St.) | 713-623-4600 | www.thecapitalgrille.com

See review in Dallas/Ft. Worth Directory.

Carmelo's *Italian* 22 | 22 | 22 | $35

West Houston | 14795 Memorial Dr. (bet. Dairy Ashford Rd. & Eldridge Pkwy.) | 281-531-0696 | www.carmelosrestaurant.com

See review in Austin and the Hill Country Directory.

Z Carrabba's Italian Grill *Italian* 22 | 19 | 22 | $28

Champions | Champions Vill. | 5440 FM 1960 W. (Champion Forest Dr.) | 281-397-8255

Galleria | 1399 S. Voss Rd. (bet. San Felipe St. & Woodway Dr.) | 713-468-0868

Northwest Houston | 7540 Hwy. 6 N. (Longenbaugh Dr.) | 281-859-9700

Upper Kirby District | 3115 Kirby Dr. (Branard St.) | 713-522-3131

West Houston | 11339 Katy Frwy. (Wilcrest Dr.) | 713-464-6595

Webster | 502 W. Bay Area Blvd. (I-45) | 281-338-0574

Kingwood | 750 Kingwood Dr. (Chestnut Ridge Dr.) | 281-358-5580

Sugar Land | 2335 Hwy. 6 S. (Southwest Frwy.) | 281-980-4433

The Woodlands | 25665 North Frwy. (Rayford Rd.) | 281-367-9423

www.carrabbas.com

For over 20 years these "dependable" "fixtures" have been "beloved by families with small children" for "solid", "midrange" Italian "without pretension" presented in "large portions"; insiders insist the Outback-controlled branches "can't compare" to the original "family-owned" outposts (Upper Kirby District and Galleria in Houston), though all locations remain "noisy" and "crowded."

Catalan Food and Wine M *American/Spanish* 24 | 21 | 21 | $43

Heights | 5555 Washington Ave. (TC Jester Blvd.) | 713-426-4260 | www.catalanfoodandwine.com

"What a wonderful addition to the neighborhood" exclaim enthusiasts of this "hip" Heights newcomer (and sib to Ibiza) where "outstanding" Spanish-inspired small plates and "cutting-edge" New American entrees are complemented by a "thoughtful" selection of wines "with some of the best prices in the city"; though the brick-arched, candlelit dining room may get "crowded" and "loud", "friendly and informed servers" ensure a "fabulous experience all around."

Cava Bistro S *American* 21 | 21 | 22 | $34

Downtown | 301 Main St. (Congress St.) | 713-223-4068 | www.bellarestaurants.com

The few who've found this often-"overlooked" Downtowner aren't cavalier about it; they praise its "innovative" New American fare served by a "friendly", "quirky" crew and dig the "cool, cavelike" wine-cellar setting with its "delightful" patio; located near a light-rail stop, this "great date" spot is also convenient for pre-theater dining.

Charivari S *Continental* 23 | 18 | 24 | $39

Midtown | 2521 Bagby St. (McGowen St.) | 713-521-7231 | www.charivarirest.com

"Step into old-world Europe" at this "quaint", "high-class" Midtowner that "truly honors" Continental cuisine with "superbly prepared" plates of Wiener schnitzel and "standout" Transylvanian specialties; "service is impeccable", although a few find the "subdued" atmosphere too "serious" and urge the owners to "loosen it up a little."

	FOOD	DECOR	SERVICE	COST
Cheesecake Factory *American*	20	20	18	$26

Galleria | Galleria | 5015 Westheimer Rd. (Post Oak Blvd.) | 713-840-0600
Sugar Land | First Colony Mall | 16535 Southwest Frwy. (Hwy. 6) | 281-313-9500
The Woodlands | Woodlands Mall | 1201 Lake Woodlands Dr. (I-45) | 281-419-3400
www.thecheesecakefactory.com

The menu's "mammoth" - and "so are the crowds" - at this "family-pleasing" chain where the "endless" American options arrive in equally "colossal" portions (ironically, "they give you so much there's no room" for their "heavenly" namesake desserts); despite "ordinary" settings, "spotty" staffing and "lots of commotion", these "well-oiled machines" are so "busy, busy, busy" that they're best accessed "off-hours" to avoid a "long wait."

	FOOD	DECOR	SERVICE	COST
Chez Georges S M *French*	24	19	21	$58

Montrose | 219 Westheimer Rd. (bet. Bagby & Taft Sts.) | 713-529-7788 | www.chezgeorgesrestaurant.com

"Experienced" chef-owner Georges Guy mans the stove while his "charming" wife, Monique, acts as maitre d' at this latest incarnation of their bistro, now set in a "small" "cottage" in the heart of Montrose - and still serving the same pricey and "excellent old-style French" staples ("try the sweetbreads and the rabbit"); though some suppers appreciate the "attractive, elegant" setting, others deem it too "doily."

	FOOD	DECOR	SERVICE	COST
Chez Nous S *French*	26	21	26	$51

Humble | 217 S. Ave. G (Main St.) | 281-446-6717 | www.cheznousfrenchrestaurant.com

"A hidden treasure" that's "worth the drive to Humble" proclaim patrons of this "special-occasion" destination set in a converted home and serving "exceptional" "classic French cooking" featuring "fresh herbs and vegetables from their own garden"; the "charming" ambiance gets a boost from "top-notch" servers who lavish "personal attention" on diners, so even if a few lament it's "slipped just a bit", most maintain it's "still an all-time favorite"; N.B. jacket suggested.

	FOOD	DECOR	SERVICE	COST
China View *Chinese*	27	16	22	$18

West Houston | 11113½ Katy Frwy. (bet. Kirkwood Rd. & Wilcrest Dr.) | 713-464-2728 | www.chinaview.us

Helmed by "creative" and "caring" chef-owner Robin Luo, this West Houston "culinary pearl" "stands out" thanks to "exquisite" Chinese dishes that utilize local produce and seafood which compensates for the somewhat "dismal setting"; add in "very friendly service" and "bargain prices" and it's no wonder fans swear they "go there at least once a week."

	FOOD	DECOR	SERVICE	COST
Chinese Café *Chinese*	22	6	13	$11

Alief | 9352 Bellaire Blvd. (Manchester) | 713-771-4330
Galleria | 5092 Richmond Ave. (Post Oak Blvd.) | 713-621-2888

Chowhounds choose these "no-frills" Chinese twins for "quick" Cantonese meals that are always "good 'n' cheap"; even if service is "sullen" and decor "nothing fancy", they're a "safe bet" for "lunch", "takeout" or a "weekday dinner."

Christian's Tailgate Bar & Grill *Burgers* 19 | 12 | 15 | $14

Heights | 7340 Washington Ave. (Katy Frwy.) | 713-864-9744 ☒
Midtown | 2000 Bagby St. (Gray St.) | 713-527-0261 ●

Some of the "best hamburgers in Texas" plus frosty mugs of beer keep the "tailgating crowd" coming to these Heights-area and Midtown "dives"; service may be "variable", but "sports on TV" and a congenial atmosphere make them fine places for "hanging out."

Z Churrascos *S American* 25 | 22 | 23 | $38

Lower Shepherd | 2055 Westheimer Rd. (Shepherd Dr.) | 713-527-8300
Southwest Houston | 9705 Westheimer Rd. (Gessner Rd.) | 713-952-1988
www.cordua.com

"The namesake steak" "melts in your mouth" at Michael Cordúa's Southwest Houston mainstays where "large portions" of "flavorful" South American cuisine are matched with "fabulous" wines and "phenomenal" desserts ("save room for the très leches cake!"); "helpful" servers work the "oversized" contemporary dining rooms, so even if tabs are a bit "pricey", boosters boast it's "always a winner" nonetheless.

Chuy's *Tex-Mex* 21 | 19 | 19 | $18

River Oaks | 2706 Westheimer Rd. (Kirby Dr.) | 713-524-1700 | www.chuys.com
Spring | 18035 I-45N (FM 1960) | 936-321-4440 ☒ M

See review in Austin and the Hill Country Directory.

Ciro's *Italian* 20 | 20 | 20 | $24

Memorial | 9755 Katy Frwy. (Bunker Hill Rd.) | 713-467-9336 | www.ciros.com

Supporters "stick with the pasta dishes" at this "popular" Memorial Italian offering "reliable" eats at modest prices; though service is "smooth" and it's often "crowded", some sticklers suggest it's "unremarkable" and add that it "lost its charisma" when it moved across the freeway to "bigger digs" in 2005.

Cleburne Cafeteria ⊄ *American* 23 | 13 | 18 | $14

West U | 3606 Bissonnet St. (Mercer St.) | 713-667-2386 | www.cleburnecafeteria.com

Size does matter at this West U "cafeteria on steroids", where the "fresh", "exceptional" Southern-style American "comfort food" comes in "gigantic" portions ("cakes the size of small dogs"); family-owned and -run, the "quaint" place is an "institution", so be prepared for "long lines after church on Sundays"; N.B. closed Saturdays.

Collina's *Italian* 18 | 12 | 17 | $17

Greenway Plaza Area | 3835 Richmond Ave. (Weslayan St.) | 713-621-8844 | www.collinas.com
Heights | 502 W. 19th St. (Nicholson Dr.) | 713-869-0492 | www.collinas.com ☒

(continued)

(continued)

Collina's

Memorial | 12311 Kingsride Ln. (Gessner Rd.) | 713-365-9497 | www.collinas.com ☒
Meyerland | 4990 Beechnut St. (Rice Ave.) | 713-349-9040 | www.collinasitaliancafe.com
Rice Village | 2400 Times Blvd. (Morningside Dr.) | 713-526-4499 | www.collinasitaliancafe.com
West Houston | 12002 Richmond Ave. (Kirkwood Dr.) | 281-679-5800 | www.collinas.com

"Fabulous" for "multigenerational groups", this "reliable" local chain turns out "down-home" Italian fare ("out-of-this-world" "gourmet pizza") in "casual" surroundings; the "best part" is that the BYOB policy, with a modest corkage fee, makes for "great value" – almost worth the "annoyance" of "haphazard" service and high decibel levels; N.B. the Meyerland and Rice Village branches are under new ownership.

Cova *American* 19 19 19 $31

West U | 5600 Kirby Dr. (Nottingham St.) | 713-838-0700 ◐
Heights | 5555 Washington Ave. (TC Jester Blvd.) | 713-868-3366
www.covawines.com

This lower Heights and West U pair of "cool", "casual" vino bars/restaurants/wine shops offers a "solid" American menu of "small" bites that work for a "light meal", "before-party pick-me-up" or "after-hours" snack; though service is "helpful", critics carp that the "extensive" list of pours "by the glass" comes at too "extravagant" a price.

Crapitto's Cucina Italiana ☒ *Italian* 21 18 22 $34

Galleria | 2400 Mid Lane St. (Westheimer Rd.) | 713-961-1161 | www.crapittos.com

"Get past the unfortunate name" – this "fine" venue in the Galleria area proffers "delicious" Italian cuisine and "well-priced" wines in a "lovely, romantic" restored 1915 house; service is generally "attentive" but generation-gappers wonder whether "anyone under 60" can find this "hidden" eatery; P.S. "request a table under the live oaks outside" on the patio.

Crú Wine Bar *American* 20 23 21 $34

The Woodlands | Market St. | 9595 Six Pines Dr. (Lake Woodlands Dr.) | 281-465-9463 | www.cruawinebar.com

See review in Dallas/Ft. Worth Directory.

Cyclone Anaya's *Mexican* 20 18 18 $23

Briargrove | 5761 Woodway Dr. (Augusta Dr.) | 713-339-4552
Heights | 1710 Durham Dr. (Inker St.) | 713-862-3209
Midtown | 309 Gray St. (Bagby St.) | 713-520-6969

"You'll have to wrestle your way in" to these "yuppified" Mexican joints (revivals of a 1960s Houston-area classic) set in "upscale" digs with exposed brick, white tablecloths and a "festive atmosphere"; "tasty" fare and "awesome margaritas" are strong points, though a few fret about "noisy" environs and tabs they find "a bit expensive."

	FOOD	DECOR	SERVICE	COST

Daily Grind *Coffeehouse* 14 | 13 | 17 | $14

Heights | 4115 Washington Ave. (Bonner St.) | 713-861-4558 | www.dailygrindunwind.com

Caffeine-crazed locals laud this "funky", "neighborhood" coffee shop in the lower Heights for its "great" java and satisfying breakfasts and lunches; the decor may be on the "shabby" side, but it's still a "comfy" place with "good people-watching" and free WiFi drawing plenty of "businesspeople" and "students on laptops."

Daily Review Café *American* 20 | 17 | 17 | $30

River Oaks | 3412 W. Lamar St. (Dunlavy St.) | 713-520-9217 | www.dailyreviewcafe.com

This "quiet and unpretentious" River Oaks eatery pleases patrons with "modestly priced" Traditional American "home cooking" (and a "great Sunday brunch") that fans favor in warm weather "when you can sit outdoors" on the "beautiful" garden patio; some quibble about "tight" quarters inside while others are left wishing that "service were better."

[Z] **Da Marco** [S] [M] *Italian* 28 | 22 | 26 | $57

Montrose | 1520 Westheimer Rd. (bet. Ridgewood & Windsor Sts.) | 713-807-8857 | www.damarcohouston.com

Aficionados "indulge" in "exemplary" Italian cuisine prepared from "the freshest ingredients" (including "superb pastas" "worth saving your carbs for") and sip wines from a "world-class" list at chef/co-owner Marco Wiles' pricey Montrose destination; its setting in a converted home cultivates a "cozy", "romantic" vibe, so even if "tables are too close together" and the "attentive" service sometimes feels "rushed", it still "stands out" as "one of Houston's finest."

Damian's Cucina Italiana [S] *Italian* 21 | 20 | 22 | $44

Midtown | 3011 Smith St. (Rosalie St.) | 713-522-0439 | www.damians.com

"Everybody is somebody" at this Midtown "fixture" where "polished, efficient" staffers proffer "old-school", "high-end" Italian cuisine and "fine" regional wines in a setting "just on the comfortable side of stuffy"; now that the "old standby" is in its third decade, however, some surveyors sigh it's "tired" and in need of an "update."

D'Amico's Italian Market Café *Italian* 21 | 15 | 18 | $22

Rice Village | 5510 Morningside Dr. (bet. Rice & University Blvds.) | 713-526-3400 | www.damico-cafe.com

Half grocery market, half Italian cafe, this "fun little" Rice Villager is a "favorite haunt" for locals who love its "straightforward" cooking ("awesome" pizza, "best-value" lunch specials); "pleasant" staffers foster a "family-friendly" vibe, so many settle in "on the patio with a glass of wine, some fresh tortellini" and the kids.

Daniel Wong's Kitchen *Chinese* 23 | 13 | 19 | $15

Bellaire | 4566 Bissonnet St. (Ave. B) | 713-663-6665 | www.danielwongskitchen.com

For over a decade, this casual, easy-on-the-wallet Bellaire eatery has been dishing up "inventive", "subtly spiced" Chinese fare that's often "healthy" thanks to its "fresh ingredients"; if fans wonder why it "isn't jam-packed during the dinner hour", it may be because, says one surveyor, "the decor and lighting are horrendous", causing some to opt for the "great" carryout.

NEW Danton's Gulf Coast Seafood Kitchen S M *Seafood* - | - | - | M

Montrose | 4611 Montrose Blvd. (Hwy. 59) | 713-807-8883 | dantonsseafood.com

This Gulf Coast-centric seafooder in Montrose plies patrons with plenty of local oysters, overstuffed po' boys, hearty seafood gumbo and plates of grilled and fried fish, as well as Louisiana classics like shrimp étouffée; its down-to-earth vibe is enhanced by the family photos and antique maps adorning the walls and welcoming staffers who are eager-to-please.

NEW Del Frisco's Double Eagle Steak House *Steak* 27 | 24 | 25 | $69

Galleria | Galleria | 5061 Westheimer Rd. (McCue Rd.) | 713-355-2600 | www.delfriscos.com

See review in Dallas/Ft. Worth Directory.

Denis' Seafood House *Seafood* 21 | 19 | 21 | $30

Memorial | 9777 Katy Frwy. (Memorial City Way) | 713-464-6900 | www.denisseafood.com

"Not flashy but excellent" seafood dishes - spiced up with "hellaciously good" sauces and "priced right" - have habitués hooked on this Cajun-accented Memorial restaurant, where "helpful" staffers "provide expert advice" on the menu as needed; adding to the appeal are "sleek" decor and live zydeco music on the patio on Thursday nights.

Dessert Gallery Bakery & Café *American/Dessert* 22 | 13 | 16 | $14

Galleria | 1616 Post Oak Blvd. (Westbriar Ln.) | 713-622-0007
Upper Kirby District | 3200 Kirby Dr. (Main St.) | 713-522-9999
NEW Sugar Land | First Colony Mall | 2260 Lone Star Dr. (Town Center Blvd.) | 281-201-4900
www.dessertgallery.com

Unsurprisingly, owing to their "overwhelming selection of delectable desserts" ("the carrot cake makes you want to eat your vegetables"), this trio of "chocoholics' dream" spots continue to be "crowd-pleasers"; surveyors who are sweet on this duo also appreciate the Traditional American meals and report that "upbeat" staffers and board games at every table help make it "fun for all ages."

Dharma Café M *Eclectic* ▽ 21 | 16 | 22 | $29

Neartown | 1718 Houston Ave. (bet. Crockett & Summer Sts.) | 713-222-6996 | www.dharmacafehouston.com

"Fresh", "simple" and "healthy" Eclectic fare (think wraps at lunch and more substantial dishes like cedar-planked salmon at dinner) is prepared with a "personal" touch at this arty neighborhood eatery recently relocated to larger digs near the edge of Neartown; "service is informal and funky" and tabs modest, meaning locals are more than content to keep it their own little "secret."

Dimassi's Mediterranean Buffet *Mediterranean* 18 | 10 | 12 | $14

Downtown | 907 Franklin St. (Travis St.) | 713-224-0588 ⊠
Galleria | 5064 Richmond Ave. (Post Oak Blvd.) | 713-439-7481
NEW **Southwest Houston** | 8236 Kirby Dr. (La Concha Ln.) | 713-526-5111
West Houston | 11335 Katy Frwy. (Kirkwood Dr.) | 713-465-8222
Sugar Land | 4654 Hwy. 6 S. (Austin Pkwy.) | 281-277-2184
The Woodlands | 1640 Lake Woodlands Dr. (Pinecroft Dr.) | 281-363-0200
www.dimassisbuffet.com

"Succulent lamb", "chunky cucumber salad" and "fresh pita" are the stars at these "wondrous" all-you-can-eat Mediterranean buffets featuring a tremendous "variety" of "honest", "reliable" Middle Eastern choices; "there's not much decor" and service is strictly "cafeteria-style", but the easy-on-the-wallet tabs offer "good bang for the buck."

divino ⊠ *Italian* 22 | 16 | 20 | $31

Lower Shepherd | 1830 W. Alabama St. (bet. Hazard & Woodhead Sts.) | 713-807-1123 | www.divinohouston.com

"Excellent-value" vinos are vaunted at this "charming", "quiet" Lower Shepherd spot, a "neighborhood favorite" for its "well-thought-out", "reliable" and "reasonably priced" Northern Italian dishes; the menu may be "limited", but portions are "sized for a human, not a horse" and service is "personal" so the roomful of "regulars" feel like they're dining "at a friend's house."

Dolce Vita Pizzeria Enoteca M *Italian* 24 | 16 | 19 | $28

Montrose | 500 Westheimer Rd. (Whitney St.) | 713-520-8222 | www.dolcevitahouston.com

Right in the middle of Montrose, this "lively", "casual cousin of Da Marco" features "amazing Italian-style" "thin-crust" pizzas topped with an "offbeat but delicious variety of toppings", resulting in some of the "best pies in town"; its "pasta specials and appetizers" are "wonderful" too, as is the "great wine list" with choices from throughout The Boot, though "pricey" tabs and service that's "not consistent" temper the experience.

Don Carlos *Tex-Mex* - | - | - | I

Sharpstown | 6500 SW Frwy. (Harwin Dr.) | 713-776-2891
Hobby | 8385 Broadway St. (Bellfort Ave.) | 713-641-2084
Neartown | 416 N. 76th St. (Sherman St.) | 713-923-1906

Free-flowing margaritas and "well-prepared" *comida* are bolstered by mariachi (on Fridays) and happy-hour specials at this earthy Tex-Mex trio; "reasonable" prices and "quick" service keep customers coming "over and over again" to all locations, though a few favor the Neartown branch for its more festive feel.

Droubi's *Mediterranean* ▽ 21 | 8 | 14 | $12

Briargrove | 2721 Hillcroft St. (Westheimer Rd.) | 713-334-1829
Southwest Houston | 7333 Hillcroft St. (Evergreen St.) | 713-988-5897

The Droubi brothers' two Med grocery-cum-sandwich shops in Briargrove and Southwest Houston remain handy for a "quick bite" according to surveyors smitten with their "tasty Middle Eastern standards" ("excellent" falafel, "great gyros", "absolute-best" fresh-baked pita) deemed a "blessed departure from the ordinary"; just expect a "complete lack of decor" and "no hugs or kisses" from the staff.

El Meson Restaurant *Pan-Latin* 19 | 13 | 18 | $23

Rice Village | 2425 University Blvd. (Morningside Dr.) | 713-522-9306 | www.elmeson.com

A "family-friendly" "neighborhood standby", this Rice Villager ropes in regulars with a variety of Cuban, Spanish and Tex-Mex options (almost "too many" say some) plus an "outstanding" collection of wines; the understated room decorated with family photos and oil paintings "isn't fancy", but service is solid and prices affordable too.

El Pueblito Place *Guatemalan/Mexican* 20 | 16 | 17 | $17

Montrose | 1423 Richmond Ave. (Loretto Dr.) | 713-520-6635

Its "backyard is reason enough to go" croon cognoscenti who are crazy about the "elaborate" "tropical" patio at this Montrose Mexican-Guatemalan; happily, its "imaginative" seafood dishes (at "modest prices") and "fine margaritas" also shine – though just like other "popular" places it can be "noisy at night", especially on weekends when there's live flamenco and salsa; N.B. check out the cabana that seats 15.

El Tiempo 1308 Cantina *Tex-Mex* 22 | 17 | 18 | $26

Montrose | 1308 Montrose (Clay St.) | 713-807-8996 | www.1308cantina.com

El Tiempo Cantina *Tex-Mex*

Greenway Plaza Area | 3130 Richmond Ave. (Eastside St.) | 713-807-1600
Memorial | 5602 Washington Ave. (Asbury St.) | 713-681-3645
www.eltiempocantina.com

The Laurenzo family (offspring of Mama Ninfa's founder) is behind these three "high-end" Tex-Mex cantinas in the Greenway Plaza area, Montrose and Memorial, where "fabulous grilled meats" and "fresh" salsas and sides embody a "refreshing fusion of flavors and textures" and service is "frantic yet friendly"; the bar scene is "excellent" for "meeting friends" or scoping out the "A-list" crowd, but be warned that the "potent" margaritas "pack a powerful punch."

Empanadas by Marini *Argentinean* ▽ 23 | 14 | 21 | $10

NEW **Southwest Houston** | Carillion Sq. | 10001 Westheimer Rd. (Briarpark Dr.) | 713-266-2729 S
Katy | 3522 S. Mason Rd. (Westheimer Pkwy.) | 281-391-4273 M
www.theoriginalmarinisempanadahouse.com

An "amazing variety" of sweet and savory "handmade Argentine-style empanadas" make for a "good lunch" or a toothsome dessert at these inexpensive order-at-the-counter Katy and Southwest Houston "mom-and-pop" shops; specialty sandwiches and salads round out the menu, while shaded patio tables provide the perfect perch at either location.

Empire Café *American* 20 | 19 | 16 | $16

Montrose | 1732 Westheimer Rd. (bet. Dunlavy & Woodhead Sts.) | 713-528-5282 | www.empirecafe.net

Yes, the New American entrees are "delicious" and the weekend breakfast specials are a "must", but at this rustic counter-service Montrose "roadside cafe" - once a gas station - it's really "all about the cake": "enormous", "delectable" desserts you can wash down with "great coffee"; "friendly" staffers and a "hip atmosphere" also help attract a "trendy crowd"; P.S. the streetside patio is "perfect for lounging in the sun" and people-watching.

Empire Turkish Grill *Turkish* ∇ 24 | 16 | 23 | $23

West Houston | 12448 Memorial Dr. (bet. Benigus & Gessner Rds.) | 713-827-7475 | www.theempireturkishgrill.com

Sultans who swing by this "find" at a West Houston strip mall savor its "flavorful", "authentic" Turkish fare, the regional artifacts on the walls and the "service with a smile"; often filled with expats at dinnertime, it feels "very much like Istanbul."

Fadi's Mediterranean *Mediterranean* 21 | 14 | 15 | $14

Briargrove | 8383 Westheimer Rd. (Dunvale Rd.) | 713-532-0666
Meyerland | 4738 Beechnut St. (W. Loop Frwy.) | 713-666-4644
www.fadiscuisine.com

"Crowds" craving "divine" Med munchies ("excellent" brick-oven pita, "exceptional lamb", lots of veggie-friendly items) gather at these two "fast" cafeteria-style spots in Briargrove and Meyerland; true, there's "not much atmosphere" but tabs are low, naturally leading to the presence of "many young children" - a fact that disappoints some who are seeking "a peaceful, quiet meal."

Farrago *Eclectic* 19 | 17 | 17 | $27

Midtown | 318 Gray St. (Bagby St.) | 713-523-6404 | www.farragohouston.com

Look for "great surprises" on the "inventive" Eclectic menu at this "super-cool", "modern" Midtown "hot spot", where a "young", "pretty" clientele gathers in the "lovely" courtyard for "perfectly mixed" cocktails, "huge burgers" "before a ballgame" or Sunday brunch ("quite a party"); prices are "reasonable" too, though service can be "awkward."

Fernando's Latin Cuisine *Pan-Latin* - | - | - | M

Sugar Land | 14135 Southwest Frwy. (William St.) | 281-494-9087 | www.fernandosrestaurants.com

Raising the level of dining in Sugar Land is this upscale Pan-Latin eatery set in a handsome wood-trimmed space evoking an old-fashioned supper club, especially on weekends when a guitarist takes to the stage; the cuisine ranges from ceviche to pastas to char-grilled steaks, which pair nicely with the wide selection of South American wines.

59 Diner *Diner* 16 | 16 | 16 | $14

Lower Shepherd | 3801 Farnham St. (Sandman St.) | 713-523-2333
Northwest Houston | 17695 Tomball Pkwy. (Gessner Rd.) | 832-237-7559
West Houston | 10407 Katy Frwy. (Sam Houston Tollway) | 713-984-2500
NEW **Stafford** | 12550 Southwest Frwy. (Kirkwood Rd.) | 281-242-5900
www.59diner.com

"Sometimes you need a diner", and at those times hungry Houstonians opt for these four "nostalgia places" in town; the Traditional American fare ("shakes that make you forget your hardening arteries", "chocolate-chip pancakes better than sex") is kid-friendly and affordable, though skeptics shrug it's just "comfort food at its worst."

Fish, The *Japanese* 20 | 17 | 15 | $37

Midtown | 309 Gray St. (Bagby St.) | 713-526-5294 | www.thefishhouston.com

"There's "eye candy aplenty" at this "trendy", moderately priced Midtown Japanese where a "young crowd" munches on "creative rolls" in a "lively" (some say "deafening") interior done up in sleek reds and blacks; skeptics say the "scene" trumps the sushi and add that service can be "inconsistent" too; N.B. the Dallas branch opened post-Survey.

Z Fleming's Prime Steakhouse & Wine Bar *Steak* 24 | 24 | 23 | $54

River Oaks | River Oaks Ctr. | 2405 W. Alabama St. (Kirby Dr.) | 713-520-5959
The Woodlands | Woodlands Mall | 1201 Lake Woodlands Dr. (I-45) | 281-362-0103
www.flemingssteakhouse.com

"Not as stuffy" as the competition, this "inviting" chophouse chain purveys "classic" steaks and sides in "relaxed", "clubby" digs conducive to both "business and romance"; "low-profile" service and an "excellent wine-by-the-glass program" add to its allure, but since "everything's à la carte", be prepared for "high-end" tabs.

Floyd's Cajun Seafood House *Cajun/Seafood* ▽ 22 | 14 | 18 | $19

Webster | 20760 Gulf Frwy. (Nasa Rd. 1) | 281-332-7474 | www.floydsseafood.com

"The Big Easy" comes to Houston via this Cajun seafooder set in boat-shaped digs on the Gulf Freeway in Webster sending out "generous portions" of fried shrimp, crab and frogs' legs that "beer drinkers" wash down with mugs of icy Abita; the "kitchen can be a little slow", but "exceptional values" keep the "crowds" happy.

Z Fogo de Chão *Brazilian/Steak* 26 | 22 | 26 | $55

Briargrove | 8250 Westheimer Rd. (Dunvale Rd.) | 713-978-6500 | www.fogodechao.com

"Paradise for Atkins diet-lovers", this churrascaria chain imported from Brazil rolls out all-you-can-eat meats on skewers for folks seeking to "embrace their inner caveperson"; the "meal-in-itself" salad bar is equally "tasty" and the drinks sure "pack a punch", but be careful and "pace yourself" to avoid the inevitable "protein swoon."

Frenchie's ☒ *Italian* 24 | 13 | 18 | $22

Clear Lake | 1041 NASA Pkwy. (El Camino Real) | 281-486-7144 | www.villacaprionclearlake.com

"Despite the name", Italian's the game at this "casual", family-owned and family-friendly Clear Lake "standard" where "NASA eats lunch" and astronaut pics adorn the walls; regulars "treasure" the "tasty" *cucina* that comes in "huge", "steaming-hot" portions, and though the "popular" place can be a "zoo", service is usually "fast."

Fung's Kitchen *Chinese/Seafood* 25 | 19 | 18 | $23

Southwest Houston | 7320 Southwest Frwy. (Fondren Rd.) | 713-779-2288 | www.fungskitchen.com

Just east of New Chinatown, this sprawling, "authentic" Southwest Houston favorite offers what may be "the best dim sum between San Francisco and New York" along with a "huge" menu of "Hong Kong-style" "fresh fish" and other "delights"; the space features chandeliers and "mini-landscapes" on the walls, and is "always crowded with Chinese patrons" and other "adventurous eaters" who don't seem to mind the often "inconsistent service."

Gaido's *Seafood* 22 | 17 | 20 | $32

Galveston | 3800 Seawall Blvd. (37th St.) | 409-762-9625 | www.gaidosofgalveston.com

"Get seated by the window" for a "great view" of the Gulf advise admirers of this Galveston "grande dame", "serving quality seafood" since "before fish had fins" (since 1911, actually); it's still "dependable" for "incredibly fresh" seafood, "generous breadbaskets" and "pecan pie to die for", along with service that's "kind" if sometimes "spotty", so though a few cutting-edge critics carp about "outdated" interiors and "overpriced" fare at this "ossified institution", most urge "don't change a thing."

Ginza *Japanese* - | - | - | M

Briargrove | 5868 San Felipe St. (bet. Chimney Rock Rd. & Fountain View Dr.) | 713-785-0332

"Japanese expats" choose this "small" spot in Briargrove for "quality" homestyle dishes like tempura, soba and udon, plus sushi so "fresh" "it nearly jumps off the plate"; traditional decor with paper screens is on the plain side, but it gets a lift from moderate prices and "pleasant" service from the staff.

Glass Wall ☒ Ⓜ *American* 25 | 22 | 22 | $42

Heights | 933A Studewood St. (bet. E. 10th & Omar Sts.) | 713-868-7930 | www.glasswalltherestaurant.com

An "inspired" menu of "seasonal" New American dishes is served in a "striking" interior decorated with river rock and aqua tile at chef-owner Lance Fegen's "high-end" surf-inspired eatery that Heights denizens are hailing as a "great new entry" in the local dining scene; "knowledgeable" servers are a definite plus, but on the downside is a room so "noisy" that some suggest "earplugs should be placed next to the silverware."

Golden Room Ⓢ *Thai* 19 | 16 | 17 | $21

Montrose | 1209 Montrose Blvd. (bet. Clay & Dallas Sts.) | 713-524-9614 | www.goldenroomrestaurant.com

According to adherents, this colorful converted cottage in Montrose - one of the oldest Thai restaurants in town - dishes up "tasty", "basic" favorites with portions of "steamed rice in the shape of Texas"; doubters deem the "cute package" more appealing than the "average" eats.

Goode Co. Hamburgers & Taqueria *Burgers* 22 | 12 | 15 | $16

West U | 4902 Kirby Dr. (Westpark Dr.) | 713-520-9153 | www.goodecompany.com

As a member of the eponymous empire, this "friendly" West U "staple" benefits from built-in Goode will ("anything that's Goode has got to be great") but holds its own with "pure-Texas" mesquite-grilled burgers, meat and fish, "delicious" Tex-Mex breakfasts (weekends only) and "nice, cold margaritas"; with its "reasonable" prices and easy counter service, this "laid-back joint" provides "great value" for "family outings."

Ⓩ **Goode Co. Texas BBQ** *BBQ* 25 | 17 | 17 | $16

West U | 5109 Kirby Dr. (bet. Bissonnet St. & Westpark Dr.) | 713-522-2530

Memorial | 8911 Katy Frwy. (Campbell Rd.) | 713-464-1901

www.goodecompany.com

Quite possibly "the gold standard in Houston BBQ", this West U "institution" dishes up "tender" mesquite-smoked meats, "fresh-baked jalapeño cornbread" and "pecan pie" that just might "make you cry" to "day workers and land barons" who "rub shoulders" at the "communal" picnic tables outside; the "spunky" counter staff keeps the lines moving "fast" at both the "larger" Memorial offshoot and the more "down-home" original.

Goode Co. Texas Seafood *Seafood* 23 | 17 | 20 | $27

West U | 2621 Westpark Dr. (Kirby Dr.) | 713-523-7154

Memorial | 10211 Katy Frwy. (Gessner Dr.) | 713-464-7933

www.goodecompany.com

Goode friends gloat this piscatory pair "proves that Texas food can be excellent even if it's not barbecue or Mexican"; the "fresh", "perfectly seasoned" fish comes in many forms ("don't leave without trying" the signature campechana) along with other Gulf Coast specialties ("good-as-it-gets" gumbo) ferried by "quick" servers; also transporting is the decor - West U's "neat old" converted train car and an "antique racing boat" at the "more upscale" Memorial location.

Grand Lux Cafe *Eclectic* 19 | 22 | 18 | $29

Galleria | Centre at Post Oak | 5000 Westheimer Rd. (Post Oak Blvd.) | 713-626-1700 | www.grandluxcafe.com

See review in Dallas/Ft. Worth Directory.

Grappino di Nino ⑧ *Italian* 20 | 23 | 19 | $34

Montrose | 2817 W. Dallas St. (La Rue St.) | 713-528-7002 | www.ninos-vincents.com

"On a nice evening" you can enjoy a glass of wine and soak up the ambiance on the "great patio" at this most casual of the three adjacent Vincent Mandola-owned Montrose eateries (Vincent's and Nino's) where live jazz Wednesday-Saturday adds to the appeal; Italian cuisine comes in "tasty" "small plates" as well as "heartier" entrees all at prices that enthusiasts assure are "reasonable" too.

Gravitas *American* 21 | 18 | 18 | $36

Neartown | 807 Taft St. (bet. Allen Pkwy. & W. Dallas St.) | 713-522-0995 | www.gravitasrestaurant.com

Co-owner-slash-"food genius" Scott Tycer lends his air of gravitas to this "hot" Neartown bistro, a "hip", "stark" space spotlighting "inventive" New American fare and "interesting" wines; prices are "reasonable" and "prospects look bright" but for now many diagnose "growing pains", as evidenced by "uneven" service and "terrible acoustics."

Grotto *Italian* 22 | 21 | 21 | $34

Galleria | 4715 Westheimer Rd. (Westcreek Ln.) | 713-622-3663
The Woodlands | 9595 Six Pines Dr. (Research Forest Dr.) | 281-419-4252
www.grottohouston.com

Though loyalists lament this Galleria/Woodlands duo has "lost its edge" since owner Tony Vallone sold it to Landry's, fans still find it "worth a visit" for "solid", "midpriced" Neapolitan-inspired dishes, "great" antipasto and "thin and crusty" pizzas ferried by a "somewhat attentive" staff; both locations thrive in "noisy", "crowded" environs with a "see-and-be-seen" vibe, especially at the bar.

NEW Grove, The *American* - | - | - | M

Downtown | Discovery Green | 1611 Lamar St. (Crawford St.) | 713-337-7321 | www.thegrovehouston.com

Chefs Robert Del Grande (Cafe Annie) and Ryan Pera (ex 17) teamed up on the ambitious American menu at this highly anticipated arrival in Downtown Houston's new Discovery Green Park inhabiting a showstopping two-story, glass-enclosed space; its moderately priced rotisserie dishes are joined by shareable items like duck meatballs and free-range deviled eggs.

Hard Rock Cafe ◐ *American* 14 | 21 | 14 | $26

Downtown | 502 Texas Ave. (bet. Bagby & Smith Sts.) | 713-227-1392 | www.hardrock.com

An "iconic part of the tourist landscape", this rock 'n' roll-themed American chain was "cool in the '80s" but many feel it's "past its sell date", citing "mundane" grub, "haphazard" service and "way too loud" acoustics; despite a "surprisingly decent burger" and all that "fun music memorabilia", it may be better to "buy the T-shirt" instead.

Hobbit Cafe *Eclectic* 21 | 13 | 15 | $16

Lower Shepherd | 2243 Richmond Ave. (Greenbriar Dr.) | 713-526-5460

"Long before Peter Jackson" brought Middle Earth to the big screen, hobbits ruled at this *Lord of the Rings*-themed cafe, an "offbeat" "geeks' paradise" now situated in an old house in Lower Shepherd; among the "cozy nooks" that are adorned with "amusing" Tolkien memorabilia, a "granola" staff feeds the "hippielike" habitués an Eclectic array of "mile-high sandwiches" and other "healthy" vegetarian-friendly vittles.

Hollywood Vietnamese & Chinese ◐ *Chinese/Vietnamese* - | - | - | I

Montrose | 2409 Montrose (Fairview St.) | 713-523-8808

Montrose denizens are delighted by the "huge" selection of "fresh and delicious" Chinese and Vietnamese items on offer at this sprawling spot that's "fun with a large crowd"; gentle prices and late hours (they're open till 2 AM on weekends) boost the appeal, as does the bamboo-bedecked patio that's especially festive.

Z Hotel Icon Bar and Restaurant *American* 24 | 25 | 23 | $61 (fka Bank)

Downtown | Hotel Icon | 220 Main St. (Congress St.) | 832-667-4470 | www.hotelicon.com

Though Jean-Georges Vongerichten and chef de cuisine Bryan Caswell have departed, this Downtown destination still lures an "expense-account" crowd thanks to its "stunning" setting nestled in the lobby of a historic bank building with 30-ft. ceilings and "beautiful" ornate furnishings; although the "staff does a marvelous job", the New American menu strikes critics as "tastefully presented", but ultimately "fairly standard" and not up to the "flashes of brilliance" of the past; N.B. after the Hotel Icon's renovation in spring 2008 they'll be known as Voice and will serve regional American cuisine.

Houston's *American* 23 | 20 | 22 | $30

Galleria | 5888 Westheimer Rd. (Fountain View Dr.) | 713-975-1947
Upper Kirby District | 4848 Kirby Dr. (Westpark Dr.) | 713-529-2386
www.hillstone.com

A "chain that doesn't feel like one", this "reliable" national franchise "clicks" thanks to a "pretty darn good" menu of "all-American comfort" items (including a notoriously "addicting spinach dip") and a "modern metropolitan" ambiance that brings in "mingling singles" after work; despite debate on the cost - "inexpensive" vs. "overpriced" - most report "solid quality" here.

Z Hugo's *Mexican* 26 | 23 | 22 | $35

Montrose | 1600 Westheimer Rd. (Mandell St.) | 713-524-7744 | www.hugosrestaurant.net

This stylish Montrose "class act" provides "gourmet, designer Mexican" that's both "innovative and traditional", making it "a great alternative" for chile-hounds "who want Latin cuisine but are tired of the old Tex-Mex"; "excellent handmade margaritas", a "great wine list", "cool setting" (though the noise-averse warn it has the "acoustics of an airplane hangar") and capable staff add to the allure; P.S. Sunday brunch is its "best-kept secret here."

Hunan ☒ *Chinese* ∇ 21 | 15 | 18 | $34

Downtown | 812 Capitol St. (Milam St.) | 713-227-8999

Tucked among the towering skyscrapers, this Downtown Sino convenient to the convention center earns kudos from fans for its "upscale" Hunan cuisine; it draws a "good lunch crowd" so those who aren't "prepared to wait" may want to opt for takeout.

Hungry's Cafe & Bistro *Eclectic* 19 | 15 | 17 | $17

Rice Village | 2356 Rice Blvd. (bet. Greenbriar & Morningside Drs.) | 713-523-8652

West Houston | 14714 Memorial Dr. (Dairy Ashford Rd.) | 281-493-1520

www.hungryscafe.com

Admirers with an appetite appreciate this Eclectic pair in Rice Village and West Houston, dubbing them "kid-friendly" "neighborhood staples" for their "healthy", "well-prepared" and "inexpensive" eats and "straightforward" decor; servers are "inexperienced but eager to please", and both locations offer home delivery for a small fee.

Z Ibiza M *Mediterranean/Spanish* 25 | 21 | 22 | $40

Midtown | 2450 Louisiana St. (McGowen St.) | 713-524-0004 | www.ibizafoodandwinebar.com

"A favorite of the 'in' crowd", this "happening" Midtown Med helmed by chef Charles Clark is famed for "imaginative", "consistently delicious" "tapas-style" dishes, though it's the "incomparable" wine list that wins the most raves with "great values" on the 500-label collection; servers are "responsive", but regulars report "it can get a little noisy", especially on "weekends", so lunch is a more "relaxing" option; N.B. they recently opened the plush, nonsmoking Ibiza Lounge Next Door offering a similarly extensive wine list plus a full bar.

India's Restaurant *Indian* 21 | 17 | 18 | $25

Galleria | 5704 Richmond Ave. (Chimney Rock Rd.) | 713-266-0131 | www.indiasrestauranthouston.com

Masala mavens hail the "constantly improving menu" at this Galleria Indian offering "seriously spiced dishes" alongside "lean" healthy heart options in serene surroundings with wall hangings and fresh flowers; a few find fault with service that needs "improving", but on the whole locals laud it as a "friendly" spot that's a "great value."

Indika M *Indian* 25 | 22 | 22 | $37

Montrose | 516 Westheimer Rd. (Whitney St.) | 713-984-1725 | www.indikausa.com

Gastronomes gush over the "delicious", "delicately spiced" Indian dishes prepared with "intelligent", "modern twists" at "charming" chef-owner Anita Jaisinghani's "upmarket" Montrose "jewel"; "gracious" servers work the "cool" and contemporary room where saffron-yellow walls and colorful curtains add a soft touch.

Irma's ⓢ *Mexican* 22 | 17 | 21 | $21

Downtown | 22 N. Chenevert St. (Ruiz St.) | 713-222-0767

At this Downtown "institution" "close to Minute Maid Park", "politicos, courthouse types" and other regulars happily step up to the plate for Irma Galvan's "uncomplicated" Mexican fare and a glass of her "legendary lemonade"; quirks of the "funky-shabby" spot include "quaint oral menus" and the "upbeat" staff's use of an "honor system" to total up the tab; N.B. closed weekends, except on days when the Astros are playing.

Irma's Southwest Grill ⓢ *Tex-Mex* 21 | 16 | 18 | $23

Downtown | 1314 Texas Ave. (Austin St.) | 713-247-9651 | www.irmassouthwest.com

"Easier to get to" and a little "pricier", this Downtown offspring of Irma's "lacks its mother's character" but the "authentic Tex-Mex" fare (including "delicious" seafood and the "signature lemonade") is just as "enjoyable"; with "efficient" service and decor that's "a bit nicer" than the original, it's equally "great before a ballgame" - especially now that it has doubled in size.

Isla Coquí Ⓜ *Puerto Rican* - | - | - | M

Heights | 1801 Durham Dr. (I-10) | 713-861-1000 | www.islacoquipr.com

"Home-cooked Puerto Rican food" (think sweet plantain-beef pie) draws an eclectic crowd to this moderately priced Heights area newbie; though the spacious room appointed with white ceiling fans is "sparsely decorated", it grooves on a festive vibe, thanks to tropical drinks and live jazz and salsa on Friday nights.

Istanbul Grill Ⓜ *Turkish* 22 | 14 | 21 | $17

Rice Village | 5613 Morningside Dr. (University Blvd.) | 713-526-2800 | www.istanbulgrill.com

This "unpretentious" Rice Village Turk provides "excellent value" with "fresh, delicious" and "authentic" Middle Eastern eats served by an "attentive staff"; the decor is "nothing much to look at", but the vibe is "casual and fun" - just know that parking can be a "nightmare."

Z Japaneiro's Sushi Bar & Latin Grill *Japanese/S American* 26 | 20 | 22 | $24

Sugar Land | Sugar Land Town Sq. | 2168 Texas Dr. (Hwy. 59) | 281-242-1121 | www.japaneiro.com

"It works!" exclaim initiates impressed by the "fusion of Japanese and Latin" at this colorful original on the Town Square in Sugar Land, where the "interesting" "balance of tastes" yields "excellent" eating and "lots of things to choose from" ("the only place I know I can get plantains and sushi"); generous portions provide "value" for the quality, and the "service is great as well."

Jarro Café ⓢ Ⓜ *Mexican* - | - | - | I

Spring Branch | 1521 Gessner (Hazelhurst Dr.) | 713-827-0373 | www.jarrocafe.com

The taco truck in front of this Spring Branch counter-service Mexican is all you need to know about its roots, which are even more evident in its "awesome tacos" and the array of "six or so salsas" (some fiery) that give the goods an authentic kick; jarringly, the frill-free interior sports decor that's more Beatlemania than taqueria.

Jasmine Asian Cuisine *Vietnamese* - | - | - | I

Alief | 9938 Bellaire Blvd. (Sam Houston Pkwy.) | 713-272-8188 | www.jasmineasiancuisine.com

Tucked into a shopping center in Alief's New Chinatown, this surprisingly spacious and stylish Vietnamese (think Indochine-era ceiling fans and lots of bamboo) offers one of the broadest menus around, including seldom-found specialties like seven courses of beef or fish; its lunch specials rank among the best deals in town.

Jasper's *American* 24 | 25 | 24 | $42

The Woodlands | Market St. | 9595 Six Pines Dr. (Lake Woodlands Dr.) | 281-298-6600 | www.jaspers-restaurant.com

See review in Austin and the Hill Country Directory.

Jax Grill *Southern* 19 | 12 | 16 | $13

Bellaire | 6510 S. Rice Ave. (Bissonnet St.) | 713-668-3606

Heights | 1613 Shepherd Dr. (Eigel St.) | 713-861-5529

This casual pair of "local grills with personality" boasts a "huge menu" of "good" "basic" Southern fare doled out "serve-yourself"-style, which helps keep prices "cheap"; "zydeco dancing on Friday and Saturday nights" is a draw at the lower Heights location, while the Bellaire outpost is "ultra-kid-friendly", which means it's "always packed on weekends and evenings" with the "soccer mom" crowd.

Jenni's Noodle House Ⓢ *Vietnamese* ▽ 21 | 10 | 16 | $15

Lower Shepherd | 3111 S. Sheperd Dr. (Alabama St.) | 713-228-3400 | www.noodlesrule.com

It's now installed in spiffier new digs in Lower Shepherd, but "yummy" "noodles in wonderfully flavorful soups" are still the main attraction at this "bargain" Vietnamese; fans find it jennuinely "cool" and "accommodating", though a few less-than-thrilled purists plead for "better instead of hipper."

Z Jimmy Wilson's Seafood & Chop House *Seafood* 26 | 20 | 23 | $30

NEW **Briargrove** | 5161 San Felipe St. (bet. Post Oak Blvd. & Sage Rd.) | 713-960-0333

Royal Oaks | 12109 Westheimer Rd. (Houston Center Blvd.) | 281-497-1110

www.jimmywilsons.com

A rep for "excellent Cajun seafood" like the trademark gumbo precedes this Royal Oaks vet, home to "the freshest" fish and a menu "chock-full of seasonal delicacies" from the Gulf and beyond; with "friendly and efficient" service, it's "like a short trip to Louisiana" even if (or maybe because) the original site's rustic room "is a little tired"; N.B. the Briargrove location is newer and unrated.

Joyce's Ocean Grill *Seafood* 19 15 20 $30

Briargrove | 6415 San Felipe St. (Winrock Blvd.) | 713-975-9902 ☒

Greenway Plaza Area | 3736 Westheimer Rd. (Willowick Rd.) | 713-850-7738

www.joycesoceangrill.com

These "friendly neighborhood" seafooders serve "fresh", "consistent" "Gulf Coast–style" cuisine and more, making them "a locals' favorite" even if the unconvinced carp "overrated"; the "old standby" in Briargrove ("tucked away in the shopping center, so look hard") has an overt marine theme, while the newer Greenway Plaza port is more nautically restrained.

Julia's Bistro ☒ *Nuevo Latino* 19 14 19 $33

Midtown | 3722 Main St. (Alabama St.) | 713-807-0090 | www.juliasbistro.com

A "modern" "urban" bistro with the MetroRail line outside its front window, this midsized Midtowner plies "innovative" Nuevo Latino cooking in a "stark, loftlike" space; most applaud the "inventive and fresh dishes" and "unusual picks" on the wine list, though holdouts hint at a "noisy background" and "erratic" service.

Kahn's Deli ☒⇏ *Deli* 23 10 18 $13

Rice Village | Village, The | 2429 Rice Blvd. (Morningside Dr.) | 713-529-2891 | www.kahnsdeli.com

This "hole-in-the-wall" Rice Village deli is a counter-service "continuation of the Kahn family tradition" featuring "generous" top-notch "NY sandwiches" for a fair price; somewhat "surly" help and wall decor that hasn't changed "since it opened" 25 years ago come with the "authentic" territory.

Kam's Fine Chinese Cuisine *Chinese* 20 13 20 $18

Montrose | 4500 Montrose Blvd. (I-59) | 713-529-5057

A "loyal local" following makes this Montrose Chinese a "neighborhood" "staple" for "quality" chow that won't break the bank; happy kampers add the "service is always friendly", and if the dark-paneled decor's "not fancy", the goods are also "spot-on to go."

Kaneyama *Japanese* ▽ 27 17 21 $36

West Houston | 9527 Westheimer Rd. (Rockyridge Dr.) | 713-784-5168 | www.kaneyama-houston.com

After a decade and a half, this West Houston Japanese "keeps its standards" with an "imaginative" menu of "great sushi" leading an "excellent" lineup that's paired with "impeccable" service; insiders sense it's "underappreciated" (maybe due to the nondescript strip-center setting), but it's a "better bargain" than many.

Z Kanomwan ☒ *Thai* 27 7 11 $18

Neartown | 736½ Telephone Rd. (Dumble St.) | 713-923-4230

Fans of this Neartown BYO stalwart (aka the 'Telephone Thai') fervently proclaim the "addictive", "intensely flavored" Siamese eats "the best" in town "hands down"; the "lackluster room" is "nothing to look at" and service is often "grumpy", but at least a trip here "won't break the bank."

Karl's at the Riverbend Ⓜ *American/Continental* ▽ 27 | 21 | 26 | $43

Richmond | 5011 FM 723 (FM 359) | 281-238-9300 | www.karlsrb.com

Those in-the-know declare it's "definitely worth the drive" to this rustic Richmond roost, a "wonderful" "find" for "traditional" American-Continental fare ("game dishes are the main attraction") matched with "reasonable wines"; the "friendly staff" is bent on creating a "relaxing" atmo and lays out "an amazing spread" for Sunday brunch.

Kasra Persian Grill *Persian* - | - | - | M

Southwest Houston | 9741 Westheimer Rd. (Gessner Rd.) | 713-975-1810

Complimentary fresh taftoon ("some of the best bread ever") kicks off the Persian excursion at this Southwest Houston strip-center standout, which grills up "large portions" of "delicious" specialties at a moderate cost; the comfy quarters are well attended, and newbies can rest assured the "staff is very helpful explaining the menu."

Katz's Deli ◐ *Deli* 19 | 15 | 16 | $18

Montrose | 616 Westheimer Rd. (Montrose Blvd.) | 713-521-3838 | www.ilovekatzs.com

See review in Austin and the Hill Country Directory.

Kenneally's Irish Pub ◐ *Pub Food* ▽ 16 | 11 | 16 | $16

Lower Shepherd | 2111 S. Shepherd Dr. (Indiana St.) | 713-630-0486 | www.irishpubkenneallys.com

"Leave it to an Irish pub" to make what many consider "the best thin-crust pizza in town" marvel mates of this Lower Shepherd tavern, which also proffers the usual "proletarian" pub grub to go with plenty of cold beer; add in a patio "for shade and relaxation", a "fun" crowd and bartenders who've "been here forever" and "what else do you need - ambiance?"; N.B. kitchen open till 1 AM nightly.

Kenny & Ziggy's New York Delicatessen *Deli* 24 | 17 | 19 | $20

Galleria | 2327 Post Oak Blvd. (Westheimer Rd.) | 713-871-8883 | www.kennyandziggys.com

"Oy, gevalt" exclaim fressers impressed by the corned beef and pastrami, "fabulous" smoked fish and other "old-fashioned Jewish comfort foods" that make this deli so "authentic" it evokes "Manhattan right in the middle of the Galleria"; also adding a "Big Apple feel" are the "crowded", "boisterous" room, "abrupt but helpful" staffers and the "NYC prices."

Khyber North Indian Grill Ⓜ *Indian* 23 | 16 | 19 | $23

Upper Kirby District | 2510 Richmond Ave. (Kirby Dr.) | 713-942-9424

Don't pass up this Upper Kirby District Indian grill urge regulars who revere its "flavorful" "food with flair" (the lunch buffet "rocks"); most praise the "warm, clubby" scene and "friendly service" as well, so though wallet-watchers find tabs rather "high", fans feel just "chatting with the owner is worth the price of admission."

Killen's Steakhouse ☒ *Steak* - | - | - | M

Pearland | 2804 S. Main St. (Hwy. 518) | 281-485-0844 | www.killenssteakhouse.com

"Wow, what a steak!" clamor carnivores who venture "outside the hustle and bustle" to this "outstanding" cow palace "in Pearland, no less", for "superb" cuts of aged prime beef bolstered by "extremely large sides"; ok, the "minimalist" setting might not strike a chord, but the "creativity goes into the food" and "until you taste it, you won't believe the hype."

Kim Son *Chinese/Vietnamese* 23 | 20 | 19 | $21

Bellaire | 10603 Bellaire Blvd. (bet. Rogerdale Rd. & Wilcrest Dr.) | 281-575-0140
Downtown | 2001 Jefferson St. (Chartres St.) | 713-222-2461
Stafford | 12750 Southwest Frwy. (Fountain Lake Dr.) | 281-242-3500
www.kimson.com

This "sprawling" Downtown landmark and its Stafford sibling offer an "extensive", even "overwhelming" menu (more than 400 items) of "good to excellent" Vietnamese and Chinese dishes - both "authentic" and "Americanized" - to suit a mixed clientele in "family-friendly", often crowded settings; on weekends the Southwest Freeway branch also serves "must-try" dim sum; N.B. the Bellaire location is buffet and dim sum only.

Kiran's *Indian* 25 | 22 | 22 | $39

Galleria | 4100 Westheimer Rd. (Midlane St.) | 713-960-8472 | www.kiranshouston.com

Chef-owner Kiran Verma "educates your palate" with "absolutely exceptional" cooking at this "high-end" Galleria-area Indian, where the cuisine introduces an "original" "mix of traditional and new"; with a "top-class" staff and "beautiful, serene surroundings" accented with antiques from the subcontinent, it's "pricey" but "worth every penny."

Kirby's Steakhouse *Steak* 24 | 22 | 23 | $50

The Woodlands | 1111 Timberloch Pl. (I-45) | 281-362-1121 | www.kirbyssteakhouse.com

See review in Dallas/Ft. Worth Directory.

Kona Grill *American* 20 | 21 | 18 | $27

Galleria | Galleria | 5061 Westheimer Rd. (Post Oak Blvd.) | 713-877-9191
Sugar Land | First Colony Mall | 16535 Southwest Frwy. (Hwy. 6) | 281-242-7000
www.konagrill.com

"Yuppies" enjoy the "see-and-be-seen" scene at these New Americans, connecting over drinks and a "wide menu" with "Hawaiian fusion" leanings shored up by "contemporary sushi"; converts claim "everything's a little surprising" here - "not bad for a chain."

Kubo's *Japanese* 25 | 20 | 21 | $31

Rice Village | Rice Village Arcade | 2414 University Blvd. (Morningside Dr.) | 713-528-7878 | www.kubos-sushi.com

Sushiphiles lavish kudos on this "true Japanese" hot spot upstairs in a retail center in Rice Village, where chefs trained in the homeland slice "super-fresh" fish of the "highest quality", including numerous more "exotic items"; the unadorned setting keeps the focus on the food, which "continues to deliver" at "top-notch" levels - "*arigato.*"

La Colombe d'Or *Continental/French* 21 | 27 | 24 | $56

Montrose | La Colombe d'Or | 3410 Montrose Blvd. (bet. Alabama St. & Westheimer Rd.) | 713-524-7999 | www.lacolombedor.com

Diners delight in the "romantic" surroundings at this Montrose mainstay housed in a "beautiful" "historically preserved" 1923 mansion-turned-hotel (it's rated No. 1 for Decor in Houston); yet while the "wonderful" flower-filled interior wins raves, detractors declare the "classic" French-Continental menu "needs invigoration" and say sometimes "spotty" service doesn't live up to the "extremely expensive" tabs.

La Griglia *Italian* 21 | 22 | 20 | $40

River Oaks | River Oaks Ctr. | 2002 W. Gray St. (bet. McDuffie St. & Shepherd Dr.) | 713-526-4700 | www.lagrigliarestaurant.com

Paesani praise this "boisterous", mural-filled River Oaks Italian for the "finest seafood" and "excellent" free pizza bread, ably served to an "elite" clientele; the "fabulous" bar is a "hot scene" as well, but din-sensitive diners should "bring earplugs"; P.S. since its sale to the Landry's empire, some find the place "about the same", yet many fret quality and service have "dropped like a lead balloon."

La Mexicana *Mexican* 19 | 12 | 17 | $17

Montrose | 1018 Fairview St. (Montrose Blvd.) | 713-521-0963 | www.lamexicanarestaurant.com

"For a hangover, take two tacos" and in an hour "you'll be ready to repeat the sins of the previous evening" report respondents who rely on the "great Mexican breakfasts" and other "old-school" *comida* at this "casual" Montrose "standby", a "neighborhood" "favorite."

Lankford Grocery & Market *Burgers* 23 | 10 | 15 | $12

Midtown | 88 Dennis St. (Boston St.) | 713-522-9555

This old, family-run, Midtown daytime "locals' dive" has surveyors swearing by its burgers and other "cheap and greasy" comfort food; they couldn't care less that staffers sometimes act like "grumpy parents" or that the space has "zero" decor.

Las Alamedas *Mexican* 20 | 25 | 22 | $33

Memorial | 8615 Katy Frwy. (Bingle Rd.) | 713-461-1503 | www.lasalamedas.com

"Intriguing interiors" with huge "windows overlooking the lush bayou" make this Memorial hacienda feel like a "beautiful oasis right beside a major freeway"; proponents praise the "classy" "gourmet" Mexican dishes - especially at the "quite nice" Sunday brunch and at happy hour with its "wonderful" free buffet - and "accommodating" staff, but critics lament that the "mediocre" fare and service are "no match for the view."

La Strada Ⓜ *Italian* 19 | 19 | 18 | $34

Montrose | 322 Westheimer Rd. (Taft St.) | 713-523-1014 | www.lastradahouston.com

Fans of this Montrose Italian dig its "excellent food", "pleasant" staff and "hip" atmosphere - especially the "debaucherous", "decadent" Sunday brunch (a "gigantic party"); critics blast the "noisy, crowded" "zoo" with its "uninspiring food" and "inattentive service": "overpriced, overdone, over"; N.B. the Galleria location has closed.

La Trattoria *Italian* ▽ 20 | 16 | 16 | $34

Briargrove | 6504 Westheimer Rd. (bet. Briargrove Dr. & Voss. Rd.) | 713-782-1324 | www.latrattoria-houston.com

A Briargrove fixture for 25 years and counting, this Northern Italian features "homemade" pastas and fresh seafood "prepared simply" in a "quiet setting" equipped with a wine cellar and a patio; "service can be spotty", but "the owner is such a character" that partisans pardon "the occasional lapses."

Laurier Café & Wine Ⓢ Ⓜ *American* 25 | 19 | 21 | $37

Greenway Plaza Area | 3139 Richmond Ave. (Eastside St.) | 713-807-1632 | www.lauriercafe.com

This "quaint, cute, cozy" cafe near Greenway Plaza pleases with "fantastic" midpriced New American cookery and bistro classics like "outstanding steak frites", accompanied by an "inspired wine list"; the "intimate setting" includes a small patio, making this a prime place for "a quiet meal with someone special."

La Vista *American/Italian* 23 | 14 | 20 | $27

Briargrove | 1936 Fountainview Dr. (San Felipe St.) | 713-787-9899
Memorial | 12665 Memorial Dr. (Broken Bough Dr.) | 713-973-7374
www.fatbutter.com

"Casual restaurants with un-casual food", this "neighborhood" New American pair is lauded for "wonderful" cooking incorporating "creative Italian" touches and a "super" BYO policy with a "more-than-fair" "$7 corkage fee" ("they now have a wine list" too); some take a dim view of the "bare-bones" spaces, but their "lively spirit" makes them "local" "favorites."

Leibman's *Deli* 21 | 16 | 16 | $15

West Houston | 14529 Memorial Dr. (Dairy Ashford Rd.) | 281-493-3663 | www.leibmans.com

Deli, "wine shop" and "gourmet foods" emporium are bundled into one at this West Houston vet, an ever-"popular" stop for its "fab selection" of overstuffed sandwiches and "made-from-scratch soups, salads and desserts"; since customers queue to "order at the counter" and seating is functional, many opt to "carry out."

Ⓩ **Le Mistral** Ⓜ *French* 26 | 18 | 22 | $43

West Houston | 1420 Eldridge Pkwy. (Briar Forest Dr.) | 832-379-8322 | www.lemistralhouston.com

"The Denis brothers bring St. Tropez to West Houston" at this "wonderful bistro", home to "fabulous" Provençal-inflected French fare proffered by "friendly" folks with an "unassuming" style; "neighborhood" Francophiles who make it a "favorite" acknowledge it's "a bit pricey, but worth it every time"; N.B. a post-Survey relocation puts the decor score into question.

Lemongrass Café *Asian Fusion* 21 | 19 | 21 | $24

Bellaire | 5109 Bellaire Blvd. (Rice Ave.) | 713-664-6698 | www.lemongrass-cafe.com

"Near-gourmet" Asian fusion fare that's "innovative" but "stays in the comfort zone" delights diners who have "discovered" this "true find" in Bellaire; there's also a "well-selected" wine list and an "eager if not expert" staff to help foster a "pleasant" atmosphere, though hearty eaters harrumph the "small portions" are too "pricey."

Lemon Tree Ⓜ *Peruvian* - | - | - | I

West Houston | 12591 Whittington Dr. (Dairy Ashford Rd.) | 281-556-0690

A "unique" niche for "excellent ceviche" and other "authentic" plates, this West Houston strip-center Peruvian's diminutive dining room is typically filled with expats; most root for the "interesting", "reasonably priced" eating even if "below-par" decor and "sometimes clueless" service strike sour notes; P.S. it's BYO only ("no corkage fee!").

Le Viet *Vietnamese* ▽ 21 | 15 | 17 | $19

Royal Oaks | 11328 Westheimer Rd. (Hayes Rd.) | 281-293-8883 | www.le-viet.com

This "unassuming" entry on Westheimer near Royal Oaks fills the neighborhood need for Vietnamese with a "great variety" of "flavorful" choices centered on seafood (the "lobster dishes are always good"); its allies appreciate the "friendly" atmo and modest cost, though the modern-esque setting could use some polishing.

Lexington Grille Ⓢ *Continental* ▽ 21 | 20 | 21 | $36

Lower Shepherd | 2005 Lexington St. (Shepherd Dr.) | 713-524-9877 | www.lexingtongrille.com

Get away from the nearby hustle and bustle at this "quaint" "little" Lower Shepherd "find", whose short but "varied menu" features Continental cooking so "delicious" it "should be illegal"; given the flattering lighting and "quiet", "romantic" vibes, romeos rank it among the "best locations for dinner with your date."

López Ⓢ *Mexican* - | - | - | I

Alief | 11606 S. Wilcrest Dr. (bet. Bellfort Ave. & Hwy. 59) | 281-495-2436 | www.vivalopez.com

Lóyal lócals say "mmm . . . is all you need to know" about this family-run Alief favorite, for three decades a "dependable" source of "solid Mexican" at a fair price; when paired with a casual, kid-friendly atmosphere and capable service, it's no surprise the sprawling setup is often packed.

Luigi's Ristorante Italiano Ⓢ *Italian* ▽ 25 | 23 | 25 | $37

Galveston | 2328 Strand St. (24th St.) | 409-763-6500

"*Grazie,* Luigi" gush grateful fans of the "authentic" Sicilian-tempered fare at this eponymous eatery nicely sited "in an old bank building" on Galveston's historic Strand; the "fresh ingredients" and "simpler-is-better" cooking are true to the classic Italian experience, as is the "outstanding service."

Luling City Market *BBQ* 23 11 13 $15

Galleria | 4726 Richmond Ave. (I-610) | 713-871-1903 | www.lulingcitymarket.com

Folks are fired up about this Galleria-area "hole-in-the-wall" barbecue joint because of its brisket ("tender as a mother's love"), ribs that "don't need sauce" and "delicious" sides, served counter-style on butcher paper; chatting with "interesting locals" at the "smoky" bar also befits the "traditional" treats but skeptics wonder what's with the "Wonder Bread" – "good Texas 'cue deserves better!"; N.B. a Midtown outpost is reportedly in the works for spring 2008.

Z Lupe Tortilla *Mexican* 21 17 17 $19

West U | 2414 Southwest Frwy. (Kirby Dr.) | 713-522-4420
North Houston | 15315 North Frwy. (Richey Rd.) | 281-873-6220
Northwest Houston | 22465 Tomball Pkwy. (Spring-Cypress Rd.) | 832-843-0004
West Houston | 318 Stafford St. (I-10) | 281-496-7580
Webster | 891 W. Bay Area Blvd. (I-45) | 281-338-2711
Sugar Land | 15801 Southwest Frwy. (Hwy. 6) | 281-265-7500
www.lupetortillas.com

"Divine" beef fajitas and "homemade tortillas" lead the lineup at this area chain of big, "crowded and loud" Mexicans, where the "relatively cheap" prices and "fun for families" ensure little ones are "everywhere"; on the flip side, there's "usually a wait" ("drop the kids in the sandbox and enjoy a 'rita") and purists posit the "yuppie" clientele and pidgin-menu shtick are "embarrassing."

Lyndon's Pit Bar-B-Q *BBQ* - - - I

Northwest Houston | 13165 Northwest Frwy. (Hollister Rd.) | 713-690-2112

Maybe it's "not a traditional Texas brisket house", but 'cue connoisseurs consider this BBQ joint's "pulled-pork approach" a "tasty" "change of pace" that's "worth a trip" to a "nondescript strip mall" in Northwest Houston; more typical touches include "fantastic" sides, reasonable prices and rustically tacky decor.

Z Lynn's Steakhouse ⊠ *Steak* 26 23 24 $53

West Houston | 955 Dairy Ashford St. (bet. I-10 & Memorial Dr.) | 281-870-0807 | www.lynnssteakhouse.com

Catering to "the expense-account crowd", this "high-end" West Houston meatery rewards the "well-heeled" with "delectable" prime beef and "first-rate" seafood complemented by "superior service" and an "extensive wine list" boasting over 500 labels; the office-park exterior belies a "warm", "intimate setting" suitable for "that romantic dinner."

Madras Pavilion *Indian* 22 11 14 $17

Upper Kirby District | 3910 Kirby Dr. (bet. Hwy. 59 & Richmond Ave.) | 713-521-2617

(continued)

Madras Pavilion

Sugar Land | 16260 Kensington Dr. (bet. Hwy. 6 & I-59) | 281-491-3672
www.madraspavilion.us

This no-frills multicity chainlet pleases "hungry" spice cadets seeking "great-tasting" South Indian eats "with a bite" ("interesting" midday buffets and "huge" dosas "are a must"); service, though, is "hit-or-miss" ("terrible" vs. "bearable"); N.B. the North Austin and Richardson branches are vegetarian, kosher and BYO.

Maggiano's Little Italy *Italian* 20 | 20 | 20 | $30

Galleria | 2019 Post Oak Blvd. (bet. San Felipe St. & Westheimer Rd.) | 713-961-2700 | www.maggianos.com

See review in Dallas/Ft. Worth Directory.

Magnolia Bar & Grill *Cajun/Seafood* ▽ 20 | 17 | 17 | $26

Briargrove | 6000 Richmond Ave. (Fountain View Dr.) | 713-781-6207 | www.magnolia-grill.com

A "reliable" stop for over 25 years and a "crawfish lover's paradise" in season, this Briargrove Cajun specializes in South Louisiana faves like Gulf seafood, étouffée and bread pudding; but though the fairly priced fare's still "consistent", the old-school setting is "getting worn around the edges."

Mai's Restaurant ◐ *Vietnamese* 23 | 11 | 17 | $17

Midtown | 3403 Milam St. (Francis St.) | 713-520-7684 | www.maisrestauranttx.com

"Terrific value" makes decor "irrelevant" at this Midtown Vietnamese "landmark" offering a "novel-size" menu of "wonderful", "spicy" specialties for "cheap"; "touch-and-go" service ranges from "quick" to "notoriously bad", but the kitchen stays open until 4 AM daily, making this "people-watching" spot "salvation" for "insomniacs", "college students" and "clubbers leaving the bars Downtown."

Mai Thai ⊠ *Thai* 23 | 16 | 23 | $19

Upper Kirby District | 3819 Kirby Dr. (bet. Hwy. 59 & Richmond Ave.) | 713-522-6707 | www.maithaihouston.com

Despite its pink-hued exterior and location in the bustling Upper Kirby District, this "tried-and-true" Thai is still "a hidden gem" serving "exemplary" Siamese classics in "quiet", "simple surroundings"; the "quality" chow and "impeccably" "polite" staff have admirers pronouncing it "a great neighborhood place."

Mama Ninfa's *Tex-Mex* 22 | 15 | 20 | $22

Hobby | 8553 Gulf Frwy. (I-45) | 713-943-3183
Bellaire | 5423 Bellaire Blvd. (Chimney Rock Rd.) | 713-432-0003
Downtown | 600 Travis St. (Texas St.) | 713-228-6200 ⊠
Galleria | 5923 Westheimer Rd. (Fountain View Dr.) | 713-781-2740
Uptown | 1650 Post Oak Blvd. (San Felipe St.) | 713-623-6060
Memorial | 9333 Katy Frwy. (Echo Ln.) | 713-932-8760

(continued)

(continued)

Mama Ninfa's

Upper Kirby District | 3601 Kirby Dr. (Richmond Ave.) | 713-520-0203

Original Ninfa's on Navigation *Tex-Mex*

Neartown | 2704 Navigation Blvd. (bet. Delano & Nagle Sts.) | 713-228-1175

www.mamaninfas.com

This "bustling" Neartown grande dame of "traditional Tex-Mex" inspired a chain of spin-offs, but consensus says "the other locations fall short" of the "awesome" "authentic" likes of its legendary fajitas, "made-by-hand" tortillas and "unmatched" Ninfaritas; the backdrop may be "ramshackle", but the "colorful atmosphere" is still "worth a trip to the neighborhood" and "a must for visitors"; N.B. the original on Navigation is now an independent operation.

Mama's Café ◐ *American* 19 | 14 | 18 | $14

Briargrove | 6019 Westheimer Rd. (bet. Fountain View & Greenridge Drs.) | 713-266-8514 | www.mamascafe.net

See review in San Antonio Directory.

Mambo Seafood *Seafood* 20 | 10 | 16 | $16

Sharpstown | 6697 Hillcroft St. (Dashwood Dr.) | 713-541-3666
Spring Branch | 10002 Long Point (Telephone Rd.) | 713-465-5009
North Houston | 10810 N. Frwy. (Kingswood Ln.) | 281-820-3300
North Houston | 6101 Airline Dr. (Dunham Dr.) | 713-691-9700
Northwest Houston | 13485 Hwy. 290 (Tidwell Rd.) | 713-462-0777
www.mamborestaurants.com

Brightly bedecked and "casual", this local chain is known for "great, cheap seafood" prepared Mexican-style and washed down with *micheladas* (spicy south-of-the-border beer drinks); in keeping with the "value" orientation, their interiors "leave something to be desired."

Mardi Gras Grill *Cajun/Seafood* ▽ 18 | 12 | 18 | $20

Heights | 1200 Durham Dr. (Nett St.) | 713-864-5600 | www.mardigrasgrill.net

"Good ol'" Cajun fin fare is the forte at this Lower Heights hideout, a "master" at crab bisque, fried seafood, seasonal boiled crawfish and other "down-home" delights; the "low-key, comfortable" digs may not evoke Bourbon Street, but they still complement the rustic eats.

Market Square Bar & Grill ☒ *American* - | - | - | I

Downtown | 311 Travis St. (Preston St.) | 713-224-6133 | www.marketsquarehouston.com

A square deal for "fine" American fare including the "best burger" around, this "locals' hangout" occupies an old brick building where the "shabby-chic ambiance" "makes everything taste better"; plus the patio out back lets desk jockeys "escape Downtown for an hour."

Z Mark's American Cuisine *American* 28 | 26 | 27 | $59

Montrose | 1658 Westheimer Rd. (bet. Dunlavy & Ralph Sts.) | 713-523-3800 | www.marks1658.com

"The old church still produces heavenly dishes" declare the faithful at this "upper-echelon" Montrose New American (voted Most

Popular and No. 1 for Food in Houston) in a "beautifully converted" fane, where "master chef" Mark Cox fuses the finest in "fresh ingredients" into "exquisite" seasonal fare that's "expensive but so worth it"; "attentive" "but not stuffy" service and a "vibrant", upscale setting "truly bring the meal to the next level", marking this one as "tops" for "special occasions."

Mary'z Mediterranean Cuisine *Mediterranean* ▽ 21 | 11 | 13 | $22

Galleria | 5825 Richmond Ave. (bet. Chimney Rock Rd. & Fountain View Dr.) | 832-251-1955 | www.maryzcuisine.com

This Galleria-area Mediterranean is an "authentic enough" source of "decent Lebanese" featuring kebabs, shawarmas and other viands of the Levant; it draws "large groups that congregate to socialize and smoke hookahs" on the expansive patio, and if "service is a bit slow", it's always "friendly."

Masala Wok *Chinese/Indian* 18 | 12 | 15 | $13

Southwest Houston | Carillion Sq. | 10001 Westheimer Rd. (Briarpark Dr.) | 713-784-8811 | www.masalawok.com

See review in Dallas/Ft. Worth Directory.

Masraff's *Continental* 23 | 24 | 24 | $50

Uptown | 1025 S. Post Oak Ln. (bet. San Felipe St. & Woodway Dr.) | 713-355-1975 | www.masraffs.com

Set in a "classy" stand-alone building, this "sophisticated" Uptowner earns wide recognition for its "superb" "Euro-American cuisine" and "especially attentive service" led by a "genial host"; a "beautiful setting" hung with Murano chandeliers creates a "fashionable atmosphere" that's a natural "for a special event" or just "to stop for a drink" and enjoy the "live piano."

Massa's Restaurant ☒ *Seafood* 19 | 14 | 18 | $31

Downtown | 1160 Smith St. (Dallas St.) | 713-650-0837

Massa's Seafood Grill ☒ *Seafood*

Downtown | 1331 Lamar St. (bet. Austin & Caroline Sts.) | 713-655-9100

www.massas.com

These family-owned Downtown seafood restaurants are fraternal, not identical, twins; the "dimly lit, relaxed" Smith Street locale offers turf as well as surf, while the amply windowed Seafood Grill cooks with a "Creole-Cajun flair", but both please their "power-lunching" patrons.

Max's Wine Dive Ⓜ *Eclectic* 21 | 15 | 17 | $32

Heights | 4720 Washington Ave. (Shepherd Dr.) | 713-880-8737 | www.maxswinedive.com

"Comfort food to the nth degree" chased with 180 "super wines by the glass" keeps this "casual", diner-ish Heights-area "hot spot" filled to the max as a "loud", "fun crowd" flocks in for "funky" Eclectic eats like fried chicken and 'haute dogs'; maybe the "service doesn't measure up to the food", but you'll still have to "come early" "if you expect to sit down."

FOOD | DECOR | SERVICE | COST

McCormick & Schmick's *Seafood*

21 | 21 | 20 | $41

Uptown | Uptown Park | 1151 Uptown Park Blvd. (Post Oak Blvd.) | 713-840-7900 | www.mccormickandschmicks.com

See review in Austin and the Hill Country Directory.

McGonigel's Mucky Duck *Pub Food*

16 | 21 | 18 | $17

Upper Kirby District | 2425 Norfolk St. (bet. Park & Revere Sts.) | 713-528-5999 | www.mcgonigels.com

"Surprisingly good pub food" shares the bill with "amazing music" at this Upper Kirby Anglo-Irish tavern, an intimate showcase where top regional acts (Alejandro Escovedo, Jack Ingram, etc.) perform most nights of the week; it's easy to duck in "for uncrowded lunches", and the "great beer selection" is poured in proper Imperial pints.

Melting Pot, The *Fondue*

21 | 20 | 21 | $43

Galleria | 6100 Westheimer Rd. (Greenridge Dr.) | 713-532-5011 | www.meltingpot.com

See review in Austin and the Hill Country Directory.

Mexico's Deli *Deli/Mexican*

- | - | - | I

West Houston | 2374 Dairy Ashford St. (Westheimer Rd.) | 281-679-7790

"This is authentic Mexican" cheer compadres of this West Houston deli, known for bounteous tortas (grilled sandwiches) that deliver hearty combos of meats and cheese at a fantastic value; the agua frescas ("fresh fruit drinks") are a "right-on" complement to the chow.

Mia Bella Trattoria *Italian*

22 | 18 | 21 | $28

Downtown | 320 Main St. (Preston St.) | 713-237-0505
Greenway Plaza Area | 2006 Lexington St. (bet. Hwy. 59 & Shepherd Dr.) | 713-523-2428
www.miabellatrattoria.com

At these two "easygoing" eateries Downtown and in the Greenway Plaza Area, Italian aficionados find the chow *bella* - "not just tomato sauce and garlic", it's "high-end fare at low-end prices"; *amici* are satisfied with the "friendly, prompt" service and "authentic" atmosphere and say the Main Street branch is "good for a quick bite" before the theater or an evening of "bar-hopping."

Michelangelo's *Italian*

24 | 22 | 23 | $36

Montrose | 307 Westheimer Rd. (Mason St.) | 713-524-7836 | www.michelangelosrestaurant.com

Nearly 40 years "hasn't changed much in the atmosphere or quality" at this "romantic" Montrose Italian, where loyalists trek for the "excellent food" and "wonderful ambiance" centered around a dining room that uniquely features a "tree growing through the roof"; it's the picture of a "charming" "date place" and a "family favorite" for brunch.

Mi Luna *Spanish*

19 | 17 | 16 | $27

Rice Village | 2441 University Blvd. (Kelvin Dr.) | 713-520-5025
The Woodlands | 6777 Woodlands Pkwy. (Kuykendahl Rd.) | 281-419-0330

The topic is tapas at this Spanish pair in Rice Village and The Woodlands where amigos come en masse to "sample a number" of "tasty", "creative" morsels and "potent" sangria; luna-tics particularly love the evenings with live music and dancing, which may be why these "informal" venues are "always festive" (aka "loud" and "chaotic") and often "crowded" with "glittery" "twentysomethings."

NEW Mint Café *Mediterranean* ▽ 19 | 13 | 16 | $18

Galleria | 2800 Sage Rd. (Alabama St.) | 713-622-3434 | www.mintcafehouston.com

Recently minted in the shadow of the Galleria, this "small", minimalist Mediterranean dishes up "plentiful" plates of Lebanese specialties ("the kebabs are great") at a moderate cost; but those not in tune with the counter-service setup demur "nothing special."

Mission Burritos *Mexican* 22 | 12 | 17 | $11

Heights | 1609 Durham Dr. (Eigel St.) | 713-426-6634
Lower Shepherd | 2245 W. Alabama St. (Greenbriar Dr.) | 713-529-0535
www.missionburritos.com

These "fast", "friendly" "counter-service" Mexicans in the Heights and Lower Shepherd "blow the doors off the bigger chains" with their "huge" "Californian-style burritos", "made to order" with "fresh" fixings at a "bargain" price; if the interiors are missin' something, there's a "great patio" at each address.

Miss Saigon Café Ⓢ *Vietnamese* 22 | 16 | 21 | $24

Rice Village | 5503 Kelvin St. (Times Blvd.) | 713-942-0108

"Small" but "clean and comfortable", this "charming" Rice Village Vietnamese wins kudos for its "simple" "home-cooked" dishes served by a "friendly" crew; though it runs a bit "more expensive" than some competitors, regulars regard this "fave" as "a sweet little date spot."

Mockingbird Bistro Wine Bar *American* 25 | 20 | 23 | $44

River Oaks | 1985 Welch St. (McDuffie St.) | 713-533-0200 | www.mockingbirdbistro.com

"Chef-owner John Sheely is a genius" twitter awestruck admirers who "consider moving closer" to this "excellent" New American "tucked away" in River Oaks, which "consistently delivers" with its "delightful" "seasonal menu" and "fabulous" 500-label wine list; it glides on the wings of "professional" service, and the "low-lit" space with medieval accents lends a "funky" feel.

Mo Mong *Vietnamese* 20 | 16 | 16 | $22

Montrose | 1201 Westheimer Rd. (Waugh Dr.) | 713-524-5664

This "swinging" "spring roll-martini nexus" in Montrose draws an "urban" clientele hungry for its "delicious", not-quite-authentic Vietnamese cuisine; "accommodating" servers are "sometimes sassy" and food is somewhat "expensive", but the "funky" scene makes some folks feel they're "in San Francisco, not Houston."

NEW Monarch *American* ▽ 21 | 25 | 24 | $55

Medical Center | Hotel ZaZa | 5701 Main St. (Ewing St.) | 713-527-1800 | www.hotelzaza.com/houston

The royal fanfare greeting the "trendy" Hotel ZaZa's debut near the Medical Center extends to this "gorgeous", "romantic" New American where "higher-end" types can "see and be seen" enjoying a "fun and functional" menu and "lovely views of the Mecom fountain" outside; but though loyal subjects find it "fabulous", others protest the "premium cost" for an operation that's "still working to get it right."

Morton's, The Steakhouse *Steak* 25 | 21 | 23 | $62

Downtown | 1001 McKinney St. (Fannin St.) | 713-659-3700
Galleria | Centre at Post Oak | 5000 Westheimer Rd. (Post Oak Blvd.) | 713-629-1946
www.mortons.com

"Consistency abounds" at this "can't-go-wrong" steakhouse chain pairing "well-prepared" chops that "hang off the plate" with "seriously powerful martinis"; "arm-and-a-leg" pricing comes with the territory, along with a "Saran-wrapped presentation" of raw meats (accompanied by an instructional "recitation" by the waiter) – a "shtick" that many find "tired."

Moveable Feast, A Ⓢ *American* ▽ 22 | 9 | 18 | $13

Memorial | 9341 Katy Frwy. (Echo Ln.) | 713-365-0368 | www.amoveablefeast.com

"Are they sure this is health food?" ask amazed admirers of this "comfortable", long-established Memorial natural foods store and cafe who assert its "variety" of "good-tasting" Traditional American eats proves such fare "doesn't have to be boring"; feasters are also moved to comment on the crew's "great hospitality."

Nelore Churrascaria *Brazilian/Steak* ▽ 20 | 19 | 25 | $42

Montrose | 4412 Montrose Blvd. (Richmond Ave.) | 713-395-1050 | www.nelorechurrascaria.com

"Only meat lovers need come (and come hungry)" to this Montrose all-you-can-eat Brazilian steakhouse, where a "caring staff" is afoot to "ensure your favorite cuts" are "only seconds away"; set in a comfy old casa with "minimal" frills, its midpriced blowout is "a whole lot cheaper" than the more upscale competition's.

New York Coffee Shop *Diner* - | - | - | I

Meyerland | 9720 Hillcroft (Braeswood Blvd.) | 713-723-8650

In "time-honored" coffee-shop "tradition", this Formica-lined Meyerland mainstay dishes up "great breakfasts", deli specials and "real NY-style bagels" that are "some of the best" in town; low prices lead to "lines on the weekends" and a regular morning crowd at the adjoining bakery; N.B. closes at 3 PM daily.

Z Nielsen's Delicatessen *Deli* 26 | 4 | 18 | $11

Galleria | 4500 Richmond Ave. (Mid Lane St.) | 713-963-8005
Spring | 26830 I-45 N. (Woodlands Pkwy.) | 281-363-3354 Ⓢ Ⓜ

After more than half a century, Nielsen ratings are still high for the "wonderful" deviled eggs, "great sandwiches" and "creamy potato salad" – all with that "famous" housemade mayonnaise – served at this "traditional" counter-service deli in the Galleria area and Spring; less of a hit is the no-frills, no-tips, no-space setting that suggests all the energy is channeled into the food: "consider carry-out" or delivery.

	FOOD	DECOR	SERVICE	COST

Niko Niko's *Greek* 23 | 13 | 16 | $15

Montrose | 2520 Montrose Blvd. (Missouri St.) | 713-528-1308 | www.nikonikos.com

"Yum yum" echo enthusiasts at this "wildly popular" Montrose "staple", an "H-town classic" where the "giant portions" of "amazing" eats are "as good as Greek gets" and the "utilitarian" "self-serve" setup is "always a full house"; it's "indispensable" to those "on a budget", and thanks to "recent renovations" the "long lines" now "move fast."

Nino's [S] *Italian* 24 | 22 | 22 | $34

Montrose | 2817 W. Dallas St. (La Rue St.) | 713-522-5120 | www.ninos-vincents.com

"It hasn't lost any of its touch over the years" say steadfast supporters of this '70s-era Montrose Italian, where the Mandola family serves up "terrific food" in a "pretty" "old house" that shares a courtyard with its sib, Vincent's; notwithstanding the rustic, "homestyle feel", this is the toniest of the three eateries on the site.

Nippon *Japanese* - | - | - | M

Montrose | 4464 Montrose Blvd. (bet. Hwy. 59 & Richmond Ave.) | 713-523-3939

For a "more authentic" sushi experience, this "real Japanese" joint in Montrose claims a 23-year history of slicing "incredibly fresh" fish to real-deal specifications (though "some excellent 'American' rolls" make the cut too); prices are fair for the quality, but some suggest the unassuming digs "need to be updated."

Nit Noi *Thai* 21 | 17 | 18 | $19

Champions | Red Oak Shopping Ctr. | 850 FM 1960 W. (Red Oak Dr.) | 281-444-7650 | www.nitnoithai.com [S]

Memorial | Woodway Sq. | 6395 Woodway Dr. (Voss Rd.) | 713-789-1711 | www.nitnoithai.com

Rice Village | 2426 Bolsover (Morningside Dr.) | 713-524-8114 [S][M]

West Houston | Royal Oaks Vill. | 11807 Westheimer Rd. (Kirkwood Dr.) | 281-597-8200 | www.nitnoithai.com

The Woodlands | 6700 Woodlands Pkwy. (Kuykendahl Rd.) | 281-367-3355 [S][M]

Now numbering five full-size restaurants, this "popular" homegrown Thai mini-chain satisfies devotees of Siamese with its "consistently" "delicious" "standards" (including "perfect" spring rolls) that can be "toned down" "for the tender of tongue" if need be; "great lunch specials" deliver added value, while service tends toward the "friendly, if not overly quick."

Noé *American* 22 | 22 | 23 | $71

Uptown | Omni Hotel Houston | 4 Riverway Dr. (Hwy. 610) | 713-871-8177 | www.noerestaurant.com

Ensconced in Uptown's Omni Hotel, this New American is deemed "fantastic" by enthusiasts of its "superb", "over-the-top" New American cuisine with a Japanese twist; most maintain that, given its "romantic" vibe and "impeccable" service, "you get more than you pay for", even though a less-impressed minority finds it a little "pretentious"; N.B. the Food score may not fully reflect the 2007 departure of chef Robert Gadsby.

Oceanaire Seafood Room *Seafood* 24 | 23 | 23 | $51

Galleria | Galleria | 5061 Westheimer Rd. (Post Oak Blvd.) | 832-487-8862 | www.theoceanaire.com

"So good that it's hard to believe it's a chain", this "exceptional" seafood franchise with outposts in Dallas and the Galleria shopping center in Houston features "all the exuberance of a steakhouse in a fish house", starting with its "bountiful menu" and "fine wine list"; "happening" bar scenes, "1930s" "ocean liner"-like settings and "big prices" reflect the overall "classy" mood.

Ocean Palace *Chinese* ▽ 23 | 14 | 19 | $18

Bellaire | Hong Kong City Mall | 11215 Bellaire Blvd. (Boone Rd.) | 281-988-8898 | www.oceanpalacerest.com

"Visitors are always impressed" with this vast Sino seafood emporium located in a busy Asian shopping mall in Bellaire; its "wonderful displays" of fin fare (especially "dinner banquets") have appeal, but the magnet for most is the "extensive" array of dim sum - on weekends, the 1,800-plus seats are "packed with Chinese families" and others "craving" the savory bites brought around via "quick carts."

Old Heidelberg *German* ▽ 21 | 16 | 19 | $28

Galleria | 1810 Fountain View (San Felipe Dr.) | 713-781-3581 | www.theoldheidelberg.com

Teutonic tastes in this burg turn to this longtime Galleria-area German for "wonderful" wursts, Wiener schnitzel and other filling fare served with a "friendly" demeanor that makes it a "family favorite"; then again, the *echt*-retro "interior needs an update" and trendsters taunt "old is the key word" here.

100% Taquito *Mexican* 18 | 14 | 15 | $11

Greenway Plaza Area | 3245 Southwest Frwy. (Buffalo Spdwy.) | 713-665-2900 | www.100taquito.com

"A real find" assert amigos of this "authentic" sit-down taqueria across the Southwest Freeway from Greenway Plaza where a variety of "mix-and-match" homey Mexican specialties make for a "fast", "fresh" meal; decor is strictly "no frills", but prices are so "cheap", that no one seems to mind.

Osaka Japanese Restaurant *Japanese* ▽ 24 | 19 | 22 | $26

Montrose | 515 Westheimer Rd. (Stanford St.) | 713-533-9098

It's "always a pleasure" to sit down to the "top sushi" at this Montrose Japanese according to adherents who appreciate the "huge" portions and "lunch specials"; the "deliciously bossy" owner charms customers, who also cheer to hear it's "open late", till 12:30 AM on weekends.

Otilia's M *Mexican* ▽ 22 | 11 | 16 | $21

Spring Branch | 7710 Long Point Rd. (Wirt Rd.) | 713-681-7203 | www.otiliasrestaurant.com

Cravers of "authentic" "interior Mexican" have a "reason to drive out to Spring Branch" to sample the "real" thing at this casual cantina, where "'no Tex-Mex' is the mantra"; *sí*, the service and decor are merely functional, but the payoff to the palate remains "very, very good" "for the price."

Ouisie's Table *Southern* 23 | 22 | 21 | $39

River Oaks | 3939 San Felipe St. (bet. Drexel Dr. & Willowick Rd.) | 713-528-2264 | www.ouisiestable.com

Loyalists love this "sophisticated" River Oaks "favorite" for its "creative menu" of "refined Southern comfort food" and "superb wine list" proffered by a "well-mannered" staff; dissenters deem the experience "uneven" and "expensive", with more than a few citing a "haughty" "attitude" from personnel that inspires "gnashing of teeth."

Palazzo's *Italian* 20 | 16 | 19 | $23

Briargrove | Briar Ridge Ctr. | 2620 Briar Ridge Dr. (Westheimer Rd.) | 713-784-8110 Ⓢ

River Oaks | 3215 Westheimer Rd. (Bammel Ln.) | 713-522-6777

West Houston | 10455 Briar Forest Dr. (Beltway 8) | 713-785-8800

www.palazzoscafe.com

Families flock to these casual Italians for "well-prepared, beautifully presented" pastas and pizzas at "great prices", even if a few feel the wine list "could be improved"; for those disturbed by "minimal decor" and uneven service ("great" vs. "abominable") there's a "convenient" solution: "they deliver!"

Palm, The *Steak* 24 | 19 | 24 | $56

Galleria | Briar Grove Plaza | 6100 Westheimer Rd. (bet. Briar Ridge & Potomac Drs.) | 713-977-2544 | www.thepalm.com

See review in San Antonio Directory.

Z Pappadeaux *Seafood* 23 | 19 | 20 | $29

(aka Café Pappadeaux)

Medical Center | 2525 S. Loop W. (S. Main St.) | 713-665-3155

Champions | 7110 W. FM 1960 Rd. (Cutten Rd.) | 281-580-5245

FM 1960 | 2226 W. FM 1960 Rd. (Kuykendahl Rd.) | 281-893-0206

Galleria | 6015 Westheimer Rd. (Greenridge Dr.) | 713-782-6310

Memorial | 10499 Katy Frwy. (Sam Houston Pkwy.) | 713-722-0221

Northwest Houston | 13080 Hwy. 290 (Hollister St.) | 713-460-1203

Upper Kirby District | 2410 Richmond Ave. (Kirby Dr.) | 713-527-9137

Seabrook | 309 Waterfront Dr. (Houston Ave.) | 281-291-9932

Stafford | 12711 Southwest Frwy. (Corporate Dr.) | 281-240-5533

The Woodlands | 18165 I-45 N. (Shenandoah Park Dr.) | 936-321-4200

www.pappadeaux.com

Additional locations throughout the Houston area

"Bring your appetite" to the Pappas clan's locally spawned seafood chain, an "uptempo" outfit known for "consistent", "nicely spiced" Louisiana-style cooking, "gaudy Cajun decor" and "huge portions" (there's "always enough to take home"); the less impressed acknowledge the "dependable, if unexciting, food" but grouse the "packed", sprawling dining rooms are "just too loud."

Z Pappas Bros. Steakhouse $ *Steak* 27 | 24 | 25 | $62

Galleria | 5839 Westheimer Rd. (Bering Dr.) | 713-780-7352 | www.pappasbros.com

"The Pappas family does it right" at these "standout" meateries in Dallas and Houston that keep "packing them in" to their "sumptuous" quarters for a "phenomenal" combo of "awesome" beef, "killer wines" and "outstanding service" that's "worth every dollar" of the "high" prices; the "warm" ambiance is "great for business dinners or a night out with the guys", so expect a strong showing of "men in suits."

Pappas Burgers *Burgers* 23 | 14 | 18 | $16

Galleria | 5815 Westheimer Rd. (bet. Augusta & Bering Drs.) | 713-975-6082 | www.pappasburger.com

The name says it all at this Galleria spot, where the "juicy", "Texas-sized" burgers and "fresh-cut" fries rank with "the best", likely since the beef comes "from their steakhouse next door"; though the order-at-the-counter setup "isn't fancy", it's "perfect" for "beer and sports."

Pappas Grill Steakhouse *Steak* ▽ 28 | 25 | 27 | $50

Stafford | 12000 Hwy. 59 S. (Wilcrest Dr.) | 281-277-9292 | www.pappasgrillhouston.com

"Despite its second-fiddle status in the Pappas steakhouse world", this "upscale" outpost in suburban Stafford "matches its glossier cousins in quality" with "fantastic" cuts of beef and a "more-than-adequate" wine lineup to ensure "you get what you pay for"; advocates add the "service is less snooty and there's rarely a wait."

Z Pappasito's *Tex-Mex* 23 | 18 | 20 | $24

Medical Center | 2515 S. Loop W. (bet. Buffalo Spdwy. & Kirby Dr.) | 713-668-5756
Briargrove | 6445 Richmond Ave. (Hillcroft Ave.) | 713-784-5253
FM 1960 | 7050 W. FM 1960 (Cutten Rd.) | 281-893-5030
Memorial | 10409 Katy Frwy. (Sam Houston Tollway) | 713-468-1913
North Houston | 15280 I-45 N. (Lockhaven Dr.) | 281-821-4505
Northwest Houston | 13070 Hwy. 290 (NW Central Dr.) | 713-462-0245
Upper Kirby District | 2536 Richmond Ave. (Kirby Dr.) | 713-520-5066
Webster | 20099 I-45 S. (NASA Rd. 1) | 281-338-2885
Humble | 10005 FM 1960 Bypass W. (Hwy. 59) | 281-540-8664
Sugar Land | 13750 Southwest Frwy. (Dairy Ashford Rd.) | 281-565-9797
www.pappasitos.com

"It's always busy" at any of the "cavernous" locations of this "mainstream" chain, but amigos are "prepared to wait" for the "generous portions" of "consistently" "solid Tex-Mex", especially the "benchmark" beef fajitas; they're "lively" (if "loud") faves "for out-of-town guests", though those who charge "quantity over quality" is the rule contend "there are better options" "for half the price."

Pappas Seafood *Seafood* 23 | 18 | 20 | $30

Sharpstown | 6894 Southwest Frwy. (Bellerive Dr.) | 713-784-4729
Almeda | 6945 I-45 S. (Woodridge Dr.) | 713-641-0318
Lower Shepherd | 3001 S. Shepherd Dr. (W. Alabama St.) | 713-522-4595
North Houston | 11301 I-45 N. (Aldine Bender Rd.) | 281-999-9928

(continued)

Pappas Seafood

Webster | 19991 I-45 S. (Bay Area Blvd.) | 281-332-7546
Humble | 20410 Hwy. 59 N. (Townsen Blvd.) | 281-446-7707
Galena Park | 12010 I-10 E. (Federal Rd.) | 713-453-3265
www.pappasseafood.com

This "family-owned chain" of "casual" but "high-quality" seafooders is reckoned a "good fallback" for "large portions" of fin fare from a "wide" "menu of Gulf Coast favorites" that includes some of the "best fried" fish around; "as with all Pappas restaurants", they're "dependable", "noisy" and "a tad pricey."

Pasha M *Turkish* ▽ 25 | 18 | 22 | $20

Rice Village | 2325 University Blvd. (bet. Greenbriar & Morningside Drs.) | 713-592-0020 | www.epasha.com

An "untapped neighborhood treasure" to those in-the-know, this "quaint little" Turk "hidden" away near Rice Village specializes in "excellent", "fresh" Mediterranean bites; posh it's not, but the "relaxing", ruby-hued setting is warmed by a "wonderfully friendly" staff and an affordable lineup of Turkish wines.

Patrenella's S M *Italian* 17 | 14 | 19 | $29

Heights | 813 Jackson Hill St. (Washington Ave.) | 713-863-8223 | www.patrenellas.net

Sited in a "cozy" house in the lower Heights, this "old-fashioned Italian" "local" is a "family-type" "standby" that dishes up "decent" red- and white-sauce dishes at a fair price; its faithful patrons can "feel the love", though more insensitive sorts scoff "mediocre."

Paulie's *Italian* 19 | 12 | 16 | $17

West U | 2617 W. Holcombe Blvd. (Kirby Dr.) | 713-660-7057
Montrose | 1834 Westheimer Rd. (bet. Driscoll & Morse Sts.) | 713-807-7271 S
www.pauliesrestaurant.com

Shortbread cookies decorated for the season are the "best thing in the place", but supporters of this self-service pair in Montrose and West U also polish off "gourmet" salads, panini and Italian entrees; "reasonable" prices and a "simple" "diner/cafeteria" setting help make this a "great place for kids."

Pei Wei Asian Diner *Pan-Asian* 19 | 15 | 16 | $15

West U | Plaza in the Park | 5110 Buffalo Spdwy. (Westpark Dr.) | 713-661-0900
Champions | Champions Vill. | 5203 FM 1960 W. (Champion Forest Dr.) | 281-885-5430
Montrose | 1005 Waugh Dr. (bet. Clay & Dallas Sts.) | 713-353-7366
Northwest Houston | 12020 FM 1960 W. (bet. Eldridge Pkwy. & Fallbrook Dr.) | 281-571-4990
Webster | 19411 Gulf Frwy. (Bay Area Blvd.) | 281-554-9876
Kingwood | Kingwood Commons | 702 Kingwood Dr. (Chestnut Ridge Dr.) | 281-318-2877
Katy | Highland Town Ctr. | 1590 S. Mason Rd. (Highland Knolls Dr.) | 281-392-1410

(continued)

(continued)

Pei Wei Asian Diner

Sugar Land | Town Center Lakeside | 16101 Kensington Dr. (Hwy. 6) | 281-240-1931
www.peiwei.com
See review in Dallas/Ft. Worth Directory.

Perbacco Cucina Caprese Ⓢ Ⓜ *Italian* ▽ 23 | 13 | 21 | $26

Downtown | 700 Milam St. (Capitol St.) | 713-335-4441

Touted as "the best Italian restaurant no one knows", this "small" hideaway in Downtown's Pennzoil Building is "not to be missed" for "garlic-laden" classics by way of the Bay of Naples at "surprisingly reasonable prices"; "quick", "personal service" renders it a "lunch favorite", and as for the "very understated room", some shrug "good food, no atmosphere."

Ⓩ **Perry's Steakhouse & Grille** *Steak* 25 | 25 | 24 | $45

Champions | 9730 Cypresswood Dr. (Cutten Rd.) | 281-970-5999
NEW Memorial | 9827 Katy Frwy. (bet. Bunker Hill & Witte Rds.) | 832-358-9000
Clear Lake | 487 Bay Area Blvd. (Rte. 3) | 281-286-8800
Sugar Land | Sugar Land Town Sq. | 2115 Town Square Pl. (Southwest Frwy.) | 281-565-2727
The Woodlands | 6700 Woodlands Pkwy. (Kuykendahl Rd.) | 281-362-0569
www.perrysrestaurants.com

"Superb for the suburbs", this locally based "chophouse chain" is a "classy but not stuffy" haven for those far from the city center that's "distinctive" for its "awesome meats" (including the "massive" "specialty" pork chop); the "sleek, stylish" space and "super service" make for a "top-notch" "night out", "especially on someone else's tab."

Pesce Ⓢ *Seafood* 21 | 23 | 21 | $52

Upper Kirby District | Upper Kirby Shopping Ctr. | 3029 Kirby Dr. (Alabama St.) | 713-522-4858 | www.pescehouston.com

Acclaimed chef Mark Holley mans the helm at this Upper Kirby District seafooder from the Landry's fleet, an upmarket harbor for "fantastic" fish served by a "very knowledgeable staff"; a "posh" backdrop featuring a "great marble bar" contributes to "the wow factor", though pesky critics call it "noisy", "pretentious" and "overpriced."

Ⓩ **P.F. Chang's China Bistro** *Chinese* 22 | 22 | 20 | $27

Galleria | Highland Vill. | 4094 Westheimer Rd. (bet. I-610 & Willowick Rd.) | 713-627-7220
Northwest Houston | Willowbrook | 18250 Tomball Pkwy. (Willow Chase Blvd.) | 281-571-4050
West Houston | 11685 Westheimer Rd. (Kirkwood Dr.) | 281-920-3553
Sugar Land | 2120 Lone Star Dr. (Hwy. 6) | 281-313-8650
The Woodlands | Woodlands Mall | 1201 Lake Woodlands Dr. (I-45) | 281-203-6350
www.pfchangs.com
See review in Dallas/Ft. Worth Directory.

Phoenicia Deli *Mediterranean* 23 | 10 | 14 | $14

Royal Oaks | 12116 Westheimer Rd. (Gray Falls Dr.) | 281-558-0416 | www.phoenicia-deli.com

The "best chicken shawarma" and other "fresh and authentic" delights make this counter-service "hole-in-the-wall" near Royal Oaks the Med deli of choice for many, including choosy "vegetarians"; its casualness and low cost keep it crowded at lunch, but as there's "no decor" there's every reason to "take away."

Piatto *Italian* 25 | 20 | 23 | $30

Galleria | 4925 W. Alabama St. (Post Oak Blvd.) | 713-871-9722 ☒

Royal Oaks | 11693 Westheimer Rd. (Cresent Park Dr.) | 281-759-7500

www.piattoristorante.com

Each of these "family-run" fraternal twins offers a "cheery environment" (the original even musters "neighborhood appeal in the middle of the Galleria") to match their "quality" Italian dishes, best prefaced by the "amazing asparagus and lump crabmeat appetizer"; champions of the "simple" style and "reasonable prices" consider them "real sleepers."

Pico's Mex-Mex *Mexican* 24 | 15 | 21 | $20

Bellaire | 5941 Bellaire Blvd. (Renwick Dr.) | 713-662-8383 | www.picos.net

"Escape from Tex-Mex" at this "out-of-the-way" Bellaire "icon", "for many years" an "exemplary" source of "real-deal" "interior Mexican" cooking (including "fresh seafood") and "awesome margaritas" in a casual roadside setting; few are piqued at the "quite plain" decor since the "value" is "well worth the trip" ("not luxurious, not expensive").

Pizzitola's Bar-B-Que ☒ *BBQ* ▽ 24 | 9 | 21 | $17

Heights | 1703 Shepherd Dr. (I-10) | 713-227-2283

The food's the thing at this no-frills lower Heights bastion of BBQ where one of the oldest working pits around smokes what some call the "best 'cue in town", including inexpensive "old-style ribs cooked the way they should be"; the "friendly staff" that "treats everyone like a regular and the regulars like family" makes up for the space, which even fans concur is "nothing pretty."

PK's Blue Water Grill *Seafood* 21 | 18 | 19 | $29

Briargrove | Woodway Sq. | 6401 Woodway Dr. (Voss Rd.) | 713-339-3663 | www.pkbluewatergrill.com

This "friendly" Briargrove seafood house reels in praise for its "tasty" preparations of "great fresh fish", served in "low-key" environs decked out in shades of navy; a few mutineers plead for a "more consistent" kitchen and opine it "needs a little pizzazz", even with live music several nights a week.

NEW **Polo's** ☒ *American* 20 | 22 | 21 | $49

Greenway Plaza Area | Sum Pla | 3800 Southwest Frwy. (Cummins St.) | 713-626-8100 | www.polosignature.com

Take a "date whom you're trying to impress" to this "inviting" Greenway Plaza New American from chef-owner Polo Becerra, where the "innovative menu", "efficient" service and "elegant supper-club" ambiance exude "a bit of the Houston social-society vibe"; meanwhile, an unmoved few maintain there's "nothing wrong, but nothing special" either, "for the price."

Post Oak Grill ⊠ *American* 21 | 19 | 21 | $38

Downtown | 1111 Louisiana St. (Lamar St.) | 713-650-1700
Galleria | 1415 S. Post Oak Ln. (Cedar Creek Dr.) | 713-993-9966
www.postoakgrill.com

"Savory" traditional fare, "dependable service" and "genteel surroundings" qualify this upscale American pair as "favorite spots for a power lunch" ("business or social"); proponents postulate they're "pricey but deliver good value", though trendsetters see a "warhorse" outfit that's "past its prime" and "needs some updating fast."

Prego *Italian* 23 | 19 | 21 | $36

Rice Village | 2520 Amherst St. (Kirby Dr.) | 713-529-2420 | www.prego-houston.com

There's a "wonderful, big-city feel" to this "bustling" trattoria in Rice Village, which keeps a "loyal" following for its "consistently strong" Italian "classics", its "fabulous" cellar and its "accommodating" service; the 100-seat spot gets "crowded" and "noisy" at peak hours, so insiders suggest large parties "ask for the wine room" for a quieter ambiance.

Pronto Cucinino *Italian* 19 | 16 | 18 | $17

NEW **Medical Center** | 3191 W. Holcombe Blvd. (Buffalo Spdwy.) | 713-592-8646
Montrose | 1401 Montrose Blvd. (Clay St.) | 713-528-8646
www.pronto-2-go.com

"What a great concept!" cheer fans of Vincent Mandola's "fast-food Italian" duo, a "casual", "convenient" supplier of "reliable" "comfort food" (including "many of the dishes from Nino's and Vincent's") at "bargain" prices; the "efficiently designed" setups are "great for families" and well-suited to "take out or eat in" - so "what's not to like?"

Quattro *Italian* 23 | 23 | 23 | $46

Downtown | Four Seasons Hotel | 1300 Lamar St. (Austin St.) | 713-276-4700 | www.fourseasons.com

You'll "forget you're in a hotel" at the Four Seasons' "sophisticated" Downtown showcase for "Italian flair", which merges a "terrific" menu and "excellent" service in a "fabulous" "modern" setting that's equally inviting for a "business meal or an intimate celebration"; but holdouts "miss the old-school" approach and deem it "overpriced"; N.B. a new executive chef assumed the top toque post-Survey.

Ragin' Cajun *Cajun* 21 | 13 | 16 | $17

Downtown | McKinney Tunnel | 930 Main St. (McKinney St. & Travis St.) | 713-571-2422 ⊠
Galleria | 4302 Richmond Ave. (West Ln.) | 713-623-6321
Southwest Houston | Woodlake Sq. | 9600 Westheimer Rd. (Gessner Rd.) | 832-251-7171

(continued)

Ragin' Cajun

Sugar Land | 16100 Kensington Dr. (Hwy. 6) | 281-277-0704
www.ragin-cajun.com

Loyalists like this counter-service Cajun mini-chain, which may well be the "closest thing to N'Awlins in Houston" thanks to "classic" po' boys and "super-spicy" crawfish (in season); the "fun", "loud" venues have "homey" decor to go with their "interactive, messy food" ("ask for seconds, but don't ask for utensils"); N.B. the Downtown Tunnel location opens only for lunch Monday–Friday.

Z Rainbow Lodge M *American* 23 | 26 | 21 | $43

Heights | 2011 Ella Blvd. (TC Jester Blvd.) | 713-861-8666 |
www.rainbow-lodge.com

Now lodged in a log cabin overlooking a creek near the Heights, this upscale, ultrarustic New American carries on a 30-year tradition ("new home, same old good food") with plenty of wild game on the "excellent" menu - as well as "mounted" on the walls; with its "beautiful gardens" and "fabulous bar", it's "worth the steep price", even if those less smitten find the eating "predictable."

NEW Rattan Pan-Asian Bistro S *Pan-Asian* - | - | - | M

West Houston | 1396 Eldridge Pkwy. (Forkland Dr.) | 281-556-9888 |
www.rattanbistro.com

This trendy West Houston arrival is already packing 'em in with its creative sushi selection and other midpriced Pan-Asian dishes; the wine program is a highlight, with an Enomatic preservation system allowing patrons to sample high-end vintages; there's also a patio for leisurely sipping.

Raven Grill *Eclectic* 21 | 19 | 19 | $26

West U | 1916 Bissonnet St. (bet. Hazard & Woodhead Sts.) |
713-521-2027 | www.theravengrill.com

"Reliable", "not overly pricey" and "popular", this kid-friendly West U Eclectic "satisfies most palates" thanks to "comfort food" with "originality"; staffers are "efficient", and the "modern" dining room and "pleasant patio" are "nice for dates or relaxing with friends."

Red Lion Pub, The ◐ *Pub Food* ▽ 19 | 16 | 15 | $21

Lower Shepherd | 2316 S. Shepherd Dr. (Fairview St.) | 713-782-3030 |
www.redlionhouston.com

"Get your English on" at this Lower Shepherd British pub where regulars lionize the "surprisingly good" grub "for a bar", from fish 'n' chips to some "unexpected" "Indian selections"; the mood's bolstered by low lighting and dark wood, and not incidentally the tip-top "selection of draught beers" comes in correct Imperial pints.

Z Red Onion Seafood y Mas S *Pan-Latin/Seafood* 26 | 22 | 22 | $28

Northwest Houston | 12041 Northwest Frwy. (43rd St.) | 713-957-2254 |
www.caferedonion.com

"One of the most original" joints in town, Rafael Galindo's seafood specialist in Northwest Houston boasts an "innovative menu" that draws on Pan-Latin inspiration ("the ceviche is fantastic!") with "consistently excellent" results; the "beautiful, upscale" decor exudes a stylishly "old-time" feel, with a pianist providing accompaniment on weekends.

NEW Red Onion Taco Cantina *Mexican* | - | - | - | I |

Northwest Houston | 13147 Northwest Fwy. (Hollister Rd.) | 713-690-1403 | www.caferedonion.com

Providing a modern twist on the traditional taqueria, Rafael Galindo's latest concept offers refined takes on Mexican street food and serves them up in an inviting crimson-colored space in a Northwest Houston strip mall; the prices may be higher than your typical cantina, but it's worth it thanks to the high-quality ingredients and incredible array of tequilas; N.B. there's also live music on Friday nights.

NEW Reef *Seafood* | 25 | 22 | 23 | $44 |

Midtown | 2600 Travis St. (McGowen St.) | 713-526-8282 | www.reefhouston.com

Ex-Bank bigwigs Bill Floyd and Bryan Caswell "have done it again" at this "happening" addition to Midtown, a "sleek", "savvy" seafooder featuring "very inventive" preparations of "stellar fish (many unheard of)" that leave diners "extremely satisfied rather than stuffed to the gills"; the "wonderful" "modern decor" and "excellent wine values" shore up the "buzz" that's netting it "a big reputation fast."

Reggae Hut *Caribbean* | - | - | - | I |

Medical Center | 4814 Almeda (Arbor St.) | 713-520-7171 | www.thereggaehut.com

"Very informal, friendly and authentic", this counter-service cafe just north of the Medical Center dishes up "real Caribbean food" like "excellent jerk and curry" chased with fruity tropical tipples; with a "laid-back" staff that "won't be rushing you out the door", it "feels like Jamaica" and costs only a fraction of a flight.

Remington, The *American* | 25 | 25 | 25 | $63 |

Galleria | St. Regis Hotel | 1919 Briar Oaks Ln. (San Felipe St.) | 713-403-2631 | www.theremingtonrestaurant.com

A "quiet" retreat for "amazing meals", this Galleria-area New American in the St. Regis Hotel is "an exceptional setting" for "a ladies' lunch" or a premium-priced dinner, providing a "stylish" backdrop and "delicious and satisfying" food; it follows through fittingly with service that's "attentive but unobtrusive"; P.S. the "busier" bar is a "great scene" with "live sounds" and dancing on weekends.

Rickshaw Far East Bistro *Pan-Asian* ▽ | 19 | 19 | 16 | $33 |

River Oaks | 2810 Westheimer Rd. (Kirby Dr.) | 713-942-7272 | www.rickshawbambu.com

An "urban", "sexy vibe" and weekend DJs who "spin music late into the night" make this contemporary River Oaks Pan-Asian a "hipster's paradise"; most report the "nouveau" eats are "terrific" ("wonderful sushi"), if "a bit costly for what you get", but service can vary.

Rioja Tapas Restaurant Ⓜ *Spanish* 24 | 22 | 23 | $32

West Houston | 11920 Westheimer Rd. (Kirkwood Dr.) | 281-531-5569 | www.riojarestaurant.com

"Wonderful tapas" are the highlight at this "authentic" West Houston Spaniard, which matches its "creative menu" with an "excellent Spanish wine list" and "very enjoyable" surroundings replete with chandeliers, glossy woodwork and a fireplace; salsa and flamenco fans add the "live music on the weekends is a nice touch."

Rio Ranch *Steak* 21 | 21 | 20 | $31

Southwest Houston | Westchase Hilton | 9999 Westheimer Rd. (Briarpark Dr.) | 713-952-5000 | www.rioranch.com

Cowhands confirm prime beef "cooked to perfection" makes for a "hearty meal" at this regionally accented steakhouse attached to Southwest Houston's Westchase Hilton, a rough-hewn hideaway with a "Texas-theme ranch" look built on Hill Country limestone and cedar; it's "a little pricey but well worth it", and some cite the Sunday spread as the "best brunch for the money" in town.

Romero's Las Brazas *Mexican* ▽ 21 | 18 | 19 | $16

Northwest Houston | 15703 Longenbaugh Dr. (Hwy. 6) | 281-463-4661 | www.romeroslasbrazas.com

Favored for "excellent" Mexican at a fair price, this "quiet, quaint" outpost in Northwest Houston is more authentic than most thanks to its homestyle Oaxacan recipes (not to mention 60-plus tequilas); with its folksy knickknacks and tiled floor, the family-friendly space's "laid-back" feel is as genuine as it gets.

Royers Round Top Café Ⓜ *American* ▽ 22 | 12 | 17 | $24

Round Top | On the Sq. | 105 Main St. (bet. FM 1457 & Hwy. 237) | 979-249-3611 | www.royersroundtopcafe.com

"Worth every dollar spent on gas" is what surveyors have to say about this "regional legend" located in Round Top, 95 miles northwest of Houston; it's a "cozy", "homey", family-run cafe that specializes in "mouthwatering" Traditional American cookery, most notably "don't-miss" "freshly baked" pies, so "pack the car and your appetite" but "leave your diet at the door"; N.B. open Thursday–Sunday only.

Rudi Lechner's *German* 23 | 18 | 24 | $22

Southwest Houston | Woodlake Sq. | 2503 S. Gessner St. (Westheimer Rd.) | 713-782-1180 | www.rudilechners.com

Guardians of Teutonic "tradition" just say "*ja*" to this "authentic German" in Southwest Houston, an "old standard" for "fantastic" "home-cooked meals", "beer in liter mugs" and even a "good salad bar"; it's "like a visit to Bavaria" complete with a "polka band" three nights a week, so even with "outdated" decor, "what's not to like?"

Rudyard's ◐ *Pub Food* - | - | - | I

Montrose | 2010 Waugh Dr. (Welch St.) | 713-521-0521 | www.rudyards.com

Besides being a "great place for darts and beer", this Montrose pub and "live music" stalwart is "actually pretty good" for all-American "bar food" according to aficionados; just be prepared for downscale digs and rudimentary service that's "inattentive to newcomers."

Ruggles Grill Ⓜ *American* 23 | 18 | 18 | $31

Montrose | 903 Westheimer Rd. (Montrose Blvd.) | 713-524-3839

Ruggles Grille 5115 Ⓢ *American*

Galleria | Saks Fifth Ave. | 5115 Westheimer Rd. (McCue Rd.) | 713-963-8067

Ruggles Cafe Bakery *American*

Rice Village | 2365 Rice Blvd. (Morningside Dr.) | 713-520-6662

www.rugglesgrill.com

Fans give the food "high marks for originality and presentation" at this "dependable" trio of New American "favorites"; there's "always a wait" at the Montrose original while the Galleria spin-off proves an "elegant" respite in the midst of Saks Fifth Avenue; the newest "order-at-the-counter" Rice Village cafe rivals "its more expensive counterparts" with "creative" burgers, salads and sandwiches and "decadent desserts" well-suited for a "for a quick lunch."

Ruth's Chris Steak House *Steak* 25 | 22 | 25 | $57

Galleria | 6213 Richmond Ave. (bet. Fountain View & Hillcroft Aves.) | 713-789-2333 | www.ruthschris.com

See review in San Antonio Directory.

NEW Saga Food & Wine *American* - | - | - | M

Midtown | 3017 Milam St. (Anita St.) | 713-523-1010 | www.sagafoodandwine.com

This Midtown fine-dining foray of Polo Becerra (Post Oak Grill and Polo's) showcases a moderately priced eclectic New American menu in a somewhat spare setting with a plant-filled patio; unusual small plates like lamb lollipops and panko-breaded asparagus augment the solid lineup of steaks and fish, and true to its name, there's also a lengthy wine list.

Sage 400 Japanese Cuisine *Japanese* 22 | 19 | 17 | $34

Galleria | 2800 Sage Rd. (Alabama St.) | 713-961-9566 | www.sage400.com

Though "it doesn't have the reputation of some others", this Galleria-area Japanese aims to please with "melt-in-your-mouth fresh" sushi and other "inventive" raw fish served in a "pretty" setting; but while it's stylish enough to be "a bit different", a few fret over "absentee servers" and "a little too much of a singles scene" barside.

Sambuca ◐ *Eclectic* 21 | 23 | 19 | $38

Downtown | 909 Texas Ave. (Travis St.) | 713-224-5299 | www.sambucarestaurant.com

See review in Dallas/Ft. Worth Directory.

Sasaki Ⓢ *Japanese* - | - | - | M

Briargrove | 8979 Westheimer Rd. (Fondren Rd.) | 713-266-5768

"Forget all those trendy" contenders urge boosters of this unassuming Briargrove Japanese, where the sushi is "phenomenally fresh" and the "atmosphere and service are as authentic as they come";

"despite its strip-center location", it's overseen by a "master" chef who honed his skills in the homeland.

Sawadee *Thai* ▽ 24 | 16 | 23 | $19

West U | 6719 Weslayan St. (Bellaire Blvd.) | 713-666-7872

A "best-kept secret", this "quiet" West U Thai is a "reliable" resource that wins raves for its "excellent" cooking ("phenomenal vegetarian fare" included); if the pedestrian decor presents less to brag about, it's readily offset by the "charming" staff and "good value."

Segari's ⊠ *Seafood/Steak* - | - | - | M

Heights | 1503 Shepherd Dr. (Maxie St.) | 713-880-2470 | www.segarisrestaurant.com

Likened to "a real speakeasy", this tiny "no-sign place" ensconced in a "pleasantly cozy" house lures insiders to the Lower Heights to partake in a "limited" menu featuring some of the "best seafood" "anywhere"; idiosyncratic founder Sam Segari's "spirit is still here", and his legacy carries on as "a great Houston secret."

Z 17 *American* 25 | 26 | 23 | $54

Downtown | Alden Houston Hotel | 1117 Prairie St. (San Jacinto St.) | 832-200-8888 | www.17food.com

This "posh" Downtown "escape" set in the boutique Alden Hotel beguiles guests with "deliciously decadent" New American "big-city fare" and a "superb wine list", both befitting a "special night out"; the "intimate", "luxuriously understated room" illuminated with "gorgeous chandeliers" is enhanced by "attentive" service, setting the scene for a truly "transporting" meal; N.B. the Food score does not reflect the recent departure of chef Ryan Pera.

Shade *American* 25 | 22 | 22 | $34

Heights | 250 W. 19th St. (Rutland St.) | 713-863-7500 | www.shadeheights.com

"Adult" diners have it "made in the shade" at this "jewel in the Heights", a "top-rate" destination for "creative" New American fare with "delightful" "seasonal variations" plus "one of the most interesting wine lists in town"; the "minimalist" setup is as "pleasing" as the "attentive" service, and the "awesome" weekend brunch rounds out an "unpretentious" but "cool" scene.

Shanghai River *Chinese* ▽ 22 | 18 | 21 | $24

River Oaks | 2407 Westheimer Rd. (Revere St.) | 713-528-5528 | www.shanghairiverrestaurant.com

Purists pooh-pooh the chow as "Americanized", but devotees still stream into this "friendly", "relaxing" River Oaks Chinese for its "delicious" "well-priced" wares ("lunch specials are a great deal"); in a "quiet", "elegant" dining room hung with Asian art, the family of proprietors makes everyone "feel at home."

Shawarma King *Lebanese* - | - | - | I

Briargrove | 3121 Hillcroft Rd. (Richmond Ave.) | 713-784-8882

For a "quick" Mideastern "munch" that's "far above fast food", this bare-bones Briargrove joint serves "very solid chicken shawarma" and other "authentic and tasty" grub right over the counter; its lieges esteem the "great prices", but since "you don't visit for ambiance" they often opt "for takeout."

Shiva Indian Restaurant *Indian* 20 | 15 | 17 | $20

Rice Village | 2514 Times Blvd. (Kirby Dr.) | 713-523-4753
Sugar Land | 16556 Southwest Frwy. (Colony Square Blvd.) | 281-494-2981
www.shivarestaurant.com

A "staple" for "all the staples", this Rice Village Indian and its Sugar Land spin-off provide "tasty" and "authentic" eats served by "attentive" staffers; some regulars rate the lunch-buffet "deal" "just ok", but dinner "doesn't disappoint" with its "good portion sizes" and dimmed lights to tone down the perfunctory decor.

Sichuan Cuisine *Chinese* - | - | - | I

Alief | 9114 Bellaire Blvd. (bet. Gessner & Ranchester Rds.) | 713-771-6868

It's "not for the faint of heart (or stomach)", but this small, spare strip-center Chinese in New Chinatown stands apart for its "incredibly authentic Sichuan" dishes, including many spiced with the "hot, hot" peppers from that region; connoisseurs are "impressed", and BYO makes it cheap to check out.

Simposio *Italian* 24 | 17 | 21 | $36

Briargrove | 8401 Westheimer Rd. (Dunvale Rd.) | 713-532-0550

Though relocated to Briargrove in late 2007, this Italian eatery still lures neighborhood patrons for a midpriced meal, albeit now in an attractive, airy setting; with the move also came a new, young chef from Tuscany, though the menu remains much the same as before with an array of Northern-area specialties, like their signature osso buco, along with with toothsome pastas and risottos.

Sinh Sinh ◐ *Chinese* - | - | - | I

Alief | 9788 Bellaire Blvd. (Corporate Dr.) | 713-541-0888

"Sinfully delicious" Sino fare marks this "hot-pot" hot spot in Alief's New Chinatown, which appeals to "seafood lovers" with an array displayed in "tanks around the restaurant"; the decor and staff are less impressive ("expect bad service and you won't be disappointed"), but seekers of the "authentic" "crave it again and again."

Skyline Bar & Grill *American* ▽ 17 | 26 | 19 | $44

Downtown | Hilton Americas Hotel | 1600 Lamar St., 24th fl. (Crawford St.) | 713-577-8325 | www.hilton.com

"If you want a view", this New American on the 24th floor of Downtown's Hilton Americas commands a "stunning" cityscape through its floor-to-ceiling windows; the "pricey" menu offers some "inventive" incentives for fine dining, though those wary of the "loud" environs may opt to just "go for a drink."

Smith & Wollensky ◐ *Seafood/Steak* 20 | 19 | 19 | $57

Galleria | Highland Vill. | 4007 Westheimer Rd. (Drexler Ave.) | 713-621-7555 | www.smithandwollensky.com

"Love the classic steakhouse atmosphere" enthuse surveyors of this Galleria outpost of an "upscale" NYC-bred chain, where "tender steaks" and "excellent seafood" are served in "enormous portions" by "helpful" servers; still, cost-watchers worry that it's "way too expensive", saying it's "best to be on an expense account" when you visit.

NEW Soma *American/Japanese* - | - | - | E

Heights | 4820 Washington Ave. (bet. Durham & Shepherd Drs.) | 713-861-2726

Chef Robert Gadsby (formerly of Noé and *Iron Chef* fame) returns to the Houston dining scene at this chic, spacious canteen in the Heights that's already packing a crowd into its showy black-and-red interior; considering it's a joint venture with the owners of Azuma, expect high-end sushi and sashimi along with a lineup of intriguing French-inspired dishes (like foie gras with tuna terrine) that showcase the top toque's skills.

Sorrento *Italian* 21 | 24 | 21 | $45

Montrose | 415 Westheimer Rd. (Whitney St.) | 713-527-0609 | www.sorrentohouston.com

"Located in restaurant alley" in Montrose, this "gracious" Italian stands apart from its neighbors with "delicious" "classical" cuisine, "personal service" and "lovely" atmospherics augmented with "live piano music"; a minority moans the kitchen is "not consistent", but fans of the "charming feel" keep it "busy"; P.S. the Sunday brunch is a "great value" for the quality.

NEW SoVino ⊠ *Eclectic* - | - | - | M

Montrose | 507 Westheimer Rd. (Whitney St.) | 713-524-1000 | www.sovinowines.com

Montrose's Restaurant Row continues to heat up with this sultry new wine bar and bistro where a sexy crowd sinks into the plush booths and nibbles various vino-friendly cheeses and charcuterie (there's also a brief selection of entrees); though the menu is global, the wine list focuses on the Southern Hemisphere, with well-priced picks from South America, New Zealand and South Africa.

Spanish Flowers ◐ *Tex-Mex* 19 | 12 | 17 | $15

Heights | 4701 N. Main St. (Airline Blvd.) | 713-869-1706 | www.spanish-flowers.com

When it's "midnight and you need a Mexican fix, this is the place" claim compadres of this Heights-area vet, which grounds its "great reputation" on "homemade tortillas", "all-day breakfasts" and "extended hours" (it's 24/7 except for Tuesdays); those not so simpatico reckon it's "unremarkable", if always wallet-friendly.

Spanish Village ⊠ Ⓜ *Tex-Mex* ▽ 19 | 15 | 20 | $21

Medical Center | 4720 Almeda Rd. (Wentworth St.) | 713-523-2861 | www.spanishvillagerestaurant.com

A "favorite of natives and old-timers", this "charmingly funky", half-century-old Medical Center mainstay serves up "basic", "consistent", "good ol'" Tex-Mex, "outstanding" margaritas and "must-have" fried chicken ("yes, fried chicken - don't ask"); still-reasonable prices and staffers "who've spent their lives there" help keep it a local "institution."

	FOOD	DECOR	SERVICE	COST

Spencer's For Steaks & Chops *Steak*

∇ 21	17	22	$64

Downtown | Hilton Americas | 1600 Lamar St. (Crawford St.) | 713-577-8325 | www.hilton.com

Meat eaters disagree about this modern steakhouse at Downtown's Hilton Americas; proponents find its "hearty" chops "terrific" but dissenters deem them just "average", so it's either "exceptionally good for a hotel restaurant" or merely "typical"; not in dispute is the 300-label wine list.

Star Pizza *Pizza*

23	12	18	$16

Heights | 77 Harvard St. (Washington Ave.) | 713-869-1241
Lower Shepherd | 2111 Norfolk St. (Shepherd Dr.) | 713-523-0800
www.starpizza.net

Experts attest "the best pizza in town" qualifies this stellar pair as an area "classic", with 30-plus years of producing "fantastic" pies (thin crust or "Chicago-style deep dish") adorned with "extremely tasty" toppings in many "original" variations; of the two, "the Shepherd location is much more hip", "but don't expect any elegance" at either.

Strip House *Steak*

24	25	23	$54

Downtown | Shops at Houston Ctr. | 1200 McKinney St. (San Jacinto St.) | 713-659-6000 | www.theglaziergroup.com

"Arguably the best steakhouse" Downtown, this "pricey" NYC "import" appeals to "biz" types with its "top-notch" beef, "fab" sides, "reasonable noise level" and "sexy" "two-martini atmosphere"; it's also noteworthy for its "risqué" "red-and-black decor" scheme, "tastefully" tarted up with "photos of vintage burlesque beauties."

Sudie's Catfish & Seafood House *Seafood*

20	15	20	$17

Pasadena | 4910 Spencer Hwy. (bet. Beltway 8 & Preston Ave.) | 281-487-0920
League City | 352 Gulf Frwy. N. (off Hwy. 518) | 281-338-5100
www.sudies.com

"If fried catfish is your thing" these "cavernous", country-style and "family-friendly" eateries in Pasadena and League City will float your boat with their "mouthwatering" all-you-can-eat catfish and other seafood specialties (plus the signature fried pickles) at "great" prices; if fried catfish is not your thing, it's all "just ok."

Sullivan's Steakhouse *Steak*

24	23	23	$53

Galleria | 4608 Westheimer Rd. (Westcreek Ln.) | 713-961-0333 | www.sullivansteakhouse.com

See review in Austin and the Hill Country Directory.

Sushi King *Japanese*

23	18	16	$34

Upper Kirby District | 3401 Kirby Dr. (Richmond Ave.) | 713-528-8998 | www.sushiking.us

Others spots have "hipper names and locations", but this Upper Kirby District Japanese boasts "better sushi than most" according to "truly impressed" admirers of its "wonderfully thick slices" and "clever, creative rolls"; sporting a contempo look and a pianist, it's "nicer on the inside" than the exterior would suggest, though "the service needs some work."

Swinging Door, The Ⓜ *BBQ* 24 | 19 | 21 | $18

Richmond | 3714 FM 359 (McCrary Rd.) | 281-342-4758 | www.swingingdoor.com

"Worth the trip" claim carnivores who congregate at this "rustic", "casual" and affordable barbecue destination in Richmond, 35 miles southwest of Houston; they "crave" the "large portions" of "best-kept-secret" ribs, chicken, brisket and "all the fixin's" ("save room" for the "divine" cobblers).

Sylvia's Enchilada Kitchen *Tex-Mex* 21 | 18 | 22 | $17

West Houston | 12637 Westheimer Rd. (Dairy Ashford Rd.) | 281-679-8300 | www.sylviasenchiladakitchen.com

"Yes, it's out of the way", but this West Houston "neighborhood" joint's "exciting takes" on Tex-Mex showcase an "astounding" selection of "delicious enchiladas" at "reasonable" prices; its "cheerful" crew is led by owner Sylvia Casares Copeland (who "even offers cooking classes" on Saturdays), and only a doubter or two "fails to see what all the fuss is about."

Taco Milagro *Mexican* 16 | 16 | 14 | $17

Champions | 7877 Willowchase Blvd. (Tomball Pkwy.) | 281-664-7070
Upper Kirby District | 2555 Kirby Dr. (Westheimer Rd.) | 713-522-1999
NEW **Webster** | 19325 Gulf Frwy. (Bay Area Blvd.) | 281-954-3070

La Mesa Mexican Bistro *Mexican*

The Woodlands | 1701 Lake Robbins Dr. (Waterway Ave.) | 281-602-7070
www.taco-milagro.com

Another brainchild of Cafe Annie chef-owner Robert Del Grande, this "popular" counter-service Mex chainlet wins friends with its "freshly made" and "budget-friendly" (if not exactly miraculous) fare and its 150-label tequila bar under a thatched-palm palapa; what makes it a "prime destination" for "young professionals", though, are the "fabulous happy hour", "excellent" patio and live music at some locations.

t'afia Ⓢ Ⓜ *American* 25 | 18 | 22 | $41

Midtown | 3701 Travis St. (bet. Alabama & Winbern Sts.) | 713-524-6922 | www.tafia.com

"A savory adventure" awaits courtesy of "genius" chef/co-owner Monica Pope at this "cutting-edge" Midtown New American, where "fresh, seasonal ingredients" are "beautifully prepared" for a "unique" "dining experience" "with a homey touch"; followers applaud the "astute" staff and "relaxed atmosphere", and though the setup "is so minimalist" it can be "a little noisy", at least "you never get bored"; P.S. the Saturday "farmer's market here is a must for serious foodies."

Tampico Seafood *Mexican/Seafood* - | - | - | I

North Houston | 10125 I-45 (West Rd.) | 281-445-2525
North Houston | 2115 Airline Dr. (Cavalcade St.) | 713-862-8425
www.tampicoseafood.com

Rightly known for "great Mexican-style seafood", this frill-free North Houston duo specializes in "very fresh grilled" dishes ("pick your own snapper and enjoy") from a lengthy menu of Gulf denizens; finatics declare it's "hard to beat" "at any price" but add "the Tex-Mex dishes don't measure up to the fish."

Tan Tan ◐ *Chinese/Vietnamese* ▽ 26 | 13 | 18 | $13

Alief | 6816 Ranchester Dr. (Bellaire Blvd.) | 713-771-1268 | www.tantanrestaurant.com

With a "tantalizing" menu offering a staggering choice of 400 items, this New Chinatown Sino-Vietnamese is a "consistent" supplier of "excellent food" that leaves loyalists with "no regrets" in spite of "questionable service" and decor; "late-night" hours on the weekends ensure the "lively vibe" lasts "even until 2 in the morning."

Taste of Texas *Steak* 24 | 21 | 23 | $44

Memorial | 10505 Katy Frwy. (bet. Beltway 8 & Gessner Dr.) | 713-932-6901 | www.tasteoftexas.com

"Texan to the core", this "popular" stalwart in "suburban" Memorial ropes in "big eaters" with "more-than-generous" slabs of Angus beef "grilled to perfection" ("love the salad bar too!") and served in a spacious setting steeped in "ranch manor" rusticity; but the "loud", "packed" room "rivals a cattle drive", and antis opine there are "classier places" "at this price level."

Teala's Mexican Restaurant *Mexican* 18 | 18 | 18 | $23

Montrose | 3210 W. Dallas St. (Rosine St.) | 713-520-9292 | www.tealas.com

Providing a "welcome break from traditional Tex-Mex", this Montrose Mexican gives its "consistently" "interesting" fare a Thai twist, as found in "top-notch" salsas and "exotic" margaritas; the "relaxed but lively" scene includes murals, a "great patio" and a "hopping" Friday happy hour.

Teotihuacan *Mexican* ▽ 24 | 13 | 20 | $13

Sharpstown | 6579 W. Bellfort St. (Fondren Rd.) | 713-726-9858
Heights | 1511 Airline Dr. (Patton St.) | 713-426-4420
Neartown | 4624 Irvington Blvd. (Cavalcade St.) | 713-695-8757

The "classic" cooking comes in "huge portions" at this "neighborhood Tex-Mex" trio, where an impressive menu of "delicious" items both familiar and less so is bolstered by "homemade corn tortillas" and "friendly" service; "don't be put off by" the modest digs, as the "flavorful" food and "great value" "will make you happy."

Terlingua *Tex-Mex* 18 | 20 | 17 | $19

NEW **West U** | 3801 Bellaire Blvd. (Southside Pl.) | 713-665-3900
Montrose | 920 Studemont St. (Washington Ave.) | 713-864-3700
www.terlinguatexasbordercafe.com

Fans find a lingering "flair for originality" at this Montrose Tex-Mex *cocina* and its "family-friendly" West U offshoot, where the wide-ranging selections are supplemented by "very potent margaritas" ("beware!"); but holdouts see "nothing spectacular" and tear into service that "can be trying at times."

	FOOD	DECOR	SERVICE	COST
Thai Bistro *Thai*	-	-	-	M
Thai Gourmet ☒ *Thai*	24	16	20	$20
Thai Pepper *Thai*	18	13	16	$22
Thai Restaurant *Thai*	▽ 20	12	21	$20
Thai Sticks *Thai*	▽ 21	22	18	$28
Thelma's Barbecue ☒ *BBQ*	▽ 21	4	11	$12
Thierry André Tellier Café & Pastry Shop ☒ *French/Swiss*	23	16	18	$20

Thai Bistro *Thai*

West U | 3241 Southwest Frwy. (Buffalo Spdwy.) | 713-669-9375

Small and "charming", this West U "gem" serves up "excellent", "reliable" Thai treats; though it's been around for years now, surveyors say it still "seems undiscovered" and note it's rarely crowded.

Thai Gourmet ☒ *Thai*

Galleria | 6324 Richmond Ave. (Hillcroft Ave.) | 713-780-7955 | www.thaigourmethouston.com

Diners get all fired up over this Galleria-area Siamese because of its "fine selection" of "wonderful", "authentic" dishes "spiced Thai-style" ("crank-up-the-heat") or "American-style"; "friendly" servers help create a pleasant atmosphere despite the eatery's "touristy location."

Thai Pepper *Thai*

Lower Shepherd | 2049 W. Alabama St. (Shepherd Dr.) | 713-520-8225 | www.tealas.com

Patrons of this Lower Shepherd Thai "favorite" (a sib of Teala's) pick it because "nothing changes, and that's a good thing"; the "cheap" fare is "spicy" and "great for a quick lunch", but those turned off by the "quiet-as-a-library" dining room advise "get it to go."

Thai Restaurant *Thai*

Galleria | 5757 Westheimer Rd. (bet. Chimney Rock Rd. & Fountain View Dr.) | 713-780-0888

A generic name belies the "fresh" preparations (with spice applied "to your liking"), "good-deal" prices and "prompt" service at this Siamese sleeper near the Galleria; meanwhile, straddlers grant it's a "reliable and fast lunch" option but "otherwise nothing special."

Thai Sticks *Thai*

Montrose | 4319 Montrose Blvd. (Richmond Ave.) | 713-529-4500

Non-locals are "wonderfully surprised" to encounter "top-tier" Thai at this "calm" enclave on Montrose, where "relaxing", upmarket vibes complement the "delicious" "fusion"-esque fare; but a few pronounce it "pricey", especially given occasionally "distracted service."

Thelma's Barbecue ☒ *BBQ*

Neartown | 1020 Live Oak St. (Lamar St.) | 713-228-2262

"You're family here" promise partialists of this "hole-in-the-wall" Neartown BBQ "shack", which plates up "rich, moist and delicious" 'cue in "outright huge" portions at a "very inexpensive" cost; but while "Thelma's a great cook, no doubt", the ultra-"informal" milieu "leaves something to be desired" and "the wait is a killer" at peak times.

Thierry André Tellier
Café & Pastry Shop ☒ *French/Swiss*

Uptown | Uptown Park | 1101 Uptown Park Blvd. (Post Oak Blvd.) | 713-877-9401

River Oaks | 2515 River Oaks Blvd. (Westheimer Rd.) | 713-524-3863 www.cafeandpastryshop.com

Francophiles favor this "charming" French-Swiss cafe/bakery in River Oaks (and its newer Uptown sib) for "nice lunches" of "wonderful" soups, salads, sandwiches and quiches, but "the real draws" are the "sophisticated" pastries "that would melt a Parisian's heart"; service can be "slow", especially when it's "crowded on weekends", but that doesn't deter the faithful who claim this "institution" is still one of Houston's "little gems"; N.B. the scores may not fully reflect a July 2007 ownership change.

This Is it *Soul Food* 21 9 12 $14

Midtown | 207 Gray St. (Bagby St.) | 713-659-1608 | www.thisisithouston.com

"If you want to get authentic", "this is it" according to aficionados of the "fatty, greasy, delicious soul food" that makes this decor-less joint near Midtown a go-to for "pure" "down-home cookin'"; though it's a "crowded", "cafeteria"-style setup ("don't argue with the line servers"), it's been keeping its customers "full and satisfied" since 1959.

Tila's Restaurante & Bar *Mexican* 21 17 18 $26

River Oaks | 1111 S. Shepherd Dr. (McDuffie St.) | 713-522-7654 | www.tilas.com

"Friendly" and whimsically decorated, this River Oaks cantina serves up "flavorful" Mexican fare that's "creative" and "reasonably priced"; service ranges from "polite" to "erratic" but parking's basically "terrible" to "impossible" ("you have to valet", but it's complimentary).

Tokyohana Grill & Sushi Bar *Japanese* 19 16 16 $26

West U | 3239 Southwest Frwy. (Buffalo Spdwy.) | 713-838-9560
North Houston | 15155 North Frwy. (Richey Rd.) | 281-877-8744
www.tokyohana.com

This Japanese pair in West U and North Houston rolls out "diverse" sushi and hibachi dishes and "decent" wines along with the usual teppanyaki chefs' tricks; the "fun" Southwest Freeway location is "extremely popular with children", even hosting magicians on Thursdays and Saturdays, though some do find it "bizarre" ("did Chuck E. Cheese and Benihana mate?"); come evening, the North Freeway location turns into a lounge, complete with DJ (Thursday-Friday).

Tony Mandola's Gulf Coast Kitchen *Seafood* 24 18 22 $37

River Oaks | River Oaks Ctr. | 1962 W. Gray St. (McDuffie St.) | 713-528-3474 | www.tonymandolas.com

"You can't go wrong" with this "dependable" River Oaks seafooder's "delectable variety" of Gulf Coast–style shellfish, "perfectly seasoned" slaw or gumbo that'll "make you weep"; "Tony runs a tight ship" in this "lively", "friendly" "hangout", so though a few find the fare "overpriced", "no one seems to care."

Z Tony's ⊠ *Continental/Italian* 27 27 27 $64

Greenway Plaza Area | 3755 Richmond Ave. (Timmons Ln.) | 713-622-6778 | www.tonyshouston.com

An undisputed "Houston classic" installed in "knockout" Greenway Plaza digs, this "world-class" tribute to "formal dining" "caters to the elite" with "the total package": "exceptional" Continental fare, the "toniest" service around (rated No. 1 in Houston) and "smart,

art-filled" surroundings; it's "expensive", but "you get what you pay for" and its "moneyed" clientele hardly objects if it's "a little stuffy."

Treebeards ☒ *Cajun/Southern* 24 | 14 | 16 | $13

Downtown | 1100 Louisiana St. (Lamar St.) | 713-752-2601
Downtown | Cloister, The | 1117 Texas Ave. (San Jacinto St.) | 713-229-8248
Downtown | Downtown Tunnel | 700 Rusk St. (Milam St.) | 713-224-6677
FM 1960 | Market Sq. | 315 Travis St. (Preston St.) | 713-228-2622
www.treebeards.com

The four locations of this "Houston classic" - open only for weekday lunch - dish up "delicious" Cajun-accented Southern "home cooking"; "courteous" service and "comfortable" cafeteria-style digs help make meals here "worth the money"; N.B. the Market Square and Cloister venues are notable - the former is in Houston's second oldest building (1870) and the latter in Christ Church Cathedral's social hall.

Trevisio ☒ *Italian* 21 | 25 | 19 | $39

Medical Center | Texas Medical Ctr. | 6550 Bertner Ave. (Moursund St.) | 713-749-0400 | www.trevisiorestaurant.com

Recuperate with a "quiet, relaxing meal" at this "underutilized" "oasis" "in the heart of the Medical Center", featuring "classy" Italian fare and a "lovely" layout with a "lush wall of water" and a "view of the expanse" of facilities below; doctors and staff appreciate the "convenience", though on the downside some diagnose "variable service."

Truluck's *Seafood* 23 | 22 | 23 | $44

Galleria | 5350 Westheimer Rd. (Sage Rd.) | 713-783-7270 | www.trulucks.com

See review in Dallas/Ft. Worth Directory.

Z Uptown Sushi ☒ *Japanese* 26 | 24 | 18 | $43

Uptown | Uptown Park | 1131-14 Uptown Park Blvd. (Post Oak Blvd.) | 713-871-1200 | www.uptown-sushi.com

"Be sure to dress to impress" for the "upscale" "social scene" at this "trendy" Uptown Japanese, but "don't let its hipness throw you off" since it follows through with "top-quality" sushi in an "elegant space"; it's a key place to "see and be seen" and accordingly "pricey", even if the "party atmosphere" is slightly offset by "hit-or-miss" service.

Van Loc *Vietnamese* 18 | 9 | 17 | $13

Midtown | 3010 Milam St. (Elgin St.) | 713-528-6441

This modest Midtowner satisfies locals via "authentic" Vietnamese "home cooking" ("excellent" spring rolls, "best pho", "well-prepared noodle dishes"); to most, the "reliable, cheap eats" "make up" for "abrupt" service and "bland" surroundings that "lack character."

Vargo's *Continental* 17 | 24 | 19 | $46

Memorial | 2401 Fondren Rd. (Westheimer Rd.) | 713-782-3888 | www.vargosonline.com

"Lovely gardens" that play "host to peacocks" provide a "serene" backdrop that surpasses the merely "good food" at this venerable Memorial-area Continental ("make reservations by the window"); it still works for "romance" and "wedding receptions", but dissenters who allege it's "ready for an update" protest paying "big money" "for too little beyond the glorious grounds."

Via Emilia *Italian* - | - | - | M

Northwest Houston | 3731 FM 1960 Rd. W. (bet. Falling Creek Dr. & Walters Rd.) | 281-587-9137

The flavor of "real Italian" awaits at this quaint, "family-owned" trattoria in Northwest Houston, where the repertoire covers favorites from osso buco to "tasty homemade pastas"; music fans note there's "great entertainment on weekends" as singers (operatic and otherwise) strut their stuff.

Z Vic & Anthony's *Steak* 26 | 25 | 24 | $61

Downtown | 1510 Texas Ave. (La Branch St.) | 713-228-1111 | www.vicandanthonys.com

It's "definitely pricey", but this "classic" Downtown steakhouse from "the Landry's empire" "ranks with the best", enticing a "power carnivore" crowd into its "opulent" "dark-oak" digs with "huge" cuts of "fabulous" beef, an "amazing wine list" and "top-of-the-line" service; sited "in the shadow of" Minute Maid Park, it's "perfect for the pre- or post-ball game" blowout.

Vieng Thai *Thai* - | - | - | I

Spring Branch | 6929 Long Point Rd. (bet. Afton St. & Silber Rd.) | 713-688-9910 | www.viengthai.com

Homestyle Thai dishes, some of them unfamiliar to American palates, rule at this modest, family-friendly Spring Branch grocery store-turned-restaurant, where the extensive, authentic menu includes signature papaya salad, basil stir fry and sticky rice with mango; N.B. its BYO policy and reasonable prices make it a downright bargain.

Vietnam Restaurant, The $ *Vietnamese* ▽ 19 | 8 | 18 | $14

Heights | 605 W. 19th St. (Lawrence St.) | 832-618-1668 | www.thevietnamrestaurant.com

Smitten surveyors appreciate this "secret" "neighborhood hangout" in a Heights strip center for its "generous portions" of "fine" Vietnamese fare (they add "just the right amount of spice") and "friendly" staff; the BYO policy "helps" the already "unbelievably low" prices.

Vietopia *Vietnamese* 20 | 21 | 19 | $22

West U | 5176 Buffalo Spdwy. (Westpark Dr.) | 713-664-7303

With "charming" "upscale" surroundings and a "helpful", "nice" staff, this "family-friendly" West U Vietnamese has won the hearts and minds of its contented clientele; the "reliable", "healthy" entrees and "fab lunch specials" are "delicious" too (if perhaps closer to "experiments in fusion" than to "authentic" South Asian vittles), but a vocal few opine this "overpriced" place is "not utopia."

Vincent's ⊠ *Italian* 22 | 20 | 21 | $34

Montrose | 2701 W. Dallas St. (Eberhard St.) | 713-528-4313 | www.ninos-vincents.com

Next door to its sibling, Nino's - with which it shares a courtyard - this "casual", "dependable" Montrose Italian still wins friends after more than two decades with its "super" signature dishes (e.g. "juicy, flavorful" rotisserie chicken, "divine veal Vincent") and "friendly", "competent" service; the unfulfilled bemoan "amazingly small" ("for Texas") portions.

Yao Restaurant & Bar *Chinese* 19 | 20 | 20 | $23

Southwest Houston | 9755 Westheimer Rd. (Gessner Rd.) | 832-251-2588 | www.yaorestaurant.com

"A real surprise" in Southwest Houston, this "upscale" "Chinese restaurant owned by an NBA star" (that's Rockets center Yao Ming) scores with "better-than-average" "traditional" cuisine and "polite, efficient service"; opponents counter it's "a little overpriced" for "ordinary" eating, but even they acknowledge that the lounge can be a "great sports bar."

NEW Yatra Brasserie ⊠ *Indian* ▽ 24 | 17 | 18 | $27

Downtown | 706 Main St. (bet. Capitol & Rusk Sts.) | 713-224-6700 | www.yatrausa.com

This newish Downtown taste of India is "worth its weight in curry" to champions of the "consistent" kitchen, which turns out dishes "flavorful" enough to "make you dance" around the stylish space; the original resides in London's ritzy Mayfair district, and its stateside sib aims to be a fashionable place to "make a night of it."

Yia Yia Mary's *Greek* 18 | 14 | 16 | $22

Galleria | 4747 San Felipe St. (I-610) | 713-840-8665 | www.yiayiamarys.com

Count on "typical Pappas quality" from this "quick", "casual" Galleria Mediterranean eatery's "tasty" "take on Greek", featuring a "traditional" lineup with "lots of things to choose from" for a "reasonable price"; meanwhile naysayers natter about "loud, loud" acoustics and chow that's "a little too Americanized" for purist palates.

Yildizlar ⊠ *Mideastern* ▽ 21 | 9 | 14 | $13

Upper Kirby District | Richmond Kirby Shopping Ctr. | 3419 Kirby Dr. (Richmond Ave.) | 713-524-7735

Globe-trotters like to graze at this Upper Kirby Middle Eastern "hole-in-the-wall" where both vegetarians and carnivores can enjoy the "authentically wonderful" fare; "try a little of everything" urge fans who frequent this cafeteria-style "quick lunch stop."

Yum Yum Cha Café *Chinese* 23 | 8 | 17 | $16

Rice Village | 2435 Times Blvd. (Kelvin Dr.) | 713-527-8455

Launched by a "charming", "personable" father-daughter team, this Chinese "little treasure" in Rice Village serves up "piping-hot", made-to-order dim sum "any day of the week at any time" ("no carts"); "be patient" counsel connoisseurs, who consider the "fresh", "upscale" fare "worth the 15-minute wait" and somewhat "slow" service; N.B. it's BYO.

Zoë's Kitchen ⊠ Ⓜ *American* ▽ 17 | 12 | 15 | $17

Upper Kirby District | 3701 S. Shepherd Dr. (Richmond Ave.) | 713-522-7447 | www.zoeskitchen.com

See review in Dallas/Ft. Worth Directory.

Zula ⊠ *American* 23 | 24 | 21 | $53

Downtown | St. Germain Bldg. | 705 Main St. (Capitol St.) | 713-227-7052 | www.zulahouston.com

This "glitzy", "extravagant", high-ceilinged Downtowner "attracts those with bling, and those who want those with bling"; fans applaud "creative", "satisfying" New American eats and appreciate staffers' "pampering", while foes shrug that this "overpriced" place "tries too hard to be hip" and now feels "dated."

HOUSTON INDEXES

Cuisines

Includes restaurant names, locations and Food ratings. Z indicates places with the highest ratings, popularity and importance.

AMERICAN (NEW)

Z Artista | **Downtown** 25
NEW Aura | **Missouri City** –
Backstreet Café | **River Oaks** 22
benjy's | **Rice Vill** 23
Bistro Lancaster | **Downtown** 20
Bistro Toulouse | **Briargrove** 20
Z Cafe Annie | **Galleria** 26
Catalan | **Heights** 24
Cava Bistro | **Downtown** 21
Cova | **multi.** 19
Crú Wine Bar | **Woodlands** 20
Empire Café | **Montrose** 20
Glass Wall | **Heights** 25
Gravitas | **Neartown** 21
Z Hotel Icon | **Downtown** 24
Jasper's | **Woodlands** 24
Kona Grill | **multi.** 20
Laurier Café | **Greenway Plaza** 25
La Vista | **multi.** 23
Z Mark's | **Montrose** 28
Max's | **Heights** 21
Mockingbird Bistro | **River Oaks** 25
NEW Monarch | **Medical Ctr** 21
Noé | **Uptown** 22
NEW Polo's | **Greenway Plaza** 20
Z Rainbow Lodge | **Heights** 23
Remington | **Galleria** 25
Ruggles | **multi.** 23
NEW Saga | **Midtown** –
Z 17 | **Downtown** 25
Shade | **Heights** 25
Skyline B&G | **Downtown** 17
NEW Soma | **Heights** –
t'afia | **Midtown** 25
Zoë's Kitchen | **Upper Kirby** 17
Zula | **Downtown** 23

AMERICAN (TRADITIONAL)

Armadillo Palace | **West U** 21
Avalon Diner | **multi.** 16
Baba Yega | **Montrose** 20
Barnaby's | **multi.** 21
Breakfast Klub | **Midtown** 23
Buffalo Grille | **multi.** 20
Z Cheesecake Factory | **multi.** 20
Christian's | **multi.** 19
Cleburne | **West U** 23
Daily Grind | **Heights** 14
Daily Review | **River Oaks** 20
Dessert Gallery | **multi.** 22
59 Diner | **multi.** 16
NEW Grove, The | **Downtown** –
Hard Rock | **Downtown** 14
Houston's | **multi.** 23
Karl's | **Richmond** 27
Lankford Grocery | **Midtown** 23
Mama's Café | **Briargrove** 19
Market Sq. | **Downtown** –
Moveable Feast | **Memorial** 22
Post Oak Grill | **multi.** 21
Royers Round Top | **Round Top** 22
Rudyard's | **Montrose** –

ARGENTINEAN

Empanadas by Marini | **multi.** 23

ASIAN FUSION

Lemongrass | **Bellaire** 21

BAKERIES

NY Coffee Shop | **Meyerland** –
Z Nielsen's | **Spring** 26
Thierry André | **multi.** 23

BARBECUE

NEW Beaver's | **Heights** –
Z Goode Co. TX BBQ | **multi.** 25
Luling City Mkt. | **Galleria** 23
Lyndon's | **NW Houston** –
Pizzitola's | **Heights** 24
Swinging Door | **Richmond** 24
Thelma's BBQ | **Neartown** 21

BELGIAN

Café Montrose | **Montrose** 22

BRAZILIAN

Z Fogo de Chão | **Briargrove** 26
Nelore | **Montrose** 20

BRITISH

Black Labrador | **Montrose** 17
McGonigel's | **Upper Kirby** 16
Red Lion | **Lower Shepherd** 19

BURGERS

Becks Prime | **multi.** 22
Bellaire Broiler Burger | **Bellaire** 21

Christian's | **multi.** 19
Goode Co. Burgers | **West U** 22
Lankford Grocery | **Midtown** 23
Pappas Burgers | **Galleria** 23

CAJUN

NEW Danton's | **Montrose** –
Floyd's | **Webster** 22
Z Jimmy Wilson's | **Royal Oaks** 26
Magnolia B&G | **Briargrove** 20
Mardi Gras | **Heights** 18
Z Pappadeaux | **multi.** 23
Ragin' Cajun | **multi.** 21
Tony Mandola's | **River Oaks** 24
Treebeards | **multi.** 24

CARIBBEAN

Reggae Hut | **Medical Ctr** –

CHINESE

(* dim sum specialist)
Café Chino | **Rice Vill** 22
Z China View | **W Houston** 27
Chinese Café | **multi.** 22
Daniel Wong's | **Bellaire** 23
Fung's* | **SW Houston** 25
Hollywood | **Montrose** –
Hunan | **Downtown** 21
Kam's | **Montrose** 20
Kim Son* | **multi.** 23
Masala Wok | **SW Houston** 18
Ocean Palace* | **Bellaire** 23
Z P.F. Chang's | **multi.** 22
Shanghai River | **River Oaks** 22
Sinh Sinh | **Alief** –
Tan Tan | **Alief** 26
Yao | **SW Houston** 19
Yum Yum Cha* | **Rice Vill** 23

COFFEEHOUSES

Brasil | **Montrose** 20
Café Artiste | **Montrose** 16
Daily Grind | **Heights** 14

COFFEE SHOPS/DINERS

59 Diner | **multi.** 16
NY Coffee Shop | **Meyerland** –

CONTINENTAL

Brownstone | **Upper Kirby** 22
Café Benedicte | **W Houston** 23
Charivari | **Midtown** 23
Karl's | **Richmond** 27
Z La Colombe d'Or | **Montrose** 21
Lexington Grille | **Lower Shepherd** 21
Masraff's | **Uptown** 23
Z Tony's | **Greenway Plaza** 27
Vargo's | **Memorial** 17

CREOLE

Z Brennan's | **Midtown** 26

CUBAN

Cafe Piquet | **Bellaire** 21

DELIS

Kahn's Deli | **Rice Vill** 23
Katz's Deli | **Montrose** 19
Kenny & Ziggy's | **Galleria** 24
Leibman's | **W Houston** 21
Mexico's Deli | **W Houston** –
Z Nielsen's | **Galleria** 26

DESSERT

Z Américas | **Galleria** 24
benjy's | **Rice Vill** 23
Z Brennan's | **Midtown** 26
Z Cafe Annie | **Galleria** 26
Z Cheesecake Factory | **multi.** 20
Z Churrascos | **multi.** 25
Dessert Gallery | **multi.** 22
Empire Café | **Montrose** 20
Quattro | **Downtown** 23
Ruggles | **Rice Vill** 23
Thierry André | **multi.** 23
Z Tony's | **Greenway Plaza** 27

ECLECTIC

Barnaby's | **multi.** 21
Black Walnut | **multi.** 20
Café Artiste | **Montrose** 16
Café Express | **multi.** 18
Dharma Café | **Neartown** 21
Farrago | **Midtown** 19
Grand Lux Cafe | **Galleria** 19
Hobbit Cafe | **Lower Shepherd** 21
Hungry's | **multi.** 19
Max's | **Heights** 21
Raven Grill | **West U** 21
Sambuca | **Downtown** 21
NEW SoVino | **Montrose** –

ETHIOPIAN

Blue Nile | **SW Houston** –

FONDUE

Melting Pot | **Galleria** 21

FRENCH

Au Petit Paris | **Lower Shepherd** -

Bistro Calais | **River Oaks** 23

Bistro Le Cep | **W Houston** 25

Bistro Provence | **W Houston** 23

Bistro Vino | **Montrose** 20

NEW Brasserie Max & Julie | **Montrose** -

Café Rabelais | **Rice Vill** 26

Chez Georges | **Montrose** 24

Chez Nous | **Humble** 26

La Colombe d'Or | **Montrose** 21

Le Mistral | **W Houston** 26

Thierry André | **multi.** 23

GERMAN

Old Heidelberg | **Galleria** 21

Rudi Lechner's | **SW Houston** 23

GREEK

Alexander | **Galleria** 24

Bibas Greek | **Heights** 18

Bibas One's | **Montrose** 18

Niko Niko's | **Montrose** 23

Yia Yia Mary's | **Galleria** 18

GUATEMALAN

El Pueblito Place | **Montrose** 20

HAWAIIAN

Kona Grill | **multi.** 20

INDIAN

Ashiana | **W Houston** 24

Bombay Brasserie | **Rice Vill** 18

India's | **Galleria** 21

Indika | **Montrose** 25

Khyber | **Upper Kirby** 23

Kiran's | **Galleria** 25

Madras Pavilion | **multi.** 22

Masala Wok | **SW Houston** 18

Shiva Indian | **multi.** 20

NEW Yatra | **Downtown** 24

ITALIAN

(N=Northern; S=Southern)

Amerigo's | **Woodlands** 22

NEW Amici | S | **Sugar Land** 24

Antica Osteria | **West U** 24

Arcodoro | S | **Galleria** 20

Arturo's | **Uptown** 19

Bice | N | **Galleria** 21

Bistro Vino | **Montrose** 20

Black Walnut | **multi.** 20

Brio | **Woodlands** 21

Carmelo's | S | **W Houston** 22

Carrabba's | **multi.** 22

Ciro's | **Memorial** 20

Collina's | **multi.** 18

Crapitto's | **Galleria** 21

Da Marco | N | **Montrose** 28

Damian's | **Midtown** 21

D'Amico's | **Rice Vill** 21

divino | N | **Lower Shepherd** 22

Dolce Vita | **Montrose** 24

Frenchie's | **Clear Lake** 24

Grappino di Nino | **Montrose** 20

Grotto | S | **multi.** 22

La Griglia | **River Oaks** 21

La Strada | **Montrose** 19

La Trattoria | N | **Briargrove** 20

La Vista | **multi.** 23

Luigi's | **Galveston** 25

Maggiano's | **Galleria** 20

Mia Bella | **multi.** 22

Michelangelo's | **Montrose** 24

Nino's | **Montrose** 24

Palazzo's | **multi.** 20

Patrenella's | **Heights** 17

Paulie's | **multi.** 19

Perbacco | S | **Downtown** 23

Piatto | **multi.** 25

Prego | **Rice Vill** 23

Pronto Cucinino | **multi.** 19

Quattro | **Downtown** 23

Simposio | N | **Briargrove** 24

Sorrento | **Montrose** 21

Tony's | **Greenway Plaza** 27

Trevisio | **Medical Ctr** 21

Via Emilia | **NW Houston** -

Vincent's | **Montrose** 22

JAPANESE

(* sushi specialist)

Aka* | **multi.** 23

Azuma/Azumi* | **multi.** 23

Benihana | **multi.** 20

NEW Blue Fin* | **W Houston** -

Café Japon* | **West U** 22

Fish, The* | **Midtown** 20

Ginza* | **Briargrove** -

Japaneiro's* | **Sugar Land** 26

Kaneyama* | **W Houston** 27

Kubo's* | **Rice Vill** 25

Nippon* | **Montrose** -

Osaka* | **Montrose** 24

Rickshaw Far East* | **River Oaks** 19

Sage 400* | **Galleria** 22

Sasaki* | **Briargrove** -
NEW Soma* | **Heights** -
Sushi King* | **Upper Kirby** 23
Tokyohana* | **multi.** 19
Z Uptown Sushi* | **Uptown** 26

JEWISH

Kahn's Deli | **Rice Vill** 23
Katz's Deli | **Montrose** 19
Kenny & Ziggy's | **Galleria** 24
NY Coffee Shop | **Meyerland** -

MALAYSIAN

Café Malay | **W Houston** -

MEDITERRANEAN

Café Benedicte | **W Houston** 23
Dimassi's | **multi.** 18
Droubi | **multi.** 21
Fadi's | **multi.** 21
Z Ibiza | **Midtown** 25
Mary'z | **Galleria** 21
NEW Mint Café | **Galleria** 19
Phoenicia Deli | **Royal Oaks** 23

MEXICAN

Berryhill Baja | **multi.** 19
Cadillac Bar | **multi.** 18
Cantina Laredo | **W Houston** 21
Cyclone Anaya's | **multi.** 20
El Pueblito Place | **Montrose** 20
Z Hugo's | **Montrose** 26
Irma's | **Downtown** 22
Jarro Café | **Spring Branch** -
La Mexicana | **Montrose** 19
Las Alamedas | **Memorial** 20
López | **Alief** -
Z Lupe Tortilla | **multi.** 21
Mexico's Deli | **W Houston** -
Mission Burritos | **multi.** 22
100% Taquito | **Greenway Plaza** 18
Otilia's | **Spring Branch** 22
Pico's | **Bellaire** 24
NEW Red Onion Taco | **NW Houston** -
Romero's | **NW Houston** 21
Taco Milagro/La Mesa | **multi.** 16
Tampico Seafood | **N Houston** -
Teala's | **Montrose** 18
Teotihuacan | **multi.** 24
Tila's | **River Oaks** 21

MIDDLE EASTERN

Cafe Lili | **Galleria** 24
Dimassi's | **multi.** 18
Droubi | **multi.** 21
Mary'z | **Galleria** 21
NEW Mint Café | **Galleria** 19
Shawarma King | **Briargrove** -
Yildizlar | **Upper Kirby** 21

NUEVO LATINO

Julia's | **Midtown** 19

PACIFIC RIM

Z Café Le Jadeite | **River Oaks** 22

PAN-ASIAN

Pei Wei | **multi.** 19
NEW Rattan | **W Houston** -
Rickshaw Far East | **River Oaks** 19

PAN-LATIN

Z Cafe Red Onion | **multi.** 24
El Meson | **Rice Vill** 19
Fernando's Latin | **Sugar Land** -
Z Red Onion | **NW Houston** 26

PERSIAN

Café Caspian | **W Houston** 22
Kasra Persian Grill | **SW Houston** -

PERUVIAN

Lemon Tree | **W Houston** -

PIZZA

Barry's | **multi.** 20
Bibas Greek | **Heights** 18
Dolce Vita | **Montrose** 24
Kenneally's | **Lower Shepherd** 16
Star Pizza | **multi.** 23

PUB FOOD

Armadillo Palace | **West U** 21
Black Labrador | **Montrose** 17
Kenneally's | **Lower Shepherd** 16
McGonigel's | **Upper Kirby** 16
Red Lion | **Lower Shepherd** 19
Rudyard's | **Montrose** -

PUERTO RICAN

Isla Coquí | **Heights** -

SEAFOOD

NEW Danton's | **Montrose** -
Denis' Seafood | **Memorial** 21
Floyd's | **Webster** 22
Fung's | **SW Houston** 25
Gaido's | **Galveston** 22
Goode Co. TX Seafood | **multi.** 23

Z Jimmy Wilson's | **multi.** 26
Joyce's | **multi.** 19
Z Lynn's | **W Houston** 26
Magnolia B&G | **Briargrove** 20
Mambo Seafood | **multi.** 20
Mardi Gras | **Heights** 18
Massa's | **Downtown** 19
McCormick & Schmick's | **Uptown** 21
Oceanaire | **Galleria** 24
Ocean Palace | **Bellaire** 23
Z Pappadeaux | **multi.** 23
Pappas Seafood | **multi.** 23
Pesce | **Upper Kirby** 21
PK's | **Briargrove** 21
Z Red Onion | **NW Houston** 26
NEW Reef | **Midtown** 25
Segari's | **Heights** -
Sudie's | **multi.** 20
Tampico Seafood | **N Houston** -
Tony Mandola's | **River Oaks** 24
Truluck's | **Galleria** 23

SMALL PLATES

(See also Spanish tapas specialist)
Catalan | Amer. | **Heights** 24
Cova | Amer. | **multi.** 19
divino | Italian | **Lower Shepherd** 22
Mi Luna | Spanish | **multi.** 19
NEW SoVino | Eclectic | **Montrose** -

SOUL FOOD

Breakfast Klub | **Midtown** 23
This Is it | **Midtown** 21

SOUTH AMERICAN

Amazon Grill | **multi.** 18
Z Américas | **Galleria** 24
Z Churrascos | **multi.** 25
Z Japaneiro's | **Sugar Land** 26

SOUTHERN

Cleburne | **West U** 23
Jax Grill | **multi.** 19
Ouisie's Table | **River Oaks** 23
Treebeards | **multi.** 24

SOUTHWESTERN

Z Brennan's | **Midtown** 26
Burning Pear | **Sugar Land** 23
Z Cafe Annie | **Galleria** 26

SPANISH

(* tapas specialist)
Catalan | **Heights** 24
Z Ibiza* | **Midtown** 25
Mi Luna* | **multi.** 19
Rioja* | **W Houston** 24

STEAKHOUSES

Benihana | **multi.** 20
Bob's Steak | **Galleria** 25
Brenner's | **multi.** 25
Burning Pear | **Sugar Land** 23
Capital Grille | **Galleria** 25
Z Churrascos | **multi.** 25
NEW Del Frisco's | **Galleria** 27
Z Fleming's Prime | **multi.** 24
Z Fogo de Chão | **Briargrove** 26
Killen's | **Pearland** -
Kirby's | **Woodlands** 24
Z Lynn's | **W Houston** 26
Morton's Steak | **multi.** 25
Palm, The | **Galleria** 24
Z Pappas Bros. | **Galleria** 27
Pappas Grill | **Stafford** 28
Z Perry's Steak | **multi.** 25
Rio Ranch | **SW Houston** 21
Ruth's Chris | **Galleria** 25
Segari's | **Heights** -
Smith & Wollensky | **Galleria** 20
Spencer's | **Downtown** 21
Strip Hse. | **Downtown** 24
Sullivan's | **Galleria** 24
Taste of Texas | **Memorial** 24
Z Vic & Antony's | **Downtown** 26

SWISS

Thierry André | **multi.** 23

TEX-MEX

NEW Armandos | **River Oaks** 14
Buffalo Grille | **multi.** 20
Cabo | **Downtown** 14
Chuy's | **River Oaks** 21
Don Carlos | **multi.** -
El Tiempo | **multi.** 22
Goode Co. Burgers | **West U** 22
Irma's SW | **Downtown** 21
Mama Ninfa's/Original Ninfa's | **multi.** 22
Z Pappasito's | **multi.** 23
Spanish Flowers | **Heights** 19
Spanish Village | **Medical Ctr** 19
Sylvia's | **W Houston** 21
Terlingua | **multi.** 18

THAI

Golden Room | **Montrose** 19
Z Kanomwan | **Neartown** 27
Mai Thai | **Upper Kirby** 23

Nit Noi | **multi.** 21

Sawadee | **West U** 24

Thai Bistro | **West U** -

Thai Gourmet | **Galleria** 24

Thai Pepper | **Lower Shepherd** 18

Thai Rest. | **Galleria** 20

Thai Sticks | **Montrose** 21

Vieng Thai | **Spring Branch** -

TURKISH

Empire Turkish | **W Houston** 24

Istanbul Grill | **Rice Vill** 22

Pasha | **Rice Vill** 25

VEGETARIAN

Brasil | **Montrose** 20

Hobbit Cafe | **Lower Shepherd** 21

Madras Pavilion | **Upper Kirby** 22

VIETNAMESE

Hollywood | **Montrose** -

Jasmine | **Alief** -

Jenni's Noodle | **Lower Shepherd** 21

Kim Son | **multi.** 23

Le Viet | **Royal Oaks** 21

Mai's | **Midtown** 23

Miss Saigon | **Rice Vill** 22

Mo Mong | **Montrose** 20

Tan Tan | **Alief** 26

Van Loc | **Midtown** 18

Vietnam | **Heights** 19

Vietopia | **West U** 20

Locations

Includes restaurant names, cuisines and Food ratings. Z indicates places with the highest ratings, popularity and importance.

Houston

ALIEF/SHARPSTOWN

Chinese Café | *Chinese* 22
Don Carlos | *Tex-Mex* –
Jasmine | *Viet.* –
López | *Mex.* –
Mambo Seafood | *Seafood* 20
Pappas Seafood | *Seafood* 23
Sichuan Cuisine | *Chinese* –
Sinh Sinh | *Chinese* –
Tan Tan | *Chinese/Viet.* 26
Teotihuacan | *Mex.* 24

ALMEDA/HOBBY/PASADENA

Don Carlos | *Tex-Mex* –
Mama Ninfa's/Original Ninfa's | *Tex-Mex* 22
Pappas Seafood | *Seafood* 23
Sudie's | *Seafood* 20

BELLAIRE/MEDICAL CENTER/WEST U

Amazon Grill | *S Amer.* 18
Antica Osteria | *Italian* 24
Armadillo Palace | *Pub* 21
Azuma/Azumi | *Japanese* 23
Bellaire Broiler Burger | *Burgers* 21
Berryhill Baja | *Mex.* 19
Buffalo Grille | *Amer.* 20
Café Japon | *Japanese* 22
Cafe Piquet | *Cuban* 21
Cleburne | *Amer.* 23
Cova | *Amer.* 19
Daniel Wong's | *Chinese* 23
Goode Co. Burgers | *Burgers* 22
Z Goode Co. TX BBQ | *BBQ* 25
Goode Co. TX Seafood | *Seafood* 23
Jax Grill | *Southern* 19
Kim Son | *Chinese/Viet.* 23
Lemongrass | *Asian Fusion* 21
Z Lupe Tortilla | *Mex.* 21
Mama Ninfa's/Original Ninfa's | *Tex-Mex* 22
NEW Monarch | *Amer.* 21
Ocean Palace | *Chinese* 23
Z Pappadeaux | *Seafood* 23
Z Pappasito's | *Tex-Mex* 23
Paulie's | *Italian* 19
Pei Wei | *Pan-Asian* 19
Pico's | *Mex.* 24
Pronto Cucinino | *Italian* 19
Raven Grill | *Eclectic* 21
Reggae Hut | *Carib.* –
Sawadee | *Thai* 24
Spanish Village | *Tex-Mex* 19
Terlingua | *Tex-Mex* 18
Thai Bistro | *Thai* –
Tokyohana | *Japanese* 19
Trevisio | *Italian* 21
Vietopia | *Viet.* 20

BRIARGROVE

Becks Prime | *Burgers* 22
Bistro Toulouse | *Amer.* 20
Cyclone Anaya's | *Mex.* 20
Droubi | *Med.* 21
Fadi's | *Med.* 21
Z Fogo de Chão | *Brazilian/Steak* 26
Ginza | *Japanese* –
Z Jimmy Wilson's | *Seafood* 26
Joyce's | *Seafood* 19
La Trattoria | *Italian* 20
La Vista | *Amer./Italian* 23
Magnolia B&G | *Cajun/Seafood* 20
Mama's Café | *Amer.* 19
Palazzo's | *Italian* 20
Z Pappasito's | *Tex-Mex* 23
PK's | *Seafood* 21
Sasaki | *Japanese* –
Shawarma King | *Lebanese* –
Simposio | *Italian* 24

CHAMPIONS

Berryhill Baja | *Mex.* 19
Café Express | *Eclectic* 18
Z Carrabba's | *Italian* 22
Nit Noi | *Thai* 21
Z Pappadeaux | *Seafood* 23
Pei Wei | *Pan-Asian* 19
Z Perry's Steak | *Steak* 25
Taco Milagro/La Mesa | *Mex.* 16

DOWNTOWN

Z Artista | *Amer.* 25
Azuma/Azumi | *Japanese* 23

- Becks Prime | *Burgers* 22
- Benihana | *Japanese/Steak* 20
- Bistro Lancaster | *Amer.* 20
- Cabo | *Tex-Mex* 14
- Café Express | *Eclectic* 18
- Cava Bistro | *Amer.* 21
- Dimassi's | *Med.* 18
- NEW Grove, The | *Amer.* –
- Hard Rock | *Amer.* 14
- Z Hotel Icon | *Amer.* 24
- Hunan | *Chinese* 21
- Irma's | *Mex.* 22
- Irma's SW | *Tex-Mex* 21
- Kim Son | *Chinese/Viet.* 23
- Mama Ninfa's/Original Ninfa's | *Tex-Mex* 22
- Market Sq. | *Amer.* –
- Massa's | *Seafood* 19
- Mia Bella | *Italian* 22
- Morton's Steak | *Steak* 25
- Perbacco | *Italian* 23
- Post Oak Grill | *Amer.* 21
- Quattro | *Italian* 23
- Ragin' Cajun | *Cajun* 21
- Sambuca | *Eclectic* 21
- Z 17 | *Amer.* 25
- Skyline B&G | *Amer.* 17
- Spencer's | *Steak* 21
- Strip Hse. | *Steak* 24
- Treebeards | *Cajun/Southern* 24
- Z Vic & Antony's | *Steak* 26
- NEW Yatra | *Indian* 24
- Zula | *Amer.* 23

FM 1960/KLEIN

- Z Pappadeaux | *Seafood* 23
- Z Pappasito's | *Tex-Mex* 23
- Treebeards | *Cajun/Southern* 24

GALLERIA/UPTOWN

- Alexander | *Greek* 24
- Z Américas | *S Amer.* 24
- Arcodoro | *Italian* 20
- Arturo's | *Italian* 19
- Berryhill Baja | *Mex.* 19
- Bice | *Italian* 21
- Bob's Steak | *Steak* 25
- Z Cafe Annie | *SW* 26
- Café Express | *Eclectic* 18
- Cafe Lili | *Lebanese* 24
- Capital Grille | *Steak* 25
- Z Carrabba's | *Italian* 22
- Z Cheesecake Factory | *Amer.* 20
- Chinese Café | *Chinese* 22
- Crapitto's | *Italian* 21
- NEW Del Frisco's | *Steak* 27
- Dessert Gallery | *Amer./Dessert* 22
- Dimassi's | *Med.* 18
- Grand Lux Cafe | *Eclectic* 19
- Grotto | *Italian* 22
- Houston's | *Amer.* 23
- India's | *Indian* 21
- Kenny & Ziggy's | *Deli* 24
- Kiran's | *Indian* 25
- Kona Grill | *Amer.* 20
- Luling City Mkt. | *BBQ* 23
- Maggiano's | *Italian* 20
- Mama Ninfa's/Original Ninfa's | *Tex-Mex* 22
- Mary'z | *Med.* 21
- Masraff's | *Continental* 23
- McCormick & Schmick's | *Seafood* 21
- Melting Pot | *Fondue* 21
- NEW Mint Café | *Med.* 19
- Morton's Steak | *Steak* 25
- Z Nielsen's | *Deli* 26
- Noé | *Amer.* 22
- Oceanaire | *Seafood* 24
- Old Heidelberg | *German* 21
- Palm, The | *Steak* 24
- Z Pappadeaux | *Seafood* 23
- Z Pappas Bros. | *Steak* 27
- Pappas Burgers | *Burgers* 23
- Z P.F. Chang's | *Chinese* 22
- Piatto | *Italian* 25
- Post Oak Grill | *Amer.* 21
- Ragin' Cajun | *Cajun* 21
- Remington | *Amer.* 25
- Ruggles | *Amer.* 23
- Ruth's Chris | *Steak* 25
- Sage 400 | *Japanese* 22
- Smith & Wollensky | *Seafood/Steak* 20
- Sullivan's | *Steak* 24
- Thai Gourmet | *Thai* 24
- Thai Rest. | *Thai* 20
- Thierry André | *French/Swiss* 23
- Truluck's | *Seafood* 23
- Z Uptown Sushi | *Japanese* 26
- Yia Yia Mary's | *Greek* 18

GREENWAY PLAZA AREA

- Collina's | *Italian* 18
- El Tiempo | *Tex-Mex* 22
- Joyce's | *Seafood* 19
- Laurier Café | *Amer.* 25

Mia Bella | *Italian* 22
100% Taquito | *Mex.* 18
NEW Polo's | *Amer.* 20
Z Tony's | *Continental/Italian* 27

HEIGHTS

NEW Beaver's | *BBQ* -
Berryhill Baja | *Mex.* 19
Bibas Greek | *Greek/Pizza* 18
Cadillac Bar | *Mex.* 18
Catalan | *Amer./Spanish* 24
Christian's | *Burgers* 19
Collina's | *Italian* 18
Cova | *Amer.* 19
Cyclone Anaya's | *Mex.* 20
Daily Grind | *Coffee* 14
Glass Wall | *Amer.* 25
Isla Coquí | *Puerto Rican* -
Jax Grill | *Southern* 19
Mardi Gras | *Cajun/Seafood* 18
Max's | *Eclectic* 21
Mission Burritos | *Mex.* 22
Patrenella's | *Italian* 17
Pizzitola's | *BBQ* 24
Z Rainbow Lodge | *Amer.* 23
Segari's | *Seafood/Steak* -
Shade | *Amer.* 25
NEW Soma | *Amer./Japanese* -
Spanish Flowers | *Tex-Mex* 19
Star Pizza | *Pizza* 23
Teotihuacan | *Mex.* 24
Vietnam | *Viet.* 19

LOWER SHEPHERD

Au Petit Paris | *French* -
Z Churrascos | *S Amer.* 25
divino | *Italian* 22
59 Diner | *Diner* 16
Hobbit Cafe | *Eclectic* 21
Jenni's Noodle | *Viet.* 21
Kenneally's | *Pub* 16
Lexington Grille | *Continental* 21
Mission Burritos | *Mex.* 22
Pappas Seafood | *Seafood* 23
Red Lion | *Pub* 19
Star Pizza | *Pizza* 23
Thai Pepper | *Thai* 18

MEMORIAL/ SPRING BRANCH

Becks Prime | *Burgers* 22
Brenner's | *Steak* 25
Buffalo Grille | *Amer.* 20
Ciro's | *Italian* 20
Collina's | *Italian* 18
Denis' Seafood | *Seafood* 21
El Tiempo | *Tex-Mex* 22
Z Goode Co. TX BBQ | *BBQ* 25
Goode Co. TX Seafood | *Seafood* 23
Jarro Café | *Mex.* -
Las Alamedas | *Mex.* 20
La Vista | *Amer./Italian* 23
Mama Ninfa's/Original Ninfa's | *Tex-Mex* 22
Mambo Seafood | *Seafood* 20
Moveable Feast | *Amer.* 22
Nit Noi | *Thai* 21
Otilia's | *Mex.* 22
Z Pappadeaux | *Seafood* 23
Z Pappasito's | *Tex-Mex* 23
Z Perry's Steak | *Steak* 25
Taste of Texas | *Steak* 24
Vargo's | *Continental* 17
Vieng Thai | *Thai* -

MEYERLAND/WESTBURY

Café Express | *Eclectic* 18
Collina's | *Italian* 18
Fadi's | *Med.* 21
NY Coffee Shop | *Diner* -

MIDTOWN

Barnaby's | *Amer./Eclectic* 21
Breakfast Klub | *Soul Food* 23
Z Brennan's | *Creole* 26
Charivari | *Continental* 23
Christian's | *Burgers* 19
Cyclone Anaya's | *Mex.* 20
Damian's | *Italian* 21
Farrago | *Eclectic* 19
Fish, The | *Japanese* 20
Z Ibiza | *Med./Spanish* 25
Julia's | *Nuevo Latino* 19
Lankford Grocery | *Burgers* 23
Mai's | *Viet.* 23
NEW Reef | *Seafood* 25
NEW Saga | *Amer.* -
t'afia | *Amer.* 25
This Is it | *Soul Food* 21
Van Loc | *Viet.* 18

MONTROSE

Baba Yega | *Amer.* 20
Barnaby's | *Amer./Eclectic* 21
Berryhill Baja | *Mex.* 19
Bibas One's | *Greek* 18
Bistro Vino | *French/Italian* 20
Black Labrador | *Pub* 17

Brasil | *Coffee* 20
NEW Brasserie Max & Julie | *French* –
Café Artiste | *Coffee/Eclectic* 16
Café Express | *Eclectic* 18
Café Montrose | *Belgian* 22
Chez Georges | *French* 24
Z Da Marco | *Italian* 28
NEW Danton's | *Seafood* –
Dolce Vita | *Italian* 24
El Pueblito Place | *Guatemalan/Mex.* 20
El Tiempo | *Tex-Mex* 22
Empire Café | *Amer.* 20
Golden Room | *Thai* 19
Grappino di Nino | *Italian* 20
Hollywood | *Chinese/Viet.* –
Z Hugo's | *Mex.* 26
Indika | *Indian* 25
Kam's | *Chinese* 20
Katz's Deli | *Deli* 19
Z La Colombe d'Or | *Continental/French* 21
La Mexicana | *Mex.* 19
La Strada | *Italian* 19
Z Mark's | *Amer.* 28
Michelangelo's | *Italian* 24
Mo Mong | *Viet.* 20
Nelore | *Brazilian/Steak* 20
Niko Niko's | *Greek* 23
Nino's | *Italian* 24
Nippon | *Japanese* –
Osaka | *Japanese* 24
Paulie's | *Italian* 19
Pei Wei | *Pan-Asian* 19
Pronto Cucinino | *Italian* 19
Rudyard's | *Pub* –
Ruggles | *Amer.* 23
Sorrento | *Italian* 21
NEW SoVino | *Eclectic* –
Teala's | *Mex.* 18
Terlingua | *Tex-Mex* 18
Thai Sticks | *Thai* 21
Vincent's | *Italian* 22

NEARTOWN

Dharma Café | *Eclectic* 21
Don Carlos | *Tex-Mex* –
Gravitas | *Amer.* 21
Z Kanomwan | *Thai* 27
Mama Ninfa's/Original Ninfa's | *Tex-Mex* 22
Teotihuacan | *Mex.* 24
Thelma's BBQ | *BBQ* 21

NORTH HOUSTON

Z Lupe Tortilla | *Mex.* 21
Mambo Seafood | *Seafood* 20
Z Pappasito's | *Tex-Mex* 23
Pappas Seafood | *Seafood* 23
Tampico Seafood | *Mex./Seafood* –
Tokyohana | *Japanese* 19

NORTHWEST HOUSTON

Z Cafe Red Onion | *Pan-Latin* 24
Z Carrabba's | *Italian* 22
59 Diner | *Diner* 16
Z Lupe Tortilla | *Mex.* 21
Lyndon's | *BBQ* –
Mambo Seafood | *Seafood* 20
Z Pappadeaux | *Seafood* 23
Z Pappasito's | *Tex-Mex* 23
Pei Wei | *Pan-Asian* 19
Z P.F. Chang's | *Chinese* 22
Z Red Onion | *Pan-Latin/Seafood* 26
NEW Red Onion Taco | *Mex.* –
Romero's | *Mex.* 21
Via Emilia | *Italian* –

RICE VILLAGE

Azuma/Azumi | *Japanese* 23
benjy's | *Amer.* 23
Black Walnut | *Eclectic/Italian* 20
Bombay Brasserie | *Indian* 18
Café Chino | *Chinese* 22
Z Café Rabelais | *French* 26
Collina's | *Italian* 18
D'Amico's | *Italian* 21
El Meson | *Pan-Latin* 19
Hungry's | *Eclectic* 19
Istanbul Grill | *Turkish* 22
Kahn's Deli | *Deli* 23
Kubo's | *Japanese* 25
Mi Luna | *Spanish* 19
Miss Saigon | *Viet.* 22
Nit Noi | *Thai* 21
Pasha | *Med.* 25
Prego | *Italian* 23
Ruggles | *Amer.* 23
Shiva Indian | *Indian* 20
Yum Yum Cha | *Chinese* 23

RIVER OAKS

NEW Armandos | *Tex-Mex* 14
Avalon Diner | *Amer.* 16
Backstreet Café | *Amer.* 22
Barnaby's | *Amer./Eclectic* 21

Berryhill Baja | *Mex.* 19
Bistro Calais | *French* 23
Brenner's | *Steak* 25
Café Express | *Eclectic* 18
☒ Café Le Jadeite | *Pac. Rim* 22
Chuy's | *Tex-Mex* 21
Daily Review | *Amer.* 20
☒ Fleming's Prime | *Steak* 24
La Griglia | *Italian* 21
Mockingbird Bistro | *Amer.* 25
Ouisie's Table | *Southern* 23
Palazzo's | *Italian* 20
Rickshaw Far East | *Pan-Asian* 19
Shanghai River | *Chinese* 22
Thierry André | *French/Swiss* 23
Tila's | *Mex.* 21
Tony Mandola's | *Seafood* 24

ROYAL OAKS

Berryhill Baja | *Mex.* 19
☒ Jimmy Wilson's | *Seafood* 26
Le Viet | *Viet.* 21
Phoenicia Deli | *Med.* 23
Piatto | *Italian* 25

SOUTHWEST HOUSTON

Amazon Grill | *S Amer.* 18
Barry's | *Pizza* 20
Benihana | *Japanese/Steak* 20
Blue Nile | *Ethiopian* -
☒ Churrascos | *S Amer.* 25
Dimassi's | *Med.* 18
Droubi | *Med.* 21
Empanadas by Marini | *Argent.* 23
Fung's | *Chinese/Seafood* 25
Kasra Persian Grill | *Mideast.* -
Masala Wok | *Chinese/Indian* 18
Ragin' Cajun | *Cajun* 21
Rio Ranch | *Steak* 21
Rudi Lechner's | *German* 23
Yao | *Chinese* 19

UPPER KIRBY DISTRICT

Aka | *Japanese* 23
Becks Prime | *Burgers* 22
Brownstone | *Continental* 22
Café Express | *Eclectic* 18
☒ Cafe Red Onion | *Pan-Latin* 24
☒ Carrabba's | *Italian* 22
Dessert Gallery | *Amer./Dessert* 22
Houston's | *Amer.* 23
Khyber | *Indian* 23
Madras Pavilion | *Indian* 22
Mai Thai | *Thai* 23
Mama Ninfa's/Original Ninfa's | *Tex-Mex* 22
McGonigel's | *Pub* 16
☒ Pappadeaux | *Seafood* 23
☒ Pappasito's | *Tex-Mex* 23
Pesce | *Seafood* 21
Sushi King | *Japanese* 23
Taco Milagro/La Mesa | *Mex.* 16
Yildizlar | *Mideast.* 21
Zoë's Kitchen | *Amer.* 17

WEST HOUSTON

Aka | *Japanese* 23
Ashiana | *Indian* 24
Becks Prime | *Burgers* 22
Bistro Le Cep | *French* 25
Bistro Provence | *French* 23
NEW Blue Fin | *Japanese* -
Café Benedicte | *Continental* 23
Café Caspian | *Persian* 22
Café Express | *Eclectic* 18
Café Malay | *Malaysian* -
☒ Cafe Red Onion | *Pan-Latin* 24
Cantina Laredo | *Mex.* 21
Carmelo's | *Italian* 22
☒ Carrabba's | *Italian* 22
☒ China View | *Chinese* 27
Collina's | *Italian* 18
Dimassi's | *Med.* 18
Empire Turkish | *Turkish* 24
59 Diner | *Diner* 16
Hungry's | *Eclectic* 19
Kaneyama | *Japanese* 27
Leibman's | *Deli* 21
☒ Le Mistral | *French* 26
Lemon Tree | *Peruvian* -
☒ Lupe Tortilla | *Mex.* 21
☒ Lynn's | *Steak* 26
Mexico's Deli | *Deli/Mex.* -
Nit Noi | *Thai* 21
Palazzo's | *Italian* 20
☒ P.F. Chang's | *Chinese* 22
NEW Rattan | *Pan-Asian* -
Rioja | *Spanish* 24
Sylvia's | *Tex-Mex* 21

Bay Area

CLEAR LAKE/LEAGUE CITY/WEBSTER

Café Express | *Eclectic* 18
☒ Carrabba's | *Italian* 22
Floyd's | *Cajun/Seafood* 22

Frenchie's | *Italian* 24
Z Lupe Tortilla | *Mex.* 21
Z Pappasito's | *Tex-Mex* 23
Pappas Seafood | *Seafood* 23
Pei Wei | *Pan-Asian* 19
Z Perry's Steak | *Steak* 25
Sudie's | *Seafood* 20
Taco Milagro/La Mesa | *Mex.* 16

KEMAH

Cadillac Bar | *Mex.* 18

SEABROOK

Z Pappadeaux | *Seafood* 23

Outlying Areas

ATASCOCITA/HUMBLE/KINGWOOD

Berryhill Baja | *Mex.* 19
Z Carrabba's | *Italian* 22
Z Chez Nous | *French* 26
Z Pappasito's | *Tex-Mex* 23
Pappas Seafood | *Seafood* 23
Pei Wei | *Pan-Asian* 19

GALENA PARK

Pappas Seafood | *Seafood* 23

GALVESTON

Gaido's | *Seafood* 22
Luigi's | *Italian* 25

KATY/BROOKSHIRE

Empanadas by Marini | *Argent.* 23
Pei Wei | *Pan-Asian* 19

MISSOURI CITY/RICHMOND/STAFFORD/SUGAR LAND

NEW Amici | *Italian* 24
NEW Aura | *Amer.* -
Avalon Diner | *Amer.* 16
Barry's | *Pizza* 20
Becks Prime | *Burgers* 22
Berryhill Baja | *Mex.* 19
Black Walnut | *Eclectic/Italian* 20
Burning Pear | *Steak/SW* 23
Café Express | *Eclectic* 18
Z Carrabba's | *Italian* 22
Z Cheesecake Factory | *Amer.* 20
Dessert Gallery | *Amer./Dessert* 22
Dimassi's | *Med.* 18
Fernando's Latin | *Pan-Latin* -
59 Diner | *Diner* 16
Z Japaneiro's | *Japanese/S Amer.* 26
Karl's | *American/Continental* 27
Kim Son | *Chinese/Viet.* 23
Kona Grill | *Amer.* 20
Z Lupe Tortilla | *Mex.* 21
Madras Pavilion | *Indian* 22
Z Pappadeaux | *Seafood* 23
Pappas Grill | *Steak* 28
Z Pappasito's | *Tex-Mex* 23
Pei Wei | *Pan-Asian* 19
Z Perry's Steak | *Steak* 25
Z P.F. Chang's | *Chinese* 22
Ragin' Cajun | *Cajun* 21
Shiva Indian | *Indian* 20
Swinging Door | *BBQ* 24

PEARLAND

Killen's | *Steak* -

ROUND TOP

Royers Round Top | *Amer.* 22

SPRING/THE WOODLANDS

Amerigo's | *Italian* 22
Becks Prime | *Burgers* 22
Benihana | *Japanese/Steak* 20
Berryhill Baja | *Mex.* 19
Black Walnut | *Eclectic/Italian* 20
Brio | *Italian* 21
Z Carrabba's | *Italian* 22
Z Cheesecake Factory | *Amer.* 20
Chuy's | *Tex-Mex* 21
Crú Wine Bar | *Amer.* 20
Dimassi's | *Med.* 18
Z Fleming's Prime | *Steak* 24
Grotto | *Italian* 22
Jasper's | *Amer.* 24
Kirby's | *Steak* 24
Mi Luna | *Spanish* 19
Z Nielsen's | *Deli* 26
Nit Noi | *Thai* 21
Z Pappadeaux | *Seafood* 23
Z Perry's Steak | *Steak* 25
Z P.F. Chang's | *Chinese* 22
Taco Milagro/La Mesa | *Mex.* 16

Special Features

Listings cover the best in each category and include names, locations and Food ratings. Multi-location restaurants' features may vary by branch. Z indicates places with the highest ratings, popularity and importance.

BREAKFAST

(See also Hotel Dining)

Avalon Diner | **multi.** 16
Barnaby's | **multi.** 21
Becks Prime | **Memorial** 22
Berryhill Baja | **multi.** 19
Black Walnut | **multi.** 20
Brasil | **Montrose** 20
Breakfast Klub | **Midtown** 23
Buffalo Grille | **multi.** 20
Café Artiste | **Montrose** 16
Z Cheesecake Factory | **Galleria** 20
El Pueblito Place | **Montrose** 20
El Tiempo | **multi.** 22
Empire Café | **Montrose** 20
59 Diner | **multi.** 16
Goode Co. Burgers | **West U** 22
Irma's | **Downtown** 22
Irma's SW | **Downtown** 21
Kenny & Ziggy's | **Galleria** 24
La Mexicana | **Montrose** 19
Lankford Grocery | **Midtown** 23
Mama's Café | **Briargrove** 19
Pico's | **Bellaire** 24
Thierry André | **multi.** 23
Tila's | **River Oaks** 21

BRUNCH

Arcodoro | **Galleria** 20
Ashiana | **W Houston** 24
Baba Yega | **Montrose** 20
Backstreet Café | **River Oaks** 22
benjy's | **Rice Vill** 23
Bistro Le Cep | **W Houston** 25
Black Labrador | **Montrose** 17
Z Brennan's | **Midtown** 26
Burning Pear | **Sugar Land** 23
Cadillac Bar | **Heights** 18
Z Cheesecake Factory | **Galleria** 20
Daily Review | **River Oaks** 20
Dharma Café | **Neartown** 21
Farrago | **Midtown** 19
Grand Lux Cafe | **Galleria** 19
Gravitas | **Neartown** 21
Hobbit Cafe | **Lower Shepherd** 21
Z Hugo's | **Montrose** 26
Hungry's | **multi.** 19
Las Alamedas | **Memorial** 20
La Strada | **Montrose** 19
Masraff's | **Uptown** 23
Max's | **Heights** 21
Michelangelo's | **Montrose** 24
Mi Luna | **multi.** 19
Ouisie's Table | **River Oaks** 23
Prego | **Rice Vill** 23
Z Rainbow Lodge | **Heights** 23
Ruggles | **Montrose** 23
Shade | **Heights** 25
Sorrento | **Montrose** 21
Vargo's | **Memorial** 17

BUFFET SERVED

(Check availability)

Ashiana | **W Houston** 24
Baba Yega | **Montrose** 20
Bistro Calais | **River Oaks** 23
Bombay Brasserie | **Rice Vill** 18
Burning Pear | **Sugar Land** 23
Cadillac Bar | **Heights** 18
Z China View | **W Houston** 27
Dharma Café | **Neartown** 21
Dimassi's | **multi.** 18
Droubi | **Briargrove** 21
Z Hugo's | **Montrose** 26
India's | **Galleria** 21
Karl's | **Richmond** 27
Khyber | **Upper Kirby** 23
Kim Son | **Bellaire** 23
Las Alamedas | **Memorial** 20
Madras Pavilion | **multi.** 22
Magnolia B&G | **Briargrove** 20
Mi Luna | **multi.** 19
Nelore | **Montrose** 20
Quattro | **Downtown** 23
Shiva Indian | **multi.** 20

BUSINESS DINING

Z Américas | **Galleria** 24
Bob's Steak | **Galleria** 25
Z Brennan's | **Midtown** 26
Brenner's | **River Oaks** 25
Z Cafe Annie | **Galleria** 26
Café Benedicte | **W Houston** 23
Capital Grille | **Galleria** 25

Carmelo's | **W Houston** 22
Z Churrascos | **multi.** 25
Z Da Marco | **Montrose** 28
Damian's | **Midtown** 21
Z Fleming's Prime | **River Oaks** 24
Z Ibiza | **Midtown** 25
Jasper's | **Woodlands** 24
Z Jimmy Wilson's | **Royal Oaks** 26
Julia's | **Midtown** 19
Z La Colombe d'Or | **Montrose** 21
Z Mark's | **Montrose** 28
Massa's | **Downtown** 19
NEW Monarch | **Medical Ctr** 21
Morton's Steak | **Galleria** 25
Nelore | **Montrose** 20
Palm, The | **Galleria** 24
Z Pappas Bros. | **Galleria** 27
Pappas Grill | **Stafford** 28
Z Perry's Steak | **multi.** 25
NEW Polo's | **Greenway Plaza** 20
Post Oak Grill | **multi.** 21
Quattro | **Downtown** 23
NEW Reef | **Midtown** 25
Remington | **Galleria** 25
Ruggles | **Galleria** 23
Ruth's Chris | **Galleria** 25
Z 17 | **Downtown** 25
Smith & Wollensky | **Galleria** 20
Strip Hse. | **Downtown** 24
Sullivan's | **Galleria** 24
Tony Mandola's | **River Oaks** 24
Z Tony's | **Greenway Plaza** 27
Trevisio | **Medical Ctr** 21
Z Vic & Antony's | **Downtown** 26
NEW Yatra | **Downtown** 24

CELEBRITY CHEFS

Z Brennan's | *Randy Evans* | **Midtown** 26
Z Cafe Annie | *Robert Del Grande* | **Galleria** 26
Catalan | *Chris Shepard* | **Heights** 24
Z Da Marco | *Marco Wiles* | **Montrose** 28
Glass Wall | *Lance Fegen* | **Heights** 25
Gravitas | *Scott Tycer/ Jason Gould* | **Neartown** 21
NEW Grove, The | *Ryan Pera* | **Downtown** -
Z Hugo's | *Hugo Ortega* | **Montrose** 26
Z Ibiza | *Charles Clark* | **Midtown** 25
Indika | *Anita Jaisinghani* | **Montrose** 25
Killen's | *Ron Killen* | **Pearland** -
Z Le Mistral | *David Denis* | **W Houston** 26
Z Mark's | *Mark Cox* | **Montrose** 28
Mockingbird Bistro | *John Sheely* | **River Oaks** 25
NEW Monarch | *Bradley Manchester* | **Medical Ctr** 21
Pesce | *Mark Holley* | **Upper Kirby** 21
NEW Reef | *Bryan Caswell* | **Midtown** 25
Shade | *Jeb Stuart* | **Heights** 25
NEW Soma | *Robert Gadsby* | **Heights** -
t'afia | *Monica Pope* | **Midtown** 25
Z Tony's | *Olivier Cieleski* | **Greenway Plaza** 27

CHEF'S TABLE

Au Petit Paris | **Lower Shepherd** -
Bice | **Galleria** 21
Bistro Calais | **River Oaks** 23
Z Brennan's | **Midtown** 26
Damian's | **Midtown** 21
Glass Wall | **Heights** 25
Masraff's | **Uptown** 23
NEW Polo's | **Greenway Plaza** 20
Quattro | **Downtown** 23
Remington | **Galleria** 25

CHILD-FRIENDLY

(Alternatives to the usual fast-food places; * children's menu available)

Amazon Grill* | **West U** 18
Avalon Diner* | **Stafford** 16
Baba Yega | **Montrose** 20
Barnaby's* | **multi.** 21
Becks Prime* | **multi.** 22
Benihana* | **multi.** 20
Berryhill Baja* | **River Oaks** 19
Black Walnut* | **multi.** 20
Breakfast Klub | **Midtown** 23
Café Express* | **multi.** 18
Café Japon | **West U** 22
Café Montrose | **Montrose** 22
Z Cafe Red Onion* | **multi.** 24
Z Carrabba's* | **multi.** 22
Z Cheesecake Factory | **Galleria** 20
Ciro's* | **Memorial** 20
Cleburne* | **West U** 23
Collina's | **multi.** 18
D'Amico's | **Rice Vill** 21
Dessert Gallery* | **multi.** 22

Droubi | **multi.** 21
El Meson | **Rice Vill** 19
El Pueblito Place* | **Montrose** 20
59 Diner* | **multi.** 16
Gaido's* | **Galveston** 22
Goode Co. Burgers* | **West U** 22
Z Goode Co. TX BBQ | **West U** 25
Grotto* | **multi.** 22
Hard Rock* | **Downtown** 14
Hobbit Cafe* | **Lower Shepherd** 21
Hungry's* | **multi.** 19
Kim Son | **multi.** 23
La Mexicana* | **Montrose** 19
Z Lupe Tortilla* | **multi.** 21
Mama Ninfa's/Original Ninfa's* | **multi.** 22
Mama's Café* | **Briargrove** 19
Moveable Feast* | **Memorial** 22
Niko Niko's* | **Montrose** 23
Nit Noi | **multi.** 21
100% Taquito | **Greenway Plaza** 18
Otilia's* | **Spring Branch** 22
Palazzo's* | **multi.** 20
Z Pappasito's* | **Upper Kirby** 23
Paulie's* | **multi.** 19
Pei Wei* | **multi.** 19
Z P.F. Chang's | **multi.** 22
Pico's* | **Bellaire** 24
Ragin' Cajun* | **multi.** 21
Raven Grill* | **West U** 21
Rio Ranch* | **SW Houston** 21
Royers Round Top* | **Round Top** 22
Rudi Lechner's* | **SW Houston** 23
Shanghai River | **River Oaks** 22
Shiva Indian | **multi.** 20
Star Pizza | **multi.** 23
Sudie's* | **multi.** 20
Swinging Door | **Richmond** 24
Sylvia's* | **W Houston** 21
Taco Milagro/La Mesa* | **Upper Kirby** 16
Tampico Seafood* | **N Houston** –
Taste of Texas* | **Memorial** 24
Teotihuacan* | **multi.** 24
Terlingua* | **multi.** 18
Thierry André | **multi.** 23
Tokyohana* | **West U** 19
Zoë's Kitchen | **Upper Kirby** 17

DELIVERY/TAKEOUT

(D=delivery, T=takeout)

Amazon Grill | T | **SW Houston** 18
Z Américas | D, T | **Galleria** 24
Z Artista | D, T | **Downtown** 25
Avalon Diner | T | **Stafford** 16
Barnaby's | T | **multi.** 21
Becks Prime | T | **multi.** 22
Berryhill Baja | D, T | **multi.** 19
Black Walnut | T | **multi.** 20
Bombay Brasserie | D, T | **Rice Vill** 18
Breakfast Klub | T | **Midtown** 23
Buffalo Grille | D, T | **multi.** 20
Cadillac Bar | T | **Heights** 18
Café Artiste | T | **Montrose** 16
Café Caspian | T | **W Houston** 22
Café Chino | T | **Rice Vill** 22
Café Express | T | **multi.** 18
Café Montrose | T | **Montrose** 22
Z Carrabba's | T | **multi.** 22
Cava Bistro | T | **Downtown** 21
Z Cheesecake Factory | T | **Galleria** 20
Z Churrascos | D, T | **multi.** 25
Chuy's | D | **River Oaks** 21
Cleburne | T | **West U** 23
Collina's | D, T | **multi.** 18
D'Amico's | T | **Rice Vill** 21
Dessert Gallery | D, T | **multi.** 22
Dimassi's | T | **multi.** 18
Droubi | T | **multi.** 21
El Tiempo | D, T | **multi.** 22
Empire Turkish | D, T | **W Houston** 24
Golden Room | T | **Montrose** 19
Goode Co. Burgers | T | **West U** 22
Z Goode Co. TX BBQ | T | **multi.** 25
Goode Co. TX Seafood | T | **multi.** 23
Grappino di Nino | T | **Montrose** 20
Gravitas | T | **Neartown** 21
Grotto | T | **multi.** 22
Hobbit Cafe | T | **Lower Shepherd** 21
Hungry's | T | **multi.** 19
India's | T | **Galleria** 21
Irma's SW | T | **Downtown** 21
Istanbul Grill | T | **Rice Vill** 22
Jenni's Noodle | T | **Lower Shepherd** 21
Kahn's Deli | T | **Rice Vill** 23
Kenneally's | T | **Lower Shepherd** 16
Kenny & Ziggy's | T | **Galleria** 24
Khyber | T | **Upper Kirby** 23
Kim Son | T | **multi.** 23

Kiran's | D, T | **Galleria** 25
Lankford Grocery | T | **Midtown** 23
La Strada | D, T | **Montrose** 19
Luling City Mkt. | T | **Galleria** 23
Lyndon's | T | **NW Houston** -
Mama Ninfa's/Original Ninfa's | D, T | **multi.** 22
Michelangelo's | T | **Montrose** 24
Miss Saigon | T | **Rice Vill** 22
Moveable Feast | T | **Memorial** 22
Z Nielsen's | T | **Galleria** 26
Niko Niko's | T | **Montrose** 23
Nit Noi | D, T | **multi.** 21
Ocean Palace | T | **Bellaire** 23
100% Taquito | T | **Greenway Plaza** 18
Palazzo's | T | **multi.** 20
Paulie's | T | **multi.** 19
Pei Wei | T | **multi.** 19
Pizzitola's | T | **Heights** 24
NEW Polo's | D, T | **Greenway Plaza** 20
Post Oak Grill | D, T | **multi.** 21
Ragin' Cajun | T | **multi.** 21
Royers Round Top | T | **Round Top** 22
Sawadee | T | **West U** 24
Shanghai River | D, T | **River Oaks** 22
Shiva Indian | T | **multi.** 20
Star Pizza | D, T | **multi.** 23
Sudie's | T | **multi.** 20
Swinging Door | T | **Richmond** 24
Sylvia's | D, T | **W Houston** 21
Taco Milagro/La Mesa | T | **Upper Kirby** 16
Thierry André | T | **multi.** 23
This Is it | T | **Midtown** 21
Treebeards | T | **multi.** 24
Van Loc | T | **Midtown** 18
Vietopia | D, T | **West U** 20
Yildizlar | T | **Upper Kirby** 21
Yum Yum Cha | T | **Rice Vill** 23
Zoë's Kitchen | D | **Upper Kirby** 17

DESSERT

Amazon Grill | **SW Houston** 18
Z Américas | **Galleria** 24
benjy's | **Rice Vill** 23
Z Brennan's | **Midtown** 26
Z Cafe Annie | **Galleria** 26
Z Cheesecake Factory | **Galleria** 20
Z Churrascos | **multi.** 25
Z Da Marco | **Montrose** 28
Dessert Gallery | **multi.** 22
Empire Café | **Montrose** 20
Quattro | **Downtown** 23
Royers Round Top | **Round Top** 22
Ruggles | **multi.** 23
Thierry André | **multi.** 23
Z Tony's | **Greenway Plaza** 27

DINING ALONE

(Other than hotels and places with counter service)

Amazon Grill | **SW Houston** 18
Barnaby's | **multi.** 21
Bellaire Broiler Burger | **Bellaire** 21
Bibas Greek | **Heights** 18
Bibas One's | **Montrose** 18
Black Walnut | **Sugar Land** 20
Z Café Rabelais | **Rice Vill** 26
Chinese Café | **multi.** 22
Christian's | **multi.** 19
Z Churrascos | **multi.** 25
Daily Grind | **Heights** 14
Dimassi's | **multi.** 18
El Meson | **Rice Vill** 19
Empanadas by Marini | **multi.** 23
59 Diner | **Stafford** 16
Golden Room | **Montrose** 19
Goode Co. TX Seafood | **multi.** 23
Hobbit Cafe | **Lower Shepherd** 21
Z Hugo's | **Montrose** 26
Hunan | **Downtown** 21
Hungry's | **multi.** 19
India's | **Galleria** 21
Indika | **Montrose** 25
Kenny & Ziggy's | **Galleria** 24
Leibman's | **W Houston** 21
Mambo Seafood | **multi.** 20
Market Sq. | **Downtown** -
Masala Wok | **SW Houston** 18
Mexico's Deli | **W Houston** -
Mia Bella | **multi.** 22
NEW Mint Café | **Galleria** 19
Mission Burritos | **multi.** 22
Z Nielsen's | **Spring** 26
Otilia's | **Spring Branch** 22
Pei Wei | **multi.** 19
Perbacco | **Downtown** 23
Pronto Cucinino | **Medical Ctr** 19
NEW Reef | **Midtown** 25
Sage 400 | **Galleria** 22
Sasaki | **Briargrove** -
Shanghai River | **River Oaks** 22

HOUSTON

SPECIAL FEATURES

Shawarma King | **Briargrove** —
Simposio | **Briargrove** 24
Sinh Sinh | **Alief** —
Taco Milagro/La Mesa | **multi.** 16
Tony Mandola's | **River Oaks** 24
Vietopia | **West U** 20
Yum Yum Cha | **Rice Vill** 23

ENTERTAINMENT

(Call for days and times of performances)

Alexander | belly dancers | **Galleria** 24
Amerigo's | piano | **Woodlands** 22
Armadillo Palace | varies | **West U** 21
Z Artista | piano | **Downtown** 25
Backstreet Café | jazz | **River Oaks** 22
Berryhill Baja | varies | **multi.** 19
Bistro Calais | jazz | **River Oaks** 23
Bistro Le Cep | accordian | **W Houston** 25
Bistro Vino | varies | **Montrose** 20
Brasil | varies | **Montrose** 20
Breakfast Klub | varies | **Midtown** 23
Z Brennan's | jazz | **Midtown** 26
Cadillac Bar | varies | **Kemah** 18
Café Artiste | band | **Montrose** 16
Z Café Le Jadeite | piano | **River Oaks** 22
Daily Review | guitar/jazz | **River Oaks** 20
Denis' Seafood | Cajun/zydeco | **Memorial** 21
El Meson | guitar | **Rice Vill** 19
El Pueblito Place | flamenco/salsa | **Montrose** 20
Grappino di Nino | jazz | **Montrose** 20
Gravitas | DJ | **Neartown** 21
Z Hugo's | Mexican | **Montrose** 26
Jax Grill | zydeco | **Heights** 19
Las Alamedas | guitar | **Memorial** 20
Masraff's | jazz/piano | **Uptown** 23
Michelangelo's | piano | **Montrose** 24
Mi Luna | jazz/Latin/soul | **multi.** 19
Ouisie's Table | jazz | **River Oaks** 23
Z Pappas Bros. | piano | **Galleria** 27
Pico's | guitar/harp | **Bellaire** 24
Z Red Onion | piano | **NW Houston** 26
Rickshaw Far East | DJ | **River Oaks** 19
Rioja | flamenco/salsa | **W Houston** 24
Rudi Lechner's | German | **SW Houston** 23
Ruggles | jazz | **Montrose** 23
Sambuca | varies | **Downtown** 21
Sullivan's | bands/jazz | **Galleria** 24
Taco Milagro/La Mesa | varies | **Upper Kirby** 16
Tokyohana | DJ | **N Houston** 19
Z Tony's | piano | **Greenway Plaza** 27
Trevisio | jazz | **Medical Ctr** 21
Via Emilia | vocals | **NW Houston** —
Z Vic & Antony's | piano | **Downtown** 26

GAME IN SEASON

Amerigo's | **Woodlands** 22
Antica Osteria | **West U** 24
Arcodoro | **Galleria** 20
Armadillo Palace | **West U** 21
NEW Beaver's | **Heights** —
Bistro Calais | **River Oaks** 23
Bistro Le Cep | **W Houston** 25
Bistro Provence | **W Houston** 23
NEW Brasserie Max & Julie | **Montrose** —
Brenner's | **Memorial** 25
Brownstone | **Upper Kirby** 22
Z Cafe Annie | **Galleria** 26
Z Café Rabelais | **Rice Vill** 26
Charivari | **Midtown** 23
Z Chez Nous | **Humble** 26
Floyd's | **Webster** 22
Glass Wall | **Heights** 25
Gravitas | **Neartown** 21
Z Ibiza | **Midtown** 25
Indika | **Montrose** 25
Karl's | **Richmond** 27
Z La Colombe d'Or | **Montrose** 21
Masraff's | **Uptown** 23
PK's | **Briargrove** 21
Z Rainbow Lodge | **Heights** 23
Rioja | **W Houston** 24
Royers Round Top | **Round Top** 22
t'afia | **Midtown** 25
Z Vic & Antony's | **Downtown** 26

HISTORIC PLACES

(Year opened; * building)

1870 | Treebeards* | **FM 1960** 24
1889 | Cava Bistro* | **Downtown** 21
1894 | Market Sq.* | **Downtown** —
1895 | Luigi's* | **Galveston** 25

1900 | t'afia* | **Midtown** 25
1911 | Gaido's | **Galveston** 22
1915 | Crapitto's* | **Galleria** 21
1924 | 17* | **Downtown** 25
1926 | Bistro Lancaster* | **Downtown** 20
1930 | Shade* | **Heights** 25
1936 | Brenner's | **Memorial** 25
1936 | Pizzitola's | **Heights** 24
1937 | Christian's | **multi.** 19
1939 | Lankford Grocery | **Midtown** 23
1941 | Cleburne | **West U** 23
1944 | Massa's | **Downtown** 19
1952 | Nielsen's | **Galleria** 26
1953 | Spanish Village | **Medical Ctr** 19
1957 | Bellaire Broiler Burger | **Bellaire** 21

HOTEL DINING

Alden Houston Hotel
Z 17 | **Downtown** 25
Four Seasons Hotel
Quattro | **Downtown** 23
Hilton Americas Hotel
Skyline B&G | **Downtown** 17
Spencer's | **Downtown** 21
Hotel ZaZa
NEW Monarch | **Medical Ctr** 21
Icon Hotel
Z Hotel Icon | **Downtown** 24
La Colombe d'Or
Z La Colombe d'Or | **Montrose** 21
Lancaster Hotel
Bistro Lancaster | **Downtown** 20
Omni Hotel Houston
Noé | **Uptown** 22
St. Regis Hotel
Remington | **Galleria** 25
Sugar Land Marriott Hotel
Burning Pear | **Sugar Land** 23
Westchase Hilton
Rio Ranch | **SW Houston** 21

LATE DINING

(Weekday closing hour)

Armadillo Palace | 12 AM | **West U** 21
Bibas One's | 24 hrs. | **Montrose** 18
Bistro Vino | 12 AM | **Montrose** 20
Brasil | 12 AM | **Montrose** 20
Cabo | 12 AM | **Downtown** 14
Café Japon | 12 AM | **West U** 22
Christian's | 12 AM | **Midtown** 19
Cova | 12 AM | **West U** 19
59 Diner | varies | **multi.** 16
Hard Rock | 12 AM | **Downtown** 14
Hollywood | varies | **Montrose** -
Katz's Deli | 24 hrs. | **Montrose** 19
Kenneally's | 1 AM | **Lower Shepherd** 16
Mai's | 4 AM | **Midtown** 23
Mama's Café | 2 AM | **Briargrove** 19
Red Lion | 2 AM | **Lower Shepherd** 19
Rudyard's | 12 AM | **Montrose** -
Sambuca | varies | **Downtown** 21
Sinh Sinh | 2 AM | **Alief** -
Smith & Wollensky | 2 AM | **Galleria** 20
Spanish Flowers | 24 hrs. | **Heights** 19
Tan Tan | varies | **Alief** 26

MEET FOR A DRINK

Z Américas | **Galleria** 24
NEW Amici | **Sugar Land** 24
Arcodoro | **Galleria** 20
Armadillo Palace | **West U** 21
NEW Armandos | **River Oaks** 14
Arturo's | **Uptown** 19
benjy's | **Rice Vill** 23
Black Labrador | **Montrose** 17
Bob's Steak | **Galleria** 25
Brasil | **Montrose** 20
Cabo | **Downtown** 14
Cadillac Bar | **multi.** 18
Christian's | **multi.** 19
Cyclone Anaya's | **multi.** 20
NEW Del Frisco's | **Galleria** 27
Dolce Vita | **Montrose** 24
El Tiempo | **Montrose** 22
Farrago | **Midtown** 19
Z Fleming's Prime | **River Oaks** 24
Grappino di Nino | **Montrose** 20
Gravitas | **Neartown** 21
Z Ibiza | **Midtown** 25
Kenneally's | **Lower Shepherd** 16
La Griglia | **River Oaks** 21
Las Alamedas | **Memorial** 20
La Strada | **Montrose** 19
Market Sq. | **Downtown** -
Max's | **Heights** 21
McCormick & Schmick's | **Uptown** 21
NEW Monarch | **Medical Ctr** 21

Palm, The | **Galleria** 24
☑ Pappadeaux | **multi.** 23
☑ Pappasito's | **multi.** 23
Pico's | **Bellaire** 24
Red Lion | **Lower Shepherd** 19
NEW Reef | **Midtown** 25
Remington | **Galleria** 25
Rickshaw Far East | **River Oaks** 19
Rudyard's | **Montrose** -
Ruggles | **Montrose** 23
Sambuca | **Downtown** 21
☑ 17 | **Downtown** 25
Smith & Wollensky | **Galleria** 20
Sorrento | **Montrose** 21
Sullivan's | **Galleria** 24
Taco Milagro/La Mesa | **Upper Kirby** 16
t'afia | **Midtown** 25
Teala's | **Montrose** 18
☑ Uptown Sushi | **Uptown** 26
NEW Yatra | **Downtown** 24

NOTEWORTHY NEWCOMERS

Amici | **Sugar Land** 24
Armandos | **River Oaks** 14
Au Petit Paris | **Lower Shepherd** -
Aura | **Missouri City** -
Beaver's | **Heights** -
Blue Fin | **W Houston** -
Brasserie Max & Julie | **Montrose** -
Danton's | **Montrose** -
Del Frisco's | **Galleria** 27
Grove, The | **Downtown** -
Mint Café | **Galleria** 19
Monarch | **Medical Ctr** 21
Polo's | **Greenway Plaza** 20
Rattan | **W Houston** -
Red Onion Taco | **NW Houston** -
Reef | **Midtown** 25
Saga | **Midtown** -
Soma | **Heights** -
SoVino | **Montrose** -
Yatra | **Downtown** 24

OUTDOOR DINING

(G=garden; P=patio; S=sidewalk; T=terrace; W=waterside)

Amazon Grill | P | **West U** 18
Arcodoro | P | **Galleria** 20
Armadillo Palace | P | **West U** 21
☑ Artista | T | **Downtown** 25
Ashiana | P | **W Houston** 24
Baba Yega | P | **Montrose** 20
Barnaby's | P | **multi.** 21
Backstreet Café | G, P | **River Oaks** 22
Becks Prime | P | **multi.** 22
Berryhill Baja | P | **multi.** 19
Bistro Vino | G | **Montrose** 20
Black Labrador | P | **Montrose** 17
Black Walnut | P | **multi.** 20
Brasil | P | **Montrose** 20
☑ Brennan's | P | **Midtown** 26
Cabo | P | **Downtown** 14
Café Express | P | **multi.** 18
Cava Bistro | P | **Downtown** 21
Chuy's | P | **River Oaks** 21
Crapitto's | P | **Galleria** 21
Crú Wine Bar | P | **Woodlands** 20
Daily Review | G, P | **River Oaks** 20
D'Amico's | P | **Rice Vill** 21
Denis' Seafood | G | **Memorial** 21
Dolce Vita | P | **Montrose** 24
El Pueblito Place | P | **Montrose** 20
El Tiempo | P | **multi.** 22
Empire Café | P | **Montrose** 20
Farrago | G | **Midtown** 19
Goode Co. Burgers | P | **West U** 22
☑ Goode Co. TX BBQ | P | **West U** 25
Grappino di Nino | P | **Montrose** 20
Grotto | P | **Woodlands** 22
NEW Grove, The | P | **Downtown** -
Hard Rock | P | **Downtown** 14
Hobbit Cafe | P | **Lower Shepherd** 21
☑ Hugo's | P | **Montrose** 26
☑ Ibiza | P | **Midtown** 25
Indika | P | **Montrose** 25
Istanbul Grill | P | **Rice Vill** 22
Jasper's | P | **Woodlands** 24
Kenneally's | P | **Lower Shepherd** 16
La Griglia | P | **River Oaks** 21
La Mexicana | P | **Montrose** 19
Lankford Grocery | T | **Midtown** 23
La Strada | P | **Montrose** 19
Market Sq. | P | **Downtown** -
Masraff's | P | **Uptown** 23
Mia Bella | P, S | **multi.** 22
Michelangelo's | P | **Montrose** 24
Niko Niko's | P | **Montrose** 23
Nino's | P | **Montrose** 24
Mama Ninfa's/Original Ninfa's | P | **Neartown** 22

Otilia's | P | **Spring Branch** 22
Ouisie's Table | G, P | **River Oaks** 23
Z P.F. Chang's | P, W | **multi.** 22
Pico's | P | **Bellaire** 24
Z Rainbow Lodge | G, P, T, W | **Heights** 23
Raven Grill | P | **West U** 21
Red Lion | P | **Lower Shepherd** 19
Sambuca | P | **Downtown** 21
Star Pizza | P | **multi.** 23
Sylvia's | P | **W Houston** 21
Taco Milagro/La Mesa | P | **Upper Kirby** 16
t'afia | P | **Midtown** 25
Teala's | P | **Montrose** 18
Thai Sticks | P | **Montrose** 21
Tila's | P | **River Oaks** 21
Tony Mandola's | P | **River Oaks** 24
Treebeards | P, T | **FM 1960** 24
Trevisio | P | **Medical Ctr** 21
Vincent's | P | **Montrose** 22

POWER SCENES

Bob's Steak | **Galleria** 25
Z Brennan's | **Midtown** 26
Brenner's | **multi.** 25
Z Cafe Annie | **Galleria** 26
Capital Grille | **Galleria** 25
Carmelo's | **W Houston** 22
Z Da Marco | **Montrose** 28
Z Hotel Icon | **Downtown** 24
Z Ibiza | **Midtown** 25
Irma's | **Downtown** 22
Jasper's | **Woodlands** 24
Z La Colombe d'Or | **Montrose** 21
La Griglia | **River Oaks** 21
Z Mark's | **Montrose** 28
Massa's | **Downtown** 19
NEW Monarch | **Medical Ctr** 21
Morton's Steak | **multi.** 25
Palm, The | **Galleria** 24
Z Pappas Bros. | **Galleria** 27
Quattro | **Downtown** 23
Remington | **Galleria** 25
Ruth's Chris | **Galleria** 25
Z 17 | **Downtown** 25
Strip Hse. | **Downtown** 24
Sullivan's | **Galleria** 24
Z Tony's | **Greenway Plaza** 27
Z Vic & Antony's | **Downtown** 26
Zula | **Downtown** 23

PRIX FIXE MENUS

(Call for prices and times)

Arcodoro | **Galleria** 20
Ashiana | **W Houston** 24
Bistro Calais | **River Oaks** 23
Bistro Vino | **Montrose** 20
Z Brennan's | **Midtown** 26
Brownstone | **Upper Kirby** 22
Chez Georges | **Montrose** 24
Z Fogo de Chão | **Briargrove** 26
Kiran's | **Galleria** 25
Z Mark's | **Montrose** 28
Masraff's | **Uptown** 23
Nelore | **Montrose** 20
Pesce | **Upper Kirby** 21
Z Rainbow Lodge | **Heights** 23
t'afia | **Midtown** 25

QUIET CONVERSATION

Amerigo's | **Woodlands** 22
Au Petit Paris | **Lower Shepherd** -
Bice | **Galleria** 21
Bistro Toulouse | **Briargrove** 20
Z Café Le Jadeite | **River Oaks** 22
Carmelo's | **W Houston** 22
Charivari | **Midtown** 23
Chez Georges | **Montrose** 24
Z Chez Nous | **Humble** 26
Crapitto's | **Galleria** 21
Damian's | **Midtown** 21
Golden Room | **Montrose** 19
Hobbit Cafe | **Lower Shepherd** 21
Z Hotel Icon | **Downtown** 24
India's | **Galleria** 21
Z La Colombe d'Or | **Montrose** 21
Z Le Mistral | **W Houston** 26
Lexington Grille | **Lower Shepherd** 21
Z Lynn's | **W Houston** 26
Mai Thai | **Upper Kirby** 23
Massa's | **Downtown** 19
Miss Saigon | **Rice Vill** 22
Ouisie's Table | **River Oaks** 23
Perbacco | **Downtown** 23
Raven Grill | **West U** 21
Ruggles | **Galleria** 23
Ruth's Chris | **Galleria** 25
Sawadee | **West U** 24
Z 17 | **Downtown** 25
Shanghai River | **River Oaks** 22
Thai Bistro | **West U** -
Thai Sticks | **Montrose** 21
Tila's | **River Oaks** 21

Vargo's | **Memorial** 17

Via Emilia | **NW Houston** -

ROMANTIC PLACES

Antica Osteria | **West U** 24

Z Artista | **Downtown** 25

Au Petit Paris | **Lower Shepherd** -

Bistro Vino | **Montrose** 20

Z Brennan's | **Midtown** 26

Z Cafe Annie | **Galleria** 26

Z Café Le Jadeite | **River Oaks** 22

Carmelo's | **W Houston** 22

Cava Bistro | **Downtown** 21

Charivari | **Midtown** 23

Chez Georges | **Montrose** 24

Z Chez Nous | **Humble** 26

Crapitto's | **Galleria** 21

Z Da Marco | **Montrose** 28

Damian's | **Midtown** 21

Z La Colombe d'Or | **Montrose** 21

Las Alamedas | **Memorial** 20

Z Le Mistral | **W Houston** 26

Luigi's | **Galveston** 25

Z Lynn's | **W Houston** 26

Z Mark's | **Montrose** 28

Masraff's | **Uptown** 23

Michelangelo's | **Montrose** 24

Z Rainbow Lodge | **Heights** 23

Remington | **Galleria** 25

Ruggles | **Galleria** 23

Skyline B&G | **Downtown** 17

Thai Sticks | **Montrose** 21

Z Tony's | **Greenway Plaza** 27

Vargo's | **Memorial** 17

Via Emilia | **NW Houston** -

SENIOR APPEAL

Bistro Lancaster | **Downtown** 20

Brownstone | **Upper Kirby** 22

Carmelo's | **W Houston** 22

Chez Georges | **Montrose** 24

Cleburne | **West U** 23

Crapitto's | **Galleria** 21

59 Diner | **Stafford** 16

Gaido's | **Galveston** 22

Lexington Grille | **Lower Shepherd** 21

Melting Pot | **Galleria** 21

NY Coffee Shop | **Meyerland** -

Z Nielsen's | **Spring** 26

Old Heidelberg | **Galleria** 21

Ouisie's Table | **River Oaks** 23

Rudi Lechner's | **SW Houston** 23

Thierry André | **River Oaks** 23

Vargo's | **Memorial** 17

SINGLES SCENES

Armadillo Palace | **West U** 21

NEW Armandos | **River Oaks** 14

Arturo's | **Uptown** 19

Berryhill Baja | **Montrose** 19

Cabo | **Downtown** 14

Cadillac Bar | **multi.** 18

Cova | **multi.** 19

Cyclone Anaya's | **multi.** 20

NEW Del Frisco's | **Galleria** 27

Dolce Vita | **Montrose** 24

El Tiempo | **Montrose** 22

Empire Café | **Montrose** 20

Farrago | **Midtown** 19

Fish, The | **Midtown** 20

La Griglia | **River Oaks** 21

La Strada | **Montrose** 19

Max's | **Heights** 21

Mi Luna | **Rice Vill** 19

Pesce | **Upper Kirby** 21

NEW Reef | **Midtown** 25

Rickshaw Far East | **River Oaks** 19

Sage 400 | **Galleria** 22

Sambuca | **Downtown** 21

Smith & Wollensky | **Galleria** 20

Sullivan's | **Galleria** 24

Taco Milagro/La Mesa | **Upper Kirby** 16

Teala's | **Montrose** 18

Z Uptown Sushi | **Uptown** 26

Zula | **Downtown** 23

SLEEPERS

(Good to excellent food, but little known)

Aka | **multi.** 23

Alexander | **Galleria** 24

Ashiana | **W Houston** 24

Bistro Calais | **River Oaks** 23

Bistro Provence | **W Houston** 23

Café Benedicte | **W Houston** 23

Charivari | **Midtown** 23

Chez Georges | **Montrose** 24

Daniel Wong's | **Bellaire** 23

Empanadas by Marini | **multi.** 23

Empire Turkish | **W Houston** 24

Frenchie's | **Clear Lake** 24

Fung's | **SW Houston** 25

Kahn's Deli | **Rice Vill** 23

Karl's | **Richmond** 27

Khyber | **Upper Kirby** 23

Laurier Café | **Greenway Plaza** 25
Luigi's | **Galveston** 25
Mai Thai | **Upper Kirby** 23
Ocean Palace | **Bellaire** 23
Pappas Grill | **Stafford** 28
Pasha | **Rice Vill** 25
Perbacco | **Downtown** 23
Remington | **Galleria** 25
Rioja | **W Houston** 24
Sawadee | **West U** 24
Sushi King | **Upper Kirby** 23
Swinging Door | **Richmond** 24
Tan Tan | **Alief** 26
Teotihuacan | **multi.** 24
Thai Gourmet | **Galleria** 24
Thierry André | **multi.** 23
NEW Yatra | **Downtown** 24

TRANSPORTING EXPERIENCES

Z Américas | **Galleria** 24
Z Artista | **Downtown** 25
Z Brennan's | **Midtown** 26
Z Cafe Annie | **Galleria** 26
Carmelo's | **W Houston** 22
Z Chez Nous | **Humble** 26
Z Da Marco | **Montrose** 28
Indika | **Montrose** 25
Z Mark's | **Montrose** 28
Z Rainbow Lodge | **Heights** 23
NEW Reef | **Midtown** 25
Shade | **Heights** 25
t'afia | **Midtown** 25
Z Tony's | **Greenway Plaza** 27

TRENDY

NEW Amici | **Sugar Land** 24
NEW Armandos | **River Oaks** 14
Z Artista | **Downtown** 25
Arturo's | **Uptown** 19
benjy's | **Rice Vill** 23
Bice | **Galleria** 21
Catalan | **Heights** 24
Cyclone Anaya's | **multi.** 20
NEW Del Frisco's | **Galleria** 27
Dolce Vita | **Montrose** 24
El Tiempo | **multi.** 22
Farrago | **Midtown** 19
Fish, The | **Midtown** 20
Glass Wall | **Heights** 25
Gravitas | **Neartown** 21
NEW Grove, The | **Downtown** -
Z Hotel Icon | **Downtown** 24
Z Ibiza | **Midtown** 25
Julia's | **Midtown** 19
La Griglia | **River Oaks** 21
La Strada | **Montrose** 19
Z Mark's | **Montrose** 28
Max's | **Heights** 21
Mi Luna | **multi.** 19
NEW Mint Café | **Galleria** 19
Mockingbird Bistro | **River Oaks** 25
NEW Monarch | **Medical Ctr** 21
Pesce | **Upper Kirby** 21
Z P.F. Chang's | **W Houston** 22
NEW Reef | **Midtown** 25
Rickshaw Far East | **River Oaks** 19
Ruggles | **Montrose** 23
Sambuca | **Downtown** 21
Shade | **Heights** 25
Smith & Wollensky | **Galleria** 20
NEW Soma | **Heights** -
Taco Milagro/La Mesa | **Upper Kirby** 16
t'afia | **Midtown** 25
Z Uptown Sushi | **Uptown** 26
Zula | **Downtown** 23

VIEWS

Z Artista | **Downtown** 25
Baba Yega | **Montrose** 20
Brenner's | **River Oaks** 25
Cabo | **Downtown** 14
Cadillac Bar | **Kemah** 18
NEW Del Frisco's | **Galleria** 27
Gaido's | **Galveston** 22
NEW Grove, The | **Downtown** -
Z La Colombe d'Or | **Montrose** 21
Las Alamedas | **Memorial** 20
NEW Monarch | **Medical Ctr** 21
Z Rainbow Lodge | **Heights** 23
NEW Reef | **Midtown** 25
Skyline B&G | **Downtown** 17
Trevisio | **Medical Ctr** 21
Vargo's | **Memorial** 17

VISITORS ON EXPENSE ACCOUNT

Z Américas | **Galleria** 24
Bice | **Galleria** 21
Bob's Steak | **Galleria** 25
Brenner's | **multi.** 25
Z Cafe Annie | **Galleria** 26
Capital Grille | **Galleria** 25
Carmelo's | **W Houston** 22
Z Da Marco | **Montrose** 28

NEW Del Frisco's | **Galleria** 27
NEW Grove, The | **Downtown** -
Z Hotel Icon | **Downtown** 24
Kirby's | **Woodlands** 24
Z La Colombe d'Or | **Montrose** 21
Z Lynn's | **W Houston** 26
Z Mark's | **Montrose** 28
Mockingbird Bistro | **River Oaks** 25
NEW Monarch | **Medical Ctr** 21
Morton's Steak | **Galleria** 25
Noé | **Uptown** 22
Palm, The | **Galleria** 24
Z Pappas Bros. | **Galleria** 27
Pesce | **Upper Kirby** 21
Quattro | **Downtown** 23
NEW Reef | **Midtown** 25
Remington | **Galleria** 25
Ruth's Chris | **Galleria** 25
Z 17 | **Downtown** 25
Smith & Wollensky | **Galleria** 20
Strip Hse. | **Downtown** 24
Z Tony's | **Greenway Plaza** 27
Z Vic & Antony's | **Downtown** 26

WINNING WINE LISTS

Z Américas | **Galleria** 24
Arcodoro | **Galleria** 20
Ashiana | **W Houston** 24
Backstreet Café | **River Oaks** 22
benjy's | **Rice Vill** 23
Z Brennan's | **Midtown** 26
Brenner's | **River Oaks** 25
Z Cafe Annie | **Galleria** 26
Z Café Rabelais | **Rice Vill** 26
Capital Grille | **Galleria** 25
Carmelo's | **W Houston** 22
Catalan | **Heights** 24
Chez Georges | **Montrose** 24
Z Churrascos | **multi.** 25
Z Da Marco | **Montrose** 28
El Meson | **Rice Vill** 19
Z Ibiza | **Midtown** 25
Kiran's | **Galleria** 25
Laurier Café | **Greenway Plaza** 25
Z Lynn's | **W Houston** 26
Z Mark's | **Montrose** 28
Mockingbird Bistro | **River Oaks** 25
Morton's Steak | **Galleria** 25
Z Pappas Bros. | **Galleria** 27
Pesce | **Upper Kirby** 21
Prego | **Rice Vill** 23
NEW Reef | **Midtown** 25
Remington | **Galleria** 25
Simposio | **Briargrove** 24
t'afia | **Midtown** 25
Z Tony's | **Greenway Plaza** 27
Z Vic & Antony's | **Downtown** 26

WORTH A TRIP

Clear Lake
Frenchie's 24
Galveston
Gaido's 22
Luigi's 25
Humble
Z Chez Nous 26
Richmond
Karl's 27
Swinging Door 24
Round Top
Royers Round Top 22
The Woodlands
Amerigo's 22

SAN ANTONIO

San Antonio Most Popular

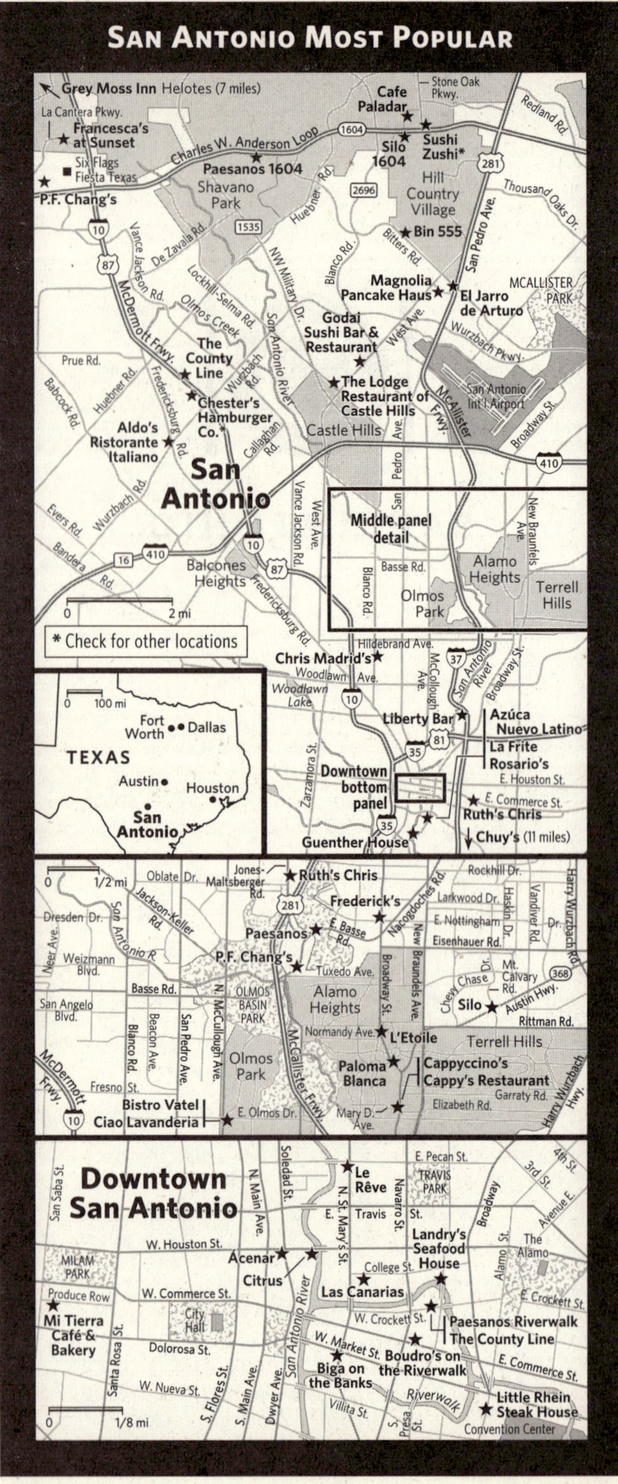

Most Popular

1. Le Rêve
2. Biga on the Banks
3. Boudro's
4. Paesanos
5. Lodge of Castle Hills
6. Liberty Bar
7. Silo
8. Cappy's
9. L'Etoile
10. Bistro Vatel
11. Paloma Blanca
12. Magnolia Pancake Haus
13. Chris Madrid's
14. Frederick's
15. Las Canarias
16. Mi Tierra Café
17. Grey Moss Inn
18. Chesters Hamburger Co.
19. Chuy's
20. Rosario's
21. Silo 1604*
22. El Jarro de Arturo
23. Ciao Lavanderia
24. Little Rhein Steak*
25. Bin 555
26. County Line*
27. Landry's
28. La Frite
29. P.F. Chang's*
30. Acenar
31. Aldo's
32. Cafe Paladar*
33. Citrus*
34. Francesca's*
35. Cappyccino's
36. Guenther House*
37. Sushi Zushi*
38. Azúca
39. Godai Sushi
40. Ruth's Chris*

It's obvious that many of the above restaurants are among the San Antonio area's most expensive, but if popularity were calibrated to price, we suspect that a number of other restaurants would join their ranks. Thus, we have added a list of 40 Best Buys on page 286. These are restaurants that give real quality at extremely reasonable prices.

KEY NEWCOMERS

Our editors' take on the most notable new arrivals of the past year. For a full list, see the Noteworthy Newcomers index on page 328.

Bistro Thyme

Chart House

Dough

Green Vegetarian

Kona Grill

Mimi's Cafe

Silo 1604

Tiago's

* Indicates a tie with restaurant above

Top Food (Based on a 30-pt. scale)

Excludes places with low votes, unless indicated by a ∇.

29 Le Rêve

28 Sandbar Fish

27 Magnolia Pancake Haus
Biga on the Banks
Godai Sushi

26 Francesca's
Lodge of Castle Hills
Frederick's
L'Etoile
Silo
Bistro Vatel
Bin 555
Silo 1604
La Frite
Las Canarias

25 Cafe Paladar
Citrus
Ruth's Chris
Chris Madrid's
Fig Tree
Sushihana*
Morton's Steak

24 Texas Farm to Table
Boudro's
Piatti
Little Rhein Steak
Palm, The
India Palace
Da Vinci Gelato
Pesca on the River*
Grey Moss Inn
Fleming's
Liberty Bar
Sawasdee Thai
Azúca

23 El Mirador
Pappadeaux
Cappy's
Korean BBQ House*
La Scala

BY CUISINE

AMERICAN (NEW)

27 Biga on the Banks
26 Lodge of Castle Hills
Silo
Bin 555
Silo 1604

AMERICAN (TRAD.)

27 Magnolia Pancake Haus
24 Texas Farm to Table
Grey Moss Inn
23 Guenther House
Chesters Hamburger Co.

CHINESE

22 P.F. Chang's
Wah Kee
Golden Wok
21 Mencius Gourmet
Formosa Garden

ECLECTIC

24 Liberty Bar
23 Cappy's
22 Grill at Leon Springs
La Tuna Grill∇
20 Eclipse Café

FRENCH

29 La Rêve
26 Frederick's
L'Etoile
Bistro Vatel
Las Canarias

ITALIAN

24 Piatti
Da Vinci Gelato
23 Sorento Ristorante
Ciao Lavanderia
Paesanos 1604*

MEXICAN

23 El Mirador
Rosario's
22 Paloma Blanca
Picante Grill*
Tiago's Cabo Grill

SEAFOOD

28 Sandbar Fish
26 L'Etoile
24 Boudro's
Pesca on the River
23 Pappadeaux

STEAKHOUSES

25 Ruth's Chris
Morton's Steak
24 Boudro's
Little Rhein Steak
Palm, The

TEX-MEX

22 Ácenar
21 Mi Tierra
Chuy's
La Hacienda/Los Barrios
La Margarita

BY SPECIAL FEATURE

BREAKFAST

27 Magnolia Pancake Haus
23 Guenther Hse.
21 Mimi's Cafe
23 El Mirador
21 Mi Tierra

BRUNCH

26 Las Canarias
25 Cafe Paladar
24 Liberty Bar
23 Cappy's
22 Guenther Hse.

BUSINESS DINING

29 Le Rêve
27 Biga on the Banks
26 Frederick's
Lodge of Castle Hills
Citrus

CHILD-FRIENDLY

25 Chris Madrid's
24 Da Vinci Gelato
23 Paesanos 1604
22 Big'z
Acenar

DINING ALONE

28 Sandbar Fish
26 Koi Kawa
23 El Mirador
Cappy's
Ciao Lavanderia

MEET FOR A DRINK

26 Silo
25 Citrus
24 Piatti
Liberty Bar
22 Grill at Leon Springs

NEWCOMERS (RATED)

26 Silo 1604
22 Tiago's
21 Mimi's Cafe

PEOPLE-WATCHING

28 Sandbar Fish
24 Boudro's
Piatti
Pesca on the River
Texas Farm to Table

POWER SCENES

28 Sandbar Fish
27 Biga on the Banks
24 Piatti
Liberty Bar
23 Paesanos 1604

QUICK BITES

28 Sandbar Fish
26 Bin 555
25 Chris Madrid's
24 Da Vinci Gelato
Texas Farm to Table

QUIET CONVERSATION

29 Le Rêve
27 Biga on the Banks
26 Francesca's
Lodge of Castle Hills
Bistro Vatel

SINGLES SCENES

24 Azúca
23 Rosario's
Paesanos 1604
22 Paloma Blanca
Grill at Leon Springs

TRENDY

27 Biga on the Banks
26 La Frite
25 Cafe Paladar
24 Liberty Bar
Texas Farm to Table

WINNING WINE LISTS

29 Le Rêve
27 Biga on the Banks
26 Francesca's
Lodge of Castle Hills
L'Etoile

BY LOCATION

ALAMO HEIGHTS

- 26 Frederick's
- L'Etoile
- 23 Cappy's
- Sorento Ristorante
- 22 Paloma Blanca

CASTLE HILLS/NORTH

- 26 Lodge of Castle Hills
- 25 Sushihana
- 23 La Scala
- 22 Chesters Hamburger Co.
- El Jarro de Arturo

DOWNTOWN

- 29 Le Rêve
- 28 Sandbar Fish
- 25 Citrus
- Morton's Steak
- 24 Palm, The

KING WILLIAM/ SOUTHTOWN

- 26 La Frite
- 24 Azúca
- 23 El Mirador
- Rosario's
- Guenther House

MEDICAL CENTER

- 24 India Palace
- 22 Chesters Hamburger Co.
- Golden Wok
- 21 Mencius Gourmet
- Aldo's

NORTH CENTRAL

- 27 Magnolia Pancake Haus
- 27 Godai Sushi
- 26 Bin 555
- 25 Ruth's Chris
- 24 India Palace

QUARRY

- 24 Piatti
- Fleming's
- 22 P.F. Chang's
- Paesanos
- 18 Canyon Café

RIVER WALK

- 27 Biga on the Banks
- 26 Las Canarias
- 25 Fig Tree
- 24 Boudro's
- Little Rhein Steak

Top Decor (Based on a 30-pt. scale)

27 Francesca's

26 Lodge of Castle Hills

25 Silo 1604
Biga on the Banks
Le Rêve

24 Ácenar
Grey Moss Inn
Citrus
Fleming's
Antlers Lodge

23 Paloma Blanca
Silo
Las Canarias
Bin 555
Cafe Paladar
La Scala

22 Reggiano's
Fig Tree
Grill at Leon Springs*
Ruth's Chris

OUTDOORS

Ácenar
Bin 555
Boudro's
Cappy's
La Hacienda/Los Barrios
Las Ramblas
Paesanos 1604
Pam's Kitchen
Pesca
Scenic Loop Café

ROMANCE

Biga on the Banks
Bistro Vatel
Bohanan's
Citrus
Francesca's
Las Canarias
Le Rêve
Lodge of Castle Hills
Oro
Silo 1604

ROOMS

Biga on the Banks
Bin 555
Bistro Vatel
Bohanan's
Cafe Paladar
Citrus
Francesca's
Liberty Bar
Lodge of Castle Hills
Silo 1604

VIEWS

Ácenar
Biga on the Banks
Bohanan's
Boudro's
Fig Tree
Grey Moss Inn
Las Ramblas
Little Rhein Steak
Mi Tierra
Scenic Loop Café

Top Service (Based on a 30-pt. scale)

27 Le Rêve

26 Frederick's
Francesca's

25 Biga on the Banks
Ruth's Chris

24 Silo 1604
Palm, The
Lodge of Castle Hills
Antlers Lodge
Bistro Vatel
Las Canarias
Silo

23 Fleming's
La Scala
Morton's Steak
L'Etoile
Fig Tree
Sandbar Fish
Little Rhein Steak
Bin 555

Best Buys

In order of Bang for the Buck rating.

1. Da Vinci Gelato
2. Magnolia Pancake Haus
3. Texas Farm to Table
4. Cheesy Jane's
5. Chris Madrid's
6. Chesters Hamburger Co.
7. Schilo's Deli
8. Taco Cabana
9. Picante Grill
10. Guenther House
11. Beto's Comida
12. Mama's Café
13. Clear Springs Café
14. Formosa Garden
15. Big'z Burger
16. Madhatters Tea
17. India Palace
18. Golden Wok
19. Mi Tierra
20. La Hacienda/Los Barrios

OTHER GOOD VALUES

Cascabel
Cove, The
Chef Chan
County Line
Demo's
Jospehine St. Cafe
La Marginal
La Tuna Grill
Little Red Barn
Mimi's Café
Pam's Patio Kitchen
Phoenix Chinese Café
Sarovar
Sea Island Shrimp House
Smokehouse, The
Sorento Rist.
Thai Taste
Tiago's Cabo Grille
Tip Top Café
Torres Taco Haven

FOOD | DECOR | SERVICE | COST

San Antonio

Ácenar *Tex-Mex*

22 | 24 | 18 | $27

River Walk | 146 E. Houston St. (St. Mary's St.) | 210-222-2362 | www.acenar.com

Locals "love the atmosphere" at this "hip", "noisy" River Walk Tex-Mex set in colorful digs with stellar "people-watching" and a shaded balcony that affords "great views" of the water; the "modern" dishes (and "excellent duck chalupas") win raves, though a few find fault with tabs that are "on the pricier side" and sometimes "inconsistent" service.

Aldaco's Mexican Cuisine ☒ *Mexican*

▽ 22 | 19 | 19 | $20

San Antonio East | 100 Hoefgen Ave. (bet. Center & Commerce Sts.) | 210-222-0561 | www.aldacos.net

"A treasure" laud loyalists of Blanca Aldaco's "slightly upscale" Mexican at Sunset Station in St. Paul Square offering cuisine with "an emphasis on fresh ingredients" and "irresistible drinks"; it's a "fun place" with patio seating and solid service making it "great for kids", though a few lament the location can be a problem when beer-infused crowds descend on the nearby Alamodome for concerts and sporting events; N.B. a second branch in Stone Oak is set to open in early 2008.

Aldino at the Vineyard *Italian*

21 | 22 | 20 | $29

Sonterra | Vineyard Ctr. | 1203 N. Loop 1604 W. (Blanco Rd.) | 210-340-0000 | www.aldinos.com

Outstripping its "strip-mall" setting, this Sonterra bastion of "imaginative", "fresh" Italian fare is a "pleasant" place to dine thanks to its spacious faux-Roman interior and "excellent patio for lingering after the meal"; in general it's considered a "great neighborhood place", though some sigh servers are "earnest" but "not well versed."

Aldo's Ristorante Italiano *Italian*

21 | 21 | 22 | $33

Medical Center | 8539 Fredericksburg Rd. (Wurzbach Rd.) | 210-696-2536

"Semi-formal" yet "homey" (it's inside a ranch house), this mid-priced Medical Center "standby" serves up "extremely consistent" "high-end" Italian fare that's "just short of great"; service can be "uneven", but the "cordial", "quiet" vibe still makes it a "solid" choice for "business meetings" and "special-occasion dinners."

Antlers Lodge ☒ *Southwestern*

23 | 24 | 24 | $56

San Antonio West | Hyatt Regency Hill Country Resort & Spa | 9800 Hyatt Resort Dr. (Rogers Rd.) | 210-520-4001 | www.hillcountry.hyatt.com

"Beautiful" rustic lodge environs – complete with antlers on the wall – and "outstanding" service draw locals and Sea World visitors to this Southwestern spot at the Hyatt Regency Hill Country resort; some say the "waiters who do magic tricks" outshine its sometimes "disappointing" and "overpriced" "hotel food", but fans insist the fare is "consistently good."

	FOOD	DECOR	SERVICE	COST

Asia Kitchen ☒ *Asian* ▽ 25 | 15 | 19 | $16

San Antonio West | 1739 SW Loop 410 (Marbach Rd.) | 210-673-0662 | www.asia-kitchen.com

An American military man and his Far Eastern wife run this "friendly" foodery in the far West offering some of "the best Asian" fare in town (i.e. "extremely spicy" Thai plus some Chinese dishes); budget-conscious types, such as "Air Force folks" from nearby bases, appreciate the "very reasonable" prices as well, though aesthetes argue the "homey-feeling" rooms "could use an overhaul."

Azúca Nuevo Latino *Nuevo Latino* 24 | 22 | 18 | $29

Southtown | 713 S. Alamo St. (bet. Durango Blvd. & Presa St.) | 210-225-5550 | www.azuca.net

Southtown partyers who "want good food and music but don't want to spend big bucks" begin and end the night at this Nuevo Latino standout, enjoying "very exciting" specialties and "the best mojitos in town" amid "lovely" "art glass" pieces from the studio next door; the "hopping" bar heats up on weekends as salsa fans shake it to live acts "ranging from the bizarre to the sublime."

Bangkok Cuisine ☒ *Thai* - | - | - | I

Northeast | 8214 Pat Booker Rd. (Village Oak Dr.) | 210-599-8884

Lunch lovers say it's "worth the trip" for a "tempting" Thai buffet at this affordable far Northeast "joint", also favored for its "awesome pad Thai" and seemingly bottomless "pot of tom yum" soup; an "always friendly" staff serves the goods, "and boy, can they spice it up!"

Barn Door, The *Steak* 19 | 16 | 19 | $25

Alamo Heights | 8400 N. New Braunfels Ave. (bet. Crownhill Blvd. & Edgehill Dr.) | 210-824-0116 | www.sawhost.com/barndoor/

Carnivores call this half-century-old steakhouse in Alamo Heights an "SA institution" because it serves up mesquite-grilled chops from its own butcher shop and "great housemade desserts" with the help of a "solid staff" that "never changes"; the same could be said of the "right-in-the-barn" decor, which fans fondly dub "down-home retro" but up-to-daters undercut as "old and tired."

Beto's Comida Latina *S American* 21 | 11 | 15 | $13

North | 8142 Broadway St. (Flamingo Dr.) | 210-930-9393 | www.betoscomidalatina.com

Hungry hombres are "hooked" on the "delicious" fish tacos and "tasty" house-specialty empanadas at this "fun", quirky Northside South American, where informal, colorful decor and a breezy backyard patio generate a casual vibe; an underwhelmed minority maintains that the food is "decent" but "never makes the grade."

Z Biga on the Banks *American* 27 | 25 | 25 | $54

River Walk | 203 S. St. Mary's St. (Market St.) | 210-225-0722 | www.biga.com

"Big, bold and beautiful" from decor to dessert, chef-owner Bruce Auden's "consistently top-notch" "jewel" makes "inspiring" use of "local and regional ingredients" to create "original" "but not complicated" New American plates that please "the eye and palate"; with "exemplary" service and "urban modern" rooms overlooking a quiet stretch of the River Walk, it's a "premier" pick for "business", romance or impressing "out-of-town guests" that's "unique in the state."

Big'z Burger Joint M *Burgers* 21 | 14 | 14 | $14

Loop 1604 | 2303 N. Loop 1604 W. (Huebner Rd.) | 210-408-2029

"Make it dirty for a dollar" by having your "juicy" half-pounder topped with a fried egg at this Loop 1604 yearling, where Le Rêve chef Andrew Weissman plies "tasty burgers with attitude" accompanied by handmade chips, "flavored" mayos and "first-class" shakes; the "family-oriented" setup sports a backyard where "kiddos can run around", but fussier sorts find the "red barn" digs "loud" and the service "slow."

Bin 555 S *American* 26 | 23 | 23 | $35

North Central | Shops at Artisans Alley | 555 W. Bitters Rd. (bet. Blanco Rd. & West Ave.) | 210-496-0555 | www.bin555.com

For an "adult evening", this North Central gem is "the chic place to be seen in SA" binging on a "diverse" seasonal assortment of New American "small plates" (courtesy of Lodge chef Jason Dady) and a "novel" wine list; equipped with an "inviting" deck and fire pit, it's a "relaxing" place to "go with a group" and "try different things" "without feeling like you have to roll out."

NEW **Bistro Thyme** *Continental* - | - | - | M
(fka Bistro Time)

Loop 1604 | 1321 N. Loop 1604 E., Ste. 105 (bet. Hwy. 281 & Stone Oak Pkwy.) | 210-495-0244 | www.bistrothymesa.com

Chef-owner Sander Edmondson is now centralized in Loop 1604 at this bright, new space, where the updated menu reflects a modern approach to American-style Continental cuisine; the signature crab cakes and reasonable wine list remain, sharing time with wild boar chili, veal burgers and wild mushroom meatloaf, not to mention colorful modern art.

Z **Bistro Vatel** S M *French* 26 | 20 | 24 | $46

Olmos Park | 218 E. Olmos Dr. (McCullough Ave.) | 210-828-3141 | www.bistrovatel.com

Damien Watel brings "Paris to San Antonio" as he "performs his magic" at his "cut-above bistro" "tucked away" in Olmos Park, serving "divine" "French soul food" with "easygoing elegance"; with its "sophisticated wine list" and "top-notch" staff, it "reaches to higher planes" with "no hype, no fuss"; N.B. the recently added chef's table offers access to an even more intimate *expérience.*

Boardwalk Bistro S *Mediterranean* ▽ 21 | 14 | 19 | $28

Near North | Boardwalk, The | 4011 Broadway St. (Thorman Pl.) | 210-824-0100 | www.boardwalkbistro.net

Locals laud this "neighborhood bistro" on an eclectic stretch of Broadway for "surprisingly tasty" Mediterranean bites like paella and "unusual fresh soups"; those lulled by the waterfall and peaceful patio appreciate that the pace "is not rushed"; N.B. the dinner prix fixe features optional wine pairings from the well-stocked cellar.

Bohanan's Prime Steak & Seafood *Seafood/Steak* 23 22 21 $55

Downtown | 219 E. Houston St. (Navarro St.) | 210-472-2600 | www.bohanans.com

"Be ready to pay" for the "quality beef" at this "high-end" steakhouse/seafooder, which "distinguishes itself" from the chains with "excellent service and an intriguing menu" presented in a "beautiful" Victorian venue overlooking Downtown's historic section; to heighten the "lovely dining experience", insiders request a window seat in early evenings to catch the sunset.

Z Boudro's on the Riverwalk *Seafood/Steak* 24 20 21 $38

River Walk | 421 E. Commerce St. (Presa St.) | 210-224-8484 | www.boudros.com

"Great people-watching" on the River Walk makes it "worth the wait" for an outside table at this "casual" steak-and-seafood favorite, known for its "enjoyable" "amalgamation of Southwest border" fare including "must-have" "guacamole made tableside" and "prickly pear margaritas"; though its rep keeps the "tight" interior "crowded" and "loud", it's always a "best bet" "if you only have one night" in town.

Cafe Paladar *Pan-Latin* 25 23 22 $39

Stone Oak | 18322 Sonterra Pl. (Loop 1604) | 210-798-7200 | www.cafepaladar.com

"Bravo!" cheer devotees of chef-owner Brian West's "sophisticated oasis" in Stone Oak, a "low-profile jewel" known for the "amazing flavor combinations" that give Pan-Latin "taste treats" like its "innovative tapas" "a personal touch"; the "warm and inviting" atmosphere (think "modern art meets Latin flair") makes its monthly wine-pairing dinners extra palatable.

Canyon Café *Southwestern* 18 20 18 $22

Quarry | Quarry Mkt. | 255 E. Basse Rd. (Jones-Maltsberger Rd.) | 210-821-3738 | www.canyoncafe.com

This Southwestern chain has "discovered the missing link" according to fans who connect with the "Santa Fe flair" of its Quarry Market outpost; the "creative menu" measures up "better than your average Tex-Mex", especially since "each meal is topped off" with a complimentary chocolate nut tamale ("mmmm").

Cappyccino's ☒ *American* 20 20 20 $20

Alamo Heights | 5003 Broadway St. (Mary D. Ave.) | 210-828-6860 | www.cappyccinos.com

"Comfort food of the yuppie sort" captures a "neighborhood" crowd at this Alamo Heights American bistro, which shares a patio with its bigger sib, Cappy's; the "cheerful service", "short menu" of standards "prepared with a gourmet touch" and "well-stocked bar" boasting "more single-malts than a man can drink" combine into a "great place to hang out."

	FOOD	DECOR	SERVICE	COST

Z Cappy's Restaurant *American* 23 | 20 | 22 | $29

Alamo Heights | 5011 Broadway (Mary D. Ave.) | 210-828-9669 | www.cappysrestaurant.com

"Imaginative creations and constant favorites" divide the wide-ranging repertoire at this rustic patch of "America, my America" in "tony" Alamo Heights, an "institution that remains fresh" for its local loyalists; capped with "unexpected pleasures" like "on-time" service and "reliably special lunch specials", it's a "quintessential" spot "to see and be seen" "in the 'hood."

Carrabba's Italian Grill *Italian* 22 | 19 | 22 | $28

Northwest | 12507 I-10 W. (De Zavala Rd.) | 210-694-4191 | www.carrabbas.com

See review in Houston Directory.

Cascabel Mexican Patio S M *Mexican* - | - | - | I

Southtown | 1000 S. St. Mary's St. (Alamo St.) | 210-212-6456

Colorful and *muy* "authentic", this indoor-outdoor "tortilla kitchen" in Southtown plies bargain bites that offer "a true expression" of interior Mexican "home cooking" (like the cup of savory chicken soup preceding every order); even amigos acknowledge "the service is slow, but maybe we need to slow down."

NEW **Chart House** *Seafood* - | - | - | M

Downtown | Tower of the Americas | 600 Hemisfair Plaza Way (bet. Durango Blvd. & Market St.) | 210-223-3101 | www.chart-house.com

A link of the nautically themed seafood chain has docked atop Downtown's iconic Tower of the Americas, offering rotating views of the cityscape from 750-feet up in the air; the moderately priced surf 'n' turf selections sate many an out-of-towner's appetite, though some may prefer to soak in the setting with a cocktail at the attached Bar 601.

Cheesecake Factory *American* 20 | 20 | 18 | $26

Loop 410 | North Star Mall | 7400 San Pedro Ave. (Loop 410) | 210-798-2222 | www.thecheesecakefactory.com

See review in Houston Directory.

Cheesy Jane's *Burgers* 19 | 16 | 18 | $11

Alamo Heights | 4200 Broadway St. (Groveland Pl.) | 210-826-0800
Northwest | HEB Ctr. | 11650 Bandera Rd. (Quincy Lee Dr.) | 210-767-9090
www.cheesyjanes.com

"Retro" types turn to this "burger joint" duo for "char-broiled" beef "any way you want it", "tater tots to die for" and creamy shakes; the "'50s diner decor" and "kid-friendly" atmo add a side of "funky fun", though a few skeptics sniff "cheesy is right."

Chef Chan Tea House *Chinese* - | - | - | I

Northwest | Autobahn Shopping Ctr. | 5545 NW Loop 410 (Evers Rd.) | 210-509-7298 | www.chefchanteahouse.com

"Phenomenal" dim sum "any time" gives Cantonese devotees "a reason to go" to this Northwest strip-center Chinese, and the "authentic" lunch carts bearing fresh morsels make it "even better on the weekends"; if the surroundings are somewhat less enchanting, they're balanced with "best-buy" prices.

Chesters Hamburger Company *Burgers* 22 | 13 | 16 | $11

Loop 410 | 1006 NE Loop 410 (New Braunfels Ave.) | 210-805-8600
Medical Center | 9980 I-10 W. (Wurzbach Rd.) | 210-669-1222
North | 16609 San Pedro Ave. (Thousand Oaks) | 210-494-3333

"Come hungry" for "burgers so big you can't get your mouth around 'em" at this "rustic" mini-chain, where the "juicy" patties are washed down with an "impressive" array of "beer from all over the world"; sure, you're obliged to "belly up to the counter" to order, but for a "consistent" chowdown "this place rocks."

Chris Madrid's Nachos & Burgers ☒ *Burgers* 25 | 13 | 17 | $12

Near North | 1900 Blanco Rd. (Hollywood Ave.) | 210-735-3552 | www.chrismadrids.com

Chris Madrid himself still oversees this Near Northside 1977-vintage beef-and-beer barn, an "institution" for "sublime", "delectably greasy" burgers sized "enormous" enough to "guarantee nobody leaves the property hungry"; with "picnic tables" inside and out, the "laid-back", "self-serve" setup is "the perfect environment", though regulars note "you'll have to take a nap" afterward.

Chuy's *Tex-Mex* 21 | 19 | 19 | $18

North | 18008 San Pedro Ave. (Loop 1604) | 210-545-0300 | www.chuys.com

See review in Austin and the Hill Country Directory.

Ciao Lavanderia ☒ *Italian* 23 | 18 | 20 | $26

Olmos Park | 226 E. Olmos Dr. (El Prado Dr.) | 210-822-3990

Sited in a "quirky" "former laundromat" just steps from his Bistro Vatel, Damien Watel's "charming" Olmos Park Italian appeals to ciao hounds with a "yummy" (if "limited") lineup of "fresh homemade pasta" and pizzas; the "value and unpretentious service" make it "great for date night" or "a quick bite" at lunch; N.B. a recent remodel has updated the space.

Citrus *American* 25 | 24 | 21 | $46

Downtown | Hotel Valencia | 150 E. Houston St. (Soledad St.) | 210-230-8412 | www.hotelvalencia.com

There's "no need to leave the hotel" for "inventive" eating thanks to this Downtown showcase for "culinary genius" Jeffrey Balfour's "top-notch" seasonal American fare, matched with "excellent service" and the "classiest" of contemporary settings; with "romantic" vibes and a River Walk view, it's suitable for "a special occasion" or when "the boss is buying."

Clear Springs Café *American* 19 | 17 | 18 | $15

Stone Oak | 606 W. Afton Oaks Blvd. (N. Loop 1604) | 210-403-3474 | www.clearspringscafe.com

Country cooking reigns supreme at this "reliable" Stone Oak link of a statewide chain of seafood specialists, "well-known" for "Texas-sized servings" of "simple" dishes like catfish, Baja shrimp and "gotta-get" onion rings; the "outdoorsy decor" is "so tacky it's great", and the child-friendly quarters spring to life on weekends.

County Line, The *BBQ* 20 | 18 | 19 | $23

River Walk | 111 W. Crockett St. (Presa St.) | 210-229-1941
Northwest | 10101 I-10 W. (Wurzbach Rd.) | 210-641-1998
www.countyline.com

BBQ buffs line up behind this regional chain and its "massive", "messy" portions of "decent" 'cue, served in "corny" rough-hewn digs that are "vigorously kid-friendly" and "perfect for out-of-town guests"; the River Walk location is "touristy", while the Northwest outpost lures locals with "family-style" feasts and toe-tapping live music Wednesday nights.

Cove, The ☒ *American* ▽ 20 | 15 | 18 | $15

Downtown | 606 W. Cypress (San Pedro Ave.) | 210-227-2683 | www.thecove.us

Nearby colleges and re-gentrified nabes create a niche clientele for this "quirky" Downtown fusion of a "friendly bar/restaurant" with a "carwash, laundromat and playground"; most covet the eclectic American eats (including "terrific" "grilled fish tacos") chased with a "fantastic beer selection", though "the young and hip" may give them second billing to "some of the best live music in town."

Crumpets Restaurant & Bakery *French* 15 | 20 | 17 | $28

Northeast | 3920 Harry Wurzbach Rd. (Oakwell Ct.) | 210-821-5454 | www.crumpetsa.com

The "peaceful, wooded setting along Salado Creek" in Northeast SA provides a "beautiful" backdrop for this "quaint" "indoor-outdoor" eatery/bakery and chef-owner Francois Maeder's "varied" array of "honest" French fare; longtime supporters salute a menu that "can still surprise", though a minority of grumps grumbles "inconsistent."

Da Vinci Gelato & Caffé *Italian* 24 | 19 | 20 | $12

Stone Oak | 18720 Stone Oak Pkwy. (N. Loop 1604) | 210-545-6686 | www.davincigelati.com

Gelati "like you'd find in Italy" draw dessert lovers to this compact strip-center cafe in Stone Oak for a taste of "authentic" ices that rank with "the best in Florence", not to mention "excellent" panini and crêpes that make it San Antonio's Best Bang for the Buck; with unusual flavors like white chocolate, guiltless fat-free/sugar-free options and the creative combo of espresso over gelato, it's a renaissance for sweet tooths.

Demo's Greek Food *Greek* 19 | 12 | 14 | $14

Near North | 2501 N. St. Mary's St. (Ashby Ave.) | 210-732-7777
North | 7115 Blanco Rd. (Lockhill-Selma Rd.) | 210-342-2772
Sonterra | Vineyard Ctr. | 1205 N. Loop 1604 W. (Blanco Rd.) | 210-798-3840
www.demosgreekfood.com

"You'll want to break a plate" to celebrate the "hearty portions" and "reasonable cost" at this longstanding Northside Greek and its two newer spin-offs, demonstrating for nearly 30 years that Hellenic eating is "more than gyros"; weekly belly dancing jiggles some sparkle into the no-frills, "no-table-service" setups.

NEW Dough S M *Italian* — | — | — | I

North Central | Blanco Junction Shopping Ctr. | 6989 Blanco Rd. (Loop 410) | 210-979-6363 | www.doughpizzeria.com

Pizza lovers are flipping over this hip, new trattoria that fashions its pies from hand-thrown dough and fresh toppings all baked together in an authentic wood-burning volcanic stone oven; featuring salads, handmade mozzarella, imported meats and a small but thoughtful wine list, it feels like a slice of Italy, even though you're actually in a North Central shopping center.

Eclipse Café M *American/Eclectic* 20 | 15 | 16 | $25

North Central | 14439 NW Military Hwy. (Huebner Rd.) | 210-408-7614 | www.eclipsecafe.biz

CIA-trained chef-owner Louis Halfant's American-Eclectic cafe pulls North Central denizens into its orbit with the "extremely good quality" of a "tried-and-true" menu backed with an "interesting array of specials" from the daily blackboard; reasonable prices offset the "plain" strip-center surroundings, though service slips cast a shadow that detractors deem "disappointing."

El Jarro de Arturo *Mexican* 22 | 18 | 22 | $21

North | 13421 San Pedro Ave. (Bitters Rd.) | 210-494-5084 | www.eljarro.com

Whether for "basic Tex-Mex" or "something more exotic", this Northside pop-spot proffers an "excellent" Mexican selection matched with "professional" service and "upscale family" environs; other attractions include the relaxing patio, live music on Friday and Saturday nights and Sunday brunch ("a must"), though some "followers come for the margaritas alone."

El Mirador *Mexican* 23 | 17 | 19 | $19

Southtown | 722 S. St. Mary's St. (Durango Blvd.) | 210-225-9444 | www.elmiradorsatx.com

The "Saturday homemade soup" specials pack 'em in to Southtown's Mexican crown jewel, which "shines" with "wonderful" "comfort" cuisine that keeps it "full of regulars" (including "local politicos at lunch"); insiders say dinner is "a SA secret" featuring "down-home Tex-Mex done well" alongside "hard-to-find" specialties that justify 40 years of loyalty.

Ernesto's Mexican Specialties & Seafood S *Mexican/Seafood* 18 | 11 | 21 | $29

North Central | 2559 Jackson-Keller Rd. (Vance Jackson Rd.) | 210-344-1248

"Not your standard beans-and-tacos" joint, this Mexican seafooder tucked into a North Central strip center specializes in "fresh fish and sauces" that strike some "more as French"; with owner Ernesto overseeing every detail and checking in at each table, the service inspires fealty even if the "bare-bones decor could use some updating."

FOOD	DECOR	SERVICE	COST

Fig Tree Restaurant, The *Continental* 25 | 22 | 23 | $55

River Walk | 515 Villita St. (Presa St.) | 210-224-1976 | www.figtreerestaurant.com

"Romantic" sorts gush over the "quaint" ambiance of this "intimate" "gem" overlooking the River Walk, a 19th-century residence in historic La Villita reconfigured for "creative" (if "not very diverse") Continental dining with "superb service"; though it's somewhat "pretentious" and "near tourist" turf, it remains "perfect for that special night out."

Fleming's Prime Steakhouse & Wine Bar *Steak* 24 | 24 | 23 | $54

Quarry | Alamo Quarry Mkt. | 255 E. Basse Rd. (Hwy. 281) | 210-824-9463 | www.flemingssteakhouse.com

See review in Houston Directory.

Formosa Garden *Chinese* 21 | 18 | 21 | $17

North Central | 1011 NE Loop 410 (New Braunfels Ave.) | 210-828-9988 | www.formosagarden.com

Thanks to "can't miss" Sino "standards" (plus "decent sushi") and "quick" service, this "modern" Mencius Group Chinese on Loop 410 is "one of the nicer Asians in town"; its North Central location is "convenient for business meals" too, so what with the sizable list of midday specials, it's no surprise this place is "very crowded at lunchtime."

Z **Francesca's at Sunset** S M *Southwestern* 26 | 27 | 26 | $56

La Cantera | Westin La Cantera Resort | 16441 La Cantera Pkwy. (Fiesta Texas Dr.) | 210-558-2442 | www.westinlacantera.com

A "wowza" view of "beautiful sunsets" (and hence the No. 1 Decor rating in San Antonio) would be reason enough for romantics to coo, but it's the "imaginative", "subtly spiced" Southwestern fare that receives "lots of oohs and ahhs" at this "pricey" venue in a La Cantera resort; add "impeccable" service to the "epicurean delight" and natives and visitors alike agree "this place has it all."

Z **Frederick's** S *Asian Fusion/French* 26 | 18 | 26 | $47

Alamo Heights | 7701 Broadway (Nottingham Pl.) | 210-828-9050 | www.frederickssa.com

"Well-heeled" types craving a "slight edge of adventure" are in for a "creative and delicious" Asian-French experience at this Alamo Heights hit, where an ex-L'Etoile chef who "knows his business" creates dishes that "open up some inventive avenues"; regulars advise "don't let the strip-mall location fool you", since if "the atmosphere leaves something to be desired", the staff "does hospitality right."

Fujiya Japanese Garden *Japanese* ▽ 19 | 19 | 17 | $23

Medical Center | 9030 Wurzbach Rd. (Gardendale St.) | 210-734-3551

"Sushi rules!" at this Japanese joint in the Medical Center area, whose authentic touches include private tatami rooms with cushioned floor seating and a separate bar for livelier times; with its heavy wood doors and trickling stream, the "attractive setting" adds to the warm welcome.

Z Godai Sushi Bar & Restaurant *Japanese* 27 | 16 | 20 | $26

North Central | 11203 West Ave. (Blanco Rd.) | 210-348-6781 | www.godaisushi.com

If "inventive", "full-flavored" sushi makes you "want to jump up and slap somebody", this busy Northside Japanese is a godsend thanks to a chef-owner "charmer" who "knows raw fish" and "entertains all night"; many maintain the "large array" of "exotic" rolls is "unquestionably the best" in town, if not "in South Texas, period."

Golden Wok Chinese Restaurant *Chinese* 22 | 19 | 19 | $17

Medical Center | 8822 Wurzbach Rd. (Gardendale Dr.) | 210-615-8282

San Antonio West | 8230 Marbach Rd. (SW Loop 410) | 210-674-2577

www.golden-wok.com

These Sino sibs in Austin and San Antonio serve "authentic" meals ordered from a "large and varied" menu and delivered by servers who are "friendly", if sometimes "a little slow"; conditions can be "crowded", but insiders insist it's "worth the wait", especially for dim sum on Sundays.

NEW Green Vegetarian Cuisine *Vegetarian* ∇ 18 | 18 | 18 | $14

Downtown | 1017 N. Flores St. (Euclid Ave.) | 210-320-5865 | www.greensanantonio.com

"Finally!" cry crunchy types who consider this "funky" Downtowner the city's "only true vegetarian option" and "a blessing" for its "cheerful" "bistro style" and "yummy" lineup of "basic" "healthy choices" "reminiscent of the '60s-'70s"; but though it's an "inviting oasis", critics cavil about "too much emphasis" on "faux meat."

Grey Moss Inn *American* 24 | 24 | 21 | $45

Helotes | 19010 Scenic Loop Rd. (bet. Babcock & Bandera Rds.) | 210-695-8301 | www.grey-moss-inn.com

"It's a long drive" to Helotes, but "awesome everything" awaits at this "classic" "country steakhouse", where generations continue to trek for a "fantastic" American menu showcasing beef from the "open mesquite grill" and "one of the best wine lists in town"; the "cozy", "Texas eclectic" interior and "romantic" patio are made for "those special occasions."

Grill at Leon Springs, The *Eclectic* 22 | 22 | 19 | $30

Leon Springs | 24116 I-10 W. (Boerne Stage Rd.) | 210-698-8797 | www.leonspringsgrill.com

This "upscale-casual" Leon Springs eatery from the L'Etoile team offers "interesting", seasonal Eclectic fare that's "delicious and priced well", plus daily specials designed for those out to "try something new"; the Dominion-proximate locale makes it "good for spotting local celebs", even if "service is a little spotty" too.

Guenther House *American* 23 | 22 | 19 | $17

Southtown | 205 E. Guenther St. (Alamo St.) | 210-227-1061 | www.guentherhouse.com

"Carb watchers beware" of the "best breakfast experience" around as the "delectable" "flour-based" "classics" tempt at this "absolutely charming" Southtown American cafe; set in the "lovely historic" home of the Pioneer Flour Mills' founders, its "kitschy museum" and gift shop help "while away the time" during the "forever-long wait" on weekends; N.B. breakfast and lunch only.

Houston Street Bistro ☒ *Continental* 22 | 20 | 23 | $31

Downtown | 204 E. Houston St. (St. Mary's St.) | 210-476-8600

A "solid" spot for Downtown business lunch by day, by night this Continental bistro just steps from the Majestic Theater becomes a "convenient" "pre-symphony" lead-in and sets the stage for "after-show cocktails and dessert" "in sophisticated comfort"; admirers applaud the "flavorful" menu, though the service is the star - "bravo!"

Hsiu Yu Chinese Restaurant *Chinese* ▽ 16 | 11 | 16 | $17

North | 8338 Broadway St. (Citadell Pl.) | 210-828-2273

Northsiders head to this longtime Sino "oasis" for "great lunch specials" and other "quick", "inexpensive" Chinese served in a friendly neighborhood setting; maybe the atmosphere's "nothing to write home about", but "in a city known for Tex-Mex", supporters shrug "hsiu me, it's good."

Ilsong Garden *Korean* ▽ 25 | 19 | 25 | $26

North Central | 6905 Blanco Rd. (Rector Dr.) | 210-366-4508 | www.onewebring.com

Partisans sing the praises of the "intriguing" possibilities at this convenient Northside niche, where "amazing" Korean specialties (including "excellent" barbecue) share the spotlight with "absolutely fabulous" sushi; the "prompt", "lovely service" and "soothing" surroundings add to its "elegant" appeal.

India Oven *Indian* ▽ 24 | 16 | 18 | $16

North Central | 1031 Patricia Dr. (West Ave.) | 210-366-1033 | www.indiaoven.com

"Reliable" and "authentic", this Northside Indian staple heats up at lunchtime owing to a popular buffet whose "quality", "good price" and "vast" array "more than make up for" any shortcomings in decor; dinner is a quieter, candlelit affair that shimmies to life with belly dancing the first Friday of every month.

India Palace *Indian* 24 | 10 | 17 | $15

Medical Center | 8440 Fredericksburg Rd. (Wurzbach Rd.) | 210-692-5262
North Central | 15909 San Pedro Ave. (Paseo Del Norte St.) | 210-403-3688
www.indiapalacesa.com

"Dazzling" lunch-and-dinner buffets that provide "spicy" "variety" at "low prices" qualify this Medical Center-area and Northside duo as hot spots for "outstanding" Indian eats; loyalists label them "a breath of fresh air" despite the rooms' "definitely lacking" looks.

	FOOD	DECOR	SERVICE	COST

Iron Cactus *Tex-Mex* 18 | 19 | 18 | $25

River Walk | 200 Riverwalk (bet. Commerce & St. Mary's Sts.) | 210-224-9835 | www.ironcactus.com

See review in Austin and the Hill Country Directory.

Josephine St. ☒ *American* 20 | 18 | 19 | $19

Near North | 400 E. Josephine St. (Ave. A) | 210-224-6169 | www.josephinestcafe.com

"If you haven't been, you're cheating yourself" out of a "real down-home" time at this "funky little" "neighborhood joint" in the Near North, where the American grub's highlight is "signature steaks and whiskey" at a "reasonable price"; the "diverse menu" means "you can also eat healthy", but its "no-nonsense" style spurs most to "stick with the basics."

Karam's Mexican Dining Room *Tex-Mex* ▽ 20 | 18 | 19 | $15

San Antonio West | 121 N. Zarzamora St. (Commerce St.) | 210-433-0111 | www.karamsrestaurant.com

Seemingly "around since Santa Ana visited the Alamo", this Westsider and its "sincere, engaging" staff continue to serve up "predictable, solid" "Tex-Mex classics" that you can eat in a courtyard adorned with mock-"Mayan ruins" or in a dining room that seems "decked out for a fiesta"; the only sour note: a few consider the neighborhood a bit iffy.

Kim Wah Chinese BBQ *Chinese* - | - | - | I

Northwest | 7080 Bandera Rd. (Huebner Rd.) | 210-520-2200

"Ask for the authentic Chinese menu" or check the handwritten "specials" board at this Northwest real-deal "favorite", where admiwahs "enjoy the adventure into" homestyle dishes like squid, duck feet and sea cucumber; but given the sparse strip-center space, they "go for the food, not the decor."

Koi Kawa Japanese Restaurant & Sushi Bar ☒ *Japanese* ▽ 26 | 22 | 22 | $23

Near North | 4051 Broadway St. (off Hildebrand Ave.) | 210-805-8111

The "consistently excellent" food makes it safe to "take the Japanese in-laws" to this gem in the Near North, a confirmed "favorite" in the eyes of sushiphiles; besides boosting the "authentic" feel, its quiet setting with a "perfect view of the unspoiled San Antonio River" is "quite a treat."

Kona Grill *American* 20 | 21 | 18 | $27

La Cantera | 15900 La Cantera Pkwy. (1604 Loop W.) | 210-877-5355 | www.konagrill.com

See review in Houston Directory.

Korean B.B.Q. House ☒ *Korean* 23 | 15 | 18 | $19

(aka Go Hyang Jib)

San Antonio East | 4400 Rittiman Rd. (Melton Dr.) | 210-822-8846

"Excellent grilled meat" leads the "variety of traditional Korean dishes" that lure seekers far East (fittingly) to this "little" "hole-in-the-wall"; cognoscenti say "ask for scissors" to cut the 'cue "bite-sized."

FOOD | DECOR | SERVICE | COST

La Focaccia Italian Grill *Italian*

FOOD	DECOR	SERVICE	COST
16	13	16	$23

Southtown | 800 S. Alamo St. (Presa St.) | 210-223-5353 | www.lafocaccia-italian-grill.com

"Ask for Luigi, the Roman owner - he'll take care of you" advise regular patrons of this Southtown eatery housed in a onetime service station (remodeled, of course, though still "nothing fancy"); as for the food, it's a split decision: fans find it "consistently good" and "relatively innovative", while foes charge the "uninspired" eats "need work."

La Fonda on Main *Mexican*

FOOD	DECOR	SERVICE	COST
-	-	-	I

Near North | 2415 N. Main Ave. (Woodlawn Ave.) | 210-733-0621 | www.lafondaonmain.com

Situated in a white-adobe converted home with a spacious tree-lined patio, local restaurateur Cappy Lawton's Near Northside centerpiece is frequented by natives who exhibit a fondness for truly authentic Tex-Mex and interior-Mexico cooking; the circa-1932 digs bolster its claim to being the oldest Mexican eatery in town.

La Frite [S] [M] *Belgian*

FOOD	DECOR	SERVICE	COST
26	19	21	$30

Southtown | 728 S. Alamo St. (Presa St.) | 210-224-7555

"The best mussels" "since dining in Brussels" and "don't-miss" frites headline the "first-rate" bill of fare at this "real" Belgian bistro in Southtown, which serves as "Bistro Vatel South" for owner Damien Watel; there's "little elbow room", but the "laid-back" "European flair" makes it a "hip" "place to hang out with the locals" ("you feel cooler just being there").

La Hacienda de Los Barrios *Tex-Mex*

FOOD	DECOR	SERVICE	COST
21	19	19	$18

North | 18747 Redland Rd. (Gold Canyon Rd.) | 210-497-8000 | www.lhdlb.com

Los Barrios *Tex-Mex*

North | 4223 Blanco Rd. (Basse Rd.) | 210-732-6017

Satisfied surveyors swear by this family-owned Tex-Mex "institution" – the "flagship" Blanco Road location's "outstanding" fajitas "continue to amaze", while the north-of-1604 offshoot draws diners in with a "beautiful patio" and what may be SA's "best margarita menu"; owing to the resulting "crowds", though, it could prove "too noisy to hear your dinner companions."

La Margarita Mexican Restaurant & Oyster Bar *Tex-Mex*

FOOD	DECOR	SERVICE	COST
21	19	19	$20

Market Square | Market Sq. | 120 Produce Row (Santa Rosa St.) | 210-227-7140 | www.lamargarita.com

A "must-visit for tourists" and locals alike, this Market Square "staple" owned by the Cortez family (Mi Tierra, Pico de Gallo) dishes out "plentiful portions" of "real SA Tex-Mex" and "potent" eponymous cocktails; staffers who "treat you well" and roving mariachis help foster a "fun, festive atmosphere", though sedater sorts bothered by "rowdy and loud" indoor goings-on may prefer sitting on the patio.

	FOOD	DECOR	SERVICE	COST
La Marginal	-	-	-	I
Landry's Seafood House on the Riverwalk	19	18	18	$40
La Scala	23	23	23	$32
Las Canarias	26	23	24	$51
Las Ramblas	▽ 21	23	21	$34

La Marginal *Caribbean/Puerto Rican*

North Central | 2447 Nacogdoches Rd. (I-410) | 210-804-2242 | www.lamarginal.com

San Juan's expats flock to this North Central canteen for "big" portions of "authentic" "homestyle Puerto Rican" (like plantains and "great Cuban sandwiches") "at great prices"; the lunch buffet's "tremendous value" means "traffic is crazy" come noon, and once the "live music" and dancing are underway, weekend "nights are wild."

Landry's Seafood House on the Riverwalk *Seafood*

River Walk | 517 N. Presa St. (College St.) | 210-229-1010 | www.landrysseafoodhouse.com

"If people-watching is your thing" "get a table by the water" at this River Walk pescatorium, a chain link that loyalists like for a "special night out"; the fin fare is "reliable" if "nothing special" and staffers are "friendly", but naysayers warn you're "charged too much for too little" ("if it weren't for the beer, the bill would have been hard to swallow").

La Scala *European*

Castle Hills | 2177 NW Military Hwy. (West Ave.) | 210-366-1515 | www.lascala.us

The "consistent quality" is "always a pleasure" at this "popular local" fixture nestled among shops and salons in a Castle Hills strip center, where the "wonderful" menu's "Euro-Italian tendencies" promise "something for every taste"; its "elegant" "pink-tablecloth" surroundings and "top-notch" service are still "special" to longtime regulars.

Las Canarias *French/Mediterranean*

River Walk | Omni La Mansión del Rio Hotel | 112 College St. (bet. Navarro & St. Mary's Sts.) | 210-518-1063 | www.lamansion.com

This "destination" restaurant lives up to "the charm and legend" of its "classy" River Walk hotel home, merging seasonal French-Med accents and an "inventive use of Texas ingredients" into "refined and delicious" plates; the follow-through includes a "lovely, relaxing" setting, an "outstanding" "European stagiere" staff that's "attentive without being overbearing" and the "wow" of a Sunday brunch flaunting a "vast" spread that's "a must" for visitors and locals alike; N.B. the Food score does not reflect the recent departure of chef Scott Cohen.

Las Ramblas *Spanish*

River Walk | Hotel Contessa | 306 W. Market St. (Navarro St.) | 210-298-8040 | www.thehotelcontessa.com

There's a "refreshing" "selection of tapas" on a hidden bend of the River Walk at this "personable" Spaniard in the Hotel Contessa, where "generous" servings of asado meats meet traditional faves like paella Valenciana; ramblers can stake out "pleasant" waterside seating or settle inside within earshot of the weekend jazz.

	FOOD	DECOR	SERVICE	COST

La Tuna Grill Ⓢ *Eclectic* ▽ 22 | 22 | 20 | $13

Southtown | 100 Probandt St. (Cevallos St.) | 210-212-5727 | www.latunagrill.com

"All types, from bankers to bikers" assemble at this Southtown standby across the yard from the like-named bar, a "true melting pot" noted for chef Mark Dortman's "surprisingly" "solid" Eclectic eats, featuring inventive sandwiches and fish tacos; the art-filled interior is right in tune with the "interesting" clientele.

Z Le Rêve Ⓢ Ⓜ *French* 29 | 25 | 27 | $110

Downtown | Historic Exchange Bldg. | 152 E. Pecan St. (St. Mary's St.) | 210-212-2221 | www.restaurantlereve.com

"A three- to four-hour culinary adventure" awaits at this rêvered Downtown "jewel" (voted San Antonio's No. 1 for Popularity, Food and Service), a showcase for "stellar" chef Andrew Weissman's "impeccable technique" via a seasonal New French prix fixe menu that "dazzles" diners and "deserves all accolades"; the "exceptional" staff and "intimate", understated room round out "the ultimate in decadence" and fully justify the ultra-"pricey" tabs; N.B. jackets and reservations well in advance are a must.

Z L'Etoile *French/Seafood* 26 | 20 | 23 | $45

Alamo Heights | 6106 Broadway (Albany St.) | 210-826-4551 | www.letoilesa.com

French cuisine "positioned between bistro and haute" leaves "multi-generational" Alamo Heights dwellers "impressed" at this venerable star among "classy places", a haven of "attentive Gallic service" set in an "elegant" "old house" reminiscent of "a bit of Paris (France, not East Texas)"; regulars single out the "always first-rate" seafood and the value-laden early-bird prix fixe.

Z Liberty Bar *Eclectic* 24 | 22 | 22 | $25

Near North | 328 E. Josephine St. (Ave. A) | 210-227-1187 | www.liberty-bar.com

You may "feel three sheets to the wind before your first drink" given the "trippy tilted floor" at this "popular" Near Northside hangout, where the "funky" circa-1890 structure is part of the "unique" "charm"; "it just gets better" with "unusual and delicious" Eclectic fare served with "no pretense" at a "reasonable price", ensuring that "visitors always ask to go back."

Little Red Barn *Steak* 17 | 18 | 20 | $18

San Antonio South | 1836 S. Hackberry St. (Rigsby Ave.) | 210-532-4235

At this Southside steakhouse, an "oldie but goodie" (since 1963), "cowboys and cowgirls" "amusingly" tricked out with prop-room six-shooters aim to provide "fast and friendly" service, fetching salads that arrive at the table when you do and "decent, cheap" beef; overall, the "down-home" "Western atmosphere" (including the menu painted on the wall) makes this place "fun for family dining" if you can swallow the "kinda corny" "faux-Texas" folderol.

	FOOD	DECOR	SERVICE	COST

Little Rhein Steak House *Steak* 24 | 21 | 23 | $52

River Walk | 231 S. Alamo St. (Market St.) | 210-225-2111 | www.littlerheinsteakhouse.com

Meat eaters who tire of "big, boisterous steakhouses" head 'em out to this "quaint" "old-time" option on the River Walk, where the prime cuts are "perfectly cooked and served" in an "attractively historic" setting; just beware of "tourists" who "overwhelm" the terrace, and "don't look at the bill."

Z Lodge Restaurant of Castle Hills, The *American* 26 | 26 | 24 | $60

Castle Hills | 1746 Lockhill Selma Rd. (West Ave.) | 210-349-8466 | www.thelodgerestaurant.com

"What a lovely setting" sigh sightseers at this "converted mansion" on tree-studded acreage in Castle Hills, "an excellent escape" enhanced by chef-owner Jason Dady's "extraordinary" New American "palate pleasers", which many rank "right up there with the best" in town; "always-on" service sways diners to go "slowly through each course" whether the occasion is a "classy" lunch with "clients" or an "intimate dinner."

Luce Ristorante e Enoteca *Italian* ▽ 20 | 23 | 20 | $49
(fka Luciano at the Strand)

Northwest | Strand, The | 11255 Huebner Rd. (McDermott Frwy.) | 210-561-9700 | www.lucesanantonio.com

"Beautifully appointed" contemporary digs set the scene for "Italian done superbly" at this corner storefront (formerly Luciano at the Strand) in a Northwest shopping center; aficionados appreciate the "wonderful entree variety" and service from a "professional" team – just make "a trip to the bank first."

Madhatters Tea *Tearoom* 20 | 20 | 17 | $16

Southtown | 320 Beauregard (Alamo St.) | 210-212-4832 | www.madhatterstea.com

"Save room" for the "deadly desserts" at this "cute", "funky" Southtown tearoom, a small counter-service spot also known for its "inventive sandwiches" and some 50 varieties of herbal brews; though a few sniff it "tries too hard to be trendy", most are smitten by this "laid-back" wonderland and say it "fits the neighborhood to a tea."

Madras Pavilion *Indian* 22 | 11 | 14 | $17

Northwest | Grandview Shopping Ctr. | 8085 Callaghan Rd. (Pinebrook Dr.) | 210-375-7766 | www.madraspavilion.us

See review in Houston Directory.

Z Magnolia Pancake Haus *American* 27 | 17 | 22 | $13

North Central | 606 Embassy Oak (West Ave.) | 210-496-0828 | www.magnoliapancakehaus.com

"If you're a breakfast person, this is your place" for all-American feasts of "divine" waffles, "pure magic" pancakes and "spectacular" omelets generous "enough for two (with leftovers)"; its roomy

North Central site sees stack-ups and "long waits" on weekends, but "no one complains because they know what's in store"; N.B. closes at 2 PM daily.

Mama's Café *American* 19 | 14 | 18 | $14

Downtown | 100 N. Main Ave. (Commerce St.) | 210-354-2233
Universal City | 7929 Pat Booker Rd. (Live Oak Crossing) | 210-653-2002
North | 14424 San Pedro Ave. (Bitters Rd.) | 210-490-1933
Northeast | 2442 Nacogdoches Rd. (NE Loop 410) | 210-826-8303
www.mamascafe.net

"Always a safe bet" from early morning till late night, these nostalgic cafes please patrons with their Traditional American eats, including "terrific" breakfasts and "night-owl comfort food"; thanks to a "fun" staff and "reasonable" prices, they're "kid-friendly", if "not much to look at" – "a typical greasy spoon."

Melting Pot, The *Fondue* 21 | 20 | 21 | $43

North Central | 14855 Blanco Rd. (Bitters Rd.) | 210-479-6358 | www.meltingpot.com

See review in Austin and the Hill Country Directory.

Mencius Gourmet Hunan *Chinese* 21 | 17 | 18 | $17

Medical Center | 7959 Fredericksburg Rd. (Medical Dr.) | 210-615-1288

"Great lunch specials" mean "there's always a line" midday at this Medical Center Hunan, where the food is "consistently" "delicious" and "everybody knows it"; the "comfortable" if "plain" dining room is satisfactory, and table service is usually "fast" and "pleasant."

NEW Merchants Grand Café *American* - | - | - | M

Alamo Heights | 5939 Broadway St. (Montclair Ave.) | 210-957-4544 | www.merchantsgrandcafe.com

Former Pesca chef Jonathan Parker is in the kitchen at this Alamo Heights newcomer set inside a renovated hardware store offering a unique approach to Traditional American pub grub utilizing fresh, local ingredients; Hill Country pâté and house-cured salmon share table space with chicken pot pie and mesquite-grilled steaks while the bar specializes in handcrafted old-fashioned cocktails.

Meson European Dining *French/Italian* ∇ 18 | 13 | 22 | $40

Northwest | 5999 De Zavala Rd. (Golden Ln.) | 210-690-5811 | www.mesoneuropeandining.com

There's "fancy attitude" "way off the beaten path" at this "lesser-known" outpost tucked into a Northwest suburban strip mall, where the "classic" French-Italian menu, "very personable host" and tableside prep pay tribute to fine dining; nonetheless, naysayers knock an "overpriced" experience that "tries to be upscale" but "doesn't measure up."

NEW Mimi's Café *American* 21 | 20 | 18 | $19

La Cantera | Rim, The | 17315 I-10W (La Cantera Pkwy.) | 210-877-5792 | www.mimiscafe.com

"Transplanted Californians" welcome this La Cantera link in the Golden State-based "comfort-food chain" as a "sure bet" for "homestyle" American fare in "plentiful portions", with special praises for the "bread baskets" and "creative muffins"; the "family-friendly" milieu makes for a "dependable" shopping break, though foes of the "big-box" approach shrug "so-so."

Mina & Dimi's Greek House ☒ *Greek* ▽ 24 | 13 | 20 | $22

San Antonio West | 7159 Hwy. 90 W. (Military Dr.) | 210-674-3464 | www.agreekhouse.com

"Air Force guys who have been to Greece love" this "lively" "mom-and-pop" establishment in a "grungy" strip center near Lackland AFB; sure, it's a bit "cramped", but the owners make "great use of spices and flavorings" in whipping up "tasty", "authentic" Hellenic dishes; "friendly, responsive" servers, "tacky" weekend belly dancers and occasional "flying plates" are all part of the "funky and fun" experience.

Mi Tierra Café & Bakery ◐ *Tex-Mex* 21 | 22 | 19 | $18

Market Square | Market Sq. | 218 Produce Row (Dolorosa St.) | 210-225-1262 | www.mitierracafe.com

Compadres cheer "hats off" to this "genuine" Tex-Mex "landmark", a 24/7 "fiesta" complete with "classic" chow, "flamboyant" decor sporting "more Christmas lights than Snoopy's doghouse" and a "good-time" soundtrack from "strolling mariachis" both inside and on the Market Square patio; the "extensive bakery" case and "baroque bar" help "pack 'em in", and even those who see "nothing to brag about" foodwise admit it's "a real blast" "to take visitors."

Mon's Thai Bistro & Sushi Bar *Thai* 17 | 14 | 16 | $22

Alamo Heights | 4901 Broadway St. (Patterson Ave.) | 210-822-3253

"Spice levels are customized for every palate" at this "informal" Alamo Heights Asian hub, which comprises "a creative take on Thai" in its montage of sushi, curries and stir-fries; most know it as a "decent" "little" "local", though a minority moans over "inconsistency."

Morton's, The Steakhouse *Steak* 25 | 21 | 23 | $62

Downtown | Rivercenter Mall | 300 E. Crockett St. (Bonham St.) | 210-228-0700 | www.mortons.com

See review in Houston Directory.

Old San Francisco *Steak* 19 | 21 | 20 | $42

North | 10223 Sahara St. (San Pedro Ave.) | 210-342-2321

This Northside "ol' timer" may be "getting long in the tooth", but its cow-palace combo of "visual stimulation" and "fill-u-up steaks" is "still going strong", especially for families and "conventioneers"; a recent ownership change has brought building renovations, a few minor menu changes and shorter hours, but current management assures that the "girl on the red velvet swing" over the bar remains the same.

Oro *American* ▽ 24 | 27 | 20 | $36

Downtown | Emily Morgan Hotel | 705 E. Houston St. (Ave. E) | 210-244-0146 | www.emilymorganhotel.com

Off the lobby of the "historic" Emily Morgan Hotel ("right across the street from the Alamo"), chef Shane Bruns strikes gold with a "trendy yet unpretentious" New American menu that's "one of the best-kept secrets Downtown"; the "classy", subtly lit space is a "relaxed" sanctuary for "a business lunch" or a "quiet and private" dinner.

Pacific Moon ☒ *Pacific Rim* 18 | 14 | 16 | $18

North | 17700 San Pedro Ave. (bet. Donella Dr. & Henderson Pass) | 210-402-3411

Whenever they're "bored with typical San Antonio fare" voters make a beeline for this simple, soothing Northside standby to enjoy eclectic Pacific Rim eats (e.g. Thai beef salad, sake-marinated pork loin) made with "extremely fresh ingredients"; the staff is "great to chat with" but that may be one reason service is sometimes "soooo slow."

Paesanos *Italian* 22 | 22 | 20 | $34

Quarry | Alamo Quarry Mkt. | 555 E. Basse Rd. (Treeline Park) | 210-828-5191

Paesanos Riverwalk *Italian*

River Walk | 111 W. Crockett St. (Presa St.) | 210-227-2782

Paesanos 1604 *Italian*

Loop 1604 | 3622 Paesanos Pkwy. (NW Military Dr.) | 210-493-1604
www.paesanos.com

"There's a reason it's always mobbed" moan regulars who nevertheless frequent this Italian "institution's" "longtime" Quarry locale for its "snob-appeal" vibe and "big plates" of "mm-mm-good" "traditional" dishes, led by the "locally famed shrimp Paesano"; the River Walk spin-off is "an oasis of quality" where alfresco lingerers can "watch the sunburned tourists with Alamo souvenirs" troop by while the Loop 1604 addition calls to mind "a Tuscan villa."

Palm, The *Steak* 24 | 19 | 24 | $56

Downtown | 233 E. Houston St. (Navarro St.) | 210-226-7256 | www.thepalm.com

"Old-school dining" is alive and well at this "distinguished" chain carnivorium, born in NYC in 1926 and drawing "movers and shakers" ever since with its "enormous" steaks and lobsters plated in "distinguished" settings adorned with celebrity "caricatures"; sure, the tabs are reminiscent of "mortgage payments" and service can careen from "top-notch" to "surly", but ultimately they're "consistently good."

Z Paloma Blanca *Mexican* 22 | 23 | 20 | $21

Alamo Heights | Cambridge Shopping Ctr. | 5800 Broadway (Austin Hwy.) | 210-822-6151 | www.palomablanca.net

"Trendy" Alamo Heights types tout this "upscale" hacienda for its "mouthwatering" mix of "authentic" Tex-Mex faves and "interior Mexico" specialties that flaunt "a bit of added Latino culinary creativity"; given the "helpful" staff and "classy, comfortable" setting (featuring original art and a "great outside patio"), consensus says "this one stands out."

Pam's Patio Kitchen ☒ Ⓜ *American* ▽ 26 | 19 | 23 | $15

North | 11826 Wurzbach Rd. (Lockhill-Selma Rd.) | 210-492-1359 | www.pamspatio.com

"Basically, everything's wonderful" gush pampered fans of this Northside "neighborhood" nook in a chic shopping strip, where the

American lineup provides "original sandwiches", soups and salads for the lunch rush and "more upscale choices" at dinner (Thursday-Saturday only); added attractions include a "super-friendly staff" and oft-unusual "art on the wall" courtesy of local talents.

Pappadeaux *Seafood* 23 | 19 | 20 | $29

Loop 410 | 76 NE Loop 410 (Jones-Maltsberger Rd.) | 210-340-7143 | www.pappadeaux.com

See review in Houston Directory.

Pasión! Latin Bistro & Bar *Nuevo Latino* 18 | 21 | 16 | $29

Loop 1604 | Vineyard Ctr. | 1401 N. Loop 1604 W. (Blanco Rd.) | 210-493-6200 | www.pasionbistro.com

Dependably "loud and festive", this Nuevo Latino on Loop 1604 stirs up some *pasión* with its "tasty and fresh" "fusion" fare; then again, the "vibrant", "crowded" bar scene caters to a "target audience" of "young singles" with "wonderful mojitos" and "live salsa" on weekends, leading some to opine eating "seems to be more of an afterthought."

Pei Wei Asian Diner *Pan-Asian* 19 | 15 | 16 | $15

North | Northwoods Shopping Ctr. | 1802 N. Loop 1604 E. (Rte. 281) | 210-507-9160

Northwest | Strand, The | 11267 Huebner Rd. (McDermott Frwy.) | 210-561-5600

Northwest | 11398 Bandera Rd. (Brae Ridge Dr.) | 210-523-0040

www.peiwei.com

See review in Dallas/Ft. Worth Directory.

Pesca on the River *Seafood* 24 | 22 | 20 | $47

River Walk | Watermark Hotel & Spa | 212 W. Crockett St. (St. Mary's St.) | 210-396-5817 | www.watermarkhotel.com

Even the "locals are circling" this "casually elegant" River Walk dock in the Watermark Hotel, a source of "excellent fresh seafood" flown in daily from around the world; many are hooked on its "cool atmosphere" and "hard-to-find" cuisine, though "pricey" tabs may dampen enthusiasm.

P.F. Chang's China Bistro *Chinese* 22 | 22 | 20 | $27

La Cantera | Shops at La Cantera | 15900 La Cantera Pkwy. (N. Loop 1604) | 210-507-6500

Quarry | Alamo Quarry Mkt. | 255 E. Basse Rd. (Hwy. 281) | 210-507-1000

www.pfchangs.com

See review in Dallas/Ft. Worth Directory.

Phoenix Chinese Café *Chinese* - | - | - | I

North Central | 11821 West Ave. (Blanco Rd.) | 210-525-1961

The Chinese menu and "specials on the blackboard" are "surprisingly authentic" at this Northside strip-center Cantonese, so those who "decipher the Chenglish" are in for "wonderful" chow from a "personable staff" that's a "bang for your buck" to boot; as for the frill-free environs, if you're "fussy about decor" it's also "great for takeout."

	FOOD	DECOR	SERVICE	COST
Piatti Locali *Italian*	24	22	23	$27

Quarry | Alamo Quarry Mkt. | 255 E. Basse Rd. (Hwy. 281) | 210-832-0300 | www.piatti.com

Shoppers show their *amore* for this Italian chain's Quarry locale, home to "addictive" dishes whose "inventive" touches and "fresh ingredients" bring to mind "a thoughtful lover, not your grandmother"; the "fancy yet familiar" setup with a "cozy bar" is a "convenient" "place to meet" that's "less crowded" than others nearby.

	FOOD	DECOR	SERVICE	COST
Picante Grill *Mexican*	22	16	19	$15

Near North | 3810 Broadway St. (Pershing Ave.) | 210-822-3797 | www.picantegrill.com

Specializing in "Mexico City-style" cuisine, this "neighborhood place" opposite the Witte Museum "thrills" amigos with "wonderful" enchiladas, fajitas, cochinita pibil and chile en nogada; affable owners and "affordable" prices add to the appeal; P.S. alfresco fans can savor the flavors while dining on the "great" plant-filled patio.

	FOOD	DECOR	SERVICE	COST
Piccolo's Italian Restaurant Ⓜ *Italian*	▽ 25	10	21	$28

Northwest | 5703 Evers Rd. (Wurzbach Rd.) | 210-647-5524

The decor may be "cheesy" ("murals of Vesuvio, oil paintings of Rome and fake grapes") but the compensations at this family-run Northwest Neapolitan are many; the "carefully prepared" Southern Italian fare is "wonderful", and "personal recognition" from the chef-owner - who "never forgets a face" - makes diners "feel special"; if the usually "efficient" servers happen to be moving "slowly", regulars urge "be patient" - "big-city tastes" await.

	FOOD	DECOR	SERVICE	COST
Pico de Gallo Restaurant *Tex-Mex*	▽ 21	16	21	$14

San Antonio West | 111 S. Leona St. (Commerce St.) | 210-225-6060 | www.picodegallo.com

Another longtimer from the Cortez family (Mi Tierra, La Margarita), this "bustling" Tex-Mex trouper west of Market Square fills up "real San Antonians" with its "fantastic" soups and "tasty" grilled-meat platters (served with "housemade tortillas" and all the trimmings); be warned that mariachis who "seem to think louder is better" may "ruin your conversation"; N.B. a post-Survey redo, which added an upstairs bar, may outdate the above Decor score.

	FOOD	DECOR	SERVICE	COST
Reggiano's *Italian/Mediterranean*	20	22	20	$34

Stone Oak | Stone Oak Plaza II | 18740 Stone Oak Pkwy. (N. Loop 1604) | 210-403-2100

An airy, "upscale feel" furnishes an apt backdrop for the "solid" Italian-Med menu at this "busy" Stone Oak staple; holdouts contend the cooking's "only so-so" and the service "a bit slow", but all agree that if you're seeking "a hopping singles scene", "this is the place."

	FOOD	DECOR	SERVICE	COST
Ristorante Grissini Ⓢ *Italian*	▽ 25	18	17	$35

Alamo Heights | Lincoln Heights Shopping Ctr. | 999. E. Basse Rd. (B'way) | 210-615-7270

After a move to a "new location" "with no loss in quality", Alamo Heights is now home to some of "the best Italian" in town courtesy of this cozy trattoria; the fireplace-equipped space is overseen by a "husband cook and wife maitre d'" team, and newfound followers only wish they would open for lunch.

Rosario's *Mexican* 23 | 19 | 19 | $20

Southtown | 910 S. Alamo St. (St. Mary's St.) | 210-223-1806 | www.rosariossa.com

"Tourists and locals mix" at this "boisterous" Southtown "favorite" for "first-rate Tex-Mex" augmented by "uncommon" specialties "usually found deep in Mexico"; owner Lisa Wong knows how to create "fun, funky" atmospherics with a "fiesta feel every day", so prepare for a "packed" and "noisy" house.

Z Ruth's Chris Steak House *Steak* 25 | 22 | 25 | $57

San Antonio East | St. Paul Sq. | 1170 E. Commerce St. (I-37) | 210-227-8847

North Central | Concord, The | 7720 Jones-Maltsberger Rd. (Shadywood Ln.) | 210-821-5051

www.ruthschris.com

"Nothing beats a steak sizzling in butter" at this "special-occasion", New Orleans-based chain where the "melt-in-your-mouth" chops are "cooked to perfection" and presented on "hot plates"; sure, reactions to decor vary - from "blah" to "old-fashioned in a good way" - but service is "attentive" and the "off-the-charts" pricing manageable "so long as your boss doesn't care how much you spend."

Z Sandbar Fish House & Market, The S M *Seafood* 28 | 20 | 23 | $34

Downtown | 152 E. Pecan St. (St. Mary's St.) | 210-222-2426

You can almost "feel the sand between your toes" at this "real seafood bar", Downtown's "island of choice" for an "amazing" extravaganza of "incredibly fresh", "artfully prepared" fin fare courtesy of über-chef Andrew Weissman; the "small", "simple" space is just around the corner but atmospherically worlds apart from his luxe flagship Le Rêve; N.B. dinner only, Tuesday-Saturday.

Sarika's Thai Restaurant *Thai* ▽ 25 | 17 | 23 | $17

Medical Center | 4319 Medical Dr. (Fredericksburg Rd.) | 210-692-3200

Sure, "the strip-mall location is nothing fancy", but this "cozy" local takes the Medical Center by tsunami with its "tasty" "basic Thai" and "lovely staff"; the modest site morphs into a lunchtime hot spot and a romantic possibility after dark, and given the "good value", supporters say you "can't go wrong."

Sarovar Indian Cuisine *Indian* ▽ 21 | 12 | 15 | $18

Northwest | 10227 Ironside Dr. (Ticonderoga Dr.) | 210-558-8289 | www.sarovar.net

"Exciting flavors" await at these Northwest San Antonio and North Austin outposts for "homestyle Indian food", which represents "many different regions" of the Raj via a well-stocked lunch buffet and an "extensive menu" at dinner; the low-key decor "isn't the best", so most focus on the "cheap" tabs.

	FOOD	DECOR	SERVICE	COST
Sawasdee Thai Cuisine	24	16	20	$18

Sawasdee Thai Cuisine *Thai*

North Central | Castle Creek Shopping Ctr. | 6407 Blanco Rd. (inside Loop 410) | 210-979-9110

"Drive your taste buds wild" with the "bold flavors" at this "Thai-rific" North Central joint, a "family-run business" where the menu's "excellent variety" is matched with "very accommodating" service; despite an unassuming location in the corner of a strip center, dee-votees declare "this place will impress you."

Scenic Loop Café *American/Tex-Mex*

19 | 20 | 20 | $28

Leon Springs | 25615 Boerne Stage Rd. (Toutant Beauregard Rd.) | 210-687-1818 | www.scenicloopcafe.com

"The hunter-gatherer in any Texan" should find what they're looking for in the "diverse" American and Tex-Mex selection at this "casual" retreat set high on the Hill Country rise of Leon Springs; besides "dependable" eating and an "awesome patio", it's "worth the ride" for a "relaxing" scene complete with a "play area" for kids and "live music" on weekends.

Schilo's Delicatessen ☒ *Deli*

21 | 15 | 19 | $14

Downtown | 424 E. Commerce St. (Presa St.) | 210-223-6692

One of the few remaining reminders of SA's influx of German immigrants, this Downtown deli founded in 1917 is as famous for its "authentic" and "homey" character as it is for its "superb" split pea soup, "killer cheesecake" and "knock-your-boots-off" housemade root beer; the "unpretentious" vibe and "good values" keep this "time warp that works" "popular" (and "overcrowded"); N.B. closes at 8:30 PM.

Sea Island Shrimphouse *Seafood*

19 | 12 | 14 | $15

Selma | Forum, The | 8223 Agora Pkwy. (I-35) | 210-658-1100
Loop 410 | 322 W. Rector St. (San Pedro Ave.) | 210-342-7771
Northwest | 11715 Bandera Rd. (N. Loop 1604) | 210-681-7000
Northwest | 4323 Amerisuites Dr. (McDeroitt Frwy.) | 210-558-8989
Northwest | 5959 NW Loop 410 (Ingram Rd.) | 210-520-3033
San Antonio South | 2119 SW Military Dr. (I-35) | 210-921-9700
www.shrimphouse.com

Locals on the lookout for "quick-fix seafood" wash up at this busy chain, a "go-to" for "fried and grilled" fish of "consistent quality", including shrimp fresh from the waters of the Gulf; aye, they're "short on decor" and patrons "stand in line" to order, but "bargain" prices make them "a family favorite."

Shiraz ☒ *Persian*

21 | 17 | 18 | $32

Olmos Park | 4230 McCullough Ave. (Olmos Dr.) | 210-829-5050 | www.dineatshiraz.com

Iranian cuisine isn't exactly common in Alamo City, but you can get it at this "small, inviting" Olmos Park Persian proffering "delicious" dishes in an "intimate", "quiet atmosphere"; service is "personal" if sometimes "slow", and a few take a dim view of the ambient "darkness" ("you need a flashlight"); N.B. though the place was named for Persia's ancient capital and not the wine, the cellar also contains many boutique bottles of the eponymous varietal.

	FOOD	DECOR	SERVICE	COST

Z Silo *American* 26 | 23 | 24 | $43

Terrell Heights | 1133 Austin Hwy. (Mt. Calvary Dr.) | 210-824-8686 | www.siloelevatedcuisine.com

"Elevate your taste buds" at this bi-level bistro in Terrell Heights, where the "superb" New American fare comes with a local twist (check out the "succulent" chicken-fried oysters) along with "prompt" service and "modern" surroundings; it also stores up a "festive bar" scene, and "though a bit pricey", its plates are portioned for "Texas-sized appetites."

Z NEW Silo 1604 *American* 26 | 25 | 24 | $43

Loop 1604 | Ventura Plaza | 434 NW Loop 1604 (bet. Blanco Rd. & Stone Oak Pkwy.) | 210-483-8989 | www.siloelevatedcuisine.com

Boosters boast this "drop-dead gorgeous" Silo spin-off on North Central's 1604 is "even better than the original" for "swanky" but "welcoming" vibes, "gourmet" New American cuisine and "attentive" service; like its forerunner, it's "costly but well worth the money", and the "bar downstairs" is likewise a "welcome addition" hosting "great live music" and "the latest singles scene."

Simi's India Cuisine *Indian* ▽ 24 | 14 | 21 | $21

Northwest | 4535 Fredericksburg Rd. (Hillcrest Dr.) | 210-737-3166

"Dependable" and "good", this Northwest Indian is known for its "delicious" subcontinental specialties ("tender lamb curry", "scrumptious saag panir") and a lunch buffet that's a "popular" "place for friends to meet" midday; the owner "greets you with a warm smile" and his staff is "attentive and respectful", so the only demerit is the unremarkable – but not quite seamy – decor.

Smokehouse, The M *BBQ* - | - | - | I

(fka Bob's Smokehouse)

San Antonio East | 3306 Roland Ave. (Rigsby Ave.) | 210-333-9548

Smoked meat mavens hungry for true "old-school" 'cue drift over to this East Side pit stop, where the "solid BBQ" is served up "like it should be" in "an often-smoky dining area with extremely basic utensils"; "despite its humble surroundings", menu standouts like homemade sausage, brisket and lamb ribs are an "undeniable" draw.

Sompong's Thai & Chinese Cuisine ⊠ *Chinese/Thai* ▽ 18 | 8 | 19 | $15

Medical Center | 8110 Fredericksburg Rd. (Datapoint Dr.) | 210-614-0845

"If you're nearby", Medical Center regulars report this longstanding Chinese-Thai hybrid is "perfect for a fast lunch" thanks to its "efficient service", "cheap" prices and ample menu of both Americanized and more authentic options; just focus on the food since the strip-center storefront is "not much on decor."

Sorrento Ristorante *Italian* 23 | 11 | 18 | $19

Alamo Heights | 5146 Broadway St. (Grove Pl.) | 210-824-0055

The "Sorrento scenes on the walls" at this Alamo Heights "neighborhood joint" may be "pure Italian kitsch", but "homemade" faves like the "well-crafted" pastas and pizzas make it a "popular" pick;

plus the "jammed", "no-frills" space creates a dining experience cognoscenti call "close to the real deal back East."

Stonewerks Big Rock Grill *American* 18 | 19 | 17 | $21

Loop 1604 | Vineyards, The | 1201 N. Loop 1604 (Blanco Rd.) | 210-764-0400

Stonewerks Caffe *American*

Quarry | Quarry Mkt. | 7300 Jones-Maltsberger Rd. (Basse Rd.) | 210-828-3508

www.stonewerks.com

It's "casual" American food "but they dress it up nice" at this "popular" pair, where the youngish "party/bar crowd" can count on a "robust beverage menu", "great patio", "big-screen" sports and "moderate prices"; both the Quarry original and its roomier 1604 spin-off werk fine for "lively (noisy)" times.

Sushihana Japanese Restaurant *Japanese* 25 | 21 | 22 | $27

Castle Hills | 1810 NW Military Hwy. (Moss Dr.) | 210-340-7808 | www.sushihanasan.com

Maybe "sushi places are popping up all over town", but this "best-kept secret" in Castle Hills "could start a revolution" according to enthusiasts who bow to the "excellent selection and presentation" of its Japanese specialties; the "thoughtful" wine list, "great service" and "very Zen" ambiance round out a repast fit for an emperor.

Sushi Zushi *Japanese* 21 | 20 | 17 | $29

Downtown | 203 S. St. Mary's St. (Market St.) | 210-472-2900

Alamo Heights | 999 E. Basse Rd. (B'way) | 210-826-8500

Northwest | Colonnade, The | 9867 I-10 W. (Wurzbach Rd.) | 210-691-3332

Stone Oak | Stone Oak Plaza II | 18720 Stone Oak Pkwy. (N. Loop 1604) | 210-545-6100

www.sushizushi.com

Even "non-sushi lovers" have a "top-notch" "variety of choices" at this "modern" chain, which augments its "huge assortment" of "fresh", "innovative" rolls with a "wide-ranging" lineup of other Japanese "favorites"; but while many hail the menu's "exciting twists", purists pan the occasionally "weird" combos as "not authentic" and "not cheap."

Taco Cabana ◐ *Mexican* 16 | 11 | 11 | $10

La Cantera | 2347 E. Southcross Blvd. (I-37) | 210-532-2422

North Central | 2908 Broadway St. (Humphrey Ave.) | 210-829-1616

North Central | 3310 San Pedro Ave. (Hildebrand Ave.) | 210-733-9332

South Central | 543 W. Malone Ave. (bet. Cottomwood & Theo Aves.) | 210-534-8533

San Antonio West | 4723 W. Commerce St. (San Augustine Ave.) | 210-436-4464

www.tacocabana.com

The "cheap eats" will cure "late-night hunger pains" "in a hurry" at this local eatery turned regional chain, home to "*puro*" Mexican served up "fast-food"-style; but choosier chowhounds lament "inconsistent service" and grub that's "nothing special."

Taipei Chinese Restaurant *Chinese* 20 | 17 | 19 | $18

Stone Oak | 18802 Stone Oak Pkwy. (N. Loop 1604) | 210-403-3316 | www.sotaipei.com

Backers boast this Stone Oak "standby" is "one of the better" "neighborhood" Chinese options, citing "great value" on a "tasty" selection that extends to a sideline in sushi; and type B's appreciate "rarely crowded" conditions that make for a less hectic lunch rush.

Texas Farm to Table Cafe *American* 24 | 16 | 19 | $13

Near North | 312 Pearl Pkwy. (Ave. A) | 210-444-1404 | www.texasfarmtotable.com

"You can't get any fresher" than the "local (and often organic) ingredients" "straight from the farm" at this "friendly, casual" Near Northside American "niche" in the revitalized Pearl Brewing complex; the "husband-and-wife chef duo" turns out "excellent", "creative" sandwiches, salads and more during daylight hours, guaranteeing "a healthy lunch" break; N.B. expansion plans are underway.

Thai-Lao Orchid ☒ *Thai* - | - | - | M

Alamo Heights | 7959 Broadway St. (Sunset Rd.) | 210-832-9889 | www.thailaoorchid.com

Regulars rely on the "seamless service, quality food and quiet" at this Alamo Heights "neighborhood" nook, where the lineup is "predominantly Thai" but takes in Vietnamese and a sushi bar too; the range of "classic dishes" helps it blossom into a "benchmark for all" in the area.

Thai Pikul *Thai* - | - | - | I

Northwest | Magic Center Plaza | 5136 Fredericksburg Rd. (Callaghan Rd.) | 210-524-9440 | www.thaipikul.com

Admittedly it's a "spare setting", but "the food speaks for itself" at this Northwest strip-center Siamese, a prime pik for Thai buffs drawn to the "great selection" of traditional tastes; for extra incentive, the free-corkage BYO policy keeps it more than affordable.

Thai Spice *Thai* ▽ 22 | 14 | 21 | $16

Northeast | Forum, The | 8327 Agora Pkwy. (bet. I-35 & Loop 1604) | 210-658-1665

The spice is right at this far Northeast outpost, where "they adjust the heat" in the "amazing" Thai specialties "according to your desire"; "impeccable" service and "terrific value" elevate it among the "best in town" – "not at all what you'd expect to find in a strip mall."

Thai Taste ☒ *Thai* - | - | - | I

Northwest | Crestview Plaza | 5520 Evers Rd. (Loop 410) | 210-520-6800

Look for minimal decor and maximum flavor at this "cheap, cheap, cheap" BYO neighborhood Thai, a popular stop for the Northwest lunch crowd; taste-testers appreciate that the dishes are scaled "from mild to very spicy", as is the clientele.

NEW **Tiago's Cabo Grill** *Mexican/Tex-Mex* 22 | 20 | 21 | $21

La Cantera | Rim, The | 17711 I-10 W. (La Cantera Pkwy.) | 210-881-2700

(continued)

Tiago's Cabo Grill

Northwest | Shops at Westpointe | 8403 Hwy. 151 (I-410) | 210-647-3600
www.tiagoscabogrille.com

This new duo of family-friendly cantinas concocts a "delicious" "blend of Tex-Mex and true Mex" featuring grilled meats, "lots of seafood choices", "unbelievable margaritas" and "awesome" chocolate cake; besides the "dependable" eating, well-wishers warm to the midrange tabs and agreeably upscale decor.

Tip Top Cafe M ⊄ *American* ▽ 25 | 15 | 23 | $13

Northwest | 2814 Fredericksburg Rd. (Santa Anna St.) | 210-732-0191 |
www.tiptopcafe.com

"Talk about Texas!" exclaim fans of this "classic" '30s-era Northwest "diner", now in its third generation of family ownership and still a "top-notch" source of "delightful" American "comfort food" à la "home-made" chicken-fried steak, onion rings and pie; if the service ("love the waitresses!") and surroundings seem stuck in time, so do the prices.

Tong's Thai Restaurant *Thai* 21 | 15 | 19 | $17

Terrell Hills | 1146 Austin Hwy. (Mt. Calvary Dr.) | 210-829-7345 |
www.tongsthai.com

Addicts who "crave the taste" of Thai turn to this "casual" Terrell Hills entry for "very fresh" dishes and "friendly" service in "cool, dark, Zen" digs; Chinese choices supplement the main menu, "and then there's the bubble tea" to tickle your tong.

Tony Roma's *BBQ* - | - | - | M

Downtown | Rivercenter Mall | 849 E. Commerce St. (Alamo Plaza) |
210-225-7662 | www.tonyromas.com

"Ribs are the specialty" of this longtime BBQ chain Downtown (that also serves seafood and steaks), though "decent prices" seem to be its strongest suit; still, many say this "dated" franchise is "past its prime", citing "tacky" decor and just "ordinary" cooking.

Torres Taco Haven *Mexican* ▽ 23 | 14 | 18 | $13

Southtown | 3119 S. Gevers St. (Greer St.) | 210-532-3049
San Antonio South | 1032 S. Presa St. (bet. Claudia & Vance Sts.) |
210-533-2171

"Pick up a coupla breakfast tacos" and "you'll never want any other" at this "cheap and fabulous" Mexican twosome that'll "knock your socks off" with their "down-home" chow; they're a "popular" "go-to" even for "local luminaries" (especially for Sunday breakfast), and visitors can count on the Torres family to "make you feel like a San Antonian."

Turquoise Turkish Grill *Turkish* - | - | - | M

Loop 410 | 3720 NW Loop 410 (Fredericksburg Rd.) | 210-736-2887 |
www.turquoisegrill.com

As the only true Turk in town, this Loop 410 eatery is a rare supplier of "spicy kebabs", a "selection of Turkish meats" and fresh-baked breads; its impressive selection of Levantine wines and Friday night belly dancing are also impossible to ignore.

FOOD | DECOR | SERVICE | COST

20nine Restaurant & Wine Bar *Californian* 18 | 22 | 20 | $35

Quarry | Quarry Mkt. | 255 E. Basse Rd. (Jones-Maltsberger Rd.) | 210-798-9463 | www.20ninewine.com

"It's all about the wine" at this "dark, intimate" Quarry destination that takes Napa Valley's Route 29 for inspiration, offering sips from an "extensive" list plus "creative flights" and artisan beers as well; though a few find the "high-end" Californian "finger food" takes a backseat to the drink selection, the "super-friendly staff" and outdoor seating area make it a "great addition" to the neighborhood nonetheless.

Van's Chinese Seafood Restaurant *Pan-Asian/Seafood* ▽ 21 | 10 | 17 | $21

Near North | 3214 Broadway St. (Mulberry St.) | 210-828-8449 | www.vansrestaurantonline.com

"Shhh, it's a well-kept secret" that "one of the largest wine cellars" in the city is hidden away at this "eclectic" Pan-Asian seafooder just north of Downtown, which is likewise advantaged with "wonderful" cooking at a "great value"; as for the decor, regulars shrug "all their taste is in their food."

Viet-Nam Restaurant *Vietnamese* - | - | - | I

Near North | 3244 Broadway St. (Mulberry St.) | 210-822-7461

"If you didn't know the place", you might overlook this tiny storefront north of Downtown and its "enjoyable and refreshing" mix of authentic Vietnamese eats; while longtime followers feel it's "a little uneven of late", they also agree it's always "worth a try."

Wah Kee Chinese Seafood Cuisine *Chinese* 22 | 16 | 20 | $18

Northwest | 2347 NW Military Hwy. (Lockhill-Selma Rd.) | 210-349-8383

Sonterra | 18360 Blanco Rd. (N. Loop 1604) | 210-497-6669

With an "extensive menu" of "real Chinese" "at its best", these Northwest and Sonterra seafood specialists qualify as "neighborhood" keepers; throw in "value prices" and "quick", "friendly" service, and few fret if "there isn't much in the way of decor."

Water Street Oyster Bar *Seafood* 18 | 15 | 16 | $23

Alamo Heights | Lincoln Heights Shopping Ctr. | 7500 Broadway St. (Basse Rd.) | 210-829-4853 | www.waterstreetco.com

SA may be "landlocked" but boosters report you can get "great Texas Gulf oysters" at this Alamo Heights seafood specialist with a "nice" bi-level interior and "relaxed" feel; however, surveyors are split on service ("wonderful" vs. "slow and sloppy"), and even admirers admit acoustics can be "way too noisy."

W.D. Deli *Deli* ▽ 21 | 18 | 18 | $11

Near North | 3123 Broadway St. (Mulberry St.) | 210-828-2322 | www.wddeli.com

Although the "funky" indoor/outdoor setup signals it's not your bubbe's deli, this "busy" Near Northside "lunch spot" raises "soups and sandwiches to a higher level" with its "wonderful" homemade goods; it's also budget-friendly, so insiders never neglect to check "the bakery case" for "a slice of heaven."

Zuni Grill *Southwestern* 19 | 18 | 16 | $29

River Walk | 223 Losoya St. (Commerce St.) | 210-227-0864 | www.joesfood.com

"Southwestern food has not gone out of style" on the River Walk, especially since this airy eatery pairs it with "a great view" and "people-watching on the patio"; the menu's "creative" combinations make it a "well-liked" spot for locals and a comparatively "interesting" option for out-of-towners.

SAN ANTONIO INDEXES

Cuisines

Includes restaurant names, locations and Food ratings. 🅉 indicates places with the highest ratings, popularity and importance.

AMERICAN (NEW)

- 🅉 Biga/Banks | **River Walk** 27
- Bin 555 | **N Central** 26
- Cappyccino's | **Alamo Hts** 20
- 🅉 Cappy's | **Alamo Hts** 23
- Citrus | **Downtown** 25
- Eclipse Café | **N Central** 20
- Kona Grill | **La Cantera** 20
- 🅉 Lodge/Castle Hills | **Castle Hills** 26
- Oro | **Downtown** 24
- Pam's Patio | **North** 26
- Scenic Loop | **Leon Springs** 19
- 🅉 Silo | **Terrell Hts** 26
- 🅉 NEW Silo 1604 | **Loop 1604** 26
- Stonewerks | **multi.** 18

AMERICAN (TRADITIONAL)

- Cheesecake Factory | **Loop 410** 20
- Cheesy Jane's | **multi.** 19
- Chesters | **multi.** 22
- Clear Springs | **Stone Oak** 19
- Cove, The | **Downtown** 20
- Grey Moss Inn | **Helotes** 24
- Guenther Hse. | **Southtown** 23
- Josephine St. | **Near North** 20
- 🅉 Magnolia Pancake | **N Central** 27
- Mama's Café | **multi.** 19
- NEW Merchants Grand Café | **Alamo Hts** -
- NEW Mimi's Cafe | **La Cantera** 21
- Texas Farm/Table | **Near North** 24
- Tip Top Cafe | **NW** 25

ASIAN

- Asia Kitchen | **San Antonio W** 25

ASIAN FUSION

- 🅉 Frederick's | **Alamo Hts** 26

BARBECUE

- County Line | **multi.** 20
- Smokehouse, The | **San Antonio E** -
- Tony Roma's | **Downtown** -

BELGIAN

- La Frite | **Southtown** 26

BURGERS

- Big'z Burger | **Loop 1604** 21
- Cheesy Jane's | **multi.** 19
- Chesters | **multi.** 22
- Chris Madrid's | **Near North** 25

CAJUN

- Pappadeaux | **Loop 410** 23

CALIFORNIAN

- 20nine | **Quarry** 18

CHINESE

(* dim sum specialist)

- Chef Chan* | **NW** -
- Formosa Gdn. | **N Central** 21
- Golden Wok* | **multi.** 22
- Hsiu Yu | **North** 16
- Kim Wah Chinese* | **NW** -
- Mencius Gourmet | **Medical Ctr** 21
- P.F. Chang's | **multi.** 22
- Phoenix Chinese* | **N Central** -
- Sompong's | **Medical Ctr** 18
- Taipei Chinese | **Stone Oak** 20
- Wah Kee | **multi.** 22

CONTINENTAL

- NEW Bistro Thyme | **Loop 1604** -
- Fig Tree | **River Walk** 25
- Houston St. | **Downtown** 22

DELIS

- Schilo's D | **Downtown** 21
- W.D. Deli | **Near North** 21

DESSERT

- Cheesecake Factory | **Loop 410** 20
- Crumpets | **NE** 15
- Da Vinci Gelato | **Stone Oak** 24
- Madhatters Tea | **Southtown** 20

ECLECTIC

- Eclipse Café | **N Central** 20
- Grill/Leon Springs | **Leon Springs** 22

La Tuna Grill | **Southtown** 22
☑ Liberty Bar | **Near North** 24

EUROPEAN

La Scala | **Castle Hills** 23

FONDUE

Melting Pot | **N Central** 21

FRENCH

☑ Bistro Vatel | **Olmos Pk** 26
Crumpets | **NE** 15
☑ Frederick's | **Alamo Hts** 26
Las Canarias | **River Walk** 26
☑ L'Etoile | **Alamo Hts** 26
Meson | **NW** 18

FRENCH (NEW)

☑ Le Rêve | **Downtown** 29

GREEK

Demo's Greek | **multi.** 19
Mina & Dimi's | **San Antonio W** 24

HAWAIIAN

Kona Grill | **La Cantera** 20

INDIAN

India Oven | **N Central** 24
India Palace | **multi.** 24
Madras Pavilion | **NW** 22
Sarovar Indian | **NW** 21
Simi's India | **NW** 24

ITALIAN

(N=Northern; S=Southern)
Aldino | **Sonterra** 21
Aldo's | N | **Medical Ctr** 21
Carrabba's | **NW** 22
Ciao Lavanderia | **Olmos Pk** 23
Da Vinci Gelato | **Stone Oak** 24
NEW Dough | **N Central** -
La Focaccia | **Southtown** 16
Luce Rist. | **NW** 20
Meson | **NW** 18
☑ Paesanos | **multi.** 22
Piatti | **Quarry** 24
Piccolo's Italian | S | **NW** 25
Reggiano's | **Stone Oak** 20
Rist. Grissini | **Alamo Hts** 25
Sorrento Rist. | **Alamo Hts** 23

JAPANESE

(* sushi specialist)
Fujiya* | **Medical Ctr** 19
☑ Godai Sushi* | **N Central** 27
Koi Kawa* | **Near North** 26
Mon's Thai* | **Alamo Hts** 17
Sushihana* | **Castle Hills** 25
Sushi Zushi* | **multi.** 21

KOREAN

(* barbecue specialist)
Ilsong Gdn. | **N Central** 25
Korean BBQ Hse.* | **San Antonio E** 23

MEDITERRANEAN

Boardwalk Bistro | **Near North** 21
Las Canarias | **River Walk** 26
Reggiano's | **Stone Oak** 20

MEXICAN

Aldaco's | **San Antonio E** 22
El Jarro de Arturo | **North** 22
El Mirador | **Southtown** 23
Ernesto's | **N Central** 18
La Fonda on Main | **Near North** -
☑ Paloma Blanca | **Alamo Hts** 22
Picante Grill | **Near North** 22
Rosario's | **Southtown** 23
Taco Cabana | **multi.** 16
NEW Tiago's | **multi.** 22
Torres Taco | **multi.** 23

NUEVO LATINO

Azúca | **Southtown** 24
Pasión! | **Loop 1604** 18

PACIFIC RIM

Pacific Moon | **North** 18

PAN-ASIAN

Pei Wei | **multi.** 19
Van's | **Near North** 21

PAN-LATIN

Cafe Paladar | **Stone Oak** 25

PERSIAN

Shiraz | **Olmos Pk** 21

PUERTO RICAN

La Marginal | **N Central** -

SEAFOOD

Bohanan's | **Downtown** 23
☑ Boudro's | **River Walk** 24
Ernesto's | **N Central** 18
Landry's | **River Walk** 19
☑ L'Etoile | **Alamo Hts** 26
Pappadeaux | **Loop 410** 23
Pesca/River | **River Walk** 24
☑ Sandbar Fish | **Downtown** 28
Sea Island | **multi.** 19
Van's | **Near North** 21
Wah Kee | **multi.** 22
Water St. Oyster | **Alamo Hts** 18

SOUTH AMERICAN

Beto's Comida | **North** 21

SOUTHWESTERN

Antlers Lodge | **San Antonio W** 23
Canyon Café | **Quarry** 18
☑ Francesca's | **La Cantera** 26
Zuni Grill | **River Walk** 19

SPANISH

(* tapas specialist)
Las Ramblas* | **River Walk** 21

STEAKHOUSES

Barn Door | **Alamo Hts** 19
Bohanan's | **Downtown** 23
☑ Boudro's | **River Walk** 24
Fleming's Prime | **Quarry** 24
Little Red Barn | **San Antonio S** 17
Little Rhein | **River Walk** 24
Morton's Steak | **Downtown** 25
Old San Francisco | **North** 19
Palm, The | **Downtown** 24
☑ Ruth's Chris | **multi.** 25

TEAROOMS

Madhatters Tea | **Southtown** 20

TEX-MEX

Ácenar | **River Walk** 22
Chuy's | **North** 21
Iron Cactus | **River Walk** 18
Karam's | **San Antonio W** 20
La Hacienda/Los Barrios | **North** 21
La Margarita | **Market Sq** 21
Mi Tierra | **Market Sq** 21
Pico de Gallo | **San Antonio W** 21
Scenic Loop | **Leon Springs** 19
NEW Tiago's | **multi.** 22

THAI

Bangkok | **NE** -
Mon's Thai | **Alamo Hts** 17
Sarika's | **Medical Ctr** 25
Sawasdee | **N Central** 24
Sompong's | **Medical Ctr** 18
Thai-Lao Orchid | **Alamo Hts** -
Thai Pikul | **NW** -
Thai Spice | **NE** 22
Thai Taste | **NW** -
Tong's Thai | **Terrell Hills** 21

TURKISH

Turquoise Turkish | **Loop 410** -

VEGETARIAN

NEW Green Veg. | **Downtown** 18

VIETNAMESE

Viet-Nam | **Near North** -

Locations

Includes restaurant names, cuisines and Food ratings. ☒ indicates places with the highest ratings, popularity and importance.

San Antonio Central

DOWNTOWN

Bohanan's | *Seafood/Steak* 23
NEW Chart House | *Seafood* -
Citrus | *Amer.* 25
Cove, The | *Amer.* 20
NEW Green Veg. | *Veg.* 18
Houston St. | *Continental* 22
☒ Le Rêve | *French* 29
Mama's Café | *Amer.* 19
Morton's Steak | *Steak* 25
Oro | *Amer.* 24
Palm, The | *Steak* 24
☒ Sandbar Fish | *Seafood* 28
Schilo's D | *Deli* 21
Sushi Zushi | *Japanese* 21
Tony Roma's | *BBQ* -

MARKET SQUARE

La Margarita | *Tex-Mex* 21
Mi Tierra | *Tex-Mex* 21

RIVER WALK

Ácenar | *Tex-Mex* 22
☒ Biga/Banks | *Amer.* 27
☒ Boudro's | *Seafood/Steak* 24
County Line | *BBQ* 20
Fig Tree | *Continental* 25
Iron Cactus | *Tex-Mex* 18
Landry's | *Seafood* 19
Las Canarias | *French/Med.* 26
Las Ramblas | *Spanish* 21
Little Rhein | *Steak* 24
☒ Paesanos | *Italian* 22
Pesca/River | *Seafood* 24
Zuni Grill | *SW* 19

SOUTHTOWN

Azúca | *Nuevo Latino* 24
Cascabel | *Mex.* -
El Mirador | *Mex.* 23
Guenther Hse. | *Amer.* 23
La Focaccia | *Italian* 16
La Frite | *Belgian* 26
La Tuna Grill | *Eclectic* 22
Madhatters Tea | *Tea* 20
Rosario's | *Mex.* 23
Torres Taco | *Mex.* 23

San Antonio East

SAN ANTONIO EAST

Aldaco's | *Mex.* 22
Korean BBQ Hse. | *Korean* 23
☒ Ruth's Chris | *Steak* 25
Smokehouse, The | *BBQ* -

SELMA

Sea Island | *Seafood* 19

UNIVERSAL CITY

Mama's Café | *Amer.* 19

San Antonio North

ALAMO HEIGHTS

Barn Door | *Steak* 19
Cappyccino's | *Amer.* 20
☒ Cappy's | *Amer.* 23
Cheesy Jane's | *Burgers* 19
☒ Frederick's | *Asian Fusion/French* 26
☒ L'Etoile | *French/Seafood* 26
NEW Merchants Grand Café | *Amer.* -
Mon's Thai | *Thai* 17
☒ Paloma Blanca | *Mex.* 22
Rist. Grissini | *Italian* 25
Sorrento Rist. | *Italian* 23
Sushi Zushi | *Japanese* 21
Thai-Lao Orchid | *Thai* -
Water St. Oyster | *Seafood* 18

CASTLE HILLS

La Scala | *Euro.* 23
☒ Lodge/Castle Hills | *Amer.* 26
Sushihana | *Japanese* 25

HELOTES

Grey Moss Inn | *Amer.*	24

LA CANTERA

Z Francesca's | *SW*	26
Kona Grill | *Amer.*	20
NEW Mimi's Cafe | *Amer.*	21
P.F. Chang's | *Chinese*	22
Taco Cabana | *Mex.*	16
NEW Tiago's | *Mex./Tex-Mex*	22

LOOP 1604

Big'z Burger | *Burgers*	21
NEW Bistro Thyme | *Continental*	-
Z Paesanos | *Italian*	22
Pasión! | *Nuevo Latino*	18
Z NEW Silo 1604 | *Amer.*	26
Stonewerks | *Amer.*	18

LOOP 410

Cheesecake Factory | *Amer.*	20
Chesters | *Burgers*	22
Pappadeaux | *Seafood*	23
Sea Island | *Seafood*	19
Turquoise Turkish | *Turkish*	-

MEDICAL CENTER

Aldo's | *Italian*	21
Chesters | *Burgers*	22
Fujiya | *Japanese*	19
Golden Wok | *Chinese*	22
India Palace | *Indian*	24
Mencius Gourmet | *Chinese*	21
Sarika's | *Thai*	25
Sompong's | *Chinese/Thai*	18

NEAR NORTH

Boardwalk Bistro | *Med.*	21
Chris Madrid's | *Burgers*	25
Demo's Greek | *Greek*	19
Josephine St. | *Amer.*	20
Koi Kawa | *Japanese*	26
La Fonda on Main | *Mex.*	-
Z Liberty Bar | *Eclectic*	24
Picante Grill | *Mex.*	22
Texas Farm/Table | *Amer.*	24
Van's | *Pan-Asian/Seafood*	21
Viet-Nam | *Viet.*	-
W.D. Deli | *Deli*	21

NORTH

Beto's Comida | *S Amer.*	21
Chesters | *Burgers*	22
Chuy's | *Tex-Mex*	21
Demo's Greek | *Greek*	19
El Jarro de Arturo | *Mex.*	22
Hsiu Yu | *Chinese*	16
La Hacienda/Los Barrios | *Tex-Mex*	21
Mama's Café | *Amer.*	19
Old San Francisco | *Steak*	19
Pacific Moon | *Pac. Rim*	18
Pam's Patio | *Amer.*	26
Pei Wei | *Pan-Asian*	19

NORTH CENTRAL

Bin 555 | *Amer.*	26
NEW Dough | *Italian*	-
Eclipse Café | *Amer./Eclectic*	20
Ernesto's | *Mex./Seafood*	18
Formosa Gdn. | *Chinese*	21
Z Godai Sushi | *Japanese*	27
Ilsong Gdn. | *Korean*	25
India Oven | *Indian*	24
India Palace | *Indian*	24
La Marginal | *Carib./Puerto Rican*	-
Z Magnolia Pancake | *Amer.*	27
Melting Pot | *Fondue*	21
Phoenix Chinese | *Chinese*	-
Z Ruth's Chris | *Steak*	25
Sawasdee | *Thai*	24
Taco Cabana | *Mex.*	16

NORTHEAST

Bangkok | *Thai*	-
Crumpets | *French*	15
Mama's Café | *Amer.*	19
Thai Spice | *Thai*	22

NORTHWEST

Carrabba's | *Italian*	22
Cheesy Jane's | *Burgers*	19
Chef Chan | *Chinese*	-
County Line | *BBQ*	20
Kim Wah Chinese | *Chinese*	-
Luce Rist. | *Italian*	20
Madras Pavilion | *Indian*	22
Meson | *French/Italian*	18

Pei Wei | *Pan-Asian* 19
Piccolo's Italian | *Italian* 25
Sarovar Indian | *Indian* 21
Sea Island | *Seafood* 19
Simi's India | *Indian* 24
Sushi Zushi | *Japanese* 21
Thai Pikul | *Thai* -
Thai Taste | *Thai* -
NEW Tiago's | *Mex./Tex-Mex* 22
Tip Top Cafe | *Amer.* 25
Wah Kee | *Chinese* 22

OLMOS PARK

Z Bistro Vatel | *French* 26
Ciao Lavanderia | *Italian* 23
Shiraz | *Persian* 21

QUARRY

Canyon Café | *SW* 18
Fleming's Prime | *Steak* 24
Z Paesanos | *Italian* 22
P.F. Chang's | *Chinese* 22
Piatti | *Italian* 24
Stonewerks | *Amer.* 18
20nine | *Calif.* 18

SONTERRA

Aldino | *Italian* 21
Demo's Greek | *Greek* 19
Wah Kee | *Chinese* 22

STONE OAK

Cafe Paladar | *Pan-Latin* 25
Clear Springs | *American* 19
Da Vinci Gelato | *Italian* 24
Reggiano's | *Italian/Med.* 20
Sushi Zushi | *Japanese* 21
Taipei Chinese | *Chinese* 20

TERRILL HEIGHTS/ TERRILL HILLS

Z Silo | *Amer.* 26
Tong's Thai | *Thai* 21

San Antonio South

SAN ANTONIO SOUTH

Little Red Barn | *Steak* 17
Sea Island | *Seafood* 19
Torres Taco | *Mex.* 23

SOUTH CENTRAL

Taco Cabana | *Mex.* 16

San Antonio West

LEON SPRINGS

Grill/Leon Springs | *Eclectic* 22
Scenic Loop | *Amer./Tex-Mex* 19

SAN ANTONIO WEST

Antlers Lodge | *SW* 23
Asia Kitchen | *Asian* 25
Golden Wok | *Chinese* 22
Karam's | *Tex-Mex* 20
Mina & Dimi's | *Greek* 24
Pico de Gallo | *Tex-Mex* 21
Taco Cabana | *Mex.* 16

Special Features

Listings cover the best in each category and include names, locations and Food ratings. Multi-location restaurants' features may vary by branch. Z indicates places with the highest ratings, popularity and importance.

BREAKFAST

(See also Hotel Dining)

El Mirador | **Southtown** 23
Guenther Hse. | **Southtown** 23
La Hacienda/Los Barrios | **North** 21
Z Magnolia Pancake | **N Central** 27
NEW Mimi's Cafe | **La Cantera** 21
Mi Tierra | **Market Sq** 21
Pico de Gallo | **San Antonio W** 21
Schilo's D | **Downtown** 21
Torres Taco | **multi.** 23
Zuni Grill | **River Walk** 19

BRUNCH

Aldino | **Sonterra** 21
Beto's Comida | **North** 21
Cafe Paladar | **Stone Oak** 25
Z Cappy's | **Alamo Hts** 23
Crumpets | **NE** 15
Guenther Hse. | **Southtown** 23
Las Canarias | **River Walk** 26
Z Liberty Bar | **Near North** 24
Madhatters Tea | **Southtown** 20
Z Paloma Blanca | **Alamo Hts** 22

BUFFET SERVED

(Check availability)

India Oven | **N Central** 24
India Palace | **multi.** 24
Las Canarias | **River Walk** 26
Las Ramblas | **River Walk** 21
Madras Pavilion | **NW** 22
Sarovar Indian | **NW** 21
Simi's India | **NW** 24

BUSINESS DINING

Aldo's | **Medical Ctr** 21
Z Biga/Banks | **River Walk** 27
NEW Bistro Thyme | **Loop 1604** -
Z Bistro Vatel | **Olmos Pk** 26
Bohanan's | **Downtown** 23
Canyon Café | **Quarry** 18
Z Cappy's | **Alamo Hts** 23
Citrus | **Downtown** 25
Fig Tree | **River Walk** 25
Z Francesca's | **La Cantera** 26
Z Frederick's | **Alamo Hts** 26
Houston St. | **Downtown** 22
La Fonda on Main | **Near North** -
Landry's | **River Walk** 19
La Scala | **Castle Hills** 23
Las Canarias | **River Walk** 26
Las Ramblas | **River Walk** 21
Z Le Rêve | **Downtown** 29
Z L'Etoile | **Alamo Hts** 26
Little Rhein | **River Walk** 24
Z Lodge/Castle Hills | **Castle Hills** 26
Luce Rist. | **NW** 20
NEW Merchants Grand Café | **Alamo Hts** -
Morton's Steak | **Downtown** 25
Oro | **Downtown** 24
Z Paesanos | **Quarry** 22
Palm, The | **Downtown** 24
Pesca/River | **River Walk** 24
Z Ruth's Chris | **multi.** 25
Z Silo | **Terrell Hts** 26
Sushihana | **Castle Hills** 25

CELEBRITY CHEFS

Z Biga/Banks | *Bruce Auden* | **River Walk** 27
Z Le Rêve | *Andrew Weissman* | **Downtown** 29
Z Sandbar Fish | *Andrew Weissman* | **Downtown** 28

CHEF'S TABLE

Z Biga/Banks | **River Walk** 27
Z Bistro Vatel | **Olmos Pk** 26
Cafe Paladar | **Stone Oak** 25

CHILD-FRIENDLY

(Alternatives to the usual fast-food places; * children's menu available)

Ácenar | **River Walk** 22
Antlers Lodge* | **San Antonio W** 23
Azúca* | **Southtown** 24
Barn Door* | **Alamo Hts** 19
Beto's Comida* | **North** 21
Big'z Burger* | **Loop 1604** 21
Bin 555 | **N Central** 26
Boardwalk Bistro* | **Near North** 21
🅩 Boudro's* | **River Walk** 24
🅩 Cappy's* | **Alamo Hts** 23
Chris Madrid's | **Near North** 25
Ciao Lavanderia | **Olmos Pk** 23
Clear Springs* | **Stone Oak** 19
County Line* | **multi.** 20
Cove, The* | **Downtown** 20
Da Vinci Gelato | **Stone Oak** 24
Demo's Greek* | **multi.** 19
El Jarro de Arturo* | **North** 22
El Mirador | **Southtown** 23
Grey Moss Inn* | **Helotes** 24
Josephine St.* | **Near North** 20
Karam's* | **San Antonio W** 20
Koi Kawa | **Near North** 26
La Focaccia | **Southtown** 16
La Hacienda/Los Barrios* | **North** 21
La Margarita* | **Market Sq** 21
🅩 Liberty Bar | **Near North** 24
Little Red Barn* | **San Antonio S** 17
Madhatters Tea | **Southtown** 20
Mama's Café* | **multi.** 19
Mina & Dimi's | **San Antonio W** 24
Mi Tierra* | **Market Sq** 21
🅩 Paloma Blanca* | **Alamo Hts** 22
Pam's Patio | **North** 26
Pei Wei* | **multi.** 19
Piatti* | **Quarry** 24
Picante Grill* | **Near North** 22
Pico de Gallo* | **San Antonio W** 21
Rosario's* | **Southtown** 23
Schilo's D* | **Downtown** 21
Tip Top Cafe* | **NW** 25
Torres Taco | **multi.** 23
Water St. Oyster | **Alamo Hts** 18
W.D. Deli | **Near North** 21
Zuni Grill | **River Walk** 19

DELIVERY/TAKEOUT

(D=delivery, T=takeout)

Ácenar | T | **River Walk** 22
Aldino | T | **Sonterra** 21
Aldo's | T | **Medical Ctr** 21
Asia Kitchen | T | **San Antonio W** 25
Azúca | T | **Southtown** 24
Bangkok | T | **NE** -
Barn Door | T | **Alamo Hts** 19
Beto's Comida | T | **North** 21
Bin 555 | T | **N Central** 26
Boardwalk Bistro | T | **Near North** 21
Cappyccino's | T | **Alamo Hts** 20
🅩 Cappy's | T | **Alamo Hts** 23
Chuy's | D | **North** 21
Ciao Lavanderia | T | **Olmos Pk** 23
County Line | T | **multi.** 20
Crumpets | T | **NE** 15
Da Vinci Gelato | T | **Stone Oak** 24
Demo's Greek | D, T | **multi.** 19
El Jarro de Arturo | T | **North** 22
El Mirador | T | **Southtown** 23
Formosa Gdn. | T | **N Central** 21
Fujiya | D, T | **Medical Ctr** 19
🅩 Godai Sushi | T | **N Central** 27
Houston St. | T | **Downtown** 22
Hsiu Yu | T | **North** 16
Ilsong Gdn. | T | **N Central** 25
India Oven | T | **N Central** 24
India Palace | D, T | **multi.** 24
Koi Kawa | T | **Near North** 26
Korean BBQ Hse. | T | **San Antonio E** 23
La Focaccia | T | **Southtown** 16
La Hacienda/Los Barrios | T | **North** 21
La Margarita | T | **Market Sq** 21
🅩 Liberty Bar | T | **Near North** 24
Madhatters Tea | T | **Southtown** 20
Mencius Gourmet | T | **Medical Ctr** 21
Mina & Dimi's | T | **San Antonio W** 24

Mi Tierra | T | **Market Sq** 21
Mon's Thai | T | **Alamo Hts** 17
Pacific Moon | T | **North** 18
Z Paloma Blanca | T | **Alamo Hts** 22
Pam's Patio | T | **North** 26
Pei Wei | T | **multi.** 19
P.F. Chang's | T | **Quarry** 22
Picante Grill | T | **Near North** 22
Piccolo's Italian | T | **NW** 25
Rosario's | T | **Southtown** 23
Sarovar Indian | T | **NW** 21
Sawasdee | T | **N Central** 24
Schilo's D | T | **Downtown** 21
Simi's India | T | **NW** 24
Sompong's | T | **Medical Ctr** 18
Sushi Zushi | D, T | **multi.** 21
Thai Pikul | D, T | **NW** -
Thai Spice | D, T | **NE** 22
Thai Taste | T | **NW** -
Tip Top Cafe | T | **NW** 25
Tong's Thai | D, T | **Terrell Hills** 21
Torres Taco | D, T | **multi.** 23
Van's | T | **Near North** 21
Viet-Nam | T | **Near North** -
Wah Kee | T | **Sonterra** 22
Water St. Oyster | T | **Alamo Hts** 18
W.D. Deli | T | **Near North** 21
Zuni Grill | T | **River Walk** 19

DESSERT

Z Biga/Banks | **River Walk** 27
Crumpets | **NE** 15
Da Vinci Gelato | **Stone Oak** 24
Grey Moss Inn | **Helotes** 24
Las Canarias | **River Walk** 26
Z L'Etoile | **Alamo Hts** 26
Madhatters Tea | **Southtown** 20
Pam's Patio | **North** 26
Pesca/River | **River Walk** 24
Z Ruth's Chris | **San Antonio E** 25
Tip Top Cafe | **NW** 25

DINING ALONE

(Other than hotels and places with counter service)

Z Bistro Vatel | **Olmos Pk** 26
Canyon Café | **Quarry** 18
Cappyccino's | **Alamo Hts** 20
Z Cappy's | **Alamo Hts** 23
Cheesy Jane's | **multi.** 19
Chesters | **multi.** 22
Ciao Lavanderia | **Olmos Pk** 23
Crumpets | **NE** 15
El Jarro de Arturo | **North** 22
El Mirador | **Southtown** 23
Ernesto's | **N Central** 18
Fig Tree | **River Walk** 25
Koi Kawa | **Near North** 26
Z Le Rêve | **Downtown** 29
Z L'Etoile | **Alamo Hts** 26
Z Liberty Bar | **Near North** 24
Z Lodge/Castle Hills | **Castle Hills** 26
Madhatters Tea | **Southtown** 20
Mon's Thai | **Alamo Hts** 17
Pei Wei | **multi.** 19
Z Sandbar Fish | **Downtown** 28
Sushi Zushi | **multi.** 21
Taco Cabana | **multi.** 16
Water St. Oyster | **Alamo Hts** 18
Zuni Grill | **River Walk** 19

ENTERTAINMENT

(Call for days and times of performances)

Ácenar | DJ | **River Walk** 22
Azúca | bands | **Southtown** 24
Beto's Comida | varies | **North** 21
Boardwalk Bistro | jazz | **Near North** 21
Crumpets | bands | **NE** 15
Demo's Greek | belly dancers | **multi.** 19
El Jarro de Arturo | bands | **North** 22
India Oven | belly dancers | **N Central** 24
Karam's | mariachi | **San Antonio W** 20
La Hacienda/Los Barrios | guitar/piano | **North** 21
La Margarita | mariachi | **Market Sq** 21
Landry's | jazz | **River Walk** 19
Las Canarias | guitar | **River Walk** 26

Madhatters Tea | contemp./folk/jazz | **Southtown** 20

Mina & Dimi's | dancers | **San Antonio W** 24

Mi Tierra | mariachi | **Market Sq** 21

Old San Francisco | piano | **North** 19

Z Paloma Blanca | guitar/vocals | **Alamo Hts** 22

Picante Grill | guitar | **Near North** 22

Pico de Gallo | keyboard/vocals | **San Antonio W** 21

Rosario's | varies | **Southtown** 23

Z Silo | bands | **Terrell Hts** 26

Water St. Oyster | blues/jazz/vocals | **Alamo Hts** 18

GAME IN SEASON

Antlers Lodge | **San Antonio W** 23

Z Biga/Banks | **River Walk** 27

Z Bistro Vatel | **Olmos Pk** 26

Citrus | **Downtown** 25

Crumpets | **NE** 15

Fig Tree | **River Walk** 25

Z Francesca's | **La Cantera** 26

Z Frederick's | **Alamo Hts** 26

Grey Moss Inn | **Helotes** 24

Las Canarias | **River Walk** 26

Z Le Rêve | **Downtown** 29

Z L'Etoile | **Alamo Hts** 26

Z Liberty Bar | **Near North** 24

Z Lodge/Castle Hills | **Castle Hills** 26

Oro | **Downtown** 24

Reggiano's | **Stone Oak** 20

20nine | **Quarry** 18

HISTORIC PLACES

(Year opened; * building)

1847 | Little Rhein* | **River Walk** 24

1853 | Fig Tree* | **River Walk** 25

1890 | Liberty Bar* | **Near North** 24

1902 | Guenther Hse.* | **Southtown** 23

1907 | Canyon Café* | **Quarry** 18

1910 | Josephine St.* | **Near North** 20

1917 | Schilo's D | **Downtown** 21

1920 | W.D. Deli* | **Near North** 21

1927 | Oro* | **Downtown** 24

1929 | Grey Moss Inn | **Helotes** 24

1930 | Le Rêve* | **Downtown** 29

1930 | Texas Farm/Table* | **Near North** 24

1932 | La Fonda on Main | **Near North** -

1938 | Tip Top Cafe | **NW** 25

1941 | Mi Tierra | **Market Sq** 21

1946 | Karam's | **San Antonio W** 20

1952 | Barn Door | **Alamo Hts** 19

1955 | El Jarro de Arturo | **North** 22

HOTEL DINING

Contessa Hotel
Las Ramblas | **River Walk** 21

Emily Morgan Hotel
Oro | **Downtown** 24

Hyatt Regency Hill Country
Antlers Lodge | **San Antonio W** 23

Omni La Mansión del Rio Hotel
Las Canarias | **River Walk** 26

Valencia Hotel
Citrus | **Downtown** 25

Watermark Hotel & Spa
Pesca/River | **River Walk** 24

Westin La Cantera Resort
Z Francesca's | **La Cantera** 26

JACKET REQUIRED

Z Le Rêve | **Downtown** 29

LATE DINING

(Weekday closing hour)

Mama's Café | 12 AM | **Downtown** 19

Mi Tierra | 24 hrs. | **Market Sq** 21

Taco Cabana | varies | **multi.** 16

MEET FOR A DRINK

Ácenar | **River Walk** 22

Azúca | **Southtown** 24

Z Biga/Banks | **River Walk** 27

NEW Bistro Thyme | **Loop 1604** -

Cappyccino's | **Alamo Hts** 20

Chuy's | **North** 21

Citrus | **Downtown** 25

Grill/Leon Springs | **Leon Springs** 22

La Fonda on Main | **Near North** –

La Hacienda/Los Barrios | **North** 21

Las Ramblas | **River Walk** 21

Z Liberty Bar | **Near North** 24

NEW Merchants Grand Café | **Alamo Hts** –

Morton's Steak | **Downtown** 25

Oro | **Downtown** 24

Z Paesanos | **Quarry** 22

Z Paloma Blanca | **Alamo Hts** 22

Piatti | **Quarry** 24

Z Silo | **Terrell Hts** 26

Sushi Zushi | **NW** 21

Taipei Chinese | **Stone Oak** 20

20nine | **Quarry** 18

Zuni Grill | **River Walk** 19

NOTEWORTHY NEWCOMERS

Bistro Thyme | **Loop 1604** –

Chart House | **Downtown** –

Dough | **N Central** –

Green Veg. | **Downtown** 18

Merchants Grand Café | **Alamo Hts** –

Mimi's Cafe | **La Cantera** 21

Z Silo 1604 | **Loop 1604** 26

Tiago's | **multi.** 22

OUTDOOR DINING

(G=garden; P=patio; S=sidewalk; T=terrace; W=waterside)

Ácenar | P, W | **River Walk** 22

Aldino | P | **Sonterra** 21

Aldo's | G, P | **Medical Ctr** 21

Azúca | P | **Southtown** 24

Beto's Comida | P | **North** 21

Z Biga/Banks | T, W | **River Walk** 27

Big'z Burger | T | **Loop 1604** 21

Bin 555 | P | **N Central** 26

Z Bistro Vatel | S | **Olmos Pk** 26

Boardwalk Bistro | P | **Near North** 21

Z Boudro's | P, W | **River Walk** 24

Z Cappy's | P | **Alamo Hts** 23

Chuy's | P | **North** 21

Ciao Lavanderia | S | **Olmos Pk** 23

Citrus | T, W | **Downtown** 25

County Line | P | **River Walk** 20

Crumpets | P, W | **NE** 15

Da Vinci Gelato | S | **Stone Oak** 24

Demo's Greek | P, S | **multi.** 19

El Jarro de Arturo | P | **North** 22

El Mirador | P | **Southtown** 23

Fig Tree | P, T, W | **River Walk** 25

Z Francesca's | T | **La Cantera** 26

Z Godai Sushi | P | **N Central** 27

Grey Moss Inn | P | **Helotes** 24

Houston St. | S | **Downtown** 22

Josephine St. | P | **Near North** 20

Karam's | G | **San Antonio W** 20

La Focaccia | P | **Southtown** 16

La Frite | S | **Southtown** 26

La Hacienda/Los Barrios | P | **North** 21

La Margarita | P | **Market Sq** 21

Landry's | P, W | **River Walk** 19

Las Canarias | T | **River Walk** 26

Las Ramblas | P, W | **River Walk** 21

Little Rhein | G, T, W | **River Walk** 24

Luce Rist. | P | **NW** 20

Madhatters Tea | P | **Southtown** 20

Mon's Thai | P | **Alamo Hts** 17

Z Paesanos | G | **multi.** 22

Z Paloma Blanca | P | **Alamo Hts** 22

Pam's Patio | P | **North** 26

Pei Wei | P, S | **multi.** 19

Pesca/River | P, W | **River Walk** 24

Piatti | S | **Quarry** 24

Picante Grill | P | **Near North** 22

Reggiano's | P | **Stone Oak** 20

Rist. Grissini | P | **Alamo Hts** 25

Scenic Loop | P | **Leon Springs** 19

Shiraz | P | **Olmos Pk** 21

Tong's Thai | P | **Terrell Hills** 21

20nine | P | **Quarry** 18

Water St. Oyster | P | **Alamo Hts** 18

W.D. Deli | P | **Near North** 21

Zuni Grill | P, W | **River Walk** 19

POWER SCENES

Aldo's | **Medical Ctr** 21
Z Biga/Banks | **River Walk** 27
Grill/Leon Springs | **Leon Springs** 22
Z Liberty Bar | **Near North** 24
NEW Merchants Grand Café | **Alamo Hts** -
Morton's Steak | **Downtown** 25
Z Paesanos | **multi.** 22
Piatti | **Quarry** 24
Z Ruth's Chris | **San Antonio E** 25
Z Sandbar Fish | **Downtown** 28

PRIX FIXE MENUS

(Call for prices and times)
Z Biga/Banks | **River Walk** 27
Z Bistro Vatel | **Olmos Pk** 26
Boardwalk Bistro | **Near North** 21
Crumpets | **NE** 15
Las Canarias | **River Walk** 26
Z Le Rêve | **Downtown** 29
Z Lodge/Castle Hills | **Castle Hills** 26
Simi's India | **NW** 24

QUIET CONVERSATION

Aldo's | **Medical Ctr** 21
Z Biga/Banks | **River Walk** 27
Z Bistro Vatel | **Olmos Pk** 26
Bohanan's | **Downtown** 23
Cappyccino's | **Alamo Hts** 20
Z Cappy's | **Alamo Hts** 23
Citrus | **Downtown** 25
Crumpets | **NE** 15
Ernesto's | **N Central** 18
Z Francesca's | **La Cantera** 26
Z Frederick's | **Alamo Hts** 26
Fujiya | **Medical Ctr** 19
Grey Moss Inn | **Helotes** 24
India Oven | **N Central** 24
La Scala | **Castle Hills** 23
Las Canarias | **River Walk** 26
Las Ramblas | **River Walk** 21
Z Le Rêve | **Downtown** 29
Little Rhein | **River Walk** 24
Z Lodge/Castle Hills | **Castle Hills** 26
Meson | **NW** 18
Oro | **Downtown** 24
Palm, The | **Downtown** 24
Pesca/River | **River Walk** 24
Rist. Grissini | **Alamo Hts** 25
Sawasdee | **N Central** 24
Shiraz | **Olmos Pk** 21
Sushihana | **Castle Hills** 25
20nine | **Quarry** 18

ROMANTIC PLACES

Aldo's | **Medical Ctr** 21
Z Biga/Banks | **River Walk** 27
Z Bistro Vatel | **Olmos Pk** 26
Bohanan's | **Downtown** 23
Citrus | **Downtown** 25
Fig Tree | **River Walk** 25
Z Francesca's | **La Cantera** 26
Grey Moss Inn | **Helotes** 24
Grill/Leon Springs | **Leon Springs** 22
La Scala | **Castle Hills** 23
Las Canarias | **River Walk** 26
Z Le Rêve | **Downtown** 29
Little Rhein | **River Walk** 24
Z Lodge/Castle Hills | **Castle Hills** 26
Meson | **NW** 18
Oro | **Downtown** 24
Shiraz | **Olmos Pk** 21
Z NEW Silo 1604 | **Loop 1604** 26
Sushihana | **Castle Hills** 25
20nine | **Quarry** 18

SENIOR APPEAL

Barn Door | **Alamo Hts** 19
Z Bistro Vatel | **Olmos Pk** 26
Boardwalk Bistro | **Near North** 21
Bohanan's | **Downtown** 23
Z Cappy's | **Alamo Hts** 23
Chef Chan | **NW** -
Crumpets | **NE** 15
El Jarro de Arturo | **North** 22
El Mirador | **Southtown** 23
Fig Tree | **River Walk** 25
Z Frederick's | **Alamo Hts** 26
Grey Moss Inn | **Helotes** 24

Grill/Leon Springs | **Leon Springs** 22
La Scala | **Castle Hills** 23
Las Canarias | **River Walk** 26
Z L'Etoile | **Alamo Hts** 26
Little Red Barn | **San Antonio S** 17
Z Lodge/Castle Hills | **Castle Hills** 26
Melting Pot | **N Central** 21
Meson | **NW** 18
Old San Francisco | **North** 19
Z Paloma Blanca | **Alamo Hts** 22
Schilo's D | **Downtown** 21
Sea Island | **Loop 410** 19
Z Silo | **Terrell Hts** 26
Sushihana | **Castle Hills** 25
Taipei Chinese | **Stone Oak** 20
Tip Top Cafe | **NW** 25
Water St. Oyster | **Alamo Hts** 18

SINGLES SCENES

Aldino | **Sonterra** 21
Azúca | **Southtown** 24
Grill/Leon Springs | **Leon Springs** 22
Kona Grill | **La Cantera** 20
NEW Merchants Grand Café | **Alamo Hts** -
Z Paesanos | **Loop 1604** 22
Z Paloma Blanca | **Alamo Hts** 22
Pasión! | **Loop 1604** 18
Reggiano's | **Stone Oak** 20
Rosario's | **Southtown** 23

SLEEPERS

(Good to excellent food, but little known)

Aldaco's | **San Antonio E** 22
Antlers Lodge | **San Antonio W** 23
Asia Kitchen | **San Antonio W** 25
Azúca | **Southtown** 24
Bohanan's | **Downtown** 23
Cafe Paladar | **Stone Oak** 25
Citrus | **Downtown** 25
Da Vinci Gelato | **Stone Oak** 24
El Jarro de Arturo | **North** 22
Fig Tree | **River Walk** 25
Golden Wok | **multi.** 22
Grill/Leon Springs | **Leon Springs** 22
Guenther Hse. | **Southtown** 23
Houston St. | **Downtown** 22
Ilsong Gdn. | **N Central** 25
India Oven | **N Central** 24
India Palace | **multi.** 24
Koi Kawa | **Near North** 26
Korean BBQ Hse. | **San Antonio E** 23
La Scala | **Castle Hills** 23
La Tuna Grill | **Southtown** 22
Mina & Dimi's | **San Antonio W** 24
Oro | **Downtown** 24
Pam's Patio | **North** 26
Pesca/River | **River Walk** 24
Picante Grill | **Near North** 22
Piccolo's Italian | **NW** 25
Rist. Grissini | **Alamo Hts** 25
Sarika's | **Medical Ctr** 25
Sawasdee | **N Central** 24
Simi's India | **NW** 24
Sushihana | **Castle Hills** 25
Texas Farm/Table | **Near North** 24
Thai Spice | **NE** 22
NEW Tiago's | **multi.** 22
Tip Top Cafe | **NW** 25
Torres Taco | **multi.** 23
Wah Kee | **multi.** 22

TRENDY

Ácenar | **River Walk** 22
Azúca | **Southtown** 24
Z Biga/Banks | **River Walk** 27
Big'z Burger | **Loop 1604** 21
NEW Bistro Thyme | **Loop 1604** -
Cafe Paladar | **Stone Oak** 25
NEW Dough | **N Central** -
Kona Grill | **La Cantera** 20
La Frite | **Southtown** 26
Z Liberty Bar | **Near North** 24
Luce Rist. | **NW** 20
NEW Merchants Grand Café | **Alamo Hts** -
Piatti | **Quarry** 24
Stonewerks | **multi.** 18
Texas Farm/Table | **Near North** 24
20nine | **Quarry** 18

VIEWS

Ácenar | **River Walk** 22
Antlers Lodge | **San Antonio W** 23
Z Biga/Banks | **River Walk** 27
Bohanan's | **Downtown** 23
Z Boudro's | **River Walk** 24
Fig Tree | **River Walk** 25
Z Francesca's | **La Cantera** 26
Grey Moss Inn | **Helotes** 24
Las Canarias | **River Walk** 26
Las Ramblas | **River Walk** 21
Little Rhein | **River Walk** 24
Mi Tierra | **Market Sq** 21
Oro | **Downtown** 24
Z Paesanos | **River Walk** 22
Pesca/River | **River Walk** 24
Scenic Loop | **Leon Springs** 19
Zuni Grill | **River Walk** 19

VISITORS ON EXPENSE ACCOUNT

Antlers Lodge | **San Antonio W** 23
Z Biga/Banks | **River Walk** 27
NEW Bistro Thyme | **Loop 1604** -
Citrus | **Downtown** 25
Fig Tree | **River Walk** 25
Z Francesca's | **La Cantera** 26
Las Canarias | **River Walk** 26
Las Ramblas | **River Walk** 21
Z Le Rêve | **Downtown** 29
Little Rhein | **River Walk** 24
Morton's Steak | **Downtown** 25
Oro | **Downtown** 24
Palm, The | **Downtown** 24
Pesca/River | **River Walk** 24
Z Ruth's Chris | **multi.** 25

WINNING WINE LISTS

Aldo's | **Medical Ctr** 21
Z Biga/Banks | **River Walk** 27
Bin 555 | **N Central** 26
NEW Bistro Thyme | **Loop 1604** -
Bohanan's | **Downtown** 23
Z Boudro's | **River Walk** 24
NEW Dough | **N Central** -
Fig Tree | **River Walk** 25
Z Francesca's | **La Cantera** 26
Grey Moss Inn | **Helotes** 24
Las Canarias | **River Walk** 26
Z Le Rêve | **Downtown** 29
Z L'Etoile | **Alamo Hts** 26
Little Rhein | **River Walk** 24
Z Lodge/Castle Hills | **Castle Hills** 26
Luce Rist. | **NW** 20
Morton's Steak | **Downtown** 25
Z Paesanos | **Loop 1604** 22
Palm, The | **Downtown** 24
Pesca/River | **River Walk** 24
Z Ruth's Chris | **multi.** 25
Z Silo | **Terrell Hts** 26
Sushihana | **Castle Hills** 25
20nine | **Quarry** 18
Van's | **Near North** 21

Wine Vintage Chart

This chart, based on our 0 to 30 scale, is designed to help you select wine. The ratings (by **Howard Stravitz,** a law professor at the University of South Carolina) reflect the vintage quality and the wine's readiness to drink. We exclude the 1991–1993 vintages because they are not that good. A dash indicates the wine is either past its peak or too young to rate. Loire ratings are for dry white wines.

Whites	88	89	90	94	95	96	97	98	99	00	01	02	03	04	05	06
French:																
Alsace	-	25	25	24	23	23	22	25	23	25	27	25	22	24	25	-
Burgundy	-	23	22	-	28	27	24	22	26	25	24	27	23	27	26	24
Loire Valley	-	-	-	-	-	-	-	-	-	24	25	26	23	24	27	24
Champagne	24	26	29	-	26	27	24	23	24	24	22	26	-	-	-	-
Sauternes	29	25	28	-	21	23	25	23	24	24	28	25	26	21	26	23
California:																
Chardonnay	-	-	-	-	-	-	-	-	24	23	26	26	25	27	29	25
Sauvignon Blanc	-	-	-	-	-	-	-	-	-	-	27	28	26	27	26	27
Austrian:																
Grüner Velt./ Riesling	-	-	-	-	25	21	26	26	25	22	23	25	26	25	26	-
German:	25	26	27	24	23	26	25	26	23	21	29	27	24	26	28	-
Reds	**88**	**89**	**90**	**94**	**95**	**96**	**97**	**98**	**99**	**00**	**01**	**02**	**03**	**04**	**05**	**06**
French:																
Bordeaux	23	25	29	22	26	25	23	25	24	29	26	24	25	24	27	25
Burgundy	-	24	26	-	26	27	25	22	27	22	24	27	25	25	27	25
Rhône	26	28	28	24	26	22	25	27	26	27	26	-	25	24	25	-
Beaujolais	-	-	-	-	-	-	-	-	-	24	-	23	25	22	28	26
California:																
Cab./Merlot	-	-	28	29	27	25	28	23	26	22	27	26	25	24	24	23
Pinot Noir	-	-	-	-	-	-	24	23	24	23	27	28	26	25	24	-
Zinfandel	-	-	-	-	-	-	-	-	-	-	25	23	27	24	23	-
Oregon:																
Pinot Noir	-	-	-	-	-	-	-	-	-	-	-	27	25	26	27	-
Italian:																
Tuscany	-	-	25	22	24	20	29	24	27	24	27	20	25	25	22	24
Piedmont	-	27	27	-	23	26	27	26	25	28	27	20	24	25	26	-
Spanish:																
Rioja	-	-	-	26	26	24	25	22	25	24	27	20	24	25	26	24
Ribera del Duero/Priorat	-	-	-	26	26	27	25	24	25	24	27	20	24	26	26	24
Australian:																
Shiraz/Cab.	-	-	-	24	26	23	26	28	24	24	27	27	25	26	24	-
Chilean:	-	-	-	-	-	-	24	-	25	23	26	24	25	24	26	-

Zagat Products

RESTAURANTS & MAPS

America's Top Restaurants
Atlanta
Beijing
Boston
Brooklyn
California Wine Country
Cape Cod & The Islands
Chicago (guide & map)
Connecticut
Europe's Top Restaurants
Hamptons (incl. wineries)
Las Vegas
London
Long Island (incl. wineries)
Los Angeles I So. California (guide & map)
Miami Beach
Miami I So. Florida
Montréal
New Jersey
New Jersey Shore
New Orleans
New York City (guide & map)
Palm Beach
Paris
Philadelphia
San Diego
San Francisco (guide & map)
Seattle
Texas
Tokyo
Toronto
Vancouver
Washington, DC I Baltimore
Westchester I Hudson Valley
World's Top Restaurants

LIFESTYLE GUIDES

America's Top Golf Courses
Movie Guide
Music Guide
NYC Gour. Shopping/Ent.
NYC Shopping

NIGHTLIFE GUIDES

Los Angeles
New York City
San Francisco

HOTEL & TRAVEL GUIDES

Beijing
Las Vegas
London
New Orleans
Montréal
Toronto
U.S. Family Travel
U.S. Top Hotels, Resorts & Spas
Vancouver
Walt Disney World Insider's Guide
World's Top Hotels, Resorts & Spas

WEB & WIRELESS SERVICES

ZAGAT TO GO℠ for handhelds
ZAGAT.com℠ • ZAGAT.mobi℠

Available wherever books are sold or at ZAGAT.com. To customize Zagat guides as gifts or marketing tools, call 800-540-9609.